Management Information Systems for the **Information Age,** Third Edition

Management Information Systems for the Information Age, Third Edition

Stephen Haag
Daniels College of Business
University of Denver

Maeve Cummings
Pittsburg State University

Donald J. McCubbrey
Daniels College of Business
University of Denver

Boston   Burr Ridge, IL   Dubuque, IA   Madison, WI   New York   San Francisco   St. Louis
Bangkok   Bogotá   Caracas   Kuala Lumpur   Lisbon   London   Madrid   Mexico City
Milan   Montreal   New Delhi   Santiago   Seoul   Singapore   Sydney   Taipei   Toronto

McGraw-Hill Higher Education

*A Division of The **McGraw-Hill** Companies*

MANAGEMENT INFORMATION SYSTEMS FOR THE INFORMATION AGE

Published by McGraw-Hill, an imprint of The McGraw-Hill Companies, Inc. 1221 Avenue of the Americas, New York, NY, 10020. Copyright © 2002, 2000, 1998 by The McGraw-Hill Companies, Inc. All rights reserved. No part of this publication may be reproduced or distributed in any form or by any means, or stored in a data base or retrieval system, without the prior written consent of The McGraw-Hill Companies, Inc., including, but not limited to, in any network or other electronic storage or transmission, or broadcast for distance learning.

Some ancillaries, including electronic and print components, may not be available to customers outside the United States.

This book is printed on acid-free paper.

2 3 4 5 6 7 8 9 0 WCK/WCK 0 9 8 7 6 5 4 3 2
2 3 4 5 6 7 8 9 0 WCK/WCK 0 9 8 7 6 5 4 3 2

ISBN 0-07-245872-0

Publisher: *George Werthman*
Senior sponsoring editor: *Rick Williamson*
Senior developmental editor: *Kelly Delso*
Senior marketing manager: *Jeff Parr*
Senior project manager: *Mary Conzachi*
Senior production supervisor: *Michael R. McCormick*
Media producer: *Greg Bates*
Coordinator freelance design: *Mary L. Christianson*
Lead supplement producer: *Marc Mattson*
Photo research coordinator: *Jeremy Cheshareck*
Cover/interior design: *Jim Fuerholzer*
Cover illustration: *© Don Baker*
Typeface: *11/13 Bulmer MT*
Compositor: *GAC, Indianapolis*
Printer: *Quebecor World Versailles Inc.*

Library of Congress Control Number: 2001092452

INTERNATIONAL EDITION ISBN 0-07-112346-6

Copyright © 2002. Exclusive rights by The McGraw-Hill Companies, Inc., for manufacture and export.

This book cannot be re-exported from the country to which it is sold by McGraw-Hill. The International Edition is not available in North America.

www.mhhe.com

DEDICATIONS

For Darian Presley and Trevor Aaron. My two lights of shining hope.

Stephen Haag

To Colin and Charlie. May they need septillions to count their joys and only fingers to count their sorrows.

Maeve Cummings

To my grandson, Paul Stuart McCubbrey, our family's miracle child.

Donald J. McCubbrey

Brief CONTENTS

CHAPTER 1
THE INFORMATION AGE IN WHICH YOU LIVE 3
Changing the Face of Business

Extended Learning Module A 33

CHAPTER 2
STRATEGIC AND COMPETITIVE OPPORTUNITIES 47
Using IT for Competitive Advantage

CHAPTER 3
DATABASES AND DATA WAREHOUSES 81
A Gold Mine of Information

Extended Learning Module B 117

CHAPTER 4
DECISION SUPPORT AND ARTIFICIAL INTELLIGENCE 127
Brainpower for Your Business

Extended Learning Module C 165

CHAPTER 5
ELECTRONIC COMMERCE 189
The End of the Beginning

CHAPTER 6
EMERGING TECHNOLOGIES 231
Innovations for Tomorrow

CHAPTER 7
DEVELOPING IT SYSTEMS 265
Bringing IT Systems to Life

CHAPTER 8
PROTECTING INFORMATION AND PEOPLE 311
Threats and Safeguards

CHAPTER 9
PREPARING FOR THE FUTURE 345
It's Your World

REAL HOT GROUP PROJECTS 362

Extended Learning Module D 375

Extended Learning Module E 399

Extended Learning Module F 411

Glossary 417
Photo Credits 425
Notes 427
Index 431

CONTENTS

CHAPTER 1

THE INFORMATION AGE IN WHICH YOU LIVE   3
Changing the Face of Business

Managing Customer Relations in an Electronic World   3

INTRODUCTION   4

THE MANAGEMENT INFORMATION SYSTEMS CHALLENGE   4
What Businesses Do   4
Customer Moment of Value   5
Team Work—Defining Customers and Their Moment of Value   6
The Role of Information Technology   6
The Global Perspective—Warehousing Customer Moment of Value   7

CHARACTERISTICS OF TODAY'S NEW BUSINESS   8
Globalization   8
The Global Perspective—Sony Wants to Be in Every Room of Your Home   9
Information as a Key Resource   9
Team Work—I Want It!   10
Electronic Commerce   10
Knowledge Worker Computing   12

INFORMATION TECHNOLOGY   12
Supporting Information-Processing Tasks   12
Supporting Decision-Making Tasks   13
Supporting Shared Information through Decentralized Computing   14
Supporting Innovation   14

INFORMATION   14
Industry Perspective (Financial Services)—Shedding Pen and Paper for Decentralized Information   15
On Your Own—Redefining Business Operations through IT Innovation   15
Industry Perspective (".com")—Free Long-Distance Phone Calls on the Internet   16
For Customer Moment of Value   16
The Flows of Information in an Organization   17
Industry Perspective (Health Care)—Intranet Telephone Directory Saves Children's Healthcare $15,000 per Year   18
What Information Describes   18

KNOWLEDGE WORKERS   19
Being an Information-Literate Knowledge Worker   19
Being a Socially Responsible Knowledge Worker   20
Industry Perspective (Entertainment & Publishing)—Internet + Entertainment = Intertainment   21
On Your Own—E-Mail: Electronic Mail or Expensive Mail?   23

Closing Case Study: How Much of Your Personal Information Do You Want Businesses to Know?   23
Knowledge Worker's Checklist   24
Real HOT: Electronic Commerce—Using the Internet as a Tool to Find a Job   26

EXTENDED LEARNING MODULE A: IT SYSTEMS IN YOUR ORGANIZATION   33

INTRODUCTION   33

ORGANIZATIONS, INFORMATION, AND INFORMATION TECHNOLOGY   34
Organizations   34
Information   34
Information Technology   35

TRANSACTION PROCESSING SYSTEMS (TPS)   36

CUSTOMER INTEGRATED SYSTEMS (CIS)   37

MANAGEMENT INFORMATION SYSTEMS (MIS)   38

WORKGROUP SUPPORT SYSTEMS (WSS)   40
Team Dynamics   40
Document Management   41
Applications Development   41

DECISION SUPPORT SYSTEMS (DSS) AND ARTIFICIAL INTELLIGENCE (AI)   42

EXECUTIVE INFORMATION SYSTEMS (EIS)   43

INTERORGANIZATIONAL SYSTEMS (IOS)   44

BUSINESS REVIEWS   45

CHAPTER 2

STRATEGIC AND COMPETITIVE OPPORTUNITIES   47
Using IT for Competitive Advantage

CAD Preps AmericaOne for the America's Cup   47

viii CONTENTS

INTRODUCTION	**48**
COMPETITIVE ADVANTAGE EXAMPLES	**48**
Federal Express	48
UPS and Fender Guitar	49
Dell Computer	50
Cisco Systems	50
On Your Own—Looking for Opportunities Close to Home	50
HOW SMART COMPANIES GET A COMPETITIVE ADVANTAGE FROM IT	**52**
The CEO's Attitude toward Information Technology	52
Bridging the Gap between Business People and Technical People	52
Industry Perspective (Manufacturing)—GE Leadership Leads the Way in Competitive IT	53
Viewing the Business Problem from Another Perspective	53
Demanding a Creative Design	54
The Global Perspective—Even Nations Can Gain a Competitive Advantage with IT	55
Looking beyond the Four Walls of the Company	56
TOOLS THAT CAN HELP	**57**
Industry Perspective (Health Care)—Just-in-Time Surgery	58
The Five Forces Model	58
The Three Generic Strategies	59
Using the Five Forces Model	59
Industry Perspective (Entertainment & Publishing)—Here Comes Electronic Ink	60
Team Work—Finding the Best IT Strategy for Your Industry	61
Industry Perspective (.com)—Keeping an Eye on the Competition	62
Using the Three Generic Strategies	62
On Your Own—Building on the State of the Art	63
The Value Chain	63
Identifying Processes That Add Value	64
Identifying Processes That Reduce Value	64
WHAT'S DIFFERENT WITH E-COMMERCE?	**65**
Mass Customization and Personalization	65
Disintermediation	67
Global Reach	68
New Technologies That Work with the Internet	68
THE U.S. AIRLINE INDUSTRY: A GREAT EXAMPLE	**69**
Airline Reservation Systems	69
Team Work—Helping the Little Guy Compete	70
Frequent Flyer Programs	70
Yield Management Systems	70
Disintermediating the Travel Agent	71
Knowledge Worker's Checklist	72
The Global Perspective—Paperless Payments	72
SUMMING IT UP	**73**
Closing Case Study: GM Tries to Lure Customers with OnStar	74
Real HOT Electronic Commerce—Ordering Products on the Internet	75

CHAPTER 3

DATABASES AND DATA WAREHOUSES — 81
A Gold Mine of Information

We Make Green Bay Packer "Cheesehead" Hats	81
INTRODUCTION	**82**
INFORMATION IN AN ORGANIZATION REVISITED	**82**
Processing Information in the Form of Transactions	82
Using Information to Make a Decision	82
The Global Perspective—Floating Databases Aboard Royal Caribbean Cruise Ships	84
Managing Information while It Is Used	84
THE DATABASE AND DATABASE MANAGEMENT SYSTEM ENVIRONMENT	**86**
What Is a Database?	86
Industry Perspective (Financial Services)—Should You Have Access to Medical Malpractice Databases?	88
What Is a Database Management System?	89
Industry Perspective (.com)—Making the Move to .com	91
Team Work—Defining Information Privileges during University Registration	95
On Your Own—DBMS Support for OLTP, OLAP, and Information Management	96
THE RELATIONAL DATABASE MODEL	**96**
THE OBJECT-ORIENTED DATABASE MODEL	**99**
DATA WAREHOUSING AND DATA MINING	**100**
What Is a Data Warehouse?	100
Team Work—Politically Correct Data Mining	101
What Are Data Mining Tools?	102
Important Considerations in Using a Data Warehouse	103
On Your Own—How Up-to-Date Should Data Warehouse Information Be?	103
Industry Perspective (Entertainment & Publishing)—We Want to Know Our Customers	105
The Global Perspective—How Many Customers Do You Really Have?	106
MANAGING THE INFORMATION RESOURCE IN AN ORGANIZATION	**106**
How Will Changes in Technology Affect Organizing and Managing Information?	106
What Types of Database Models and Databases Are Most Appropriate?	107
Who Should Oversee the Organization's Information?	107
Industry Perspective (Health Care)—Cracking the Human Genetic Code	108
Is Information Ownership a Consideration?	108

What Are the Ethics Involved in Organizing and Managing Information?	108
How Should Databases and Database Applications Be Developed and Maintained?	109
Closing Case Study: Mining Dining Data	109
Knowledge Worker's Checklist	110
Real HOT Electronic Commerce—Searching Online Databases and Information Repositories	112

EXTENDED LEARNING MODULE B: BUILDING A DATABASE AND ENTITY-RELATIONSHIP DIAGRAMMING 117

INTRODUCTION 117

DESIGNING AND BUILDING A RELATIONAL DATABASE 118
Step 1: Defining Entity Classes and Primary Keys 118
Step 2: Defining Relationships among Entity Classes 118
Step 3: Defining Information (Fields) for each Relation 121
Step 4: Using a Data Definition Language to Create Your Database 123

CHAPTER 4

DECISION SUPPORT AND ARTIFICIAL INTELLIGENCE 127
Brainpower for Your Business

Continental Airlines Flies High with Decision Support 127

INTRODUCTION 128

DECISIONS, DECISIONS, DECISIONS 128
Types of Decisions You Face 128
How You Make a Decision 130

DECISION SUPPORT SYSTEMS 130
Components of a Decision Support System 131
Industry Perspective (Health Care)—Doctor's Little Helper Is Just a Click Away 134
Ethical Questions in Decision Support Systems 134

GROUP DECISION SUPPORT SYSTEMS 135
The Team Decision-Making Process and You 136
Key Components in a Group Decision Support System 136
Meetings: A Fact of Life in Business 137
Industry Perspective (Manufacturing)—Finding What to Fix at IBM 137
Meetings When and Where You Want to Be 138

Team Work—Hold Virtual Meetings to Complete a Project	139
The Global Perspective—GIS Put South Africans on an Election Map	140

GEOGRAPHIC INFORMATION SYSTEMS 140

ARTIFICIAL INTELLIGENCE 143

EXPERT SYSTEMS 144
The Global Perspective—Expert System Gets Goods Safely across the Border 144
Components of an Expert System 146
Industry Perspective (".com")—Look Ma, No Hands! 148
What Expert Systems Can and Can't Do 148
Ethical Questions in Expert Systems 149
Team Work—Traffic Lights Revisited 150

NEURAL NETWORKS 150
Training a Neural Network 150
Ethical Questions in Neural Networks 151

GENETIC ALGORITHMS 151

INTELLIGENT AGENTS 152
Find-and-Retrieve Agents 152
On Your Own—Go Bargain Hunting Online 153
User Agents 153
Monitoring and Surveillance Agents 153
Industry Perspective (Financial Services)—Just How Good Is Your Web Site? 154
Data-Mining Agents 154
Components of an Intelligent Agent 154
On Your Own—Which AI Software Should You Use? 155

Knowledge Worker's Checklist 156
Closing Case Study: Are You Green, Yellow, or Red on Your Bank's Computer? 157
Real HOT Electronic Commerce—Finding Investment Opportunities on the Internet 159

EXTENDED LEARNING MODULE C: NETWORK BASICS 165

HOME NETWORKS 165
Connecting to the Internet—The King of Networks 165
A Simple Home Network—Peer to Peer 167

BUSINESS NETWORKS 171
Client/Server—A Business View 171
Client/Server—A Physical View 175

COMMUNICATIONS SERVICE PROVIDERS 176
Public Network 178
Private Network 178
Value-Added Network 178
Virtual Private Network 179

CONTENTS

NETWORK TECHNOLOGIES	**179**
Types of Networks by Distance and by Topology	179
Telecommunications Media—The Paths over Which Information Travels	181
Processors	185
Protocols	186
This Is Really Only the "Basics"	186

CHAPTER 5

ELECTRONIC COMMERCE — 189
The End of the Beginning

Buying Pepsi Online	189
INTRODUCTION	**190**
THE GROWTH OF GLOBAL E-COMMERCE	**190**
Global E-Commerce Growth Projections	191
The Digital Divide	191
BUSINESS TO CONSUMER E-COMMERCE	**192**
The Advantages of B2C E-Commerce	192
Industry Perspective (Retail)—The Right Tool for Ace Hardware	194
On Your Own—B2C Services	195
Team Work—Broadband Services: Where Do You Place Your Bets?	195
The End of the Beginning in B2C E-Commerce	196
Industry Perspective (Manufacturing)—Toyota Gets Moving on Web Initiatives	198
Lessons Learned: What Works and What Doesn't Work	198
The Global Perspective—Europe to Lead World in Online Grocery Sales	199
BUSINESS TO BUSINESS E-COMMERCE	**205**
Corporate Purchasing Segments	206
Purchasing of Direct Materials	206
Industry Perspective (".com")—Dairy Industry Gets Set for B2B Exchange	207
Team Work—What Should Allright Distributors Do?	208
Purchasing of Indirect Materials (MRO)	211
On Your Own—A Range of Possibilities for New EDI	211
Industry Perspective (Transportation)—BNSF: Making the Trains Run on Time	212
B2B Marketplaces	212
Intranets and Extranets	213
THE ROLE OF GOVERNMENT IN PROMOTING E-COMMERCE	**214**
E-COMMERCE PAYMENT SYSTEMS AND DIGITAL CASH	**215**
Traditional and Next-Generation EDI	215
Credit Cards and Smart Cards	215
Electronic Bill Presentment and Payment	216
SECURITY AND PRIVACY ISSUES	**216**
Security	216
Privacy	218
The Global Perspective—European Privacy Laws	219
Knowledge Worker's Checklist	220
Closing Case Study: Who Needs Disappearing Inc.?	220
Real HOT Electronic Commerce—Getting Your Business on the Internet	222

CHAPTER 6

EMERGING TECHNOLOGIES — 231
Innovations for Tomorrow

High-Tech Hollywood Creates High-Quality Films	231
INTRODUCTION	**232**
EMERGING TECHNOLOGIES FOR ALL THE SENSES	**233**
3-D	233
Automatic Speech Recognition	234
Industry Perspective (Retail)—Growing Up with Speech Recognition	237
Virtual Reality	237
On Your Own—Understanding the Speed of Automatic Speech Recognition	238
Industry Perspective (Health Care)—Virtual Reality for the Betterment of People and Society	239
Biometrics	241
Some Final Thoughts about Emerging Technologies for All the Senses	241
THE INTERNET EXPLOSION	**241**
Electronic Cash	242
Team Work—Finding Electronic Cash on the Internet	244
Free Internet Telephone Use	244
Industry Perspective (IT & Telecommunications)—EZfone Makes Internet Phone-Calling "EZ"	245
High-Speed Internet Access	245
Internet Appliances	246
Industry Perspective (".com")—Storage Space and Software for Rent/Free on the Internet	247
THE WIRELESS REVOLUTION	**248**
The Global Perspective—Buy Soft Drinks with Your Phone? They Do in Finland	249
On Your Own—Which Internet Appliance Is Right for You?	249
Global Positioning System	250
Industry Perspective (Manufacturing)—OnStar Is Always Onboard while You Drive	250

Wireless Local Area Networks	251
Addressing the "Ility" Issue of Wireless Technologies	252

EMERGING TECHNOLOGIES FOR YOUR PERSONAL LIFE — 252
Smart Cards	252
Intelligent Home Appliances	253
Team Work—Finding Home Appliances with a Brain	253
The Global Perspective—Staying in Touch with Your Home from Around the World	254
Your Internet-Connected Home	254
Closing Case Study: Self-Scanning, Multimedia, and Wireless Grocery Shopping	255
Knowledge Worker's Checklist	256
Real HOT Electronic Commerce—Finding Freeware and Shareware on the Internet	257

CHAPTER 7

DEVELOPING IT SYSTEMS — 265
Bringing IT Systems to Life

HomeBase Buys Software to Move beyond EDI — 265

INTRODUCTION — 266

IT SYSTEMS — 266
Gathering All Proposed IT Systems	267
Considering Proposed IT Systems in Light of Organizational Goals	267
Evaluating Proposed IT Systems	267
Planning for What You Can't Live Without	268
The Goal—The IT Systems Plan	269

SYSTEMS DEVELOPMENT IS A QUESTION-AND-ANSWER SESSION — 269
Why Is Your Participation Important?	269
Industry Perspective (Financial Services)—Disaster Recovery Plans Are More than One Plan	270
Systems Development	271

INSOURCING AND THE TRADITIONAL SYSTEMS DEVELOPMENT LIFE CYCLE — 272
Industry Perspective (Retail)—For Sears, Planning for the Future Was Essential	273
Step 1: Planning	274
Step 2: Scoping	274
Photo Essay 7-1—ITW Enterprises at Work	276
Step 3: Analysis	278
Step 4: Design	280
Step 5: Implementation	282
Step 6: Support	283
The Global Perspective—Hiring Programmers from around the World	284
Team Work—Your Responsibilities during Each Step of the SDLC	284

SELFSOURCING AND PROTOTYPING — 286
Prototyping	286
Industry Perspective (Manufacturing)—Prototyping with Software Is a Must in Manufacturing	287
The Selfsourcing Process	289
On Your Own—How Have You Selfsourced?	291

OUTSOURCING — 292
The Outsourcing Process	293
On Your Own—A Request for Proposal and the Systems Development Life Cycle	295
The Advantages and Disadvantages of Outsourcing	295
The Global Perspective—Outsourcing at a Global Level	296

ENTERPRISE RESOURCE PLANNING AND ENTERPRISE SOFTWARE — 297
The Reality of Enterprise Resource Planning and Enterprise Software	298
Industry Perspective (".com")—JD Edwards' OneWorld Enterprise Software Prepares Your Organization for the Web	299
Team Work—Matching IT Systems to the Who of Systems Development	299
Knowledge Worker's Checklist	300
Closing Case Study: Codeveloping Enterprisewide Systems in the Medical Field	302
Real HOT Electronic Commerce—Building the Perfect Web Page	303

CHAPTER 8

PROTECTING INFORMATION AND PEOPLE — 311
Threats and Safeguards

Payless—Shoes with Information behind Them — 311

INTRODUCTION — 312

PEOPLE — 312
Ethics	312
Team Work—What Would You Do?	314
Intellectual Property	315
Privacy	316
Industry Perspective (Manufacturing)—Don't Send Suggestive E-Mail from Your Place of Work!	317
Industry Perspective (Health Care)—Employee Monitoring That Makes People Happy	318
On Your Own—Who Knows about You?	319
The Global Perspective—Britain's E-Mail Privacy—RIP	321
Cultural Diversity	321
On Your Own—Is Your Computer a Health Hazard?	323
Ergonomics	323
The Global Perspective—Going to College without Going to College	324

INFORMATION — 324
The Role of Information	324

CONTENTS

Team Work—Could You Work a Help Desk?	325
Security	325
Industry Perspective (Entertainment & Publishing)—Bounce and Toy Story 2: Playing Digitally at a Cinema Near You	326
Industry Perspective (".com")—eCampus is Security Conscious	333
Disaster Recovery	333
Industry Perspective (Financial Services)—The Bank Was in Danger of Collapse	335
Knowledge Worker's Checklist	336
Closing Case Study: Arriving for Work in Your Fuzzy Slippers	336
Real HOT Electronic Commerce—Making Travel Arrangements on the Internet	338

CHAPTER 9

PREPARING FOR THE FUTURE 345

It's Your World
Will You Allow History to Repeat Itself? 345

INTRODUCTION 346

WHAT ARE THE JOBS OF THE FUTURE? 346
On Your Own—What's Your Future Job and the Skills You Need? 347

WILL B2C DOT-COMS SURVIVE? 348

WHEN WILL WE ACHIEVE TRANSPARENCY? 348
The Unreliability of Technology 349
Industry Perspective (".com")—Who's Afraid of the Big, Bad Dot-Coms? 350
Industry Perspective (Hospitality & Leisure)—Backup Servers Serve Up Domino's Pizza 350
The Last-Mile Bottleneck Problem 351
Industry Perspective (IT & Telecommunications)—Using Wireless Fiber Optics to Solve the Last-Mile Bottleneck Problem 352

ANY LAST PREDICTIONS? 352
Will We Close the Digital Divide? 352
Will Technology Truly Become "Intelligent"? 352
Will Coins and Cash Disappear? 352
Will Wireless Be the Only Way? 352
Team Work—Gaze into Your Crystal Ball 352

WHAT WILL THE KEY FUTURE BUSINESS RESOURCE BE? 352

Knowledge Worker's Checklist 354
Closing Case Study: You and Your Information 354
Real HOT Electronic Commerce—Continuing Your Education Through the Internet 356

REAL HOT GROUP PROJECTS 362

CASE 1 ASSESSING THE VALUE OF INFORMATION: TREVOR TOY AUTO MECHANICS 362

CASE 2 ASSESSING THE VALUE OF INFORMATION: AFFORDABLE HOMES REAL ESTATE 363

CASE 3 EXECUTIVE INFORMATION SYSTEM REPORTING: B&B TRAVEL CONSULTANTS 364

CASE 4 BUILDING VALUE CHAINS: STARLIGHT'S CUSTOMERS DEFINE VALUE 365

CASE 5 USING RELATIONAL TECHNOLOGY TO TRACK TECHNOLOGY: REMO FASHIONS 367

CASE 6 BUILDING A DECISION SUPPORT SYSTEM: CREATING AN INVESTMENT PORTFOLIO 368

CASE 7 ADVERTISING WITH BANNER ADS: HIGHWAYSANDBYWAYS.COM 369

CASE 8 EVALUATING REQUESTS FOR PROPOSALS: ITW ENTERPRISES 370

CASE 9 DEMONSTRATING HOW TO BUILD WEB SITES: WITH HTML 372

CASE 10 MAKING THE CASE WITH PRESENTATION GRAPHICS SOFTWARE: INFORMATION TECHNOLOGY ETHICS 372

EXTENDED LEARNING MODULE D: HARDWARE AND SOFTWARE 375

COMPUTER HARDWARE: PHYSICAL DEVICES 376
Capturing Information: Input Technologies 376
Photo Essay: Input Technology Tools 378
Conveying Information: Output Technologies 381
Photo Essay: Output Technology Tools 382
Creating Information: Computer Brain 384
Cradling Information: Storage Technology 385
Photo Essay: Storage Technologies 386
Communicating Information: Telecommunications Technology 389

COMPUTER SOFTWARE: INTELLECTUAL INTERFACES 390
System Software: Technology Management 390
Application Software: Your Productivity 391

HARDWARE AND SOFTWARE WORKING TOGETHER: PERFECT HARMONY — 393

BUYING YOUR PERSONAL COMPUTER SYSTEM: WHAT DO YOU REALLY NEED? — 397
Buy as Much RAM as You Can — 397
Buy as Fast a CPU as You Can — 397
Buying Personal Productivity Software in a Suite — 397
Standard Input Devices Are Usually Enough — 397
Consider the Quality of Your Printer — 397
Buy the Fastest Modem You Can — 397
Desktop versus Laptop—Who Knows? — 397
Buying a Used Computer—Beware — 398
Consider Ergonomics — 398
Questions and Projects — 398

EXTENDED LEARNING MODULE E: THE INTERNET AND THE WORLD WIDE WEB — 399

PHOTO ESSAY: A TOUR OF THE INTERNET — 400
Types of Computers on the Internet — 401

THE WORLD WIDE WEB — 402
Interpreting Addresses — 403

NAVIGATING THE WEB WITH WEB BROWSER SOFTWARE — 404

FINDING SITES WITH A SEARCH ENGINE — 406

SCAVENGER HUNTS — 408

EXTENDED LEARNING MODULE F: OBJECT-ORIENTED TECHNOLOGIES — 411
Photo Essay: What Does It Mean to Be Object-Oriented? — 412
Photo Essay: Why Are Object-Oriented Concepts and Techniques Becoming So Popular? — 414

SO WHY ARE OBJECT-ORIENTED CONCEPTS AND TECHNIQUES IMPORTANT TO YOU? — 416

GLOSSARY — 417
PHOTO CREDITS — 425
NOTES — 427
INDEX — 431

PREFACE

It is the information age, truly a time when knowledge is power. More so than ever before, businesses all over the world are focusing on information as a key resource. And those businesses have entered the 21st century with an even greater focus on information. Even to a greater extent, businesses are focusing on customers, business partners, and processes that provide vitally important information. That's why you constantly see such terms as ***competitive intelligence, knowledge worker, competitive scanning,*** and ***business geography*** in the business trade press.

Business leaders today understand that technology plays many roles in an organization, not the least of which is capturing and organizing information. We wrote this text to help your students take their respective places in the business world as leaders. Information technology (or IT) can be used simply to make an organization more efficient, either by cutting costs, time, and/or energy spent. This is still a significant contribution that IT can and will continue to make. IT can also be used to make an organization more effective, by supporting the analysis of information to support decision-making tasks. We have a long way to go in this arena, but technologies such as ***decision support systems, artificial intelligence,*** and ***data-mining agents*** are definitely paving the way.

IT can also be used today as a "point of business," enabling an organization to be innovative in the products and services it offers, how it reaches its customers, and even in deciding which customers to target. Many of today's successful Internet businesses—what we call ***pure plays***—don't have physical locations; rather they exist in cyberspace, reaching and serving customers solely through electronic means.

Whatever the case, business today is different from business yesterday. And your students today need to be prepared to deal with business tomorrow, which will most certainly be different than today's business.

We've written the third edition of this text—***Management Information Systems for the Information Age***—specifically to address the changing role of information technology in organizations today. It truly is the information age; IT, information, and people are key competitive tools for all organizations. With respect to IT, the word "information" is the most important part of the terms *information* technology and management *information* systems.

In this third edition, we focused a great deal of our efforts in updating the entire text, while, at the same time, making it more modular. This edition is leaner and shorter than the previous edition and includes nine chapters and six *Extended Learning Modules*. You can quite literally cover any of the *Extended Learning Modules* any time you want, or perhaps not at all. This gives you great flexibility in not only choosing what material you want to cover but also in what order you want to cover it.

For the third edition, we continue our tremendous Web support. As a matter of fact, we've increased the Web support. At http://www.mhhe.com/haag, you'll find topics such as intelligent agents, data warehousing products and reviews, and XML. You'll also find over 1,000 links your students can use to complete the *Real HOT Electronic Commerce* projects.

More Flexible Organization of the Text

To help you present the ever-changing role of IT and MIS to your students, we've created a modular organization to this text. The material, in sequence, is still in the same order as the second edition. However, we've packaged some of the material so that you can cover it whenever you want or not all. To achieve this, we've created *Extended Learning Modules*. You can cover these modules according to the particular needs of your students.

For example, *Extended Learning Module B* covers how to design the correct structure for a database and how to perform entity-relationship diagramming. If that material is not important to your students, you can omit it completely—it will not affect your ability to cover the chapter on databases and data warehouses (Chapter 3). As well, you can cover the technical module on networks *(Extended Learning Module C)* before or after the chapter on electronic commerce (Chapter 5). And you still have the option of not covering it at all.

As you can see from the figure on the next page, we've placed the *Extended Learning Modules* within the text according to where you would most likely cover them. But, again, you cover them when you want. For example, you may choose to cover *Extended Learning Module E* (The Internet and the World Wide Web) during the first week of class.

Content Changes for the Third Edition

In the third edition, you'll find that the ordering of the material is very similar to that in the second edition;

Chapters	Modules
1 The Information Age	A IT Systems in Your Organization
2 Strategic and Competitive Opportunities	
3 Databases and Data Warehouses	B Building Databases and ER Diagramming
4 Decision Support and AI	
	C Network Basics
5 Electronic Commerce	
6 Emerging Technologies	
7 Developing IT Systems	
8 Protecting Information and People	
9 Preparing for the Future	
	D Hardware and Software
	E The Internet and the World Wide Web
	F Object-Oriented Technologies

we've simply combined, collapsed, and pulled out certain material to give you greater flexibility in covering it. Below, we highlight specific content changes to the chapters and modules.

- *Chapter 1: The Information Age in Which You Live* This chapter has retained its overall focus on businesses serving their customers at their moment of value (time, location, and form). In doing so, it still recognizes that people, information technology, and information are three important and key organizational resources. It also expands the coverage of and introduction to information technology and information. For IT, Chapter 1 now includes such topics as **online transaction processing (OLTP), online analytical processing (OLAP),** and **shared information** through **decentralized computing.** For information, Chapter 1 now includes such topics as the flows of information in an organization and what information describes.
- *Extended Learning Module A: IT Systems in Your Organization*
  While evaluating the second edition, our reviewers noted the importance of categorizing IT systems such as transaction processing systems, management information systems, executive information systems, and so on. However, our reviewers requested a more compact presentation of those systems. So, second-edition Chapter 2 has been refined and placed in this *Extended Learning Module*. It includes a short, but thorough,

presentation of ***TPSs, CISs, MISs, WSSs, DSSs*** and ***AI, EISs,*** and ***IOSs.*** There is also extensive Web support for this *Extended Learning Module* in the form of numerous business examples.

- *Chapter 2: Strategic and Competitive Opportunities* Chapter 2, which is second-edition Chapter 3, has been greatly refined. While its focus on the strategic and competitive opportunities enabled by IT remains the same, the new chapter centers much of its discussions around such topics as ***first mover advantage, distribution chains, B2B and B2C electronic commerce, innovation, creative designs, Porter's five forces model, value chain analysis, global reach,*** and ***disintermediation,*** just to name a few. It concludes with an in-depth analysis of the airline industry in its quest to use IT for competitive advantage.
- *Chapter 3: Databases and Data Warehouses* The chapter on databases and data warehouses remains largely intact in the third edition. Its focus on the competitive use of technologies such as databases and data warehouses, as opposed to their technical implementation details, has always been regarded as a key feature of the text.
- *Extended Learning Module B: Building a Database and Entity-Relationship Diagramming* This *Extended Learning Module* includes the steps that a person would go through to define database requirements and then ensure the correct structure of the database through normalization. As with other parts of the text, there is extensive Web

support for this content including projects and assignments that your students can complete to further refine their ability to define the correct structure of a database.

- *Chapter 4: Decision Support and Artificial Intelligence*
While still maintaining a strong focus on the ethical use of DSS and AI technologies, this chapter includes two major changes over the second edition. First, our reviewers stated that too much time was being spent on the process of building or buying these technologies. So, we've refined and shortened much of that material. Second, we've provided new material in the area of **intelligent agents** including **buyer agents, shopping bots, user agents, monitoring** and **surveillance agents,** and **data-mining agents.**

- *Extended Learning Module C: Network Basics*
This *Extended Learning Module* expands the coverage of technical network terminology that appeared in second-edition Chapter 6. The four sections of this *Extended Learning Module* include: home networks (**modems, DSL, cable modems, peer-to-peer, Cat 3** and **Cat 5, network hubs,** and **Bluetooth**); business networks (**client/server,** business views, and physical views); **communications service providers** (**public networks, private networks, VANs, VPNs, Internet VPNs,** and **international VPNs**); and network technologies (types of networks by distance and topology, **telecommunications media, bandwidth, processors,** and **protocols**).

- *Chapter 5: Electronic Commerce*
Chapter 5 is perhaps the most exciting and dynamic change to the third edition. It provides a strong and in-depth look at the world of electronic commerce. In it, you'll find topics such as **global e-commerce, demand aggregation,** the **digital divide,** the **advantages of B2C e-commerce, e-tailers, micropayments, click-throughs** and **banner ads, viral marketing, B2B e-commerce, EDI, XML, B2B marketplaces, intranets** and **extranets, supply chain management systems, electronic bill presentment and payment,** and **security** and **privacy.**

- *Chapter 6: Emerging Technologies*
Chapter 6 on emerging technologies has changed dramatically from the second edition and will continue to change each edition. In the third-edition chapter, we've included new topics such as **biometrics, Internet telephone systems, high-speed Internet access, Internet appliances,** and the **Internet-connected home of the future.** No longer appearing in this chapter are such topics as multimedia, which we now consider to be a stable and necessary technology.

- *Chapter 7: Developing IT Systems*
This updated chapter on the development of IT systems contains both the second-edition chapters on planning for and developing IT systems. The "planning for" material has been collapsed and refined according to our reviewer requests. Further, we have added new topics including **enterprise resource planning** and **enterprise software.**

- *Chapter 8: Protecting Information and People*
This updated chapter reflects a new view of the information covered in Chapter 10 of the second edition. This chapter now centers around the protection of information and people within an organization. It includes such topics as **ethics, intellectual property, fair use doctrine, e-mail encryption, cultural diversity, ergonomics, hackers, cyber crimes, denial-of-service attacks, risk management,** and **disaster recovery plans.**

- *Chapter 9: Preparing for the Future*
Chapter 9 concludes the formal text and presents a thought-provoking view of the future. It includes discussions centering around jobs of the future, what it will take for B2C dot-coms to survive, the perceived unreliability of technology, overcoming the **last-mile bottleneck problem,** and how your students can better prepare to be the most important resource in an organization.

- *Extended Learning Module D: Hardware and Software*
This *Extended Learning Module* provides an overview of various hardware and software technologies. While reducing its coverage of specific personal productivity software such as word processing and presentation graphics, it now provides a better discussion of how hardware and software work together in an IT system.

- *Extended Learning Module E: The Internet and the World Wide Web*
This *Extended Learning Module* now contains a more technical flavor in addition to its practical-use focus contained in the second edition. It includes new topics such as **Internet backbone, network access points, network service providers, Internet server computers, Web servers, mail servers, ftp servers, Internet relay chat servers,** navigating with a Web browser, and finding sites

with different types of search engines. It also includes six different Internet scavenger hunts (always popular with your students).
- *Extended Learning Module F: Object-Oriented Technologies*
This final *Extended Learning Module* focuses on object-oriented technologies and how they differ from traditional views of separating information from procedures.

The Key Pedagogical Components of This Text

Regardless of the topic or body of material, the most effective learning tool is always an interactive environment in which both students and teachers actively participate. In IT and MIS, we expand that interactive environment even further to include technology itself as an important role player. To help you create the most successful and dynamic learning environment, we've provided several pedagogical components to foster the interactivity between (1) you as the instructor and your students and (2) your students and technology.

Real HOT Electronic Commerce Projects

From the first edition on, the Real HOT Electronic Commerce projects have always been well received by both students and teachers. **"Real HOT,"** in this case, stands for **"Real Hands-On Technology"** because your students are literally required to roll up their sleeves and actively participate in electronic commerce as it exists on the Internet.

This component (which appears at the end of each chapter) focuses on how individuals and businesses can and do use the Internet for electronic commerce. As your students work through these projects, they will become "electronic commerce consumers." However, many of the questions they must answer encourage them to consider various aspects of becoming an "electronic commerce provider." Even further, the project at the end of Chapter 5 focuses specifically on helping your students go through the process of opening their own pure play electronic commerce Web site.

The Real HOT Electronic Commerce projects by chapter include:

- Using the Internet as a Tool to Find a Job
- Ordering Products on the Internet
- Searching Online Databases and Information Repositories
- Finding Investment Opportunities Using the Internet
- Getting Your Business on the Internet
- Finding Freeware and Shareware on the Internet
- Building the Perfect Web Page
- Making Travel Arrangements on the Internet
- Continuing Your Education through the Internet

To support these projects, we've provided over 1,000 links on the Web site for this text.

Real HOT Group Projects

As with the Real HOT Electronic Commerce projects, the Real HOT Group projects have been a valuable teaching tool in previous editions. These projects, once again, require your students to literally roll up their sleeves and use technology and technology-related tools to solve a problem or take advantage of an opportunity. For example, one project provides your students with a spreadsheet that contains click-through information on an organization's customers. Your students must use that information to determine on what Web sites (if any) the organization should advertise. As well, your students must determine what Web sites the organization should approach in an effort to have those Web sites buy advertising space on its Web site.

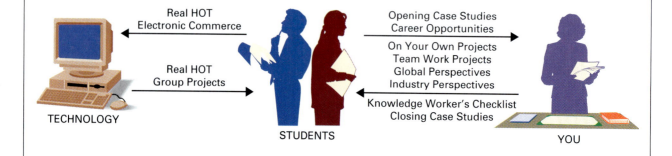

As most of the Real HOT Group projects require your students to use existing electronic files, we provide those in a variety of ways including: (1) on the instructor's CD so you can place them on a network and (2) on the Web site that supports this text so your students can download them.

Opening Case Studies

Each chapter begins with a case study that covers many of the topics introduced in the chapter. These opening case studies provide you with a mechanism for addressing the practical and business uses of the chapter material.

Industry Perspectives

Each chapter includes four or five different Industry Perspectives components. These components address the business use of certain technologies as they are applied to various industry settings. These industries include dot-com, entertainment and publishing, financial services, hospitality and leisure, health care, IT and telecommunications, manufacturing, retail, and transportation. These are particularly helpful for your students, especially for those who have already determined a specific industry in which they hope to find employment.

Career Opportunities

Within the chapter text, we take the time to break away from traditional textbook prose and really speak to your students about their career opportunities and why the covered material is so important. These Career Opportunities will definitely help you answer this question for your students—"Why am I reading this material?"

On Your Own and Team Work Projects

Throughout each chapter, you'll find several projects to be completed by individual students (On Your Own projects) and by groups of students (Team Work projects). Many of these projects can be completed in class and make great break-out exercises, while others require some outside work. We have placed these projects within the text so you can easily integrate them into your presentation and so your students can more easily identify the chapter material that relates to each project.

Global Perspectives

A constant theme you'll find throughout this text is that business is now global—competitors, distributors, suppliers, and customers for any business now exist all over the world. To reinforce this, we've included two Global Perspectives features in each chapter that discuss specific concepts within the context of a global business environment.

Knowledge Worker's Checklist

At the close of each chapter, we address the learning objectives list to summarize the material for your students. This is consistent with the teaching adage of "Tell them what you're going to tell them, tell them, and then tell them what you told them."

Closing Case Study

Each chapter includes a closing case study which will help your students apply what they just learned. These case studies profile an actual business and then require your students to use the chapter material to answer a variety of questions.

The Web Site and Online Learning Center (http://www.mhhe.com/haag)

To help keep our text as up-to-date as possible and create interactivity among you, your students, and technology, we've created a Web site that both you and your students will find invaluable.

Specifically for your students, the Web site contains:

- Real HOT Group project hints
- Real HOT Group project files
- Over 1,000 links for completing the Real HOT Electronic Commerce projects
- On Your Own project hints
- Team Work hints
- Product reviews for ASR, data warehousing tools, O-O databases, and much more
- Online and real-time quizzes for preparing for exams

For you, the Web site contains new On Your Own and Team Work projects and all the instructor's resource material in downloadable form, including sample syllabi, pop quizzes, and teaching tips and suggestions for presenting each chapter or module.

The Support Package

As both authors and teachers, we realize that no textbook is complete without a well-rounded teaching support package. To facilitate your efforts in the classroom, we've provided five components in the support package for this text. In creating these, it was our sincere goal to support your unique teaching efforts and teaching style. The support package for this textbook includes an Instructor's Resource Guide, Instructor's Manual, a test bank, a PowerPoint slide presentation, and our Web site.

- **Instructor's Resource Guide**
  - A wealth of material to help instructors prepare to teach the IT/MIS course
  - Sample syllabi for 5 week, 10 week, and 15 week terms
  - Recommended uses of the various pedagogical features
  - Recommended uses of the various support package features such as the PowerPoint slides
  - Sample testing mechanisms for (1) two exams and a final exam and (2) a midterm exam and a final exam
  - Sample group and class project ideas
- **Instructor's Manual**
  - Teaching tips and suggestions for presenting each chapter
  - How to use the various pedagogical features such as the opening and closing case studies
  - Pop quizzes for each chapter
  - Solutions to the Real HOT Group and Electronic Commerce projects
  - Guidelines for implementing the On Your Own and Team Work projects
- **Test Bank (authored by Margaret Trenholm-Edmunds of Mount Allison University)**
  - Completely automated
  - Over 1,500 true/false, fill-in-the-blank, multiple choice, and short-answer questions
  - Facilities for generating exams and adding your own questions
- **PowerPoint Slide Presentation (authored by Laurette Poulos Simmons, Ph.D., Loyola College in Maryland)**
  - Approximately 50 slides per chapter
  - Supplemental in-text art work files for you to choose from
- **Web Site**
  - At http://www.mhhe.com/haag
  - An invaluable resource for both you and your students
  - Coverage of the latest uses of technology
  - Coverage of new technology advancements
  - Over 1,000 great links for completing the Real HOT Electronic Commerce projects
  - All the files your students need to complete the Real HOT Group projects

Acknowledgments

It has been our privilege once again to work with a host of talented individuals, all of whom wanted this book to be as successful as possible. Unfortunately, we don't have space to name everyone; in reality, we probably don't know the names of absolutely everyone involved. To those behind the scenes and whose names we never heard—our deepest and most heartfelt regards.

We would like specifically to mention a few people. They include; Scott Scheidt, Mary Conzachi, and Jeremy Cheshareck; Christine Wright, our developmental editor; and Rick Williamson, our editor who brought the book to life. Without the encouragement and support of each of these people, our efforts would not be nearly as successful.

Our gratitude is also extended to helpful reviewers of the manuscript. They took on a thankless job that paid only a portion of its true worth. We had the best. They include:

Noushin Ashrafi, University of Massachusetts—Boston
Jack D. Becker, University of North Texas
Alicia Fetters, Des Moines Area Community College
Alice Jacobs, University of Phoenix
Ronald S. Lemos, California State University—Los Angeles
Ron Lenhart, Mohave Community College
Teresita S. Leyell, Washburn University
Stephen L. Loy, Eastern Kentucky University
Ross A. Malaga, University of Maryland—Baltimore County
B. Dawn Medlin, Appalachian State University
John Melrose, University of Wisconsin—Eau Claire
Fui Hoon Nah, University of Nebraska—Lincoln
Harold Palmer, Ferris State University
Tony Polito, University of Northern Iowa
Mahesh S. Raisinghani, University of Dallas
Michael D. Reimann, University of Texas—Arlington
Stephanie Robbins, University of North Carolina—Charlotte

Roberta M. Roth, University of Northern Iowa
William David Salisbury, Mississippi State University
Laurette Poulos Simmons, Loyola College in Maryland
Sumit Sircar, University of Texas—Arlington
Kala Chand Seal, Loyola Marymount University
Laleh Smec, Towson University
Jayne Stasser, Miami University

Mani R. Subramani, University of Minnesota
Thomas Triscari, Rensselaer Polytechnic Institute
Qiang Tu, Montclair State University
Douglas Turner, State University of West Georgia
Craig K. Tyran, Oregon State University
Bennie D. Waller, Francis Marion University
Connie E. Wells, Nicholls State University
Dennis Williams, Cal Poly—San Luis Obispo
Myung H. Yoon, Northeastern Illinois University

From Stephen Haag...

Over the past 17 years, I've been proud to be a part of the creation of 14 books, with 17 more coming in 2001 and 2002. My co-authors and everyone else associated with these books have made each experience truly one that is unforgettable and exhilarating. I would not trade those experiences for anything in the world. To all of you, I offer my gratitude.

On a more personal note, I've experienced the joy of childbirth with my wife, Pam, twice in the last couple of years. I now have Darian and Trevor crawling underneath my desk and begging for attention. They've seen fit to make sure I've had many sleepless nights—it was on those nights, between putting a child back to sleep, that I completed much of this text. Daddy loves both of you boys very much.

From Donald McCubbrey...

The joy of this profession is working with students. Thanks go to them for keeping me current by getting better every year. Thanks to my colleagues at the Daniels College of Business for creating an atmosphere of excellence. Special thanks go to my friends from academe, industry, and government from many countries around the world. You know who you are because most of us meet each year in Bled, Slovenia. Our first annual Electronic Commerce Conference was held there in 1988. Thanks to Maeve and Stephen who were kicks to work with. Thanks to my wife, Janis, who puts up with me and is a kick to live with.

From Maeve Cummings...

I'm indebted to Stephen Haag, who is the dynamic force behind this book. His boundless energy and inexhaustible dedication make working with him an awesome and exhilarating experience. Our editor Rick Williamson and all the other committed people at McGraw-Hill/Irwin made the process as smooth and pleasant as possible.

Many others contributed directly and indirectly to this project. Cort Buffington and my husband, Slim, supplied a major portion of the material in the network module. Melanie Buffington gave unstintingly of her time and talent in helping me proof and copy edit. Kem Marcum and Bob Roth of Payless ShoesSource; Karen Wagaman of QuVIS; and Jennifer Thomas of Freeman Hospitals and Health System were most helpful and, despite busy schedules, were very generous with their time and expertise.

Numerous people at Pittsburg State University provided me with support and assistance. Kevin Bracker, Barbara Clutter, Felix Dreher, and Malcolm Turner all contributed in various and invaluable ways. Last, but by no means least, I am, as ever, grateful to have been able to draw continuously from my husband's bottomless well of support and patience.

ABOUT THE AUTHORS

Stephen Haag is a professor and Chair of Information Technology and Electronic Commerce and the Director of Technology in the University of Denver's Daniels College of Business. Stephen holds a B.B.A. and M.B.A. from West Texas State University and a Ph.D. from the University of Texas at Arlington. Stephen has published numerous articles appearing in such journals as *Communications of the ACM, The International Journal of Systems Science, Applied Economics, Managerial and Decision Economics, Socio-Economic Planning Sciences,* and the *Australian Journal of Management.*

Stephen is also the author of 13 other books including *Interactions: Teaching English as a Second Language* (with his mother and father), *Case Studies in Information Technology, Information Technology: Tomorrow's Advantage Today* (with Peter Keen), and *Exceling in Finance.* Stephen is also the lead author of the soon-to-be-released *I-Series,* which includes 17 books. Stephen lives with his wife, Pam, and their four sons, Indiana, Darian, Trevor, and Elvis, in Highlands Ranch, Colorado.

Donald J. McCubbrey is a Professor in the Department of Information Technology and Electronic Commerce and Director of the Center for the Study of Electronic Commerce in the Daniels College of Business at the University of Denver. He holds a BSBA in Accounting from Wayne State University, a Master of Business from Swinburne University of Technology in Victoria, Australia, and a Ph.D. in Information Systems from the University of Maribor, Slovenia.

Prior to joining the Daniels College faculty in 1984, he was a partner with Andersen Consulting/Arthur Andersen & Co. He has published articles in *Communications of the Association for Information Systems, Information Technology and People* and *MIS Quarterly,* and co-authored the systems analysis and design text entitled *Foundations of Business Systems.* He lives in the Colorado foothills with his wife, Janis.

Maeve Cummings is a professor of Information Systems at Pittsburg State University. She holds a B.S. in Mathematics, and an M.B.A. from Pittsburg State University; and a Ph.D. in Information Systems from the University of Texas at Arlington. She has published in various journals including the *Journal of Global Information Management* and the *Journal of Computer Information Systems.* She is on the editorial board of several journals including the *Journal of Global Information Technology Management* and the *Midwest Quarterly.*

Maeve is the co-author of *Case Studies in Information Technology* and a soon-to-be-released two-book series titled *Computing Concepts.* Maeve lives in Pittsburg, Kansas with her Husband, Slim.

Management Information Systems for the **Information Age,** Third Edition

CHAPTER OUTLINE

INDUSTRY PERSPECTIVE

Financial Services — 15
Shedding Pen and Paper for Decentralized Information

".com" — 16
Free Long-Distance Phone Calls on the Internet

Health Care — 18
Intranet Telephone Directory Saves Children's Healthcare $15,000 per Year

Entertainment and Publishing — 21
Internet + Entertainment = Intertainment

IN THE NEWS

- **4** Knowledge workers in the United States outnumber all other workers by more than a four-to-one margin.
- **5** Customer movement of value means providing service when, where, and how the customer wants it.
- **8** Top 50 world industrial leaders by country from 1975 to 2000 (Figure 1.3).
- **10** Would you pay $500 for a birthday cake for your pet? Some people do.
- **11** Over 25 million people in the United States telecommute, and that figure is expected to grow by 20 percent over the next several years.
- **13** The five categories of information-processing tasks include capturing, conveying, creating, cradling, and communicating information (Table 1.1).
- **19** An East Coast retail store manager stocks diapers and beer on the same aisle to increase sales.
- **20** Are you a professional, expert, or innovator?
- **22** It's estimated that one of every two copies of software in use in the world today is a pirated copy (Figure 1.10).

FEATURES

- **6** **Team Work** Defining Customers and Their Moment of Value
- **7** **The Global Perspective** Warehousing Customer Moment of Value
- **9** **The Global Perspective** Sony Wants to Be in Every Room of Your Home
- **10** **Team Work** I Want It!
- **15** **On Your Own** Redefining Business Operations through IT Innovation
- **23** **On Your Own** E-Mail: Electronic Mail or Expensive Mail?
- **26** **Electronic Commerce** Using the Internet as a Tool to Find a Job

KNOWLEDGE WORKER'S CHECKLIST

In The Information Age, Knowledge Workers Understand . . .

1. *The Management Information Systems Challenge* and management information systems
2. Important factors shaping the new business
3. The role of information technology in the new business
4. Information as a key business resource
5. Their role as information-literature knowledge workers

WEB SUPPORT

http://www.mhhe.com/haag

- Job Databases
- Searching Newspapers for Job Ads
- Locating Internships
- Interviewing and Negotiating Tips
- Organization Sites and Job Postings
- Employment Opportunities with the Government

The Information Age in Which You Live

Changing the Face of Business

CHAPTER 1

CASE STUDY

Managing Customer Relations in an Electronic World

One of the hottest topics today in the business world is electronic commerce. It's all about performing business (commerce) electronically, and includes giving customers the ability to order products and services over the Internet and connecting with other organizations electronically to exchange such information as sales invoices and purchase orders. It even includes moving money electronically—electronic funds transfer for organizational use and electronic or digital cash for personal use.

In this electronic world, it's often easy to lose touch with your customers. You may not ever see or speak with them. If they order products from a Web site, they can become just another number to you. That's one of your challenges in today's business world—retaining your customer focus and managing your relationship with your customers.

When Cleanscape software launched a newly acquired line of products, Brent Duncan, Cleanscape's marketing manager, explained, "One of the first things we wanted to do was to set up a process to manage and maintain our relationship with our customers. We wanted to unite functions of our company under a single, relational database: marketing, sales, service, accounting—even engineering."

Cleanscape chose to do this not by avoiding the pitfalls of Internet-based business but rather by capitalizing on its advantages. So, Cleanscape implemented a customer relationship management (CRM) system that resides solely on the Internet. Anywhere there's an Internet connection, salespeople, managers, marketing specialists, or even accountants can access and use Cleanscape customer information and even update it. All that's needed is a computer, a modem, and simple Web browser software.

Today's new business world that includes such facets as electronic commerce and customer relationship management is certainly an exciting one with many challenges. Those challenges include making the best use of information, information technology tools and the people within your organization. And that's what management information systems is all about.[1] ❖

Introduction

It is the *information age*—a time when knowledge is power. Today, more than ever, businesses are using information to gain and sustain a competitive advantage. You'll never find a business whose slogan is "What you don't know can't hurt you." Businesses understand that what they don't know can become an Achilles heel and a source of advantage for their competitors.

Think about your major. Whether it's marketing, finance, accounting, human resource management, or any of the many other specializations in a business program, you're preparing to enter the business world as a knowledge worker. Simply put, a *knowledge worker* works with and produces information as a product. According to *U.S. News & World Report*, knowledge workers in the United States outnumber all other workers by more than a four-to-one margin.[2]

Sure, you may work with your hands to write notes or use a mouse and keyboard to produce a spreadsheet, but what you've really done is use your mind to work with, massage, and produce more information. Accountants generate profit and loss statements, cash flow statements, statements of retained earnings, and so on, some of which appear on paper. But you wouldn't say that an accountant produces paper any more than you would say Michelangelo was a commercial painter of churches.

In the information age, *management information systems* is an important topic. Why? Because management information systems deals with the coordination and use of three very important organizational resources—information, information technology, and people. Formally, we define MIS as follows:

> **Management information systems (MIS)** deals with the planning for, development, management, and use of information technology tools to help people perform all tasks related to information processing and management.

In that definition, you can find three key resources—information, information technology, and people.

As we move forward in this chapter, let's first delve into the challenges organizations face with respect to MIS in today's information-based environment. Then, we'll explore today's changing business world and some factors which literally require organizations to use information technology just to survive (with the ultimate goal of beating the competition). Finally, we'll more closely explore information, information technology, and people—three invaluable organizational resources.

The Management Information Systems Challenge

Some people will tell you that information technology is the solution to all your problems. Not true. Information technology (IT) is a set of tools for working with information. If we weren't in the information age, IT would probably not be as important. Indeed, many of us would not even carry around laptop computers and PDAs, much less have a computer at home. For IT to be successful in your organization, you must carefully coordinate its use with information and with other knowledge workers. And that's what MIS is all about.

To help you better understand the role of IT and MIS in an information-based organization, we have created **The Management Information Systems Challenge (The MIS Challenge)** that *all* businesses must strive to meet (see Figure 1.1). Notice that we emphasize the word *all* and stress that all business—whether service- or product-oriented, whether large or small—must address the challenge of MIS to be successful. Let's take a closer look at *The MIS Challenge*, and see what it involves.

There are three aspects of *The MIS Challenge*, including

1. What businesses do
2. Customer moment of value
3. The role of information technology

Let's look at these three aspects in more detail.

What Businesses Do

Businesses serve their customers, it's that simple. And it doesn't matter whether you own a business that makes dog treats, are employed by an organization that provides telecommunications services around the world, or work at a school that gives students an education, the goal of the business (and the only reason it will continue to stay in business) is to serve its customer base. Consider MCI and its goal of completely customized calling plans.

Most telephone service providers have a handful of calling plans, from which you must choose one. But MCI wants to change all that. By sifting through over 1 trillion bytes of information about its customers, MCI plans to offer each individual customer his or her own calling plan. MCI's plan is an example of mass customization through technology. And it's an example of

FIGURE 1.1

Business is in the business of serving its customers. Whether it's building cars, mowing lawns, or providing telecommunications around the world, a business will only survive if it provides perfect service to its customers.

Perfect service occurs at the customer's moment of value. That is, perfect service occurs when the customer wants it (time), where the customer wants it (location), how the customer wants it (form), and in a manner that is guaranteed to the customer. We call the guarantee to the customer "perfect delivery."

Today perfect service is only possible if a business has the right information in the hands of the right people at the right time; this occurs through the appropriate use of information technology. Therefore the challenge facing any business is to plan for, develop, manage, and use its three most important resources—information, information technology, and people—to provide perfect service at the customer's moment of value. The planning for, development, management, and use of these three fall within the function of management information systems, or MIS.

The Management Information Systems Challenge

a business striving to serve each individual customer according to his or her unique needs.[3]

Customer Moment of Value

Serving the needs of customers extends beyond just providing products and services—it includes providing perfect service to the customer, which occurs at the customer's moment of value. **Customer moment of value** is defined as providing service

1. When the customer wants it (time)
2. Where the customer wants it (location)
3. How the customer wants it (form)
4. In a manner guaranteed to satisfy the customer (perfect delivery)

The first three characteristics of customer moment of value—time, location, and form—are the basis by which many organizations today are succeeding in retaining their current customer base and attracting new customers. Consider these examples.

Amazon Says, "Customers Want to Do Business All the Time" Amazon.com is one the first and still most talked about Web sites on the Internet. Amazon's goal was simple—let customers do business any time they want. Today (and at any time), you can visit Amazon and send free greeting cards, read about new car releases, and buy almost anything from books and movies to wireless phones to health and beauty products. Business no longer operates from 8 to 5—just ask anyone buying and selling products on the Internet.

Ford Says, "Location, Location, Location" In the United States it may still be the big 3—Ford, Chrysler, and General Motors—but in Asia it's "Oh what a Toyota." For every Ford sold in Asia, almost 10 Toyotas are sold. So, Ford decided the best way to sell cars in Asia was to make them there (an example of location customer moment of value). In the past five years, Ford has invested over $1 billion in manufacturing plants throughout Asia. In this instance, "location" means reaping the advantages of making the product in the home country of the consumer.[4]

Dreyer's Says, "Ice Cream Flavors Will Win the Battle" "Ice cream is fragmented to the *n*th degree, and there is the opportunity," according to Rick Cronk, cofounder of Dreyer's Grand Ice Cream Inc. And the opportunity lies in having information about the whimsical desires of the consumer market. Dreyer's reps enter a grocery store armed with handheld computers and track inventory levels (even for its competitors). That information is sent to headquarters where it's carefully poured over and analyzed by product specialists. Dreyer's found that markets dominated by older people prefer more sugar-free varieties, whereas most urban consumers prefer coffee flavors. And providing the right ice cream flavor to the right market meets the *form* (how the customer wants it) customer moment of value.[5]

CAREER OPPORTUNITY

Many businesses today have forgotten about the customer. Some have tried but failed to regain their customer-service perspective and are now out of business. In your career, take every opportunity to make your customers number 1—*they* are the reason you're in business. And you can keep your customers and gain new ones by focusing on their *moment of value*.

The final characteristic of a customer's moment of value deals with providing the first three—time, location and form—in a manner guaranteed to satisfy the customer (what we call ***perfect delivery***). In business, perfect delivery amounts to saying "We know our customers' moment of value according to time, location, and form, and we're willing to guarantee that we can meet those characteristics." This guarantee of perfect delivery comes in many forms. For example, if an auto parts store doesn't have a part you need, it may be willing to call around town to help you find the part. That same store may even have someone deliver it to you so you don't have to drive across town (*location* perfect delivery). Pizza delivery businesses may also guarantee perfect service by giving you a free pizza if delivery does not occur within a given amount of time (*time* perfect delivery).

The Role of Information Technology

An organization's ability to provide perfect service at customer moment of value depends on three things:

1. Knowing the time at which the customer's moment of value occurs
2. Knowing the location where the customer's moment of value occurs
3. Knowing the form in which the customer's moment of value occurs

CAREER OPPORTUNITY

Achieving perfect service at the customer's moment of value is of great importance to all businesses today. And perfect service is difficult; in fact, it's sometimes impossible to achieve every time you deal with a customer. But that doesn't mean you shouldn't try. What if you owned a business—would you rather have employees who always tried to provide perfect service or employees who attempted to just "get by" while providing your customers with a product or service? You'd obviously want the first set of employees—so do the businesses that might someday be your employer.

Defining Customers and Their Moment of Value

In reality, businesses have many sets of customers. Consider a plastics manufacturing firm. It has customers who consume or use its products, the community from which it draws employees, stockholders and financial institutions who have invested money in it, and various government agencies that regulate certain aspects of its business. These are all "customers" expecting to be served.

Your school is no different. It too has many sets of customers to whom it must provide perfect service at the appropriate moment of value.

1. Define each set of customers for your school.
2. For each customer set, define the products and services your school provides.
3. For each customer set, define the moment of value in terms of time, location, form, and perfect delivery.

As a student, how does your school use technology to provide you with products and services at your moment of value? How else can your school use technology to better provide you with products and services according to your moment of value? ❖

THE GLOBAL PERSPECTIVE

Warehousing Customer Moment of Value

Customer moment of value is not a concept that the business world merely pays lip service to. It is an absolute must for staying competitive. Consider USCO Logistics, a third-party logistics provider. Headquartered in Naugatuck, CT, USCO operates 41 warehouse facilities in the United States, Canada, and Mexico. It also serves South America, Europe, and Asia through licensed partnerships.

In 2000, USCO Logistics was awarded the third annual international Warehouse of the Year award. It has also seen revenues triple from 1997. As Bob Auray, CEO of USCO, noted when he joined the company, "Employees understood who their customers were. . . . When we see a storage account we look at it as an opportunity to add value: How do we increase the velocity of that product so it's better for the customer and for us? Our whole operating culture allows us to add more value."

For example, USCO helped Sun Microsystems develop an Internet-based solution. That solution allows maintenance parts to be delivered much faster—often within an hour of a service call.

The warehousing industry is changing—from just moving products to moving information as well. Using state-of-the-art technology, USCO is one of the premier warehousing specialists. Its focus on adding value to its customers is second to none.

If you want to be number 1, focus on your customers and their moment of value. Focus on adding ever more value to them at that moment they need it. If you do, you may very well triple your revenues within three years.[6]

All these can be summed up easily—it's having **knowledge,** and **knowledge comes from having information.** Gaining knowledge through information is the role of IT in today's information-based business. IT is a set of tools that can help provide the right people with the right information at the right time. This will help those people make the best decisions possible about the time, location, and form of the customer's moment of value.

From that you might say, "Okay, let's provide an IT structure that will allow people to share and use information. Then we'll be successful." Unfortunately, that's only part of the solution, and a small one at that. The real solution lies in fundamentally changing the way an organization works and the processes it undertakes so that people will share and use information (through IT) as a natural part of their respective jobs. Says Daniel Shubert of Electronic Data Systems Corp., "The problem is not with the technology, but with the corporate processes. Companies must fundamentally change the way they do business, and that's hard."[7] The article in which that statement appears goes on to say, "You can't assume people will share information, just because the network allows them to. . . ." Indeed, it's far easier to develop a complex IT system for supporting information sharing than it is to get people to change the way they think about business processes and share information as naturally as they would expect a paycheck at the end of each month.

As you move forward in this text, you'll see that we always focus on what it takes to meet *The MIS Challenge*—how to plan for, develop, and manage the coordinated use of information technology and information by people. Sometimes a chapter or an *Extended Learning Module* focuses specifically on one of the three key organizational resources (information technology, information, or the people using them). For example, *Extended Learning Modules B* through *F* and Chapters 3 and 4 focus most of their attention on information technology, while Chapters 7 and 8 examine your role as a knowledge worker while planning for, developing, and managing IT in your organization. Whichever the focus, meeting *The MIS Challenge* is always the context of and underlying purpose for our discussion.

We encourage you always to consider the "big picture" as you read through this text—keep your focus on "putting it all together" to provide the customer's moment of value. Neither, information, information technology, nor people is a business panacea alone. All three key resources must work together for your organization to survive and win.

Characteristics of Today's New Business

In preparing to enter today's fast-paced, ever-changing, and exciting business environment, you need to understand the new thinking in business. To do that, let's examine some of the most important factors shaping today's business and the many changes that have come about as a result of those factors. Figure 1.2 shows four such factors: globalization, information as a key resource, electronic commerce, and knowledge worker computing. These and other factors have created dramatic changes in the workplace. Some are external forces that have provided outside pressure and have forced organizations to change within. Others are simply internal results of external pressure.

Why is it important for you as a knowledge worker to understand these new factors? Simply put, they translate into a substantial opportunity for you, if you understand them and prepare yourself through your education to take advantage of them.

Globalization

Take a look around your home or room. How many of the products that you see are wholly domestic? It might surprise you to learn that many of them are "foreign." For example, the pencil you're taking notes with may have come from Japan, and the paper on which this text is printed may have come from Canada. Business today is global business. Even if you own a small business and have suppliers and customers who are wholly domestic, you probably have some sort of foreign competition.

Consider the graph in Figure 1.3. It charts the world's industrial leaders from 1975 to 2000. Notice the gradual and consistent increase in the number of companies outside the United States. But don't let the numbers scare you. Although it's true that there are many

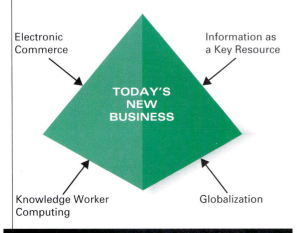

FIGURE 1.2

Factors Changing the Landscape of Business Today

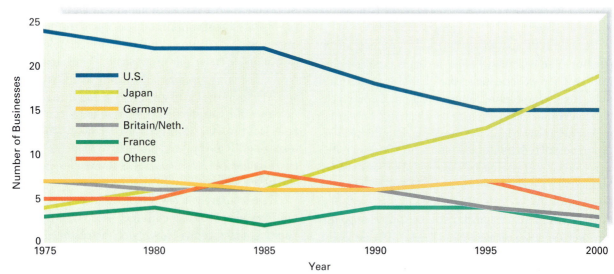

FIGURE 1.3

Where the Big Companies Are[8]

THE GLOBAL PERSPECTIVE

Sony Wants to Be in Every Room of Your Home

It's simple—Sony wants to create a broad range of electronic products that will be in every room of your home and can connect to each other to create your own personal network. Nobuyuki Idei, president and CEO of Sony, wants you to be able to use your TV remote control to open the garage door, turn on the sprinklers, and even turn off the lights in rooms throughout your home.

Sony is launching headlong into a product development campaign that will yield connectable and networkable TVs, home and portable audio systems, telephones, computers, Sony Play Stations, and Internet appliances. That home network of your future will be connected to the Internet, supporting your access to millions of different Web sites. It may even connect your intelligent Internet-based toilet to your doctor's office.

Does this seem far-fetched or futuristic? Sony can't wait until technologies are proven or already developed by other organizations. If you want to compete and survive in today's economy, you have to be on the leading edge of technology. As Nobuyuki explains it, ". . . we can't merely follow the dot-com companies or Microsoft or anybody else. We have to take advantage of everything the technology and the new economy provides. We have to prepare while we still have time."

Maybe that philosophy is why Japan now has 19 of the 50 largest companies in the world, all of which are technology oriented.[9] ❖

---

foreign companies competing for consumer dollars in the U.S. market, U.S.-based companies enjoy marketing their products and services throughout most of the world. So, while foreign companies are competing for the dollars in the United States of some 275,000,000 consumers, U.S. companies are selling products and services to a market of more than 6,118,000,000 (that's over 6 billion) consumers worldwide.

Globalization, a factor shaping today's business, is a result of many factors, including privatization, deregulation, improved worldwide transportation and telecommunication, the emergence of transnational firms, and trade blocs. Think about trade blocs for a moment. The three that dominate the world today are the World Trade Organization (formally known as the General Agreement on Trades and Tariffs, or GATT), the European Union (EU), and the North American Free Trade Agreement (NAFTA). NAFTA, alone, has opened a market of 134,000,000 people in Chile, Canada, and Mexico to U.S. businesses. For you, globalization represents a substantial career opportunity. In fact, you may have taken courses in international finance, international marketing, global logistics, or international business. Even if you haven't you should realize that most large businesses operate as *transnational firms*—firms that produce and sell products and services in countries all over the world. Think of how much better your resume would look if you could speak a foreign language or had knowledge in subjects relating to all aspects of international commerce.

> **CAREER OPPORTUNITY**
> Remember, the optimist sees the donut, whereas the pessimist sees the hole. Today's optimistic knowledge worker sees globalization as an opportunity to expand internationally; the pessimistic knowledge worker sees globalization as a threat to the "home front." Which are you?

Information as a Key Resource

In the introduction to this chapter, we alluded to the importance of information in today's business environment. This truly is a time when knowledge is power, and knowing your competition as well as your customers will define the success of your organization. Every day, you can pick up any business magazine such as *Forbes, Business Week,* or *Fortune* and read about the many information-based success stories of businesses in all industries. But why is information so important—why must businesses have information to be successful?

Again, there are many reasons; one such reason is that we now operate in a wants-driven economy. Some

TEAM WORK

I Want It!

Tennis shoes with lighted heels are just one of the many wants-based products that have recently surfaced. Take a walk around a mall, see how many wants-based products you can find, and then fill in the table below. Critically think about what information a business must know about its customers to identify potential buyers. Also, stay away from foods—we need very few actual food products, but our taste buds deserve variety.

Now that you've identified a few wants-based products, consider how technology could help you capture and process information relating to people who buy those products. Where would that information come from? Could you use technology to capture that information? Once you have the information, what technologies could you use to process that information? ❖

Product	Price	Why People Want It	What Kind of People Buy It

---

30 years ago that wasn't true—people mainly purchased only what they needed. Not so today, when wants often exceed needs and consumers are more than willing to spend their money on products and services they want rather than spend their money on just what they need. Consider a seemingly trivial example: tennis shoes in which the heels light up with the pressure of each footstep. Now, how many people do you think really **need** tennis shoes with rear lights? Very few, if any, but if that's what they want, that's what they'll buy.

Consider another example: dog bakeries, some of which even offer dog birthday cakes that range in price from $150 to $500. Now, if you ask a dog, it would probably say (that is, if it would speak) that dog treats (mail carrier cookies that taste like beef, fire hydrant cookies that taste like chicken, and so on) are very necessary. But in reality, neither people nor dogs need to eat treats—some dog owners simply want to indulge their pets.

For business, this requires a dramatic shift in thinking, marketing, and product research and development. Businesses can no longer base product decisions on what people need. Businesses must do their research and find out what people want, or figure out how to make people want a product they're producing. This need to capture and record information about what people want has led to the many IT-based databases and data warehouses of which businesses are now boasting. These databases and data warehouses contain valuable information detailing customers' wants and desires.

Electronic Commerce
The New Business Horizon

Electronic commerce is certainly the hottest topic in business today, and we've devoted all of Chapter 5 to it. Electronic commerce will forever change the landscape of business. But what exactly is electronic commerce and what does it enable an organization to do? Formally defined,

Electronic commerce is commerce, but it is commerce accelerated and enhanced by IT, in particular, the Internet. It enables customers, consumers, and companies to form powerful new relationships that would not be possible without the enabling technologies.

- For businesses, electronic commerce includes
- Performing transactions with customers over the Internet for purposes such as home shopping, banking, and electronic cash use

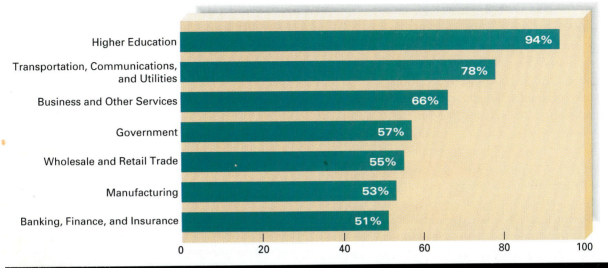

FIGURE 1.4

Attention Knowledge Workers! Work from Home[10]

- Performing transactions with other organizations through the use of electronic data interchange (EDI)—the direct computer-to-computer transfer of transaction information contained in standard business documents such as invoices and orders
- Gathering information relating to consumer market research and competitors (called competitive scanning)
- Distributing information to prospective customers through interactive advertising, sales, and marketing efforts

Electronic commerce is the great new business horizon, and we have yet to realize its full potential. For 1999, electronic commerce on the Internet was estimated to be about $31 billion. By 2003, that number is expected to rise to $380 billion. But $380 billion is only a very small, small portion of the world's total commerce. And electronic commerce will make serious winners out of some and losers out of others. Indeed, many early ".com" companies are going out of business today because of their failure to implement electronic commerce correctly. In short, you can't simply create a Web site and expect your customers to beat a virtual path to you. You must still follow sound business principles and guidelines. Some of those have certainly changed for an electronic environment, but they do still exist.

Electronic commerce is also giving rise to many "best business practices," such as telecommuting and the virtual workplace (see Figure 1.4). Telecommuting and the virtual workplace go hand in hand:

> **Telecommuting** is the use of communications technologies (such as the Internet) to work in a place other than a central location.
>
> The **virtual workplace** is a technology-enabled workplace. No walls. No boundaries. Work anytime, anyplace, linked to other people and information you need, wherever they are.[11]

Today, it's estimated that over 25 million people in the United States telecommute, and that figure is expected to grow by 20 percent over the next several years.[12] Telecommuting and the virtual workplace are—in reality—internalized electronic commerce. After all, some of your customers exist within your organization. So why not communicate and interact with them electronically?

At the end of each chapter, you'll find a section entitled *Real HOT Electronic Commerce*. In these sections, you'll learn how businesses are performing (and how you can perform) electronic commerce functions such as accepting orders over the Internet, competitive scanning, finding business opportunities, and finding investors. In the *Real HOT* section at the end of this chapter, you'll learn how to perform an electronic commerce function vitally important to you—that of finding a job on the Internet.

Knowledge Worker Computing

In every organization today, you'll find people sitting at powerful workstations and PCs doing their own information processing. Some of these people may be performing simple tasks, such as writing letters and generating graphs, but others are developing sophisticated order-entry systems that run on a network or three-dimensional drawings to demonstrate certain product features. All these are examples of knowledge worker computing. **Knowledge worker computing** places technology, technology power, software, information, and technology knowledge in the hands of those who need it—knowledge workers. So, knowledge worker computing involves you in more than just developing a budget using spreadsheet software, creating a presentation using presentation graphics software, or using a system that someone else has developed. It requires you to take an active role in developing systems that support your specific needs or the needs of a team. Knowledge worker computing might involve

- Giving you telecommuting tools so that you can work wherever and whenever needed
- Letting you develop personal database applications so you can maintain information for your own processing needs
- Setting up networks that allow departments to develop and maintain their own applications
- Setting up Web sites so customers can order products and services
- Giving access to information to those people who need it so they can make the right decisions at the right time

The list of possibilities is endless. But the most important thing to know about knowledge worker computing is that it places *technology knowledge* in your hands. As a knowledge worker, your responsibilities may very well include using telecommuting tools, setting up a personal database, evaluating hardware technologies to determine the best one for a given situation, and so on.

Information Technology
Its Role in the New Business

Information technology, as both an industry and business resource, is still in its infancy. In the 1950s, businesses embarked on the first widespread use of computers primarily as tools for recording and processing accounting transactions. Thus IT has only really been a part of business for about the last 40 years. Nonetheless, IT is one of the most important resources in today's business environment, and successful businesses are investing heavily in IT. But what exactly is information technology, or IT, and how are businesses using information technology?

Formally defined, **information technology (IT)** is any computer-based tool that people use to work with information and support the information and information-processing needs of an organization. IT includes keyboards, mice, screens, printers, modems, payroll software, word processing software, and operating system software, just to name a few. And how are businesses using IT? They use IT in four ways to support (1) information-processing tasks, (2) decision-making tasks, (3) shared information through decentralized computing, and (4) innovation.

Supporting Information-Processing Tasks

First and foremost, businesses are using IT to support basic information-processing tasks. These tasks range from computing and printing payroll checks, to creating presentations, to setting up Web sites from which customers can order products.

As you consider information-processing tasks, you can easily categorize various IT tools according to their purpose. To help you remember the categories of IT tools, we've created the 5 Cs of information-processing tasks (see Table 1.1). These include

1. **Capturing information**—at its point of origin with input devices
2. **Conveying information**—in its most useful form with output devices
3. **Creating information**—to obtain new information with the CPU and internal memory (RAM)
4. **Cradling information**—for use at a later time with storage devices
5. **Communicating information**—to other people or another location with telecommunications technologies.

You can consider each of these information-processing tasks individually, but eventually you have to combine them to create a system that handles all the tasks. Why? Because any particular business function—whether finance, marketing, human resource manage-

TABLE 1.1 The 5Cs: Categories of Information-Processing Tasks and IT Tools

Information-Processing Task	Description	IT Tools
Capturing information	Obtaining information at its point of origin	Input technologies: • Mouse • Keyboard • Bar code reader
Conveying information	Presenting information on its most useful form	Output technologies: • Screen • Printer • Monitor
Creating information	Processing information to create new information	Computer's brain: • CPU • RAM
Cradling information	Storing information for use at a later time	Storage technologies: • Hard disk • CD-ROM • DVD
Communicating information	Sending information to other people or another location	Telecommunications technologies: • Modem • Satellite • Digital pager

ment, or distribution—always involves these five information-processing tasks. We would encourage you to read through *Extended Learning Module D* to learn more about the specific IT tools within each category.

You may notice that software is not included in the 5 Cs. That's because software is a fundamental part of each information-processing task. For example, if you use automatic speech recognition, you're using a variety of IT tools including software that distinguishes your spoken words to form sentences. No matter what information-processing task you perform, software is always involved.

Supporting Decision-Making Tasks

When businesses use IT to process information such as payroll or a sales order, we refer to it as online transaction processing. ***Online transaction processing (OLTP)*** involves gathering input information, processing that information, and updating existing information to reflect the gathered and processed information. Businesses also use IT to support decision-making tasks, what we call online analytical processing. ***Online analytical processing (OLAP)*** is the manipulation of information to support decision making.

OLAP can range from performing simple queries on a database to determine which customers have overdue accounts to employing sophisticated artificial intelligence tools such as neural networks and genetic algorithms to solve a complex problem or take advantage of an opportunity. So, we say that OLTP supports efficiency (doing things the right way—the cheapest, the fastest, and so on) while OLAP support effectiveness (doing the right things or making the right decisions).

Chapter 4 is devoted entirely to decision support systems and artificial intelligence—IT tools that support decision-making processes. You can also perform OLAP by using databases and data warehouses, which we discuss in Chapter 3.

Supporting Shared Information through Decentralized Computing

At Bass Brewery—one of England's largest beer manufacturers—variety is the spice of life that guarantees a high level of sales in a market that demands widely varying products and batch sizes.[13] Bass produces more than 50 types of beer in more than 150 different packages. To support this, Bass uses an automated state-of-the-art networked computer system. With this networked computer system, Bass has reduced product transition time from hours to just a few minutes.

With the touch of a computer screen, the production manager can view outstanding orders then switch all the production facilities from one type of beer to another. This includes starting cleaning fluid throughout the brew house and electronically sending recipes to the brew house vats and information about bottling sizes and labels to the packaging hall. The key for Bass is twofold—decentralized computing and shared information (see Figure 1.5).

Decentralized computing is an environment in which an organization splits computing power and locates it in functional business areas as well as on the desktops of knowledge workers. This is possible because of the proliferation of less expensive, more powerful, and smaller systems including desktop computers, laptop computers, and minicomputers. ***Shared information*** is an environment in which an organization's information is organized in one central location, allowing anyone to access and use it as they need to.

Today, most organizations are like Bass—they have created decentralized computing structures while bringing together the entire spectrum of the organization's information in an orderly fashion so that it can be accessed and used by anyone who needs it. This structure of information is most often a database, which is designed to directly support the concept of shared information. Throughout the organization, people now use software to provide specific updates to databases and have access to powerful software that lets them sift through the database to find any information they need.

At Signet Corp., sifting through a database is big business.[14] According to Richard Fairbank, "It's all about collecting information on 150 million prospective customers, and on the basis of data alone, making credit and marketing decisions." What Signet is looking for are good credit risks who don't pay off their balances each month. Many of these people carry balances near $5,000 and pay interest at annual rates ranging from 13 to 17 percent. Credit cards, interest rates, and shared information—they all go hand in hand in the credit world.

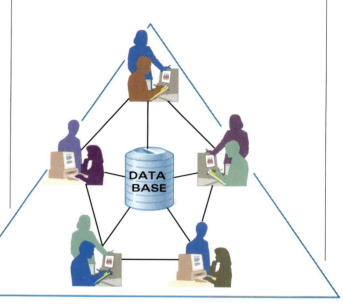

FIGURE 1.5
Shared Information through Decentralized Computing

Supporting Innovation

IT tools not only support information-processing tasks, decision-making tasks, and shared information through decentralized computing, they also enable innovation. Consider FedEx—the first package freight company to offer package delivery software that its customers can use to electronically request package pickup and check the status of packages during delivery. All the other major package delivery services (including the U.S. Postal Service) were forced to quickly develop similar software or risk losing their customer base to a company that provided a more innovative and efficient way to handle information-processing tasks related to delivering packages.

Throughout this text, you'll find literally hundreds of examples of the innovative use of technology to gain and sustain a competitive advantage. If you want some everyday examples that touch your own life, complete the *On Your Own* project on the next page.

Information
A New Key Business Resource

Information is one of the three key business resources in *The MIS Challenge*, and it is the basis on which many

INDUSTRY PERSPECTIVE

Financial Services

Shedding Pen and Paper for Decentralized Information

Making the transition from pen and paper to technology can be both challenging and rewarding. At Provident Mutual Life, regional vice presidents until recently used paper, pencils, and notebooks to maintain contact lists for brokers, dealers, and agent reps. As Frank Constantino, Provident's systems vice president, explained, "Even if what the regional vice presidents had didn't work particularly well, many of them were wed to it. Key for any change was having something really easy to use, something that would show significant improvement early on."

So, Provident chose to implement an Oracle relational database for maintaining contact information. Says Frank, "We wanted to have a common platform and a centralized database that would house all the information." The Oracle database certainly provides for sharing information, but decentralized computing was also key.

Several times a day, Provident's people can easily synchronize information on their laptops with information in the central database. And they can do this in just a few minutes with a simple phone call.

Many organizations today have latent and hidden knowledge throughout their structure. The key lies in centralizing all that information, while still giving people access to it whenever and wherever they need it. These are the concepts of decentralized computing and shared information. Decentralized computing provides people with the flexibility to handle their own specific information-processing tasks. Information sharing, on the other hand, guarantees everyone in the organization—regardless of location—access to and use of any needed information.[15] ❖

---

organizations operate in today's business environment, which brings us to an interesting question. What *is* information exactly? You can't really put your hands on it, which means that it's intangible and its value is extremely difficult to measure. But today's businesses are banking on their information, so it must be important.

To understand the nature of information and exactly what it is, you must understand another term—data. **Data** are raw facts or observations that describe a particular phenomenon. For example, the current temperature, the cost of a part, and your age are all data. **Information,** then is simply data that have a particular meaning within a specific context. For example, if you're trying to decide what to wear, the current temperature is *information* because it's pertinent to your decision at hand (what to wear)—the cost of a part, however, is not. Information may be data that have been processed in some way or presented in a more meaningful fashion. In business, for instance, the cost of a part may be information to a sales clerk, but it may represent only data to an accountant who is responsible for determining the value of current inventory levels. For the accountant, the cost of the part and current quantity on hand represent data the he or she uses to calculate

ON YOUR OWN

Redefining Business Operations through IT Innovation

FedEx and its customer-oriented package delivery software is just one of hundreds of examples of IT innovation that you'll find in business every day and in your personal life. Below we've listed several different business environments that have used IT for innovation to change the way you live your life. For each, define its innovation through IT.

1. Airline
2. Banks
3. Grocery stores
4. Phone companies
5. Hotels
6. Fuel stations
7. Utility companies
8. Cable TV providers

Can you think of any other types of businesses that have found innovation through IT and changed the way you live your life? ❖

INDUSTRY PERSPECTIVE

".com"

Free Long-Distance Phone Calls on the Internet

Innovative uses of technology are all around you. And the ones to come will forever change how you live your life. Consider using the Internet to make long-distance phone calls. And consider using the Internet to make free long-distance phone calls.

One such dot-com company that offers you this ability is Net2Phone at http://www.net2phone.com. You can sign up for free and make all the U.S. long-distance phone calls you want for free. The person you're calling doesn't even have to own a computer.

On your end, you can use a special phone provided by Net2Phone or the microphone and speakers that probably came with your computer when you bought it. So, you connect to the Internet and then to Net2Phone's Web site and make your call. It's that simple—and it's free, except for the monthly fee that your ISP charges you. But you're already spending that money any way. So, why not use it to make free long-distance phone calls?

This innovative use of technology will affect not only your life but the entire telecommunications industry as well. Large telephone service providers such as AT&T and MCI are no longer including long-distance revenues in their long-term projections, even international long distance. Right now, you have to pay 7 cents a minute to Net2Phone to make a call to Europe or Japan. But that will someday be free as well. ❖

---

the current value of inventory for that part. The current value of inventory for that part is the information the accountant derives from the two pieces of data.

For Customer Moment of Value

Information Time, Location, and Form

As you consider information, you can do so in terms of customer moment of value. After all, what you'll produce as a knowledge worker is information, and you'll pass that information to someone else (your customer). And it doesn't matter if that person is a true "customer" of your organization or another employee within your organization—he or she is still your customer. So, as you create information you should consider your customer's moment of value—time, location, and form (see Figure 1.6).

The Time Dimension

The time dimension of information encompasses two aspects—(1) providing information when your customer wants it and (2) providing information that describes the time period your customer wants. The first really deals with timeliness. Information can in fact become old and obsolete. For example, if you want to make a stock trade today, you need to know the price of the stock right now. If you have to wait a day to get stock prices, you may not survive in today's turbulent securities market.

TIME
- When your customer wants it
- Describing the right time period

LOCATION
- Access it wherever your customer wants

FORM
- Audio, text, video, etc.
- Free of errors

FIGURE 1.6

Customer Moment of Value for Information

The second time aspect deals with providing information that describes the appropriate time period. For example, most utility companies provide you with a bill that not only tells you of your current usage and the average temperature but also compares that information to last month and perhaps the same month last year. This type of information can help you better manage your utilities or simply understand that this month's high utility bill was caused by inclement weather.

The Location Dimension

The location dimension of information deals with providing information to your customer where he or she wants it. This simply means that your customers should have access to the information they need regardless of where they are—on a plane, in a hotel room, at home, at work, or even driving down the road. Of course, there are many technologies that support the location dimension of customer moment of value, most notably the Internet. Today, you can be almost anywhere in the world and use the Internet to access almost any information you need.

To keep certain information private and secure while accessing it remotely, many organizations are creating intranets. An *intranet* is an internal organizational Internet that is guarded against outside access by special security software called a firewall. Intranets look and work just like the Internet. So, if your organization has an intranet and you want to access information on it while away from the office, all you need is Web browser software, a modem, and the password that will allow you through the firewall.

US West has created an intranet called the *Global Village*.[16] Employees can connect to the *Global Village* and meet in online chat rooms, exchange documents, and discuss ongoing projects, even with employees located in remote geographical areas. While doing this, the firewall ensures that no one outside US West can gain access to the intranet information.

The Form Dimension

The form dimension of information deals with a variety of aspects. One of them is simply providing information to your customers in a form they want—audio, text files, video, animation, graphical, and others. It also deals with accuracy. So, the information you provide must always be free of errors. Think of information as you would a physical product. If you buy a product and it's defective, you become an unsatisfied customer. Likewise, if you receive information that is incorrect, you're very unhappy as well. Information is a valuable resource and also a commodity you provide to customers. Make sure it's always correct and error free.

The Flows of Information in an Organization

Up, Down, Horizontal, and Out

Because of the nature of shared information through decentralized computing, information in an organization flows in four directions—up, down, horizontally, and outward. To consider these flows, let's first briefly look at the structure of an organization. Most people view a traditional organization as a pyramid with four levels and many sides (see Figure 1.7). At the top is *strategic management,* which provides an organization with overall direction and guidance. The second level is often called *tactical management,* which develops the goals and strategies outlined by strategic management. The third level is *operational management,* which manages and directs the day-to-day operations and implementations of the goals and strategies. Finally, the fourth level of the organization comprises nonmanagement employees who actually perform daily activities, such as order processing, developing and producing goods and services, and servicing customers.

Information that flows upward, or the *upward flow of information*, describes the current state of the organization based on its daily transactions. When a sale

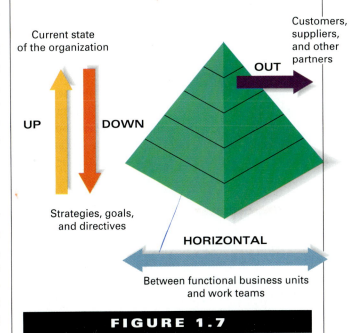

FIGURE 1.7

An Organization and Its Information Flows

INDUSTRY PERSPECTIVE

Health Care

Intranet Telephone Directory Saves Children's Healthcare $15,000 per Year

It's true. By placing its organization-wide telephone directory on an intranet, Children's Healthcare of Atlanta saves over $15,000 per year. But that's not the real reason why Children's won *CIO Magazine's 2000 Web Business 50/50* award. Its intranet, called *Careforce Connection*, provides much more.

Careforce Connection maintains a managed care database that provides detailed information on the managed care plans in which the hospital participates as well as which doctors are involved in what plans. Doctors use the intranet to verify which plans cover different types of drugs. Nurses use the intranet to determine which tests must be sent to outside labs. Overall, the intranet has even helped reduce the number of managed care claims rejected because of inaccurate or incorrect information.

Children's averages about 3,500 user sessions per day on its intranet, spread among its 4,500 employees. Those employees can look up a variety of information ranging from simple telephone numbers to educational courses taught in-house. As Camille Evans, Children's director of electronic communications, explains, "It's a wonderful tool for connecting everyone." And the intranet is completely secure and private, ensuring that no one outside Children's can gain access to *Careforce*.[17] ❖

---

occurs, for example, that information originates at the lowest level of the organization and then is passed up through the various levels of management. IT plays a vital role in the upward flow of information. Information gathered as part of the everyday operations is consolidated by IT and passed upward to decision makers who monitor and respond to problems and opportunities.

The *downward flow of information* consists of the strategies, goals, and directives that originate at one level and are passed to lower levels. For example, in 2000 General Motors decided to phase out its line of Oldsmobile automobiles. This strategic management decision was passed down to tactical management, which determined how to restructure the organization. Those decisions were passed to car dealers, who determined how to rid their inventory and what incentives to offer. Incidentally, GM is still going through this process, which will probably take several years.

Information that flows horizontally, or the *horizontal flow of information*, is between functional business units and work teams. The concept is quite simple—why reinvent the wheel? Throughout an organization, there is much knowledge and expertise, and much of it needs to be shared across departmental and unit barriers. IT tools such as intranets and databases definitely play a role in the horizontal flow of information.

Finally, the *outward flow of information* consists of information that is communicated to customers, suppliers, distributors, and other partners outside the organization for the purpose of doing business. This outward flow of information (and its corresponding inward flow of information) is really what electronic commerce is all about. Today, no organization is an island, and you must ensure that your organization has the IT tools to communicate outwardly with all types of business partners.

What Information Describes

Internal, External, Objective, and Subjective

Different jobs need different information, so different people in your organization need different types of information. Information may be internal, external, objective, subjective, or some combination of the four. *Internal information* describes specific operational aspects of the organization, whereas *external information* describes the environment surrounding the organization. *Objective information* quantifiably describes something that is known; *subjective information* attempts to describe something that is unknown.

Consider a bank that faces the decision of what interest rate to offer on a CD. That bank will use internal information (how many customers it has who can afford to buy a CD), external information (what other banks are offering), objective information (what is today's prime interest rate), and subjective information (what prime interest is expected to be several months down the road).

Knowledge Workers
Information and Technology Users

To this point, we've looked at *The MIS Challenge,* characteristics of today's new business, information technology, and information as a new business resource. We have done so to give you a broad overview of the nature of business and the role of IT and information. Let's now turn our attention to the most important resource in business—you as a knowledge worker. Recall that, as a knowledge worker, you work with and produce information as a product. And it really doesn't matter if you use a high-powered workstation or a calculator, you're still a knowledge worker, responsible for processing information that your business needs to survive.

To succeed as a knowledge worker in today's information-based business environment, you need to understand the true nature of information, what it means to be an information-literate knowledge worker, and the ethical responsibilities of working with information.

Being an Information-Literate Knowledge Worker

In the Information Age

Knowing the appropriate time, location, and form dimensions of your information needs is a major step toward becoming an information-literate knowledge worker in the information age. But it doesn't stop there—knowing what you need is only part of the information equation. You also need to know such things as how and where to obtain that information and what the information means once you receive it. Let's consider the following definition for an information-literate knowledge worker:

> An ***information-literate knowledge worker*** can define what information is needed, knows how and where to obtain that information, understands the meaning of the information once received, and can act appropriately, based on the information, to help the organization achieve the greatest advantage. In all instances, an information-literate knowledge worker always uses information according to ethical and legal constructs.

It may seem like a mouthful of a definition, but if you look at it closely it's actually composed of five distinct charges to you. These include

- **Charge 1**—You must define what information you need.
- **Charge 2**—You must know how and where to obtain information.
- **Charge 3**—You must understand the meaning of the information.
- **Charge 4**—You must act appropriately based on the information.
- **Charge 5**—You must use information adhering to both legal and ethical constructs.

In the next section, we'll address the fifth charge (ethical and legal considerations regarding the use of information); right now let's focus on the first four.

Consider a unique, real-life example of an information-literate knowledge worker. Several years ago, a manager of a retail store on the East Coast received some interesting information—diaper sales on Friday evening accounted for a large percentage of total diaper sales for the week. Most people in this situation would immediately jump to charge 4 and decide to make sure that diapers are always well stocked on Friday or run a special on diapers during that time to increase sales, but not our information-literate knowledge worker. She first looked at the information and decided it was not complete. That is, she needed more information before she could act.

She decided the information she needed was why a rash of diaper sales occurred during that time and who was buying them (charge 1—define the information you need). That information was not stored within the system, so she stationed an employee in the diaper aisle on Friday evening who recorded any information pertinent to the situation (charge 2—know how and where to obtain information). The store manager learned that young businessmen purchased the most diapers on Friday evening. Apparently, they had been instructed to buy the weekend supply of diapers on their way home from work (charge 3—understand what the information means). Her response, which is charge 4, was to stock premium domestic and imported beer near the diapers. Since then, Friday evening is not only a big sale time for diapers but also for premium domestic and imported beer.

These four charges of becoming an information-literate knowledge worker in the information age are actually all about problem solving. That is, understanding the problem (or in the diaper case, opportunity) and determining what information you need to solve the problem or take advantage of the opportunity; knowing where and how to get the information you need to make a decision; evaluating the information once it's received and formulating several alternatives to address the problem or opportunity; and finally, acting appropriately based on the information.

IT tools are great for helping you through this problem-solving or advantage-realizing process. In fact, many IT-based systems are designed specifically to help you solve a problem or take advantage of an opportunity. We call these decision support systems and artificial intelligence, and you'll learn more about them in Chapter 4, including group decision support systems, expert systems, neural network, and genetic algorithms.

> **CAREER OPPORTUNITY**
> While you're working with information, never jump to conclusions. Always stop for a moment and ask yourself, "What does this information really mean?" "Do I have all the information I need to make a decision?" That's what our East Coast retail store manager did, and it definitely paid off.

Charges 1 and 2 are usually related to the task you're trying to perform. For example, if you're trying to decide where to build a new store, it's up to you to decide what information you need as well as where that information might be located and in what way you need to go about getting it. Charges 3 and 4 are related not only to the task you're trying to perform, but also to your ability to see what's "not there" or "around the corner" and be innovative and creative in choosing the right alternative. Your abilities to do this will measure what we refer to as your **level of information literacy**. Levels of information literacy include being a professional, an expert, or an innovator (see Figure 1.8). In the previous diaper example, these three levels might look like this:

- Professional—"I'm aware that diaper sales increase on Friday evenings, so let's make sure that diapers are well stocked during that time."
- Expert—"I understand that diaper sales increase on Friday evenings and that we could capitalize on that by keeping diapers well stocked and running a sale during that time to increase revenue."

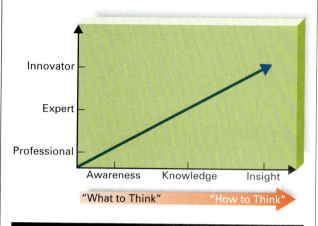

FIGURE 1.8
Levels of Information Literacy

- Innovator—"The majority of diaper sales can be attributed to businessmen coming home from work. Let's make sure diapers are always well stocked but, more important, let's place premium beer near the diapers to entice the businessmen to purchase a product with a high gross margin."

Notice also from Figure 1.8 that as a professional and expert you deal mainly with "what to think," and that's what your curriculum is designed to do. In this textbook for example, you'll learn about the various issues involved in MIS (awareness) and the potential ramifications of those issues and how you deal with them (knowledge). What neither we nor any other text or instructor can teach you is how to gain insight from your knowledge. We can teach you "what to think" but not "how to think." Your ability to learn how to think will define you as a true innovator.

Being a Socially Responsible Knowledge Worker

In the Information Age

The first four changes in becoming an information-literate knowledge worker challenge you to learn how to use information to benefit your organization. But you must also realize that you have certain social responsibilities as well. A college athletic coach, for instance, is charged with creating a winning team for the school. At the same time, however, he or she is also charged with making certain the athletes succeed in their studies and do not take any drugs (such as steroids) that might improve their performance, but harm them.

INDUSTRY PERSPECTIVE

Entertainment & Publishing

Internet + Entertainment = Intertainment

The young generation now growing up with technology looks at computers much differently from the way older generations view them. Young people think if you can't play a game on it then it's not a computer. If this seems trivial, it's not. Technology today is not just for work—people see a computer as an entertainment or relaxing tool. Even if you use your computer just to surf the Internet or perhaps bid on auction items at eBay, you're using your computer for relaxation or entertainment.

Consider what's happening right now in the hand-held or personal digital assistant market. Originally, these devices were developed with business purposes in mind—appointment books, calendering functions, address books, note taking, and the like. Today, PDA companies are including all of those functions but developing and marketing their PDAs as hand-held "wireless intertainment centers." Cybiko is one such product. Using a wireless modem, you can easily connect to the Internet for e-mail, but you can also download games and music. Cybiko even comes with many built-in games including word find and the standard solitaire.

This really makes sense when you think about it. The previous (and still current) craze among young people is video games that you play on your TV. The natural extension of that is hand-held video game systems that include Internet access so you can download and play whatever game you want.

Technology is not just for business—it's also for intertainment.[18] ❖

As a knowledge worker, your charge is similar. You're charged with using information in the best possible way, but you're also charged with using that information in a socially responsible way. The last charge—use information adhering to both legal and ethical constructs—falls into the general category of ethics. **Ethics** are the principles and standards that guide our behavior toward other people.

Ethical conduct is a key concern in business today, especially in the use of information and IT. As a knowledge worker, you need to understand that ethics are different from laws. Laws require or prohibit some action on your part, whereas ethics are more a matter of personal interpretation. Consider the following examples:

1. Copying software you purchased or making copies for your friends and charging them for copies
2. Making an extra backup of your software just in case both the copy you are using and the primary backup fail for some reason
3. Giving out the phone numbers of your friends and family to MCI for its Friends & Family calling plan, without asking them for permission

Each of these is either ethically or legally incorrect. In the second example, you may have been ethically correct in making an extra backup copy (because you did not share it with anyone), but according to most software licenses you're prohibited by law from making more than one backup copy.

To help you better understand the relationship between ethical and legal acts (or the opposite), consider Figure 1.9. The table is composed of 4 quadrants and you always want to remain in quadrant I. If all your actions fall in that quadrant, you'll always be acting legally and ethically, and thus in a socially responsible way.

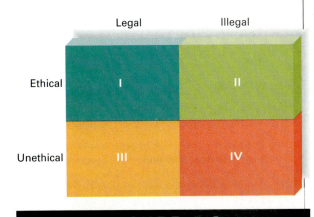

FIGURE 1.9

Acting Ethically and Legally[19]

In business, the question of ethics is an overriding concern because of the widespread use of IT to capture information. For example, if a business invests money to capture information about you as you make a purchase, does that information then belong to the business that captured the information or do you still have privacy rights regarding its distribution? Here are a few more examples to ponder:

- If you find a coin in a pay telephone, does it belong to you, should you turn it over to the phone company, or should you try to find the person who last used the phone?
- Does a business have the right to read your e-mail if it explicitly reserved that right in the employment contract you signed? Is the business then financially and legally responsible for any flaming e-mail you distribute? *Flaming* is the distribution of an online communication that offends someone because of the use of obscene, derogatory, or inappropriate language.
- Do organizations have the right to generate mailing lists of their customers and sell those lists to other businesses?
- If you see a physician for lower back pain that turns out to be nothing more than a result of bad sitting posture and then later apply for health insurance, does the physician have the right to notify the insurance carrier of your previous problem?
- If you find a money clip in the parking lot of a mall, are you required to take it to the lost and found and turn it in? What if it contains $2? $100? $1000?
- If you receive an unsolicited product in the mail along with a bill, can you keep the product without paying for it? Should you send it back? Was the company acting ethically or legally in sending you an unsolicited product and then asking you to pay for it?

Throughout this textbook, you'll read about becoming a socially responsible knowledge worker with respect to the use of IT and information. Many of our discussions will focus on various IT crimes such as viruses, hacking, and violating the privacy rights of individuals. The ethical and legal aspects of using information and IT are not only important for business, but also expensive—whether violating ethical standards (as with Chevron—see the *On Your Own* box) and laws or taking measures to avoid unethical and illegal acts.

For example, it's estimated that one of every two copies of software in use in the world today is a pirated copy (see Figure 1.10). Imagine how much money software manufacturers are losing to pirated software. Their sales and net revenues would easily double if pirated software were nonexistent.

We've written this text specifically for you as you prepare to become a knowledge worker in today's information age and to introduce you to management information systems within a business environment. It doesn't matter if you plan to be a financial analyst, a tax accountant, a marketing specialist, a compensation

PIRATED SOFTWARE LOSERS AND USERS

TOP LOSERS		TOP USERS	
Revenues Lost by Software Publishers (in billions)		Percentage of Illegally Acquired Software	
Japan	$1.31	China	98
United States	$1.05	Russia	95
France	$0.48	Thailand	92
Italy	$0.26	India & Pakistan	87
United Kingdom & Ireland	$0.24	Czech & Slovak Republics	84
WORLD TOTAL	$8.08	WORLD AVERAGE	49

FIGURE 1.10

Pirates on the Prowl[20]

ON YOUR OWN

E-Mail: Electronic Mail or Expensive Mail?

In February 1995, an employee at Chevron came across what he thought was an interesting and funny list—"25 Reasons Why Beer Is Better Than Women." He quickly logged into his e-mail and distributed the list to many people. The only problem was that one of the people who received the e-mail was a woman, and she was offended by it. What followed was a lot of legal mumbo jumbo and an eventual out-of-court settlement worth $2 million that Chevron had to pay to the offended employee—definitely an example of when e-mail becomes expensive mail.

Most people agree that the original sender should not have distributed the list. It was mail that was potentially embarrassing and offensive to some people and, therefore, should not have been distributed as a matter of ethics. What people don't agree on, however, is whether or not the company was at fault for not monitoring and stopping the potentially offensive mail. What are your thoughts? Before you decide, follow the accompanying diagram and consider the consequences of your answers.[21]

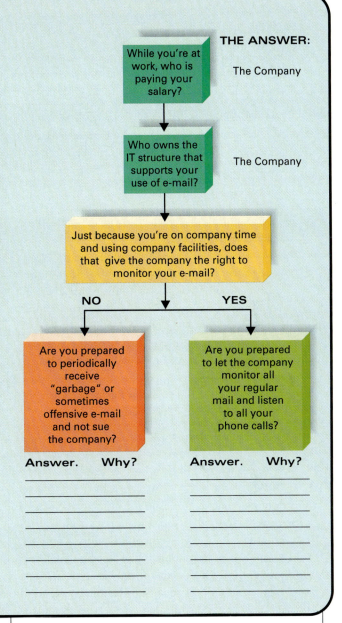

---

director, or a computer programmer, this text will help you understand that the use of technology in any organization will be successful only if **you** help plan for, develop, manage, and use the three most important business resources in *The MIS Challenge*. Those three resources are information, information technology, and people. Without all three working together in a coordinated and meaningful fashion, IT will not be successful, the right information will not be made available to the right people at the right time, and the organization will ultimately suffer.

Your career opportunity lies in making these three resources work together effectively. To do that, you need to learn about information, information technology, people, and the issues involved in bringing these together. We will help you do just that in the rest of this book.

CLOSING CASE STUDY

How Much of Your Personal Information Do You Want Businesses to Know?

The information age has brought about great debates with respect to information availability and privacy.

KNOWLEDGE WORKER'S -LIST

***The Management Information Systems Challenge* and Management Information Systems.** *The Management Information Systems Challenge* addresses three aspects:

1. *What businesses do:* Serve their customers.
2. *Customer moment of value:* Providing service when the customer wants it (time), where the customer wants it (location), how the customer wants it (form), and in a manner guaranteed to the customer (perfect delivery).
3. *The role of information technology:* To supply a set of tools that provide the right people with the right information at the right time.

Management information systems (MIS) deals with the planning for, development, management, and use of information technology tools to help people perform all tasks related to information processing and management. No matter what career path you choose, you will be responsible for some portion of the MIS function.

Important Factors Shaping the New Business. There are many factors shaping today's new business environment. They represent a significant career opportunity for you if you understand them and are prepared to take advantage of them in the workplace. Some of the factors include

1. *Globalization:* The opportunity to expand internationally and reach a market of over 6 billion consumers.
2. *Information as a key resource:* Knowledge is power, and knowledge comes from having information.
3. *Electronic commerce:* The performance of all functions related to business in an electronic fashion.
4. *Knowledge worker computing:* The placement of technology, technology power, software, information, and technology knowledge in the hands of those who need it—knowledge workers.

The Role of Information Technology in the New Business. Information technology (IT) is one of the three key resources in *The MIS Challenge*. Formally defined, ***information technology (IT)*** is any computer-based tool that people use to work with information and support the information and information-processing needs of an organization. For you, the role of IT is

---

For example, most counties in the United States provide searchable Internet-based databases with real estate information. You can type in an address and see what a family paid for a home, when they bought it, and often even how it's financed. You can also type in a person's name and find the same information. Is that good or bad? Probably depends on your perspective. Consider these other examples.

Mitchells of Westport

Mitchells is an upscale old-fashioned clothing retailer that's exploiting technology and information to create one-to-one customer service. With a database of more than 50,000 customers and 10 years of transaction data, Mitchells can sift through information to better serve its customers. As CEO Jack Mitchell explains, "What that means in real terms is that we can look at historical preferences of our customers, and, for instance, see if a customer who used to buy American suits likes a more contemporary European look in his clothing."

Mitchells even tracks information on its high-revenue customers such as the company they work for, their position, birthdays, anniversaries, and kids' name and ages. Mitchells uses this type of information to constantly communicate with its customers and create a very real one-to-one relationship.

Acxiom Corp.

Most people have never heard of Acxiom Corp., but it is most certainly aware that you exist, even to the extent that it may know your height and weight. Acxiom specializes in providing information to organizations that want to market products and services. Since the mid-1980s, Acxiom has been gathering information and building a special file called InfoBase. InfoBase contains some or all of the following facts on 195 million Americans: home ownership, age, estimated income, cars owned, occupation, buying habits, types of credit cards used, children, and even height and weight.

For a fee, you can buy any or all of this information from Acxiom on any customer demographic (perhaps

1. *To support information-processing tasks*—using IT tools to capture, convey, create, cradle, and communicate information
2. *To support decision-making tasks*—through technology-enabled online analytical processing
3. *To support shared information through decentralizing computing*—organizing all information in one location and providing knowledge workers with the IT tools to access that information
4. *To support innovation*—determining how IT can significantly alter what your business does to achieve the greatest advantage

Information as a Key Business Resource. Information is one of the three key business resources in *The MIS Challenge*, and it is the basis by which many organizations operate in today's business environment. **Information** is data that have a particular meaning within a specific context, and **data** are any raw facts or observations that describe a particular phenomenon.

Information considerations include:

1. *Customer moment of value*—the time when your customer wants information, the location where your customer wants information, and the form in which your customer wants information
2. *Flows of information in an organization*—up, down, horizontal, and out
3. *What information describes*—internal, external, objective, and subjective information

Their Role as Information-Literate Knowledge Workers. Knowledge workers outnumber all other types of workers by a four-to-one margin. This simply means that businesses rely on information and, more important, on knowledge workers who understand the nature of information and how to use it. Knowledge workers who can do this are called information-literate knowledge workers. As an information-literate knowledge worker, you understand

1. *The dimensions of information*—according to time, location, and form.
2. *Your charges*—(1) defining what information you need, (2) knowing how and where to obtain information, (3) understanding the meaning of information, and (4) acting appropriately based on information. Meeting these four charges will define your ability to be a true innovator.
3. *Your charge as an ethical user of information*—being socially responsible as you manage and use information. ❖

---

just the people who live in your neighborhood). And Acxiom does sell this information to other organizations. For example, Allstate Corp. buys information concerning insurance applicants' credit reports, driving records, claims histories, and family relationships (just in case you have a relative who likes to speed) from Acxiom.

In today's world, information is big business, and the use of it is definitely enabled by information technology.[22,23]

◄ Questions ►

1. What is the role of information technology at Acxiom? Could it still maintain and provide such a wealth of information without using IT? Acxiom's InfoBase holds 350 terabytes of information. How much information is that? How many double-spaced pages of text would it take to hold all that information?
2. Acxiom and Mitchells have two entirely different sets of customers—one markets to organizations while the other markets to consumers. For each, define their customer moment of value concerning information. How do they differ? How are they the same?
3. What are the ethical and legal issues relating to the fact that Acxiom may know your height and weight and is certainly willing to sell that information to the highest bidder? Can Acxiom legally own that information and sell it to any and every organization?
4. From where do you think Acxiom gathers its information? Could it establish a partnership with other organizations such as Mitchells and buy personal information? How do you feel about this?
5. Many people dream of having a close personal relationship with a clothing retailer such as Mitchells. You simply walk in and the salesperson seems to know everything about you (and remembers you well). However, Mitchells communicates extensively with its customers by e-mail. Would you ever get tired of receiving e-mails

that solicit your business? How many of those e-mails do you receive now on a weekly basis? What steps can you take to avoid them?

6. Overall, what's your view of the information age in which we live? Are we better off because we have access to a wealth of information, including personal information? Should organizations such as Acxiom and Mitchells exploit their information for all its worth? Should they consider your feelings? ❖

Electronic Commerce
Business and You on the Internet

Using the Internet as a Tool to Find a Job

Electronic commerce is a great new business horizon. And it's not "just around the corner" any more. Electronic commerce is already here and businesses all over the world are taking advantage of it. Today, information technology can help you land a job. You can use your knowledge of IT and IT itself to help you find potential employers, place your resume in their hands, locate summer internships, and learn the art of selling yourself during the interview and negotiation process. How? By simply cruising the Internet and using online job database and service providers as well as accessing information about how to prepare for an interview (among other things).

Are you taking advantage of the Internet to find a job? If you're not, we'd like to help you by introducing you to just a few of the thousands of Web sites that can help you find a job. In this section, we've included a number of Web sites related to finding a job through the Internet. On the Web site that supports this text (http://www.mhhe.com/haag, select "Electronic Commerce Projects"), we've provided direct links to all these Web sites as well as many, many more. These are a great starting point for completing this *Real HOT* section. We would also encourage you to search the Internet for others.

Job Databases

There are—quite literally—thousands of sites that provide you with databases of job postings. Some are better than others. Some focus on specific industries; others offer postings only for executive managers. For the best review of job Web sites, connect to two different places. The first is Web21's *100 Hot Jobs and Careers* at http://www.100hot.com/jobs. This site ranks the most popular job Web sites according to traffic (number of hits). The second is the *Career Resources Homepage* at http://www.rpi.edu/dept/cdc/homepage.html. This site provides the most comprehensive list of the available job Web sites. There, you'll find a list of over 1,000 job Web sites.

Think for a moment about the job you want. What would be its title? In which industry do you want to work? In what part of the country do you want to live? What special skills do you possess? (For example, if you're looking for an accounting job, you may be specializing in auditing.) Is there a specific organization for which you would like to work?

Connect to a couple of different databases, search for your job, and answer the following questions for each database.

A. What is the date of last update?

B. Are career opportunities abroad listed as a separate category or are they integrated with domestic jobs?

C. Can you search for a specific organization?

D. Can you search by geographic location? If so, how? By state? By city? By zip code?

E. Does the site provide direct links to e-mail addresses for those organizations posting jobs?

F. Can you apply for a position online? If so, how do you send your resume?

G. Can you search by a specific industry?

Creating and Posting an Electronic Resume

Most, if not all, job databases focus on two groups—employers and employees. As a potential employee, you search to find jobs that meet your qualifications and desires. Likewise, employers search job databases that contain resumes so they can find people (like you) who meet their qualifications and desires. In this instance, you need to build an electronic resume (e-resume) and leave it at the various job database sites as you perform your searches. That way, organizations performing searches can find you.

What you need to understand first is that building an e-resume is quite different from creating a paper resume. It really is! An e-resume (and the search for an e-resume) is built on key words. For example, if you put "tele-marketing experience" in your e-resume and a potential employer searches for "telemarketing experience," your e-resume may not appear as a match. Likewise, if a potential employer is looking for someone who can start work during the first of the summer and you enter your first available date as June 15, is that a match? So, building an e-resume is an important process and one that you should not take lightly.

Almost all the job database sites we've listed give you the ability to create and post an electronic resume. Visit two new job database sites (different from those you visited to find a job). In each, go through the process of creating an e-resume, posting it, and making some sort of modification to it. As you do, answer the following questions for each of the sites.

A. Do you have to register as a user to build an e-resume?

B. Once a potential employer performs a search that matches your e-resume, how can that employer contact you?

C. What valuable tips for building a good e-resume are available?

D. Once you build your e-resume, can you use it to perform a job search?

E. When you modify your e-resume, can you update your existing e-resume or must you delete the old one and create a new one?

F. How many key terms concerning your qualifications can you include in your e-resume?

G. For what time frame does your e-resume stay active?

Searching Newspapers the New-Fashioned Way

One of today's most popular ways to find a job is to search the classified sections of newspapers. Each Sunday (if your library is open) and Monday you can visit your local library and find a gathering of people searching through the classified sections of the *LA Times*, *Boston Herald*, and *Dallas Morning News* in the hope of finding a job. Most of these people are attempting to find a job in a specific geographic location. For example, a person looking in the *Dallas Morning News* is probably most interested in finding a job in the Dallas/Ft. Worth area. And as you might well guess, newspapers are not to be left off the Internet bandwagon. Today you can find hundreds of online editions of daily newspapers. And the majority of these provide their classified sections in some sort of searchable electronic format. Pick several newspapers, perform an online search for a job that interests you at each newspaper, and answer the following questions.

A. Can you search by location/city?

B. Can you search back issues or only the most recent issue?

C. Does the newspaper provide direct links to Web sites or provide some other profile information for those organizations posting jobs?

D. Does the newspaper provide direct links to e-mail addresses for those organizations posting jobs?

E. Is the newspaper affiliated with any of the major job database providers? If so, which one(s)?

Locating That "All Important" Internship

Have you ever noticed that a large number of jobs require experience? That being the case, how does someone gain such experience through a job when experience is required to get the job? As it turns out, that's always been a perplexing dilemma for many college students, and one way to solve it is by obtaining an internship. Internships provide you with valuable knowledge about your field, pay you for your work, and offer you that valuable "experience" you need to move up in your career.

At the end of this section, we've provided you with a number of Web sites that offer internship possibilities—visit a few of them. Did you find any internships in line with your career? What about pay—did you find both paying and nonpaying internships? How did these internship sites compare to the more traditional job database sites you looked at earlier? Why do you think this is true?

Interviewing and Negotiating

The Internet is a vast repository of information—no doubt more information than you'll ever need in your entire life. During the job search process however, the Internet can offer you very valuable specific information. In the area of interviewing and negotiating, for example, the Internet contains over 1,500 sites devoted to interviewing skills, negotiating tips, and the like.

Interviewing and negotiating are just as important as searching for a job. Once you line up that first important interview, you can still not land the job if you're not properly prepared. If you do receive a job offer, you may be surprised to know that you can negotiate such things as moving expenses, signing bonuses, and allowances for technology in your home.

We've provided Web sites for you on the next page that address the interviewing and negotiating skills you

need in today's marketplace. Review some of these sites (and any others that you may find). Then, develop a list of do's and don'ts for the interviewing process. Finally, develop a list of tips that seem helpful to you that will increase your effectiveness during the negotiation process. Once you've developed these two lists, prepare a short class presentation.

Going Right to the Source— The Organization You Want

Today, many organizations are posting positions they have open on their own Web sites. Their idea is simple. If you like an organization enough to visit its Web site, you might just want to work there. For example, if you connect to the *Gap* at http://www.gap.com and buy clothes online, you might consider working there if the opportunity is right.

Choose several organizations that you'd be interested in working for. For each organization, connect to its Web site, look for job opportunities, and answer the following questions:

A. Are you able to find job opportunities?

B. How difficult is it to find the job opportunities?

C. Are positions grouped or categorized by type?

D. Is a discussion of career paths included?

E. How do you obtain an application form?

F. Are there international opportunities available? Do the job descriptions include a list of qualifications?

G. Are there direct links to e-mail addresses for further questions?

Web Sites for Finding a Job

Service	Address
American's Job Bank	http://www.ajb.dni.us
NationJob	http://www.nationjob.com
Monster.com	http://www.monster.com
Headhunter.net	http://www.headhunter.com
JobOptions	http://www.joboptions.com

Newspapers	Address
LA Times	http://www.latimes.com
Minneapolis Star Tribune	http://www.startribune.com
Dallas Morning News	http://www.dallasnews.com
Denver Post	http://www.denverpost.com
New York Times	http://www.nytimes.com

Internship Sites
http://www.internships.wetfeet.com
http://www.studentadvantage.lycos.com
http://www.internships.com
http://www.jobweb.com/catapult/jintern.htm
http://www.rsinternships.com

Interviewing and Negotiating Sites
http://www.getinterviews.com
http://www.job-interview.net
http://www.interviewcoach.com
http://www.brassringcampus.com
http://www.collegegrad.com/intv

Organization	Address
IBM	http://www.ibm.com
Ford	http://www.ford.com
General Mills	http://www.generalmills.com
United Airline	http://www.ual.com
Hertz	http://www.hertz.com

Go to the Web site that supports this text: **http://www.mhhe.com/haag** and select "Electronic Commerce Projects."

We've included links to over 100 Web sites for using the Internet as a tool to find a job as well as Employment with the Government.

KEY TERMS AND CONCEPTS

Customer Moment of Value, 5
Data, 15
Decentralized Computing, 14
Electronic Commerce, 10
Ethics, 21
External Information, 18
Flaming, 22
Globalization, 9
Information, 15
Information Age, 4
Information-Literate Knowledge Worker, 19
Information Technology (IT), 12
Internal Information, 18
Intranet, 17
Knowledge Worker, 4
Knowledge Worker Computing, 12
Levels of Information Literacy, 20
Management Information System (MIS), 4
Management Information Systems Challenge, 4
Objective Information, 18
Online Analytical Processing (OLAP), 13
Online Transaction Processing (OLTP), 13
Operational Management, 17
Perfect Delivery, 6
Shared Information, 14
Strategic Management, 17
Subjective Information, 18
Tactical Management, 17
Telecommuting, 11
Transitional Firm, 9
Virtual Workplace, 11

SHORT-ANSWER QUESTIONS

1. What is a knowledge worker?
2. What is management information systems (MIS)? What are the three key resources of MIS?
3. What are the three aspects of *The Management Information Systems Challenge?*
4. What are important factors shaping today's business?
5. What is the difference between data and information?
6. What are the five charges of being an information-literate knowledge worker?
7. What are ethics?
8. What are the four characteristics of customer moment of value?
9. How is a wants-driven economy related to information as a key resource in the new business?
10. What is knowledge worker computing? Why is it important to you?

SHORT-QUESTION ANSWERS

For each of the following answers, provide an appropriate question:

1. Time, location, and form.
2. What we are in right now.
3. What I will be in the work place.
4. Tools for working with information.
5. Commerce enhanced and accelerated by IT.
6. What OLAP supports.
7. An internal organizational Internet.
8. The highest level of management.
9. External.
10. Ethics.

DISCUSSION QUESTIONS

1. Knowledge workers dominate today's business environment. However, many industries still need workers who do not fall into the category of knowledge workers. What industries still need skilled workers? Can you see a time when these jobs will be replaced by knowledge workers?

2. Put yourself in the shoes of a bank CEO and focus specifically on customers with checking and savings accounts. What is their moment of value in terms of time, location, form, and perfect delivery? How have banks already used IT to deliver perfect service at the customer's moment of value? In what ways could banks further exploit IT to achieve greater customer satisfaction?

3. The three key resources in *The Management Information Systems Challenge* are information, information technology, and people. Which of these three resources is the most important? Why? The least important? Why?

4. We identified four important factors that are changing business today. What other factors are also causing changes? Has IT had some sort of involvement in their presence?

5. Telecommuting is like all things—it has a good side and it has a bad side. What are some of the disadvantages or pitfalls of telecommuting? How can these be avoided?

6. As an information-literate knowledge worker for a local distributor of imported foods and spices, you've been asked to prepare a customer mailing list that will be sold to international cuisine restaurants in your area. If you do, would you be acting ethically? If you don't consider the proposal ethical, what if your boss threatened to fire you if you didn't prepare the list? Do you believe you would have any legal recourse if you didn't prepare the list and were subsequently fired?

7. How is your school helping you prepare to take advantage of knowledge worker computing? What courses have you taken that included teaching you how to use technology? What software packages were taught?

IT Systems in Your Organization   33

EXTENDED LEARNING MODULE A

IT Systems in Your Organization

Introduction

The focus of this *Extended Learning Module* is on the seven different types of information technology systems (IT systems) used by organizations today. Some provide for the basic processing of transactions, while others enable customers, suppliers, and distributors to interact with your organization through various telecommunications systems such as the Internet.

The phrase "information technology systems in an organization" is composed of four distinct parts: (1) an organization, (2) information in an organization, (3) information technology, and (4) information technology systems in an organization. So, we'll perform a quick review of an organization, information, and information technology, and then we'll describe the seven different IT systems. As we do, we'll differentiate them according to

- Online transaction processing (OLTP) versus online analytical processing (OLAP)
- The 5 Cs of information-processing tasks—capture, convey, create, cradle, and communicate
- What information describes—internal, external, objective, or subjective

The seven IT systems we'll discuss here include:

1. Transaction processing systems (TPS)
2. Customer integrated systems (CIS)
3. Management information systems (MIS)
4. Workgroup support systems (WSS)
5. Decision support systems (DSS) and artificial intelligence (AI)
6. Executive information systems (EIS)
7. Interorganizational systems (IOS)

Organizations, Information, and Information Technology

All organizations today—regardless of their size or configuration—use information technology as a set of tools to work with information.

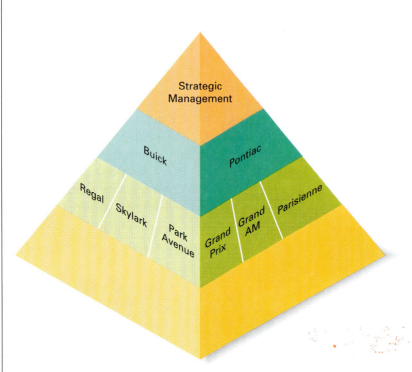

FIGURE A.1
General Motors with Many Levels and Sides

Organizations

Most people view a traditional organization as a pyramid with four levels and many sides (see Figure A.1). At the top is *strategic management,* which provides an organization with overall direction and guidance. The second level is often called *tactical management,* which develops the goals and strategies outlined by strategic management. The third level is *operational management,* which manages and directs the day-to-day operations and implementations of the goals and strategies. Finally, the fourth level of the organizations comprises nonmanagement employees who actually perform daily activities, such as order processing, developing and producing goods and services, and servicing customers.

In Figure A.1, you can see the four levels of General Motors (GM) as well as two of its sides. In this case, the sides are defined by the various major product lines offered by GM.

Information

In today's information-based environment, information is indeed a key resource for all organizations.

What Information Describes Information may be internal, external, objective, subjective, or some combination of the four. *Internal information* describes specific operational aspects of the organization. *External information* describes the environment surrounding the organization. *Objective information* quantifiably describes something that is known. *Subjective information* attempts to describe something that is currently unknown.

Of the seven IT systems we'll discuss in a moment, some are designed to work with internal as opposed to external information. Others are designed to work with objective as opposed to subjective information. Still others can work with some combination of the four.

Flows of Information Information in an organization flows in four directions—up, down, horizontally, and outward (see Figure A.2). The *upward flow of information* describes the current state of the organization based on its daily transactions. The *downward flow of information* consists of the strategies, goals, and directives that originate at one level and are passed to lower levels. The *horizontal flow of information* is the flow of information that occurs between functional business units and work teams. The *outward flow of information* consists of information that is communicated to customers, suppliers, distributors, and other partners outside the organization for the purpose of doing business.

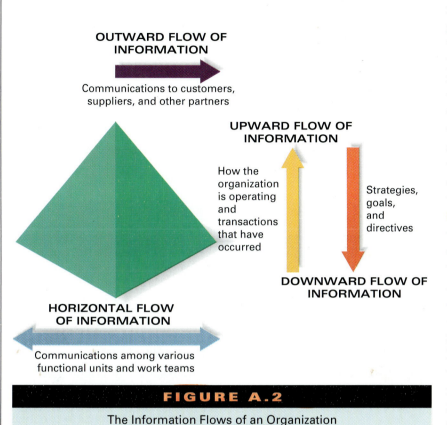

FIGURE A.2

The Information Flows of an Organization

Information for Customer Moment of Value Whenever you generate information and pass it to someone else, that person is your customer. It doesn't matter if that person is a true "customer" of your organization or if that person is another employee within your organization—he or she is still your customer. Customer moment of value considerations for information are: time, location, and form. *Time* deals with two aspects (1) providing information when your customer wants it and (2) providing information that describes the time period your customer is interested in. *Location* deals with providing information to your customer where he or she wants it. *Form* deals with providing information in a form that your customer wants it in—narrative, tabular, graphical, sound, image-based, and so on.

Information Technology

Because information is so important today, organizations use information technology tools to work with that information.

The 5 Cs of Information-Processing Tasks The five categories of information-processing tasks in an organization are capturing, conveying, creating, cradling, and communicating information. *Capturing* information is obtaining information at its point of origin. *Conveying* information is presenting information in its most useful form. *Creating* information is processing information to obtain new information. *Cradling* information is storing information for use at a later time. *Communicating* information is sending information to other people or locations.

Each of the seven IT systems we'll discuss in a moment is designed to handle some or all of the 5 Cs of information-processing tasks. Each IT system has primary information-processing tasks but may address all of the 5 Cs in some fashion.

OLTP versus OLAP As you create or process information with technology, you can do so in two ways—online transaction processing and online analytical processing. ***Online transaction processing (OLTP)*** involves gathering input information, processing that information, and updating existing information to reflect the gathered and processed information. ***Online analytical processing (OLAP)*** is the manipulation of information to support decision making.

Several of the IT systems we'll discuss in a moment focus on OLTP, while the others focus mainly on OLAP.

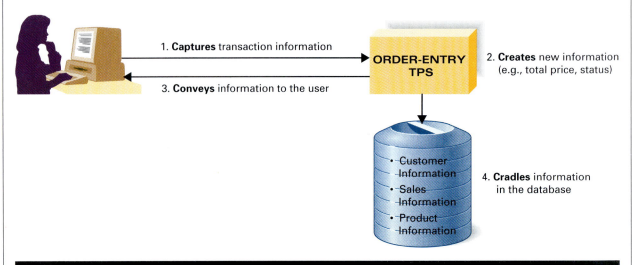

FIGURE A.3

Order-Entry TPS

Transaction Processing Systems (TPS)

At the heart of every organization are IT systems whose primary responsibilities are to capture transaction information, create new information based on the transaction information, cradle the transaction information and newly created information, and convey the results to the user. Among these IT systems are transaction processing systems and customer integrated systems.

A *transaction processing system (TPS)* is exactly what its name implies—a system that processes transactions that occur within an organization. In Figure A.3, you can see an order-entry TPS. In this instance, the clerk is using the TPS to capture the transaction information (e.g., credit card information, product information, and so on). The TPS then creates new information (e.g., total price and applicable tax), updates information within the database, and finally conveys the newly created information to the clerk.

Typical TPSs include order-entry (which we just illustrated), payroll, accounts receivable, inventory ordering, and a number of other basic systems you'll find in any organization. TPSs support OLTP (as opposed to OLAP), are primarily responsible for capturing, conveying, creating, and cradling information, and work almost solely with internal and objective information.

OLTP vs. OLAP

INFORMATION- PROCESSING TASKS
- Capture
- Convey
- Create
- Cradle
- Communicate

WHAT INFORMATION DESCRIBES
- Internal
- External
- Objective
- Subjective

Customer Integrated Systems (CIS)

A *customer integrated system (CIS)* is an extension of a TPS that places technology in the hands of an organization's customers and allows them to process their own transactions. Automated teller machines (ATMs) are perhaps the most common example of a CIS. ATMs provide you with the ability to do your own banking anywhere at any time (two key aspects of customer moment of value). What's really interesting is that ATMs actually do nothing "new," but they give you greater flexibility in accessing and using your money.

CISs further decentralize computing power in an organization by placing that power in the hands of customers (see Figure A.4). For that reason, CISs are also responsible for communicating information (as well as the other four information-processing tasks). Because CISs are extensions of TPSs, they support OLTP (and not OLAP) and work almost exclusively with internal and objective information.

CISs are the new popular IT system today. You can use a CIS to scan your groceries at a grocery store and pay for fuel at the pump instead of going inside. And you can find thousands of CISs all over the Internet that let you do everything from ordering concert tickets to making reservations on a cruise ship.

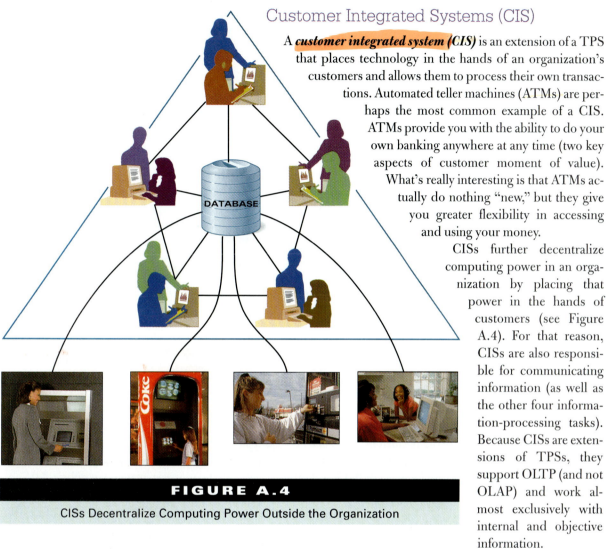

FIGURE A.4
CISs Decentralize Computing Power Outside the Organization

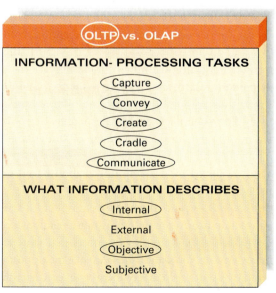

MANAGEMENT INFORMATION SYSTEMS . . .

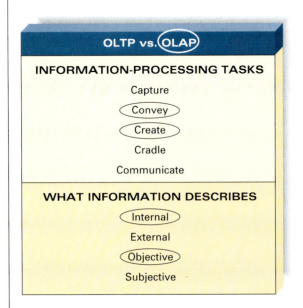

FIGURE A.5

Management Information Systems at Work

Management Information Systems (MIS)

Once TPSs and CISs capture, process, and store information in a database, people all over the organization need access to it. Among the different IT systems that help people access that information are management information systems. A *management information system (MIS)* is a system that provides periodic, predetermined, and/or ad hoc reporting capabilities (see Figure A.5). Most often, MIS reports summarize or aggregate information to support decision-making tasks. So, MISs are systems that have information-processing responsibilities that include creating information (through OLAP) and conveying information to whoever needs it.

MISs are often called *management alerting systems* because they "alert" people (usually management) to the existence (or potential existence) of problems or opportunities. This is an important distinction between an MIS and other systems that support management efforts. MISs are designed primarily to summarize what has occurred and point people toward the existence of problems or opportunities. Reports generated by MISs rarely tell someone why a problem or opportunity exists or offer solutions.

MISs provide reports in many different forms. MISs reports can be periodic, summarized, exception, comparative, and ad hoc. *Periodic reports* are reports that are produced at a predetermined time interval—daily, weekly, monthly, yearly, and so on. *Summarized reports* are simply those reports that aggregate information in some way. For example, sales by salespeople, defective returns by product line, and number of students enrolled in a class are all MIS reports. *Exception reports* show only a subset of available information based on some selection criteria.

Comparative reports show two or more sets of similar information in an attempt to illustrate a relationship. Finally, *ad hoc reports* are those reports that you can generate whenever you want. These are just the opposite of periodic reports which come to you consistently within a given time frame.

MAXIMUM OFFICE PRODUCTS
For Period Ending January 31, 2002

Customer	0–10 Days*	11–30 Days	31–60 Days	61–90 Days	91–120 Days	Past 120 Days
ACME Hardware		$2,400				
Bellows Meats		700	$300			
Darin Publicity						$2,000
Federal Inc.	$1,400					
Jake's Fidelity	7,000					
Malloy Realty		1,600				
P. J.'s Floral				$600	$200	
Shann Landscape						
Whitt Federal						1,500
Yellow Truck	9,500					
Zeno Fishery		6,000				
Totals	$17,900	$10,700	$300	$600	$200	$3,500
Total sales:	$33,200					
% of total	53.9%	32.2%	0.9%	1.8%	0.6%	10.5%

*Terms are given 2/10, net 30. $358 total discounted for payments within 10 days.

FIGURE A.6

An Aging Schedule MIS Report

In Figure A.6, you can see an example of an MIS report that is summarized, exception, and comparative. It could also be considered periodic (notice the title). But you may be able to generate it whenever you want, making it an ad hoc report. In accounting, this type of report is often called an "aging schedule." It is a summary report because it shows total credit sales by customer. It is an exception report because it lists when payments were made (the selection criteria). It's also a comparative report because it provides footnotes that compare percentage of total sales receipts within specific periods.

Because MISs generate reports from a database of TPS and CIS information, they usually work with internal and objective information only.

Workgroup Support Systems (WSS)

A *workgroup support system (WSS)* is a system that is designed specifically to improve the performance of teams by supporting the sharing and flow of information. The foundation of any WSS is *groupware*—the popular term for the software component that supports the collective efforts of a team. Popular groupware suites include Lotus Notes/Domino, Microsoft Exchange, Novell Groupwise, and NetSys WebWare.

A WSS can be used in a variety of business settings and for a variety of reasons. For example, a team may use a WSS as it decides how best to provide additional capital funding for an organization. In this instance, the team will gather internal, objective, subjective, and external information and perform OLAP. On the other hand, another team may use a WSS to support its processing of inventory requests. In that instance, the team will primarily perform OLTP on internal and objective information. Whatever the case, WSSs are responsible for the cradling, conveying, and communicating of information.

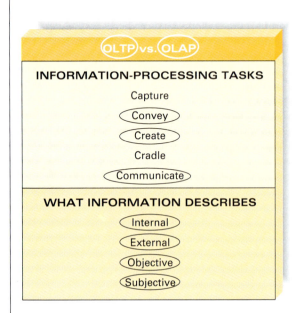

FIGURE A.7 The Groupware Environment

Groupware contains software components for supporting the following three functions (see Figure A.7):

1. Team dynamics
2. Document management
3. Applications development

Team Dynamics

Team dynamics is the most basic and fundamental support provided by groupware. Team dynamics includes any communications among team members and the facilitation and execution of meetings. For communications, groupware suites include such technologies as e-mail and electronic bulletin boards.

Electronic meeting support is the component of groupware that helps you schedule meetings and carry out those meetings. Electronic meeting support includes:

- *Group scheduling software*—provides facilities for maintaining the daily calendars of team members and evaluating those calendars to determine optimal meeting times. Some group scheduling software will even help you reserve a certain room and any equipment you may need.

- ***Electronic meeting software***—lets a team have a "virtual" meeting through IT. This software helps you develop an agenda and then distribute it to all team members. Each team member can then respond to any agenda item, with the software distributing the response to all other team members. In many instances, these types of virtual meetings may take place over a period of several weeks.
- ***Videoconferencing software***—allows a team to have a "face-to-face" meeting when members are geographically dispersed. Basically, videoconferencing software uses microphones and video cameras to capture team members in one location and then display them in another location to other team members.
- ***Whiteboard software***—allows you to make a presentation to your team members and electronically captures any notes you may write on a large whiteboard. So you can make a PowerPoint presentation, write notes on certain slides, and have the whiteboard software capture your writing and distribute those notes to each team member.

Document Management

Perhaps the most critical component of any groupware suite is document management, which is achieved through a group document database. A *group document database* is a powerful storage facility for organizing and managing all documents related to specific teams. The complete group document database will contain documents from many different teams (see Figure A.8). Because of this, group document databases support levels of security to control access to database documents, authenticate the identity of people creating new documents or making changes to existing documents, and guard against wrongful use.

A team can store, access, track, and organize a wealth of information inside a group document database. This information can be in many forms—traditional database tables, text files, sound, and even video. Within your group document database area, you can perform full searches that will completely analyze all the information, regardless of form.

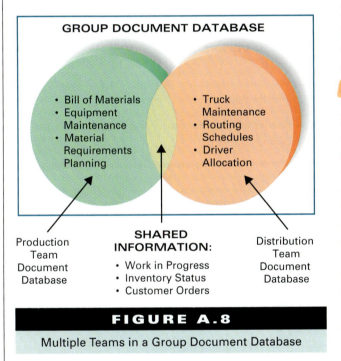

FIGURE A.8
Multiple Teams in a Group Document Database

Applications Development

The final component of a groupware environment is that of applications development. In groupware, *applications development facilities* constitute a wealth of basic building blocks that you can use to create applications quickly, so teams can literally "get to work." These basic building blocks include prewritten applications and programming tools that developers can use to create customized applications.

Prewritten applications include those software systems that are ready for immediate use. For example, most groupware suites include customer management, billing, and payroll applications. Groupware suites also include programming tools. You can use these programming tools to make modifications to the prewritten applications or create completely new applications.

In this text, we've devoted Chapter 7 to applications development. There, you'll find more discussions of the process of developing applications (or modifying existing applications).

Decision Support Systems (DSS) and Artificial Intelligence (AI)

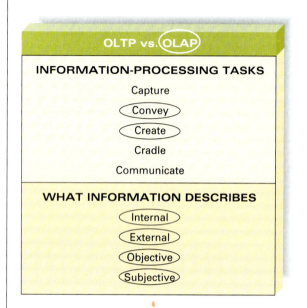

Decision support systems (DSS) and artificial intelligence (AI) are IT systems that help you create information through OLAP to facilitate decision-making tasks that require significant effort and analysis. For example, if you were considering different locations for a new distribution center, your decision would be affected by the quality of the workforce, projected fluctuations in interest rates, tax incentives offered by each location, proximity to other warehouses and distribution centers, proximity to major transportation outlets, and so on.

That is not a simple decision. And to make it, you'll be using a variety of information that describes internal, external, objective, and subjective facets. So, DSSs and AI (in general) help you perform OLAP on all types of information to make a decision.

In this text, we've devoted all of Chapter 4 to these vitally important systems. Here, we'll simply provide some definitions for you.

- ***Decision support system (DSS)***—highly flexible and interactive IT system that is designed to support decision making when the problem is not structured.
- ***Group decision support system (GDSS)***—type of decision support system that facilitates the formulation of and solution to problems by a team.
- ***Geographic information system (GIS)***—a decision support system designed specifically to work with spatial information.
- ***Artificial intelligence (AI)***—the science of making machines imitate human thinking and behavior.
- ***Expert system***—an artificial intelligence system that applies reasoning capabilities to reach a conclusion.
- ***Neural network***—an artificial intelligence system which is capable of learning to differentiate patterns.
- ***Genetic algorithm***—an artificial intelligence system that mimics the evolutionary, survival-of-the-fittest process to generate increasingly better solutions to a problem.
- ***Intelligent agent***—is software that assists you, performing repetitive tasks and adapting itself to your preferences.

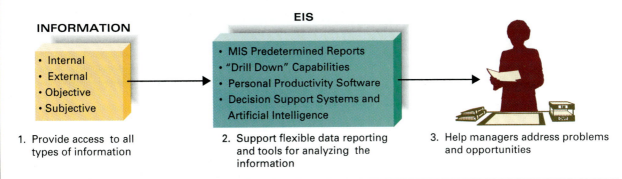

FIGURE A.9

Executive Information Systems at Work

Executive Information Systems (EIS)

An ***executive information system (EIS)*** is a highly interactive MIS combined with decision support systems and artificial intelligence for helping managers identify and address problems and opportunities (see Figure A.9). Similar to an MIS, an EIS allows managers to view information from different angles. Additionally, it provides managers with the flexibility to easily create more views to better understand the problem or opportunity.

And, similar to DSSs and AI, an EIS provides tools for further analyzing information and creating strategies for solving a problem or taking advantage of an opportunity. So, an EIS is primarily responsible for the information-processing tasks of creating information through OLAP and conveying that information to the user. As well, EISs work with all types of information—internal, external, objective, and subjective.

EISs have several unique features. Among those are:

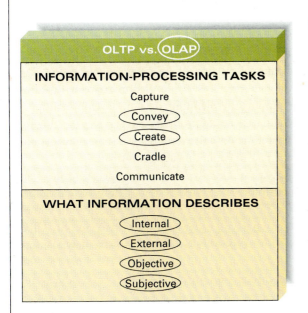

- **Drill down capabilities**—from a reporting perspective, an EIS would allow you to start with a highly summarized graph (say, sales by year) and then click on any part of that graph to see more detail (e.g., click on a year and the EIS would show sales for that year by region).
- **Identification of information responsibility**—EISs identify the person responsible for information. For example, if you had drilled down as far as the EIS allowed and still needed more information, your EIS would identify the person in your organization who could provide more.
- **Use of DSS and AI tools**—EISs include many DSS and AI tools that can help you understand why a problem or opportunity exists and develop strategies. For example, within an EIS you can import information into a spreadsheet and perform a "what-if" analysis to determine the effect of future events.

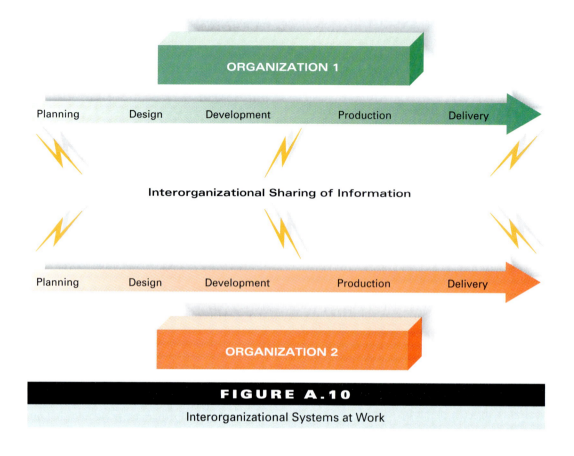

FIGURE A.10
Interorganizational Systems at Work

Interorganizational Systems (IOS)

In Chapter 1 we discussed electronic commerce as an important factor shaping the landscape of business today. Electronic commerce supports a "virtual" market in which product manufacturers, service suppliers, wholesalers, retailers, and customers gather to do business. To do this effectively, businesses must provide first-rate technologies that support the flow of information among all parties involved—we call these technologies interorganizational systems. An *interorganizational system (IOS)* automates the flow of information between organizations to support the planning, design, development, production, and delivery of products and services (see Figure A.10). Therefore, IOSs are responsible for the information-processing task of communicating information.

In fact, we've already looked at a special form of an IOS—a customer integrated system. These systems allow an organization to electronically communicate with you as a customer while you order a product or service. So, CISs are essentially a type of IOS that supports the flow of information between an organization and its customers for the purpose of directly supporting the delivery of products and services.

Just as business-to-consumer IOSs can provide an organization with significant competitive advantage, so can business-to-business IOSs. Business-to-business IOSs support not only the delivery of products and services, but

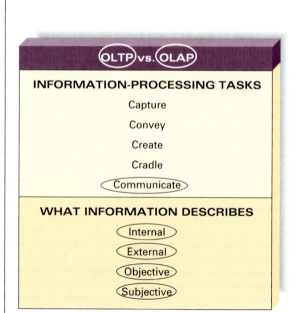

also support the timely exchange of information throughout the entire product cycle—from planning to delivery. For this reason, it's difficult to generalize about IOSs and say they always support OLAP or OLTP (or, for that matter, work with only certain types of information). For example, IOSs that support product ordering and delivery support OLTP, while IOSs that support product planning probably include support for OLAP.

In this text, we've devoted all of Chapter 5 to electronic commerce. There, you'll deal extensively with IOSs and their role in shaping the new business landscape today.

Business Reviews

If you'd like to learn how specific organizations are taking advantage of the seven IT systems we introduced in this module, visit the Web site for this text at http://www.mhhe.com/haag. Here's just a few of the organizations you'll find there.

- Vanity Fair
- US West
- Avon
- Bergen Brunswig
- Johnson & Johnson
- IBM
- Hilton Hotels
- R.J. Reynolds
- World Insurance Network
- Marriott
- Bank of America
- Union Pacific
- London Stock Exchange
- Hechinger Stores
- National Jewish Center
- Texas Commerce Bank
- General Electric
- IBM, Apple, and Motorola
- Caterpillar
- AlliedSignal

CHAPTER OUTLINE

INDUSTRY PERSPECTIVES

Manufacturing
54
GE Leadership Leads the Way in Competitive IT

Health Care
58
Just-in-Time Surgery

Entertainment and Publishing
60
Here Comes Electronic Ink

".com"
62
Keeping an Eye on the Competition

IN THE NEWS

- **49** UPS and Fender Guitar have teamed to create an information partnership.
- **54** Amazon.com's "one-click" purchasing process saves users time when checking out.
- **58** Switching costs make customers reluctant to switch to another product or service.
- **63** mysimon.com can compare prices for you at numerous web sites.
- **64** Can you tell which processes are value-added and which are value-reducing?
- **65** Electronic commerce supports mass customization and personalization.
- **67** What organizations will electronic commerce disintermediate?
- **69** The U.S. airline industry is a great example of using information technology for competitive advantage.

FEATURES

- **50** **On Your Own** Looking for Opportunities Close to Home
- **55** **The Global Perspective** Even Nations Can Gain a Competitive Advantage with IT
- **61** **Team Work** Finding the Best IT Strategy for Your Industry
- **63** **On Your Own** Building on the State of the Art
- **70** **Team Work** Helping the Little Guy Compete
- **72** **The Global Perspective** Paperless Payments
- **75** **Real Hot Electronic Commerce** Ordering Products on the Internet

KNOWLEDGE WORKERS CHECKLIST

In the Information Age, Knowledge Workers Understand . . .

1. How the creative use of information technology can give an organization a competitive advantage
2. How to generate ideas for using information technology in innovative ways, and tools that can help
3. How e-commerce technologies "up the stakes" and give organizations even more opportunities
4. How one specific industry has consistently used information technology for competitive advantage
5. How to use information technology for competitive advantage in their organizations

WEB SUPPORT

http://www.mhhe.com/haag

- XML
- E-Books
- Auction Houses
- Books and Music
- Clothing and Accessories
- Computers
- Automobiles

Strategic and Competitive Opportunities

Using IT for Competitive Advantage

CHAPTER 2

CASE STUDY

CAD Preps AmericaOne for the America's Cup

The America's Cup is the oldest trophy in international sport. Design of the competing sailboats is a critical success factor, since one small advantage gained by a design innovation can separate winners from losers. AmericaOne, the San Francisco-based challenger for the America's Cup, began the competition months before the race. They relied on computer-aided design (CAD), Internet collaboration tools, and a passion for sailing and design to build two of the world's fastest sailboats.

Competitors hold off on actually building their boats for as long as they can. The idea is to spend a lot of time considering the many possibilities for design and innovation before starting to build the boat. Designing a sailboat is both an aerodynamic and a hydrodynamic problem, sort of like trying to design an airplane that is half underwater and half out of the water. Of course, the boat has to be completed and tested in time for the race.

AmericaOne had 40 naval architects, fluid dynamists, research scientists and structural analysts working on their design. The project team was located in many parts of the world, from California to New Zealand. Their work was coordinated using the Internet and software products like Autodesk Inc.'s AutoCAD and Volo View Internet collaboration tools. This approach gave AmericaOne's backers the ability to assemble a project team of world class experts in their fields no matter where they were located, and ensure that they worked together almost as if they were all in the same physical location. For example, drawings and concepts could be shared in real time with team members located in several different countries.

Designing a boat moves in a sequential fashion, starting with the hull, then the keel, and finally the sail. The design work was typically done independently by design experts in each area, with very little communication between them. If a project had been done using old methods, the team could evaluate only six designs before they would have to start building the boat. Team members would have to gather in one place to evaluate their options or rely on communication by telephone or fax. Such methods often led to poor communications and misunderstandings.

Using the new software and the Internet for design and collaboration, the team was able to consider literally thousands of design alternatives before starting to build the boat. For example, the team was able to very quickly agree on an innovation to the sail, which affected the positioning of the mast and the weight of the keel.

When the 2000 America's Cup race was held off the coast of Auckland, New Zealand, AmericaOne lost to the Italian Prada Challenge team's Luna Rossa by seconds. Team New Zealand ultimately won the Cup.

Even though their efforts fell short this time, the U.S. team fully realized just how much they had accomplished in an incredibly short period of time. They also realized that design and collaboration software and the Internet have forever changed the way that racing sailboats will be designed and built.[1] ❖

Introduction

There are many examples of creative ways that organizations have used information technology to give themselves a competitive advantage. A company gains a *competitive advantage* by providing a product or service in a way that customers value more than the competition's. We'll give you some examples in a moment. First, it's important for you to get the right perspective on it. It's not the technology that gives a company a competitive advantage; it's the way that people use the technology that makes the difference. Let's assume there is a Porsche parked outside and there are two people available to drive it, a trained professional racecar driver and a senior citizen who usually drives a six-year-old Buick. Although both human beings would have access to the same technology, there's probably no question in your mind that the professional racecar driver would do a better job of utilizing the technology embodied in the Boxster.

In a way, it's the same with information technology. With the widespread availability and ever-decreasing cost of computers, telecommunications, and the Internet, the same technology is available to just about everyone. The real difference comes in the way that different people use the technology. Those who are well trained, proficient, and creative in its use are going to get the most out of it and give their organizations a competitive advantage.

Competitive Advantage Examples

Seeing competitive advantage in action is perhaps the best way for you to learn how to implement it in your organization. As we look at the following examples, we'll introduce you to some "best business practices" as well.

Federal Express

It used to be that if you wanted to track a package you'd shipped somewhere via FedEx you had to call an 800 number and listen to some music for a while until a customer service representative came on the line. Then you had to give him or her the tracking number from your receipt, which would be entered into the computer system that would access a database containing up-to-date information on the whereabouts of your package. You could find out if it had been delivered and, if so, who had signed for it.

Someone at FedEx got the idea that with today's technology you could make life easier for the customer, so they designed a system which lets you access the database through your Internet connection and browser. Now, all you have to do is to go to the FedEx Web site and key in your tracking number. The system will respond by giving you the same information you used to get from a human being (see Figure 2.2).

This is an example of a win-win system. It's better for the customer because it's easier and faster. No more waiting in voice mail jail. It's better for FedEx because it's cheaper. It doesn't need nearly as many telephone customer service repre-

FIGURE 2.1
Who Can Get the Most Out of the Boxster S?

Competitive Advantage Examples **49**

FIGURE 2.2

FedEx Package Tracking Screen

sentatives. Plus, it gains a competitive advantage by delivering superior customer service, at least until the competition develops a similar system of its own—as UPS did.

UPS and Fender Guitar

FedEx's competitor, UPS, liked what it saw in the FedEx customer-controlled tracking system and quickly developed a similar system of its own. This illustrates an important point about using information technology for competitive advantage. The advantage usually turns out to be temporary because your competitors soon figure out that they have to offer a similar system to their customers or lose them to you. Even a temporary advantage can make a difference, however, because the first mover usually makes some gains at the expense of the competition. A ***temporary advantage*** simply means that whatever you do, sooner or later the competition duplicates what you've done, or even leapfrogs you with a better system. Despite this, the ***first mover,*** the company first to market with a new IT-based product or service, may well capture new customers it never gives up, and is often viewed as an innovative market leader.

Another characteristic of information systems that gives a competitive advantage is that they tend to be interorganizational systems (refer back to *Extended Learning Module A* for a discussion of these). Instead of an information system that is designed just for a company's internal needs (such as a payroll system) an interorganizational system links the computer systems of independent companies.

A good illustration of this is the way that Fender Guitar and UPS partner to make things easier for themselves and their customers. All Fender guitar shipments are routed through the UPS shipping hub in the Netherlands. While there, they are tuned. This avoids the need to have them sent to a Fender location for tuning, lets the customer play the guitar right out of the box, and saves Fender 9 percent in costs. The process is managed by a computer system that lets information on customer orders flow seamlessly between UPS and Fender.[2] Arrangements such as this are called information partnerships. An ***information partnership*** lets two or more companies cooperate by integrating their IT systems, thereby providing customers with the best of what each can offer.

The Information Partnership

What is an information partnership?	■ An information partnership is an agreement between organizations for the sharing of information to strengthen each partner organization.
What does an information partnership do?	■ It creates organizational synergy from complementary resources at participating organizations.
How is an information partnership IT-enabled?	■ EDI forms the bedrock of the information partnership. ❖

Dell Computer

Dell computer has a direct sell model that gives it a huge advantage over any competitor still using a traditional model of selling through retailers. The traditional way that PC manufacturers get their product to customers is to build a bunch of PCs and ship them to wholesalers and distributors, or maybe directly to retailers. The PCs sit on the retailers' shelves or in a warehouse until you come in and buy one. If you looked at a typical distribution chain you would see that there are a lot of PCs in inventory. (A ***distribution chain*** is simply the path followed from the originator of a product or service to the end consumer.) In a typical distribution chain you'd find inventory at the manufacturer's warehouse, at the wholesalers, at the distributors, and at the retailers. Holding on to all of this inventory costs money, because whoever owns the inventory has to pay for it and pay for the operation of the warehouses or stores while waiting for someone to buy it.

Dell's model is different.[3] It sells computers directly from its Web site. Dell makes it easy for you to log on and configure a computer just the way you want it. Once you've done that and given Dell your credit card number, you click to order and your computer arrives in a few days. Shortly after you click to order, Dell has your money! Then it gets busy sending electronic orders to other companies, alliance partners, who assemble and ship your computer. An ***alliance partner*** is a company that you do business with on a regular basis in a cooperative fashion, usually facilitated by IT systems. Dell pays its alliance partners for their efforts a bit later. It's another win-win situation. You win because you get a computer made expressly for you, which arrives in good shape in a few days. Dell wins because all this occurred without it having to tie up a lot of money in inventory in the distribution chain. The differences between Dell's "sell, source, and ship" model and the traditional "buy, hold, and sell" model are illustrated in Figure 2.3.

CAREER OPPORTUNITY

Think competitive advantage. Clarifying a company's advantage to you as a customer helps you to evaluate the company's value to you as a customer. If the company's competitive advantage is fast product delivery, you can decide if that's important to you as a customer. In this way, you become a wiser consumer, whether purchasing for yourself or for your company.

Cisco Systems

Dell Computer is in both the B2B and B2C space. This is shorthand for "Business to Business" and "Business to Consumer." ***Business to Business (B2B)*** refers to companies whose customers are primarily other businesses while ***Business to Consumer (B2C)*** is the term used for companies whose customers are primarily individuals. (Some companies, such as Dell Computer, have both B2B and B2C lines of business.)

Cisco Systems sells switches and routers, machines that manage information flowing through telecommunications networks in the B2B space. Cisco has been a leader in utilizing the direct sell model over the Internet. It currently sells over $1 billion a month in this way. Customers like the system because it lets them log on to a home page that they can customize to reflect the particular way that they deal with Cisco. Then, they can order Cisco products and configure them to their exact specifications. Cisco likes the system because it puts the management of the customer order process in the hands of the customer, thus freeing up Cisco employees for other tasks.

Recently, Cisco announced a partnership with Ariba, one of the leading suppliers of Web-based purchasing tools.[4] Ariba's software, which manages buying, selling and e-commerce processes, will be combined with Cisco Web-based ordering tools, which provide pricing and configuration capabilities. Cisco says that its newly streamlined order entry process will increase customer productivity by as much as 20

ON YOUR OWN

Looking for Opportunities Close to Home

You don't have to be a part of a traditional for-profit organization in order to get into the habit of looking for ways to use IT for competitive advantage. Not for profits and governmental agencies can get benefits from IT as well. For example, most universities are considered to be not for profit. See if you can come up with ways that your college or university could get a competitive advantage from the way it uses IT. You might try taking the customer's perspective (yours) as a point of departure. ❖

Competitive Advantage Examples   **51**

BUY — PC Retailer Buys from Manufacturer or Distributor

HOLD — PCs Are Sent to Retailer Warehouse

PCs Are Placed on Retailer's Shelves

SELL — Finally, a PC Is Sold

SELL

SOURCE — Monitor Supplier, PC Case Supplier, Keyboard Supplier, CPU Supplier — Dell Sends Orders to Its Alliance Partners

Assemble PC

SHIP

FIGURE 2.3
Buy-Hold-Sell versus Sell-Source-Ship

percent. So, as you can see, Cisco has found a couple of ways to get a competitive advantage through the creative use of information technology. First, Cisco made it easy to turn the management of the customer ordering process to the customers themselves, and then it formed a software alliance with Ariba to increase the productivity of the customer ordering process even more. As you might expect, both Cisco and its customers are pleased with the results.

How Smart Companies Get a Competitive Advantage from IT

If getting a competitive advantage through the creative use of information technology can give such great benefits, then why isn't every company doing it? The reason is that it's easier said than done. We're talking about using technology in a creative way to solve a business problem, and that means innovation. ***Innovation*** is the process of devising ways to do things in new and creative ways. Using information technology to tackle a business problem in the way that other companies have been doing is certainly not going to give a company a competitive advantage. Some of the things that are important in coming up with creative technology-based solutions are

1. The CEO's attitude toward information technology
2. Bridging the gap between business people and technical people
3. Viewing the business problem from another perspective
4. Demanding a creative design
5. Looking beyond the four walls of the company

Let's examine each of these points in a little more detail.

The CEO's Attitude toward Information Technology

The CEO's vision can influence the way that managers think about lots of things within their company, including information technology. Often, the background of the CEO influences her or his perspective. For example, if most of her corporate experience was in financial management, you can be sure that the financial planning and control processes in the company will be in great shape. If his experience was mostly in manufacturing, you might find that a request to modernize a plant would receive a favorable hearing. Compared with the other functional areas of a company, the IT function is relatively new. More than that, it has been changing very rapidly and continues to do so. Many CEOs had very little experience in managing IT when they were rising through the company ranks, and those who did were no doubt managing IT environments that are very different from today's and tomorrow's. If getting a competitive advantage from information technology is low on the CEO's priority list you can bet that IT initiatives will have difficulty in getting a favorable hearing. On the other hand, if the CEO understands that IT can be a powerful competitive weapon, a message is sent to the entire organization that coming up with creative IT ideas is important.

Bridging the Gap between Business People and Technical People

Designing an information system that gives a competitive advantage requires at least two things. First, it requires an understanding of the business problem you are trying to solve. Second, it requires an understanding of available technologies to know which ones to use in designing a creative solution for the business problem. This is why studying management information systems (MIS) is so important. MIS emphasizes both business processes and technical solutions.

But think of a company at which the technical people are all computer science majors and the business people all have degrees in marketing or accounting, with little training in MIS. Then, let's say, that the biggest business problem for the company is to increase the number of repeat buyers on its B2C Web site. It's able to get first-time buyers with special discounts, but is finding it hard to convert those first-time buyers into repeat customers. If we turned this problem over to a computer scientist, he might not know (or care) enough about buyer behavior to be able to come up with a solution that works (see Figure 2.4).

If we turned the problem over to the marketing manager, she might know lots about buyer behavior but not have a clue about how to make the company's Web site "sticky." Usually this problem is solved by forming a project team to come up with a solution that draws the best knowledge of the business problem from the busi-

How Smart Companies Get a Competitive Advantage from IT   53

FIGURE 2.4

When Managerial and Technical Perspectives Differ[5]

ness people and the best technical solution from the technical people. A ***project team*** is a team designed to accomplish specific one-time goals which is disbanded once the project is complete. When this process works well, the business people on the project team learn more about the technology and what it can do, and the technical people learn more about the business issues involved, and working together, they come up with a great solution. When it doesn't work, companies find that the business people and the technical people simply can't communicate with each other well enough to focus their respective strengths on solving the problem.

If you want a better appreciation of what we're talking about, just think about the last time you asked one of your favorite geeks a technical question and he tried to snow you with his answer. See what we mean?

CAREER OPPORTUNITY

Poor communication between business people and technical people causes many IT projects to fail. Your career opportunity is to focus on bridging the communications gap between these two groups so that an IT solution can be developed that really solves the business problem in a creative way. To do this well, you will need to understand the unique set of values each group has.

Viewing the Business Problem from Another Perspective

Too often, when project teams try to come up with the design of an information system, they view the business

INDUSTRY PERSPECTIVE

Manufacturing

GE Leadership Leads the Way in Competitive IT

Jack Welch, General Electric's (GE) Chairman and CEO has earned wide recognition as an outstanding corporate manager. During his 20 years at the helm of GE, he raised the corporation's profits from $1.6 billion to more than $10 billion on revenues of $110 billion. Under his leadership, GE created a business culture that is widely regarded as the best in the world. GE has become the envy of many for its ability to run a global company efficiently and profitably.

While a lot of executives and traditional businesses have been slow to react to the competitive advantages made possible by the Internet, Jack Welch and GE have not been among them. He recognized that the potential of the Internet would bring new threats and opportunities that GE could not afford to ignore.

He urged his managers to examine their competitive positions and think "destroyyourbusiness.com". In other words, he asked them to see how a competitor could use the Internet to make inroads into their markets or gain a competitive advantage over them. Thinking that way, GE managers would be able to innovate and change their businesses before a new competitor arrived on the scene.

He also has been leading by example, unlike many of his peers at other companies. He assigned young mentors to himself and 3,000 other top GE executives to teach them how to use the Web.

Welch is serious about changing the culture at GE from a traditional one to one that is Internet-driven. He sees the potential for using the Web to eliminate unnecessary layers of middle management, promote teamwork, improve customer service, and make GE more competitive.

Jack Welch is a great example of the kind of vision, leadership, and understanding that winning corporations need from their CEOs if they are going to be able to thrive in the information economy.[6, 7] ❖

---

problem from their own internal perspective rather than from the perspective of the people the system is primarily designed to serve. Instead, it's often more effective to put yourself in the place of the primary user of the system and to try to come up with ways in which that user would be not just served but delighted by the system. So, take the perspective of a customer of the company and ask, How could the information system be designed so that it enhances the customer's experience?

The Federal Express online tracking system we discussed earlier in this chapter is a good example. Amazon.com gets good marks in this area as well. Its site is easy to navigate and gives personalized purchase suggestions to users, and its patented "one-click" purchasing process saves users time when checking out.

Demanding a Creative Design

One of the biggest mistakes people make when designing new information systems is to come up with a design that is ordinary, something very similar to what other companies are doing. You want to think about information systems development as having two distinct phases: design and construction. In a way, it's similar to building a house, and what the design team does is similar to what an architect does. In both cases, you have a right to demand a creative design. A *creative design* of an IT system is one that solves the business problem in a new and highly effective way rather than the same way others have solved it.

Let's say you won the lottery, and you decided to spend $3 million on that dream house you always wanted. One way to do it would be to look at existing houses that are on the market, buy one that you like, and then make any necessary modifications to tailor it to your needs. Another way to do it would be to hire a talented architect to design your house from scratch.

If you hired an architect, one of the first things he would do is interview you to discover what sort of house you want. How many bedrooms, how many bathrooms, what does the kitchen and family room need to have? What sort of entertaining space do you need, and what sort of space do you want for work and

THE GLOBAL PERSPECTIVE

Even Nations Can Gain a Competitive Advantage with IT

Using IT for competitive advantage is not restricted to companies. Singapore is proving that a nation can use IT for competitive advantage as well.

As a small island nation with little in the way of natural resources, Singapore concluded that its most valuable resource was its people. At the beginning of the 1990s the government decided that the wave of the future was IT, and that it should invest in training a cadre of IT workers and focus on becoming what they called "The Intelligent Island." Singapore subsequently became well-known for the way it used IT to speed up the flow of goods through its port facilities by replacing cumbersome paperwork processes with e-commerce techniques.

This is the way Singapore's Economic Development Board (EDB) expresses its current vision on its Web site:

- "Building on its early successes with IT, the EDB's economic blueprint, called Industry 21 or I 21, aims to develop Singapore into a vibrant and robust global hub of knowledge-driven industries. Singapore's manufacturing and services sectors will be further developed with a strong emphasis on technology, innovation, and capabilities. Singapore will also be made more attractive for multinational companies to anchor more of their key knowledge-intensive activities here. At the same time, local companies will be encouraged to embrace more knowledge-intensive activities, with promising local companies evolving into world-class players."

- "Singapore will also leverage on other hubs for ideas, talent, resources, capital and markets, while developing its own world-class capabilities and global reach. The overall goal is for Singapore to be a leading centre of competence in knowledge-driven activities and a choice location for company headquarters, with responsibilities for product and capability charters. Ultimately this will create high value-added jobs for knowledge and skilled workers."[8, 9] ❖

---

for quiet times? How about decks, a home theater, an indoor squash court or an outdoor swimming pool? To finish up, he would want to see the lot you had selected, let us suppose, in the foothills of Colorado, with a snow-capped mountain view.

With this information, he would go away and design a home to meet your needs. He would go out to the site and check the views, noting where the sun rises and sets. He would make sure that your requirements were met, but would also strive to meet them creatively, with a pleasing design. (For $3 million, you wouldn't want a house that looks like every other house!) He probably would build a model of the house, or use computer-aided design tools to help give you an appreciation of what your house would be like after it was built. If you didn't like the model, you would reject the design, and ask the architect to make changes until you were absolutely satisfied. Then, when you were, you would give him your approval to begin the construction phase, upon which someone would begin digging the foundation, carpenters and electricians and other skilled trades people would be called in and the house built just the way you wanted it. Figure 2.5 shows how one prominent IT author looks at this issue.

We said that this was similar to the process of designing and building information systems. If you bought an existing house, it would be like buying a pre-coded application software package, like one of Siebel Systems' eBusiness applications, for example.[10] If you decided that you didn't like any of the existing available applications, you would appoint a project team to design a custom system for you, similar to the way you would hire an architect to design your house. If the project team came to you with an ordinary design, you can be almost certain that it would not give you a competitive advantage. Worse yet, the system could be obsolete by the time it was put into operation because in all likelihood the competition would not be standing still. So, in order to get your money's worth from your investment, you have every right to send your design team

> *The error of today's architects is that they work in offices with T-squares.*
> *They might as well be working in factories.*
> *They plan houses as if they were making the same Ford car over and over....*
> *I cannot build a preconceived house...*
> *I must understand the land...*
> *feel the cold at night...*
> *feel how the winds blow...*
> *see how the sun moves and the birds fly...*
> *think about the history of the place and the people....*
>
> *The personality of the owner is very important....*
> *I need someone who can help me—through his personality—build a house.*
> *The owner must consider architecture a work of art.*
> *He is my collaborator.*
>
> I find these ideas to be extremely relevant to our systems development efforts. While some might say, "It's just common sense," we tend to forget why we do the things we do. Perhaps more importantly, we lose track of what to emphasize among all our activities. An important theme of this book is that the analyst must "go to the land" to get really in touch with the users, their problems, and their objectives. Working in some back room using memos and the telephone, the analyst will get only a second-hand view of the problem.
>
> The back-room approach is not a substitute for firsthand data gathering. The analyst must touch, feel, and have extensive, personal contact with the environment. By doing so, the analyst will be able to obtain sufficient information to test the validity of preconceived notions. Furthermore, he will open the lines of communication with the user community. The most successful projects are truly joint efforts in which both analysts and users make significant contributions: Users bring to the problem an indispensable business expertise; analysts bring objectivity, technical expertise, and analytical skills. They need each other's perspective and cooperation to do the best possible job.

Source: Allen Carter, "Primitive Sophistication on the Costa de Careyes," *Architectural Digest*, Vol. 33, No. 1 (July/August 1976), pp. 45–48. Reprinted from *Architectural Digest*. Copyright John C. Brasfield Publishing Corp., 1976.

FIGURE 2.5
Primitive Sophistication on the Costa de Careyes[11]

"back to the drawing board" until they come up with a design that delights you. That's the design that is likely to give you a competitive advantage.

Looking beyond the Four Walls of the Company

We talked about interorganizational systems a little earlier in this chapter. Another well-known example is Wal-Mart. With some small exceptions, if you expect to do business with Wal-Mart, they expect you to be able to connect your information systems with theirs and do business electronically. Instead of Wal-Mart sending you a paper purchase order through the mail, it will send you an electronic purchase order over a telecommunications network. If you can't do this, you'll have to sell your product to someone else because Wal-Mart won't buy from you. Wal-Mart's written policy is shown in Figure 2.6.

As you can see, it uses a technology called Electronic Data Interchange (EDI) to support interorganizational communications. We discuss EDI in more detail in Chapter 5, but what you need to know about EDI now is that it drives time, costs, and errors out of the exchange of standard business documents between companies by using computer-to-computer communications instead of paper documents and the postal service. EDI is one of the earliest examples of e-commerce and is still widely used today to support such applications as just-in-time (JIT) manufacturing inventory control systems.

Just-in-time is an approach that produces or delivers a product or service just at the time the customer wants it. Automobile assembly plants, for example, rely on their suppliers to deliver the right quantities of needed parts to the assembly line just shortly before they are needed. JIT can greatly reduce the amount of money that manufacturers need to spend to maintain inventories at their factory sites.

Wal-Mart is known for its "Always Low Prices." One of the most important strategies for achieving this is managing its supply chain processes. A ***supply chain*** consists of the paths reaching out to all

Electronic Data Interchange (EDI) (Product Suppliers)

EDI has proven to be the most efficient way of conducting business with our product suppliers. This system of exchanging information purchases orders, invoices, etc., allows us to improve customer service, lower expenses, and increase productivity. Wal-Mart expects its merchandise suppliers to be able to participate in EDI transactions once they become Wal-Mart suppliers and are assigned a specific Supplier Number. EDI packages range in price from minimal expense to highly sophisticated systems.

If you become a Wal-Mart supplier and do not currently have EDI capability, Wal-Mart will work with you to determine the EDI package that best meets your business needs, while also meeting our EDI requirements. If you already have an EDI system in place when you become a Wal-Mart supplier, Wal-Mart will perform tracking tests to make sure your current system is compatible with Wal-Mart's EDI.

Supplier Proposal Packet

If you are a supplier who would like to initiate a potential business relationship with Wal-Mart Stores Inc., please download and read the proposal packet carefully. Then fill out the forms following the checklist on page 18.

[Download the proposal packet in Adobe Acrobat format.](#)

FIGURE 2.6

Wal-Mart Wants All of Its Suppliers to Use EDI

---

of the suppliers of parts and services to a company. A supply chain consists not only of a company's suppliers, but of its suppliers' suppliers as well. Wal-Mart buys at the lowest possible prices, and then, working with members of its supply chain, makes sure that the steps undertaken by everybody from that point on are accomplished as efficiently as possible. As you might expect, the creative use of information technology is an important part of making this strategy a reality.

Manufacturers of consumer goods and retailers are now working together on a process known as "Collaborative Planning, Forecasting, and Replenishment."[12] ***Collaborative planning, forecasting, and replenishment (CPFR)*** is a concept that encourages and facilitates collaborative processes among members of a supply chain. Participants in the CPFR effort realized that inefficiencies in the supply chain could be improved if they collaborated with each other in the way they exchanged information.

In the past, retailers would track their sales and place orders from time to time, perhaps once a week, when their stock levels reached a certain level. One of the techniques used in CPFR is to have retailers share sales data for products obtained from store check-out scanners with manufacturers on a daily basis. This provides manufacturers much more current and accurate data with which to schedule their production. Excess inventories are eliminated from manufacturers' warehouses, retail distribution centers, and store shelves. Stock-outs are reduced, as are total costs in the supply chain. The chief beneficiary of this is you, the consumer. With CPFR, the item you want is more likely to be on the retailer's shelf, and at a lower cost.

Tools That Can Help

Professor Michael Porter's frameworks have been widely accepted by business people as useful tools for

INDUSTRY PERSPECTIVE

Health Care

Just-in-Time Surgery

Don't tell Joe, but some 200 items for his coronary bypass surgery didn't arrive at the hospital until just as Joe was being rolled into the operating room. Joe, and many other patients like him, are experiencing, firsthand, the just-in-time delivery system called ValueLink, employed by Baxter International of Deerfield, Illinois. As a supplier of medical products, Baxter relieves hospitals from the cost of carrying inventory. With the costs of health care rising fast, Baxter customers, such as Dr. Bruce Capehart at Duke University Medical Center, find the just-in-time system appealing. He says, "We're not simply slowing the rate of increase in the cost of health care. We've achieved a real decrease."

Still, Baxter has extended the concept of just-in-time delivery by entering into risk-sharing agreements. Each year, Baxter and its risk-sharing partners split any cost savings they achieve—or jointly cough up for overruns. So far, the agreements have generated savings for Baxter's customers by standardizing the items required for surgical procedures. For example, in the case of arthroscopic knee surgery, Baxter persuaded eight Duke physicians to eliminate excessive variety and use more of the same items. That move reduced the cost per operation by 25 percent. Before the agreement, Duke's supply costs had risen 31 percent from 1991 to 1994. Using this approach, both Duke and Baxter benefit. Duke's medical supply costs drop because of reduced variety and reduced inventory. Baxter achieves a higher level of customer satisfaction while the reduced product variety eases the task of just-in-time delivery.[13] ❖

---

thinking about business strategy. Several of Porter's colleagues, Professor Warren McFarlan among them, have shown how Porter's frameworks can also be applied to using information technology for competitive advantage. Porter's three frameworks are:

1. The Five Forces Model
2. The Three Generic Strategies
3. The Value Chain

The Five Forces Model

The *five forces model* was developed to determine the relative attractiveness of an industry. Porter's intention was that it be used as a tool for business managers when they were trying to decide if they should enter a particular industry or expand their operations if they were already in it. As illustrated in Figure 2.7, the five forces are

1. **Buyer Power**. *Buyer power* is high when buyers have many choices of whom to buy from, and it's low when their choices are few. If the buyers in a particular industry hold a lot of the power, the industry is less attractive to enter. For example, wheat farmers have no choice but to sell to a very small number of large agricultural conglomerates. This gives the individual wheat farmer very little control over the price he can expect to receive for his crop.

2. **Supplier Power**. *Supplier power* is high when buyers have few choices of whom to buy from, and low when there are many choices. If the suppliers in a particular industry hold a lot of the power, the industry is also less attractive to enter. When there is excessive supplier power, the suppliers can make life difficult for companies who need their product or service. An extreme example of supplier power is a producers' cartel, such as the Organization of Petroleum Exporting Companies (OPEC), which, by limiting the supply of crude oil, can cause worldwide energy prices to rise.

3. **Threat of Substitute Products or Services**. If there are very few alternatives to using the product or service the *threat of substitute products or services* is low, and it is an advantage to the supplier. Or, if there are switching costs associated with the product or service, it is an advantage to the supplier as well. *Switching costs* are costs that can make customers reluctant to switch to another product or service. For example, you may decide

to keep your virus protection software even if a slightly better one becomes available because you don't want to invest the time and money to install and learn the new package. So, even if there are substitute products or services, if there are significant switching costs associated with moving to it, customers may think twice about changing.

4. **Threat of New Entrants**. The *threat of new entrants* is high when it is easy for competitors to enter the market. If it's easy, that's not good, for pretty soon you'll have a ton of competitors going after your customers. If it's difficult for others to enter the market, that's good news for those who are already there.

5. **Rivalry among Existing Competitors**. An industry is less attractive when the *rivalry among existing competitors* is high and more attractive when it is low. Competition is more intense in some industries than in others. The intensity of competition in the industry is another factor that you should consider before entering an industry. What sort of ball game will you be competing in? Is this industry for amateurs or professionals?

The Three Generic Strategies

Porter says that a business should adopt only one of *three generic strategies*: cost leadership, differentiation, or a focused strategy. As illustrated in Figure 2.8, a focused strategy can focus on either cost leadership or differentiation. According to Porter, trying to follow more than one of these strategies at the same time is almost always unsuccessful.

Taking examples from retailing, Wal-Mart is following a broadly targeted cost leadership strategy. Nordstrom's, with its emphasis on superior customer service and in-store experience, is following a broadly targeted differentiation strategy. Rite-Aid is pursuing a cost leadership strategy, but is focused on drugstore items. Red Envelope's (http://www.redenvelope.com) unique selection and presentation of gift items gives it a differentiated focus in this category.

Using the Five Forces Model

Warren McFarlan had the idea that a company could use information technology to alter one or more of the five forces in its favor, or could use IT to reinforce one of the three generic strategies. When he shared this idea with business people, they quickly found that it worked. Some good examples of where it worked are

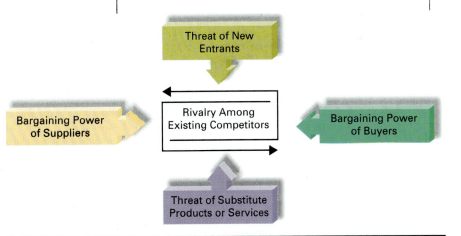

FIGURE 2.7

The Five Forces Model

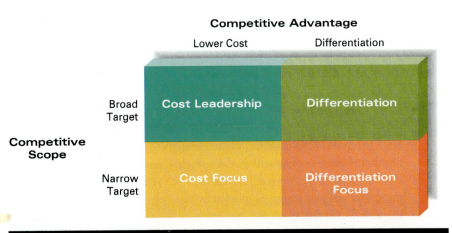

FIGURE 2.8

The Three Generic Strategies[14]

60 CHAPTER TWO Strategic and Competitive Opportunities

INDUSTRY PERSPECTIVE

Entertainment & Publishing

Here Comes Electronic Ink

Cambridge, Massachusetts-based E Ink Corp. is one of the leaders in the development of a new technology that has the potential to replace today's newspapers and books. The company is developing electronic ink and "paper" that can be linked with wireless communications networks. Imagine reading an electronic book that can be replaced with a new one when you are finished with it. Imagine a newspaper that updates itself with breaking news while you are reading it. Imagine a sign in the supermarket offering a special on bananas that lowers the price automatically when the computers in the stockroom think bananas are not selling fast enough.

As devised by E Ink, Electronic ink is a clear, liquid plastic made up of microcapsules that contain white color chips in a blue dye. The microcapsules are suspended in a liquid that is similar to the consistency of vegetable oil. The white chips carry an electrical charge so that they will react to an electrical stimulus that produces visible print.

Electronic ink can be placed on a variety of different surfaces, from walls to computer screens. The writing surface is a sheet of plastic film laminated to a layer of circuitry.

Developers hope that they can ultimately develop surfaces for electronic ink that will have the look and feel of paper. In the short run, however, new signs, books, and newspapers that can be used for electronic ink will be bulkier than their paper counterparts.

E Ink has a more detailed explanation of its product on its Web site, www.eink.com. You might also be interested in seeing how e-content is and will be distributed by looking at Digital Goods' Web site at www.digitalgoods.com. Say goodbye to that heavy backpack![15] ❖

---

1. **Buyer Power**. Business travelers have many hotels to choose from in most large cities. Because there are many hotel chains and even independent hotels vying for the business traveler's business, buyers have many choices, and therefore hold power over the suppliers of hotel rooms. To counteract this, many hotel chains have created loyalty programs which give points for each stay that can be cashed in for free hotel stays at one of their resort hotels or for other rewards. The hotel chains created reward "plateaus" so that the more a traveler stays at any of the chain's hotels the more instant rewards a customer receives. Examples of instant rewards include a free upgrade to a room on the executive floor or even a suite if one is available at check-in. Such programs have the effect of increasing the likelihood that a traveler will stay at a single chain, thus reducing buyer power. There are many such programs available today, supported by state-of-the-art information systems.

2. **Supplier Power**. One of the best ways to decrease supplier power is to locate alternative sources of supply. The B2B marketplaces on the Internet can have the effect of doing this. A ***B2B marketplace is an*** Internet-based service which brings together many buyers and sellers. One recent example is the cooperative Internet purchasing venture established by the automotive industry, Covisint. It will use Internet technology to "speed the flow of material through the supply chain, increase response to consumer demand, and deliver new products to market faster than ever before." Covisint will try to achieve supply chain efficiencies by making it easier for automotive manufacturers and their suppliers to collaborate over the Internet.[16] Another way of reducing supplier power is to find a way to put more information in the hands of the buyer. The Internet has played a huge role in this in many industries. Probably the best example is the automobile industry. It used to be that when you wanted to buy a new car you really put yourself at the mercy of the dealer. The new-car salesman knew what the new car cost the dealer, knew how much your trade-in was really worth, and knew how much money the dealership could make on optional

Tools That Can Help **61**

Finding the Best IT Strategy for Your Industry

Regardless of which of Michael Porter's tools you select to use in developing IT solutions, selecting ones that are appropriate for your organization is crucial. To simplify the selection process even further, you might consider which tools work best with the various industries profiled in the Industry Perspectives boxes in each chapter of this book. Match the tool on the left with the most appropriate industry across the top. Each tool can match more than one industry. For each match, write at least one reason why this match is appropriate. ❖

Porter's Tools	Hospitality & Leisure	Financial Services	Health Care	Retail	IT & Telecommunications	Transportation	.com	Entertainment & Publishing	Manufacturing
Reduce buyer power									
Reduce supplier power									
Increase switching costs									
Increase entry barriers									
Switch to a cost leader strategy									
Switch to a differentiated strategy									
Switch to a focused strategy									
Enhance value-added activities									
Lower value-reducing activities									

equipment, extended warranties, and financing. You probably went in to the dealer knowing what kind of car you wanted and how much you wanted to pay per month and not much more. This put all the bargaining power in the hands of the dealer and is why, to most people, negotiating for a new car was not a pleasant experience. Now, all of the information the dealer has is freely available on the Internet. The new-car buyer can thus begin negotiations having roughly the same information the dealer has. Supplier power is effectively reduced.

3. **Threat of Substitute Products or Services.** Many professionals find that their normal way of making a living is threatened by the introduction of new information technology–enabled products or services. One example is that of the local certified public accountant who made a good portion of her living by doing tax returns for individuals. Her income from tax return preparation was reduced substantially after inexpensive and easy-to-use tax return software packages such as TurboTax® hit the market. Individuals who had personal computers found that they could get the equivalent of a professionally prepared tax return for $39.95 rather than $500. One of the challenges for professionals is to find a way to counter information technology–based threats to their livelihoods. Can you think of other professionals who might be threatened by information technology–based alternatives?

4. **Threat of New Entrants.** It is not a good thing to be trying to survive in an industry in which it is very easy for others to enter. After all, how many choices do you need for places to buy pet food on the Internet? One of the reasons behind the demise of many dot-com companies in the year 2000 was that it was so easy to enter a market that too many companies who were poorly prepared for the competitive environment did so. Ultimately, many of them failed. Successful companies try to use information technology to erect what are called

INDUSTRY PERSPECTIVE ".com"

Keeping an Eye on the Competition

If you're a retailer in the bricks and mortar world, it's important to keep an eye on what your competition is doing. For example, if you walk into the conference room of a supermarket's office, you'll likely find the walls plastered with their newspaper ads side by side with those of their competitors. The managers want to be sure their prices are not too far out of line with everyone else's. It's a bit more difficult if you're a retailer on the Web. Since the Web has global reach, you could have thousands of competitors offering the same products as you. Trying to keep track of what thousands of competitors are doing is next to impossible.

One answer could be RivalWatch.com. For $150,000 a year, they will monitor the activities of as many Web-based competitors as a company can identify. They inform their clients on the competition's pricing, product assortment, availability, and even promotional activities.

Lest they be accused of spying on the competition, a RivalWatch.com executive is careful to point out that all of the information they gather on behalf of their clients is publicly available. It's just that most clients don't have the software power to gather and analyze the information for themselves. Some companies are asking RivalWatch.com to monitor as many as 1,000 products from 12 to 15 competitors each day.[17]

---

entry barriers. An ***entry barrier*** is a product or service feature that customers have come to expect from companies in a particular industry. Entry barriers make it more difficult for competitors to enter a particular market. A good example of an entry barrier is what we have come to expect from our bank. When we consider where it is that we might like to do our banking, we want to be sure they can offer us an ATM card that works at lots of locations locally and even around the world. We'd also like to be able to access our account on the Internet so that we can see if a deposit was recorded or if a check has cleared. We might also want to be able to pay bills from the bank's Internet site. When one bank in a region first introduced such information technology services, they gained a competitive advantage. Other banks saw that they had to introduce similar services or face the loss of some of their customers to the bank that was more advanced. Now, such services are entry barriers to anyone who thinks of starting a new bank. They will have to make the investment in information technology to offer services customers have come to expect from a bank. Otherwise, they will be at a competitive disadvantage.

5. **Rivalry among Existing Competitors.** There are many ways that information technology can make one company better prepared than its rivals in an intensely competitive setting. For example, many retailers compete on the basis of price, particularly with commodity-like products. Whether you buy a six-pack of Diet Pepsi at a convenience store or at a discount chain, it will taste the same. Price will be the difference. One of the reasons it could be cheaper at the discount chain store is because the chain store uses information systems to be more efficient, much like Wal-Mart. So, if you have the time and other things to buy, you'll most likely buy that six-pack of Pepsi at the discount chain. For a retailer, having information systems to be more efficient and lower costs so that it can compete with lower prices is a definite advantage.

Using the Three Generic Strategies

The three generic strategies and information technology are usually used together in the following way. Companies use information technology to change the basis of competition in ways that are favorable to them. For example, if they find that they are embroiled in a fierce competitive marketplace where all of the players

ON YOUR OWN

Building on the State of the Art

It's good to get into the habit of noticing the ways that companies are using or not using IT effectively. You can start to build up your own catalog of ideas for your own organization. It's always good to use to use a state-of-the-art application and see if you can build on it to come up with something even better. Pick a company that you think is getting a competitive advantage from IT and try to suggest ways that it could be improved. This is the time to let your imagination run free and to consider using some of the new emerging technologies. ❖

---

are competing on the basis of price, they could use information technology to develop and support a strategy based on differentiation. Amazon.com deals with many commodity-like products for which competition (as we saw with Diet Pepsi) is usually based on lowest price. New books, CDs, and videos are all commodity-like products. It doesn't really matter where you buy them, they will all be the same.

You may have noticed, however, that while Amazon.com has good prices, their price is often not the lowest. (If you want to check this out, log on to http://www.mysimon.com and compare the prices at Amazon.com with those of other Internet retailers for a book, CD, or video you're thinking of buying.) What Amazon.com has done well, however, is to make our buying experience a pleasurable one by making the site informative and easy to navigate and by using sophisticated software to personalize the site for each individual customer. The more we shop at Amazon.com, the more personalized it can make our customer experience. It has used information technology to permit it to pursue a differentiated strategy in what would otherwise be simply a low-cost marketplace.

The Value Chain

Once you understand how IT can help you develop and sustain a business strategy, the next thing to see is how IT can support important business processes. A *business process* is a standardized set of activities that accomplishes a specific task, such as processing a customer's order. One important graphic tool to identify important processes is Michael Porter's value chain.

The *value chain* views the organization as a chain—or series—of processes, each of which adds value to the product or service for the customer. Adding value is what your organization does to deliver a more perfect product or service to the customer. If you view your organization as a value chain, you can identify the processes that add value for customers and, thus, identify IT systems that can support those value-adding processes.

Figure 2.9 on the next page depicts the components of a value chain. The primary value processes along the bottom half of the chain make, deliver, market and sell, and service your organization's products or services. Processes along the top half of the chain, such as management, accounting, finance, legal, human resources, research and development, and purchasing, support the primary value processes. Your organization requires these support value processes to ensure the smooth operation of the primary value processes in its value chain.

All value processes process an individual value. However, these processes combined have a total value greater than the sum of their individual values. We call this additional value *value-added,* and it's depicted on the far right of the value chain. The larger the value-added, the more value customers place on an organization's product or service. To the organization, this can mean a competitive advantage and often greater profits. Let's look at how a firm might use the value chain to identify both value-added and value-reducing processes.

If you've ever purchased a necktie, you may have heard of the Robert Talbott company of Carmel Valley, California.[18] Talbott is the premier necktie manufacturer in the United States, providing one of every two ties sold in a Nordstrom department store. Talbott has always shunned technology—all of its tie orders, historically, were written on paper forms.

That used to work fine, because Talbott's has always ensured added value by utilizing high-quality workmanship, unique designs, and fine fabrics. However, customer "wants" drive their demands, and so those demands are always changing. Today, customers want constantly updated styles and more of them. In fact, Talbott now creates four neckwear lines for Nordstrom each year with up to 300 designs per line. Keeping up with all those necktie designs has become increasingly difficult for Talbott. Given this situation, how could the value chain help Talbott plan for a better way of meeting customer demands? Well, it would begin by identifying both value-added and value-reducing processes. Let's look at the identification of value-added processes first.

Identifying Processes That Add Value

Talbott should begin by looking at the firm's business processes and identifying, with help from customers, those processes that add the most value. These include manufacturing high-quality ties and purchasing quality materials at Talbott. Then Talbott should graphically depict the customer responses on a value chain. Figure 2.10 is one possible result. Notice how the processes are sized to depict the value that customers attribute to those processes. The largest value-added source is the high-quality manufacturing process. Still, a close second is the purchasing process that provides access to high-quality silks and other fabrics. As these processes are the ones that are most visible to the customers, they will quickly add even more value when supported by new IT systems. Therefore, Talbott created a computer-aided design system to reduce the time it takes to create and manufacture new ties.

Identifying Processes That Reduce Value

In addition to identifying *value-added* processes, it's important to identify those processes that *reduce* value for the customer. Using the same technique to gather this information from the customers, Talbott should create a value-reducing value chain. Talbott identified the sales process as the process that reduced value the most, as shown in Figure 2.11 on page 66. It found sales were lost because salespeople were promising neckties that were out of stock. It often took up to three days to discover the out-of-stock status and communicate that fact to the customers. Customers were beginning to lose faith in Talbott's ability to deliver high-quality ties. They saw this process failure as one that reduced Talbott's value to them as customers.

To correct the sales process deficiencies, Talbott implemented a new IT system to get timely product information to the sales force. Using laptop computers,

The value chain is composed of primary value and support value processes. From left to right, and along the bottom half of the chain, the organization creates its product or service through primary value processes. Along the top half of the chain, the support value processes provide the organization support in performing those primary value processes. When all processes are combined they have a total value greater than the sum of their individual values, called "value-added," and it's depicted on the far right of the value chain. Greater value-added means a competitive advantage and, often, greater profits.

FIGURE 2.9

The Components of a Value Chain

the sales force now carries product-line custom CD-ROMs on the road with them. They place orders over their computers from their hotel rooms and receive inventory updates at the same time. As a result, customers have new faith in an old friend who now adds more value than ever.

What's Different with E-Commerce?

The big difference between the new economy and the old economy is the Internet. We have discussed some examples of companies that have created competitive advantage through the creative use of IT. In recent years, however, the Internet and, in particular, the World Wide Web have created a burst of new entrepreneurship, new ways to reach out to customers and suppliers, new businesses using business models never seen before. It has been a time of experimentation with some spectacular successes, and also failures.

The Internet is global, can now be found everywhere, and is either free or quite inexpensive in many countries. Companies searching for competitive advantage should keep in mind three Internet capabilities.

1. Mass Customization and Personalization
2. Disintermediation
3. Global Reach

Let's examine how each of these works.

Mass Customization and Personalization

Mass customization and personalization are two different concepts that are sometimes confused. With *mass customization*, a business gives its customers the opportunity to tailor its product or service to the

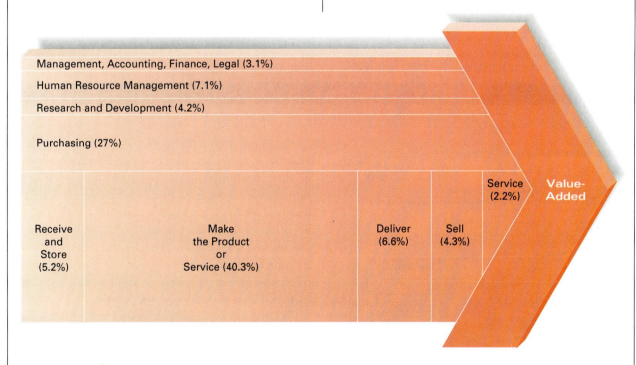

Talbott asked its customers to quantify how much value each process added to the products and services they received. Using a total of 100 points for the value chain, each customer distributed those points among Talbott's processes. The results from all customers were tallied and used to size each process in the value chain. Process percentages total 100 percent for the value chain.

The results showed that the high-quality production process (Make the Product or Service) adds the most value for the customer at 40.3 percent. Also highly valued is the process that purchases unique, high-quality fabrics (Purchasing, 27%). As these processes are most visible to customers, they will quickly add even more value when supported by new IT systems.

FIGURE 2.10

The Value-Added View of a Necktie Manufacturer

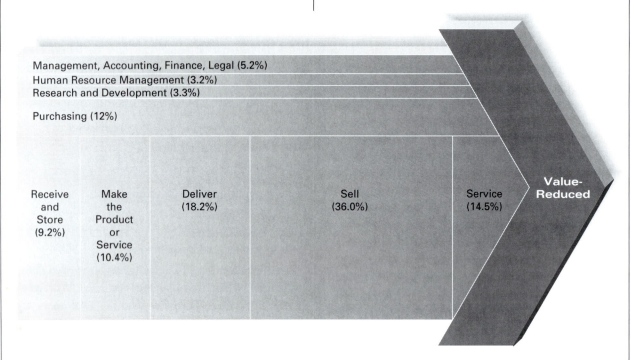

Talbott asked its customers to quantify how much each process reduced the value of the products and services they received. Using a total of 100 points for the value chain, each customer distributed those points among Talbott's processes. The results from all customers were tallied and used to size each process in the value chain. Process percentages total 100 percent for the value chain.

The results showed that the selling process (Sell) reduces the value for the customer the most at 36.0 percent. Any process that significantly reduces value to customers is a target for improvement and support by IT systems. For most firms, including Talbott, they just cannot afford to allow a process to endanger their relationships with customers.

FIGURE 2.11

The Value-Reduced View of a Necktie Manufacturer

FIGURE 2.12

Create Your Own Custom CD at CDNow

customer's specifications. For example, if you order an automobile from the factory, you can have it made with exactly the list of options and colors you wish. An example of mass customization in an Internet business is the customized CDs you can order through http://www.cdnow.com. Usually when you buy a CD there are about 12 tracks on it and you're lucky if you like three of them. So, you end up playing the tracks you like and skipping past the ones you don't. CDNow and others let you create your own CD containing only tracks you like as illustrated in Figure 2.12. You pick them and then the CD is created for you.

Personalization takes a different twist. The idea of ***personalization*** is that an Internet site can know enough about your likes and dislikes that it can fashion offers that are more likely to appeal to you. Think about personalization this way. What if you could open up the daily newspaper and the only ads you saw were ads for products or services that you were really interested in. No more ads for mattresses, wireless phones, or sofas. Personalization techniques try to do the same thing, get offers in front of you that you are much more likely to find interesting. One of the best examples is the books that Amazon.com will suggest to you when you log

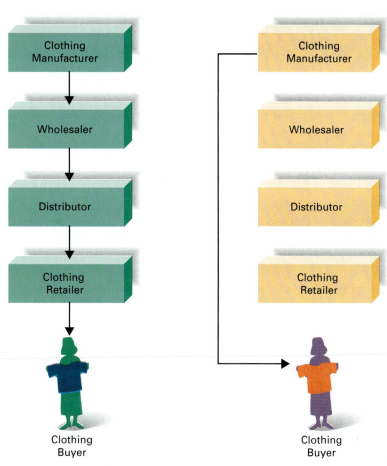

Disintermediation occurs when one or more intermediaries in the supply chain are bypassed. For example, if you buy clothing directly from a manufacturer, such as Lands' End, wholesalers, distributors, and retailers who are normally in the supply chain are by-passed.

FIGURE 2.13

Disintermediation at Work

onto their site. Using a technique called collaborative filtering, it keeps track of your taste in books. ***Collaborative filtering*** is a technique to enable a Web site to support personalization. Based on buying patterns you establish over time, the Web site places you in an affinity group of people who like the same sort of topics. Then, it tracks the buying patterns of the affinity group as well as yours, and make suggestions to you for books the affinity group is buying that you have not yet bought. With the creative use of IT, it can give you the personal service you might expect from a small, owner-managed bookstore in your home town where the owner knew your tastes and could suggest books you would be interested in reading.

Disintermediation

Disintermediation simply means that with the Internet as a delivery vehicle, intermediate players in a distribution channel can be bypassed, as illustrated in Figure 2.13. For example, if you buy a book from Amazon.com, the bookstore on Main Street is bypassed. Many Internet business models have taken advantage of the ability to bypass intermediaries such as wholesalers and retailers to reach the consumer directly. Good advice for businesses occupying an intermediary position in a distribution channel is to think through how an e-business might enter the market and take customers away from them. There are scores of examples of this happening to stockbrokers, insurance agents, real estate agents, mortgage brokers, as well as to merchants selling commodity-like items such as books, videos, and CDs.

One interesting example is Egghead Software (http://www.egghead.com). Egghead Software used to have stores in strip malls in many cities. It soon found that it was being disintermediated by the Internet. Customers who might have normally come into an Egghead store and buy a shrinkwrapped software package off the shelf were finding that it was more convenient to buy software from a Web site and have it downloaded immediately. What did Egghead finally do? They closed their brick and mortar stores and set up shop in cyberspace.

Global Reach

Sausage Software (http://www.sausagetools.com) is a software developer located outside Melbourne, Australia. They make a pretty good web editor called Hot Dog. If you want to try it out, you can log on to their Web site and download a trial copy that you can use free for 30 days, as shown in Figure 2.14.

At the end of the 30-day trial period, if you want to continue to use Hot Dog, you'll have to log on to the Web site and give your credit card number. Sausage will send you a coded string of numbers by email that you key into Hot Dog. The code opens up the software for you to use forever, just as if you had bought it off the shelf at CompUSA. Think about what just happened. You bought a piece of software, had it delivered to your home computer and paid for it, all over the Internet. Without the Internet, if Sausage wanted to reach you in the United States, it would have had to put someone on an airplane for Los Angeles, find a software retailer like CompUSA, and convince the buyers to add copies of Hot Dog to their stores' shelves. Since shelf space is limited and Hot Dog is not well known, Sausage probably would have to pay the retailer $20,000 or so as a "stocking fee" just to get Hot Dog on the shelves of a few stores so the retailer could see how it sells. The Internet gives even small companies like Sausage Software *global reach,* the ability to extend their reach to customers anywhere there is an Internet connection, and at a much lower cost. So much the better if the product is digital, for then it can be both sold and delivered over the Internet.

New Technologies that Work with the Internet

One the most exciting things about working in the IT field is that new and better technologies are always being introduced. This makes it possible for bright people to figure out how the new technologies can be used to give their organization a competitive advantage. Some of the new and emerging technologies that are becoming important are:

1. Wireless communications
2. Broadband communications
3. XML
4. Peer to peer networking

We'll talk more about these technologies and how they will be used in e-commerce applications elsewhere in this text. For now, let's just take a look at how wireless communications could be used for competitive advantage.

The trend is for the global positioning system to be integrated with wireless devices, either cellular telephones, PDAs, or pagers. The satellite-based global positioning system (GPS) enables the location of a receiving device anywhere on Earth to be pinpointed. By late 2001, the U.S. Federal Communications Commission has mandated that cellular telephones in the United States have GPS capability.[19] The reason for adding this capability is to be able to locate people during a 911 emergency. If you call 911 from your home telephone, emergency response personnel can quickly find out where you live from a database, because your

FIGURE 2.14
Downloading Hot Dog

Taking Advantage of Emerging Technologies

Emerging Technologies are technologies that are still in the research and development stage and may or may not prove to be important in a few years. A well-managed company in the information age will have a group of people who focus on emerging technologies. Some of the things they do include:

- Environmental Scanning. Keep in touch with research and development efforts going in industry and university research labs.
- Select specific technologies that may have business benefit for the company.
- Begin to pilot test the technologies in-house in cooperation with business units.
- Select pilot applications for the new technologies.
- If successful, migrate them to other appropriate business units.

See Chapter 6 for some specific emerging technologies. ❖

---

home telephone number appears on their equipment and is always associated with the same location. It's not the same with your cell phone, however. If you dial 911 from your cell phone, you could be calling from anywhere. With GPS capability integrated with your cell phone, emergency response personnel will be able to locate you accurately to within an area the size of a tennis court. This capability, of course, will be very useful to anyone who is unfortunate enough to drive into a ditch on a rainy night on a dark, unfamiliar, country road.

Once GPS is integrated with wireless, numerous possibilities open up for marketers. You recall the importance of personalization in e-commerce, and how effective personalization messages can give your organization a competitive advantage. Well, now marketers will know not only who you are, but where you are. Imagine walking through the mall when your cell phone rings. It's the Ralph Lauren store calling. They know you're walking right by them and that you would be interested in a special reduction on sweaters. (Of course, you can turn your cell phone off, but Ralph Lauren hopes you'll wish to turn it on while shopping.)

Of course you don't want your phone going off all the time with offers that you're not interested in, so marketers will use permission marketing. ***Permission marketing*** simply means that marketers will get your permission to send your way only offers you're very likely to find attractive. Can you think of other applications for cell phones with GPS capability?

The U.S. Airline Industry: A Great Example

To give you a feel for how much of what we have been discussing in this chapter can come together in a single industry, it's hard to think of a better example than the U.S. air travel industry. The large U.S. airlines, in particular, have given ample evidence over a number of years that they know how to use information technology for competitive advantage. Let's show you what we mean.

Airline Reservation Systems

The airlines really got started using IT in a significant way when American Airlines and United Airlines

FIGURE 2.15
One Scenario for Wireless M-Commerce

introduced the first airline reservations systems, SABRE and APOLLO. At the time they pretty much divided up the market between them. They marketed the reservation systems to travel agents who got a special computer terminal from either SABRE or APOLLO when they signed up. Typically, a travel agent signed up for one or the other system, but not both. Airline companies who did not have their own reservation systems, Frontier Airlines, for example, paid for the privilege of being a "co-host" on SABRE or APOLLO, which permitted their flights to be listed on the systems and available to travel agents. American and United got a tremendous competitive advantage from being the owners of the reservation systems. First, the systems were very profitable. Second, American and United had access to information on the sales volumes of their competitors such as Frontier because it was all available in the reservation systems database. If Frontier wanted to have special competitive analyses prepared it could request special reports, but had to pay for them and wait for them to be prepared.

SABRE and APOLLO were accused by their co-hosts of "screen bias."[20] This meant that when a travel agent keyed in a request, available flights between Chicago and San Francisco, for example, the first flights shown were those of the airline who owned the reservation system. Flights of co-hosts such as Frontier were shown later.

Frequent Flyer Programs

When the airlines introduced frequent flyer programs (the airline industry's form of loyalty program), it was to increase the likelihood that their most valued customers, their frequent business travelers, would fly them instead of the competition. Until frequent flyer programs were introduced, business people had no particular incentive to fly the same airline all the time.

After frequent flyer programs came into being, with their mileage and other perks, air travelers saw that it made sense to concentrate their travel with a single airline as much as possible in order to get free trips and upgrades to first class. Frequent flyer programs became very popular and now almost every airline in the world has some sort of program. Frequent flyer programs require complex computer systems to handle all the record keeping and reporting. They are a good example of using IT to alter Porter's five forces in the airlines' favor. They reduced buyer power by making it less likely a traveler would choose another airline; they reduced the threat of substitute products or services by increasing switching costs; and they erected entry barriers by making a frequent flyer program a practical necessity for any airline to compete effectively.

Yield Management Systems

Yield management systems are designed to maximize the revenue that an airline generates on each flight. Basically, what they do is alter the price of available seats on a flight minute by minute as the date of the flight approaches, depending on the number of seats that have been sold compared to an estimate of what was expected. So, if fewer seats have been sold, more low-cost seats are made available for sale. If more seats have been sold than what was estimated, fewer low-cost seats will be made available for sale. The objective is to have the airplane take off full at the highest possible average cost per seat, as illustrated in Figure 2.16. (Airlines would

Helping the Little Guy Compete

Assume that a friend of your family owns a small travel agency located in a neighborhood shopping center. The business has provided a comfortable living for him and his family for over 20 years. With the recent changes in the air travel distribution industry, however, he is becoming concerned about whether or not he can survive in the new competitive environment. Airline companies have reduced commissions paid to travel agents, and at the same time have encouraged members of their frequent flyer programs (the best customers) to bypass travel agents and deal with airlines directly. In addition, new competition has arisen from Internet-based travel sites. Using IT-enabled techniques such as E-tickets seems to be part of a never-ending process to squeeze travel agents. With new technologies being introduced all the time, your friend is concerned that there is no way he can survive.

See if you can come up with some suggestions for how he could use IT to improve his ability to compete. ❖

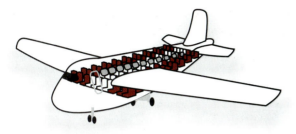

Average seat = $420
Yield = $50,400

120 seats occupied at average price of = $420 per seat = $50,400 total yield for the flight.

Average seat = $325
Yield = $65,000

200 seats occupied at average price of = $325 per seat = $65,000 total yield for the flight.

FIGURE 2.16

The Payoff from Yield Management

rather make something on a low-cost seat than make nothing on an empty seat.)

Yield management systems are the reason that an airfare you're quoted over the phone can be $100 higher when you call back an hour later. Yield management systems are also why you should never ask your seatmate what she paid for her ticket unless you're prepared to be disappointed. They're a good example of how the *value chain* concept used IT to add value to the sales and marketing process.

Disintermediating the Travel Agent

Travel agents get a commission from the airlines on every ticket they sell. Airlines, realizing that agents' commissions were their third-highest cost after payroll and fuel, decided to reduce travel agents' commissions, and at the same time, make it easier for air travelers to make reservations directly with the airlines either through a Web site or by using a toll-free 800 number. They encouraged their frequent flyers to bypass the travel agents by doing three additional things:

1. They offered up to 1,000 frequent flyer miles to travelers who made their reservations on the Web.

2. They gave out restricted toll-free 800 numbers to members of frequent flyer "elite" groups, with shorter waiting times and specially trained reservationists.

3. They introduced "e-tickets" which eliminated the need for a paper ticket. One of the travel agent's most valued functions was to see that the traveler had his or her ticket well in advance of the flight. With the introduction of e-tickets, the paper ticket disappeared, replaced by a digital record in the airlines' computer systems.

Expert surveys have estimated that the number of travel agents in the United States will be sharply reduced as a result of these and other moves by the airline companies.[21]

Note, however, that the competitive landscape in the air travel industry continues to change as tech-savvy entrepreneurs come up with new business ideas. Internet-based travel services such as Expedia, Travelocity, and Trip.com, have entered the market, as has Priceline.com, where customers can name their own price. Last-minute deals to make sure all those seats are filled are sent out by personalized e-mails on Wednesday of each week. You've told the airline's Web site that you want to know when there are last-minute bargain fares to New York, and given the airline permission to send you those e-mails. Auction sites such as bid4vacations.com are another approach. Wireless applications are on the way. It will not be long before your airline will call your cell phone and tell you to sleep in for another hour because your flight has been delayed.

You can see how the airlines have employed Michael Porter's frameworks as well as some of the other approaches discussed in this chapter: taking the customer's perspective, demanding creativity, personalization, disintermediation, and coming up with new ways to relate to customers and suppliers.

KNOWLEDGE WORKER'S -LIST

How the Creative Use of Information Technology Can Give an Organization a Competitive Advantage. Smart companies spend a lot of time, money, and effort in designing and installing IT systems because they realize a competitive advantage when IT systems deliver creative solutions to business problems. A *competitive advantage* can be gained by providing a product or service in a way that customers value more than the competition's. Some concepts related to IT systems are

- *Temporary advantage*—whatever you do, sooner or later the competition duplicates what you've done, but a temporary advantage can linger in customers' minds and have lasting effects.
- *First mover*—first to market with a new IT-based product or service can gain competitive advantage.
- *Information partnership*—two or more companies acting in cooperation by integrating their IT systems provide customers with the best of what each can offer.
- *Alliance partner*—companies that you do business with on a regular basis in a cooperative fashion.
- *Business to Business (B2B)*—IT-enabled business with other businesses.
- *Business to Consumer (B2C)*—IT-enabled business with individual customers.

How to Generate Ideas for Using Information Technology in Innovative Ways, and Tools That Can Help. Creating an IT system that gives you a competitive advantage is not merely a technical challenge. Important considerations include:

1. The CEO's attitude toward information technology
2. Bridging the gap between business people and technical people
3. Viewing the business problem from another perspective
4. Demanding a creative design
5. Looking beyond the four walls of the company

Concepts to remember and tools that can help include:

1. *The five forces model*
    - *Buyer power*
    - *Supplier power*
    - *Threat of substitute products or services*
    - *Threat of new entrants*
    - *Rivalry among existing competitors*
2. *Three generic strategies*
    - *Cost leadership*
    - *Differentiation*
    - *Focused strategy*
3. *The value chain*—a view of the organization as a chain—or series—of processes, each of which adds value to the product or service for the customer

THE GLOBAL PERSPECTIVE

Paperless Payments

Many organizations today ask the same, nagging question: When will we get paid? For some who do business with governments slow to pay, the question can loom quite large. Pharmacists working with the British Columbia Ministry of Health used to wait as long as 60 days to get word of when they would get paid. Today, however, pharmacists receive the same decision within 20 seconds—online. In the old prescription claim system, claims were paper-based and all were processed manually. The new online system eliminates the need for paper claims and saves the ministry the equivalent of 30 full-time jobs. Communicating information electronically has other benefits as well. In addition to filing claims online, pharmacists can check prescription histories for 2.8 million people within seconds. This allows the pharmacist to ensure new prescriptions won't create adverse side effects with existing prescriptions. Providing benefits to the pharmacist users of the system encourages system use. The pharmacists benefit and the ministry benefits by encouraging pharmacists to avoid paper claims. All told, this paperless system will pay for itself in just 6 months. So, now, the ministry isn't the only one who knows when pharmacists get paid.[22, 23] ❖

How E-Commerce Technologies "Up the Stakes" and Give Organizations Even More Opportunities. E-Commerce makes it even more important for you to focus on competitive advantage. The main reason for this is that the Internet and related technologies provide new capabilities to establish more effective information partnerships along the supply and distribution chains and to forge closer relationships with customers. This can be achieved through:

- *Mass customization*—when a business gives its customers the opportunity to have its product or service tailored to the customer's specifications
- *Personalization*—when an Internet site can know enough about your likes and dislikes that it can fashion offers that are more likely to appeal to you (supported by techniques such as *collaborative filtering*)
- *Disintermediation*—with the Internet as a delivery vehicle, intermediate players in a distribution channel can be bypassed
- *Global reach*—the ability to extend reach to customers anywhere there is an Internet connection, and at a much lower cost

How One Specific Industry Has Consistently Used Information Technology for Competitive Advantage. The U.S. air travel industry is a good industry for you to study to see how companies can consistently use IT for competitive advantage over a period of many years to both reduce costs and create differentiation. For example, the airlines' frequent flyer programs increase customer loyalty by encouraging frequent flyers to take most or all of their flights on a single airline. Using Porter's five forces framework, frequent flyer programs reduce buyer power and increase switching costs. And frequent flyers like them! Because they do, frequent flyer programs also are also an example of an entry barrier. If you want to be in the airline business you pretty much have to have a frequent flyer program. Frequent flyer programs also illustrate how a competitive advantage is often only temporary as competitors race to duplicate innovative IT systems. Other examples of the use of IT for competitive advantage include the airline reservation systems, yield management systems, and the airline companies' e-commerce initiatives.

How to Use Information Technology for Competitive Advantage in Their Organizations. Try to get into the habit of looking for ways that IT could be used to solve a business problem in your organization. Work with IT professionals to get their ideas and look around to see what the state of the art is, not only in your industry, but in others as well. Keep in mind that you are operating in a competitive environment and that it will be useful for you to try to anticipate what your competition's next move in the IT arena might be. Remember that the nature of a competitive environment is that there are winners and losers. IT <u>can</u> give you a competitive advantage, but "if you snooze, you'll lose!" ❖

Summing It Up

We've talked about ideas for using IT for competitive advantage, discussed tools companies use to generate such ideas, and given several examples of IT systems that have given their organizations a competitive advantage. Now, we'll summarize some of the most important things you should keep in mind as you work to bring an IT competitive advantage to your organization.

First, remember that what you are trying to do is to make your organization more efficient and more effective. That means that you should be applying IT to solving an important business problem. It's the difference between doing something right and doing the right thing. IT resources are limited in most organizations so it's important that they be applied to solving the most important business problems or exploiting the opportunities with the highest potential payoff.

Second, remember that your organization is in a competitive environment. The reason we emphasize competitive advantage is that you and your competitors are both trying to attract and retain the same customers. You are all competing for that customer's business. We all tend to buy from the company that gives us the best product or service at the price we want to pay and the customers of your organization are no different. Companies should strive to "delight the customer" by giving them more value than what they were expecting to receive. Keep that in mind when you're reviewing proposals for new IT systems. Will they help you to delight your customers? It's always smart to try to anticipate how your competitor might use IT for competitive advantage. Why let them get a first-mover advantage?

Third, in addition to the other suggestions we made in this chapter, if an IT system is going to give you a competitive advantage it must push the state of the art.

In order to push the state of the art, you must find out what a state-of-the-art IT system is for the business problem you are trying to solve. Do a little research to find out which company has the best solution and then try to surpass it. And don't restrict your search to just your industry. A state-of-the-art system for a hospital, for example, might find some ideas in a manufacturing control system. Don't let your imagination be limited by just considering technologies that are currently available, or discard currently available technologies because they are too expensive. If you place artificial boundaries like these on candidate solutions you may inhibit creativity unnecessarily. You can always bring an overly ambitious solution back to reality, but if you don't evaluate it, the opportunity will be lost.

One other point worth reemphasizing is that using IT for competitive advantage usually provides only a temporary advantage. This is because your competitors are forced to duplicate (or to better) what you have. This means that your organization must be continually looking for ways to use IT for competitive advantage so you stay ahead of, or don't fall behind, the competition.

That may sound like a lot of work, and a never-ending cycle, but the reassuring reality is that there will be continuing opportunities for you to come up with creative IT solutions to business problems.

CLOSING CASE STUDY

GM Tries to Lure Customers with OnStar

General Motors Corp. has suffered a loss in market share in the United States in the past few years. Partly this is because many of its cars are viewed as boring by consumers. GM recently added an in-car Internet and cellular service to many of its cars in an attempt to update its image and increase sales.

The service is called OnStar and was originally offered in Cadillacs in 1996 as an emergency concierge and road service. It uses a global positioning system (GPS) combined with a cellular telephone and a 24 hour call center. Fees for the OnStar service start at $195 for an annual subscription. You may have seen ads on television for OnStar, showing a driver who is calling the OnStar call center because he has locked his keys in his car. The OnStar call center operator tells him not to worry and unlocks his car doors with a remote signal from the center. Problem solved. OnStar subscribers can also get emergency roadside assistance and driving directions. The integrated GPS combined with cellular connection to the call center provides assurance that a vehicle can be located no matter what. As one example, emergency assistance is automatically dispatched if the OnStar system detects that the car's airbags have been deployed.

GM also has plans to upgrade the onboard cellular system into a platform for delivering Web-based e-mail and content, as well as voice-activated calling to its OnStar menu.

Industry analysts have commented that adding services like OnStar is something GM had to do in order to improve its brands' images in the minds of consumers. GM is betting that being the leader with an onboard technology like OnStar will show that it is once again technology leader rather than a follower.

It used to be a dealer-installed option, but OnStar now comes standard in GM vehicles. It's one of the many small ways that GM President Rick Wagoner wants to keep the company innovative. Estimates are that the cost to develop OnStar was considerably less than the $500 million or more that it costs to develop a new vehicle.

GM expects to have an embedded OnStar system installed in at least 1 million vehicles in 31 different models by the end of 2000. It currently has about 150,000 subscribers and are adding over 5,000 each month. Still, some industry analysts remain skeptical about the OnStar initiative. They agree that OnStar offers some interesting features that will be valued by consumers. On the other hand, they point out that if GM doesn't do something about its fundamental problem, the style of its cars, it will not be able to pull out of its downward spiral in market share. They go on to say that the most important thing that GM should focus on is sharpening up its design and manufacturing. It needs to build vehicles that young people want to buy.[24] ❖

◄ Questions ►

1. The chapter discussed several examples of companies that have used IT for competitive advantage. Is there anything about the OnStar system that makes it a good example as well? Is OnStar a feature that is likely to give GM a competitive advantage for an extended period of time or is it likely to give, if anything, a temporary advantage?

2. Evaluate the OnStar system from the perspectives of the five forces model and the three generic strategies. Explain how OnStar might alter the five

forces in GM's favor. Where would you place the OnStar system in the three generic strategies grid illustrated in Figure 2.8?

3. Is OnStar a good example of a company incorporating emerging technologies into its product strategies? Why or why not? What features do you think a system such as OnStar might offer five years from now? Is GM taking any risks by placing such a large bet on OnStar's being accepted by the marketplace? What are those risks, if any?

4. If you were a product designer for Ford Motor Company, what would your reaction be to GM's rollout of OnStar? Do you think that systems such as OnStar will become an entry barrier? Log on to the Internet and see if you can find out what the other major automobile manufacturers, both U.S. and non-U.S., are doing in response to the OnStar system. Draw a conclusion as to which responses you think will be most effective.

5. What would your reaction to OnStar be if you were a marketing strategist for a cell-phone, Internet Portal, or GPS service provider? Would you consider OnStar to be a competitive threat to your company? If so, why, and what would your response be? If you would not consider OnStar to be a threat, why not?

6. What additional applications could you suggest to GM as areas it could focus on to use IT for competitive advantage that might give it an equal or better payoff than what it is hoping to get from OnStar? Can you think of applications that would let it gain manufacturing or supply chain efficiencies? Can you think of applications that would give it efficiencies in distribution? Could GM go to a mass-customized, direct-sell model like Dell Computer's and deal directly with its customers, bypassing dealers the way the airlines have bypassed travel agents?

Electronic Commerce
Business and You on the Internet

Ordering Products on the Internet

For most people, electronic commerce is all about business-to-consumer (B2C). That is, most of us think of electronic commerce as an essential enabler for allowing businesses to interact with its individual consumers (you and me). The B2C aspect of electronic commerce certainly dominates the Internet right now. On the Internet, you (as an individual consumer) can purchase groceries, clothes, computers, automobiles, music, antiques, books, and much more. If you want to buy it, there's probably an Internet site selling it. Even more, there are probably hundreds of Internet sites selling what it is you want, giving you the opportunity to shop for the best buy.

We would offer a couple of words of caution before you begin this project. Those words are "caveat emptor" or "let the buyer beware." You can indeed find almost anything you want to buy on the Internet. However, you should carefully consider the person or organization from whom you're making the purchase. This is especially true if you have to provide a credit card number to make the purchase.

Books and Music

Books and music make up one category of products you can readily find to purchase on the Internet. One of the most widely known and acclaimed Internet sites performing electronic commerce is Amazon.com at

http://www.amazon.com. Amazon boasts over 3 million book and music titles for sale.

Of course, as with all products you buy on the Internet, you need to consider price and the amount you'll save on the Internet compared to purchasing books and music from local stores. Sometimes, prices are higher on the Internet, and you can certainly expect to pay some sort of shipping and handling charges. So don't blindly purchase any product on the Internet without first checking local stores.

Make a list of books, music CDs or cassettes that you're interested in purchasing. Find their prices at a local store. Next, visit three Web sites selling books and music and answer the following questions.

A. What are the books or music albums you're interested in?

B. What are their prices at a local store?

C. Can you find them at each Internet site?

D. How does each site categorize its books and music?

E. Are the local prices higher or lower than the Internet prices?

F. How do you order and pay for your products?

G. How long is the shipping delay?

H. What is the shipping charge?

I. Overall, how would you rate your Internet shopping experience compared to your local store shopping experience?

Clothing and Accessories

It might seem odd, but many people purchase all types of clothing on the Internet—from shoes to pants to all kinds of accessories (including perfume). The disadvantage in shopping for clothes on the Internet is that you can't actually try them on and stand in front of the mirror. But if you know exactly what you want (by size and color), you can probably find and buy it on the Internet.

Connect to several clothing and accessory sites and experience cyber-clothing shopping. As you do, consider the following. How do you order and pay for merchandise? What sort of description is provided about the clothing—text, photos, perhaps 3D views? What is the return policy for merchandise that you don't like or doesn't fit? Can clothing retail stores expect to see a decline in sales as more people shop on the Internet? Finally, is shopping for clothes on the Internet as much fun as going to the mall? Why or why not?

Computers and Accessories

It only makes sense that the Internet (a computing-based environment) is full of online stores where you can purchase anything computing-related. And what's really great is that most of these sites provide product reviews, the ability to customize your own system, and technical support once you make your purchase. To see how purchasing a computer on the Internet works, think about the system you'd like to have—CPU speed, internal memory size, storage peripherals, and monitor characteristics.

Connect to three different computer-related sites (definitely consider connecting to Dell, Gateway, HP, or cdw.com) and evaluate their effectiveness in allowing you to shop for a computer system. As you do, answer the following questions for each site.

A. What is the cost of your "dream" system?

B. How do you specify the characteristics of your system?

C. How do you order your system?

D. What packaged software—if any—comes with your system?

E. Does the site offer any financing?

F. Does the site offer any "special" already-built systems?

G. What sort of technical support is provided once you purchase your system?

H. How long does it take for your system to be shipped to you?

Many of the sites you visited may offer product reviews and recommendations concerning how to configure the best system. What they probably don't do is provide a list of pricing alternatives comparing other

Web sites. Before you buy a computer online, you should definitely do some competitive pricing. Fortunately, there are some sites devoted to providing you with that information. At Price Scan (http://www.pricescan.com), for example, you can obtain a great review of competitive pricing on almost any technology-related product. If you search around the Internet (using search terms such as "computer" and "buyers guide"), you'll undoubtedly find a great number of sites that provide similar information.

Internet Auction Houses

As you search for products on the Internet, you'll find a lot of individuals and traditional organizations such as The Gap selling their wares. You'll also come across a variety of Internet auction houses. These auction houses act as clearing stations on which you can sell your products or purchase products from other people in an auction format (essentially, Consumer to Consumer or C2C electronic commerce). Auction houses represent some serious electronic commerce on the Internet. EBay, one of the more popular auction houses, boasts an amazing 10 million items for sale.

It works quite simply. First, you register as a user at a particular auction house. Once you do, you'll have a special user ID (perhaps your e-mail address or a special name you give yourself) and password that allow you to post products for sale or bid on other products. When the auction is complete for a particular product (auction houses set time limits that last typically from one to 10 days), the auction house will notify the seller and the winning bidder of the final price. Then, it's up to you and the other person to exchange money and merchandise.

So, think of a product you'd like to buy or sell—perhaps a rare coin, a computer, a hard-to-find Beanie Baby, or a car. Connect to a couple of different Internet auction houses and answer the following questions for each.

A. What is the registration process to become a user?
B. Do you have to pay a fee to become a user?
C. Is your product of interest listed?
D. How does the auction house categorize products?
E. How do you bid on a product?
F. What does the auction house charge you to sell a product?
G. What is the duration of a typical auction?
H. Can you set a minimum acceptable bid for a product you want to sell?
I. How does the auction house help you evaluate the credibility of other people buying and selling products?

Automobiles

On the Internet, you'll find a lot of products for sale that almost don't seem to fit the "electronic commerce" environment. We've already discussed clothes and perfume—you can't try them out, but you can buy them on the Internet. How about groceries? There are actually several sites where you can place grocery orders and have those orders shipped to your doorstep. You can also buy real estate from photos.

Another product category that you may not expect to find on the Internet is automobiles. That's right—on the Internet you can find literally any automobile you'd be interested in purchasing. Muscle cars, Jaguars, Rolls Royces, Hondas, and thousands more are for sale on the Internet.

Try connecting to a few of these sites and browse for an automobile you'd like to own. As you do, think about these issues. What variety can you find (color, engine size, interior, etc.)? Are financing options available? How do you "test drive" a car for sale on the Internet? What happens if you buy a car and then don't like it? What about used cars—can you trust people selling a used car on the Internet? How do you pay for a car, typically a relatively large purchase?

And just as you could when buying a computer, you can find a variety of sites that provide competitive pricing information concerning cars. Many of these sites are for all cars in general, not just those for sale on the Internet. One of the best sites is AutoSite at http://www.autosite.com/. If you're ever shopping for a new or used car, you should definitely check out that site.

CHAPTER TWO Strategic and Competitive Opportunities

Web Sites for Ordering Products

Book and Music Stores	Address
Amazon	http://www.amazon.com
Barnes and Noble	http://www.barnesandnoble.com
Borders	http://www.borders.com
Book Zone	http://www.bookzone.com
varsitybooks.com	http://www.varsitybooks.com

Clothing and Accessory Stores	Address
Fashionmall.com	http://www.fashionmall.com
L.L. Bean	http://www.llbean.com
Birkenstock Express	http://www.footwise.com
Eddie Bauer	http://www.eddiebauer.com/home/
Lands' End	http://www.landsend.com

Computer Stores	Address
CDW	http://www.cdw.com
Cyberian Outpost	http://www.outpost.com
Hewlett-Packard	http://www.hp.com
Dell	http://www.dell.com
Gateway	http://www.gateway.com

Auction Houses	
bid4vacations.com	http://www.bid4vacations.com
eBay	http://www.ebay.com
HaggleOnline	http://www.haggle.com
SportingAuction.com	http://sportingauction.com
UBID	http://www.ubid.com

Go to the Web site that supports this text:
http://www.mhhe.com/haag
and select "Electronic Commerce Projects."

We've included links to over 100 Web sites for ordering products on the Internet, including automobiles.

KEY TERMS AND CONCEPTS

Alliance Partner, 50
Business to Business (B2B), 50
B2B Marketplace, 60
Business to Consumer (B2C), 50
Business Process, 63
Buyer Power, 58
Collaborative Filtering, 67
Collaborative Planning, Forecasting, and Replenishment (CPRF), 57

Competitive Advantage, 48
Creative Design, 54
Disintermediation, 67
Distribution Chain, 50
Entry Barrier, 62
First Mover, 49
Five Forces Model, 58
Global Reach, 68
Information Partnership, 49

Innovation, 52
Just-In-Time, 56
Mass Customization, 65
Permission Marketing, 69
Personalization, 66
Project Team, 52
Rivalry among Existing Competitors, 59
Supplier Power, 58

Supply Chain, 56
Switching Cost, 58
Temporary Advantage, 49
Threat of New Entrants, 59
Threat of Substitute Products or Services, 58
Three Generic Strategies, 59
Value Chain, 63

SHORT-ANSWER QUESTIONS

1. Why are competitive advantages achieved through IT usually only temporary?
2. What are "interorganizational systems?"
3. What is meant by B2B and B2C?
4. Why is it important to view the business problem from another perspective?
5. What is CPFR? How do companies who use it get a competitive advantage?
6. What is the *value chain?* How is it used?
7. What is the difference between mass customization and personalization? See if you can give some examples not included in the chapter.
8. What is meant by *global reach?* Why might it be important for an importer in Lincoln, Nebraska, to be concerned about it?
9. What are airline companies trying to do with their yield management systems? Why is IT important in making them effective?

SHORT-QUESTION ANSWERS

For each of the following answers, provide an appropriate question.

1. No. It's the way that people use the technology in creative ways to solve a business problem.
2. The FedEx tracking system.
3. It's a way to bridge the communications gap between the business people and the technical people.
4. Send them back to the drawing board.
5. Buyer power, supplier power, barriers to entry, threat of substitute products or services, rivalry among existing competitors.
6. Mass customization and personalization, disintermediation, and global reach.
7. GPS.
8. Permission marketing.
9. Loyalty programs.

DISCUSSION QUESTIONS

1. What is meant by the term "competitive advantage"? Why is it important? Give some examples of companies you deal with which you think have achieved competitive advantage.
2. How does Dell get a competitive advantage from its "sell, source, and ship" model?
3. Why is the CEO's perspective important if an organization hopes to gain a competitive advantage from IT?
4. The chapter states that it is important to view the business problem from another perspective if you are to develop an IT system that gives your organization a competitive advantage. Why is this important? What are some of the other perspectives that you could use?
5. Give additional examples of companies who have used Porter's five forces model to gain competitive advantage.
6. Give additional examples of companies in each category of Michael Porter's three generic strategies model as illustrated in Figure 2.8.
7. Can you think of why a process in the value chain would be value-reducing? Do you really think that organizations operate with processes that are value-reducing? How could that happen?
8. Assume you are in business as a real estate agent. Should you feel threatened by the possibility of being disintermediated? If you think so, what are some of the things you can do about it?
9. Think of other good examples of industries in which companies have used IT for competitive advantage the way the U.S. airline industry has. Can you think of industries that are way behind the curve?

CHAPTER OUTLINE

INDUSTRY PERSPECTIVES

Financial Services
88
Should You Have Access to Medical Malpractice Databases?

".com"
91
Making the Move to .com

Entertainment and Publishing
105
We Want to Know Our Customers

Health Care
108
Cracking the Human Genetic Code

IN THE NEWS

- **84** Bank of America submits 2,000 daily queries against 800 gigabytes of information.
- **85** Do you look up names in a phone book by page number or alphabetically?
- **89** Ritz-Carlton hotels use databases to put chocolates on your pillow.
- **91** Microsoft Access lets you use binoculars to find information in a database.
- **97** Which types of databases are the most popular? See Figure 3.13.
- **97** Blue Plus saves lives with a database.
- **100** Data warehousing and data mining—prospecting for gold in information.
- **103** Sega uses a data warehouse to sell its video games.
- **107** If the Internet had been around in 1912, the *Titanic* might not have gone down.

FEATURES

- **84** **The Global Perspective** Floating Databases Aboard Royal Caribbean Cruise Ships
- **95** **Team Work** Defining Information Privileges during University Registration
- **96** **On Your Own** DBMS Support for OLTP, OLAP, and Information Management
- **101** **Team Work** Politically Correct Data Mining
- **103** **On Your Own** How Up-to-Date Should Data Warehouse Information Be?
- **106** **The Global Perspective** How Many Customers Do You Really Have?
- **112** **Electronic Commerce** Searching Online Databases and Information Repositories

KNOWLEDGE WORKER'S CHECKLIST

In the Information Age, Knowledge Workers Understand...

1. The importance of separating the logical from the physical concerning the organization of information
2. The role of databases and database management systems in an organization
3. The basic concepts of the relational database model
4. The role of data warehouses and data mining tools in an organization
5. Key issues in managing the information resource

WEB SUPPORT

http://www.mhhe.com/haag

- Data Warehousing Tools
- Financial Aid Resources
- Libraries
- Consumer Information
- Demographics
- Real Estate

Databases and Data Warehouses

A Gold Mine of Information

CHAPTER 3

CASE STUDY

We Make Green Bay Packer "Cheesehead" Hats

Well, not the actual hats, but rather the dispersion resins that go in them, according to Ken Smith, CIO at PolyOne Corp., a $3.5 billion manufacturer of chemical compounds for making plastics. PolyOne, located in Avon Lake, Ohio, is a leading manufacturer of chemicals, and it's also leading the way in which chemical companies use IT. And, yes, it is a leader in the innovative uses of its products (including the resins that go into Green Bay Packer "Cheesehead" hats).

PolyOne recently embarked on creating a data warehouse of customer and product information. A data warehouse is a large collection of information that supports business analysis activities and decision-making tasks. Using the data warehouse, PolyOne employees can easily and quickly see what products have been purchased, when, in what volume, at what prices, and by individual customer or customer segment. According to Ken, "It allows us to have a more meaningful relationship with our customers and provide them with total solutions, not just sell them products."

That's a powerful statement. In today's e-commerce world, personal relationships with customers (and suppliers) can get lost in the "electronic shuffle." That is, if your customers are ordering electronically, you may not ever speak to them in person. So, e-commerce requires focused attention on developing close, personal relationships with customers. And PolyOne is using its data warehouse to do just that.

Inside the data warehouse, PolyOne employees can "slice and dice" their way through various dimensions of information. For example, they can view customer purchasing histories by season. This gives them the ability to better anticipate customer needs according to time of year.

And PolyOne isn't ignoring e-commerce; instead it's aggressively pursuing e-commerce activities while cultivating customer relationships. After just a few short months of implementing its Web site with order-placing capabilities, PolyOne had generated over $10 million in sales. All of the order information from its Web site goes directly into PolyOne's data warehouse. So, its Web site not only generates sales but also provides vitally important customer information to the data warehouse that is used to maintain customer relationships.[1] ❖

Introduction

Imagine that you're the inventory manager for a multimillion dollar firm and that you can accurately predict selling trends by the week, territory, salesperson, and product line. Imagine that you own an accounting firm and can accurately predict which and how many of your clients will file for tax extensions. Imagine that you're an accounts manager and can accurately determine creditworthy risks. Sound impossible? Not really—it's quite possible that you could make these predictions with a 95 percent accuracy rate, or even higher. How? Obviously your education has something to do with it. But so does access to and the ability to work with a resource that every organization owns today—information. *Access to* information implies that it's organized in such a way that you can easily and quickly get to it. *Working with* information implies that you have the right information-processing tools. That's what this chapter is all about—organizing information and having the right tools to work with that information.

Most people believe that working with information—especially while making a decision—is much more difficult than organizing it. And who knows, perhaps it is. But unless you organize your information in a way that is easily accessed with your tools, those tools are useless. To organize information today, most organizations rely on databases and data warehouses. To work with that information, all organizations use software. As applied to databases and data warehouses, the software tools are called database management systems and data mining tools, respectively.

Throughout this chapter, we will focus on (1) databases and data warehouses—the most popular methods for organizing and managing information and (2) database management systems and data mining tools—the software you use to work with information in databases and data warehouses. We have also included *Extended Learning Module B* to help you learn how to develop your own personal database application. Knowing how to develop a personal database application is an important part of the concept of knowledge worker computing and a substantial career opportunity for you.

Information in an Organization Revisited

Up to this point, we've viewed various aspects of and perspectives on information, including dimensions, flows, what information describes, and shared information. In Chapter 1, specifically, we addressed the issue of creating information by looking at transaction and analytical processing. Keeping those concepts in mind, let's now address this question: "What do organizations do with information as an important resource?" Basically, organizations do three things with information: (1) process information in the form of transactions, (2) use information to make decisions, and (3) manage information while using it.

Processing Information in the Form of Transactions

First, organizations process information in the form of transactions, as we discussed in Chapter 1. Consider your school's registration system. It processes information by capturing your registration requests and processing those requests to create your class schedule and tuition bill and update the various classes for which you've registered. In capturing and processing that information, your school's registration system is supporting the concept of online transaction processing. *Online transaction processing (OLTP)* involves gathering input information, processing that information, and updating existing information to reflect the gathered and processed information. Most organizations today use databases and database management systems to support OLTP. Databases that support OLTP are most often referred to as *operational databases*.

Using Information to Make a Decision

Once your organization captures and processes information, many people need to analyze that information to perform various decision-making tasks. In your registration system, for example, an administrator may wish to know, "How many senior-level marketing majors have not taken statistics?" This is a form of online analytical processing. *Online analytical processing (OLAP)* is the manipulation of information to support decision making. OLAP is essentially an IT-based extension of creating information through analytical processing, which we also discussed in Chapter 1.

At Mervyn's, a subdivision of Dayton Hudson Corp., OLAP is a must and a definite improvement over the way things used to work. According to Sid Banjeree, "Mervyn's had people who spent hours pouring over shopping carts full of paper reports . . ." to gather product information by units, by dollars, by a single store, by season, by region, and by ad zone. Now, those same people spend just a few seconds to perform the same tasks with OLAP and a data warehouse. As Sue Little, Mervyn's manager of merchandise planning and logistics systems, points out, "We're finally comparing apples to apples, and now we're spending only 10 percent of our time gathering data and 90 percent acting upon it, rather than the other way around."[2,3]

A data warehouse is, in fact, a special form of a database that contains information specifically for supporting decision-making tasks. Data warehouses differ from most other types of databases, because they are designed chiefly to support OLAP and not OLTP. Figure 3.1 provides examples that distinguish between OLTP and OLAP.

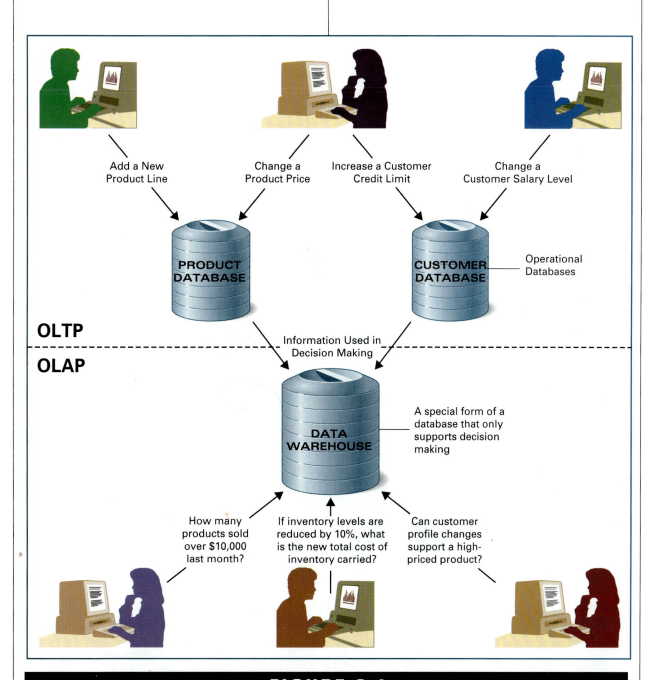

FIGURE 3.1

Online Transaction and Analytical Processing

THE GLOBAL PERSPECTIVE

Floating Databases Aboard Royal Caribbean Cruise Ships

Databases are not a "land-locked" technology, as anyone at Royal Caribbean Cruises will tell you. With floating hotel-like structures that include restaurants, casinos, duty-free shops, and Internet cafes, Royal Caribbean has sophisticated database technologies aboard each ship. According to Thomas Murphy, Royal Caribbean CIO, "The technology is becoming so much more important in running a cruise ship. Customer satisfaction depends on it, but so does the basic operation of the ship."

Aboard a cruise ship, databases track everything including general customer information, customer complaints and inquiries, on-demand movie requests, Internet café use, shopping purchases, meal purchases, and even pay-for-use services such as massages and hair cuts. The system even tracks male customers according to what size of tuxedo they reserve. That information can be used again if the same passenger takes another cruise on a Royal ship.

Royal Caribbean is also planning to build a centralized land-based data warehouse. Each ship, as it records information in its database, will use wireless telecommunications technologies to upload information into the data warehouse. Service planners will then be able to better predict what types of services will be needed on future cruises. For example, by time of year and cruise destination, service planners will know what sizes of tuxedos to stock and approximately how many massages will be performed.

What fields of information would you have in a "massage" record?[4] ❖

Managing Information while It Is Used

Your organization must manage its information at the same time its knowledge workers are using it. Managing information is no small task. Indeed, for most organizations it's quite a challenge. Many large organizations today track hundreds of thousands of pieces of information that must be organized and stored in a way that allows immediate access by each knowledge worker whenever he or she requires it. Let's look at Bank of America for example.[5] In 1986, its data warehouse consisted of 15 gigabytes of information and was accessed only five times a day, but each of those five queries cost Bank of America $2,430. Today, Bank of America's data warehouse has grown to 800 gigabytes, and roughly 2,000 inquiries are submitted daily at a cost of $24 each. When Robert Menicucci, senior vice president, goes to work, he can easily ask such questions as, "How many Silicon Valley residents own Acura Legends and golf club memberships?" Queries of this sort give Bank of America a competitive advantage, because it can better define its customers' lifestyles, which allows Bank of America to tailor its services and products to customer needs and wants.

Managing information includes a variety of tasks such as determining who can view or use what information, specifying how to back up information, determining how long to retain information, and identifying what storage technologies to use. Most important, managing information includes choosing the appropriate technology to organize information so that knowledge workers can *logically* use it without having to know anything about its physical organization. The difference between logical and physical is key. In managing information, *physical* deals with the structure of information as it resides on various storage media, whereas *logical* deals with how knowledge workers view their information needs. In the optimal information-based environment, knowledge workers need to know nothing about the physical characteristics of information storage. They simply need to know the logical characteristics of their information needs. In Figure 3.2, you can see the difference between logical and physical information organization. On the physical side, technology manages information according to where it resides on various storage media and includes such terms as bits, bytes, and words. On the logical side, knowledge workers view information as logical collections of characters, fields, records, files, databases, and data warehouses.

For a knowledge worker, the smallest logical unit of information is a ***character***. A logical grouping of characters is called a ***field*** (a person's name, a product number, price, and so on). A logical grouping of fields is a ***record***. For example, all fields associated with a

Information in an Organization Revisited 85

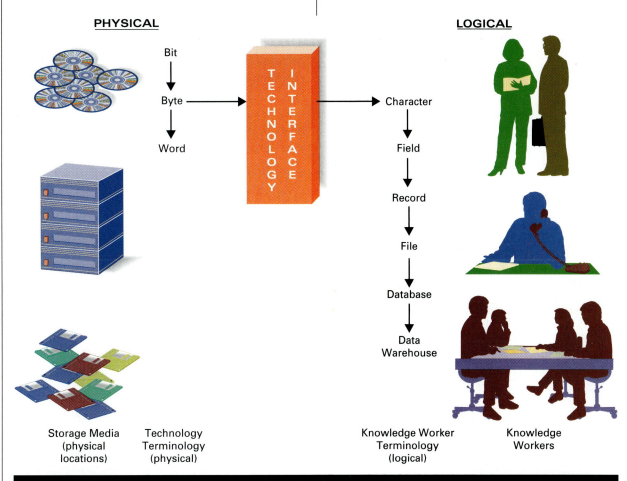

FIGURE 3.2

The Difference between Logical and Physical Information Organization

particular product are the product record. All logically associated records comprise a *file*. For example, all product records constitute the product file. When you bring together logically associated files, you create a *database*. A product database, for example, would include a product file, an order file, and a distributor file, among others.

CAREER OPPORTUNITY

We cannot stress enough the importance of separating logical from physical when talking about information management. If you have to spend time trying to find the location of information, you have in fact **wasted** time. As a knowledge worker, you should spend all your time dealing with information logically, not physically. Need a simple example? How about a phone book. It's logically organized (alphabetically). When looking up a phone number, people don't care about page numbers—they care only about spelling.

The most recent addition to this logical view of information is a data warehouse. Data warehouses are composed of information from several databases and are central to today's logical view of information. Data warehouses bring together a wide spectrum of information from various databases to support the decision-making information needs of knowledge workers and decision makers in the form of OLAP.

Again, the key is to separate the logical from the physical. Knowledge workers should only have to know the logical characteristics of the information they need. The technology interface should then take over and convert logical information requests into their physical equivalent. If your organization does this correctly, knowledge workers can spend more time dealing with information logically as opposed to physically. To create this separation between logical and physical, tools such as databases, database management systems, data warehouses, and data mining tools provide the technology interface that allows knowledge workers to logically

The Database and Database Management System Environment

In most organizations, databases and database management systems provide the foundation for organizing, managing, and working with information. In a database and database management system environment, the database contains the information, and the database management system is the collection of software tools that supports management of a database and performance of OLTP and OLAP functions (see Figure 3.3). Employees throughout your organization—whether knowledge workers or IT specialists, such as database programmers—interact with a database by using database management system software tools.

What Is a Database?

The term "database" is perhaps one of the most overused and misunderstood terms in today's business environment. Many of the people who will tell you they have a database, in fact, have only files. Others simply refer to a gathering of information as a file. In reality, many of these files are probably databases. Consider these definitions of a database:

- Collection of data organized to serve many applications
- Collection of related files
- Integrated collection of computer data
- Collection of files
- Superset of related files

You can see why it's easy to misunderstand the database concept. Each definition refers to a database as a "collection," but describes the collection differently. Let's adopt the following definition of a database:

> A **database** is a collection of information that you organize and access according to the logical structure of that information.

work with information without having to know its physical details. This technology interface is vitally important.

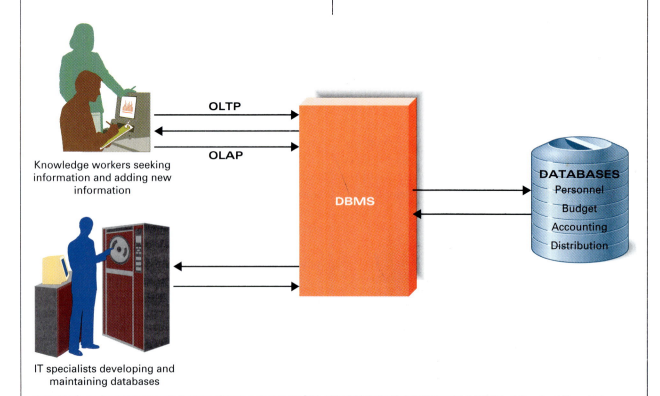

FIGURE 3.3

Databases and Database Management Systems

The Database and Database Management System Environment

So you can see that a database is actually composed of two distinct parts: (1) the information itself and (2) the logical structure of that information. Let's look at a portion of an inventory database to further explore the characteristics of a database.

Important Characteristics of a Database

A Collection of Information In Figure 3.4 we've created a view of a portion of an *Inventory* database. Notice that the *Inventory* database contains two files: *Part* and *Facility*. (In reality, it would contain many more files including *Orders*, *Distributors*, and so on.) A facility is simply a storage place for parts (similar to a warehouse). Most often, a database contains two or more files with related information (although some databases may contain only one file). The *Part* and *Facility* files are logically related for two reasons. First, parts are stored in various facilities, so each file contains a common field—*Facility Number*. Second, you would use both files to manage your inventory, a common function in almost any business.

A Logical Structure Using a database, you organize and access information according to its logical structure, not its physical position. A **data dictionary** contains the

... is composed of

PART FILE

Part Number	Part Name	Cost	Percentage Markup	Facility Number	Bin Number
1003	50' Tape Measure	$11.90	40.00%	291	2988
1005	25' Tape Measure	$9.95	40.00%	291	3101
1083	10 Amp Fuse	$0.07	50.00%	378	3984
1109	15 Amp Fuse	$0.07	50.00%	378	3983
2487	25 Amp Fuse	$0.08	50.00%	378	3982
2897	U.S. Socket Set	$29.75	25.00%	411	8723
3789	Crimping Tool	$14.50	30.00%	411	3298
3982	Claw Hammer	$9.90	30.00%	291	2987
4101	Metric Socket Set	$23.75	25.00%	411	4123
5908	6" Pliers	$7.45	25.00%	411	4567
6743	8" Pliers	$7.90	25.00%	411	4385

FACILITY FILE

Facility Number	Facility Name	Phone Number	Street Location	Manager Name
291	Pegasus	378-4921	3578 W. 12th St.	Greg Nelson
378	Medusa	379-2981	4314 48th Ave.	Sara Wood
411	Orion	298-8763	198 Red Ln.	James Riley

FIGURE 3.4

A Portion of an Inventory Database

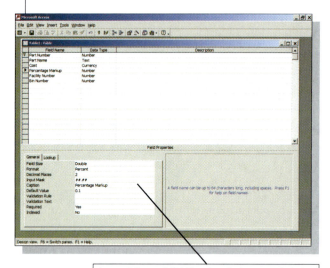

As you define each field in a data dictionary, you include certain properties that describe its logical structure. The properties given here are for the field *Percentage Markup*.

FIGURE 3.5

Defining the Logical Structure of a Database

logical structure of information in a database. When you create a database, you first create the data dictionary. The data dictionary contains important information or logical properties about your information. The screen in

Figure 3.5 shows how you can build the data dictionary for the *Part* file using Microsoft Access (a popular personal database package). Notice that the data dictionary identifies all field names, type (Currency for *Cost*, for example), size, format, default values, and so on.

This is quite different from other ways of organizing information. For example, if you want to access the information in a certain cell in most spreadsheet applications, you must know its physical position—row number and column character. With a database, however, you need only know the field name of the column of information (for example, *Percentage Markup*) and its logical row, not its physical row. As a result, in our *Inventory* database example, you could easily change the percentage markup for part number 1003, without knowing where that information is physically stored (by row or column).

Logical Ties in the Information In a database environment, you create ties or relationships in the information that show how files relate to each other. Before you can create these relationships among files, you must first specify the primary key for each file. A ***primary key*** is a field in a database file that uniquely describes each record. In our Inventory database, *Part Number* is the primary key for the *Part* file and *Facility Number* is the primary key for the *Facility* file.

INDUSTRY PERSPECTIVE

Financial Services

Should You Have Access to Medical Malpractice Databases?

In 1990, a database was established listing doctors who had qualification reviews or investigations of medical malpractice. To date, it has been used only by licensing boards, medical societies, hospitals, and other health care entities.

But some people and politicians want to change all that. They want the database released to the public. They believe that customers have the right to research physicians and medical practitioners with respect to disciplinary action and medical malpractice payment information.

However, according to Lawrence Smith, president of the Physician Insurers Association of America (PIAA), the PIAA "... does not feel the information should be made available to the public. This information was never collected with that purpose in mind.... It was not designed to measure the quality of medical care delivered."

What are your thoughts? In today's information-based environment, you can find almost any information you want. But should you really have access to all of it? Should you be able to look up instructors according to their student-evaluation rankings? Will this always help you determine which class to take? Should instructors be able to look up all your grades? Can an instructor use that information to decide whether to let you enroll in his or her class?

Is there such a thing as too much information? Can too much information actually be detrimental?[6] ❖

From Figure 3.4, you can also see that *Facility Number* also appears in the *Part* file. This creates the logical relationship between the two files and is an example of a foreign key. A *foreign key* is a primary key of one file that also appears in another file.

Built-in Integrity Constraints By defining the logical structure of information in a database, you're also developing *integrity constraints*—rules that help ensure the quality of the information. For example, by stating that *Facility Number* is the primary key of the *Facility* file and a foreign key in the *Part* file, you're saying that a part (in the *Part* file) cannot be assigned to a facility number that does not exist in the *Facility* file. Also, because you've identified *Part Number* as the primary key of the *Part* file, you're saying that no two parts can have identical part numbers.

In 1994, *Consumer Reports* rated the Ritz-Carlton first among luxury hotels.[7] Why? It's simple—Ritz-Carlton has created a powerful guest preference database to provide customized, personal, and high-level service to guests at any of its hotels. For example, if you leave a message at a Ritz-Carlton front desk that you want the bed turned down at 9 P.M., prefer no chocolate mints on your pillow, and want to participate in the 7 A.M. aerobics class, that information is passed along to the floor maid and also stored in the guest preference database. The next time you stay in a Ritz-Carlton hotel, in Palm Beach for example, your information travels with you and the hotel staff immediately knows of your desires.

For the management at Ritz-Carlton, achieving customer loyalty starts first with knowing each customer individually. That includes your exercise habits, what you most commonly consume from the snack bar in your room, how many towels you use daily, and whether you like a chocolate on your pillow. The guest preference database contains all this information, and employees use it to fill your every need (or whim).

What Is a Database Management System?

When you use word processing software, you develop and work with a document. When you use spreadsheet software, you develop and work with a workbook or spreadsheet. When you use personal information management software, you develop and work with a phone book or appointment calendar. The same is true in a database environment—you use software to develop and work with a database. A *database management system (DBMS)* is the software you use to specify the logical organization for a database and access it. A DBMS contains five important software components (see Figure 3.6 on page 90):

1. DBMS engine
2. Data definition subsystem
3. Data manipulation subsystem
4. Application generation subsystem
5. Data administration subsystem

DBMS Engine
Providing the Logical-to-Physical Bridge

The DBMS engine is perhaps the most important—yet seldom recognized—component of a DBMS. The *DBMS engine* accepts logical requests from the various other DBMS subsystems, converts them to their physical equivalent, and actually accesses the database and data dictionary as they exist on a storage device. Therefore, the DBMS engine allows you to work with database information from a logical point of view, without having to worry about physical and technical details. Again, the distinction between *logical* and *physical* is important in a database environment. The *physical view* of information deals with how information is physically arranged, stored, and accessed on some type of secondary storage device, such as a magnetic hard disk or CD-ROM. The *logical view* of information, on the other hand, focuses on how you as a knowledge worker need to arrange and access information to meet your particular business needs.

Databases and DBMSs provide two really great advantages in separating the logical from the physical view of information. First, the DBMS handles all physical tasks. So you, as a database user, can concentrate solely on your logical information needs. Second, although there is only one physical view of information, there may be numerous knowledge workers who have different logical views of the information in a database. That is, according to what business tasks they need to perform, different knowledge workers logically view information in different ways. The DBMS engine can process virtually any logical information view or request into its physical equivalent.

Data Definition Subsystem
Defining the Logical Structure of a Database

The *data definition subsystem* of a DBMS helps you create and maintain the data dictionary and define the structure of the files in a database. Recall that a data dic-

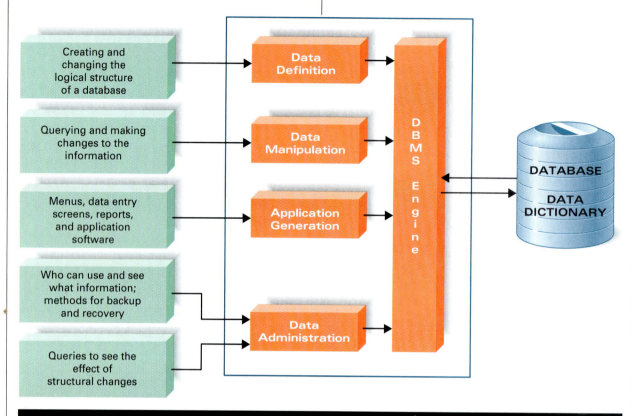

FIGURE 3.6

Software Subsystems of a Database Management System

tionary contains the logical structure of information in a database. The data definition subsystem of a DBMS is often called the "data definition language" or DDL. Figure 3.5 on page 88 contains a DDL screen for the *Part* file.

The most important function of the data definition subsystem is that it supports your ability to define the logical structure or properties of the information when you first create a database. Once again, as you do this the DBMS engine, not you, is responsible for developing the physical structure of the information as it will appear on a storage device. Logical structures of information include the following:

**Logical Structures
(Properties)**   **Example**
Name   *Part Number, Bin Number*
Type   Alphabetic, numeric, date, time, etc.
Form   Is an area code required for a phone number?
Default value   If no percentage markup is entered, the default is 10%.
Validation rule   Can percentage markups exceed 100%?
Is an entry required?   Must you enter a *Facility Number* for a part or can it be blank?
Can there be duplicates?   Primary keys cannot be duplicates, but what about percentage markups?

Once you've created a database, the data definition subsystem also allows you to define new fields, delete fields, or change field properties. For example, you could easily add a new field—*Price*—to the *Part* file and define it as *Cost* * (1 + *Percentage Markup*).

Data Manipulation Subsystem
Mining and Changing Information in a Database

The ***data manipulation subsystem*** of a DBMS helps you add, change, and delete information in a database and mine it for valuable information. Software tools within the data manipulation subsystem are most often

The Database and Database Management System Environment **91**

INDUSTRY PERSPECTIVE — On the Web

Making the Move to .com

Perhaps the world's largest traditional information service has now gone Web-wild. Who is it? It's LEXIS-NEXIS at http://www.nexis.com. LEXIS-NEXIS has long been the preferred information service of libraries all over the world. Now it's at your fingertips on the Web.

On the Web, it includes access to billions of documents from thousands of full-text newspapers, journals, magazines, newsletters, news wires, broadcast transcripts, and other news sources. When you subscribe to LEXIS-NEXIS online (it's not free unfortunately), you have access to all that information and much more functionality.

You can build and customize your own LEXIS-NEXIS home page. So, when you log on, you see exactly what you want in the form of local news, market news, and sources you frequently search and read. You can even request that customized late-breaking news be sent to you via e-mail.

You can also build your own source list. So, you can easily perform searches of just certain magazines—no longer do you have to read thousands of search results from obscure and meaningless (to you) sources. You can find articles from only the sources you choose.

You can also get up-to-the-minute market news and other news-related items from around the world. You can build a portfolio of stocks you want to track and read press releases on a daily basis from those companies.

If you spend a great deal of time on the Web finding information, LEXIS-NEXIS may be just what you're looking for. You can research term papers. You can read the news online instead of subscribing to a newspaper. Whatever information you need, LEXIS-NEXIS probably has it.[8] ❖

---

the primary interface between you as a user and the information contained in a database. In most DBMSs, you'll find a variety of data manipulation tools, including views, report generators, query-by-example tools, and structured query language.

Views Views are perhaps the simplest tools to use when you want to mine information from a database or change information contained in a database. A *view* allows you to see the content of a database file, make whatever changes you want, perform simple sorting, and query to find the location of specific information. The screen in Figure 3.7 shows a view in Microsoft Access for the *Part* file of our *Inventory* database. At this point, you could click on any specific field and change its content. You could also point to an entire record and click on the cut icon (the scissors) to remove a record. If you want to add a record, simply click the *Part Number* field of the first blank record and begin typing. Notice, we've sorted the file in ascending order by *Part Number*. You can easily achieve this by clicking on the A → Z sort button in the view window. If you

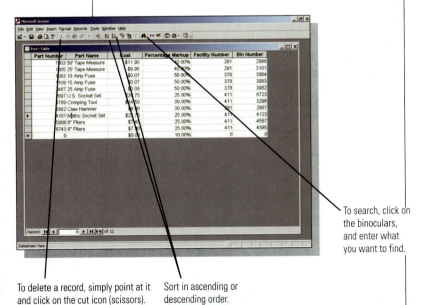

To delete a record, simply point at it and click on the cut icon (scissors).

Sort in ascending or descending order.

To search, click on the binoculars, and enter what you want to find.

FIGURE 3.7

A View in Microsoft Access

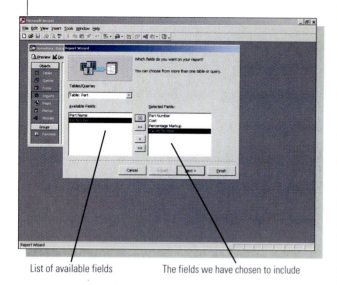

List of available fields   The fields we have chosen to include

FIGURE 3.8

Specifying Fields for a Report

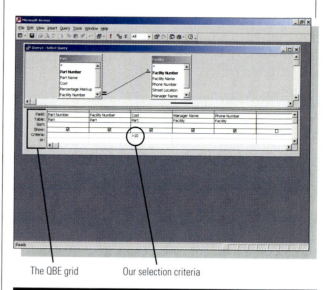

The QBE grid   Our selection criteria

FIGURE 3.10

Specifying Information for a Query-by-Example

Parts by Facility Location
09-Jun-96

Part Number	Cost	Percentage Markup	Facility Number
1005	$9.95	40.00%	291
1003	$11.90	40.00%	291
3982	$9.90	30.00%	291
1083	$0.07	50.00%	378
1109	$0.07	50.00%	378
2487	$0.08	50.00%	378
2897	$29.75	25.00%	411
3789	$14.50	30.00%	411
4101	$23.75	25.00%	411
5908	$7.45	25.00%	411
6743	$7.90	25.00%	411

FIGURE 3.9

The Completed Report

you want to see in a report. Once you define a report, you can simply view it on the screen or print it. Figure 3.8 shows an intermediate screen in Microsoft Access that allows you to specify which fields of information are to appear in a report. We have chosen to include all fields in the report except *Part Name* and *Bin Number*. Following a simple and easy-to-use set of screens, we went on to specify that sorting should take place by *Facility Number* and that the name of the report should be "Parts by Facility Location." The completed report is shown in Figure 3.9. Notice that it only displays those fields we requested, that it's sorted by *Facility Number*, and that the title is "Parts by Facility Location."

Query-by-Example Tools *Query-by-example (QBE) tools* help you graphically design the answer to a question. In our *Inventory* database, for example, "What are the names and phone numbers of the facility managers who are in charge of parts that have a cost greater than $10?" The question may seem simple considering that we have only 3 facilities and 11 parts in our database. However, can you imagine trying to answer that question if 100 facilities and 70,000 parts were involved? It would not be fun.

Fortunately, data manipulation tools such as QBE can help you answer questions or perform queries in a matter of seconds. In Figure 3.10, you can see a QBE screen that answers our question. When you perform a QBE, you (1) identify the files in which the information is located, (2) drag any necessary fields from the identi-

want to sort in descending order by *Percentage Markup*, simply point to any *Percentage Markup* field and click the Z → A sort button. You can also perform searches within views. For example, if you want to find all parts that have the term "pliers" in the *Part Name* field, simply point anywhere in that column, click on the "find text" button (the binoculars) and enter "pliers." Access will respond by highlighting each *Part Name* field where the word "pliers" appears.

Report Generators *Report generators* help you quickly define formats of reports and what information

Part Number	Facility Number	Cost	Manager Name	Phone Number
4101	411	$23.75	James Riley	298-8763
3789	411	$14.50	James Riley	298-8763
1003	291	$11.90	Greg Nelson	378-4921
2897	411	$29.75	James Riley	298-8763

FIGURE 3.11

The Results of Our Query-by-Example

fied files to the QBE grid, and (3) specify selection criteria.

For names and phone numbers of facility managers in charge of parts with costs over $10, we first identified two files—*Part* and *Facility*. Second, we dragged *Part Number*, *Facility Number*, and *Cost* from the *Part* file to the QBE grid and dragged *Manager Name* and *Phone Number* from the *Facility* file to the QBE grid. Finally, we specified in the Criteria box that we wanted to view only those parts with costs exceeding $10. Access did the rest and provided the information in Figure 3.11. If you find that you consistently use a certain query such as the one above, you can save it. When needed later, you would simply specify the name of the query, and it would automatically be performed.

Structured Query Language *Structured query language (SQL)* is a standardized fourth generation query language found in most database environments. By standardized, we mean that a committee has developed a set of guidelines stating how SQL should work, no matter which hardware or DBMS software you use. Standardized languages, such as SQL, are of great benefit to you because once you learn them for a particular system you don't have to relearn how they work for other systems. This is not true for views, QBE, and report generators which operate differently for different DBMSs.

SQL performs the same function as QBE, except that you perform the query by creating a statement instead of pointing, clicking, and dragging. In other words, SQL is sentenced-based rather than graphics-based. The basic form of an SQL statement is

SELECT . . . FROM . . . WHERE . . .

After the SELECT, you list the fields of information you want; after the FROM, you specify in what files those fields are located; and after the WHERE, you specify any selection criteria. If we consider the query performed above using QBE, the SQL statement would be:

SELECT   DISTINCTROW Part.[Part Number], Part.[Facility Number], Part.Cost, Facility.[Manager Name], Facility.[Phone Number]
FROM   Part INNER JOIN Facility ON Part.[Facility Number] = Facility.[Facility Number]
WHERE ((Part.Cost>10));

This SQL statement is identical to the previous QBE example and provides the same results. Consider the SELECT clause. It requests *Part Number*, *Facility Number*, and *Cost* from the *Part* file (the file name is given before each field name followed by a period). It also requests *Manager Name* and *Phone Number* from the *Facility* file. The FROM clause creates a join between the fields listed for the two files and matches the joining information when *Facility Number* is a match. Finally, the WHERE clause states that the only desired information is when *Cost* exceeds $10.

As you can tell, QBE is much simpler and easier to use than SQL for answering simple questions or performing simple queries. However, QBE becomes limited when you want to gather information from more than two files. SQL, on the other hand, will allow you to build a query that may include information from as many as 10 different files.

Application Generation Subsystem

Developing Database Applications

The *application generation subsystem* of a DBMS contains facilities to help you develop transaction-intensive applications. These types of applications usually require that you perform a detailed series of tasks to process a transaction. Application generation subsystem facilities include tools for creating data entry screens, programming languages specific to a particular DBMS, and interfaces to commonly used programming languages that are independent of any DBMS. In Figure 3.12, you can see a sample data entry screen for entering new parts into our *Inventory* database. This data entry screen is much more visually appealing and easier to use than a view. We could also add other helpful features to this data entry screen, including a pull-down list in the *Facility Number* field that would let the user choose from a list of available facilities in which to store the new part.

Each DBMS also comes with its own programming language that you can use to write transaction-intensive applications. In the personal database environment, for example, Microsoft Access has its own programming language as do other popular DBMS packages like Paradox, FoxPro, and dBASE. DBMS packages for larger systems such as DB/2 also provide their own programming languages.

Because databases are such an integral part of today's business environment, most DBMS packages support an interface to today's more popular general-purpose programming languages. In COBOL for example—the most widely used programming language for business applications—SQL statements can be embedded to quickly and rapidly access database-stored information. Other languages such as C++ and Java also support embedded SQL statements.

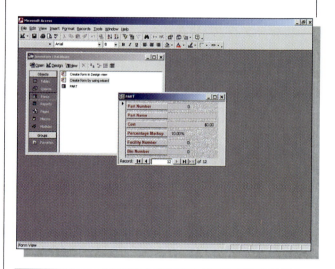

FIGURE 3.12
A Sample Data Entry Screen

> **CAREER OPPORTUNITY**
> Knowledge workers always ask the same question about data manipulation subsystem tools: "Which are best?" Unfortunately, the answer is, "It depends on what you're trying to do." If you're working with only a few files that contain only a few records, views and QBE are great. If you just want to generate reports and not change any information, report generators are the way to go. If, on the other hand, you're trying to perform complex queries using numerous files with large amounts of information, SQL is probably best. What does all this mean for you? Learn how to use all the data manipulation tools available to you.

Data Administration Subsystem
Managing the Database

The ***data administration subsystem*** of a DBMS helps you manage the overall database environment by providing facilities for backup and recovery, security management, query optimization, reorganization, concurrency control, and change management. The data administration subsystem is most often used by a data administrator or database administrator—people responsible for assuring that the database environment meets the entire information needs of the organization.

Backup and recovery facilities provide a way for you to (1) periodically back up information contained in a database and (2) restart or recover a database and its information in case of a failure. These are important functions you cannot ignore in today's information-based business environment. Organizations that understand the importance of their information in a database take precautions to preserve it by running backup databases, a DBMS, and storage facilities parallel to the primary database environment. These backup systems can immediately take over if the primary system fails, often without interrupting service to the users and application software.

> **CAREER OPPORTUNITY**
> Some of the figures in this section are screen captures from a personal DBMS package called Microsoft Access. What's really great about databases and DBMSs is that the concepts are the same whether you're using a personal DBMS package or a large mainframe DBMS package. For example, all DBMS environments support the concepts of primary and foreign keys, and they all use SQL, QBE tools, data entry screens, and views. Your advantage is that, once you learn database and DBMS concepts while using a personal DBMS package, you can apply your knowledge directly to business environments where other DBMS packages may be used.

TEAM WORK

Defining Information Privileges during University Registration

Suppose your school supports complete online paperless registration of classes—from class scheduling by the faculty, to class selection approval by advisers, to actual registration by you. In this type of environment, people need different types of information access privileges. As a student, for example, you need "view" privileges of available classes but not the privilege of adding a new class.

Consider further that the registration environment is restricted to four groups of information—Student, Course, Class, and Courses Taken (similar to your transcript). In this instance, we define a class as a scheduled course. For example, a course may be Introduction to Financial Markets, while scheduled instances of that course (called classes) would be section I at 9:00 on MWF and section II at 8:00 on TTH.

1. For each of these four groups of information, identify specific pieces of information that would need to be stored. For example, Student information would include Student I.D., Name, Major, and so on.

2. After you've identified specific pieces of information for each group, determine the access privileges for the following people. For each of the people, identify whether they should have "view," "add," "change," or "delete" privileges.

   Students   Instructional Faculty
   Deans   Department Chairs
   Director of Registration   Director of Housing
   Director of Financial Aid President/Provost

If you want, you can build a grid. To do so, list the people above in the columns and the pieces of information in the rows. Then, in the appropriate cells, place a "V" for view privileges, an "A" for add privileges, a "C" for change privileges, and/or a "D" for delete privileges.

What would be the potential impact if these access privileges were not properly controlled by the DBMS administration subsystem? ❖

Security management facilities allow you to control who has access to what information and what type of access those people have. In many database environments, for example, some people may need only "view" access to database information, but not "change" privileges. Still others may need the ability to add, change, and/or delete information in a database. Through a system of user-specification and password levels, the data administration subsystem allows you to define which users can perform which tasks and what information they can see. At car dealership JM Family Enterprises (JMFE), security management facilities are an absolute must because its technology environment is highly decentralized and includes many users of mobile technologies.[9] JMFE's system supports encryption and passwords to protect databases, files, and many hardware resources. The system even supports automatic log-offs after a certain amount of time if users accidentally leave their system running.

Query optimization facilities often take queries from users (in the form of SQL statements or QBEs) and restructure them to minimize response times. In SQL, for example, you can build a query statement that might involve working with as many as 10 files. Fortunately, you don't have to worry about structuring the SQL statement in the most optimized fashion. The query optimization facilities will do that for you and provide you with the information you need in the fastest possible way.

Reorganization facilities continually maintain statistics concerning how the DBMS engine physically accesses information. In maintaining those statistics, reorganization facilities can optimize the physical structure of a database to further increase speed and performance. For example, if you frequently access a certain file by specific order, the reorganization facilities may maintain the file in that presorted order or create an index that maintains the sorted order of the file.

Concurrency control facilities ensure the validity of database updates when multiple users attempt to access and change the same information. This is crucial in today's networked business environment. In an airline

ON YOUR OWN

DBMS Support for OLTP, OLAP, and Information Management

In the table below, we've listed the various DBMS subsystems or tools. For each of these, identify whether it supports online transaction processing, online analytical processing, both online transaction and analytical processing, or the management of a database. ❖

DBMS Tool	OLTP	OLAP	Both	Management
DBMS engine				
View				
Report generator				
QBE				
SQL				
Data entry screen				
DBMS programming language				
Common programming language				
Data administration subsystem				

reservation system, for example, if two reservation agents attempt to simultaneously reserve the same seat on a flight for two different passengers, who gets the seat? What happens to the person who did not get his or her requested seat? These are important questions that must be answered and, once answered, defined in the database environment using concurrency control facilities.

CAREER OPPORTUNITY

Which DBMS software component or subsystem is most important? The answer is that they all are equally important. No matter what you're trying to do, the DBMS engine, data definition, data manipulation, application generation, and data administration subsystems are vital. To create a successful database in your organization, you must exploit each of these subsystems fully. Your career opportunity lies in understanding the major tasks each subsystem performs. Although you may never personally be involved in backing up a database, having information backed up may become crucial to you if your primary database fails.

Change management facilities allow you to assess the impact of proposed structural changes to a database environment. For example, if you decide to add a character identifier to a numeric part number, you can use the change management facilities to see how many files will be affected. Recall that *Part Number* would be the primary key for a *Part* file and that it would also be a foreign key in many other files. Sometimes, structural changes may not have much effect on the database (adding a four-digit zip code extension), but others can cause widespread changes that you must assess carefully before implementing.

The Relational Database Model

When your organization decides to create a database environment, one of the most important questions to answer is which database model to adopt. There are actually four database models in use today—the hierarchical, network, relational, and object-oriented database models. The hierarchical and network database models are the oldest of the four and the least used. In this section, we concentrate on the most widely used model—the relational database model; in the next section we'll look at the object-oriented database model—the newest of the four.

The relational database model is the most widely used model for modeling information in a database, for both personal and business environments (see Figure

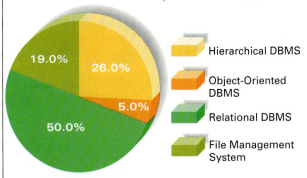
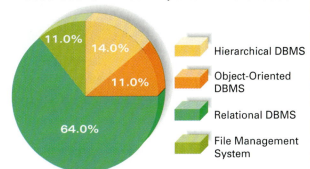

FIGURE 3.13

Database Models and Their Use in 1993 and 1995

3.13). The *relational database model* uses a series of two-dimensional tables or files to store information. The term **relation** describes each two-dimensional table in the relational model (hence its name *relational database model*).

Our previous example of the *Inventory* database is in fact a relational database. It maintains part information in a two-dimensional table and maintains facility information in another two-dimensional table. Each table or relation in a relational database model stores information pertaining to a particular entity class. An **entity class** is a concept—typically people, places, or things—about which you wish to store information and that you can identify with a unique key (called the primary key).

Entity classes are easy to find. At your college or university, for example, entity classes would include students, classes, courses, rooms, faculty, departments, and so on. You are an *instance* of the "student" entity class. That is, an **instance** is an occurrence of an entity class that can be uniquely described (for you, it would be with your student I.D. number or social security number).

Let's consider another example—a video rental store—and look more closely at the relational model. In Figure 3.14 on the next page, you can see the relational database model for a small video rental store. Notice that there are four relations that contain information pertaining to four different entity classes—*Customer*, *Video*, *Video Rental*, and *Distributor*. The information in each of these four relations is logically related to other relations by the presence of foreign keys—primary keys of one relation that exist in another relation.

For example, *Dist Num* is the primary key of the *Distributor* relation that uniquely identifies each distributor from which the video rental store buys videos. *Dist Num* also appears as a foreign key in the *Video* relation—this allows you to define which videos were purchased from which distributor. If you look closely at the *Video Rental* relation, you'll notice that two fields make up the primary key—*Cust ID* and *Video Num*. In this particular instance, the primary key of the *Video Rental* relation is a **composite primary key**—a primary key that uses more than one field to create a unique description (a primary key that uses only one field is an **atomic primary key**). The composite key is necessary because a customer can rent many videos, and a video can be rented by many different customers (at different times). So the composite primary key for the *Video Rental* relation is composed of two foreign keys—the primary key *Cust ID* in the *Customer* relation and the primary key *Video Num* in the *Video* relation.

The greatest advantage of the relational database model is that it's built on the relatively simple concept of representing information in two-dimensional tables (relations). Most people can easily identify entity classes and then create and work with simple two-dimensional tables that contain information describing those entity classes.

Blue Plus, an HMO of Blue Cross and Blue Shield, uses a relational database for information-based preventive programs. It has developed a mammography program called *A Decision for Life*. The database that supports the program contains information on over 300,000 women aged 50 to 75. Using various data manipulation tools, Blue Plus sends reminders to those women, urging them to have a mammogram. Those reminders are paying off—the number of Blue Plus patients aged 50 and older coming in for mammograms increased from 68 to 84 percent in just two years. The entire health care industry will spend in excess of $10 billion this year on technologies such as databases that can save lives.[10,11]

CHAPTER THREE Databases and Data Warehouses

Customer Relation

Cust ID	Name	Phone	Address
47857	Jake Stevens	237-6871	2352 8th Ave.
47952	Abigail Green	237-2310	124 Northland
67098	C. J. Smerud	239-7101	P.O. Box 124a
97832	Devin Cash	446-7987	1372 Ivanhoe

Primary key | Foreign key | Primary keys

Video Rental Relation

Cust ID	Video Num	Date Rented	Date Returned
97832	1111-2	3-11-97	3-13-97
47952	4371-1	4-14-97	4-17-97
47952	4781-2	4-14-97	

Foreign key

Video Relation

Video Num	Name	Type	Dist Num	Days	Rental Price
1111-1	Tides Gone Bad	Drama	457	2	$3.00
1111-2	Tides Gone Bad	Drama	457	2	$3.00
2356-1	Horror Night	Horror	235	2	$1.50
4371-1	The Alien	Sci Fi	381	2	$3.00
4781-1	Phobia	Horror	457	1	$3.00
4781-2	Phobia	Horror	457	1	$3.00

Primary key

Because *Dist Num* is the primary key of the *Distributor* relation and also appears in the *Video* relation, it's a foreign key in the *Video* relation.

Primary key

Distributor Relation

Dist Num	Name	Phone
235	Hughes Films	(800) 234-8000
986	ABC Enterprises	(212) 543-9822
457	North Film Works	(800) 320-2000
381	NBC Capitol	(800) 632-9721

FIGURE 3.14

A Relational Database Model for a Video Rental Store

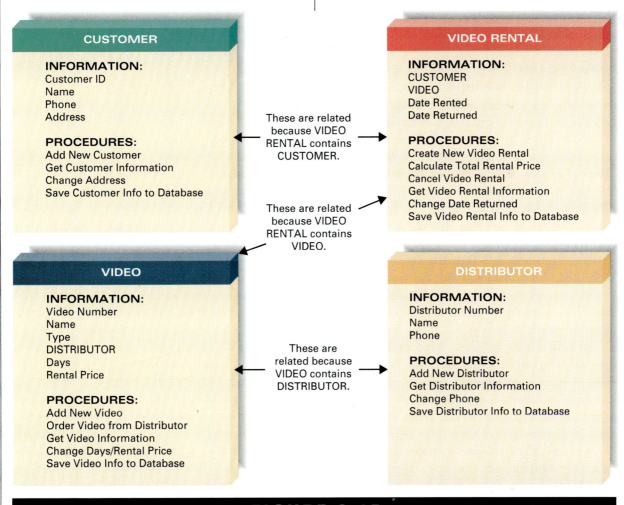

FIGURE 3.15

An Object Representation for a Video Rental Store

The Object-Oriented Database Model

Technology—its abilities, how you use it, and how you perceive its use in business—is changing every day. The same is certainly true for database technologies. In past years, the network and hierarchical database models were the most widely used; today it's the relational model. A new database model, however, has emerged that very well may define how the majority of tomorrow's databases will look and work. That new database model is the object-oriented database model.

The object-oriented database model cannot be properly defined without some understanding of its underlying foundation—an object. An *object* is a software module containing information that describes an entity class along with a list of procedures that can act on the information describing the entity class. In this instance, an entity class is the same as for the relational database model. So an object includes (or encapsulates) both information about a specific entity class and the software instructions (procedures) to work with that information.

In Figure 3.15, you can see the four object representations for the video rental store (the relational representation for the video rental store is in Figure 3.14). Notice that each object contains both information and procedures. For example, the VIDEO RENTAL object contains *Date Rented* and *Date Returned* as well as the procedures for updating those two fields—*Create New Video Rental* (which would specify today's date as *Date Rented*) and *Change Date Returned*. Notice also that the VIDEO RENTAL object contains two other objects—

CUSTOMER and VIDEO. This is necessary because the transaction is called a video rental when a customer rents a video.

Now that you understand something about objects, let's return to object-oriented databases. An *object-oriented database* (*O-O database* or *OODB*) is a database model that brings together, stores, and allows you to work with both information and procedures that act on the information. An *object-oriented database management system* (*O-O DBMS* or *OODBMS*) is the DBMS software that allows you to develop and work with an object-oriented database. Unlike the relational database model, which stores information in a two-dimensional table separate from the procedures that act on that information, an O-O database combines both.

In *Extended Learning Module F*, we cover object-oriented technologies in more detail. But from our example here, you can see several key features that have led many people to believe that object-oriented technologies will become the foundation for how organizations will store and work with information in the future. First, combining information and procedures more closely models how an organization works as opposed to the relational database model. When you consider the inventory function in a typical business for example, you don't think only about information (quantity on hand, reorder points, cost, price, and so on), and you don't think only of procedures (back ordering, processing invoices, and so on). Instead, you actually consider information and procedures together as a series of business processes. Again, other database models, such as the relational model, actually require you to consider and model information separately from procedures.

The second key feature of object-oriented technologies is that of reuse. *Reuse* simply means that, once you define a set of procedures for a given object, those procedures can also be used by other objects. For example, in Figure 3.15 you can see that the VIDEO RENTAL object contains the CUSTOMER object. So, while a clerk is in the process of checking out a video to a customer (using the VIDEO RENTAL object), the customer could request that his or her address be changed. Because the VIDEO RENTAL object contains the CUSTOMER object (which would include all information and procedures), the clerk can easily make the address change without having to stop the video rental process, go to another part of the system, change the customer's address, and return to the video rental process.

Data Warehousing and Data Mining
Prospecting for Gold in Information

As a manager at Victoria's Secrets, suppose you wanted to know the total revenues generated from the sale of shoes last month. That's a simple query, which you could easily implement using either SQL or a QBE tool. But what if you wanted to know, "By actual versus budgeted, how many size 8 shoes in black did we sell last month in the southeast and southwest regions, compared with the same month over the last 5 years?" That task seems almost impossible, even with technology. And, if you were actually able to build an SQL query for it, you would probably bring the organization's operational database environment to its knees.

People today need to know answers to that type of question and many others that may be even more complex. For your organization to succeed (and survive), users must have (1) a way to easily develop the logical structure of such questions and (2) the needed information presented to them quickly without sacrificing the speed of various operational systems and databases. To support such intriguing, necessary, and complex queries, many organizations are building data warehouses and providing data mining tools. A data warehouse is simply the next step (beyond databases) in the progression of representing an organization's information logically, and data mining tools are the tools you use to mine a data warehouse for valuable information. Let's consider each in turn.

What Is a Data Warehouse?

Data warehouse is one of the newest and hottest buzz words and concepts in the IT field and the business environment. A ***data warehouse*** is a logical collection of information—gathered from many different operational databases—that supports business analysis activities and decision-making tasks. Sounds simple enough on the surface, but data warehouses represent a fundamentally different way of thinking about organizing and managing information in an organization. Consider these key features.

Data Warehouses Combine Information from Different Databases Data warehouses combine information—by summarizing and aggregating—from different

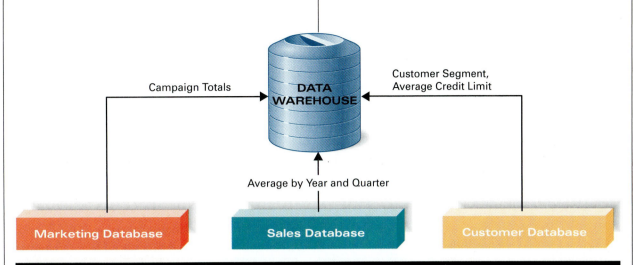

FIGURE 3.16
Building a Data Warehouse from Operational Databases

operational databases in your organization. As you extract information from various operational databases to create a data warehouse, you gather only required information for decision making (see Figure 3.16). This "required information" is defined by users according to their logical decision-making information needs. So a data warehouse contains only information relevant to user needs for decision making.

Data Warehouses Are Multidimensional In the relational database model, information is represented in a series of two-dimensional tables. Not so in data warehouses—most data warehouses are multidimensional, meaning that they contain layers of columns and rows. For this reason, most data warehouses are really *multidimensional databases*. The layers in a data warehouse represent information according to different dimensions. This multidimensional representation of information is referred to as a *hypercube*.

In Figure 3.17 on the next page, you can see a hypercube that represents product information by product line and region (columns and rows), by year (the first layer), by customer segment (the second layer), and by credit sales (the third layer). Using this hypercube, you can easily ask, "According to customer segment A, what percentage of total sales for product line 1 in the south-

Politically Correct Data Mining

Suppose your group is in charge of a political campaign for a candidate running for mayor in your town. Your job includes two primary tasks: (1) developing marketing material and (2) advising the candidate concerning which groups of people feel strongly for or against certain issues. Suppose also that you wanted to build a voter data warehouse to support your information needs. Address the following issues and perform the following tasks:

1. What information would you include by what dimension?
2. Design a hypercube that would incorporate the various dimensions you indicated.
3. Graphically, what would it look like?
4. For each piece of information, specify where you would obtain this information. ❖

west territory were credit sales?" You should also notice that the information in Figure 3.17 is a summary of information located in one or more operational databases.

Data warehouses are a special form of databases. Recall that a database is a collection of information that you organize and access according to the logical structure of the information. The same is true for a data warehouse. Users of a data warehouse express their information needs logically and are not concerned about row, column, or layer. Data warehouses also have a data dictionary. Data warehouse data dictionaries maintain the logical structure of the information and include two additional important characteristics—origin and method. That is, a data warehouse data dictionary always tracks from which operational databases information originated and by which method (total, count, average, standard deviation, and so on).

Data Warehouses Support Decision Making, Not Transaction Processing In an organization, most databases are transaction-oriented. That is, most databases support online transaction processing (OLTP) and, therefore, are operational databases. Data warehouses are not transaction-oriented—they exist to support various decision-making tasks in your organization. Therefore data warehouses support online analytical processing (OLAP).

What Are Data Mining Tools?

Data mining tools are the software tools you use to query information in a data warehouse. These data mining tools support the concept of OLAP—the manipulation of information to support decision-making tasks. Data mining tools include query-and-reporting tools, intelligent agents, and multidimensional analysis tools (see Figure 3.18). Essentially, data mining tools are to data warehouse users what data manipulation subsystem tools are to database users.

Query-and-Reporting Tools *Query-and-reporting tools* are similar to QBE tools, SQL, and report generators in the typical database environment. In fact, most data warehousing environments support simple and

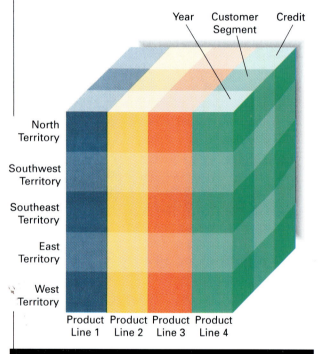

FIGURE 3.17

The Multidimensional Aspect of Data Warehouses

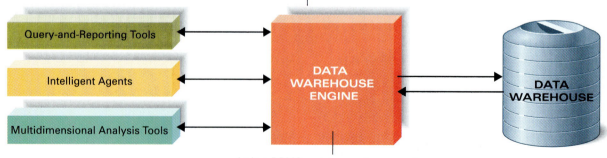

As in a DBMS, a data warehouse system has an engine responsible for converting your logical requests into their physical equivalent.

FIGURE 3.18

The Data Miner's Tool Set

easy-to-use data manipulation subsystem tools such as QBE, SQL, and report generators. Most often, data warehouse users use these types of tools to generate simple queries and reports.

Intelligent Agents *Intelligent agents* utilize various artificial intelligence tools such as neural networks and fuzzy logic to form the basis for "information discovery" in OLAP. For example, Wall Street analyst Murray Riggiero uses OLAP software called Data/Logic, which incorporates neural networks to generate rules for his highly successful stock and bond trading system.[12] Other OLAP tools, such as Data Engine, incorporate fuzzy logic to analyze real-time technical processes.

Intelligent agents represent the growing convergence of various IT tools for working with information. Previously, intelligent agents were considered only within the context of artificial intelligence and were seldom thought to be a part of the data organizing and managing functions in an organization. In Chapter 4, we'll explore artificial intelligence techniques such as intelligent agents.

Multidimensional Analysis Tools *Multidimensional analysis (MDA) tools* are *slice-and-dice techniques* that allow you to view multidimensional information from different perspectives. For example, if you completed either of the two recommended Real HOT group projects for Chapter 1, you were using spreadsheet software to literally slice and dice the provided information.

Sega of America, one of the largest publishers of video games, uses a data warehouse to effectively distribute its more than $50+ million a year advertising budget. With its data warehouse, product line specialists and marketing strategists "drill" into trends of each retail store chain. Their goal is to find buying trends that will help them better determine which advertising strategies are working best and how to reallocate advertising resources by media and territory. Sega definitely benefits from its data warehouse, and so do retailers such as Toys "R" Us, Wal-Mart, and Sears—all good examples of customer relationship management through technology.[13,14]

Important Considerations in Using a Data Warehouse
Do You Need a Data Warehouse?

If you ask most people in the business world if they need a data warehouse, they'll immediately say yes. But they may be wrong. Although data warehouses are a great way to bring together information from many different databases and data mining tools are a great way to manipulate that information, they're not necessarily the best technologies for all businesses.

Why? Three reasons. First, there's the expense associated with a data warehouse. Building a data warehouse takes considerable time, and time is money. Data mining software is also not exactly inexpensive. You

How Up-to-Date Should Data Warehouse Information Be?

Information timeliness is a must in a data warehouse—old and obsolete information leads to poor decision making. Below is a list of decision-making processes that people go through for different business environments. For each, specify whether the information in the data warehouse should be updated monthly, weekly, daily, or by the minute. Be prepared to justify your decision.

1. To adjust class sizes in a university registration environment
2. To alert people to changes in weather conditions
3. To predict scores for professional football games
4. To adjust radio advertisements in light of demographic changes
5. To monitor the success of a new product line in the clothing retail industry
6. To adjust production levels of foods in a cafeteria
7. To switch jobs to various printers in a network
8. To adjust CD rates in a bank
9. To adjust forecasted demands of tires in an auto parts store ❖

must also be prepared to spend money in training potential data warehouse users.

Second, and perhaps most important, some organizations simply don't need data warehouses and data mining tools. For these organizations, users can easily extract needed information from operational databases without sacrificing performance. To support the multidimensional analysis of information as it resides in a relational database, organizations can choose from a variety of data mining tools called *relational OLAP technologies.* Relational OLAP technologies allow you to view and query relational database information from many dimensions. Relational OLAP technologies include Axsys by Information Advantage, Beacon by Prodea Software, and Metacube by Stanford Technology.

> **CAREER OPPORTUNITY**
> Your choice of data warehousing tools is an important one. All offer similar features, but each also offers some unique functionality. Some of today's more popular data warehousing tools include BusinessMiner by Business Objects, Decisionhouse by Quadstone Limited, Enterprise Miner by SAS, Data Mine by Red Brick, Cognos Business Intelligence Software by Cognos, DSS Suite by MicroStrategy, and Knowledge Access Suite by Information Discovery. Visit our Web site at http://www.mhhe.com/haag for a review of these tools and others.

Finally, many IT departments suffer from supporting too many applications and application tools. If your organization chooses the data warehouse route, it must be prepared to provide support. Says David Tanaka, a DSS manager at Hospital Health Plan Management Corp., "Right now, we are support-strapped. If we introduce something like OLAP, we will have to give it a lot of support."[15] Every organization must carefully ask itself if there truly is an information need for such technologies and if it can devote time toward developing and supporting those technologies. If the answer is no, then a data warehouse is inappropriate.

Do You Already Have a Data Warehouse?
Many organizations already have data warehouses in place and provide users with data mining tools. Where? Most commonly, EISs use a form of data warehouse and data mining tools. Recall from *Extended Learning Module A* that an EIS makes use of a special database that contains information from other databases. This EIS database, in fact, may be a data warehouse. If this is the case, then you should consider expanding the EIS so other users can have access to it.

In some instances, an organization may choose to abandon its EIS and develop a completely new data warehouse that can be used throughout the organization. That's what Blue Cross/Blue Shield of Maryland decided to do. Says Mark Max, director of financial systems, "Adopting OLAP allowed Blue Cross/Blue Shield of Maryland to better examine its volume of data and stay competitive in the health care industry."[16] Staying competitive sounds like a good idea, doesn't it?

Who Will the Users Be?
To build the best data warehouse, you must understand the information requirements. To determine those information requirements, you have to know who the users will be. Only data warehouse users can define the logical information requirements. As with all types of technology, data warehouses will serve no meaningful purpose unless you ask users what they need.

Sometimes knowing your users is extremely difficult. Think about MasterCard International and its data warehouse, MasterCard On-Line.[17] What makes this data warehouse unique—besides the fact that it will be the world's largest data warehouse when in full production—is that MasterCard plans to let its 22,000 banks, retailers, restaurants, and other partners mine it for valuable information. If you were working for a restaurant and wanted to give away airline tickets as part of a promotional campaign, MasterCard would allow you to build OLAP queries such as, "What are the preferred flight destinations of people who frequent our restaurant at least twice a month?"

These types of data warehouses—those that people outside the providing organization can use—fall into the category of interorganizational systems (IOSs from *Extended Learning Module A*). That is, they allow many organizations to share vitally important market and customer information. By the way, MasterCard's data warehouse will contain 1 terabyte (trillion) of information concerning 8.5 million daily credit and debit card transactions.

Do All Your Employees Need the Whole Data Warehouse?
Data warehouses are often perceived as organization-wide, containing summaries of all the information that

INDUSTRY PERSPECTIVE

Entertainment & Publishing

We Want to Know Our Customers

Business is not usually singular. That is, most organizations today have several organizations within them and multiple outlets. Tracking customer information across all these can be difficult—but not if you use a data warehouse. Just ask the Borders Group Inc.

Composed of Borders Books, Borders Music superstores, and Waldenbooks stores, Borders Group Inc. also sells to many of its customers through its Web site at http://www.borders.com. To track customers and their buying habits, the Borders Group gathers information from all its operational databases and loads it into a 1-terybyte data warehouse.

The Borders Group wants to use its data warehouse to build better customer relationships through increased access to information. And it has to do this to compete effectively against its biggest rival, Amazon.com. Amazon's industry-leading data warehouse contains over 3 terabytes of customer information. The Borders Group can compete against Amazon, but it can do so only through information technologies such as a data warehouse.[18] ❖

---

an organization tracks. However, some people need access to only a portion of that data warehouse information as opposed to all of it. In this case, an organization can create one or more data marts. A ***data mart*** is a subset of a data warehouse in which only a focused portion of the data warehouse information is kept.

Lands' End first created an organizationwide data warehouse for everyone to use, but soon found out that there can be "too much of a good thing."[19] In fact, many Lands' End employees wouldn't use the data warehouse because it was simply too big, too complicated, and included information they didn't need access to. So, Lands' End created several smaller data marts. For example, Lands' End created a data mart just for the merchandising department. That data mart contains only merchandising-specific information and not any information, for instance, that would be unique to the finance department.

Because of the smaller, more manageable data marts, knowledge workers at Lands' End are making better use of information. If some of your employees don't need to access organizationwide data warehouse information, consider building a smaller data mart for their particular needs.

How Up-to-Date Must the Information Be?

Data warehouses contain information from other databases. From an operational perspective, it's important to consider how often you should extract information from those databases and update the data warehouse. Instantaneously is usually not feasible in most organizations because of communication costs and performance considerations. So some organizations take "snapshots" of databases every 30 minutes and update the data warehouse, whereas other organizations perform updates nightly.

At DowElanco, for example, a joint venture of The Dow Chemical Company and Eli Lilly and Co., every needed transaction in any Dow Chemical company as well as DowElanco is passed nightly to DowElanco's data warehouse. As that information is passed, it is summarized into monthly views to help sales analysts determine which products customers really need.[20] This issue goes back to knowing the information requirements of users. Some users, because of the time sensitivity of their decision-making tasks, may need almost continuously updated information. Others may not. Whatever the case, updating is an issue to be taken seriously.

What Data Mining Tools Do You Need?

User needs determine which data mining tools are necessary—query-and-reporting tools, multidimensional analysis tools, intelligent agents, or some combination of the three. This is where training comes in. It's important for your organization to make users aware of the potential of all data mining tools, so they can best describe the software they'll need to mine the data warehouse for valuable information.

THE GLOBAL PERSPECTIVE

How Many Customers Do You Really Have?

Recently, a financial institution in the United Kingdom attempted to determine just how many different customers it really had. From a wide range of different computer systems with different databases, the company determined that the number of customers was 25 million. But after combining information from those different databases and using duplicate-elimination software, it found that it really had only 7 million customers. That's quite a difference.

According to various studies, companies in the insurance sector (a part of the overall financial services industry) can boost profits by 100 percent just by retaining 5 percent more of their customers for a single year. But if you don't know how many customers you have or who those customers are, that might prove to be difficult.

As you consider the use of databases and data warehouses in your organization, you must consider the whole picture. You can't develop information repositories without considering what other parts of the organization might have or need the same information. That's why the role of a chief information officer (CIO) is so important. Your CIO is responsible for maintaining a view of the big picture of your organization's information needs.

Good CIOs are actually few and far between. If you're thinking of a career in the technology field, you might want to set your sights on being a CIO. Although you can't start as a CIO right out of school, you can work toward that goal. How? By fully and completely understanding how your organization works and the information needs of your organization in each and every department.[21] ❖

Managing the Information Resource in an Organization

As you prepare to enter today's fast-paced, exciting, and information-based business world, you must be prepared to help your organization manage and organize its information. After all, you will be a knowledge worker—a person who works primarily with information. Your organization will be successful, in part, because of your ability to organize and manage information in the way that best moves the organization toward its goals. Below is a list of questions that you should keep in mind. The answers to some are definitely moving targets. As business and technology changes, your answers may have to change as well.

How Will Changes in Technology Affect Organizing and Managing Information?

If there ever has been a moving target that businesses are trying to hit, it's most probably information technology. It seems every day that businesses are faced with new technologies that are faster, better, and provide more capabilities than the technologies of yesterday. Chasing technology in a business environment can be very expensive. For example, converting a relational database application to an object-oriented approach can cost your organization millions of dollars, not to mention many years.

What you have to remember is that technology is simply a set of tools for helping you work with information, including organizing and managing it. As new technologies become available, you should ask yourself whether those technologies will help you organize and manage your information **better**. You can't simply say, "A new technology is available that will allow us to organize and manage our information in a different way, so we should use it." The real question is whether that different way of organizing and managing information is better than what you're currently doing. If the answer is yes, you should seriously consider the new technology in light of the strategic goals of the organization. If the answer is no, stay with what you've got until a tool comes along that allows you to do a **better** job.

One of the greatest technological changes that will occur over the coming years is a convergence of different tools that will help you better organize and manage information. Environment Canada's Ice Services, for example, is providing a combination of a data warehouse and Internet-based information resources that seafarers can use.[22] This new system gathers ice charts stored in the Internet and logically organizes them in the form of a data warehouse. Using this new system, seafarers can obtain updated maps and charts that reflect changing ice conditions every 4 hours instead of every 12 hours. Who knows—the *Titanic* might still be here today if this system had been available in 1912!

What Types of Database Models and Databases Are Most Appropriate?

Successful use of database and database applications depends on many factors, including type of database model and type of database. Today most organizations use the relational and object-oriented database models, but the choice between the two is not clear. Functional requirements play an important part in determining which database model is best.

The same is true for type of database. In the box titled "Types of Databases Found in Organizations," you can read about different types of databases, including centralized, distributed (partitioned and replicated), external or online, operational, data warehouses (analytical databases), and knowledge worker. Here again, the choice depends on the application. If you need applications that use information gathered outside the organization, an external or online database may be best. If you need to support transaction-intensive basic business functions, an operational database is probably best.

This may not be a major consideration in the future of business. Today's data warehouses—designed to bring together the full spectrum of information in an organization—may eliminate several types of databases. But, then again, they may not.

Who Should Oversee the Organization's Information?

In organizations today, you can find **chief executive officers (CEO)**, chief operating officers (COO), and chief financial officers (CFO). You can also find another title—chief information officer. The **chief information officer (CIO)** is responsible for overseeing an organization's information resource. A CIO's responsibilities may range from approving new knowledge worker project development to monitoring the quality and use of an organizational data warehouse.

Two important functions associated with overseeing an organization's information resource are data and database administration. **Data administration** is the function in an organization that plans for, oversees the development of, and monitors the information resource.

Types of Databases Found in Organizations

- **Centralized databases**—databases that maintain all database information in one location.
- **Distributed databases**—databases in which information is distributed to various locations. The two main forms of a distributed database are partitioned and replicated. A **partitioned database** maintains certain files of information in different locations—usually where that information is most often used. A **replicated database** maintains multiple copies of information in different locations.
- **External** or **online databases**—databases that exist outside an organization. Examples of external or online databases include Dow Jones QuickSearch (current stock quotes), CENDATA (U.S. census statistical data), and MEDIS (medical journal reference).
- **Knowledge worker databases**—databases designed and maintained by knowledge workers to support their personal information needs.
- **Operational databases**—databases designed specifically to support online transaction processing (OLTP). Examples include an inventory database, an accounts receivable database, and a personnel database.
- **Data warehouses**—a logical collection of information gathered from many different operational databases that supports business analysis activities and decision-making tasks. Data warehouses therefore support online analytical processing (OLAP) and not online transaction processing. ❖

INDUSTRY PERSPECTIVE

Health Care

Cracking the Human Genetic Code

Years ago, most people thought it would be impossible to crack and understand the human genetic code. Three billion bases pair up to form a single piece of our genetic message. Most people truly believed it was impossible to capture, store, track, and understand that much information.

But Human Genome Project (HGP) statisticians never gave up hope. And they turned to technology for help. Specifically, they chose SAS Institute and its Enterprise Miner data warehousing tool. HGP plans for its research eventually to reveal what genetic patterns cause diseases, with the possible cures to follow.

"This is where data mining comes in," explains Dr. Bruce Weir, a statistician at North Carolina State University, who works on the HGP. "We're going to look at data, like a million bits of information per person, maybe a thousand people—some of which have a disease and some of whom don't—and then we'll compare those patterns."

SAS Institute has developed some unique tools for the HGP to use. These tools filter false alarms or "noise" that may look like abnormalities but really aren't. SAS Institute has built a special data mining tool as well that helps factor in family history patterns.

Once the genome project is complete, physicians will be able to match drugs to specific gene types. That's a lofty goal that the medical community has long worked toward. It is hoped that technology will help to alleviate and possibly even eliminate diseases such as Alzheimer's.[23] ❖

It must be completely in tune with the strategic direction of the organization to assure that all information requirements can be met.

Database administration is the function in an organization that is responsible for the more technical and operational aspects of managing the information contained in organizational databases. Database administration functions include defining and organizing database structures and contents, developing security procedures, developing database and DBMS documentation, maintaining DBMS software, and approving and monitoring the development of databases and database applications.

In organizations of any great size, both functions are usually handled by a steering committee rather than a single individual. These steering committees are responsible for their respective functions and reporting to the CIO. It's definitely a team effort to manage most organizational resources—information is no different.

Is Information Ownership a Consideration?

Information sharing in your organization means that anyone—regardless of title or department—can access and use whatever information he or she needs. But information sharing brings to light an important question—does anyone in your organization own any information? In other words—if everyone shares information, who is ultimately responsible for providing that information and assuring the quality of the information? Information ownership is a key consideration in today's information-based business environment. Someone must accept full responsibility for providing specific pieces of information and ensuring the quality of that information. If you find that the wrong information is stored in the organization's data warehouse, you must be able to determine the source of the problem and whose responsibility it is.

This issue of information ownership is similar to other management functions. If you manage a department, you're responsible for the work in the department as well as expenses and people. The same is true for information. If information originates in your department, you essentially own that information because you're providing it to those who need it and ensuring its quality.

What Are the Ethics Involved in Organizing and Managing Information?

Throughout this text, we address many ethical issues associated with information and information technology. Many of our discussions focus on your organization's societal obligations with respect to customers. Within the organization, those same issues are a concern. By bringing together vast amounts of information into a single place (a database or data warehouse) and providing software (a DBMS or data mining tools) that anyone can use to access that information, ethics and privacy become important concerns.

For example, as a manager of marketing research, should you be able to access the salaries of people in distribution and logistics? Should you be able to access medical profiles of those in accounting? Should you be able to access counseling records of those in manufacturing? The answer to some of these questions is obviously no. But how does an organization safeguard against the unethical use of information within the organization?

While most DBMS packages provide good security facilities, it's far easier for someone within your organization to obtain information than it is for someone outside the organization. So what's the key? Unfortunately we don't know the answer and neither does anyone else. But it all starts with each person always acting in the most ethical way with respect to information. Ethics, security, and privacy will always be great concerns. You can do your part by always acting ethically. Remember, being sensitive to ethics is an important part of becoming an information-literate knowledge worker.

How Should Databases and Database Applications Be Developed and Maintained?

There are many ways your organization can go about developing and maintaining databases and database applications. Which to choose is always a function of what you're trying to do. For example, if a workgroup responsible for building a new distribution center needs a database, then you should consider a workgroup support system such as Lotus Notes, which contains a group document database structure and built-in templates that will help you develop applications quickly.

If, on the other hand, you're interested in developing transaction-intensive applications such as payroll, you may decide to follow an organizational development process and choose the DBMS environment most suited to your organization as a whole. Many organizations are even choosing to outsource these functions for noncritical databases and applications. Whatever the case, the choice of *how* to develop and maintain databases and database applications is an important one for any organization.

CLOSING CASE STUDY

Mining Dining Data

Restaurants, fast-food chains, casinos, and others use data warehouses to determine customer purchasing habits and what products and promotions to offer and when to offer them. Some of the leading data warehouse users include AFC Enterprises (operator and franchiser of more than 3,300 Church's, Popeyes Chicken and Biscuits, Seattle Coffee Company, Cinnabon, and Torrefazione outlets worldwide); Red Robin International (a 135-unit casual-dining chain); Harrah's Entertainment (owner of 18 U.S. casinos); Pizzeria Uno; and Einstein/Noah Bagel (operator of 428 Einstein's and 111 Noah's NewYork Bagels).

AFC Enterprises

AFC cultivates loyal clientele by slicing and dicing its data warehouse to strategically configure promotions and tailor menus to suit local preferences. AFC's data warehouse helps it better understand its core customers and maximize its overall profitability. AFC tracks customer-specific information from name and address to order history and frequency of visits. This enables AFC to determine exactly which customers are likely to respond to a given promotion on a given day of the week.

AFC also uses its data warehouse to anticipate and manipulate customer behavior. For example, AFC may use its data warehouse to determine that coffee is added to the tab 65 percent of the time when a particular dessert is ordered and 85 percent of the time when that dessert is offered as a promotional item. Knowing that, AFC may run more promotions for certain desserts figuring that customers will respond by ordering more desserts and especially more coffee (coffee is a high-margin item in the restaurant business).

Red Robin International

Red Robin's terabyte-size data warehouse tracks hundreds of thousands of POS transactions, involving millions of menu items and over 1.5 million invoices. As Howard Jenkins, Red Robin's vice president of information systems, explains it, "With data mining in place, we can ask ourselves, 'If we put the items with high

KNOWLEDGE WORKER'S -LIST

The Importance of Separating the Logical from the Physical Concerning the Organization of Information. The *physical view* of information organization deals with how information is physically arranged, stored, and accessed on some type of secondary storage device. The *logical view* of information organization, on the other hand, focuses on how knowledge workers need to arrange and access information to meet a particular business need. Separating the logical from the physical is key in information management. The less time knowledge workers have to be concerned with the physical aspects of information organization, the more time they can spend determining their logical information needs.

The Role of Databases and Database Management Systems in an Organization. A *database* is a collection of information that you organize and access according to the logical structure of the information. Databases today represent the most popular way of organizing information. Databases contain two distinct parts—the information itself and the logical structure of the information, which is called a *data dictionary*.

A *database management system (DBMS)* is the software you use to specify the logical organization for a database and access it. A DBMS contains software components for providing the logical to physical bridge (*DBMS engine*), defining the logical structure of a database (*data definition subsystem*), mining and changing information in a database (*data manipulation subsystem*), developing transaction-intensive applications (*application generation subsystem*), and managing the database environment (*data administration subsystem*).

Although databases and DBMSs support online analytical processing through views, QBE tools, report generators, and SQL, they are mostly designed to support online transaction processing.

The Basic Concepts of the Relational Database Model. The most popular database model is the relational database model. The *relational database model* uses a series of two-dimensional tables or files to store information. The term *relation* describes each two-dimensional table in the relational model.

Each relation stores information about an *entity class*—a concept (typically people, places, or things)—about which you wish to store information that you can identify with a unique primary key. A *primary key* is a field in a file (relation) that uniquely describes each record. A primary key of one file that also appears in another file is called a *foreign key*. Foreign keys create the logical relationships between two files (relations).

The Role of Data Warehouses and Data Mining Tools in an Organization. A *data warehouse* is a logical collection

---

margins in the middle of the menu, do we sell more versus putting it at the top or bottom, [and if so], to whom and where?' We can also tell if something cannibalizes the sale of other items and can give the marketing department an almost instant picture of how promotions are being sold and used."

The placement of items on a menu is strategic business, just as the placement of promotional items in a grocery store can mean increased sales for one item and reduced sales for another. The job of finding the right mix is definitely suited to mining a data warehouse.

Harrah's Entertainment

Harrah's uses its data warehouse to make decisions for its highly successful "Total Gold" customer-recognition program. Depending on their spending records, Total Gold members often receive free vouchers for dining, entertainment, and sleeping accommodations. Knowing which rewards to give to which customers is key.

John Boushy, senior vice president of entertainment and technology for Harrah's, says, "We can determine what adds value to each customer and provide that value at the right time." Dining vouchers or free tickets for shows are awarded to day visitors, not sleeping accommodations. Customers who consistently visit a particular restaurant and order higher-end foods receive free dinners and cocktails, not vouchers for free (and cheaper) breakfasts.

Pizzeria Uno

Pizzeria Uno uses its data warehouse to apply the "80/20" rule. That is, it can determine which 20 per-of information gathered from many different operational databases that is used to support business analysis activities and decision-making tasks. Therefore data warehouses are designed to support online analytical processing and not online transaction processing. Data warehouses are multidimensional, meaning that they represent many dimensions of information in the form of a hypercube.

Data mining tools are the software tools you use to query information in a data warehouse. Data mining tools include *query-and-reporting tools* such as QBE and SQL, *intelligent agents* or certain forms of artificial intelligence such as neural networks that support "information discovery," and *multidimensional analysis (MDA) tools* that let you slice and dice information to view it from different perspectives.

Key Issues in Managing the Information Resource. *How will changes in technology affect organizing and managing information?* Changes in technology occur every day. The key is to decide whether those changes provide better ways of organizing and managing information. If they do, seriously consider them. If they don't, wait for one that will.

What types of database models and databases are most appropriate? The two popular database models include the relational database model and the object-oriented database model. By type, databases include *centralized databases* that maintain information in one location, *distributed databases* that allocate information to different places, *external* or *online databases* that rest outside the organization, *knowledge worker databases* that support personal information needs, *operational databases* that support online transaction processing, and *data warehouses* that support online analytical processing. The choice is important.

Who should oversee the organization's information? Today, the responsibility for an organization's information rests with the *chief information officer (CIO)*, who is responsible for *data administration* (planning, overseeing the development of, and monitoring the information resource) and *database administration* (the technical and operational aspects of managing information contained in organizational databases).

Is information ownership a consideration? Information ownership deals with who is responsible for providing specific information and assuring the quality of that information. Ultimately, information ownership must rest with someone.

What are the ethics involved in organizing and managing information? Internally, organizations must still protect the privacy and information rights of their employees. It's far easier for someone inside the organization to gain access to information than for someone outside the organization. We must all do our part to act ethically regarding the use of information.

How should databases and database applications be developed and maintained? Database and database applications can be developed and maintained in a variety of ways including knowledge worker development, development and maintenance from an organizational point of view, and outsourcing. The choice is a key one. ❖

cent of its customers contribute to 80 percent of its sales and adjust menus and promotions to suit top patron preferences. These changes can often lead to converting some of the other 80 percent of Pizzeria Uno's customers to the more profitable 20 percent.

Einstein/Noah Bagel

Einstein/Noah Bagel uses its data warehouse in real-time to maximize cross-selling opportunities. For example, if data warehouse information reveals that a manager in a given store might be missing a cross-selling opportunity on a particular day, an e-mail is automatically sent out to alert managers to the opportunity. Salespeople can then respond by offering the cross-selling opportunity ("How about a cup of hot chocolate with that bagel since it's so cold outside?") to the next customer.[24] ❖

◂ Questions ▸

1. Consider the issue of timely information with respect to the businesses discussed in the case. Which of the businesses must have the most up-to-date information in its data warehouse? Which business can have the most out-of-date information in its data warehouse and still be effective? Rank the five businesses discussed with a "1" for the one that needs the most up-to-date information and a "5" for the one that is least sensitive to timeliness of information. Be prepared to justify your rankings.

2. Harrah's Entertainment tracks a wealth of information concerning customer-spending habits. If you were to design Harrah's Entertainment's data warehouse, what dimensions of information would you include? As you develop your list of

dimensions, consider every facet of Harrah's business operations, including hotels, restaurants, and gaming casinos.

3. AFC Enterprises includes information in its data warehouse such as customer name and address. Where does it (or could it) gather such information? Think carefully about this, because customers seldom provide their names and addresses when ordering fast food at a Church's or Popeyes. Is AFC gathering information in an ethical fashion? Why or why not?

4. Visit a local grocery store and walk down the breakfast cereal aisle. You should notice something very specific about the positioning of the various breakfast cereals. What is it? On the basis of what information do you think grocery stores determine cereal placement? Could they have determined that information from a data warehouse or from some other source? If another source, what might that source be?

5. Suppose you're opening a pizza parlor in the town where you live. It will be a "take and bake" pizza parlor in which you make pizzas for customers but do not cook them. Customers buy the pizzas uncooked and take them home for baking. You will have no predefined pizza types but will make each pizza to the customer's specifications. What sort of data warehouse would you need to predict the use of toppings by time of day and day of the week? What would your dimensions of information be? If you wanted to increase the requests for a new topping (such as mandarin oranges), what information would you hope to find in your data warehouse that would enable you to do so?

REAL HOT
Electronic Commerce
Business and You on the Internet

Searching Online Databases and Information Repositories

The world of information is at your fingertips on the Internet. As you've already seen in the *Real Hot* project in Chapter 1, you can search the Internet for jobs and leave your resume for employers to find. Almost any type of information you want you can find on the Internet.

As you find sites on the Internet that provide information, many of them will do so in the form of a database—a searchable grouping of information that allows you to find specific information by entering key words and key phrases. These words and phrases are in fact some sort of key (similar to primary and foreign keys we discussed in this chapter) that are used as matching criteria in a field of the database.

In this section, you'll explore a variety of information topics that you can find on the Internet. To help you, we've included a number of Web sites related to searching online database and information repositories. On the Web site that supports this text (http://www.mhhe.com/haag), we've provided direct links to all these Web sites as well as many, many more. These are a great starting point for completing this *Real HOT Electronic Commerce* section.

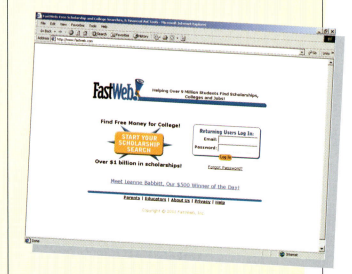

Financial Aid Resources

On the Internet, you can find valuable databases that give you access to financial aid resources as you attend school. These resources can be in the form of scholarships, money you don't have to pay back, and standard student loans. And there are a variety of financial aid lenders, ranging from traditional banks and the government to private parties wanting to give something back to society.

Find at least three Web sites that provide a financial aid database and answer the following questions for each.

A. Do you have to register as a user to access information?

B. Do you have to pay a fee to access information?

C. Can you build a profile of yourself and use it as you search?

D. Can you apply for aid while at the site or must you request paper applications that you need to complete and return?

E. By what sort of categories of aid can you search?

F. Does the site seem sincere in offering aid to you?

Libraries

Just as you learned in this chapter about LEXIS-NEXIS going online, many libraries and archives are doing so also. Many libraries and other such sites even offer full books online for you to read. You may never have to go to the "physical" library again.

Think for a moment about a term paper you're currently writing or may have to write soon. What is the major topic? Now connect to a couple of different library sites and try to find some of the information you'll need. As you do, answer the following questions for each site.

A. What organization supports the site? Is the organization reputable?

B. Do you have to pay a subscription fee to access the information provided?

C. How good are the search capabilities?

D. How can you obtain printed versions of information you find?

E. Are you able to search periodicals? If so, how up-to-date are the issues?

F. Is finding information in libraries on the Internet easier or more difficult than finding information in a traditional library?

Consumer Information

Many consumer organizations also provide databases of information on the Internet. At those sites, you can read about the latest product reviews, search for new pharmaceuticals that cure diseases (or alleviate symptoms of them), and access safety information for products such as automobiles and children's toys.

Connect to several consumer organization sites and do some digging around. As you do, think about a product you're considering buying or perhaps have just bought. Is the information helpful? Is the information opinion only, completely factual, or a combination of the two? How important will this type of consumer information become as electronic commerce becomes more widespread on the Internet?

Demographics

Recall from Chapter 1 that we characterized our economy today as "wants-driven." That is, a large portion of purchases are made based on what people *want* and not necessarily what they need. This presents a real marketing and product development challenge.

For organizations focusing on meeting those wants or desires, the demographic makeup of the target audience is key. It's simple—the more you know about your target audience, the better equipped you are to develop and market products based on wants.

And you can find all sorts of demographic information on the Internet. Connect to a couple of different demographic-related Web sites and see what they have to offer. As you do, answer the following questions for each.

A. Who is the target audience of the site?

B. Who is the provider of the site?
C. Is the provider a private (for-profit) organization or a not-for-profit organization?
D. How often is the demographic information updated?
E. Does the site require that you pay a subscription fee to access its demographic information?
F. How helpful would the information be if you wanted to start a new business or sell various types of products?

Real Estate

You can't actually live on the Internet, although some people may seem as though they want to try. But you can find real estate for sale and rent. You can find sites that take you through a step-by-step process for buying your first home, that provide mortgage and interest rate calculators, that offer financing for your home, and that even offer crime reports by neighborhood.

Connect to several real estate–related sites and see what they have to offer. As you do, answer the following questions for each.

A. What is the focus of the site (residential, commercial, rental, and so forth)?
B. Does the site require you to register as a user to access its services?
C. Can you request that e-mail be sent to you when properties become available that you're interested in?
D. How can you search for information (by state, by zip code, by price range, by feature such as swimming pool)?
E. Does the site offer related information such as loans and mortgage calculators?

Web Sites Containing Online Databases and Information Repositories

Financial Aid	Address
FastWeb	http://www.fastweb.com
FinAid	http://www.finaid.org
CollegeNET	http://www.collegenet.com
Collegeboard.com	http://www.collegeboard.com
Scholarships.com	http://www.scholarships.com

Library	Address
The Internet Public Library	http://www.ipl.org
New York Public Library	http://www.nypl.org
Library of Congress	http://www.lcweb.loc.gov
The British Library	http://portico.bl.uk
IFLANET	http://www.ifla.org

Consumer Information	Address
Consumer Reports Online	http://www.consumerreports.org
Consumer World	http://www.consumerworld.org
Consumer Information Center Catalog	http://www.pueblo.gsa.gov
Better Business Bureau	http://www.bbb.org
Consumer Law Page	http://www.consumerlawpage.com

Demographic Information	Address
Acxiom	http://www.acxiom.com
U.S. Census Bureau	http://www.census.gov
Mediamark Research	http://www.mediamark.com
American Demographics	http://www.demographics.com
Maritz Inc.	http://www.maritz.com

Real Estate	Address
REALTOR.com	http://www.realtor.com
Homes.com	http://www.homes.com
All Real Estate Search	http://www.allre.com
Real Estate Center	http://www.recenter.tamu.edu

 Go to the Web site that supports this text: **http://www.mhhe.com/haag** and select "Electronic Commerce Projects." We've included links to over 100 Web sites concerning online databases and information repositories, including a review of general Internet search tools such as Yahoo! and WebCrawler.

KEY TERMS AND CONCEPTS

Application Generation Subsystem, 93
Atomic Primary Key, 97
Centralized Database, 107
Character, 84
Chief Information Officer (CIO), 107
Composite Primary Key, 97
Composite Relation, 121
Data Administration, 107
Data Administration Subsystem, 94
Database, 86
Database Administration, 108
Database Management System (DBMS), 89
Database Management System Engine (DBMS Engine), 89
Data Definition Subsystem, 89
Data Dictionary, 87
Data Manipulation Subsystem, 90
Data Mart, 105
Data Mining Tool, 102
Data Warehouse, 100
Distributed Database, 107
Entity Class, 97
Entity-Relationship (E-R) Diagram, 118
External Database, 107
Field, 84
File, 85
Foreign Key, 89
Instance, 97
Integrity Constraint, 89
Intersection Relation, 121
Knowledge Worker Database, 107
Logical View, 89
Multidimensional Analysis (MDA) Tool, 103
Normalization, 120
Object, 99
Object-Oriented Database (O-O Database or OODB), 100
Object-Oriented Database Management System (O-O DBMS or OODBMS), 100
Online Analytical Processing (OLAP), 82
Online Database, 107
Online Transaction Processing (OLTP), 82
Operational Database, 82
Partitioned Database, 107
Physical View, 89
Primary Key, 88
Query-and-Reporting Tool, 102
Query-by-Example (QBE) Tool, 92
Record, 84
Relation, 97
Relational Database Model, 97
Replicated Database, 107
Report Generator, 92
Structured Query Language (SQL), 93
View, 91

SHORT-ANSWER QUESTIONS

1. What is the difference between online transaction processing (OLTP) and online analytical processing (OLAP)?

2. Why is separating logical from physical important in information organization?

116   CHAPTER THREE   Databases and Data Warehouses

3. What is a database? What are the two distinct parts of a database?
4. What are the five subsystems of a database management system? For what are they responsible?
5. What tools can you use to query a database?
6. What are the primary differences between the relational and object-oriented database models?
7. What are the various types of databases that can be found in an organization?
8. What is a data warehouse? How does it differ from traditional, operational databases?
9. What are the tools used to mine a data warehouse?
10. How does a data mart differ from a data warehouse? How are they the same?

SHORT-QUESTION ANSWERS

For each of the following answers, provide an appropriate question.

1. Subset of a data warehouse.
2. What creates the logical relationship between two files in the relational database model.
3. A combination of information and software that acts on that information.
4. Slicing and dicing.
5. The manipulation of information to support decision making.
6. How you should always work with information.
7. Bits, bytes, and words are examples.
8. What describes the structure of information in a database.
9. The subsystem of a DBMS that contains such tools as views, report generators, QBE, and SQL.
10. Multidimensional, for example.

DISCUSSION QUESTIONS

1. Of the seven IT systems we discussed in *Extended Learning Module A*, which primarily support the concept of online transaction processing (OLTP)? Which primarily support the concept of online analytical processing (OLAP)? Are there some IT systems that really support neither? Which are they and why?
2. Object-oriented technologies are used widely in organizations to reengineer processes. Why do you think this is true? If object-oriented technologies are indeed the best way to model business processes, why are organizations still using relational database technologies?
3. Some people believe that data warehouses will eventually replace most other types of databases, including operational ones. If this is to occur, how must data warehouses and data mining tools change? What do you see as the greatest drawback(s) to data warehouses' replacing operational databases?
4. Of the online databases you explored in the electronic commerce section of this chapter, which databases do you think were relational and which were object-oriented? Were any of those databases really data warehouses in disguise?
5. Knowledge worker computing databases are created on desktops every day in business around the globe, mostly because of the readily available, easy-to-use DBMSs on the market. Many of these knowledge workers have not been exposed to logical modeling techniques such as those described in *Extended Learning Module C*. What do you think are the most common mistakes or omissions made by these people?
6. Databases and data warehouses clearly make it easier for people to access all kinds of information. This will lead to great debates in the area of privacy. Should organizations be left to "police" themselves with respect to providing access to information or should the government impose privacy legislation? Answer this question with respect to (1) customer information shared by organizations, (2) employee information shared within a specific organization, and (3) business information available to customers.

EXTENDED LEARNING MODULE B

BUILDING A DATABASE AND ENTITY-RELATIONSHIP DIAGRAMMING

Introduction

As you learned in Chapter 3, databases are quite powerful and can aid your organization in both transaction and analytical processing. But you must carefully design and build a database for it to be effective. Relational databases are similar to spreadsheets in that you maintain information in two-dimensional files. In a spreadsheet, you place information in a cell (the intersection of a row and column). To use the information in a cell, you must know its row number and column character. For example, cell C4 is in row #4 and Column C.

Databases are similar and different. You still create rows and columns of information. However, you don't need to know the physical location of the information you want to see or use. For example, if cell C4 in your spreadsheet contained sales for Able Electronics (one of your customers), to use that information in a formula or function, you would reference its physical location (C4). In a database, you simply need to know you want sales for Able Electronics. Its physical location is irrelevant—that's why we say databases work with information according to logical location, while spreadsheets work with information according to physical location.

So, you do need to carefully design your databases for effective utilization. In this module, we'll take you through the process of designing and building a database. There are well-defined rules to follow, and you need to be aware of them.

A Note to Both Instructors and Students

This module is designed to offer you a good overview of the process of designing and building a database. As authors, we believe this is a vitally important task. Entire books have been written on the process of designing and building a database. So, we can't tell you everything there is to know in the coming few pages.

If you'd like to learn more about this topic and try your hand at several exercises and projects, we encourage you to visit the Web site for this text at http://www.mhhe.com./haag (then choose "Building Databases"). There, we offer many more examples, as well as several exercises and projects.

For those of you teaching this course, you can find solutions and additional teaching material for building databases in the Instructor's Manual.

Designing and Building a Relational Database

Using a database amounts to more than just using various DBMS tools. You must also know how to actually build a database. "Knowing how" falls within the concept of knowledge worker computing, because knowledge worker computing includes placing technology knowledge in your hands.

So let's take a look at how you would go about building a database. The four steps include:

1. Defining entity classes and primary keys
2. Defining relationships among entity classes
3. Defining information (fields) for each relation
4. Using a data definition language to create your database

Let's assume you own a small business and are interested in tracking employees by the department in which they work, job assignments, and number of hours assigned to each job. Each of your employees can be assigned to only one department, and a department may have many employees (a department, however, may not have any employees assigned to it). Further, each employee can be assigned to any number of jobs and a job can have many employees assigned to it. But it's not necessary that any employees be assigned to a certain job. Figure B.1 contains a sample Employee Report you would like to generate.

Step 1: Defining Entity Classes and Primary Keys

The first and most important step in developing a relational database is to define the various entity classes and the primary keys that uniquely define each instance within each entity class. Recall that an ***entity class*** is a concept—typically people, places, or things—about which you wish to store information and that you can identify with a unique key (called the primary key). A ***primary key*** is a field in a database file that uniquely describes each record or instance. An ***instance*** is an occurrence of an entity class that can be uniquely described.

From the employee report you want to generate, you can easily identify the entity classes *Employee*, *Job*, and *Department*. Now, you have to identify their primary keys. For most entity classes, you cannot use names as primary keys because duplicate names may exist. For example, you have two employees with the last name Jones. However, our sample report does show that each employee has a unique *Employee ID*. So, *Employee ID* should be the primary key for the *Employee* entity class.

Employee ID	Name	Department Num	Department Supervisor	Num of Employees	Job Number	Job Name	Hours	Job Number	Job Name	Hours
1234	Jones	43	Halston	3	14	Acct	4	23	Sales	4
2345	Smith	15	Dallas	1	14	Acct	8			
6548	Joslin	43	Halston	3	23	Sales	6	46	Admin	2
9087	Mills	43	Halston	3	23	Sales	5	14	Acct	3
8797	Jones	69	Irving	1	39	Maint	8			

FIGURE B.1

A Sample Report for Your Employee Database Environment

Likewise, the *Department* entity class has a unique identifier (*Department Num*), as does the *Job* entity class (*Job Number*).

Step 2: Defining Relationships among the Entity Classes

The next step in developing a relational database is to define the relationships among the entity classes. To help you do this, we'll use an entity-relationship diagram. An ***entity-relationship (E-R) diagram*** is a graphic method of representing entity classes and their relationships. An E-R diagram includes seven basic symbols:

1. A rectangle to denote an entity class
2. A diamond to denote a relationship between two entity classes
3. A line to connect symbols
4. A "1" to denote a single relationship
5. An "M" to denote a multiple relationship
6. A "|" to denote a required relationship
7. An "O" to denote an optional relationship

In Figure B.2, you can see the E-R diagram for your database using these symbols. Let's take some time to explore how to create and read an E-R diagram.

In creating an E-R diagram, simply draw rectangles on a piece of paper for all your entity classes (and place an entity class name inside each rectangle). Then, you have to decide where among the entity classes logical relationships exist. You can do this by asking some simple questions. For example, is there a relationship between employees and departments? The answer is yes because employees are assigned to departments. Likewise, employees are assigned jobs (another relationship). However, there is no logical relationship between departments and jobs. So, we drew diamonds between *Employee* and *Department* and between *Employee* and *Job* and connected the symbols.

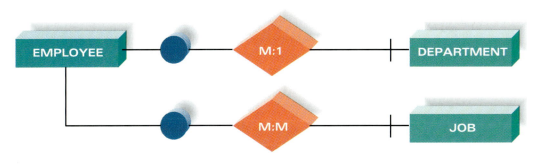

ENTITY-RELATIONSHIP DIAGRAM SYMBOLS

A rectangle denotes an entity class.	A line connects symbols.	**M** An M denotes a multiple relationship	A circle denotes an optional relationship.
A diamond denotes a relationship between two entity classes.	**1** A 1 denotes a single relationship.	A dash denotes a required relationship.	

FIGURE B.2

An Entity-Relationship Diagram

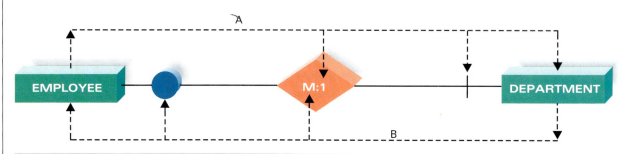

FIGURE B.3

Reading an Entity-Relationship Diagram

Now, you need to define the exact relationships using "1," "M," "|," and "O." Consider the portion of your E-R diagram in Figure B.3. To help you read the symbols, we've added dashed lines and arrows. Following the arrows marked "A," you would read the E-R diagram as, "An *Employee* is assigned to one and must be assigned to one *Department*." So, that part of the E-R diagram states that the logical relationship between *Employee* and *Department* is that an *Employee* must (the "|" symbol for a required relationship) be assigned to one *Department* and that no *Employee* can be assigned to more than one *Department* (the "1" symbol to denote a single relationship).

Following the arrows marked "B," you would read the E-R diagram as, "A *Department* may have many *Employees* assigned to it but is not required to have any *Employees* assigned to it." So, that part of the E-R diagram states that the logical relationship between *Department* and *Employee* is that a *Department* may have many (the "M" symbol to denote a multiple relationship) *Employees* in it but may also not have any *Employees* in it (the "O" symbol to denote an optional relationship).

Now, go back to Figure B.2 and notice the relationship between *Employee* and *Job*. Below, write the logical relationships for *Employee* and *Job* and *Job* and *Employee* (your instructor has the answers and can help you through this).

Employee to *Job*:

___

Job to *Employee*:

___

After developing the initial E-R diagram, it's time to begin the process of normalization. **Normalization** is a process of assuring that a relational database structure can be implemented as a series of two-dimensional tables. The complete normalization process is extensive and quite necessary for developing organizationwide databases. For our purposes, we will focus on the following three rules of normalization:

1. Eliminate repeating groups or M:M relationships
2. Assure that each field in a relation depends only on the primary key for that relation
3. Remove all derived fields from the relations

Building a Database And Entity-Relationship Diagramming   **121**

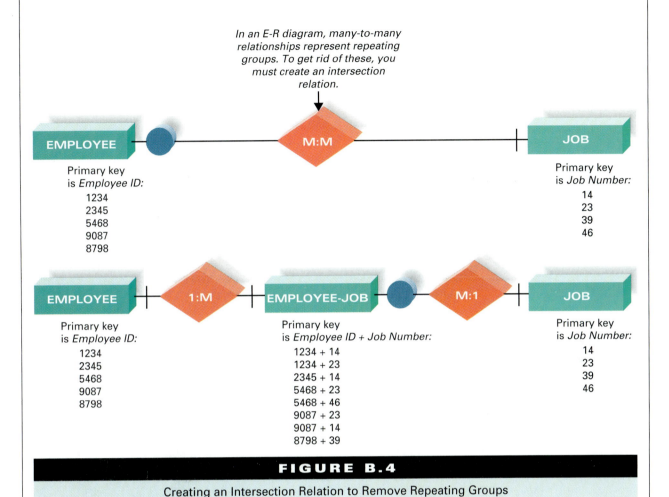

FIGURE B.4
Creating an Intersection Relation to Remove Repeating Groups

The first rule of normalization states that no repeating groups can exist in an entity class (or that an M:M relationship cannot exist between two entity classes). Repeating groups are fields of information that appear more than once in an entity class. You can find repeating groups in two ways. First, look in your employee report in Figure B.1. Note that three fields—*Job Number*, *Job Name*, and *Hours*—appear twice as columns of information. Second, the presence of an M:M (many-to-many) relationship in an E-R diagram also identifies a repeating group. You can look at the E-R diagram in Figure B.2 and see that there is a many-to-many relationship between *Employee* and *Job*. To develop the best relational database model, you cannot have repeating groups or many-to-many relationships between entity classes. Let's look at how to eliminate the repeating group in your E-R diagram.

In Figure B.4, we've developed the appropriate relationships between *Employee* and *Job* by removing the repeating groups. Notice that we started with the original portion of the E-R diagram and created a new relation between *Employee* and *Job* called *Job Assignment*, which is an intersection relation. An **intersection relation** (sometimes called a **composite relation**) is a relation you create to eliminate a repeating group. It's called an intersection relation because it represents an intersection of primary keys between the first two relations. That is, an intersection relation will have a composite primary key that consists of the primary key fields from the two intersecting relations. The primary key fields from the two original relations now become foreign keys in the intersection relation. When combined, these two foreign keys make up the composite primary key for the intersection relation.

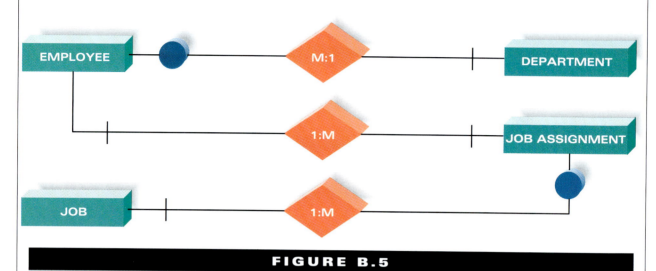

FIGURE B.5
The Completed E-R Diagram for Your Database

For your database, the intersection relation *Job Assignment* represents which employees are assigned to each job. If you read the relationship between *Employee* and *Job Assignment*, it states that an *Employee* can have many *Job Assignments* and that an *Employee* must have at least one *Job Assignment*. The relationship in reverse (between *Job Assignment* and *Employee*) states than an employee found in *Job Assignment* must be found and can be found only one time in *Employee*. Figure B.5 shows the complete E-R diagram after you remove the many-to-many relationship.

Step 3: Defining Information (Fields) for Each Relation

Once you've completed steps 1 and 2, you must define the various pieces of information that each relation will contain. Your goal in this step is to make sure that the information in each relation is indeed in the correct relation and that the information cannot be derived from other information—the second and third rules of normalization.

In Figure B.6, we've developed a view of the relations based on the new E-R diagram with the intersection relation. To make sure that each piece of information is in the correct relation, look at each and ask, "Does this piece of information depend only on the primary key for this relation?" If the answer is yes, the information is in the correct relation. If the answer is no, the information is in the wrong relation.

Let's consider the *Employee* relation. The primary key is *Employee ID*, so each piece of information must depend only on *Employee ID*. Does *Name* depend on *Employee ID*? Yes — so that information is in the correct relation. Does *Department Num* depend on *Employee ID*? Yes, because each employee's department designation depends on the particular employee you're describing. What about *Department Supervisor*? The answer here is no. The supervisor for a particular department doesn't depend on which employee is in that department.

So the question becomes, "In which relation should *Department Supervisor* appear?" The answer is in the *Department* relation, because *Department Supervisor* depends on the primary key (*Department Num*) that uniquely describes each department. Therefore, *Department Supervisor* should not be in the *Employee* relation, but, rather, in the *Department* relation.

Now, take a look at the intersection relation *Job Assignment*. Notice that it includes the field called *Hours*. *Hours* is located in this relation because it depends on two things—the employee

step 3

EMPLOYEE RELATION

Employee ID	Name	Department Num	Department Supervisor
1234	Jones	43	Halston
2345	Smith	15	Dallas
5468	Joslin	43	Halston
9087	Mills	43	Halston
8798	Jones	69	Irving

JOB RELATION

Job Number	Job Name
14	Acct
23	Sales
39	Maint
46	Admin

DEPARTMENT RELATION

Department Num	Department Supervisor	Num of Employees
15	Dallas	1
43	Halston	3
69	Irving	1

repeating

JOB ASSIGNMENT RELATION

Employee ID	Job Number	Hours
1234	14	4
1234	23	4
2345	14	8
5468	23	6
5468	46	2
9087	23	5
9087	14	3
8798	39	8

Hours belongs in this relation because it depends on a combination of who *(Employee ID)* is assigned to which job *(Job Number)*.

FIGURE B.6
A First Look at the Relations in Your Database

you're describing and the job to which he or she is assigned. So, *Hours* does depend completely on the composite primary key *Employee ID* and *Job Number* in the *Job Assignment* relation.

If you follow this line of questioning for each relation, you'll find that all other fields are in their correct relations. Now you have to look at each field to see whether you can derive it from other information. If you can, the derived information should not be stored in your database. When we speak of "derived" in this instance, we're referring to information that you can mathematically derive—counts, totals, averages, and the like. Currently, you are storing the number of employees (*Num of Employees*) in the *Department* relation. Can you derive that information from other information? The answer is yes—all you have to do is count the number of occurrences of each department number in the *Employee* relation. So, you should not store *Num of Employees* in your database.

EMPLOYEE RELATION

Employee ID	Name	Department Num
1234	Jones	43
2345	Smith	15
5468	Joslin	43
9087	Mills	43
8798	Jones	69

JOB RELATION

Job Number	Job Name
14	Acct
23	Sales
39	Maint
46	Admin

DEPARTMENT RELATION

Department Num	Department Supervisor
15	Dallas
43	Halston
69	Irving

JOB ASSIGNMENT RELATION

Employee ID	Job Number	Hours
1234	14	4
1234	23	4
2345	14	8
5468	23	6
5468	46	2
9087	23	5
9087	14	3
8798	39	8

FIGURE B.7

The Correct Structure of Your Database

Once you've completed step 3, you've completely and correctly defined the structure of your database and identified the information each relation should contain. Figure B.7 shows your database and the information in each relation. Notice that we have removed *Department Supervisor* from the *Employee* relation (following the second rule or normalization) and that we have removed *Num of Employees* from the *Department* relation (following the third rule of normalization).

Step 4: Using a Data Definition Language to Create Your Database

The final step in developing a relational database is to take the structure you created in steps 1 to 3 and use a data definition language to actually create the relations. In this step, you'll develop a *data dictionary*, which is the logical structure of the information and files in your database. This step also includes such specific functions as defining the various relations, their primary keys, properties of each of the fields, and how the relations are logically related (through foreign keys). We won't cover any specific DBMS package here, because they all look and work a little differently. However, we would encourage you to start your preferred DBMS package and create the database we just developed.

In the *Real HOT Group projects* at the end of this text, we've included a couple of different projects that deal with building databases. You should try your hand at them and see how you do.

And don't forget, you can learn even more about designing and building databases at http://www.mhhe.com/haag. We've also included numerous exercises and projects on our Web site.

CHAPTER OUTLINE

INDUSTRY PERSPECTIVES

Health Care
134
Doctor's Little Helper Is Just a Click Away

Manufacturing
137
Finding What to Fix at IBM

".com"
148
Look Ma, No Hands!

Financial Services
154
Just How Good Is Your Web Site?

IN THE NEWS

- **127** Continental Airlines comes back from the brink of extinction with decision support.
- **134** The house burns down. Who goes to jail—you or the DSS?
- **134** Medical students learn with a DSS so that they won't kill real patients.
- **139** Your team members are on different continents? That's no reason not to have meetings!
- **143** Should public schools be near toxic waste sites?
- **144** When you cross the border, you'd better have all your paperwork in order.
- **150** Neural networks can find bombs in baggage, cancerous tissue in people, and fraud in credit card usage.
- **151** Ethics: Should we examine people as though they were ants?
- **151** Genetic algorithms: evolution provides the solution.

FEATURES

- **139** **Team Work** Hold Virtual Meetings to Complete a Project
- **140** **The Global Perspective** GIS Put South Africans on an Election Map
- **144** **The Global Perspective** Expert System Gets Goods Safely across the Border
- **150** **Team Work** Traffic Lights Revisited
- **153** **On Your Own** Go Bargain Hunting Online
- **155** **On Your Own** Which AI Software Should You Use?
- **159** **Electronic Commerce** Finding Investment Opportunities on the Internet

KNOWLEDGE WORKER'S CHECKLIST

In the Information Age, Knowledge Workers Understand . . .

1. Categories of decisions and the process of decision making
2. The various types of decision support systems and their respective roles in effective decision making
3. The different types of artificial intelligence systems and how they contribute to better decision making
4. How to choose an IT system to suit your decision

WEB SUPPORT

http://www.mhhe.com/haag

- Groupware
- Learning About Investing
- Researching Companies
- Sources of Company Financials
- Making Trades Online
- Retrieving Stock Quotes
- Intelligent Agents

Decision Support and Artificial Intelligence

Brainpower for Your Business

CHAPTER 4

CASE STUDY

Continental Airlines Flies High with Decision Support

In 1992, things looked bleak for the major airlines. The weather was very bad and they lost $4.8 billion. In 1999, the weather was bad again AND labor costs were higher AND jet-fuel prices were higher. However, that year, the airlines had *earnings* of $4.8 billion. The problems were greater in 1999, but the business decisions were better—largely because of decision support systems.

Continental Airlines is a case in point. In 1993 Continental Airlines didn't even have e-mail. In 1994, a new team of executives took control after bankruptcy reorganization, and hired IT specialists to develop decision support software.

For years Continental executives had made decisions based on the information that employees dutifully compiled, by hand, from paper tickets—information that was weeks old. While they were copying numbers from one bit of paper to another, market conditions (fares, demand for tickets, competition) were changing all around them.

Then information technology came to the rescue. Continental's new decision support systems provide up-to-the-minute information on each flight. Continental can now analyze that information together with other variables such as the daily cost of jet fuel. Continental has discovered lots of new information, such as the fact that 18 percent of its flights were operating at a loss. Continental was under the impression that its hub in Greensboro, North Carolina, had made a profit in 1993, but with more detailed information and decision support analysis, they found out that the hub was actually losing money—to the tune of $60 million per year.

Continental has about 2,200 flights a day with 30,000 possible routings. Its decision support system can analyze whether a seat on a particular flight should be sold for $100 or should be held back in case a last-minute business traveler wants the seat, and will pay $1,000 for it. Sometimes it may actually make more sense to sell to the low-paying customer if there's a high likelihood of even higher-paying passengers showing up at a stop-over location. The part of the system that figures this out by itself raised Continental's revenue by about $50 million.

Another decision support system calculates the cost of cancelled or delayed flights. Yet another shows the amount of revenue "aboard" each flight, even before it takes off, and makes suggestions such as holding a flight for high-paying customers whose connection is late.

No detail is too small for decision support. The system can flag planes full of cheap-ticket vacationing passengers and assign snack sacks, while planes that show a significant proportion of business travelers get hot meals.[1] ❖

Introduction

In the opening case study, Continental Airlines turned what industry analysts had forecast as a very bleak future into a very profitable one with decision support systems. The role of IT was to help Continental's management make decisions that would decrease costs, take full advantage of opportunities, and thereby increase revenues. In the frantic world of air travel, time was of the essence. A great analysis delivered today pointing to what management should have done yesterday is worse than useless.

People in business everywhere regularly make decisions as complex as those that Continental faces. Information technology can help in the decision-making process, regardless of whether you're running an airline or a doggie grooming business.

The big winners in tomorrow's business race will be those organizations, according to *Management Review*, that are "big of brain and small of mass."[2] For example, with only 35 people, the Adtrack company is able to track 10 million records (in a data warehouse) of information pertaining to newspaper and magazine ads. These 35 people perform complex tasks to provide newspapers and ad agencies with information on their relative position against competitors.[3,4]

For many years, computers have been crunching numbers faster and more accurately than people can. A computer can unerringly calculate a payroll for 1,000 people in the time it takes a pencil to fall from your desk to the floor. Because of IT, knowledge workers have been freed of much of the drudgery of manually handling day-to-day transactions. And now IT power is augmenting brainpower and thought processes in ways previously seen only in science fiction. In some cases, IT power is actually **replacing** human brainpower to a limited degree.

Businesses, like individuals, use brainpower to make decisions, some big, some small, some relatively simple, and some very complex. As an effective knowledge worker, you'll have to make decisions on issues such as whether to expand the workforce, extend business hours, use different raw materials, or start a new product line. IT can help you in most, if not all, of these decisions. The extended brainpower that IT offers you as a decision maker comes in the form of decision support systems and artificial intelligence.

Whether to use a decision support system (there are several variations) or some form of artificial intelligence depends on the type of decision you have to make and how you plan to go about making it. So let's first look at different types of decisions and the process you go through to make a decision. Then we'll discuss decision support systems and artificial intelligence—IT brainpower (see Figure 4.1).

Decisions, Decisions, Decisions

Decision making is one of the most significant and important activities in business. Organizations devote vast resources of time and money to the process. In this section, we'll consider different decision types and the phases of decision making to help you better understand how IT can benefit that process.

Types of Decisions You Face

Some decisions are easier to make than others. Consider, for example, that you're making a pizza and need mozzarella cheese. So you go to the store and buy the cheapest mozzarella cheese you can find. The decision as to which brand to buy is simple since it depends only on cost.

Now contrast buying cheese with the decision you would face if you were offered four jobs that were equally attractive for different reasons. Which one do you choose? How do you decide? No doubt you'll base your decision, in part, on the salary. A salary offer below a certain threshold knocks the job out of contention. On the other hand, if it's within an acceptable salary range, less tangible criteria become important. If the jobs are in different cities, you'll weigh your personal preferences for each place. You'll also want to consider other intangible aspects of each job, such as opportunities for

Decisions, Decisions, Decisions   129

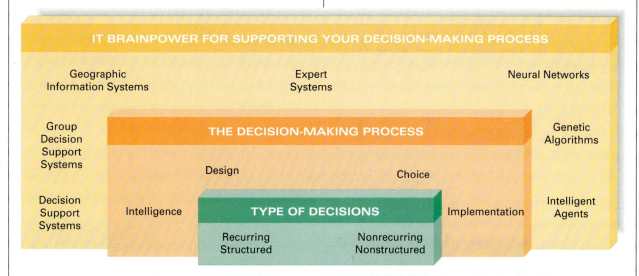

FIGURE 4.1

Your Focus for This Chapter

advancement and personal growth prospects. These characteristics are harder to quantify and compare.

Choosing the right job is definitely more complex than buying mozzarella cheese because it has multiple decision criteria and not all of which are quantifiable. So it's much more difficult to select the "best" of the alternatives. Buying cheese is an example of a structured decision, whereas choosing the right job is an example of a decision with nonstructured and structured elements.

A *structured decision* involves processing a certain kind of information in a specified way so that you will always get the right answer. No "feel" or intuition is necessary. These are the kinds of decisions that you can program—if you use a certain set of inputs and process them in a precise way, you'll arrive at the correct result. Calculating gross pay for hourly workers is an example. If hours worked is less than or equal to 40, then gross pay is equal to hours times rate of pay. If hours worked is greater than 40, then gross pay is equal to 40 times rate of pay plus time and a half for every hour over 40. You can easily automate these types of structured decisions with IT.

A *nonstructured decision* is one for which there may be several "right" answers and there is no precise way to get a right answer. No rules or criteria exist that guarantee you a good solution. Deciding whether to introduce a new product line, employ a new marketing campaign, or change the corporate image are all examples of decisions with nonstructured elements.

In reality, most decisions fall somewhere between structured and nonstructured. The job choice decision is an example (see Figure 4.2). In choosing the right job, the salary part of the decision is structured, whereas the other criteria involve nonstructured aspects (for example, your perception of which job has the best advancement opportunity). Stock market investment analysis is another example of "somewhere in between" because you can calculate financial ratios and use past performance indicators. However, you still have to consider nonstructured aspects of the companies, such as projected prime interest rate, unemployment rates, and competition.

Another way to view decisions is by the frequency with which the decision has to be made. The decision

FIGURE 4.2

Viewing Structured versus Nonstructured Decision Making as a Continuum

as to which job to take is the sort of decision you don't make on a regular basis—this is a nonrecurring, or ad hoc, decision. On the other hand, determining pay for hourly employees is a routine decision that businesses face periodically. Therefore determining gross pay for hourly employees is a recurring decision.

A *recurring decision* is one that happens repeatedly, and often periodically, whether weekly, monthly, quarterly, or yearly. You will usually use the same set of rules each time. When you calculate pay for hourly employees, the calculation is always the same regardless of the employee or time period. A **nonrecurring**, or **ad hoc, decision** is one that you make infrequently (perhaps only once) and you may even have different criteria for determining the best solution each time. A company merger is an example. These don't happen often—although they are becoming more frequent. And if the managers of a company need to make the merger decision more than once, they will most likely have to evaluate a different set of criteria each time. The criteria depend on the needs of the companies considering the merger, the comparability of their products and services, their debt structure, and so on.

How You Make a Decision

Decision making has four distinct phases (see Figure 4.3):[5]

- *Intelligence* (find what to fix): Find or recognize a problem, need, or opportunity (also called the diagnostic phase of decision making). The intelligence phase involves detecting and interpreting signs that indicate a situation which needs your attention. These "signs" come in many forms: consistent customer requests for new-product features, the threat of new competition, declining sales, rising costs, an offer from a company to handle your distribution needs, and so on.
- *Design* (find fixes): Consider possible ways of solving the problem, filling the need, or taking advantage of the opportunity. In this phase, you develop all the possible solutions you can.
- *Choice* (pick a fix): Examine and weigh the merits of each solution, estimate the consequences of each, and choose the best one (which may be to do nothing at all). The "best" solution may depend on such factors as cost, ease of implementation, staffing requirements, and timing. This is the prescriptive phase of decision making—it's the stage at which a course of action is prescribed.

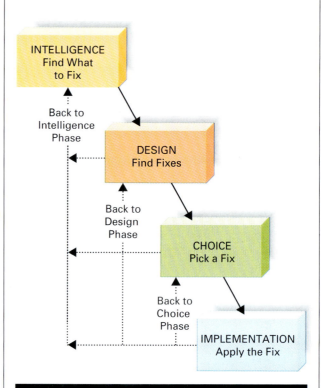

FIGURE 4.3

Four Phases of Decision Making

- *Implementation* (apply the fix): Carry out the chosen solution, monitor the results, and make adjustments as necessary. Simply implementing a solution is seldom enough. Your chosen solution will always need fine-tuning, especially for complex problems or changing environments.

These four phases are not necessarily linear—you'll often find it useful or necessary to cycle back to an earlier phase. When choosing an alternative in the choice phase, for example, you might become aware of another possible solution. Then you would go back to the design phase, include the newly found solution, return to the choice phase, and compare the new solution to the others you generated.

Decision Support Systems

Help in Deciding What to Do

In Chapter 3, you saw how data mining can help you make business decisions by giving you the ability to slice and dice your way through massive amounts of information. Actually, a data warehouse with data mining tools is a form of decision support. The term decision support system, used broadly, means any computerized system that helps you make decisions. However, there's also a more restrictive definition. It's rather like the term medicine. Medicine can mean the whole health care industry or it can mean cough syrup, depending on the context.

Narrowly defined, a *decision support system (DSS)* is a highly flexible and interactive IT system that is designed to support decision making when the problem is not structured. A DSS is an alliance between you, the decision maker, and specialized support provided by IT (see Figure 4.4). IT brings speed, vast amounts of information, and sophisticated processing capabilities to help you create information useful in making a decision. You bring know-how in the form of your experience, intuition, judgment, and knowledge of the relevant factors. IT provides great power, but you—as the decision maker—must know what kinds of questions to ask of the information and how to process the information to get those questions answered. In fact, the primary objective of a DSS is to improve your effectiveness as a decision maker by providing you with assistance that will complement your insights. This union of your know-how and IT power makes you better able to respond to changes in the marketplace and to manage resources in the most effective and efficient ways possible. Following are some examples of the varied applications of DSSs:

- Baylor University Medical Center uses a DSS called MediSource which analyzes the interaction between drugs that are prescribed for a patient. This DSS covers about 98 percent of the most commonly prescribed drugs in medicine.[6]
- Hallmark Cards, Inc., of Kansas City, uses information from its point-of-sale scanners in a DSS to analyze sales trends and to forecast demand for products.[7]
- Hormel Foods Corporation uses a DSS to evaluate sales by brand and to measure the success of its marketing efforts. Hormel's DSS has contributed to a dramatic 46 percent increase in sales.[8]

What You Bring	Advantages of a DSS	What IT Brings
Experience	Increased productivity	Speed
Intuition	Increased understanding	Information
Judgment	Increased speed	Processing capabilities
Knowledge	Increased flexibility	
	Reduced problem complexity	
	Reduced cost	

FIGURE 4.4
The Alliance between You and a Decision Support System

Components of a Decision Support System

DSSs vary greatly in application and complexity, but they all share specific features. A typical DSS has three components (see Figure 4.5): data management, model management, and user interface management.

Before we look at these three components individually, let's get a quick overview of how they work together. When you begin your analysis, you tell the DSS, using the user interface management component, which model (in the model management component) to use on what information (in the data management component). The model requests the information from the data management component, analyzes that information, and sends the result to the user interface management component, which in turn passes the results back to you.

The *data management* component performs the function of storing and maintaining the information that you want your DSS to use. The data management component, therefore, consists of both the DSS information and the DSS database management system (see Figure 4.5). The information you use in your DSS comes from one or more of three sources:

- *Organizational information:* You may want to use virtually any information available in the organization for your DSS. What you use, of course, depends on what the decision is and what information you need and whether it's available. You can design your DSS to access this information directly from your company's databases and data

132 CHAPTER FOUR Decision Support and Artificial Intelligence

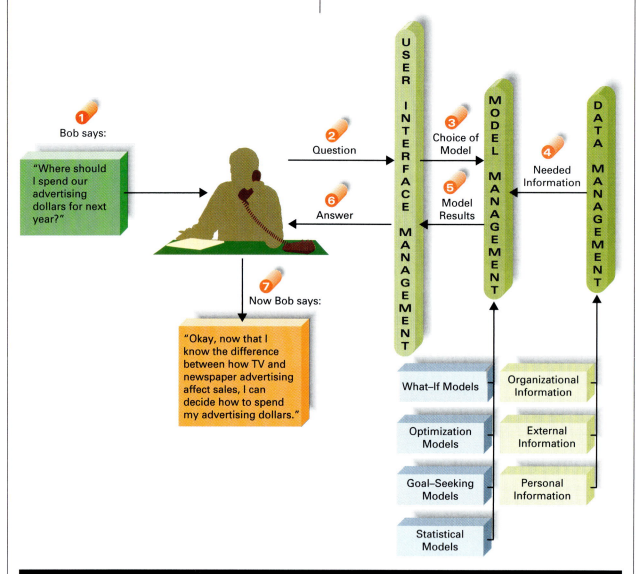

FIGURE 4.5
Components of a Decision Support System

warehouses. However, specific information is often copied to the DSS database to save you time in searching through the organization's databases and data warehouses.

- *External information:* Some decisions require input from external sources of information. Various branches of the federal government, Dow Jones, Compustat data, and the Internet, to mention just a few, can provide additional information for use with a DSS.
- *Personal information:* You can incorporate your own insights and experience—your personal information—into your DSS. You can design your DSS so that you enter this personal information only as needed, or you can keep the information in a personal database that's accessible by the DSS.

The ***model management*** component consists of both the DSS models and the DSS model management system. A model is a representation of some event, fact, or situation. Because it's not always practical, or wise, to experiment with reality, people build models and use them for experimentation. Models can take various forms. Consider these examples:

- The police force uses cardboard cutouts to represent criminals and bystanders in a crisis situation to train police officers to react appropriately and not shoot the good guys. Thus, the cutouts form a model that represents a real-life situation.

- Your local video arcade most probably has a racecar game, which is a simulation (or model) of real racecar driving. You can experiment with this representation of reality without exposing yourself to the hazards of the Indy 500.

- Airlines use sophisticated flight simulators to train pilots to fly passenger planes. Commercial pilots have to periodically undergo testing in a simulator. The simulator artificially creates loss of engine power, fire in the cabin, and other crisis situations to ensure pilots are able to deal with such problems before lives are at stake. Again, a model (the simulator) allows experimentation and provides information without risk to life or limb.

Businesses use models to represent variables and their relationships. For example, you would use a statistical model called analysis of variance to determine whether newspaper, TV, and billboard advertising are equally effective in increasing sales. DSSs help in various decision-making situations by utilizing models that allow you to analyze information in many different ways. The models you use in a DSS depend on the decision you're making and, consequently, the kind of analysis you require. For example, you would use what-if analysis to see what effect the change of one or more variables will have on other variables, or optimization to find the most profitable solution given operating restrictions and limited resources. Spreadsheet software such as Excel can be used as a simple DSS for what-if analysis. Figure 4.6 is an example of a spreadsheet DSS you might build to compare how much you'd pay for a house at different interest rates and payback periods.

The model management system stores and maintains the DSS's models. Its function of managing models is similar to that of a database management system. The model management component can't select the best model for you to use for a particular problem—that requires your expertise—but it can help you create and manipulate models quickly and easily.

The **user interface management** component allows you to communicate with the DSS. It consists of the user interface and the user interface management system. This is the component that allows you to com-

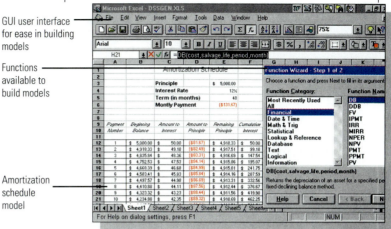

FIGURE 4.6

A DSS Up Close

bine your know-how with the storage and processing capabilities of the computer. The user interface is the part of the system you see—through it you enter information, commands, and models. This is the only component of the system with which you have direct contact. If you have a DSS with a poorly designed user interface—if it's too rigid or too cumbersome to use—you simply won't use it no matter what its capabilities. The best user interface uses your terminology and methods and is flexible, consistent, simple, and adaptable.

For an example of the components of a DSS, let's consider the DSS that Lands' End, a catalog sales company, uses.[9] Lands' End has tens of millions of names in its customer database. It sells a wide range of women's, men's, and children's clothing, as well as various household wares. To match the right customer with the right catalog, Lands' End has identified 20 different specialty target markets. Customers in these target markets receive catalogs of merchandise that they're likely to buy, saving Lands' End the expense of sending catalogs of all products to all 20 million customers. To predict customer demand, Lands' End needs to continuously monitor buying trends. And to meet that demand, Lands' End must accurately forecast sales levels. To accomplish these goals, it uses a DSS which performs three tasks:

- *Data management:* The DSS stores customer and product information. In addition to this organizational information, Lands' End also needs external information, such as demographic information and industry and style trend information.

INDUSTRY PERSPECTIVE

Health Care

Doctor's Little Helper Is Just a Click Away

They're in the business of curing ill people—and they use a decision support system to do it. Nearly 200 years old, the Massachusetts General Hospital (MGH) is the oldest and largest teaching hospital of Harvard Medical School. It's the third-oldest general hospital in the United States, and is one of the most prestigious. The hospital handles about 36,000 inpatients and more than 1 million outpatients, and that's not counting the 65,000 emergency visits every year.

MGH hasn't survived this long without being able to harness the most modern techniques and tools. DXplain is one such tool developed at the venerable old hospital. DXplain is a clinical diagnostic decision support system to help doctors make an effective diagnosis. For 12 years, thousands of physicians and medical students have used DXplain either to help with diagnosis or as a learning tool.

DXplain has a database of more than 2,000 different illnesses, their symptoms, and corresponding laboratory test results. It's both an electronic medical textbook and a medical reference library with fast, easy access.

To use this medical decision support system, physicians and medical students need only a PC with Internet access. First they type in personal information about patients, such as age and gender. Next, they choose the appropriate symptoms from the lists presented by DXplain. Then, the DSS suggests possible causes. The system also provides etiology and pathology on each disease and even gives the doctor links to relevant references from the Medline database at the National Library of Medicine.[10] ❖

- *Model management:* The DSS has to have models to analyze the information. The models create new information that decision makers need to plan product lines and inventory levels. For example, Lands' End uses a statistical model called regression analysis to determine trends in customer buying patterns and forecasting models to predict sales levels.

- *User interface management:* A user interface enables Lands' End decision makers to access information and specify the models they want to use to create the information they need.

Ethical Questions in Decision Support Systems

Ethical behavior means that you consider the results of your actions—this is called *accountability*. The higher the risk of potential damage, the more important accountability becomes. Consider this hypothetical situation.

Let's say a small town used a DSS to plan fire protection for its inhabitants. Using a commercially available DSS, the town council projected the number of fire trucks the town would need, the location of the fire stations and hydrants, and so on. The town council believed that the system would be wholly adequate because the DSS software had been used correctly. However, one day, a little boy was playing with matches and set a sheet of paper on fire. He heard his mother coming and quickly hid the burning paper under the bed. The house was rapidly engulfed in flames. Firefighters were dispatched. When they arrived at the site, the nearest hydrant was out of reach of their hoses. By the time they retrieved extra hoses and started the water flowing, the little boy's house and those on either side were gutted. Whose fault was it that the fire department was unable to render adequate assistance? Do the DSS developers bear any responsibility for creating a faulty program? Should the city administrators have relied on the results they obtained from the DSS? Should they have cross-checked their results?

Consider another situation. A social club for retired railroad workers and surviving spouses has extensive information on members, including age, address, phone number, income level, and number of people in the household. Using a DSS, the officers of the organization generate a list containing the names of potentially gullible people and sell the list to a shady insurance company, knowing that the insurance company plans to take advantage of club members. The social club doesn't tell its members that it has sold the list. This is perfectly legal because, in general, private organizations are bound by very few laws concerning the use of the information they collect (as long as the information is not copyrighted or otherwise protected). Of course, being legal is not the same as being ethical.

"Legal" means that a law doesn't prohibit an action. "Ethical" means that your concept of what is right will dictate an action. Because the law offers little or no direction, how you use information pertaining to clients and customers depends on your ethics and your organization's ethical culture. You're accountable ethically, if not always legally, for information that you have on customers and clients. In the absence of legal guidelines, many professional organizations, including the legal and medical professions, have adopted strict ethical guidelines on the use of client information. The Association of Information Technology Professionals (AITP) is among several organizations that have established guidelines for IT specialists. To be an ethical decision maker, you must consider how information is collected and how it will be used.

Group Decision Support Systems
IT Power for Team Meetings

Let's say you and nine classmates in an archeology class are planning a field trip to a dig site. Each of you has a computer and individually considers alternative sites, analyzing cost and time demands, transport considerations, and so on. After that, you get together and discuss your ideas, narrowing the alternatives. Then you return to your computers and analyze the revised list of possibilities.

Let's revisit this scenario, but this time we'll augment your IT with telecommunications and specialized groupware. Now you and your team(classmates) are connected by a computer network, and everyone can view everyone else's suggestions. Furthermore, you have software to help the team gather, consolidate, analyze, and rank the suggestions. You can now collectively suggest dig sites, keep the suggestions that have promise, analyze the cost and benefit of each one, and form a plan of action.

CAREER OPPORTUNITY
Many claims are made about DSSs. It's important that you understand not only the benefits of DSSs but also their limitations. A little skepticism is often a good thing. Some early research will save you lots of time and trouble later on. If you're considering buying a fully developed DSS or a DSS generator, find other people who are already using the system and ask their opinion. You can find interest groups all over the country that specialize in various types of software or problems. Contacting one of these groups is a good way to get information. The Internet is a good place to start looking.

In this revised scenario, you and your team used a group decision support system. A *group decision support system (GDSS)* is a type of decision support system that facilitates the formulation of and solution to problems by a team. A GDSS facilitates team decision making by integrating (1) groupware, (2) DSS capabilities, and (3) telecommunications (see Figure 4.7).

The more complex and the less structured the decision a team has to make, the more a GDSS can help. For example, the Department of Energy's Emergency Preparedness Team uses a GDSS to develop a strategic

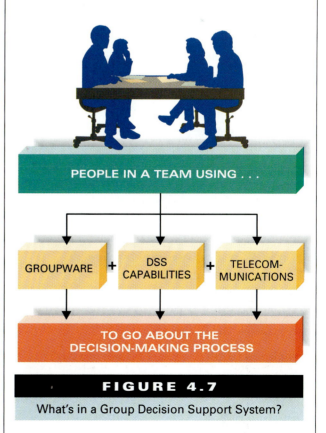

FIGURE 4.7
What's in a Group Decision Support System?

defense plan against nuclear bomb threats. Working in the desert near Las Vegas, the team uses its GDSS to pool ideas to generate the most effective disaster plan.[11]

In our discussion of GDSSs and how they can help you and your organization, we'll explore the team decision-making process, the components of a GDSS, and the types of team meetings a GDSS can support.

The Team Decision-Making Process and You

You can use a GDSS to support a team engaged in any one or more of the first three phases of decision making: intelligence, design, or choice. But, whatever the objective of the meeting, you usually go through three distinct steps.

1. *Brainstorming:* Your team members generate ideas in this step. Your team could be identifying the strengths, weaknesses, opportunities, or threats faced by your organization. Or you could be considering or choosing possible solutions to a problem. Avoid discussing the merits or drawbacks of the ideas that other team members contribute at this stage, simply note them.
2. *Issue categorization and analysis*: During this step, you and your team members arrange ideas into manageable classifications. Then you further discuss those ideas, clarify any unresolved issues, and evaluate the worth of each idea.
3. *Ranking and voting:* When your team has seen, discussed, and analyzed the ideas, each member assigns weights to each idea. After prioritizing them, the team votes on the final ranking.

These three steps constitute the process of team decision making. In GDSS-enhanced meetings, existing IT is combined with specialized groupware to improve productivity by helping team members simultaneously contribute and view suggestions and ideas, review the ideas, and reach a consensus.

Key Components in a Group Decision Support System

Like all IT systems, a GDSS is an important alliance between people and IT tools.

People in a GDSS	IT Tools in a GDSS
Team	Groupware
Facilitator	DSS capabilities
	Telecommunications

People in a GDSS

People have one of two roles in a GDSS. The first role is a member of the team working on a problem. The team consists of people united by a common goal.

The second role is that of the facilitator who helps the team reach its goals. A group facilitator has two roles, one nontechnical and one technical. The nontechnical role involves planning and running the meeting, providing advice on the formulation of a meeting agenda, determining the format of the meeting, and conducting the meeting without participating in the discussion. The facilitator's nontechnical skills often affect the outcome of a GDSS meeting. The facilitator's technical role involves handling the administrative and technical details of GDSS meetings. These include responsibility for the operation of the computers and the network, the DSS capabilities, and the groupware. The facilitator's technical skills enable the team to be efficient and productive.

IT Tools in a GDSS

IT tools are a very important part of a GDSS. These tools consist of groupware, DSS capabilities, and telecommunications. Groupware is the umbrella term for any kind of software that allows teams to communicate and share documents. GDSS groupware is a special kind of groupware designed to accommodate team decision making. It has capabilities that support the three phases of team decision making:

- *Brainstorming*: This part of GDSS groupware allows you and your team members to enter comments and suggestions simultaneously and anonymously. The GDSS groupware then collects the various contributions and displays them either on a viewing screen or on the individual team members' computers.
- *Issue categorization and analysis:* Based on key words, the GDSS software sorts and classifies the team's ideas. Each set of ideas then goes into a separate electronic folder. You can open any or all of the folders and add your comments. You can also refine and reorganize the topics in the folders.
- *Ranking and voting:* You assign weights to the various ideas, and then the GDSS groupware calculates the outcome and shows these results numerically or graphically to the team.

GDSS groupware was originally developed for meetings in which all participants are in the same room. Today, however, GDSS groupware supports other types of meetings. Team members need not be in the same room, or even in the same building. Later in this chapter, we'll discuss the various types of meetings made possible by IT.

Specialized GDSS groupware is not the only kind of groupware you can use to improve your team meetings. You can, in fact, use any type of groupware that facilitates communication and decision making including, but not limited to, electronic mail, electronic bulletin boards, videoconferencing, and language translation groupware. Document management groupware is particularly helpful because it allows the team to collaborate on documents, spreadsheets, and other projects.

The DSS capabilities that you use depend on the type of decision you're making. So you must consider which method of analysis—whether statistical, what-if, or another—must be applied to your information to render the most informed decision. Each member of your team must be able to formulate suggestions and analyze those of others. Without the ability to analyze alternatives, you can't adequately assess them and, therefore, cannot contribute fully to the meeting.

The cornerstone of a GDSS-enhanced meeting is a telecommunications network—the hardware and software that connect computers.

The GDSS concept supports many different types of meetings. In addition to improving the productivity of traditional meetings, IT can also provide new, more flexible meeting formats. Let's now consider the nature of meetings and how the GDSS concept can help.

Meetings: A Fact of Life in Business

A large part of business involves decision making; and a large part of decision making involves groups of people working collaboratively. Cooperation is the keystone to innovation and creativity in business. Cooperation, however, involves meetings, and meetings consume a large proportion of work time—35 percent for tactical management and between 50 and 80 percent for strategic management. Thus meetings use two of the most valuable assets an organization has—time and people.

Because IT systems save time and increase employee productivity, the most effective organizations in

INDUSTRY PERSPECTIVE — Manufacturing

Finding What to Fix at IBM

"**W**hat's the problem?" It was asked time and time again by IBM's manufacturing shop floor manager. Everyone seemed to have a different idea—poor equipment maintenance, low-quality raw materials, inadequate communication with production planning, lack of sufficient shop floor space, and so on.

This is a problem all businesses face—not why shop floor control has gone haywire—but rather what problem is causing **any** malfunction. This is the first stage in decision making—finding what to fix (intelligence).

To find the exact problem (and not simply the symptoms), IBM's shop floor manager worked with a group facilitator to develop an agenda, announced the upcoming meeting, and gathered key personnel in a GDSS decision room for some serious and productive brainstorming. The meeting proceeded as follows:

1. The team spent 35 minutes offering 635 ideas and insights.
2. The team spent the next 30 minutes consolidating those ideas and insights into a list of key issues.
3. During the last 45 minutes of the meeting, the team ranked the key issues and voted on their relative importance.

After just 2 short hours, IBM's shop floor manager had a complete report of the team's comments, consolidated and prioritized.

In decision making, the most important stage is intelligence—finding what to fix. That's probably why it's the first step. One of the most wasteful activities in business—and one of the most costly—is fixing the wrong problem.[12, 13, 14] ❖

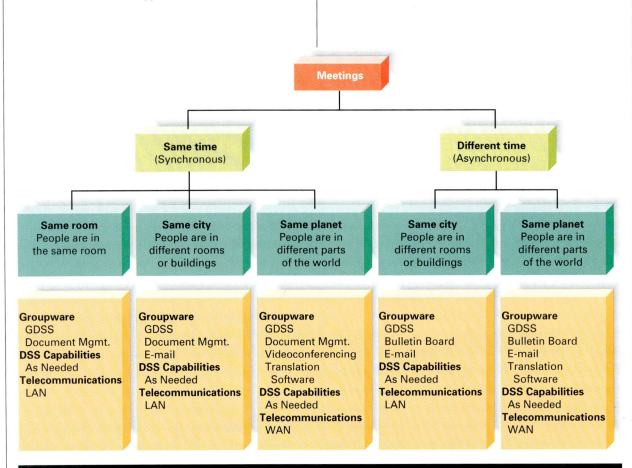

FIGURE 4.8

Types of Team Meetings

the information age will be those that use IT systems to connect people and their ideas. A GDSS is one such IT system. A GDSS will help your organization get the most from its meetings by directly addressing the two biggest problems associated with meetings—too much time spent and too little productivity achieved. GDSSs exist to maximize the positive effects of team decision making—the synergy of collective effort—and minimize the negative effects of wasted time and energy.

Traditional face-to-face meetings are notoriously time-inefficient. Meetings without IT support are sequential—everyone takes a turn speaking—and that takes a lot of time. A GDSS changes the form of the meeting so that participants can offer their contributions simultaneously. A GDSS-enhanced meeting reduces the likelihood of digressing into less important or irrelevant topics. And a GDSS-enhanced meeting allows you to access needed information during the meeting.

The effectiveness, or productivity, of meetings also declines with an increase in the size of the team. Meetings of 3 to 5 people work well but, after that, the more people participating in a meeting, the less productive the meeting becomes. Decisions are often biased by the presence of influential members, conflict between members, and groupthink. *Groupthink* arises when individual members of the team are discouraged from thinking independently. A GDSS-enhanced meeting induces a greater level of independent thought and a greater degree of anonymity, minimizing the unwillingness of many people to express or support controversial opinions.

Meetings When and Where You Want to Be

Because IT connects people and computers, it supports not only traditional face-to-face meetings that occur in the same place at the same time, but also a wide variety of other meeting formats. We can classify meetings into two main categories: Same-time meetings and different-time meetings. The GDSS concept adjusts groupware, DSS capabilities, and telecommunications components to the meeting type (see Figure 4.8).

Group Decision Support Systems

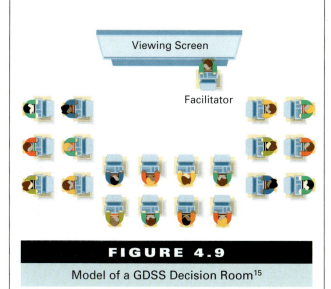

FIGURE 4.9
Model of a GDSS Decision Room[15]

Same-Time Meetings (Synchronous Meetings)

Same-time, or *synchronous*, meetings require team members to interact directly with one another simultaneously. Such meetings can occur while participants are in the same room, the same city, or scattered around the planet.

- **Same Room.** A *same-room* meeting implies that all the team members meet in the same room. Most GDSS groupware has been developed for same-room meetings where project teams get together to solve a problem or make a decision. Same-room GDSS meetings usually take place in a GDSS *decision room*, which has telecommunications in the form of a local area network that connects the team members. Each computer in the room is equipped with GDSS groupware and DSS capabilities. You and your team members enter your ideas at your computers and your comments are displayed on a public viewing screen, making them visible to the entire team (see Figure 4.9).

- **Same City.** In *same-city* meetings, team members are located within a small geographic area, such as a building, block, or city. They do not meet in the same room. They may choose to participate in the meeting from their respective offices rather than gather in a decision room. Some court proceedings are conducted this way. More than 200 state courthouses use videoconferencing for proceedings involving prisoners. The practice not only cuts costs by reducing the need to transport inmates to courthouses but also reduces the opportunity for escapes and injuries to guards.[16]

Hold Virtual Meetings to Complete a Project

Many e-businesses have been hit with denial of service attacks. *Denial-of-service* attacks cause thousands of computers to try to access a Web site at the same time, overloading the target site and shutting it down. The objective is to flood the online company—the target—with so many access attempts as to overload the system, and prevent legitimate customers from getting into the site to do business.

With your partner or partners, hold a series of online meetings to write a two-page paper on denial of service attacks. You can use e-mail, set up a chat room, or any other electronic form of contact to write the paper—just don't discuss the project face-to-face. ❖

- **Same Planet.** A *same-planet* meeting takes place when the team members are dispersed geographically and meet electronically. As companies spread across the country and around the world, face-to-face meetings become more difficult, but the pressure to reach decisions quickly in an increasingly competitive world becomes more intense. The more dispersed the team members, the more costly and inconvenient it is to bring them together in a single room. First, the meeting can be similar to a same-city meeting, using telecommunications and groupware. Second, it can resemble a same-room meeting if it uses videoconferencing, which allows team members in each location to see and hear the other teams. Desktop videoconferencing can turn your monitor into a TV set, showing your discussion partners. Sun Microsystems even uses desktop videoconferencing to meet with its customers.[17]

Different-Time Meetings (Asynchronous Meetings)

Teams whose members are located in the same city (or even the same building) may not find it convenient or efficient to meet at the same time. When team members are dispersed around the planet, same-time meetings may be even more difficult to achieve. For example,

THE GLOBAL PERSPECTIVE

GIS Put South Africans on an Election Map

The world was watching as South Africa held its second postapartheid election, and Mandla Mchunu, chief electoral officer at the Independent Electoral Commission of South Africa (IEC), knew it. The population of South Africa was more than 43 million, nearly three times that of Florida. Many citizens had no permanent addresses and were unable to read or write. The country had no infrastructure that could gather and transmit electoral information. Yet, with less than a year to go, the IEC was expected to compile voter lists, oversee voter registration, conduct the elections, and deliver the results.

So Mr. Mchunu turned to decision support for assistance and, along with his IT team, developed and implemented a very effective GIS to meet the daunting historic challenge.

As the international community watched closely, the IEC saw to it that the election was democratic, fair, and fast. They did it with the help of a geographic information system and a satellite-based wide-area network. Using their customized GIS the team brought together all the necessary information, including 1994 census data, to determine the 14,500 voting districts. They then registered voters into the GIS database over the network. On the first weekend, 9.7 million people registered.

On election day, 16.2 million people voted in a period of 14 hours. During and after the election, the team publicized the results on large-scale GIS maps so that all interested parties could follow the election's progress.[18] ❖

---

time differences mean that daytime in the United States is nighttime in Asia.

However, the dispersed team members can still meet in a *different-time* or *asynchronous* meeting that could last days, weeks, or even months. In this type of meeting, your team would use an electronic bulletin board, a central database, or e-mail. In different-time meetings, the schedule is flexible, and each team member can contribute as appropriate and feasible. A different-time meeting would have all the elements of a same-time meeting, but it would take longer to complete the meeting. For example, you could send the agenda to your team members through e-mail; then members could post suggestions to an electronic bulletin board, or they could distribute them to the other members through e-mail. At a later stage, they could explore and clarify issues to reach a consensus.

Geographic Information Systems

Words and Pictures

Suppose you've decided to go on a two-week vacation that will include camping, sightseeing, and mall touring in Minnesota (after all, Minneapolis boasts the largest shopping mall in the United States—The Mall of America). What maps should you buy? Some will show roads for traveling from one place to another; others will show campgrounds in the state that boasts 10,000 lakes; others will pinpoint historic landmarks; and still others will detail hotels around The Mall of America as well as the locations of the hundreds of stores in the mall.

To get a truly comprehensive picture of your proposed vacation, you'd have to buy each map, redraw them to make a single map, then note on it where you'll go and how you'll get there. Of course, you could choose to carry all the maps and use them only when needed. But what about a business that needs to analyze different maps with geographic, demographic, highway, and other information to decide where to build a new distribution facility?

Fortunately there's a special type of DSS for just this kind of problem—it's called a geographic information system. A ***geographic information system (GIS)*** is a decision support system designed specifically to work with spatial information. Spatial information is any information that can be shown in map form, such as roads, the distribution of bald eagle populations, sewer systems, and the layout of electrical lines. Today GISs are helping businesses perform such tasks as

- Identifying the best site to locate a branch office based on number of households in a neighborhood
- Targeting pockets of potential customers in a particular market area
- Repositioning promotions and advertising based on sales
- Determining the optimal location of a new distribution outlet

When businesses combine textual information and spatial information, they are creating a new type of information called *business geography*. GISs are well-suited to storing, retrieving, and analyzing business geography to support the decision-making process. Healthdemographics, a San Diego–based company, sells such a business geography–based GIS to nursing home providers.[19] Using Healthdemographics' GIS system, nursing home providers can store, retrieve, and analyze information from many external databases containing national demographic information, combining it with information from operational databases within nursing home organizations.

Nursing home providers make decisions based on supply and demand. Supply is the nursing home providers serving the area. Demand is simply those geographic areas that have populations in need of long-term care and assisted living. Healthdemographics' GIS system helps nursing home administrators visually correlate and analyze these supply-and-demand characteristics.

In England, the Lecestershire Constabulary uses a GIS to see patterns in the time, location, and method of crimes. The GIS allows officers to see all this information in overlays giving them the whole picture. The result has been that the police have been able to intervene to stop crime when they saw a predictable pattern and can make better decisions concerning the deployment of officers.[20]

If you need spatial information for a GIS, you can obtain that information from a variety of sources, including government agencies and commercially available spatial information databases. For example, the U.S. Census Bureau can provide you with demographic information, the Bureau of Labor Statistics can give you employment information, and polling companies such as Scarborough Research Corp. have consumer-habit information.

A GIS is actually a combination of sophisticated graphics and database technology. Using a GIS, you can logically link textual and spatial information. For example, you could gather geographic information about the distribution of customers who buy yachts (spatial information). You could also gather information about their color preferences (textual information) and link it to the spatial information. Then, using queries similar to those illustrated in Chapter 3, you could analyze both the spatial and textual information, generating output in the form of maps, graphs, or numeric tables. Some GISs let you load thousands of rows of information from a spreadsheet.

A GIS database represents information thematically. That means that a GIS map is composed of many separate, overlapping information layers, each of which has its own theme. For example, the first layer might be roads, the next might be utilities (water, electricity, etc.), the third school-age children, and the fourth homes within a certain price range. In reviewing Figure 4.10, notice how the information structure resembles a cube much like the multidimensional nature of a data warehouse. You can use a GIS to slice and dice information as you need it, in the same way you'd use data mining.

A GIS not only processes spatial information, but also presents information spatially. To understand the importance of this feature, imagine asking a friend for directions to a mall. If the directions are given to you in an oral or written form, you probably won't find the mall as readily as you would have if you'd been given a map complete with landmarks and compass directions. Business geography is no different—a picture is still worth a thousand words. Figure 4.11 is a map of toxic release sites and schools in Bronx County, New York City. Thus, the possible exposure of school children is clear. For other such maps look at Mapinfo's Web site at www.mapinfo.com. Following are some other examples of GIS applications:

- Sears uses a GIS to plan the daily routes that Sears drivers nationwide must take when delivering appliances and other merchandise to customers' homes. Sears saves millions of dollars annually on its 4 million home deliveries with its GIS. The 52 distribution centers use the GIS to reduce the time it takes to map out a delivery route from 2.5 hours to about 20 minutes.[21]
- Relocate, a real estate service firm in Manhattan, uses GIS maps to analyze the real estate market. For example, to determine why an office building remains vacant at $25 per square foot, Relocate asks the GIS to display a map showing all the buildings in that class. If the average rent is $23, it

142 CHAPTER FOUR Decision Support and Artificial Intelligence

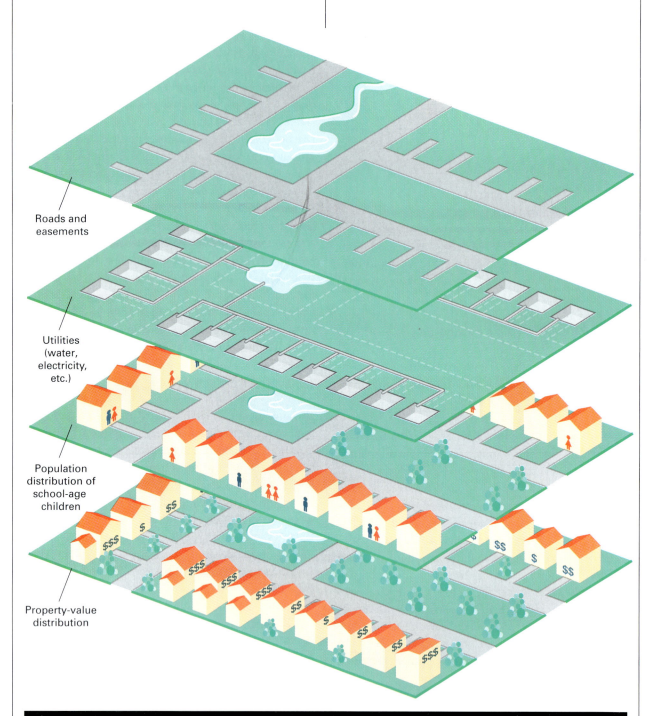

FIGURE 4.10

Thematic Mapping in a Geographic Information System

becomes instantly obvious why the $25-per-square-foot building remains vacant.[22]

- Boise, Idaho, has grown rapidly over the last several years. The sheriff's office maintains a 900-page map book which department dispatchers on the 911 lines use to help police officers, firefighters, and paramedics locate emergency scenes. The county sheriff's department used to update the map book every two years by drafting and copying updated pages individually. The map sections have very detailed information including street names, rights of way, address ranges, and hydrants. Since

Artificial Intelligence

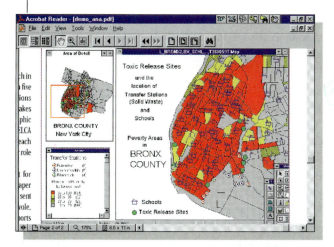

FIGURE 4.11

Are the Children in Danger?

installing a GIS, the sheriff's department can plot a page within 15 minutes, or the whole map book within a few weeks. Updates are now made every two weeks, keeping the maps current, which is crucial for this fast-growing urban area. Each department can also get a specialized map. For example, the fire department needs the location of hydrants, but the paramedics don't.[23]

Artificial Intelligence

Where No Machine Has Gone Before

DSSs, GDSSs, and GISs are IT systems that augment business brainpower. IT can further expand business brainpower by means of artificial intelligence—the techniques and software that enable computers to mimic human behavior in various ways. Financial analysts use a variety of artificial intelligence systems to manage assets, invest in the stock market, and perform other financial operations.[24] Hospitals use artificial intelligence in many capacities, from scheduling staff, to assigning beds to patients, to diagnosing and treating illness.[25] Many government agencies use artificial intelligence, including the IRS and the armed forces. Credit card companies use artificial intelligence to detect credit card fraud, and insurance companies use artificial intelligence to ferret out fraudulent claims.[26] Artificial intelligence lends itself to tasks as diverse as airline ticket pricing, food preparation, oil exploration, and child protection.

Artificial intelligence (AI) is the science of making machines imitate human thinking and behavior. For example, an expert system is an artificial intelligence system that makes computers capable of reasoning through a problem to reach a conclusion. We use the process of reasoning to find out, from what we already know, something that we don't know. The Marion County Department of Public Welfare uses an expert system to help evaluate cases of child abuse, standardizing the set of questions and relative importance of the answers so that critical aspects of the situation are not neglected.[27] With 600 cases a month and an 80 percent employee turnover rate (because of the low pay and nature of the work), consistency is a problem. Now when a complaint is called in the caseworker asks pertinent questions, then feeds the answers into an expert system. The system applies reasoning techniques to reach a conclusion, then makes a recommendation on what action the caseworker should take.

Today computers can see, hear, smell, and, important for business, think—in a manner of speaking. Robots are a well-known form of AI. A *robot* is a mechanical device equipped with simulated human senses and the capability of taking action on its own (in contrast to a mechanical device such as an automobile which requires direction from the driver for its every action). Robots are in use in many industries. For example, Piedmont Hospital's Pharmacy Dosage Dispenser is a robotic prescription-filling system. Using bar code technology, this pharmaceutical robot receives medication orders online, retrieves prepackaged doses of drugs, and sends them to hospital patients.[28] One of the most exciting new areas of research in robotics is the development of microrobots that can be introduced into human veins and arteries to perform surgery.

A recent U.S. Commerce Department survey reported that 70 percent of the top 500 companies use artificial intelligence as part of decision support, and the sale of artificial intelligence software is rapidly approaching the $1 billion mark. The artificial intelligence systems that businesses use most can be classified into the following major categories:

- Expert systems, which reason through problems and offer advice in the form of a conclusion or recommendation

- Neural networks, which can be "trained" to recognize patterns

- Genetic algorithms, which can generate increasingly better solutions to problems by generating many, many solutions, choosing the

- best ones, and using those to generate even better solutions
- Intelligent agents, which are adaptive systems that work independently, carrying out specific, repetitive or predictable tasks

Expert Systems
Following the Rules

Suppose you own a real estate business, and you generate over 40 percent of your revenue from appraising commercial real estate. Consider further that only one person in your firm is capable of performing these appraisals. What if that person were to quit? How do you replace that expertise? How fast can you find someone else? How much business would you lose if it took you a month to find a suitable replacement?

In business, people are valuable because they perform important business tasks. Many of these business tasks require expertise, and people often carry expertise in their heads—and often that's the only place it can be found in the organization. AI can provide you with an expert system that can capture expertise, thus making it available to those who are not experts so that they can use it, either to solve a problem or to learn how to solve a problem.

An **expert system**, also called a **knowledge-based system**, is an artificial intelligence system that applies reasoning capabilities to reach a conclusion. Expert systems are excellent for diagnostic and prescriptive problems. Diagnostic problems are those requiring an answer to the question "What's wrong?" and correspond to the intelligence phase of decision making. Prescriptive problems are those that require an answer to the question "What to do?" and correspond to the choice phase of decision making.

An expert system is usually built for a specific application area called a *domain*. You can find expert systems in the following domains:

- Accounting—for auditing, tax planning, management consulting, and training
- Medicine—to prescribe antibiotics where many considerations must be taken into account (such as the patient's medical history, the source of the infection, and the price of available drugs)

THE GLOBAL PERSPECTIVE

Expert System Gets Goods Safely across the Border

If you think you have to fill out a lot of paperwork to go to school, just wait until you try to trade with countries outside the United States. Legally speaking, some countries are easier to trade with than others.

For example, the North American Free Trade Agreement (NAFTA) created a trading alliance among the United States, Canada, and Mexico. It opened up avenues of trade that had not been available before. But NAFTA also brought with it a huge tangle of rules and regulations with which any business importing or exporting within NAFTA has to comply. Companies moving goods in and out of any of the three NAFTA countries must process and integrate vast amounts of information to maintain compliance, such as Rules and Certificates of Origin, detailed audit trails, and so on.

Sony Electronics Inc., trying to simplify the procedure as much as possible, turned to an expert system to aid in its North American import-export operations. Sony uses Origin Pro™, an expert system from SmartSource.com, which analyzes and interprets the complex process of international trade and customs compliance. The expert system software identifies areas of noncompliance and provides help with filling in the gaps. The software performs the two tasks that expert systems are best at: figuring out what's wrong (diagnostic) and what to do about it (prescriptive).

Sony is encouraging its suppliers throughout the NAFTA region to also adopt the use of Origin Pro to improve its supply chain management. With Origin Pro, importers and exporters can save valuable time and be confident that their shipments won't be delayed because they forgot to include a form or fill out the necessary paperwork.[29] ❖

- Process control—for example, to control offset lithographic printing
- Human resource management—to help personnel managers determine whether they are in compliance with an array of federal employment laws
- Financial management—to identify delinquency-prone accounts in the loan departments of banks
- Production—to guide the manufacture of all sorts of products, such as aircraft parts, and so on
- Forestry management—to help with harvesting timber on forest lands

A DSS sometimes incorporates expert systems, but an expert system is fundamentally different from a DSS. To use a DSS, you must have considerable knowledge or expertise about the situation with which you're dealing. As you saw earlier in this chapter, a DSS *assists* you in making decisions. That means that you must know how to reason through the problem. You must know which questions to ask, how to get the answers, and how to proceed to the next step. However, when you use an expert system, the know-how is in the system—you need only provide the expert system with the facts and symptoms of the problem for which you need an answer. The know-how, or expertise, that actually solves the problem came from someone else—an expert in the field. What does it mean to have expertise? When someone has expertise in a given subject, that person not only knows a lot of facts about the topic, but also can apply that knowledge to analyze and make judgments about related topics. It's this human expertise that an expert system captures.

Let's look at a very simple expert system that would tell a driver what to do when approaching a traffic light. Dealing with traffic lights is the type of problem to which an expert system is well-suited. It is a recurring problem, and to solve it you follow a well-defined set of steps. You've probably gone through the following mental question-and-answer session millions of times without even realizing it (see Table 4.1).

When you approach a green traffic light, you proceed on through. If the light is red, you try to stop. If you're unable to stop, and if traffic is approaching from either side, you'll probably be in trouble. Similarly, if the light is yellow, you may be able to make it through the intersection before the light turns red. If not, you will again be faced with the problem of approaching traffic.

Let's say that you know very little about what to do when you come to a traffic light, but you know that there are experts in the field. You want to capture their expertise in an expert system so that you can refer to it whenever the traffic light situation arises. To gain an understanding of what's involved in the creation and use of an expert system, let's now consider the components of an expert system individually with the traffic light example in mind.

TABLE 4.1 Traffic Light Expert System

Rule	Symptom or Fact	Yes	No	Explanation
1	Is the light green?	Go through the intersection.	Go to Rule 2.	Should be safe if light is green. If not, need more information.
2	Is the light red?	Go to Rule 4.	Go to Rule 3.	Should stop, may not be able to.
3	Is the light likely to change to red before you get through the intersection?	Go to Rule 4.	Go through the intersection.	Will only reach this point if light is yellow, then you'll have two choices.
4	Can you stop before entering the intersection?	Stop.	Go to Rule 5.	Should stop, but there may be a problem if you can't.
5	Is traffic approaching from either side?	Prepare to crash.	Go through the intersection.	Unless the intersection is clear of traffic, you're likely to crash.

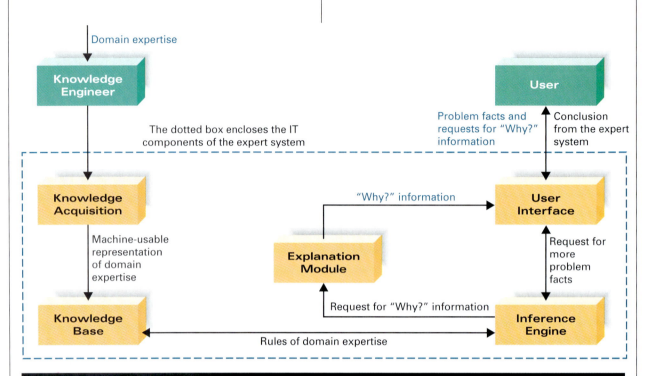

FIGURE 4.12

Expert System Components

Components of an Expert System

An expert system, like any IT system, combines information, people, and IT components.

Information Types	People	IT Components
Domain expertise	Domain expert	Knowledge base
"Why?" information	Knowledge engineer	Knowledge acquisition
Problem facts	Knowledge worker	Inference engine
		User interface
		Explanation module

These components and their relationships are shown in Figure 4.12. Dotted lines enclose the expert system's IT components.

Information Types

The traffic light *domain expertise* is the core of the expert system, because it's the set of problem-solving steps—the reasoning process that will solve the problem. You'll also want to ask the expert system how it reached its conclusion, or why it asked you a question. The *"Why?" information* included in the expert system allows it to give you the answers. It's information that's provided by the expert—the traffic expert in our example. With the domain expertise and the "Why?" information, the expert system is now ready to solve traffic light problems. So now you need to enter the *problem facts,* which are the specifics of your traffic light situation. Problem facts are the symptoms of and assertions about your problem. You'll enter these problem facts as answers to the expert system's questions during your consultation.

People

Three separate roles must be filled in the development and use of an expert system. The first role is that of the domain expert, who knows how to solve the problem. The ***domain expert*** provides the domain expertise in the form of problem-solving strategies. In our traffic light expert system, the domain expert could be an official from the department of motor vehicles. This official, turned domain expert, would also be able to indicate where to gather further domain expertise, and might direct you to the local police station or give you a booklet with the rules of the road. Eventually, the

Domain Expertise Captured as Rules by the Knowledge Engineer

Rule 1:   IF   The light is green
                THEN   Go through the intersection.
                REASON   If light is green, should be safe. If not, need more information.

Rule 2:   IF   The light is red
                THEN   Go to Rule 4 else go to Rule 3.
                REASON   Should stop, may not be able to. ❖

---

combination of these sources will produce the five steps that you saw in Table 4.1.

The domain expert usually works with an IT specialist, a **knowledge engineer**, who formulates the domain expertise into an expert system. In this case, the knowledge engineer might consider it best to represent the five steps in the form of rules, making a **rule-based expert system**. The knowledge engineer will see to it that the rules are in the correct order and that the system works properly. See the box entitled "Domain Expertise Captured as Rules" for an example of how the knowledge engineer might formulate the rules.

The *knowledge worker* or user—that's you—will then apply the expert system to the problem of what to do when approaching a traffic light. When you face the traffic light problem, you would run a *consultation* (see Figure 4.13) and provide the expert system with the problem facts. You would answer the questions as they appear on the screen, with the expert system applying the appropriate rules and asking you more questions.

This process continues until the expert system presents you with a conclusion (telling you what to do) or indicates that it can't reach a conclusion (telling you that it doesn't know what you should do).

IT Components

When the knowledge engineer has converted the domain expertise into rules, the **knowledge base** stores the rules. All the rules must be in place before a consultation, because the expert system won't be able to offer a conclusion in a situation for which it has no rules. For example, if the traffic light is broken and has been replaced by a four-way stop sign, the expert system, as it stands, would not be able to reach a conclusion. The knowledge engineer could, of course, go back to the domain expert and enter rules about four-way stops. The knowledge engineer uses the **knowledge acquisition** component of the expert system to enter the traffic light rules. The domain expertise for the rules can come from many sources, including human experts, books, organizational databases, data warehouses, internal reports, diagrams, and so on.

The **inference engine** is the part of the expert system that takes your problem facts and searches the knowledge base for rules that fit. This process is called *inferencing*. The inference engine organizes and controls the rules—it "reasons" through your problem to reach a conclusion. It delivers its conclusion or recommendation based on (1) the problem facts of your specific traffic light situation and (2) the rules that came from the domain expert about traffic light procedures in general. The **user interface** is the part of the expert system that you use to run a consultation. Through the user interface, the expert system asks you questions, and you enter problem facts by answering the questions. In the traffic light expert system, you would enter "yes" or "no." These answers are used by the inference engine to solve the problem.

Is the light green (Yes/No)?   No.

Is the light red (Yes/No)?   No.

Is the light likely to change to red before you get through the intersection (Yes/No)?   Why?

Will only reach this point if light is yellow, and then you'll have two choices.

Is the light likely to change to red before you get through the intersection (Yes/No)?   No.

Conclusion: Go through the intersection.

FIGURE 4.13

Running a Consultation

INDUSTRY PERSPECTIVE ".com"

Look Ma, No Hands!

Imagine telling your computer, verbally, that you want to buy a new car. Say you're looking for a new Subaru Forester. Just tell the Web site what options you want and let it show you all the cars meeting your criteria. Now, say you find what you want and would like information on financing. Again, you speak to the site and it will lead you through its many financing options.

Autobytel.com, one of the most recognizable online car shopping services, is making that possible. This site is the first to let you find information and buy products by talking into a headset, bypassing the mouse and keyboard entirely.

Autobytel.com has teamed up with One Voice Technologies, the company that sells software called One Voice. One Voice is an intelligent voice recognition system, which consists of an expert system, a database, and natural language processing capabilities.

You'll find many voice-recognition systems on the market for word processing. What makes this product different is that it enables interactive dialog—you can basically chat with Autobytel.com about purchasing a car. The expert system provides One Voice with the questions to ask and can tell it what to do with the answers.

Autobytel.com has even bigger plans for its voice-recognition system. Eventually the company wants to allow people with Web-enabled cellular phones to buy cars too.[30] ❖

The domain expert supplies the "Why?" information, which is entered by the knowledge engineer into the ***explanation module***, where it is stored. During a consultation, you—as the knowledge worker or user—can ask why a question was posed and how the expert system reached its conclusion. If you're using the expert system as a training tool, then you'll be very interested in how it solved the problem.

In Figure 4.14 you can clearly see the distinction between the development and use of an expert system. The domain expert and the knowledge engineer develop the expert system, then the knowledge worker can apply the expert system to a particular set of circumstances.

What Expert Systems Can and Can't Do

An expert system uses IT to capture and apply human expertise. For problems with clear rules and procedures, expert systems work very well and can provide your company with great advantages. An expert system can:

- Handle massive amounts of information
- Reduce errors
- Aggregate information from various sources
- Improve customer service
- Provide consistency in decision making
- Provide new information
- Decrease personnel time spent on tasks
- Reduce cost

You can, however, run into trouble in building and using an expert system.

1. Transferring domain expertise to the expert system is sometimes difficult because domain experts cannot always explain how they know what they know. Often experts are not aware of their complete reasoning processes. Experience has given them a feel for the problem, and they just "know."

2. Even if the domain expert can explain the whole reasoning process, automating that process may be impossible. The process may be too complex, requiring an excessive number of rules, or it may be too vague or imprecise.

3. In using an expert system, keep in mind that it can solve only the problems for which it was designed. It cannot deal with inconsistency or a newly encountered problem situation. An expert system can't learn from previous experience and can't apply previously acquired expertise to new problems the way humans can.

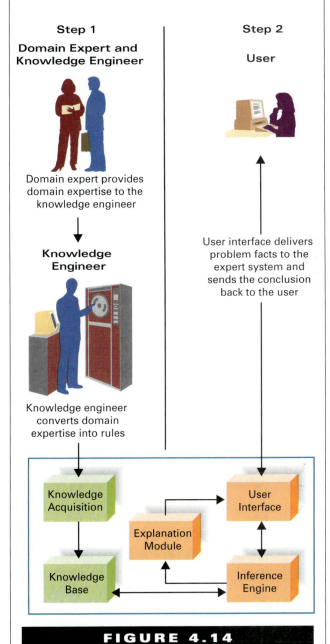

FIGURE 4.14

Developing and Using an Expert System

4. An expert system has no common sense or judgment. One of the early expert systems built into an F-16 fighter plane allowed the pilot to retract the landing gear while the plane was still on the ground and to jettison bombs while the plane was flying upside down, both highly dangerous actions.

Ethical Questions in Expert Systems

Expert systems can diagnose mechanical problems with automobiles and suggest scheduling plans for production, but they have also been developed to provide conclusions that affect lives. An expert system can recommend that someone get a loan from a bank or be admitted to a university. For any IT system that affects people, we must consider the ethical dimension. Let's examine three questions:

1. Will an expert system act ethically?
2. What kind of decisions should you let an expert system make for you?
3. Should you accept the decision of an expert system without question?

You already know the answer to the first question! An expert system will act the way it's programmed to act. So, if a system was programmed with domain expertise that was biased in some way, then the expert system's conclusion will be biased too. The question becomes whether the decisions you're making with an expert system reflect your ethical standards. You will especially want to know this if your decisions will affect lives.

For the second question—What decisions should an expert system make?—let's suppose you have an expert system that processes job applications and makes recommendations as to whether an applicant is suitable. One advantage of an expert system is that it's consistent (which can be helpful if you find yourself called upon to defend your decision in court). The consistency of an expert system ensures that criteria are not weighed differently for different applicants. For example, an expert system will not, cannot, give preference to a lower GPA because the applicant is better looking. Choosing an employee, like many decisions you make in business, is one of those complicated tasks that requires a choice not between "good" and "bad" but between "good" and "better," and "better" is a matter of judgment. You have an ethical responsibility to your organization and its shareholders to choose the most qualified person, and you have a responsibility to the applicants to treat them fairly. Therefore, when you're considering which decisions to allocate to an expert system, you would do well to keep in mind the ethical implications of your decision and the question whether an expert system can adequately consider every aspect of the problem.

Our third question asks whether you should question the conclusions of an expert system. An expert system (or any IT system) is only as good as the people who developed it. Always view any computer-generated results carefully and critically.

Traffic Lights Revisited

Create a table similar to Table 4.1 to extend the traffic light expert system. Include the following situations in the table:

1. There is a wreck in the middle of the intersection.
2. You are turning left at the intersection.
3. You are turning right at the intersection.
4. A pedestrian is crossing in front of you.
5. A dog has wandered into the intersection.
6. A ball belonging to children playing near the intersection has rolled into the street.
7. The car in front of you has stalled. ❖

Neural Networks

They Learn by Example

Suppose you see a breed of dog you've never encountered before. Would you know it's a dog? For that matter, would you know it's an animal? Probably so—in both instances. You know from experience that the creature is an animal that's classified as a dog. A neural network simulates this human ability to classify things. A *neural network* is an artificial intelligence system which is capable of learning to differentiate patterns.

CAREER OPPORTUNITY

How does a neural network really work? What does it look like inside? How does it develop patterns? If you want answers to these questions, we recommend that you pick up a good book devoted to neural networks. In those books, you'll find hundreds of pages of discussions about how neural networks work. Your career opportunity, however, lies not in learning how neural networks work, but rather in learning what types of problems neural networks are well-suited for. Neural networks work best on pattern-recognition problems for which a vast amount of historical information is available. Without this information, you'll never be able to properly train a neural network—and if you can't train a neural network, it will never be able to recognize patterns on its own.

Neural networks are useful to a variety of applications. For example, many airports use a neural network called SNOOPE to detect bombs in luggage. Because chemical compounds have distinct patterns, SNOOPE can easily detect the compounds inside the luggage as they pass through a checking system.[31] In medicine, neural networks check 50 million electrocardiograms per year, check for drug interactions, and detect anomalies in tissue samples that may signify the onset of cancer and other diseases. In business, neural networks are very popular for securities trading, fraud detection, credit evaluation, real estate appraisal, and even handwriting recognition. Neural networks are most useful for identification, classification, and prediction when a vast amount of information is available. By examining hundreds, or even thousands of examples, a neural network detects important relationships and patterns in the information. For example, if you provide a neural network with the details of numerous credit card transactions and tell it which ones are fraudulent, eventually it will learn to identify suspicious transaction patterns.

Training a Neural Network

Bradford Lewis, a stock fund manager for Fidelity Investments, manages a fund that is consistently one of the best performing in the industry. Using a neural network, Bradford feeds 180,000 attributes (profits, per share earnings, book value, and so on) of 2,000 stocks into a neural network to look for patterns. He is "trying to capture as much of the historical cause and effect of the stock markets" as he can.[32] His first step is to show the neural network examples of "good" stocks. From these, the neural network "learns" the characteristics of a good stock. The neural network then practices identifying examples of good and bad stocks. The characteristics that repeatedly appear in the good stocks are assigned more weight by the neural network. For example, suppose that the stocks of businesses that have been in operation for more than 10 years always appear as good stocks. The neural network will assign this characteristic more weight than, say, the current price of the stock, which fluctuates. After lots of practice, the neural network can recognize good stocks on its own.

Here are some examples of companies that use neural networks:

- Citibank uses neural networks to find opportunities in financial markets.[33] Using a neural network to carefully examine historical stock market data, Citibank financial managers learn of interesting coincidences or small anomalies (called market inefficiencies). For example, it could be that whenever IBM stock goes up, so does Unisys stock. Or it might be that a U.S. Treasury note is selling for 1 cent less in Japan than it is in the United States. These snippets of information can make a big difference to Citibank's bottom line in a very competitive financial market.
- Chase Manhattan Bank uses a neural network internally to evaluate commercial loans. Many banks also use neural networks to decipher the numbers at the bottom of checks which are often blurred, off-center, or incomplete.[34,35]
- Fraud detection is one of the areas in which neural networks are used the most. MasterCard, and many other credit card companies, use a neural network to spot peculiarities in individual accounts. MasterCard estimates neural networks save them $50 million annually.[36]
- Cigna Corp. Healthcare Group Inc. has a neural network to identify variations in the claims submitted by physicians. The system searches for patterns in billing charges, laboratory tests, and frequency of office visits. A claim for which the diagnosis was a sprained ankle and which included an electrocardiogram would be flagged for the account manager.[37]
- Doctors use neural networks to find problems. Neural networks find the distinctive patterns left in the blood when tumors invade healthy tissue. They analyze pap smears and can find a few abnormal cells on a slide with a half-million cells. Neural networks can detect heart attacks and even differentiate between the subtly different symptoms of heart attacks in men and women.[38,39,40]

Ethical Questions in Neural Networks

Neural networks pose an interesting ethical problem because you can apply pattern recognition just as easily to other human behavior as to credit card use. For example, the Chicago Police Department uses a neural network to analyze information pertaining to its 12,500-person police force to identify officers who may be prone to misconduct.[41] So far, the neural network has identified 91 officers, half of whom were already enrolled in misconduct counseling programs. Is this reasonable? Are police officers different from civilians because they are the guardians of society and have powers that ordinary citizens do not possess, such as the power to enforce search and arrest warrants? Is it necessary, desirable, ethical, or even legal to monitor them more closely?

Even more disturbing is a case in England in which neural networks are analyzing the behavioral patterns of children in the hope of forecasting potential criminals.[42] Such a system has grave civil liberties implications. Should a child be classified early in life as a potential troublemaker? Many experts believe that a child will meet the expectations of adult guardians. Is it better to identify troubled children early in an effort to help them, or is it detrimental to label them so early?

Genetic Algorithms

It's a Matter of Breeding

Have you ever wondered how chefs around the world create recipes for great-tasting foods? For example, how did the Chinese discover that cashew nuts and chicken taste good when combined? How did Mexican chefs arrive at combining tomatoes, onions, cilantro, and other spices to create pica de gallo? How did British chefs decide to combine lamb and mint jelly? All those great recipes came about through *evolutionary processes.* Someone literally decided to put together a few ingredients and taste the result. Undoubtedly, many of those combinations resulted in unpalatable concoctions that were quickly discarded. Others were tasty enough to warrant further experimentation of combinations.

Today significant research in AI is devoted to creating software capable of following similar evolutionary processes. This software is called a genetic algorithm. A *genetic algorithm* is an artificial intelligence system that mimics the evolutionary, survival-of-the-fittest process to generate increasingly better solutions to a problem. Genetic algorithms use three concepts of evolution:

- *Selection*—or survival of the fittest. The key to selection is to give preference to better outcomes.
- *Crossover*—or combining portions of good outcomes in the hope of creating an even better outcome.
- *Mutation*—or randomly trying combinations and evaluating the success (or failure) of the outcome.

Genetic algorithms are best-suited to decision-making environments in which thousands, or perhaps millions, of solutions are possible, and each of those solutions must be carefully evaluated. As you might imagine, businesses face decision-making environments such as these every day. Genetic algorithms are good for these types of problems because they use selection, crossover, and mutation as methods of exploring countless solutions and the respective worth of each. For example, US West uses a genetic algorithm to determine the optimal configuration of fiber-optic cable in a network that may include as many as 100,000 connection points. By using selection, crossover, and mutation, the genetic algorithm can generate and evaluate millions of cable configurations and select the one that uses the least amount of cable. At US West, this process used to take an experienced design engineer almost two months. US West's genetic algorithm can solve the problem in two days and saves the company $1 million to $10 million each time it's used.[43]

In a genetic algorithm, there is really no "intelligence" behind selection, crossover, and mutation. Genetic algorithms simply use these concepts to produce and evaluate numerous solutions. You have to tell the genetic algorithm what constitutes a "good" solution. That could be low cost, high return, etc., since many solutions are useless or absurd. If you created a genetic algorithm to make bread, for example, it might try to boil flour to create moistness. That obviously won't work, so the genetic algorithm would simply throw away that solution and try something else. Other solutions would eventually be good, and some of them would even be wonderful. According to David Goldbert, a genetic algorithm pioneer at the University of Illinois at Urbana-Champaign, evolution is the oldest and most powerful algorithm there is, and "three billion years of evolution can't be wrong!"[44]

Intelligent Agents

Tireless Assistants

Do you have a favorite restaurant? Is there someone there who knows you and remembers that you like Italian dressing, but not croutons, on your salad; and ice cream and a slice of cheddar cheese on your apple pie? Does this person familiar with your tastes put a glass of diet cola on your favorite table when you come in the door? If so, he or she has the qualities that artificial intelligence scientists are working on incorporating into intelligent agents. An *intelligent agent* is software that assists you, performing repetitive tasks and adapting itself to your preferences.

You may not realize it, but you're probably already familiar with a primitive type of intelligent agent—the shifty-eyed paper clip that pops itself up when you're using Word. For example, if your document looks as if it is going to be a business letter—that is, you type in a date, name, and address—the animated paperclip will offer helpful suggestions on how to proceed. Another example of a primitive intelligent agent is the software on Amazon.com's Web site that suggests books to you on the basis of your previous purchases and those of people who bought the books you did.

You can find hundreds of intelligent agents, or bots, for a wide variety of tasks. The BotSpot and SmartBot Web sites at http://www.botspot.com and http://www.smartbots.com are good places to look for the different types of agents available.

Essentially there are four types of intelligent agents:

- Find-and-retrieve agents
- User agents
- Monitor and surveillance agents
- Data-mining agents

Find-and-Retrieve Agents

The find-and-retrieve agents travel around a network (very likely the Internet) finding information and bringing it back to you. For example, if you're looking for a particular vintage car, you might send a bot out to find one for you. These would be *buyer agents* or *shopping bots,* which are intelligent agents that look on the Web for the product of your choice and bring the information back to you. These agents work very efficiently for commodity products such as CDs, books, electronic components, and other one-size-fits-all products.

Intelligent Agents   **153**

Go Bargain Hunting Online

Try out shopping bots for yourself. Choose three items to search for: one music item, one item of clothing, and one household item. Search for them with each of the following sites.

- Bottom Dollar at http://www.bottomdollar.com
- MySimon at http://www.mysimon.com
- R U Sure at http://www.rusure.com
- Yahoo Shopping at http://shopping.yahoo.com
- Prescan at http://www.prescan.com

Answer these questions . . .

- How many hits did you get at each site for each item?
- Are tax, postage, and handling charges included in the quoted price?
- Can you sort in order of price?
- Does the Shopping site specialize in a particular kind of item? ❖

Shopping bots make money by selling advertising space, special promotions in cooperation with merchants, or click-through fees, which are payments to the site that provided the link to the merchant site. Some shopping bots give preference to certain sites for a financial consideration.

MySimon.com is the most successful shopping bot to date with more than a million visitors a month according to Nielsen/NetRatings. MySimon searches for millions of products on thousands of Web sites.[45]

Government sites have search-and-retrieve agents you can use to get the information you need. FERRET (Federal Electronic Research and Review Extraction Tool) was developed jointly by the Census Bureau and the Bureau of Labor Statistics. With FERRET you can find information on employment, health care, education, race and ethnicity, health insurance, housing, income and poverty, aging, and marriage and family.

User Agents

User agents are intelligent agents that help an individual perform computer-related tasks. Intelligent agents usually work in the background, so your computer is still available to you for use. In this category belong those intelligent agents that check your e-mail, sort it according to priority (your priority), and alert you when good stuff comes through—like college acceptance letters.

If you're a gamer, you might want to have a bot that will patrol game areas for you or act as your opponent. For your daily news requirements, you might want to bypass the TV and newspaper altogether with a news bot. There are several versions of these. A CNN Custom News bot will gather news from CNN on the topics you want to read about—and only those. Others search all types of sources for news on your chosen subjects.

You can find many other types of user agents including

- Agents that fill out forms on the Web automatically for you. They even store your information for future reference.
- Agents that scan Web pages looking for and highlighting the text that constitutes the "important" part of the information there.
- Chat agents that will discuss topics with you from your deepest fears to sports.

Monitoring and Surveillance Agents

Monitoring and surveillance agents are intelligent agents that perform continuous and repetitive tasks, that keep working in the background, alerting you when they find something of interest. This type of agent is essential in push technology, which means sending information to your computer without a specific request for it. E-mail is a good example of push technology since you mostly don't request that a particular e-mail arrive with specific information at a prearranged time.

Agents that monitor large networks for potential problems belong in this category. For example, Computer Associates International (CA) has a monitoring agent that watches their huge network 24 hours a day. Every five seconds, the agent measures 1,200 data points and can predict a system crash 45 minutes

INDUSTRY PERSPECTIVE

Financial Services

Just How Good Is Your Web Site?

If you had an e-commerce Web site up and running, wouldn't you want to know how effective it was? If you say, Yes, you're not alone. Most Web sites would like to be able to measure how their site stacks up against the competition.

Chase Manhattan Bank is no exception. The bank uses WebCriteria, software with intelligent agent capabilities that finds Chase's Web site's deficiencies and offers help in solving the problem. WebCriteria replicates the consumer's online experience and reports back.

WebCriteria performs two services: site analysis and task analysis. Site analysis measures

- The length of time it takes for a page to load
- How long it takes the average person to navigate
- The content on each page

The intelligent agent software then compares your Web site to as many competitor Web sites as you specify. WebCriteria also has a database of hundreds of Web sites that you can compare yours against. You can compare your site to small competitors and to the leading Web sites. You can even download the information to Excel to do your own analysis.

The task analysis portion of the software gives you a measure of your site's effectiveness. You can use it to tell how long it takes a user to find information or purchase something from your site.[46] ❖

---

before it happens. NASA's Jet Propulsion Laboratory has an agent that monitors inventory, planning, and scheduling equipment ordering to keep costs down.[47]

Other monitoring agents work on the manufacturing shop floor, finding equipment problems and locating other machinery that will do the same job.

Some further types of monitoring and surveillance agents include

- Agents that watch your competition and bring back price changes and special offer information
- Agents that monitor Internet sites, discussion groups, mailing lists, and so on, for stock manipulation, insider training, and rumors that might affect stock prices
- Agents that monitor sites for updated information on the topic of your choice
- Agents that watch particular products and bring back price or term changes
- Agents that monitor auction sites for products or prices that you want

Data-Mining Agents

A *data-mining agent* operates in a data warehouse discovering information. A data-mining agent may detect a major shift in a trend or a key indicator. It can also detect the presence of new information and alert you. Volkswagen uses an intelligent agent system that acts as an early-warning system about market conditions. If conditions become such that the assumptions underlying the company's strategy are no longer true, the intelligent agent alerts managers.[48] For example, the intelligent agent might see a problem in some part of the country that is or will shortly cause payments to slow down. Having that information early lets managers formulate a plan to protect themselves.

Components of an Intelligent Agent

To be truly "intelligent" systems, intelligent agents must have three qualities: autonomy, adaptivity, and sociability.[49]

- *Autonomy* means that they act without your telling them every step to take. Many of the intelligent agents in use today have this quality. They check networks, index Web pages, retrieve football scores from any information source, tell you when a competitor has an offer you should be aware of, and so on.

- *Adaptivity* is discovering, learning, and taking action independently. This means that the intelligent agent learns about your preferences and makes judgments by itself. If you were to fly to Chicago to visit your mother the last weekend of

Which AI Software Should You Use?

What type, or types, of decision support would be appropriate for each of the following situations? Note why you think that those you choose are appropriate.

The decision support alternatives are

- DSS
- GDSS
- GIS
- Expert System
- Neural Network
- Genetic algorithm
- Intelligent agent

Problem	Type of Decision Support
Marketing executives on two continents want to develop a marketing strategy.	
A CEO is trying to determine why customer satisfaction levels have dropped.	
Filling out a long tax form.	
Determining where to put a new shopping center.	
Determining which of many thousands of insurance claims are fraudulent.	
Finding the shortest route you could take to visit all the states in the contiguous United States.	
Franchisees want to decide on a new sandwich to offer in their restaurants.	
Trying to determine what qualities you need to get accepted as a player on a TV game show.	

every month, the intelligent agent would discover that it needed to start looking for cheap fares to Chicago at least three weeks ahead of time. It would then do this without your intervention.

- *Sociability* is conferring with other agents. For example, a buyer agent, or shopping bot, might go out looking for a product or service. At various branches of a retail store there might be a store agent that knows the merchandise and prices in its own store. The store agents would communicate with each other and the buyer agent to produce results for you. These agents communicate with each other using the Knowledge Query and Manipulation Language (KQML), which has become the de facto standard for interagent communications.

At the moment no intelligent agent software has these qualities. Various agents are autonomous, and some are adaptive with a reasonable amount of success. Sociability is a very hot research area at the moment and more a goal than a reality. Some artificial intelligence scientists believe that lots of one-purpose agents working together are the way to create a very sophisticated artificial intelligence system.

CAREER OPPORTUNITY

The future holds many innovations that will be useful for business, but keeping track of all the new developments is a daunting task. You need a plan. For example, read technology-based publications on a regular basis. Many good publications are available in varying degrees of specialization. *Informationweek* is a good magazine that focuses on technology in business. Most business-related publications such as *Newsweek, Time,* and *The Wall Street Journal* have technology sections.

KNOWLEDGE WORKER'S -LIST

Categories of Decisions and the Process of Decision Making. Decisions can be categorized as structured or nonstructured and recurring or nonrecurring. A *structured decision* involves processing a certain kind of information in a specified way so that you will always get the right answer. A *nonstructured decision* is one for which there may be several "right" answers, and there is no precise way to get a right answer. Most decisions have structured and nonstructured elements.

A *recurring decision* is one that happens repeatedly, and often periodically, whether weekly, monthly, quarterly, or yearly. A *nonrecurring decision* is one that you make very infrequently (perhaps only once) and you may even have different criteria for determining the best solution each time.

The decision-making process follows four steps.

Intelligence (find what to fix) is the first stage, and this is when you establish the nature of the problem or opportunity.

Design (find fixes) is the next step, and here you find all the solutions you can.

Choice (choose a fix) is the third step and the one when you decide on a plan to address the problem or opportunity.

Implementation (apply the fix) is the final stage in which you put your plan into action. These steps are not always sequential. You often cycle back to earlier steps.

The Various Types of Decision Support Systems and Their Respective Roles in Effective Decision Making. A *decision support system (DSS)* is a highly flexible and interactive IT system that is designed to support decision making when the problem is not structured. A typical DSS has three components: data management, model management, and user interface management. The development and use of a DSS usually require your active participation.

For making decisions as part of a team you would utilize a *group decision support system (GDSS)* which consists of groupware, DSS, and telecommunications to help teams formulate and solve problems. The groupware, DSS, and telecommunications vary according to the nature of the meeting. The three phases of team decision making are brainstorming, issue categorization and analysis, and ranking and voting.

Meetings belong to one of two major categories. A *same-time meeting (synchronous meeting)* is a meeting at which the team members interact, offering ideas and suggestions during an appointed time period. They may be in a decision room where they can see each other, or they may be in different locations, perhaps connected by videoconferencing. The type of IT support varies depending on the situation.

A *different-time meeting (asynchronous meeting)* takes place over a period of days or weeks. Team members do not interact directly but exchange ideas and suggestions by sending them to some central location such as a bulletin board or database to be reviewed as the schedules of the team members allow.

A *geographic information system (GIS)* is a decision support system designed specifically to work with spatial information. Spatial information is any information that can be shown in map form. A GIS helps your decision making by making it easy to manipulate spatial information and to display results graphically.

The Different Types of Artificial Intelligence Systems and How They Contribute to Better Decision Making. *Artificial intelligence (AI)* is the science of making machines mimic human thought processes and behavior. Four types of AI systems are widely used in business: expert systems, neural networks, genetic algorithms, and intelligent agents.

TABLE 4.2 AI Systems Compared

AI System	Problem Type	Based on	Starting Information
Expert systems	Diagnostic or prescriptive	Strategies of experts	Expert's know-how
Neural networks	Identification, classification, prediction	The human brain	Acceptable patterns
Genetic algorithms	Optimal solutions	Biological evolution	Set of possible solutions
Intelligent agents	Specific and repetitive tasks	One or more AI techniques	Your preferences

An ***expert system*** is an artificial intelligence system that applies reasoning capabilities to reach a conclusion. An expert system captures and makes available to you the expertise of a human expert. Expert systems solve problems by mimicking the reasoning process of a human expert to reach a conclusion. The problem-solving strategy of a *domain expert,* the *domain expertise,* is transferred to the ***knowledge base*** by the ***knowledge engineer*** using the ***knowledge acquisition*** component. Then you, the ***knowledge worker*** or user, supply the *problem facts* using the ***user interface,*** and the ***inference engine*** reasons through your problem facts and the domain expertise in the knowledge base to reach a conclusion. If you have a question about how the expert system reached its conclusion, you can ask for the *"Why?" information* from the ***explanation module.***

A ***neural network*** is an artificial intelligence system that is capable of learning because it's patterned after the human brain. After lots of practice, a neural network can recognize patterns without human intervention. You develop and train a neural network for a specific problem area. When the neural network has been trained, you provide it with a new pattern and it can give you information about that pattern.

A ***genetic algorithm*** is an artificial intelligence system that mimics the evolutionary, survival-of-the-fittest process to generate increasingly better solutions to a problem. It uses the evolutionary concepts of selection, crossover, and mutation to generate new solutions or strategies. ***Selection*** is the process of choosing good solutions, ***crossover*** is the process of combining portions of good solutions, and ***mutation*** is the process of randomly changing parts of a solution. When fed a set of possible solutions, a genetic algorithm can generate many, many more solutions.

An ***intelligent agent*** is an artificial intelligence system that can move around your computer or network performing repetitive tasks independently, adapting itself to your preferences. An intelligent agent is a combination of the most modern software technologies.

How to Choose an IT System to Suit Your Decision. In order to find the right kind of decision support for your problem, you must know which IT systems support decision making, what they can do, and what you have to do.

A ***DSS*** is used to analyze information for problems that are not structured, either recurring or nonrecurring. You must have the expertise to solve the problem, know which model to use, and be able to interpret the results. A DSS can be used for any or all of the first three stages of decision making—intelligence, design, and choice.

A ***GDSS*** exists to help teams meet more efficiently and effectively by providing an integration of groupware, DSS, and telecommunications. A GDSS-enhanced meeting is especially helpful for nonstructured decisions and can benefit any or all of the first three phases of decision making.

A ***GIS*** is helpful for generating, analyzing, and displaying spatial information.

AI systems provide you with software that has know-how of its own. You don't have to do the problem solving yourself; you provide the AI system with information and let it carry on from there.

The most widely used AI system in business is an ***expert system***, which is well-suited to recurring diagnostic and prescriptive problems in which the solution process is well-defined and concrete.

A ***neural network*** works well for identification, classification, and prediction problems. A neural network is good for problems for which lots of information must be integrated to produce an overall pattern.

A ***genetic algorithm*** will generate an optimal solution from generations of solutions. A genetic algorithm must be given criteria specifying what constitutes a "good" solution.

An ***intelligent agent*** is helpful in performing repetitive, predictable tasks, such as sending faxes or e-mail, or searching and monitoring networks. An intelligent agent adapts itself to your preferences. ❖

CLOSING CASE STUDY

Are You Green, Yellow, or Red on Your Bank's Computer?

Would your banker give you an A, a B, or a C? What about your supermarket? You know you're being graded in your classes, but did you know that you're also being graded by businesses?

Special treatment for certain customers is not new. Airline customers who fly first class have always received preferential treatment, even when flights were cancelled or delayed. You won't find them napping on a stone floor with their back packs as pillows. This makes business sense to the airlines, since these are the customers who are most profitable.

Networks, databases, and data warehouses make the segmenting of customers possible to a degree unheard of just a few years ago. Neural network software allows businesses to see which category customers fit into according to how they affect the company's bottom line and thus to gauge whether it is worth the trouble of making them happy.

First Union Bank

First Union Bank classifies customers as red, green, or yellow. If you're a green customer, you get little extras such as reduced credit card rates or a waiver of fees. If you're a red customer you're considered to be expendable since you bring little or no value, i.e., you're costing the bank more than you're bringing in. This classification system has increased the productivity of the service representatives at the bank by 18 percent.

Visa

Visa has saved millions of dollars using neural network software to spot fraud and to determine which of their customers might default or go bankrupt. Neural networks are good at spotting patterns, and if your profile looks like that of people who have defaulted, you'll be tossed into that category.

Catalina Supermarkets

It's not only financial institutions that are using this categorizing software. Catalina Supermarkets keeps track of which customers buy which products, how frequently, and at what price. The supermarket chain has increased its percentage of high-value customers by offering services such as free home delivery. The low-value customers don't get the good deals and are not offered the special services.

Twentieth Century Fox

Even the movie business is getting in on the act. Twentieth Century Fox uses box-office information to determine the most popular movies, actors, and plots in certain theaters, cities, and areas of the country. By not sending a movie that will not be very popular into a certain neighborhood, Twentieth Century avoids a loss. On the other hand, the result may be that people in certain areas will not get the chance to see certain movies.

There was a time when certain neighborhoods or geographic regions were redlined. That meant that banks and other businesses wouldn't deal with anyone who lived there. Some people think that this sort of market segmentation is a new form of redlining.[50] ❖

◀ Questions ▶

1. A neural network learns to recognize patterns based on past information. One set of people is judged by the behavior of another. Is this fair or reliable? How accurate is it for a business to predict the future behavior of customers on the basis of historic information? Don't people change? Have you ever changed your behavior in the course of your life?

2. Customers are not likely ever to see the information that companies are using to pigeonhole them. Even the company executives may not know what criteria the neural network uses. How important are the assumptions underlying the software (i.e., the facts that the neural network are given about customers)? Even the IT specialists who design neural networks can't vouch for their accuracy or specify exactly how the neural network reaches its conclusions. Is this safe for businesses? What are the possible business consequences of using neural networks without assurances of their reliability?

3. Businesses can use segmenting to suggest products and services to you, or if you request it, to prevent your getting junk mail you don't want. Is that good? Would receiving wanted information or avoiding junk mail be worth the price of being categorized?

4. Say you run a business that supplies medical equipment (not prescription drugs)—wheelchairs, hospital beds, heating packs. You're trying to determine which customers you should give preferential treatment to. What assumptions or variables would you use (for example, age, income, and so on) to segment your customer population?

5. Do you think that this segmentation practice is fair? First, consider the business stockholders, then consider the customers. Does it matter whether it's fair or not? Why or why not? Should there be laws against it, or laws controlling it, or none at all? Explain and justify your answer.

6. Does the practice make business sense? If you owned stock in a company, how would you feel about this practice? Do you think you should get better treatment if you're a better customer? Do you think people who are not such good customers should get the same deal that you get? Would it

make any difference whether the company collected the information and did the neural network analysis itself, or bought the information or the whole package from a third party?

7. Is this the same as redlining, or is it OK because it looks at behavior and classifies people rather than assuming characteristics based on membership in a particular group?

Electronic Commerce
Business and You on the Internet

Finding Investment Opportunities on the Internet

When you buy stock in a company, you're betting on the success of that firm. Sometimes that bet is a good one, and sometimes it's not. Finding a company that's a good bet involves lots of research. To further complicate matters, some people prefer investing in large, safe companies, whereas others prefer the higher return of a small, more risky firm. So how do you make sense of all the options? Well, now you have access to financial information that professional investors use to evaluate stocks. The Internet brings together information-hungry investors with companies that have been anxiously looking to reach out to investors online. Over 900 companies now offer investment information on the World Wide Web, and the number is increasing rapidly. Remember, though, you must proceed with caution. Do your best to verify the source of any information.

Throughout this *Real HOT Electronic Commerce* exercise you'll find tables of Web site addresses that relate to each topic. In addition to those listed here, you'll find many other Web site addresses on the Web site that supports this textbook (http://www.mhhe.com/haag, and select "Electronic Commerce Projects").

Learning about Investing

Investing can be as simple as finding a company that performs well financially and buying some of their stock. Or, if you want to spread your investment over a number of stocks and you don't want to personally select each stock, you can invest in a mutual fund. Of course there are thousands of mutual funds with all types of investment objectives. So, any way you go you must pick your investment wisely. To help you get up to speed quickly, you'll find many helpful Web sites on the Internet.

For starters, you might explore the National Association of Securities Dealers (NASD) at http://www.nasdr.com. Check out their Investor Resources with its Education and Tools. You might want to retrieve more general information from the online versions of traditional print media such as *The Wall Street Journal* or *Money* magazine. In the table below, we've provided a list of investment reference sites that will help bring you up to speed on investing.

Pick three of the investment reference sites from the table on page 162, explore what information is available, and answer the following questions.

A. Is the site designed for first-time investors or those that are more experienced?

B. Can you search for a specific topic?

C. Are specific stocks or mutual funds reviewed or evaluated?

D. Does the site provide direct links to brokerage or stock quoting sites?

E. Is a forum for submitting questions available? If so, are frequently asked questions (FAQs) posted?

F. Who sponsors the site? Does it seem as if the sponsor is using the site to advertise its own products or services?

G. Can you download reference documents to read later?

Researching the Company behind the Stock

One excellent way to pick a stock investment is to research the company behind that stock. Focusing on items such as sales revenues and profits to pick a stock is called *fundamental research*. So you might choose to invest in Hughes stock because you've discovered their sales revenues have been climbing steadily for the last three years. Or you might initially consider buying some Disney stock but change your mind when you find that EuroDisney revenues have been below expectations.

Now that you're ready to research a stock investment, connect to four different company sites using the table on page 162. The Web site that supports this text includes a list of many other company sites. As you connect to the four sites, look up each company's financials and answer the questions that follow. You'll probably want to include at least two companies with which you are familiar and two that are new to you. In addition to reviewing company financials, look around each company site and see to what degree the site is investor-oriented.

A. Do all the company sites offer financial information?

B. Is the information targeted at investors? How can you tell?

C. Can you download financial information to your computer and use it in a spreadsheet?

D. Can you download the company's annual report? Is it a full-color version?

E. Does the site provide direct links to e-mail addresses for requesting additional information?

F. Do the companies provide comparisons to others in their industry?

G. Does the site provide stock quotes as well as financials?

H. Can you search the site for financial-related information such as press releases?

I. Was there a charge for retrieving the financial information?

Finding Other Sources of Company Financials

Searching for a company's financials may be a bit more difficult than you may have first imagined. First you must determine the Internet address for the company either by guessing the address and typing it in or using one of the many search engines available. Both of these methods are fraught with error. For example, if you guessed that http://www.amex.com was the address for American Express you'd be wrong. And even if you did guess a company's address, many companies don't provide their financials on their company-sponsored Web site. Take Adidas Corporation, for example, at http://www.adidas.com. No financials are available at this site. You'll find that many company Web sites lack information for investors.

The reason many companies don't provide financials on their Web sites is that they view the primary purpose of their web sites as reaching consumers not investors. So, many companies elect to post their financials on a financial provider site or simply to let investors view the company's submissions to the Securities and Exchange Commission at the SEC's Web site.

On page 162, we've provided a list of five Web sites that list or distribute financial information on companies. Pick three providers of financial information, access their Web sites and answer the following questions.

A. Is there a charge for retrieving the information?

B. Do you have a choice about the information's format?

C. Are companies listed alphabetically?

D. Does the site offer more than just annual reports?

E. Are there direct links from the site to the desired company's page?

F. Can you find more companies at the site than by searching for individual company Web pages?

G. How many companies are available on each Web site?

H. Are the represented companies mostly large and established or small and relatively unknown?

Making Trades Online

If you want to invest in securities, you might do what a lot of people do, go to a stockbroker. However, many of the same services offered by stockbrokers are now available on the Internet.

Virtually all of the stockbrokers with offices you can visit have Web sites that support online investing and more. These services include account information, financial planning, and online investing services. Before we go online to look at some of these stockbrokers we should be sure we understand the difference between a full-service brokerage house and a discount brokerage house. As the names imply, the full-service brokerage offers many more services than does the discount brokerage. And it's important to understand that the price for many of these services is built into the fees to buy and sell stocks and mutual funds. So you pay for having these services available even if you don't use them at a full-service brokerage. So, let's venture online and see what the various brokerages have to offer us. In the table below you'll find a list of brokerages and where you can find them on the Internet.

Pick three of the brokerages from the table, examine what it takes to conduct an online investment transaction, and answer the following questions.

A. Must you already have an investment account with the brokerage to purchase stocks or mutual funds?
B. Which sites are full-service brokerages and which are discount brokerages? How can you tell?
C. Is online research available? Is it free?
D. Can you retrieve stock price quotes for free?
E. If you already have an account with the brokerage, do they offer special services for these customers? What kind of services are offered?
F. Is the site aimed at experienced investors or new investors?
G. If you are investing for the first time, would you feel comfortable using online investing? If so, why?

Retrieving Stock Quotes

Once you find the right stock to buy, you'll then be asking yourself, "How much will this stock cost me?" Stocks and mutual funds are both offered by the share and so you can easily buy as much or as little of the stock or mutual fund as you like. Still, some individual shares are priced in the hundreds or thousands of dollars and that alone might make the purchase undesirable to you.

In addition to pricing individual shares to assess the affordability of an investment, you'll probably want to see how the price has varied over time. Even though most financial advisors will tell you that historical price variations provide no indication of future performance, most everyone uses price history to get a feel for whether the investment is trading at all-time highs or lows. So finding a chart of a stock price online might be helpful when making your purchase.

And even after you've made your purchase, you'll probably want to follow how your investment is doing. The thrill of realizing a "paper profit" is enough to keep many investors checking their investments daily. Of course, realizing a "paper loss" can be equally disappointing. And even if daily tracking isn't for you, you'll certainly want to check on your investments regularly and doing so online can be quick and painless. In the table below you'll find a list of online stock and mutual fund quoting services and where you can find them on the Internet.

Pick three of the stock quoting services from the table on page 162, examine what it takes to retrieve a stock or mutual fund quote, and answer the following questions.

A. Are the quotes provided free of charge or for a fee?
B. Does the site require a "ticker" symbol (the abbreviation used by experienced investors) or can you type in a company name?
C. Are the quotes "real-time" or are they "delayed" (15–20 minutes old)?
D. Does the site require registration?
E. Are historical prices available?
F. Are price charts available? Can you customize the chart display?
G. Can you create and save a personal portfolio of stocks?

162 CHAPTER FOUR Decision Support and Artificial Intelligence

Web Sites for Finding Investment Opportunities

Investment References	Address
The Basics of Investing	http://www.investor.nasd.com/ni_module_menu.html
Microsoft Money Insider	http://moneyinsider.msn.com/home.asp
Investing Basics	http://www.aaii.com/invbas
CBS MarketWatch Investor's Primer	http://cbs.marketwatch.com/news/primer
The Syndicate	http://www.moneypages.com/syndicate/index.html

Companies	Address
Disney	http://www.disney.com/investors
Coca-Cola	http://www.coca-cola.com/co
Century 21 Real Estate	http://www.century21.com
Boeing	http://www.boeing.com/company offices/financial
Hughes	http://www.hughes.com/invest.html

Providers	Address
Investors Relations Information Network (IRIN)	http://www.irin/com
Securities and Exchange Commission (SEC)	http://www.sec.gov/edgarhp.htm
Barron's Annual Report Service	http://www.icbinc.com/cgi-bin/barrons.pl
Hoover's Online	http://www.hoovers.com
Tana Interactive Annual Reports List	http://www.tanagraphics.com/ti/ar_list

Brokerages	Address
Merrill Lynch	http://www.ml.com
Charles Schwab	http://www.schwab.com
American Express Financial Advisors	http://www.americanexpress.com/financial
Smith Barney	http://www.smithbarney.com
E*Trade	http://www.etrade.com

Quoting Services	Address
Yahoo Finance	http://quote.yahoo.com
PC Quote Online	http://www.pcquote.com
CNN Financial News Stock Quotes	http://cnnfn.com/markets/quotes.html
Microsoft Investor	http://investor.msn.com
Wall Street City	http://www.wallstreetcity.com

Go to the Web site that supports this text: **http://www.mhhe.com/haag** and select "Electronic Commerce Projects."

We've included links to over 100 Web sites for finding investment opportunities on the Internet.

KEY TERMS AND CONCEPTS

Adaptivity, 154
Ad Hoc Decision, 130
Artificial Intelligence (AI), 143
Autonomy, 154

Buyer Agent, 152
Choice, 130
Crossover, 152
Data Management, 131

Data-Mining Agent, 154
Decision Support System (DSS), 131
Design, 130

Domain Expert, 146
Expert System, 144
Explanation Module, 148
Genetic Algorithm, 152
Geographic Information System (GIS), 140
Group Decision Support System (GDSS), 135
Implementation, 130
Inference Engine, 147
Intelligence, 130
Intelligent Agent, 152
Knowledge Acquisition, 147
Knowledge Base, 147
Knowledge-Based System, 144
Knowledge Engineer, 147
Model Management, 132
Mutation, 152
Neural Network, 150
Nonrecurring Decision, 130
Nonstructured Decision, 129
Recurring Decision, 130
Robot, 143
Rule-Based Expert System, 148
Selection, 152
Shopping Bot, 152
Sociability, 155
Structured Decision, 129
User Agent, 153
User Interface, 147
User Interface Management, 133

SHORT-ANSWER QUESTIONS

1. What are the four types of decisions discussed in this chapter? Give an example of each.
2. What are the four steps in making a decision?
3. What is a DSS? Describe its components.
4. What are the problems that arise when more than five people meet to make a decision?
5. What different types of meetings can you have involving time and place?
6. What is a geographic information system used for?
7. How is information represented in a geographic information system?
8. What is artificial intelligence? Name the artificial intelligence systems used widely in business.
9. What are the components of an expert system?
10. What are five advantages of an expert system?
11. How does a neural network work?
12. What three concepts of evolution are used by the genetic algorithm?
13. What are intelligent agents? What tasks can they perform?

SHORT-QUESTION ANSWERS

For each of the following answers, provide an appropriate question:

1. A decision that you face every day.
2. The part of a DSS where the models are stored.
3. It has Groupware, DSS capabilities, and telecommunications.
4. It shows information thematically.
5. Any system that simulates human senses and can act on its own.
6. A domain expert must provide the rules for this AI system.
7. Classification is the strong suit of this AI system.
8. This AI system takes its cue from evolution.
9. It can find the best price for a product on the Internet.
10. Adaptivity and sociability are two of its qualities.

DISCUSSION QUESTIONS

1. Some experts claim that if a business gets 52 percent of its decisions right, it will be successful. Would using a decision support system guarantee better results? Why or why not? What does the quality of any decision depend on?
2. Early systems researchers called expert systems "experts in a box." Today, in most situations, people who consult expert systems use them as assistants in specific tasks and not to totally replace human experts. What sorts of tasks would you feel comfortable about having expert systems

accomplish without much human intervention? What sorts of tasks would you *not* be comfortable having expert systems handle independently? Give examples.
3. Consider the topic of data warehouses in Chapter 3. In the future, AI systems will be increasingly applied to data warehouse processing. Which AI systems do you think might be helpful? For which tasks, or situations, might they best be applied?
4. Consider the differences and similarities among the four AI techniques discussed in this chapter. Name some problems that might be amenable to more than one type of AI system.
5. AI systems are relatively new approaches to solving business problems. What are the difficulties with new IT approaches in general?
6. Neural networks recognize and categorize patterns. If someone were to have a neural network that could scan information on all aspects of your life, where would that neural network potentially be able to find information about you? Consider confidential (doctor's office) as well as publicly available (department of motor vehicles) information.
7. What type of AI systems could your school use to help with registration? Intelligent agents find vast amounts of information very quickly. Neural networks can classify patterns instantaneously. What sort of information might your school administration be able to generate using these (or other AI systems) with all of its student information?

EXTENDED LEARNING MODULE C

NETWORK BASICS

When you connect computers so that they can share information, software, and/or hardware, you've created a network. A ***computer network*** (which we simply refer to as a network) is two or more computers connected so that they can communicate with each other and share information, software, peripheral devices, and/or processing power. To have a network you need only two computers, but many networks have dozens, hundreds, or even thousands of computers.

In this module we'll discuss

- Home networks
- Business networks
- Communications service providers
- Network technologies

Home Networks

Since the Internet is the biggest network on the face of the earth, and because for most people it's the most familiar, we'll start with ways that your computer can connect to it. You can read more about the Internet in *Extended Learning Module E*.

Connecting to the Internet—The King of Networks

If you want to connect your computer to the Internet, you need a hardware device that serves as a connection from your computer or home network to another network, that is, the Internet. You have several choices. You can use

- A telephone modem
- Digital Subscriber Line (DSL) modem
- A cable modem
- A satellite modem

Telephone Modem Simply put, a telephone modem is a telephone for your computer. You use a traditional telephone to talk to other people with their own phones. A computer uses a modem to communicate with other computers. A ***telephone modem*** is a device that connects your computer to your phone line so that you can access another computer or network. If you want to connect to the Internet, you use your modem to first access your Internet Service Provider (ISP). Your ISP then connects you to the Internet. Most people refer to a telephone modem simply as a "modem." A modem is a device that converts the digital signals from your computer into analog form (by modulating the signal) that can be transmitted over a phone line, and then converts the analog signal back to digital signals (by demodulating the signal) for the computer at the receiving end of the transmission (see Figure C.1). In other words, a modem **mo**dulates and then **dem**odulates transmissions.

A telephone modem is the slowest type of Internet connection you can get. The fastest a telephone modem can go is 56 Kbps (or 56 thousand bits per second). The other three types of connections are much faster.

Digital Subscriber Line (DSL) A ***Digital Subscriber Line (DSL)*** is a high-speed Internet connection using phone lines, which allows you to use your phone for voice communication at the

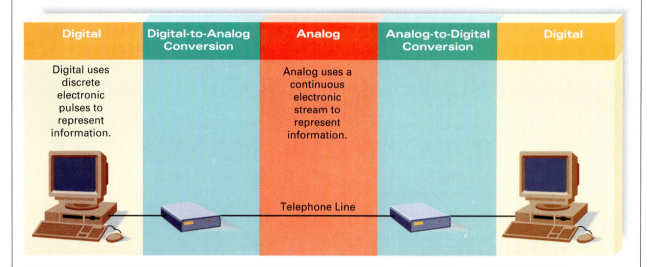

FIGURE C.1
The Role of a Telephone Modem

same time. There are many kinds of DSL systems (ADSL or asymmetric DSL, SDSL or symmetric DSL, HDSL or high-bit-rate DSL, to name a few). One type of DSL system, ADSL, divides your phone line into three channels. One is for sending information, one receives information, and the last is your regular voice phone line. That means that you can talk on the phone while you're surfing the Internet using the same phone line (see Figure C.2).

A DSL modem has three big advantages over a regular phone modem.

1. DSL is much faster—up to 100 times faster than a phone modem.
2. DSL is an "always-on" connection giving you instant Internet access—you don't have to dial into your ISP first.
3. You can still use the same phone line for voice connections.

The big drawback with DSL is that you have to live within a certain distance of the proper telephone company equipment. The distance will depend on the type and speed of DSL service that your phone company offers.

Cable Modem If you have cable television, you know that it comes into your home on a coaxial cable that connects to

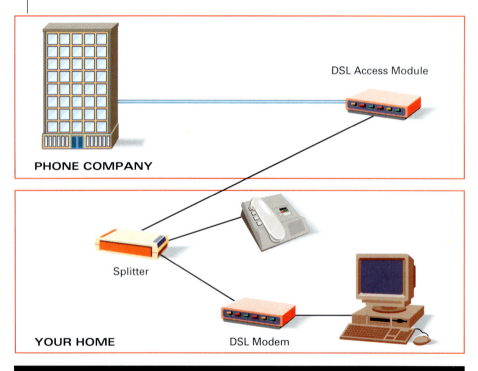

FIGURE C.2
DSL System

Network Basics **167**

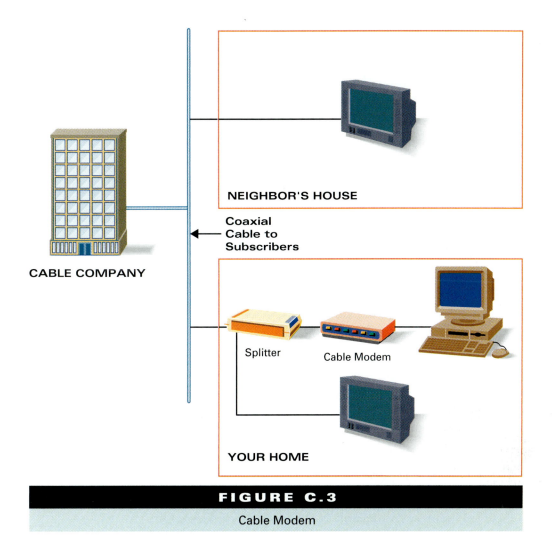

FIGURE C.3

Cable Modem

your TV set. This same cable can connect you to the Internet too. Both cable TV signals and your Internet connection travel from the cable company on one wire.

A splitter inside your home separates the TV transmission and the Internet access parts. The Internet access part goes to your cable modem. A *cable modem* is a device that uses your TV cable to deliver an Internet connection (see Figure C.3). The cable from the cable modem attaches to either an Ethernet card (an expansion card that connects your computer to a network) or to a USB port in your computer. The speed of transmission with a cable modem is between 20 and 100 times as fast as a phone modem. It's also an "always-on" connection and doesn't use a phone line at all.

Satellite Modem You can also get Internet access using a satellite dish. A *satellite modem* is a modem that allows you to get Internet access from your satellite dish. You'll need the right type of antenna (i.e. the satellite dish). You can get an antenna for Internet access alone or one that gives you both Internet access and TV reception. Satellite modems are among the newest types of connections to the Internet. We expect them to be widely used in the near future.

A Simple Home Network—Peer-to-Peer

The simplest kind of network is a peer-to-peer network. Say you have a computer with a printer attached and then you get another computer and connect it to the first so that both computers can use the same printer. What you've created is a peer-to-peer network. A *peer-to-peer network* is a network in which a small number of computers share hardware (such as a printer), software,

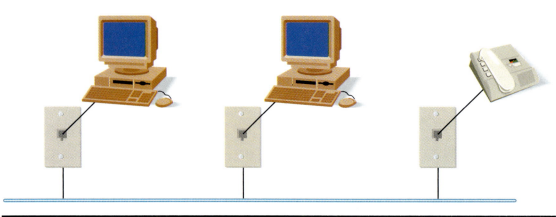

FIGURE C.4
PNA Home Network

and/or information. Each computer independently stores its own software and information, but can access the information on the other computers.

You can set up a peer-to-peer network one of two ways—either using your existing phone wiring, or with Ethernet cards and dedicated network cabling.

Home Network with Existing Phone Wiring A relatively new technology called **Home PNA**, which stands for Home Phoneline Networking Alliance, allows you to network your home computers using telephone wiring. You'll need

- PNA adapter cards
- A phone jack for each computer
- Phone wire (also known as Category 3 or, more simply, Cat 3)

First, you must install a PNA adapter card in each computer. A *PNA adapter card* is an expansion card that you use to network multiple computers with ordinary phone cable. The PNA adapter card has a connector for a telephone jack (RJ-11 connector) into which you plug one end of a Cat 3 cable. *Cat 3*, or *Category 3*, cable is ordinary phone cable. You plug the other end into an extra phone jack in the wall (see Figure C.4).

Home Network with Ethernet Cards and Dedicated Network Cable To set up this type of network you need

- Network interface cards
- Network cables

Two Computers. Connecting two computers with a peripheral device, such as a printer, is the easiest. First, you install a network interface card in each computer. A *network interface card (NIC)* is an expansion card or a PC Card (for a laptop) that connects your computer to a network and allows information to flow between your computer and the rest of the network. An NIC has a connector called an RJ-45 that looks very like a telephone connector, except that it's a little larger (see Figure C.5).

An *Ethernet card* is the most common type of network interface card. An Ethernet card will plug into either an ISA or PCI expansion slot. You would connect the computers to each other with Cat 5 twisted pair cable (similar to phone cable except it's thicker) or coaxial cable (the kind of cable used to transmit cable TV signals). *Cat 5* or *Category 5* is a better-constructed version of the Cat 3 twisted-pair cable used for the telephone system. The ends of the cable plug into the

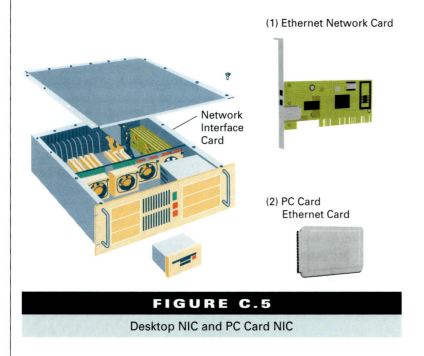

FIGURE C.5

Desktop NIC and PC Card NIC

Ethernet cards on the two computers. You connect the printer to one computer, but both computers can access it now that they are networked.

The Windows operating system (we recommend Windows 98 or newer), installed on each computer, provides you with the network operating software you need for your peer-to-peer network—whether you have two or more computers. It's comparatively easy to install and use. To make files available to another computer, you have to turn on the file-sharing option in Windows. When you do that, the files on one computer will appear as additional folders on the other computer.

More than Two Computers. If you have more than two computers in your home network you'll need a hub or switch. A *network hub* is a device that connects multiple computers into a network but which allows only one communication link at a time. A hub is like a telephone party line—only one conversation can take place at a time. A *switch* is a device that connects multiple computers into a network in which multiple communication links can be in operation simultaneously. It's like a modern phone system in which multiple communication threads are possible simultaneously.

If your little home network isn't connected to any outside network, such as the Internet, there's no possibility of anyone from the outside accessing the network. However, if you want your home network to have Internet access, you can do so in any one of the four ways described in the previous section on connecting to the Internet. If you do connect your home network to the Internet, you would be well advised to use a home router, such as a LinkSys Cable/DSL router. This is a small device that acts as a smart hub. It connects computers together into a network, but also has the advantage that it separates your home network from any other network it's connected to—such as the Internet. In other words, it acts as a firewall, giving you much better security. A firewall is software or hardware that protects your network from intruders.

See Figure C.6 for a typical home network with Internet access. This network has either a cable or a DSL modem. Internet access comes in through a home router, which serves both to connect the computers and as a firewall. All computers on the network can use the same printer.

Wireless Home Networks Infrared and radio signal systems are the most popular types of wireless networks for home and small businesses. One such low-cost home or business network uses Wireless Network Access Point devices. A *Wireless Network Access Point,* or *Wireless Access Point,* is a device that allows computers to access a wired network using radio waves. WAPs are also called wireless bridges. Each device has a receiver, a transmitter, and antennas to provide for bidirectional information flow. Each computer (or other device) that's to be part of the wireless network must have a wireless adapter. A wireless adapter would be either an expansion card for the desktop computer or a PC Card for a laptop computer.

In Figure C.7, you can see a more sophisticated home network, which would also work for a small business that wants a peer-to-peer network. It uses a cable or DSL modem, again coming into a router. The router, in turn, connects to a hub for the networked computers. It also connects to a WAP for a wireless computer, usually a laptop.

170 EXTENDED LEARNING MODULE C

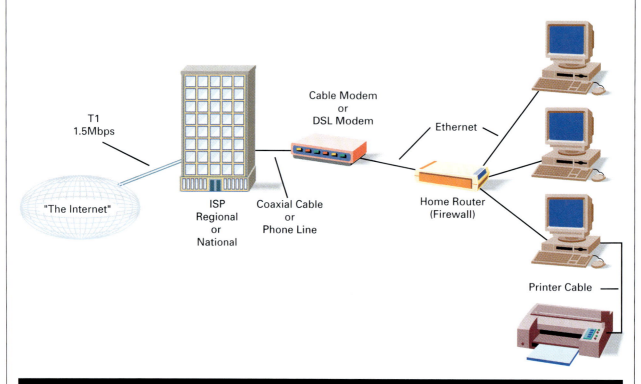

FIGURE C.6
A Typical Home Network

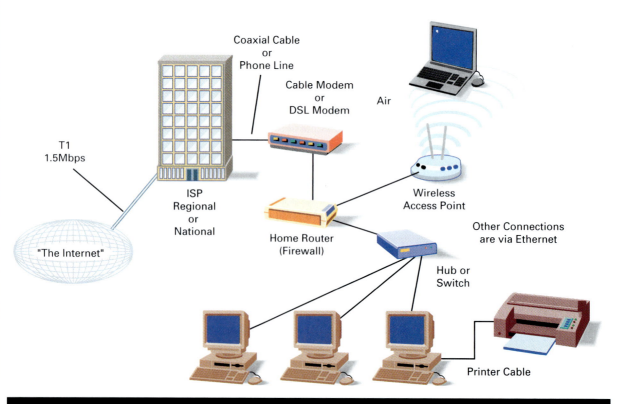

FIGURE C.7
Peer-to-Peer Home or Small Business Network with Wireless Access Point

A relatively new wireless technology for short-range wireless connections is called Bluetooth. Named for a Viking king, ***Bluetooth*** technology provides entirely wireless connections for all kinds of communication devices. For example, Bluetooth could replace the cable connecting a laptop computer to a cellular telephone. Palm, the company that makes palmtop computers, is incorporating Bluetooth into its PalmV to work with printers and cellular phones.[1] Virtually all digital devices, such as keyboards, joysticks, printers, and so on, can be part of a Bluetooth system. Eventually even household appliances will be adaptable to the network. So, in the future you'll be able to start the dishwasher from your computer.

Business Networks

In the peer-to-peer home networks described above the computers were all equal. Each one had its own files and devices, which it can share with the other computers. But, unless you're a business with very few computers, you'd probably use a client/server network instead of a peer-to-peer network. A ***client/server network*** is a network in which one or more computers are servers and provide services to the other computers which are called clients. The server or servers have hardware, software, and/or information that the client computers can access. Servers are usually powerful computers with large storage systems. Depending on the network, the server could be a high-end PC or a minicomputer.

The servers can also control the use of application software. You would usually install application software on the server and the clients would access it from there. This way, client computers don't need to have all the software on their hard disks. Large companies often have several servers, each of which may provide services to different parts of the company.

Client/Server—A Business View

The term client/server network can mean a network structure, that is, one or more computers providing services to other computers. However, client/server is a term that also describes a business model. As a business model, client/server describes distributed processing. That is, it describes where processing takes place. Different companies have different processing needs. For example, if your school has an online system on which you can check your grades, you'll probably find that you can't change grades at your end—access to that kind of processing is severely restricted. On the other hand, a bank employee would need to be able to process a loan at his or her computer.

You can use one of five basic client/server implementation models. Which one you use depends on your business environment and where you want processing implemented.

Client/server networks differ according to three factors (see Figure C.8):

1. Where the processing for the presentation of information occurs, that is, where the information that you see on the screen or printout is formatted, and the editing of information as you enter it.

2. Where the processing of logic or business rules occurs. *Logic* deals with the processing that the software implements. For example, in a payroll application, the logic would dictate how to handle overtime, sick leave, and vacation time.

3. Where the data management component (DBMS) and information (database) are located. Or, put another way, how the information in the database is stored and retrieved.

Client/Server Model 1: Distributed Presentation In this first model, the server handles almost all functions, including a major portion of the presentation. The only processing that the client does is to help with formatting of the information you see on the screen or printout.

Client/Server Model 2: Remote Presentation In the second model, the client handles all presentation functions. The processing of business rules happens on the server as does data management.

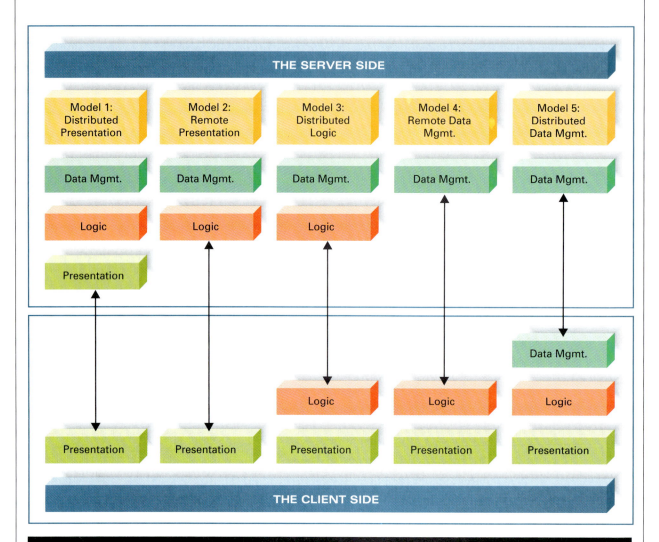

FIGURE C.8
The Five Implementation Models for Client/Server[2]

Client/Server Model 3: Distributed Logic In this model, the server handles all data management and the client handles all presentation formatting, but the logic processing is shared between the server and the client.

Client/Server Model 4: Remote Data Management In the fourth model, duties are fully separated again. The server handles data management only, and the client processes business rules and formats the presentation of results.

Client/Server Model 5: Distributed Data Management In this final model, the client handles all presentation formatting and business rule processing, and both the server and client share data management duties.

Which model you choose depends on the organization of your business and where you want processing to occur. To help you understand how these client/server models work, let's consider two examples—one for model 3 and one for model 5.

Client/Server Implementation: Model 3 In model 3—distributed logic—the server handles the entire data management function, the client handles the entire presentation function, and server and client share in the processing or application of business rules.

Suppose you're the manager of the manufacturing division of an organization and need to give pay raises to each of your employees. You use the following divisional and organizational rules for determining pay raises.

Divisional Rules

1. Each manufacturing employee begins with a base raise of $2,500.
2. No manufacturing employee can receive less than a $2,000 raise.
3. If loss of time because of injury is longer than three days, then deduct $500 from the pay raise.
4. If the employee worked less than five days of overtime, then deduct $500 from the pay raise.

Organizational Rules

1. No employee with less than five years of experience can receive a pay raise that exceeds $2,500.
2. Each employee's pay raise must be within 20 percent of last year's raise.
3. Each employee who has taken three or more business-related trips in the last year gets an extra $500 raise.

The following process would then determine the exact pay raise for each employee (see Figure C.9).

1. You would request information for the employee.
2. Your client workstation would send that request to the server.
3. The server would retrieve the employee information from the employee database.
4. The server would return the employee information to your client workstation.
5. Your client workstation would execute the divisional manufacturing business rules (or logic) that apply to pay raises for manufacturing employees.
6. Your client workstation would format and present the information pertaining to the employee and the appropriate pay raise.
7. You would submit the proposed pay raise for processing.
8. Your client workstation would send that information to the server.
9. The server would execute the organizational business rules or logic relating to pay raises for all employees.
10. The server would return the employee's pay raise (modified according to the organizational business rules) to your work station.
11. Your client workstation would format and present the modified pay raise.
12. You would submit the finalized pay raise for final processing.
13. Your client workstation would send that information to the server.
14. The server would update the employee database to reflect the employee's pay raise.

In this example the server was responsible for data management (retrieving and updating employee information) and executing the business rules or logic that apply to all employees for pay raises. Your client workstation is responsible for editing your entry of information, formatting the presentation of information to you, and executing the business rules or logic that apply to pay raises for manufacturing employees.

When you take the process of distributed logic apart as we did in this example, it seems very complex and tedious. And if you're writing the software to do it, it is. However, as a knowledge worker, the process is completely transparent, meaning that you don't know (or care) how data management, logic, and presentation are handled.

174 EXTENDED LEARNING MODULE C

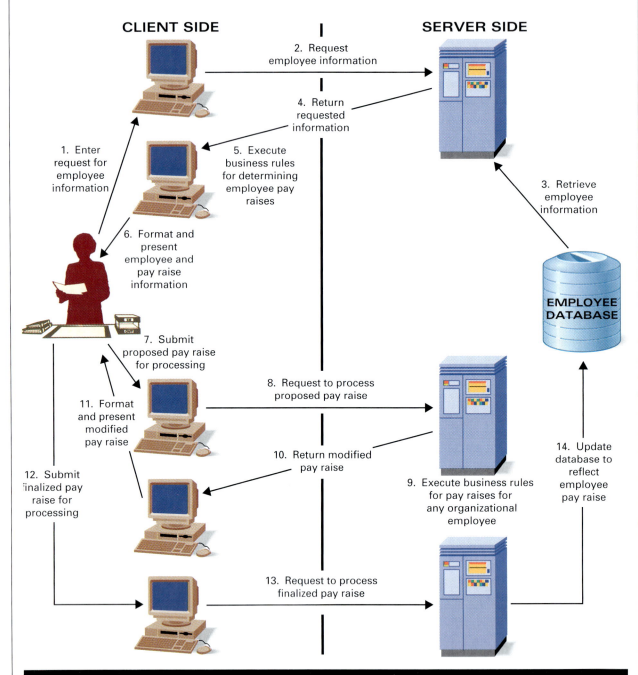

FIGURE C.9
Model 3: Client/Server Implementation for Employee Pay Raises

From a management point of view, client/server is a very tidy, organized, and flexible way to make information that all managers need available to them, while keeping information and processing that individual departments need local to the appropriate office.

Client/Server Implementation: Model 5 Model 5—distributed data management—is simpler than Model 3. In this case the server's only duty is to help with data management; the client does everything else.

Say you have a data warehouse with information on sales over the past five years (see Figure C.10). Your client workstation gets its information from your company's OLTP (online trans-

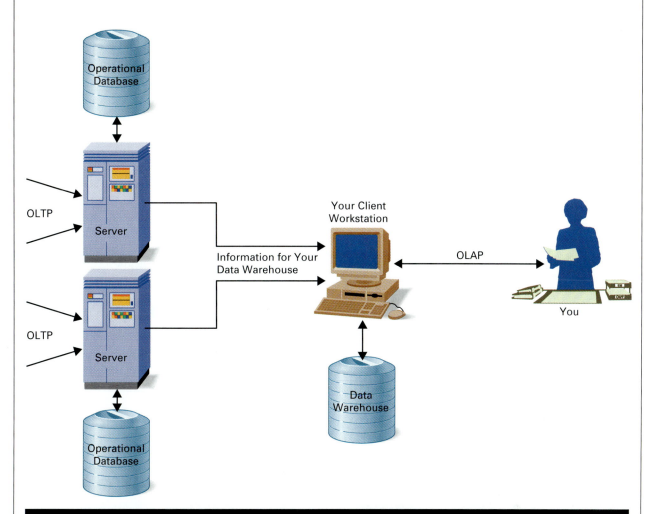

FIGURE C.10

Model 5: A Personal Data Warehouse in a Client/Server Implementation

action processing) servers. Software on the servers extract the information you need and transfer it to your client workstation. Your client workstation then builds the data warehouse according to your requirements and you can use your data warehouse for the OLAP (online analytical processing) you need.

In this example, we again see a separation of duties to suit particular business needs. The servers process company-wide OLTP software on transaction information, and copy to your workstation the information you want to have. Your client computer has, and processes, only the information that you need.

Client/Server—A Physical View

There are more physical implementations of client/server networks than cars on the road. Figure C.11 shows a typical Ethernet configuration for a medium-sized business. You can see that, in this network, the company has a dedicated phone circuit (discussed later in this module), which is necessary for the amount of traffic that a medium-sized business would have. A router connects the company's network to the ISP which provides Internet access. A hub or switch serves to connect the smaller company networks to the server or servers, which will have control over the organizational databases, and there might also be a wireless network connection for people with laptops. One or more servers are also available to all the computers in the network. One server would most likely provide Internet and e-mail services.

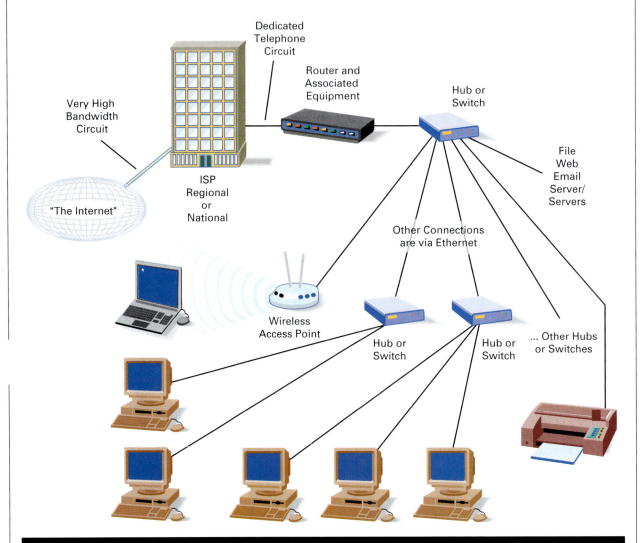

FIGURE C.11
A Typical Client/Server Network for a Medium-Sized Business

Figure C.12 is an example of an enterprisewide network. Such a network might have mainframes and older, legacy networks that must be tied to the more modern network. The various smaller networks may be scattered all over the country, or even the world. Parts of the network would need high bandwidth or high-capacity communications media (which we'll discuss later). There would probably be multiple servers on such a large network, probably one for each of the smaller networks.

Communications Service Providers

You can set up your own cabling and so on and have your own communications network, or you can get a third party to provide it for you. Which strategy you take determines network ownership. Network ownership determines

- Rights to the network
- Cost
- Availability
- Services provided
- Speed
- Security

Network Basics | **177**

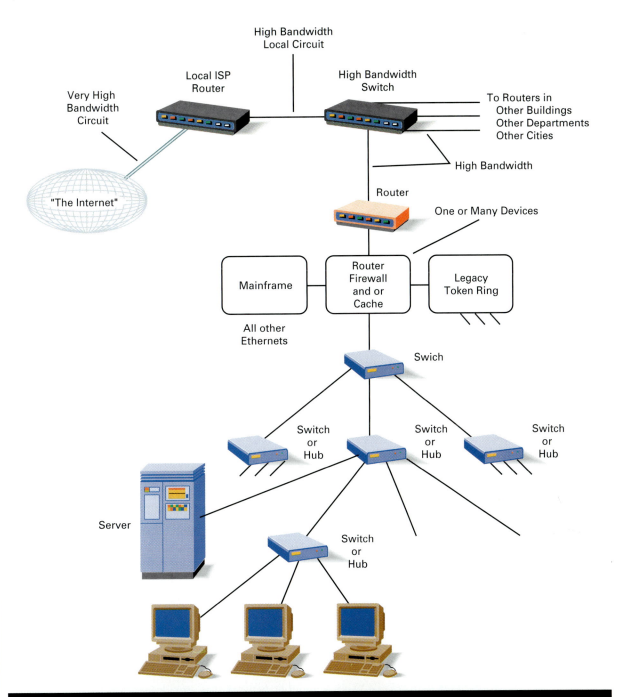

FIGURE C.12

A Typical Enterprise-Wide Network

Small networks within an office building are almost always private. That means that the company buys, installs, and maintains the network. Therefore that company has exclusive rights to the use of the network.

The following discussion deals with networks that cover a large geographic area and require ***communications service providers***, third parties who furnish the conduit for information. You can support your network with a public network, a private network, a value-added network, or a virtual private network (see Table C.1).

TABLE C.1 Comparison of Types of Network Ownership

Cost	Availability	Services	Speed	Security
Public Pay-as-you-go	Compete for time and use	Moves information only	Slower than private network	Little or none guaranteed
Private Pay for all of it Or Pay flat fee for leased line	No competition for use	Can have additional services	Faster than public networks	Higher than that of public networks
Value-Added Network Pay-as-you-go	Little or no competition for use	VAN provider offers additional services	Faster than public networks	Much better than public networks
Virtual Private Network Flat fee per month plus usage fee	Compete for use	VPN owner provides some additional services	Slower than equivalent public network	Better than public networks

Public Networks

A *public network* is a network on which your organization competes for time with others. The telephone system is a public network. You're not guaranteed that you'll be able to get a line when you want to make a call—as you may have found out if you unsuccessfully tried to call your mother on Mother's Day. When all the lines are busy you get a recorded message to that effect. And when you dial into the Internet you're competing with others for access, and you'll find that the speed of getting to Web sites varies greatly.

Private Networks

A *private network* consists of the communications media that your organization owns or exclusively leases to connect networks or network components. You can lease dedicated lines from a communications service provider.

Value-Added Networks

A *value-added network (VAN)* is a semipublic network that provides services beyond the movement of information from one place to another. The "value-added" part of this type of network is what makes it attractive. For example, if you need EDI (electronic data interchange) capabilities to automate the exchange of standard business documents between your organization, your suppliers, and customers, you might hire a communications service provider to set up a network and provide EDI capability. VAN providers also offer security and auditing services and translate between different versions of EDI systems.

General Electric Information Services offers VAN services. If you buy their VAN, all you have to do is develop an interface between (1) your system and GE's VAN and (2) your customers' and suppliers' systems and GE's VAN. GE will do the rest.

Of course, you could do all this yourself. You could build a private network, and develop software to handle the conversions that you'll need for EDI. Most companies don't adopt this strategy. It's too complex and expensive.

Virtual Private Networks

A *virtual private network (VPN)* is a public network that promises availability to your organization, but doesn't provide you with a dedicated line or communications media. Your information travels with information from other organizations. A VPN usually offers additional services such as data encryption.

VPNs are prevalent on the Internet as organizations move into electronic commerce functions across the Internet. An **Internet virtual private network** gives you a way to establish a *virtual* Internet network that consists of you, your customers, and suppliers. This arrangement is often called an *extranet*.

Practically every national phone service provider (Baby Bells, AT&T, MCI, and so on) offers domestic VPN services. If you need to transmit information further abroad, you can use an **international virtual private network (International VPN)**—virtual private networks that depend on services offered by phone companies of various nationalities. Two current examples are Phoenix and Worldpartners. Phoenix is an alliance between Deutsche Telekom AG (Germany), France Telecom, and Sprint. Worldpartners is the largest international VPN and consists of AT&T, Kokusai Denshim Denwa (Japan), Singapore Telecom, and Unisource, which is itself an alliance of telecommunications providers from Spain, the Netherlands, Sweden, and Switzerland.

Network Technologies

Connecting hundreds, maybe thousands, of computers is a complicated task for which you'll need IT network specialists. In this section we discuss some of the hardware and protocols that that they'll consider when setting up your network.

Types of Networks by Distance and by Topology

Many, many types of networks exist today. Earlier in this module we discussed peer-to-peer and client/server. A peer-to-peer network is one in which all the computers are equal and share information and hardware. A client/server network has one or more computers that provide services to the others.

However, this isn't the only way you can classify computer networks. Two other ways are by geographic distance and by physical configuration.

Classification of Networks by Geographic Distance There are two basic types of networks in this category: LANs and WANs. **Local area networks (LANs)** cover a limited geographic distance, such as an office, office building, or a group of buildings in close proximity to each other. **Wide area networks (WANs)** cover large geographic distances, such as a state, a country, or even the entire world. A wide area network is essentially a network of smaller networks. The Internet is the biggest WAN on the planet. When a company's LAN is connected to the Internet, the LAN becomes part of a WAN.

An example of a company WAN is Metropolitan Life Insurance Co., which uses a WAN to connect its LANs[3] (see Figure C.13). At Met Life, a central server makes the organization's pension database available to employees who work all over the country. The database has information on all current and prospective clients, as well as information about competitors. Each LAN also has its own server with a database of client and product information for that particular area. As updates are made at each LAN site the LAN servers communicate those updates to the central WAN server. Likewise, the central server updates all appropriate information on the LAN site servers nightly. When Met Life sales associates are on the road, they can dial into the central server to receive whatever updates they need.

Classification of Networks by Physical Structure—Topologies You can also describe networks according to how the computers are physically connected. **Network topology** refers to the physical arrangement of computers in a network. Here, we'll discuss bus, ring, and star topologies. Most

180 EXTENDED LEARNING MODULE C

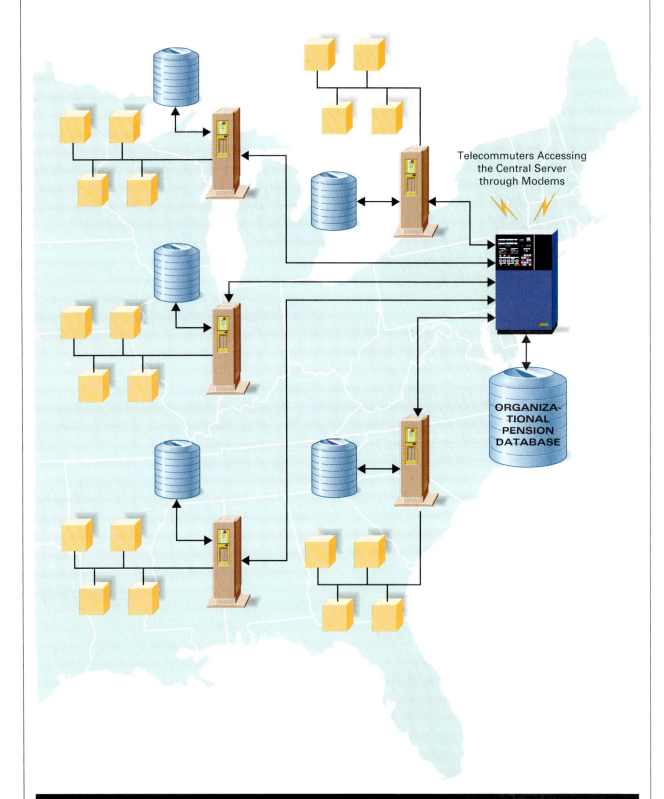

FIGURE C.13

Local and Wide Area Networks at Metropolitan Life Insurance Co.

Network Basics

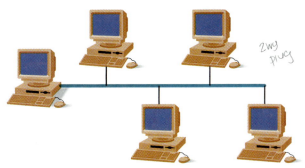

(a) A bus topology connects all computers to a single communications medium over which all communications travel.

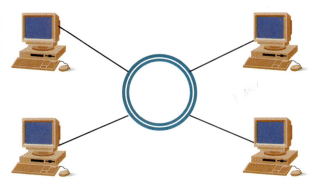

(b) A ring topology connects all computers to a single communications medium that is connected on both ends to form a closed loop.

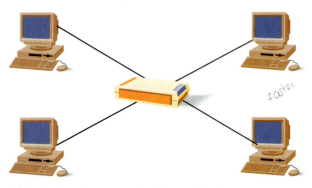

(c) A star topology connects all computers to a central computer.

FIGURE C.14

Bus, Ring, and Star Network Topologies

networks are a lot more complicated and are in fact hybrids of two or all three of the network topologies.

- ***Bus topology***: All computers are connected to a single communications medium over which all communications travel (see Figure C.14a). The common communications medium in a bus topology is called the "bus." If you send a message to another computer in a bus topology, that message (along with a unique address for the destination computer) travels the entire bus. Each computer reads the address to determine if it's the intended recipient. If it is, that computer accepts the message; if not, the computer simply disregards the message.

- ***Ring topology***: All computers are connected to a communications medium, which forms a closed loop (see Figure C.14b). Usually, there are two loops, one for backup in case the other one goes down. As with the bus topology, all communications travel the entire communications medium, and each computer must read the address and determine if it's the intended recipient.

- ***Star topology***: This arrangement has a central hub or switch from which all computers radiate (see Figure C.14c). If you send a message to another person's computer, the message goes through the hub or switch, which in turn interprets the address and sends the communication to the right computer.

Telecommunications Media— The Paths over Which Information Travels

The objective of networks and telecommunications is to move information electronically from one place to another. This may be as simple as sending information to the office next door, or as far-reaching as sending a message to the other side of the world. Whatever the case, information must travel over some path from its source to its destination. ***Communications media*** are the paths, or physical channels, in a network over which information travels from one place to another.

All communications are either wired or wireless. ***Wired communications media*** transmit information over a closed, connected path. ***Wireless communications media*** transmit information through the air. Forms of wired and wireless communications media include:

Wired
- Twisted-Pair Cable
- Coaxial Cable
- Fiber Optic Cable

Wireless
- Microwave
- Satellite
- Infrared

Bandwidth Before discussing the various types of communications media we should first address bandwidth. ***Bandwidth*** or ***capacity***, for our purposes, refers to the amount of information that a communications medium can transfer in a given amount of time. You measure the capacity of a communications medium in bits per second (bps), thousands of bits per second (Kbs), or millions of bits per second (Mbps). For example, if a particular communications medium has a maximum capacity of 16 megabits per second (Mbps), up to 16 million bits of information can be transmitted in a single second. The bandwidth is comparable to the size of a drinking straw. The fatter the straw, the more liquid you can drink in a given period of time.

Wired Communications Media Wired communications media are those which tie devices together with cables of some kind. Twisted pair, coaxial cable, and optical fiber are the types of cabling you'd find in computer networks (see Figure C.15).

Twisted-Pair. Twisted-pair cable comes in two varieties – Cat 3 and Cat 5, both of which you already saw in connection with home networks earlier in this module. Cat 3 and Cat 5 are types of unshielded twisted-pair cable (UTP). Most of the world's phone system is twisted pair and since it's already in place, it's an obvious choice for networks.

Cat 3 cabling provides a slow, fairly reliable path for information at up to 64 kilobits per second (Kbps). However, distance, noise on the line, and interference tend to limit its reliability. For human speech communication, this is not much of a problem. If there's a crackle on the line, you can usually still understand what your conversation partner is saying. Digital information communication across a network, however, requires much greater accuracy. For example, a crackle that changes a credit card number from 5244 0811 2643 741 to 5244 081**0** 2643 741 is more than a nuisance; in business it means retransmitting the information or applying a charge to the wrong person's credit card.

Cat 5 or Category 5 is another version of twisted-pair cabling, which provides a much

Twisted-Pair Cables
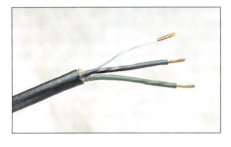

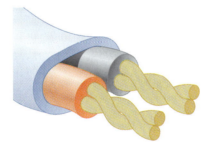

Coaxial Cables

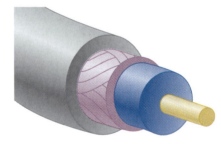

Optical Fibers
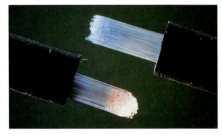

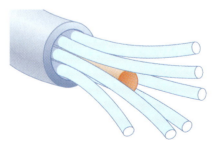

FIGURE C.15

Wired Communications Media

higher bandwidth. It's the most widely used cabling for data transfer in today's LANs. Cat 5 can carry information at a much higher rate than Cat 3, at least for distances up to approximately 100 yards. It costs relatively little and is fairly easy to install and maintain. However, if you need a high level of security, twisted-pair cabling of any kind might not be a good idea, since it's relatively easy to tap into the cables and intercept the information. It's even possible to access the information by simply detecting the signals that "leak" out.

Coaxial Cable. An alternative to twisted-pair cable is ***coaxial cable (coax)***, which is one central wire surrounded by insulation, a metallic shield, and a final case of insulating material. (Coax is the kind of cable that delivers cable television transmissions.) While coaxial cable was once the cable of choice for internal LAN wiring, it has been almost completely replaced by twisted-pair cable. Coaxial cable is capable of carrying at least 500 Mbps, or the equivalent of 15,000 voice calls, simultaneously. Because of its shielded construction, coaxial cable is much less susceptible to outside interference and information damage than twisted-pair cable. However, coaxial cable is generally more expensive than twisted-pair and is more difficult to install and maintain. Security is about the same with coaxial cable as with twisted-pair, except that the radiation, or leaking, of information is much less. Coax is commonly used for leased line private networks.

Optical Fiber. The fastest and most efficient medium for wired communication is ***optical fiber***, which uses a very thin glass or plastic fiber through which pulses of light travel. Transmission through optical fiber is similar to flashing code with a light through a hollow tube. Optical cable's advantages are size (one fiber has the diameter of a human hair); capacity (exceeding 1,400 Mbps); much greater security; and no leakage of information. It's very hard to "tap" into optical fiber. Attempts are pretty easy to detect since installing a tap disrupts service on the line—and that's noticeable. However optical fiber is very expensive and very difficult to install and maintain.

Wireless Communications Media For many networks, wired communications media are simply not feasible, especially for telecommunication across rugged terrain, great distances, or when one or more parties may be in motion. For whatever reason, if wired communications media don't fit your needs, wireless may be the answer. Wireless communications radiate information into the air, either very narrowly beamed or in many directions like ripples from a pebble tossed into a pond. Since they radiate through the air, they don't require direct cable connections of any kind. Obviously, security is a big problem since the information is available to anyone in the radiation's path. However, wireless encryption methods are good, and getting better.

Short Distances. Infrared is the oldest type of wireless communication. ***Infrared*** uses a red light that's below what your eye can see. Infrared is probably what your remote control uses to change the channel on your television set or turn up the heat in your gas-fired fireplace.

You can use infrared to connect hand-held devices, such as pocket PCs, to peripheral devices such as printers. Wireless keyboards and mice are usually connected to your PC with an infrared link. Infrared communication is totally line-of-sight, meaning that you can't have anything blocking the path of the signal, or it won't work. Infrared transmission has very limited bandwidth (typically 1 Mbps).

Another method of short-distance wireless communications is omnidirectional (all directions) microwave transmission. ***Microwave transmission*** is a type of radio transmission. You can choose one of two systems—Bluetooth, which you saw earlier in this module, and WiFi. ***WiFi (Wireless Fidelity)*** is well established as a medium for local network access. WiFi used to be called IEEE standard 802.11b. To add WiFi to your network, you'd connect a wireless access point to the wired network, which would then act as a receiver for messages coming into the network and a transmitter for messages going out to the wireless device. The wireless computer—either laptop, hand-held, or desktop—has a companion receiver and transmitter, and can access the network as if it were cable connected. You can even extend the reach of wireless networks to cover an entire neighborhood by increasing the power of the transmitters and by elevating the antenna. The higher the antenna is, the greater the area it can cover. But bandwidth is somewhat limited.

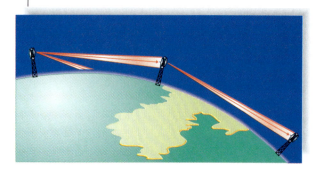

FIGURE C.16
Microwave

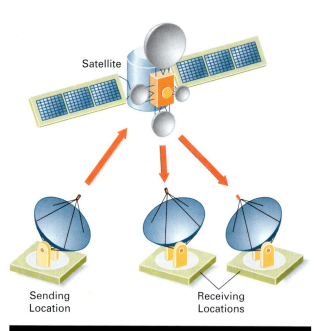

FIGURE C.17
Satellite

Medium Distances. Microwaves may be transmitted very directionally with a parabolic dish antenna or can be radiated in a wide curved path for broader use. Microwave transmission is a line-of-sight medium. That is, the microwave signal cannot follow the curved surface of the earth. So to send the information over a distance of more than about 20 miles you'd have to use *repeaters*, which take the message, strengthen it, and pass it along. Microwave signals have difficulty getting through walls or trees or other solid objects, so there must be a clear path from sender to receiver (see Figure C.16).

Long Distance Microwave. *Communications satellites* are microwave repeaters in space. Since satellites are so high, they can cover essentially the whole earth. As with the range extending land-based repeaters, satellites receive information from one location and relay it to another. You'd usually use satellite communications to connect land-based networks in far-flung locations or to connect moving vehicles (see Figure C.17).

Satellite communications are cost effective for moving large amounts of information, especially when there's a large number of receiving sites. For example, Kmart and other retailers place very small aperture terminal (VSAT) satellite dishes on the roofs of their stores. The VSATs allow individual stores to transmit information to the home office, and the home office, in turn, can transmit information to all the stores simultaneously.

The traditional satellite service to homes and businesses has always been television delivery. But as you already know from the discussion earlier on types of Internet access, you can now get Internet access via satellite. The biggest problem is delay, since signals must travel about 22,000 miles into space and the same distance back again. Another new application of satellite service is the delivery of digital radio nationwide. That means that if you have a favorite radio satellite radio station, you'll never be out of range again—no matter how far you drive.

Key Considerations for Communications Media Communications media technology is vitally important in a network. To determine the most appropriate communications medium, you must consider the capacity, reliability, cost, and distance that your network covers as well as the mobility of your network users.

- *Capacity* or *Bandwidth* determines (1) how much information can travel over the communications medium at once, and (2) how fast the information can travel. Twisted-pair has the lowest capacity, and optical fiber the highest.
- *Reliability* is a measure of how much you can depend on your network. If you need a network with the greatest reliability, you probably won't choose wireless communications because wireless networks are the most susceptible to outside interference.

- *Cost* is always a very important consideration in the building and maintenance of a network. Your choice of capacity and reliability will usually affect the cost.
- *Distance* is a consideration in what medium you choose. Infrared, for example, works only over small distances, whereas optical fiber and satellite work well over great distances.
- *Mobility* may be important to your organization. If so, you may want to investigate wireless communications so that connectivity becomes mobile within a building. For larger distances, you'll need cellular phones to give you an alternative to land phone lines for connecting to the network when out of the office.

Processors

In a network, **communications processors** are the hardware devices that facilitate the flow of information between networks or computers. The most simple and common form of a communications processor is a modem. You've already seen how a modem gets you Internet access. A modem is a device that connects you to your ISP and from there to the Internet.

Most networks have other types of processors that perform a wide range of functions. These include multiplexors and various internetworking units.

Multiplexors *Multiplexors* collect the transmissions from several communications media and send them over a single line that operates at a higher capacity. You use multiplexors in pairs; one combines the messages from all the computers at one end, and bundles them all together into one line. The other multiplexor separates out the different messages again and sends them to the computers at the other end (see Figure C.18).

Internetworking Units Most networks of any size are actually combinations of smaller networks. Many of the smaller networks may be similar to each other or of different types. Three common types of internetworking units are bridges, routers, and gateways. The choice of which internetworking unit to use depends on the similarities and differences of the networks you need to connect.

A **bridge** connects two networks of the same kind, such as two IBM networks that use a ring topology. A bridge passes messages between the networks. A **router** connects networks that are somewhat similar. A router could connect star and bus topology networks. It separates the traffic within each network so that all information doesn't travel to every computer. A **gateway** connects networks that are very dissimilar. For example, a gateway would connect an Apple local talk LAN to an SNA LAN.

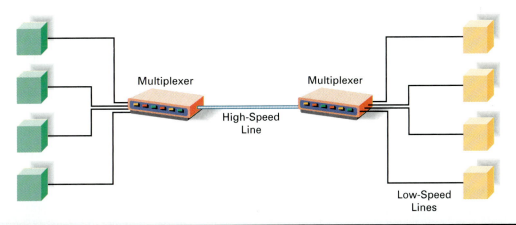

FIGURE C.18

Multiplexor

Protocols

For computers to communicate, they must speak the same language, just as people must if they want to understand each other. These "languages" for computer communication are called *protocols*. Here are a few of the most widely used protocols.

TCP/IP TCP/IP is a protocol you've probably heard of. ***Transmission control protocol/Internet protocol (TCP/IP)*** is the primary protocol for transmitting information over the Internet. TCP/IP was originally developed for our Internet's predecessor—ARPANET. It's proved to be so popular, in fact, that it has spread to LANs, where it's now used a lot, especially for intranets.

Ethernet *Ethernet* is the most common protocol for connecting components in a LAN. We discussed Ethernet cards for home networks earlier in this module. Ethernet uses a shared communications medium (such as a bus topology). In a shared Ethernet network, each component constantly monitors the communications medium for traffic. When one computer sends out a message, each of the other computers checks to see if it's the intended recipient. If so, it accepts the message; if not, it disregards it. When a component wants to send a message, it listens to see if there's traffic on the line. If not, it sends its message. If the line is busy, it waits until the line is available.

ATM ***Asynchronous transfer mode (ATM)*** is a transmission protocol that divides long messages into smaller units called cells. The cells are then sent over the network, and reassembled at their destination. For example, if you're using a multimedia application stored on a server, the server might break the application into cells containing video, text, and sound. The server would transmit the cells to you, and your client computer would reassemble the message.

ISDN ***Integrated services digital network (ISDN)*** is both a plan and an international communications protocol for converting the world's public telephone system from analog to digital. The objective is to be able to transmit all forms of information (voice, video, text, and so on) simultaneously over twisted-pair phone lines. Most of the world's phone systems are severely limited in the amount of information they can transmit, the speed of the transmission, their reliability, and the services they provide. ISDN is the blueprint for transmitting all forms of information 10 to 30 times faster than current speeds, and handling multiple applications on the same line at the same time.

ANSI X12 and EDIFACT ***ANSI X12*** (also referred to a ***X.12***) and ***EDIFACT*** are both protocols for transmitting commonly formatted information in electronic data interchange (EDI) transactions. EDI is how businesses exchange transaction information such as purchase orders. Businesses in the United States, Canada, and Australia tend to use ANSI X12, while Europe favors EDIFACT.

We have by no means presented all the protocols in existence. We've left out SNA, X.400, X.25, X.12, SONET, FDDI, ISO 7498, and Frame Relay, to name some of them. It's not necessary that you know all of these protocols (unless you want to be a network specialist). What you do need to understand is that there are many ways to send information across a network. Your job is to effectively communicate your business needs to a network specialist. As in any other area of information technology, business needs should drive technical specifications.

This Is Really Only the "Basics"

What you've just read is really only the "basics" of networks, how they work, and the hardware and software involved. Volumes have been written about how networks work. What's most important for you to remember is what we stated in the previous paragraph. You need to understand your business needs. You must effectively communicate those needs to network specialists. Then and only then will your organization be successful in its development of a network infrastructure that supports its business processes.

CHAPTER OUTLINE

INDUSTRY PERSPECTIVES

Retail
194
The Right Tool for Ace Hardware

Manufacturing
198
Toyota Gets Moving on Web Initiatives

".com"
207
Dairy Industry Gets Set for B2B Exchange

Transportation
212
BNSF: Making the Trains Run on Time

IN THE NEWS

- **191** As of November 2000, there were an estimated 407 million people online in the world.
- **191** Urgent action is needed to slow the "digital divide."
- **196** Nearly 25 million U.S. consumers purchased gifts online during the (2000) holiday season.
- **197** Analysts predicted that many dot-com companies would run out of cash in the year 2000. Were they right?
- **204** Most online retailers failed to keep promises to consumers about when packages would arrive.
- **205** Many companies do not pay enough attention to the way they seek out and maintain strategic relationships.
- **217** A *New York Times* article portrayed employees as the biggest threat to a company's security.
- **218** Do you need a honeypot?

FEATURES

- **195** **On Your Own** B2C Services
- **195** **Teamwork** Broadband Services: Where Do You Place Your Bets?
- **199** **The Global Perspective** Europe to Lead World in Online Grocery Sales
- **209** **Teamwork** What Should Allright Distributors Do?
- **211** **On Your Own** A Range of Possibilities for New EDI
- **219** **The Global Perspective** European Privacy Laws
- **222** **Electronic Commerce** Getting Your Business on the Internet

KNOWLEDGE WORKER'S CHECKLIST

In the Information Age, Knowledge Workers Understand . . .

1. The growth of global e-commerce
2. Business to Consumer (B2C) business models. What works and what doesn't work
3. The variety of options for Business to Business (B2B) business models
4. The role of government in promoting e-commerce
5. E-commerce payment systems
6. The importance of security and privacy issues

WEB SUPPORT

http://www.mhhe.com/haag

- Competitive Intelligence
- Storefront Software
- Hosting Services
- Marketing the Site
- Privacy Issues
- Getting Funding
- Product and Price Comparison Sites

Electronic Commerce

The End of the Beginning

CHAPTER 5

CASE STUDY

Buying Pepsi Online

Cans of soda are probably one of the last things we would think of buying online. They're available on every street corner.

Despite this, Pepsi-Cola Co. has a number of Internet initiatives underway, from music sites to banner ads to Internet sweepstakes. And more are on the drawing board. Even though it is currently spending only 3 percent of its $400 million ad budget on the Internet, Pepsi is placing a lot of emphasis on the medium as an effective way of reaching the most desirable customers. For example, in a deal put together with Yahoo!, Pepsi agreed to put the Yahoo Logo on 1.5 billion cans of Pepsi. In return, Yahoo encouraged their visitors to visit the *Pepsi Stuff* site.

Three million consumers logged on to *Pepsi Stuff* and provided Pepsi with detailed demographic information about themselves. Pepsi's sales volume was up by 5 percent as a result of the promotion at a cost of about one-fifth of a traditional mail-in project.

Pepsi intends to keep using the Web as its medium of choice because it is also the medium of choice for its target market—those under 25. They simply decided that it makes sense to flash the Pepsi logo where their target customers hang out.

As it moves forward, Pepsi will expand its Web-centric marketing efforts. While banner ads and other more traditional methods have had some success, it's the creation of engaging Pepsi Web sites that has given the brand the best results online. As the technology expands, Pepsi expects the creative potential of what can be done on the Web to explode.[1] ❖

Introduction

You've probably heard the ancient Chinese curse, "May you live in interesting times." It's a curse because it is often easier to live in times that are not so interesting, when things move along pretty much as expected, as they always have. The past few years of the new economy introduced by the World Wide Web have certainly been interesting. There has been an entrepreneurial frenzy unlike anything the world has ever seen. Fortunes have been made and lost. Dot-com millionaires and billionaires were created. Some have seen their fortunes increase while others have watched their dot-com business wonders turn into "dot-bombs." Some of them even had to sell their Ferraris.

We called this chapter the "end of the beginning" because most observers of the e-commerce scene believe that the revolution in business promised by the Internet has just begun. One has said it's "…like we're in the first minute of the first period of a hockey game." We have some hint of how e-commerce is going to unfold. We are learning what works and what doesn't work. But there is much about the new economy that is yet to be discovered. And much of it will be discovered by people like you.

The Growth of Global E-Commerce

Maybe we ought to start with a definition, because there are many definitions of e-commerce. We like this one. "**E-commerce** is commerce, but it is commerce accelerated and enhanced by IT, in particular the Internet. It enables customers, consumers, and companies to form powerful new relationships that would not be possible without the enabling technologies."

But let's not forget that, fundamentally, it's all still about commerce, people buying and selling products and services from and to each other. The Internet facilitates commerce by its awesome ability to move digital information at low cost.

As illustrated in Figure 5.1, there are four main perspectives for e-commerce, Business to Business (B2B), Business to Consumer (B2C), Consumer to Business (C2B), and Consumer to Consumer (C2C). We will

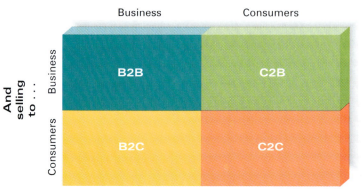

FIGURE 5.1

Four Categories of E-Commerce[2]

focus on B2C and B2B in this chapter. Government's role in e-commerce is also important, as we discuss in a later section of this chapter.

B2C is what you read about the most in the popular press. These are the e-commerce sites that sell products and services, or provide information services directly to consumers. They include such well-known sites as Yahoo, Amazon.com, and LandsEnd.com.

Even though most of the media's attention is focused on B2C, the dollar volume of e-commerce is widely expected to be concentrated in the B2B segment. This is because the B2B segment is so much larger, regardless of whether we're talking about e-commerce or traditional commerce.

The C2C sector is where consumers deal with each other, either through an auction site such as eBay or directly in one of the peer to peer networking applications (see Gnutella at http://www.gnutella.wego.com for trading music and other digital files).

Finally, the C2B sector is the one in which the Internet makes it possible for many consumers who want to buy the same or similar products to band together in order to obtain volume discounts from a business. This process is known as demand aggregation. **Demand aggregation** combines purchase requests from multiple buyers into a single large order which justifies a discount from the business. While it's possible to aggregate demand on the Internet, the best-known company to try it, Mercata (http://www.mercata.com), was unsuccessful and went out of business. Demand aggregation, of course, is also possible in the B2B sector (see http://www.mobshop.com for an example).

Global E-Commerce Growth Projections

As shown in Table 5.1, there were an estimated 407 million Internet users worldwide in November 2000. Matrix.net estimates that the number of Internet users is currently doubling every 18 months.[3] While growth cannot continue at such a pace for very long, the ultimate number of Internet users worldwide will clearly be an impressive figure.

In a survey released in October 2000, Forrester Research predicted that worldwide e-commerce sales will account for 8.6 percent of total sales of goods and services in the year 2004. Forrester also estimated the United States will lead the world with Internet sales of $3.2 trillion, followed by Western Europe at $1.5 trillion.[4] The Gartner Group estimates that worldwide e-commerce will reach $4.4 trillion by 2003, 90 percent of it in the B2B space.[5]

You must use growth projections such as the ones cited here with caution, because they are, in fact, estimates. Nevertheless, the consensus of knowledgeable observers of the e-commerce scene are consistent in their expectations that it has nowhere to go but up (and up).

The Digital Divide

You will notice from Table 5.1 that the number of Internet users varies from region to region in the world. Less-developed regions have fewer users than more-developed regions. This phenomenon is called the "digital divide." The phrase the *digital divide* expresses the fact that different peoples, cultures, and areas of the world or within a nation do not have the same access to information and telecommunications technologies. For example, Finland and the other Scandinavian countries have a high population online. These small countries are affluent, with a tradition of good telecommunications systems. Just the opposite is true in Africa and Latin America, as another example. Many of these areas have large populations, are poor, and do not have state of the art computer and telecommunications infrastructures, thus creating a global digital divide. The *global digital divide* is the term used specifically to describe differences in IT access and capabilities between different countries or regions of the world. It should be a concern to e-commerce policy experts that the global digital divide threatens to restrict the benefits of global e-commerce to just the wealthy nations.

Many people are calling for collective action to help countries and regions on the wrong side of the global digital divide to develop the capabilities to participate in global e-commerce (see box entitled "UN Urged to Close Global Digital Divide"). This challenge will re-

TABLE 5.1 How Many Online?[6]

Based in Dublin, Ireland, NUA is an Internet thought leader and consultancy that is perhaps best known for its Internet surveys. Its Web site (http://www.nua.com) is a good source of information on Internet demographics and activity. Here is NUA's "educated guess" as to the number of users online worldwide in November 2000.

	Millions Online
Africa	3.11
Asia/Pacific	104.88
Europe	113.14
Middle East	2.40
Canada and United States	167.12
Latin America	16.45
World Total	407.10

UN Urged to Close Global Digital Divide

United Nations Secretary General Kofi Annan has called for urgent action to close the "digital divide" that separates rich countries from poor ones.

A panel of IT experts that the UN Secretary General appointed recommended that everyone in the world have access to a computer and the Internet by 2005. The panel told the UN General Assembly that the longer poor countries are excluded from the Internet revolution, the more difficult it will be for them to catch up. Thus, unless something is done, and done soon, poor countries face the risk of being "completely bypassed" from global e-commerce.[7] This has grave implications for the whole world. ❖

quire large investments in technical infrastructure and education, and will not be easily met, but it is one of our most important tasks for the future.

> **CAREER OPPORTUNITY**
> Helping in some way to close the digital divide either within your own country or between your country and less-developed countries not only would be a contribution to humanity but could be an exciting adventure and even a very satisfying career. Whether through college or business, there will be many opportunities for young people trained in e-commerce to share their knowledge with others in all parts of the world.

Business to Consumer E-Commerce

We noted earlier in this chapter that B2C e-commerce was relatively small compared to B2B e-commerce. It is also small compared to other forms of retail commerce. For example, in 1999, B2C sales were just 1 percent of total retail sales in the United States, while catalog sales amounted to 10 percent of all retail sales. But B2C sales are expected to grow dramatically in the next few years. Goldman Sachs estimates that they could be 15 to 20 percent of total U.S. retail sales by the year 2010.[8]

The Advantages of B2C E-Commerce

In addition to the opportunity to employ the techniques of mass customization and personalization we discussed in Chapter 2, several current and potential advantages over the traditional retailing channels of "brick-and-mortar" stores and catalog sales are offered by the Internet.

1. Shopping can be faster and more convenient.
2. Offerings and prices can change instantaneously.
3. Call centers can be integrated with the Web site.
4. Broadband telecommunications will enhance the buying experience.

Shopping on the Internet Can Be Faster and More Convenient

Some brick-and-mortar stores are open 24 hours a day, seven days a week, but most are not. Internet sites are open all the time. You've probably experienced the frustration of going from one store to another, from one shopping mall to another, fighting traffic, trying to find a place to park, looking for that one certain item. Then, when you finally locate it at the fourth store you visit, you have to find a clerk who will take your money, or stand in a long checkout line.

Catalog shopping avoids some of the irritations of brick-and-mortar shopping by letting you pick out the item you want from a catalog, dial a toll-free telephone number, and order the item from a customer service rep. Many catalog retailers such as Lands' End and Eddie Bauer are open 24 hours a day, seven days a week, but others are not. Although the service of some catalog retailers is very good, with others you are put on hold and have to listen to music you don't like until the customer service rep comes on the line to take your order. In order to comparison shop, you must hope you have all the right catalogs, and then page through them in a cumbersome fashion.

When you shop on the Internet, it can be faster and more convenient. If you don't find what you want at the right price on one e-tailer's Web site, a click of the mouse will take you to a competitor's site. The term *e-tailer* has come to be used to describe an Internet retail site. E-tailers are further divided into pure plays and clicks-and-mortar sites. *Pure plays* are Internet retailers such as Amazon.com that have no physical stores. *Clicks-and-mortar* retailers are like Nordstrom, which has both an Internet presence and physical stores. They can often have catalogs as well. Clicks-and-mortar retailers are also called "bricks-and-clicks." As far as we know, no one has invented a term to describe catalog retailers such as Lands' End that have an Internet presence but no physical store. Can you think of one that might describe such businesses? (See Figure 5.2 for a depiction of these alternative sales channels.)

Compare the convenience of shopping on the Internet to driving from one store to another. Compare the convenience of shopping on the Internet to shopping from catalogs, where it is time-consuming to flip from catalog to catalog if you want to do product and price comparisons. On the Internet, not only can you go from site to site with the click of a mouse, but there are many sites that offer product and price comparisons for you as well. Some of these are shown in Table 5.2.

One of the applications suggested for m-commerce relates to price comparisons. *M-commerce* is the term used to describe e-commerce conducted over a wireless device such as a cell phone or personal digital assistant (PDA). Let's say you're in an electronics store and you

Business to Consumer E-Commerce   193

TABLE 5.2 Product and Price Comparison Sites

Site Name	Web Address
DealTime	http://www.dealtime.com
mySimon	http://www.mysimon.com
PriceGrabber.com	http://www.pricegrabber.com
StoreRunner	http://www.storerunner.com

notice a CD player at what seems to be a good price. With m-commerce, you'll be able to find the price at other merchants for the same item simply by using your wireless device. Internet-based services will search the Web and tell you whether the price you see on the item in front of you is a good deal or not. It will be similar to what you can do now sitting in front of your PC.

If the product you want to buy is digital, such as software, music, and books, it can be delivered <u>immediately</u> over the Internet. This, of course, represents a tremendous advantage over both stores and catalog retailers. Besides, Internet pure play retailers do not kill trees to make catalogs.

Offerings and Prices Can Change Instantaneously

Another advantage e-tailers have is that product offerings and prices can be changed instantaneously in response to customer demand. One of the most difficult aspects of managing a retail operation, particularly with high-fashion goods, is to know how much to order at the beginning of the selling season. You also need to have enough information to re-order early if sales are better than expected, and to reduce prices early if sales are not up to your expectations.

Children's toys, for example, fall into this category because toys can be "hot" during the critical holiday selling season. One year it's Pokemon and the next year it's the PlayStation. In March or April of each year, retail merchandisers try to estimate the number of each item they will sell in November and December, because that's when orders must be placed with the manufacturer. When the selling season arrives, actual sales are measured against estimated sales. If sales are taking off, an early order to the manufacturer will make it more likely that more of the hot product can be shipped. If the retailer waits too long, none will be available be-

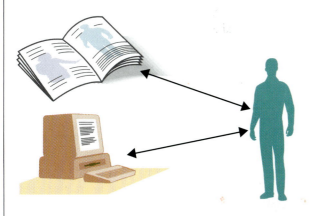

FIGURE 5.2

Alternative Channels for Selling to Consumers

INDUSTRY PERSPECTIVE

Retail

The Right Tool for Ace Hardware

In most small hardware stores, there's a gray-haired guy who can answer any question you might have. For example, if you say you want to put a bird feeder on a pole, the wise old guy says, "You need a flange fastener." Or, if you want to hang shutters he'll tell you, "You need pintles." He knows all the doohickeys: T-joints, pan head screws, toggle bolts, rheostats, turnbuckles, ball valves. He also knows where they are in the store.

That's great for the customers, but where could the Ace Hardware dealers themselves turn when they needed some advice on how to run their businesses better?

Up to now, Ace's dealers were out of luck. They met to compare notes only a couple of times a year, at conventions. Many had little further contact with each other, or even with Ace headquarters because dealers operate as independents. They sell some Ace products but don't work for Ace and are free to offer goods made by other suppliers.

Recently, Ace began deploying a Web site that illustrates the power of a Web-based community by demonstrating that "Nobody is as smart as everybody." While some information and advice is available on the site, the main attraction for Ace's 5,000 dealers is that they can discuss do's, don'ts, and doohickeys with each other.

Ace and its dealers are delighted with the site. Although Ace won't get too specific, it does say that the exchange of ideas and information by the online community has increased sales so much that it achieved a 500 percent return on its investment in the first six months.[9] ❖

---

cause everyone has ordered more and the manufacturer either cannot keep up with the incoming orders or they've moved on to produce products for sale after the holiday season. If sales are slower than expected, the retailer must react quickly to reduce the product's price, or there will be piles of unsold products on the shelves. As you know, sometimes an unpopular item is hard even to give away.

Think about the advantage e-tailers have in managing this process. They can obtain real-time information on how sales are going against expectations. More important, they can adjust prices immediately if sales are not going as well as expected. In a way, it's similar to the yield management systems of the airlines we discussed in Chapter 2, but it is a tremendous advantage for the e-tailer. Many e-tailers have "clearance" areas on their sites to alert their customers to last minute bargains.

If a catalog retailer wants to reduce its price what does it have to do? Produce more mountains of catalogs to mail to its customers. If a traditional retailer wants to advertise a sale, the expense and delay of newspaper advertising is the answer. E-tailers not only can change prices across the board instantly, but, if they wish, can offer special pricing to their best customers by using the personalization techniques we discussed in Chapter 2.

Call Centers Can Be Integrated with the Web Site

The retailing space has seen some interesting developments since B2C e-commerce began. One of the more innovative adaptations has been Web sites that give customers the ability to contact a customer service representative through the site. If you log on to http://www.Flooze.com, for example, you can contact a customer service representative for help via interactive chat. *Interactive chat* lets you engage in real-time typed exchange of information between you and one or more other individuals over the Internet. LandsEndLive™, on the Lands' End site (http://www.landsend.com), gives you an option of communicating with a customer service representative using either interactive chat or the telephone. If you choose to use the telephone, you will need a second line on which the customer service representative can call you back or a direct Internet connection. Soon, you'll be able to connect directly to the customer service representative using Internet telephony as long as your computer has a microphone and speakers. Internet telephony is a combination of hardware and software that uses the Internet as the medium for transmission of telephone calls in place of the networks of traditional telephone service providers.

ON YOUR OWN

B2C Services

Just about any product you can imagine is offered for sale to consumers over the Internet—books, videos, CDs, automobiles, clothes, groceries. Not only can you buy products over the Internet, you can buy services. There are sites where you can get financial advice, medical advice, weather reports, and more. See if you can come up with at least 10 sites offering services (not products) on the Internet. Many of the sites offering services are free. Make 5 of the 10 sites on your list sites where the consumer must pay for the service. ❖

TEAMWORK

Broadband Services: Where Do You Place Your Bets?

Assume that your Aunt Millie has just died and left you $10 million in her will. Because you're young, adventurous, and technologically astute, you decide to invest the entire $10 million in stocks of companies in sectors that will be sure to benefit from the coming surge in broadband telecommunications supporting B2C e-commerce applications.

Because there is intense competition in the industry, and several competing technologies, you decide to consult some of your classmates to decide how to allocate the $10 million. You have the option of keeping all or a portion of the $10 million in T-bills while you wait to see how things unfold.

Allocate the $10 million among the following broadband technologies (or T-bills). Which technologies do you feel will be most successful for B2C e-commerce applications in the United States? Pick one other country and do the same. Be prepared to justify your decisions, and feel free to add other technologies:

ISDN
DSL
Cable
Satellite
Fixed wireless
Fiberless optics
Other
T-bills ❖

Before long, speech recognition software will reach the point where the need for call center representatives will be reduced, particularly for routine inquiries. Speech recognition is a branch of computer science that lets computers identify spoken words (discussed in more detail in the next chapter). If you'd like to see how a speech recognition service works in providing information services to consumers, just dial 800-555-tell in the United States. You'll be connected with *Tell Me*, a service that can respond to your spoken commands and provide information on a variety of topics: weather, stock quotes, movie guides, and even driving directions.

Broadband Telecommunications Will Enhance the Buying Experience

When broadband telecommunications become widely available the buying experience will be greatly enhanced. You'll be able to purchase a full-length feature film, for example, and have it downloaded in about 45 minutes. This will sure beat driving to Blockbuster and waiting in line. The inventory of available films will not be limited to what a video store is able to stock on its shelves. You'll be able to choose any film that has ever been made and it will always be available.

Travel sites will offer full-motion video tours of vacation destinations that will let you get a better appreciation of what that beachfront resort in Costa Rica will really be like before you book accommodations at it. Automobile buying sites will be able to offer virtual test drives to let you narrow down your choices before you take the time to visit an auto dealership. Think of what will be possible with virtual reality (basically, a 3-D simulation in which you physically participate—discussed in more detail in the next chapter). You will indeed be able to experience "Costa Rica" without spending as much time and money as to actually go there! (Unfortunately—or not—it's unlikely that the relatively inexpensive virtual experience will ever completely match an actual experience.) Can you think of other ways that broadband technologies will enhance the retail e-commerce buying experience?

Holiday Shoppers Like Their Old Favorites

During the 2000 holiday season, nearly 25 million U.S. consumers purchased gifts online. Even so, shoppers concentrated their buying on just a few Web sites, according to a survey conducted by the Gartner Group.

Consumers tended to stay loyal to sites they had used before, and 87 percent of those polled said they shopped at no more than three Web sites.

Amazon.com was by far the most popular e-tailer, with 28 percent of all respondents shopping there. Amazon.com attracted twice as many shoppers as any other site in the survey.

A separate report from the NPD Group also named Amazon.com as the most popular Web site for the holiday season. Next in line were eBay, Barnesandnoble.com, JCPenney.com, and Etoys.com.[10]

The End of the Beginning in B2C E-Commerce

When it first became apparent that the Internet provided a powerful new channel to reach consumers, there was a burst of activity to establish new B2C ventures on the Web. There was also plenty of venture capital available to fund them and, when the new companies had been established long enough to be able to show some growth in revenues and customers, their stock was offered to the public in an initial public offering (IPO).

The prevailing wisdom was that companies did not have to show a profit. That would come in time as they built up their customer databases. It was described as a "land grab"—the important thing was to establish your brand and build your customer database. Analysts and investors justified the soaring market capitalizations of dot-com companies that were not expected to show a profit for months or even years by looking at new measures of financial performance. Instead of looking at conventional measures such as price–earnings ratios (the dot-coms had no earnings) or the present value of a future stream of earnings (again, no earnings), new valuation measures were invented. Comparing the cost of acquiring a new customer against the lifetime value of a customer became a popular measure.

From the beginning, there was a minority of observers who said that a shake-out was coming. There would be very few winners and many losers among the dot-coms. The reason for this prediction was that by its very nature, the Internet encourages information sharing. The identity of the e-tailer providing the best overall customer value will get passed around very quickly. For example, there are well over 1,000 Web sites that sell books, but most people can think of only two: Amazon.com and BN.com. Once word gets around, the "swarm" tends to go to the best-known site. On the book jacket of Evan I. Schwartz's book *Digital Darwinism* is this observation:

> Natural selection is already occurring, weeding out the start-ups and on-line ventures that fail to keep pace with evolving technology and customer needs.[11]

The box entitled "Holiday Shoppers Like Their Old Favorites" shows how this played out during the 2000 Christmas selling season in the United States.

The end of the beginning for B2C e-commerce really began with the sell-off in the Nasdaq markets in the Spring of 2000. Concern among the investor community was raised by articles that began appearing in financial newspapers such as *Barron's,* which looked at the financial statements of prominent e-tailers and predicted how many more months they could last before they ran out of cash. They looked at the amount of cash companies had on hand, their "burn rates" (how much money they were spending each month), and how much sales revenues were expected. As illustrated in Table 5.3, the number of months before the company ran out of cash could be estimated. When you have the opportunity, look up these companies and see if they're still in business.

Investors became leery of throwing more money at start-ups as they saw Digital Darwinism at work. Although at the beginning, it was relatively easy for people to get a business plan funded, at "the end of the beginning" it was becoming increasingly clear that while a thousand flowers might bloom, 998 of them would die. Investors began to demand that dot-com entrepreneurs show them the P2P, or "path to profitability." While the new ways of valuation were not completely abandoned, the more traditional ways that had been set aside came back into favor. It was time to "show me the money."

TABLE 5.3 Who Survived the Shakeout?[12]

At the end of 1999, Pegasus Systems International estimated the time when 51 Internet companies would run out of cash. It was analyses like this that got the attention of dot-com investors in the spring of 2000. Pegasus was right on some, but not on others.

March 2000	July 2000	November 2000
Pilot Ntwk Services	Intraware	LifeMinders.com
CDNow	Interliant	SmarterKids.com
	MyPoints.com	Drugstore.com
	Egghead.com	Ashford.com
	MotherNature.com	NorthPoint Comm.
	ImageX.com	
	BigStar Entmt	
	Mail.com	

April 2000	August 2000	December 2000
Secure Computing	Gybercash	EarthWeb
	Applied Theory	NetObjects
	WorldTalk Corp	Tickets.com
	Primix Solutions	
	Newsedge	

May 2000	September 2000	January 2001
Peapod	FTD.com	Salon.com
VerticalNet	ShopNow.com	Amazon.com
MarketWatch.com	Beyond.com	PurchasePro.com
	Healtheon	

June 2000	October 2000	February 2001
Drkoop.com	E Loan	Cobalt Group
Infonautics	Interactive Pictures	Multex.com
Medscape	Ask Jeeves	EToys
Intelligent Life	LoisLaw.com	Kana Comms
Digital Island	PlanetRX.com	E-Stamp
Splitrock Services		
VitaminShoppe.com		

INDUSTRY PERSPECTIVE

Manufacturing

Toyota Gets Moving on Web Initiatives

Toyota Motor Sales USA is surging ahead on its Web initiatives. Toyota's efforts to streamline its business processes with its dealers and supply chain partners are similar to earlier initiatives by rivals General Motors Corp. and Ford Motor Co. But Toyota is one of the first automakers to use the Web to connect with its dealerships in a virtually paperless communications network across the country.

Many observers believe that success in the highly competitive global market for automotive vehicles will depend on which carmakers use the Internet to capture and use information most effectively—particularly in such areas as supply chain and customer relationship management.

Toyota's latest project, scheduled to go live by 2002, should cut its transportation costs by 25 percent and reduce the current day's supply of total inventory by 50 percent. Passing some or all of these savings along to consumers will enable Toyota to be even more competitive.

The new system will permit dealers to precisely and instantly locate the car model a customer wants—whether it's in a warehouse, on a truck, or in a factory—and deliver it faster. This is a challenge other carmakers are currently wrestling with, say analysts.

Though it's not quite the build-to-order model that Dell Computer Corp. uses to sell its PCs, Toyota's approach should greatly reduce the cycle time for customers to get their cars and, at the same time, drive time and cost out of Toyota's interorganizational business processes.[13] ❖

Lessons Learned: What Works and What Doesn't Work

It is important to reflect on what lessons have been learned in the beginning so that new B2C entrepreneurs (perhaps you and a group of classmates) can increase their chances of being successful. Some of the most important lessons are

1. Commodity-like items work best.
2. Digital products are the best of all.
3. Attracting and retaining customers is key.
4. Remember the importance of merchandising.
5. You must execute well.
6. Pick your sector carefully.
7. Watch the competition.

We'll discuss each of these points in more detail in the following sections.

Commodity-Like Items Work Best

People tend to be more comfortable buying items on the Internet that are commodity-like, that is, uniform. You're comfortable buying a book on the Internet because you know it will be just like the one you'd get if you bought it from your local bookstore. You might be less comfortable buying "high touch" products such as furniture. When you buy a chair, you probably want to sit in it to be sure it feels the way you want it to feel. PCs are commodity-like. When you log on to Dell Computer's Web site and configure a computer the way you want it, you can count on its being identical to one configured in the same way by another buyer miles away.

Two industries that will be interesting to watch in this context are automobiles and groceries. In the case of automobiles, it really doesn't matter where you buy that Porsche Boxster pictured in Chapter 2. You could buy it from a local dealer, you could buy it from a dealer hundreds of miles away, or you could order it built the way you want it, go to the Porsche factory in Germany, and watch it roll off the assembly line. In theory, because an automobile is commodity-like, you could also log on to the Porsche site, configure your car just the way you want it, and have it built to your specifications and then delivered to your home. A substantial part of the cost of the automobile you buy is the cost of distribution, in particular the cost of inventories of completed automobiles on manufacturers' or dealers' lots. If

Business to Consumer E-Commerce   **199**

THE GLOBAL PERSPECTIVE

Europe to Lead World in Online Grocery Sales

A recent study predicts that adding an online channel will be key to the success of traditional supermarkets in the future. Europe will be the leader in online grocery sales, with a value of 55 billion euros ($51.18 billion) by the year 2003.

The study found that the U.K. leads Europe in online groceries as the result of the pilot projects of companies Tesco and Iceland. The study predicts that 7 percent of grocery sales in the U.K. will be made online by 2005. The main users of Net grocery stores now are high earning, urban, and young. The handicapped and elderly are likely to find online grocery shopping a welcome blessing.[14] ❖

---

we could get to the point where we could log on and order a car built to our specifications the way we log on and order a computer from Dell, perhaps some of the cost savings could be passed along to us.

The reason grocery sales over the Internet will be interesting to watch is that the things we buy in grocery stores are a mixture of commodity and noncommodity items. Examples of commodity items are laundry detergents or breakfast cereals. Examples of noncommodity items are produce and fish or meat. You might not mind having someone else pick a box of breakfast cereal off the shelf for you, but you might prefer to choose your own tomatoes or steaks. Among some well-known dot-com grocers that are trying to find their path to profitability, Webvan and Peapod are best known. It will be interesting to see if they will be successful or not.

Digital Products Are the Best of All

The reasons we say that digital products are best suited for B2C e-commerce are the following:

1. They are commodity-like products.
2. They can be mass-customized and personalized.
3. They can be delivered at the time of purchase.
4. They foster disintermediation.
5. They have global reach.

We first introduced some of these digital ideas in Chapter 2 when we gave customized CDs and downloaded software as examples. There are, of course, many other examples, videos (when the necessary bandwidth becomes available) and any text product such as books, newspapers, articles, or manuscripts.

Now, much of the information available on the Internet is free. You can go to the Web sites of many newspapers and magazines and get current information and search the online archives of back issues. At the present time, such sites are either losing money or attempting to support their sites with advertising. Some, such as the online version of *The Wall Street Journal* charge an annual subscription fee. Others, such as *Business Week*, make some information free and restrict access to other stories to their print subscribers.

> **CAREER OPPORTUNITY**
> If you've ever thought of starting your own B2C e-commerce business, you might want to consider selling information over the Internet rather than products. Some people think that this is where a lot of opportunities have yet to be exploited.

Many observers forecast that, in time, you'll be asked to pay for much of the information you now get for free. One technology that will hasten this is called micro-payments. ***Micro-payments* are techniques to facilitate the exchange of small amounts of money for an Internet transaction.** Most B2C transactions today are paid for by credit card. It is not practical to process small payments on credit cards (less than $2) because of credit card transaction processing costs. With micro-payments, however, a newspaper in London could charge you 5 cents for a detailed local weather report or theater timetable. If you were on your way to London and wondering whether or not to take a raincoat and which play to see, you might find that 5 cents was a bargain. And for the newspaper, 5 cents here and 5 cents there could soon add up to some real money. We'll talk more about micro-payments later in this chapter when we discuss smart cards.

Attracting and Retaining Customers Is Key

Designing an attractive Web site that is easy to use is one of the key factors in the success of a B2C venture. As previously mentioned, and as you well know, it's very easy for potential customers to leave your site for your competitor's site with a click of the mouse. So, once they've found your site, it's important to keep them there until they purchase something, and once they've purchased something, you need to give them an incentive to return. You must not turn them off with an unattractive or customer-unfriendly Web site. Some tips from a professional Web site designer are listed in Table 5.4.

No retailer is going to make money if they don't have customers. The same thing is true with B2C e-commerce. Because entry barriers can be lower on the Internet than in traditional retailing, there can be many Web sites competing for the same customers. Successful B2C businesses have learned that attracting and retaining customers is the key.

Of course, with a B2C Web site, it's not enough to simply "build it and they will come." You have to find a way to let potential customers know that you are there and that, among the many choices they have, your Web site is the one they should choose to visit. Your Web site needs to be marketed.

There are entire books written on the subject of marketing and promoting Web sites; a detailed description of the various techniques that are used is beyond the scope of this text. Instead, we'll present a brief overview of the topic in this section.

When marketing professionals consider how to market and promote a business, they talk about the marketing mix. **Marketing mix** is the set of marketing tools that the firm uses to pursue its marketing objectives in the target market.[15] Brick-and-mortar retailers have traditionally used a combination of techniques such as newspaper advertising, direct mail, radio, and television to attract customers to their stores. If you were in charge of the marketing budget for a retail store, one of your tasks would be to decide how much of your budget should be spent on each one of the possible marketing techniques. In order to do this, you would need some way of estimating which combination of techniques would generate the most sales. Traditional marketing techniques are used by dot-com companies. Most of us have seen magazine ads with the company's URL prominently displayed, or seen television ads for a dot-com company.

In the B2C e-commerce space, there are additional techniques for attracting customers available using the Internet itself. Some of these include:

1. Registering with search engines
2. Banner ads
3. Viral marketing
4. Affiliate programs
5. Selling to existing customers

TABLE 5.4 Do's and Don'ts of Web Site Design[16]

Toni Will-Harris has 10 do's and don'ts for Web site design. A condensed version appears here. The complete version can be found on her Web site: http://www.efuse.com/Design/top_10_do_s_and_don_ts.html.

1. Keep graphic files small. The longer a graphic file takes to load, the higher the probability the user will leave before it's done.
2. Keep text files small for the same reason.
3. Design text and backgrounds for easy reading.
4. Design for 256 colors and 640 × 480 resolution. It's the lowest common denominator for older computers.
5. Use "ALT" tags on graphics. ALT text appears before the graphic does, or in place of the graphic for users who have turned graphics off for speed.
6. Include your company name, address, e-mail address, and your phone and fax numbers on every page.
7. Keep your site fresh. It's important to change content frequently so people have something to come back for.
8. Be generous. The more detail you offer, the more reason you give people to visit your site.
9. Be backward compatible. Using cutting edge technology may shut out some readers.
10. Test your site as visitors will see it, using all versions of the popular browsers.

Registering with Search Engines According to Microsoft bCentral, 85 percent of all Web surfers use search engines to find what they need.[17] So, one of the first things you should do is to register with the various search engines. There are two types of search engines—directories and true search engines. ***Directories*** organize listings into hierarchical lists. Yahoo! is probably the best example. If you search on weather for example, you start with the world, get to regions, then countries, and then cities. Log on to Yahoo! sometime and look for the weather in Ljubljana, the capital of Slovenia. You will click first on Europe, then on Slovenia, and finally on Ljubljana. And as you do, you'll see the descending directories displayed on the page, as illustrated in Figure 5.3.

True search engines use software agent technologies to search the Internet for keywords and place them into indexes. Then for example, when you key in weather and Ljubljana, the search engine will go to its indices, stored in a database, and come up with a list of URLs of Web sites which contain the keywords weather and Ljubljana. Try keying in "weather Ljubljana" at http://www.altavista.com if you want to see how it works.

You can register your site with the directory search engines by filling out some forms. There are services that will do this for you for a fee. For true search engines, it is important to put the keywords people will be using in their search arguments in the Web site text or meta tags. ***Meta tags*** are part of a Web site text not displayed to users but accessible to browsers and search engines for finding and categorizing Web sites.

Banner Ads Banner ads are another way of driving traffic to your Web site. ***Banner ads*** are the little ads that appear on Web sites. For example, Figure 5.4 shows the opening screen at the travel site, TRIP.com. Notice the banner ads for bid4vactions.com, Skyteller, and Jetvacations.com. They are there because the advertisers believe that people who visit TRIP.com are likely to also be interested in the products or services they offer.

If you click on the banner ad for bid4vacations.com, you'll end up at the site, an auction site for vacations. Bid4vacations.com may have paid TRIP.com for placing the banner ad on the TRIP.com site, or it might compensate TRIP.com on the basis of click-throughs or some other measure of effectiveness. ***Click-throughs*** are simply a count of the number of people who visit one site and click on a banner ad and are taken to the site of the advertiser. Software is able to determine the source of visitors to bid4vacations.com and give an accurate count of the number who clicked through from TRIP.com so that TRIP.com can be compensated. Similar arrangements will be made by TRIP.com with the other advertisers on its site. As with most things involving the Internet, there is a wide variety of arrangements that can be made between cooperating Web sites. As illustrated in Figure 5.5, sometimes the arrangements are reciprocal. In this case, if you click on the Skyteller.com ad on the TRIP.com site, you'll be taken to the Skyteller site. There, you'll notice that there is a

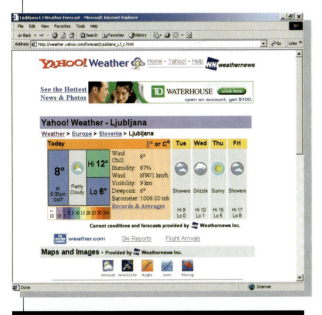

FIGURE 5.3

What's the Weather Like in Ljubljana?

FIGURE 5.4

Web Site Banner Ads

FIGURE 5.5

Reciprocal Web Site Banner Ads

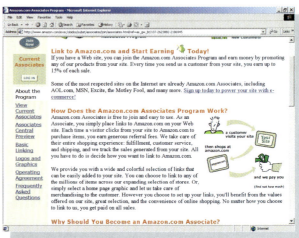

FIGURE 5.6

Become an Amazon.com Associate!

banner ad for TRIP.com. It could be that no cash will be exchanged between the two dot-coms for placing banner ads on each other's sites.

E-Mail and Viral Marketing E-mail marketing has proven to be especially effective for B2C e-commerce. Sites have various ways of asking for your e-mail address. Most commonly, you supply it when you order something so that the site can send you an e-mail confirmation of your order and let you know when your order has been shipped. Most sites, at the same time, will ask your permission to send you occasional e-mails announcing special sales or information that may be of interest to you about specials from other B2C companies. The more the dot-com knows about you, the more e-mail offers can be personalized to appeal to you. Much of what makes B2C e-commerce potentially so effective is the ability of companies to build customer databases and then use sophisticated data mining software to help in crafting personal appeals. Most people don't like to receive "spam" and immediately delete it from their e-mail inboxes without taking the time to read it. **Spam** is unsolicited e-mail from a company we have never done business with. Viral marketing is a technique that gets around spam.

Viral marketing encourages users of a product or service supplied by a B2C company to ask friends to join in as well. A good example is the arrangement that many information services such as Computerworld.com have to let us e-mail a copy of an article to a friend. In the e-mail, there is usually an invitation to visit the site to get acquainted with the products and services it offers. The e-mail also contains the name of the person who sent the article and permits the addition of a personal message. People are more likely to respond to an invitation that was initiated by a friend than one that comes from a company they are not familiar with.

Affiliate Programs *Affiliate programs* are arrangements made between e-commerce sites that direct traffic from one site to the other and by which, if a sale is made as a result, the originating site receives a commission. Usually this is done using a banner ad. So, for example, if the TRIP.com site and Bid4Vacations.com had an affiliate arrangement, TRIP.com would receive a commission on a sale made to a customer who clicked on the Bid4Vacation.com banner ad on the TRIP.com site. Amazon.com has over 500,000 associates. This means that there are over 500,000 Web sites with Amazon.com banner ads directing customer traffic to the Amazon.com site. Every time a customer clicking on the Amazon.com banner ad on an associate's Web site buys something at Amazon.com, the associate receives a commission of up to 15 percent of the amount of the sale. Information on Amazon.com's associate program is available on its Web site, part of which is reproduced in Figure 5.6.

Selling to Existing Customers One of the keys to success in the B2C space is to encourage customers to continue to buy from you. As do traditional businesses, B2C entrepreneurs call this "repeat business." It doesn't do you much good to spend a lot of money on marketing programs if customers buy from you only once. One of the most effective ways of generating repeat business is to build a customer database and use it for

Business to Consumer E-Commerce   203

eBags builds its customer database through frequent flyer mileage sweepstakes and viral marketing.

FIGURE 5.7

Viral Marketing on the eBags Site

FIGURE 5.8

RedEnvelope's Home Page—A Very Well-Designed Site

e-mail permission marketing (defined in Chapter 2). In pursuing its path to profitability, one prominent B2C retailer, eBags.com (http://www.eBags.com), is using the following strategy:

1. It uses many of the marketing techniques previously described in this chapter to attract customers to its Web site including banner ads, affiliate programs, and ads in traditional media.

2. Its Web site is well-designed and easy to use, content-rich, with multi-view photos of products, detailed product descriptions, and customer ratings.

3. It is building a database of customers and asks for permission to e-mail them information on special offerings at reduced prices. As shown in Figure 5.7, it uses a frequent flyer mileage sweepstakes and viral marketing to help build the database.

4. As customers return to the site, eBags analyzes their usage patterns and learns which products they're most interested in. It adds this information to its database and uses a powerful data mining tool to help personalize offers to its customers.

5. It keeps track of the conversion rate and the amount of the average sale. **Conversion rate** is the percentage of customers who visit the site who actually buy something.

6. Knowing the number of visits it receives each day, as well as the conversion rate and average sale amount, eBags can easily project sales revenue per day. Knowing its costs, it is able to determine where the breakeven point lies. It can also quickly forecast the effect on profits if it's able to increase the number of visitors to the site, increase the conversion rate, or increase the average sale amount.

Remember the Importance of Merchandising

Remember that a B2C business must do an effective job of merchandising. That means it must understand its customer base well enough to be able to select products that will appeal to them and that are attractively displayed. An example of a company that does this well is RedEnvelope (http://www.redenvelope.com), as shown in Figure 5.8. RedEnvelope is a site that specializes in gifts. It takes its name from the Asian tradition of presenting gifts in a red envelope to signify good fortune, love, and appreciation. It is a site worth visiting to see how an e-tailer has combined attractive design, ease of use, and skillful product selection. It offers a wide variety of products for the gift-giver. One of its most creative features is a category called "Express Gifts," designed to serve procrastinators. If you order a gift from this category before midnight, RedEnvelope guarantees that it will be delivered the next day.

You Must Execute Well

Executing well simply means that when a customer places an order on your Web site, you have to follow through and execute the necessary business processes to get the item to the customer in a timely fashion. Some of the things good B2C sites do are to immediately send an e-mail acknowledgement of the order, containing all of the order details and an estimated ship date. This reassures the customer that the order was received and is in process. An order number and instructions for follow-up with customer service are also included. When the order is shipped, the customer receives another e-mail giving details on the shipment such as a carrier tracking number and expected delivery date. Making it easy to return unwanted items is also important. Some B2C companies include easy cost-free instructions for returning items along with each shipment. Clicks-and-mortar companies have an advantage in this respect if they permit online customers to return items to the local store. Part of the shake-out among online toy retailers began during the holiday selling season in 1999, when toys were not delivered in time for Christmas morning. The reputations of some retailers suffered so much by their failure to execute well that they never recovered. (See the box entitled "Order Fulfillment Execution Can Be a Differentiator.")

Pick Your Sector Carefully

One of the reasons a company such as eBags is successful is that it picked its sector carefully. It was started by several executives from Samsonite Corporation who really understood the suitcase and bag business. In addition, this particular space was not overcrowded with competitors. By contrast, see what *Business Week* recently said about online pet stores:

> Only a few months ago, online pet-supply retailers were all the rage among investors. But if the past week's events are any indication, selling kibble and kitty litter in cyberspace is shaping up as a doggy business. Late last week, Petstore.com announced that it had laid off an "undisclosed number" of its 200 employees. The company declines to elaborate. This despite the fact that the site has raised $150 million in venture capital, most of which came from Discovery Communications, owner of the Animal Planet cable station. That announcement came just after a merger between two of the smaller players, Allpets.com and PetQuarters.com.
>
> Meanwhile, Petplanet.com announced that it has hired an investment banking firm to help "study the company's capital requirements," leading some analysts to predict it may be facing a money crunch. And Pets.com's stock, which was offered at $11 a share, continues to fall. It now trades around $2.
>
> Analysts aren't surprised. "Everyone and his uncle knew this was an overcrowded space," says Matt Stamski, a senior analyst for Gomez Advisors. The question is: Who's going to survive?[18]

Watch the Competition

Watching the competition is good advice for any business, but it's especially important for B2C businesses. The reason for this is that, as we have previously dis-

---

Order Fulfillment Execution Can Be a Differentiator

A study conducted during the 2000 holiday season found that 67 percent of items ordered online were not received as ordered, and 12 percent were not received in time for Christmas.

The study also found that orders placed at sites operated by traditional retailers and mail-order catalogers were on time 7 percent more often than those from pure play online retailers. Large companies outperformed smaller ones in areas such as order time, delivery date information, and percent of on-time deliveries.

One advantage that traditional retailers have shown over pure plays is that their return policies are less time-consuming and complex. For example, just 51 percent of pure plays provided preprinted labels; nearly 80 percent of traditional retailers and catalogers provided them.

Some sites executed well. Amazon.com, Gap.com, Godiva, Lands' End, LL Bean, Nordstrom, and OfficeMax were rated highly for performance in order time, delivery time, and on-time delivery.[19]

cussed, retaining customers is obviously one of the keys to e-commerce success. Because it is so easy to lose a customer to a competitor who comes up with a better idea, it's important to be alert to what the competition is up to. You should try to "get inside the heads" of your competitors as a way of anticipating what their next move might be. Put yourself in their place. What would you do next if you were them?

Business to Business E-Commerce

B2B e-commerce is the term used to define e-commerce that takes place between business organizations. As we mentioned earlier in this chapter, B2B is where the most money will be spent in e-commerce. This is what you should expect would be the case, because most business transactions take place between businesses as they buy and sell from and to each other. Manufacturers buy parts from their suppliers and services from accounting and law firms, consulting companies, and suppliers of office equipment. Retailers buy products to put on their shelves from manufacturers, wholesalers, and distributors. Trade is global; companies do business with other companies in countries all over the world. You probably have an idea how common this is, if you look at the tag inside your blouse or shirt and see Malaysia, Sri Lanka, Peru, or Mongolia.

Common estimates are that somewhere between 85 and 90 percent of trade dollars are in the B2B space and that 85 to 90 percent of e-commerce dollars will also be spent in the B2B space. The Gartner Group estimates that global e-commerce will total $7.3 trillion by the year 2004, and that 90 percent of it will be in the B2B space.[20] Clearly, B2B e-commerce is worth learning more about.

One of the most important ways that B2B e-commerce contrasts with B2C e-commerce is in the importance of relationships. In B2C e-commerce, establishing a relationship with your customer is important because you want customers to return to your Web site to buy from you again, rather than lose them to a competitor. In the B2B space, relationships are even more important. Businesses tend to form longer-term relationships with some of their most trusted trading partners. Suppose you're the manager of production in a manufacturing firm when you suddenly get an unexpectedly large rush order from one of your best customers. It will be much easier for you to order the necessary materials you need to build and fill that order if your suppliers are people you've done business with over a period of years. They know you, you know them, and just like a friend, you can count on them to step in and help you out when you need it. Think of how difficult obtaining those needed materials would be if you tried to obtain them quickly from companies you had never done business with before. Relationships do matter.

One of the things Peter Keen and Mark McDonald point out in their book *The E-Process Edge* is that in the world of e-commerce, innovation counts for nothing if you can't execute your business processes in an exceptional fashion. They note that e-commerce ". . . more and more involves a complex network of relationships to operate between the enterprise, its customers, intermediaries, complementors and suppliers."[21] This is illustrated in Figure 5.9. ***Intermediaries*** add services that can be provided better by a specialist company

The Importance of Relationships in the B2B Space

Relationships are important in the B2B space, but many companies do not pay enough attention to the way they seek out alliance partners and then maintain their relationships.

Relationship mismanagement will become a bigger problem as alliances and partnerships become an essential part of the B2B landscape. In the past, companies often took pride that they were vertically integrated and did not have to rely on other companies. Now, companies have seen the value of focusing on their core competencies, the things they do best, and outsourcing non–core operations to alliance partners with world-class competencies in areas such as computer processing or logistics.

But even as companies focus on core competencies, the outsourced functions still need to be performed. This requires that the outsourced relationships be well managed. You don't have to own a function in order to manage it.[22] ❖

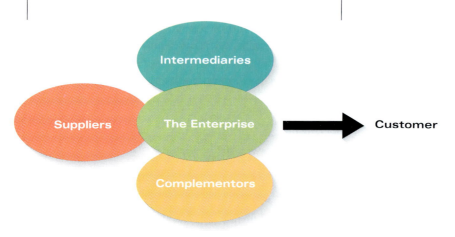

FIGURE 5.9

The Value Network[23]

than by the enterprise itself. Examples include such categories as information services and fulfillment. **Complementors** provide products and services that complement the offerings of the enterprise and thereby extend its value-adding capabilities to its customers. Yahoo!, for example, has 10,000 complementors providing services such as weather information, financial news, general news, and so forth that add value to the Yahoo! site. Keen and McDonald go on to emphasize the importance of trading partner relationships in forming a company's value network. A *value network* is all of the resources behind the click on a Web page that the customer doesn't see, but that together create the customer relationship–service, order fulfillment, shipping, financing, information brokering, and access to other products and offers. Some of these resources are provided by software, some are outsourced to trusted trading partners, some are provided by electronic links to alliance partners, and others are handled by enhanced internal business processes—exception handling, for example. The point is that managers in the e-commerce world have many more choices in how to deliver products and services at their customers' moment of value. If a trusted trading partner can perform an essential function better than your company can internally, you have the potential for a winning combination for yourself, your trading partner, and your customer.

Corporate Purchasing Segments

In the B2B space, the most attention has traditionally been given to the ways that e-commerce could stream-line the purchasing of materials. This does not mean that e-commerce applications such as in sales, transportation, and payments are not important and growing areas; it simply means that attention has been devoted to purchasing because this is where the most money is being spent. Purchasing applications are usually divided into three segments:

1. Purchasing of direct materials
2. Purchasing of indirect materials (MRO)
3. Purchasing of services

Direct materials are materials that are used in production in a manufacturing company or are placed on the shelf for sale in a retail environment. They are called direct because they have a direct relation to the company's primary business. *Indirect materials* (commonly called MRO materials) are materials that are necessary for running a modern corporation, but do not relate to the company's primary business activities. *MRO* is the acronym for **m**aintenance, **r**epair, and **o**perations materials. Examples of MRO materials include everything from ballpoint pens to printer toners, three-ring binders, repair parts, and lubricating oil.

Finally, services might be corporate travel, consulting services, hiring of part-time workers, and the like. Although there are B2B solutions for the purchase of services, most activity in the B2B space is focused on either direct materials or MRO, so this is where we'll focus our discussion.

Purchasing of Direct Materials

One of the most important contributions to a company's effectiveness made by its purchasing department is in the purchase of direct materials—searching out reliable sources of supply, negotiating issues such as price, quality, and delivery performance expectations, and monitoring supplier performance. In the typical setting, a purchasing department reaches an agreement with a supplier based on an estimate of quantity required over the course of a year. Then, as goods are needed to satisfy production requirements, the supplier will be asked to ship a certain amount to one or more

INDUSTRY PERSPECTIVE ".com"

Dairy Industry Gets Set for B2B Exchange

If buyers and sellers of dairy products can't find each other quickly enough, the products could spoil. That presented an opportunity for a B2B exchange called Dairy.com, owned and operated by MomentX Corp. in Dallas. Dairy.com plans to operate a B2B exchange that will let dairy product producers and processors buy and sell raw dairy products using a spot-market model.

Currently, spot market transactions for liquid dairy products such as skim milk and cream are made through phone calls and faxes. This is a risky and inefficient process since dairy products have to be delivered and used while they're fresh. In contrast, Dairy.com's business model promises to match buyers and sellers and let them complete a transaction in a matter of minutes.[24] ❖

---

factory or store locations. The requested quantity will be determined by the purchasing company's current needs, often by a Just-in-Time (JIT) or Collaborative Planning, Forecasting, and Replenishment (CPFR) system, as we discussed in Chapter 2.

Electronic Data Interchange

The foundation of B2B e-commerce, the most important form of B2B e-commerce today in dollar volume, is Electronic Data Interchange, which we introduced to you in Chapter 2. *Electronic data interchange (EDI)* is the direct computer-to-computer transfer of transaction information contained in standard business documents such as invoices and purchase orders, in a standard format. EDI replaces paper documents with digital records exchanged between trading partners' computers. Although EDI can be and is used to support MRO purchasing, it is most commonly used to support the purchase of direct materials.

While there are other ways to exchange digital information between businesses, EDI practitioners say that if it doesn't meet the three criteria above it is not EDI.

1. *Computer-to-computer exchange* means just that. It must travel from one company's computer system to another's over a telecommunications network of some sort, be it a private network, a VAN, or the Internet. (For more discussion on network options, please see *Extended Learning Module C.*) Computer to a fax machine does not count.

2. *Standard business documents* means that EDI is restricted to standard business forms such as purchase orders, purchase releases, advance shipping notices, invoices, and the like, and not free-form business correspondence such as business letters.

3. *Standard format* means that trading partners have agreed that the digital information exchanged will be in a standard format so that the computer systems at either company can interpret what is being transmitted and use it for further processing without human intervention.

When you think about it, EDI is really a pretty simple idea. If a large company such as General Motors sent a paper purchase order to one of its suppliers, for instance Gates Rubber Company, it would probably have printed the purchase order as output from a computer system that determined the quantity needed, the date the material was needed, the plant to send the material to, and so forth. Then someone would have stuffed the purchase order into an envelope with the proper postage and mailed it via the U.S. Mail in Detroit. Three or four days later, the purchase order would have arrived at Gates Rubber Company in Denver, Colorado, the envelope opened and the purchase order information entered into Gates's order entry computer system. Since the purchase order information was in GM's computer and ended up in Gates's computer, it would be faster, cheaper and more accurate to simply send the order from GM's computer to Gates's computer directly. Essentially, this is what EDI does. It drives paper out of the interorganizational business process of buying and selling materials between trading partners.

EDI has been in use for over 30 years. It has spread by what is called a "hub and spoke" manner. (See Figure 5.10.) For example, a large company such as GM (the hub) decides to use EDI to support a JIT manufacturing

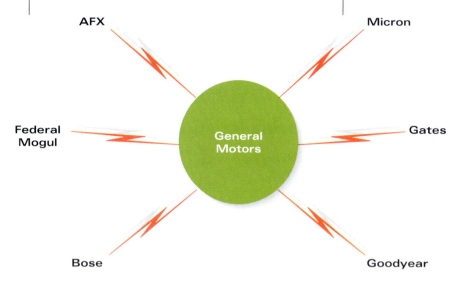

In a typical EDI "hub and spoke" arrangement, the large company, in this case GM, is the hub. It mandates EDI relationships with its smaller trading partners, called spokes. A large hub such as GM will have thousands of trading partners as EDI spokes.

FIGURE 5.10

An EDI Hub and Spoke Arrangement

process at its assembly plants. The purchasing department at GM notifies its parts suppliers (such as Gates—the spoke) that it expects Gates to be able to accept and transmit standard business documents using EDI from now on. Often, the message was conveyed to the spoke company in terms that made it clear the spoke company had no choice but to accept EDI transactions from the hub if it expected to continue to do business with them. In early systems, spokes had to accept orders from hubs in data formats that were proprietary to the hub, and not standard. This meant that Gates, for example, had to accept a purchase order from GM in one data format, another from Ford in Ford's proprietary format, and another from Toyota in Toyota's format.

Today, Gates has over 600 EDI trading partners. If each one sent EDI transactions to Gates in a proprietary format, you can imagine what a mess it would be for Gates's IT programmers to translate each hub's transactions into the data format Gates needs for its internal computer systems.

To address the concerns of the spokes, industry groups developed industrywide standards for EDI transactions, so that a purchase order, for example, had the same format no matter which hub it came from. It soon became apparent that cross-industry standards made more sense, inasmuch as industry members did business with companies in other industries as well. Cross-industry standards called ANSI X12 and, later, another one called EDIFACT were developed and adopted. ANSI X12 is most popular with EDI users in the United States, while EDIFACT is more widely used in Europe and in international trade generally.

Value-added networks (VANs) make it easier for trading partners to establish telecommunications links with each other. Rather than sending EDI transactions directly from a hub company to a spoke company, or vice versa, companies usually send a stream of orders to many trading partners directly to a VAN. This eliminates the requirement for a company to establish an individual computer-to-computer connection with each one of its trading partners. (For a company with hundreds or thousands of trading partners, this could get complicated.) Instead, all EDI transactions are sent to a VAN and the VAN places them in an electronic mail box for each trading partner. Other trading partners do the same thing. Then, once or twice a day, for example, Gates's computer connects with the VAN and downloads all EDI transactions from all of its trading partners at one time, as illustrated in Figure 5.11. VANs also provide translation services between different versions of EDI standards, audit services, and control services, and will even translate EDI messages from hubs to fax messages for smaller spokes who are not prepared to conduct true EDI. Translating from EDI to fax and vice versa makes it appear to the hub company that a small trading partner is using EDI and is thus not a cause for exception processing at the hub.

Next-Generation EDI

Although EDI is very effective, it has not had widespread acceptance beyond hub companies. Typically, smaller companies use EDI only because it is a requirement forced upon them by their larger trading partners (recall Wal-Mart's EDI policy from Figure 2.6 in Chapter 2). The primary reason EDI is shunned by smaller companies is that it can be complicated to set up and administer. Typically, resources must be devoted to es-

What Should Allright Distributors Do?

Allright Distributors is a small distributor of electronic parts and supplies located in Canton, Michigan. Sales are about $20 million annually. They have a LAN-based system using Pentium III PCs to support an integrated order entry, inventory control, billing, and accounts payable system. The system was installed about two years ago and replaced a much more cumbersome and expensive system that operated on an IBM AS400 mid-range computer.

One of its major customers is MichCon, the local natural gas distribution company, which is in the process of implementing a strategic EDI Program. Under the program, MichCon has a goal of getting the 20 percent of its suppliers who represent 80 percent of its purchases into an EDI-based trading relationship by mid-year. The impetus behind MichCon's effort is to obtain the benefits of speed, accuracy, and cost reduction it has realized from its early EDI implementations from suppliers who represent the majority of its purchase dollar volume.

MichCon has approached Allright and asked them to consider converting their trading relationship to one that is based on EDI using ANSI X12 standards. The MichCon implementation would be Allright's first EDI application. Janis Rowlison, Allright's sales manager, to whom the request was directed, is anxious to comply with MichCon's request since MichCon is Allright's single largest customer.

Janis has turned to the IS Director, Paul Stuart, and asked for his help in identifying the steps they would have to take in order to develop an EDI capability. Paul has done a little research and was appalled by the uncertainties surrounding EDI standards, VANs versus the Internet, security issues, the need for translation software, and the like. He has also learned that the specific format of each EDI message to be used has to be agreed upon by each set of trading partners before they can begin to use EDI. He can foresee that the MichCon initiative would require him to be involved in meetings to get the MichCon message formats completely understood so that he could handle them correctly. He sees that VANs and translation software would make his life easier, but that they would cost money. He also sees that the MichCon scenario is only the tip of the iceberg. Soon, there would be other customers who would want to use EDI with Allright. There could be meetings with each one of them as well, and more meetings was the last thing he felt he needed.

Paul tells Janis and the president, Heather Cadwell, that he does not see how Allright can accommodate MichCon's request. He goes on to suggest that setting up an EDI relationship with MichCon could cost more than it was worth.

Janis is furious. Her income is largely commission-based, and she has no intention of risking the loss of all of MichCon's business. She tells Heather that Paul should be fired, that the company should find an IS director who can be responsive to the demands of the business, or pretty soon there won't be any business!

Heather sees that she needs to deal with the issue quickly, and decides that the controller, Marie Zayots, might have some valuable input. She also wonders if it might not be time to call in an outside expert for some advice....

Discuss the Allright situation with your team and see if you can help Heather reach the best decision for her company. ❖

---

tablishing precise procedures under which EDI transactions will be exchanged between two companies. These procedures include transaction formats, exception procedures, and so on. Once the procedures are documented, two trading partners exchange test transactions to be sure everything works well before live transactions are exchanged. All of this takes a significant commitment of time and resources, and in many cases smaller companies do not see benefits from EDI flowing to them (other than keeping the hub company as a customer).

There are many efforts under way now to create a new generation of EDI for B2B transactions that would be easier to set up and use, and would therefore be more

210 CHAPTER FIVE Electronic Commerce

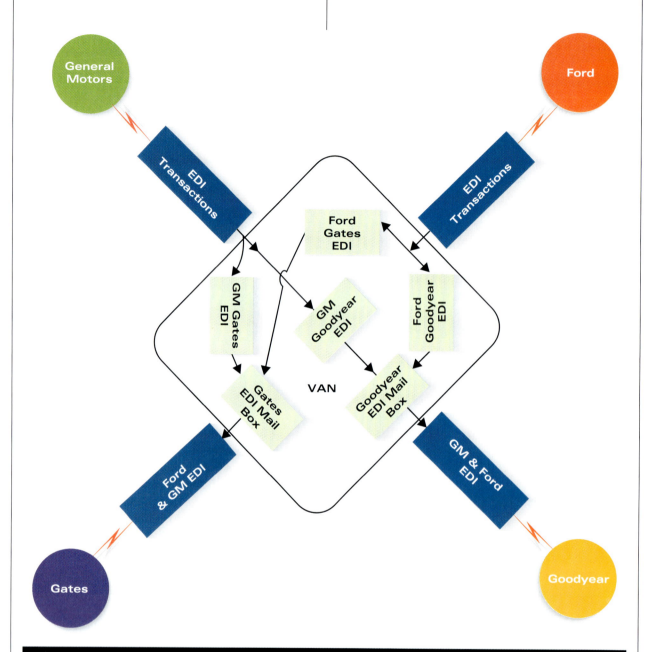

FIGURE 5.11

How Value-Added Networks Facilitate EDI

attractive to smaller companies. The vision for next-generation EDI is that a company could create a purchase order on a PC Web form, and send it out over the Internet to a company it has never done business with before. The transaction would contain within itself access to the intelligence for a computer at the receiving company to interpret it and begin to process it, much the same as if it were a purchase order received in the mail and opened by a human. Most of these efforts involve the Internet as a substitute for private networks or VANs because the Internet is cheaper. Many of them are built around an emerging technology for the Internet called XML. ***XML (eXtensible Mark-up Language)*** is a language coming into use for the production of Web documents and as the basis for the exchange of business documents.

You know HTML as the coding language used to create Web pages. HTML uses tags to control the way that text and images are represented on Web pages. XML is related to HTML because they are both subsets of a language called SGML (Standardized Graphi-

```
<PersonName>
    <PersonNameTitle>Ms</PersonNameTitle>
    <PersonFirstName>Wanda</PersonFirstName>
    <PersonMiddleName>Wilma</PersonMiddleName>
    <PersonLastName>Worthington</PersonLastName>
</PersonName>
```

In XML, unlike HTML, the names within the tags tell you the meaning of the data.

FIGURE 5.12

XML Example

ON YOUR OWN

A Range of Possibilities for New EDI

Below are links to Web sites of groups that are working on alternatives to traditional EDI where XML plays a role. Take a look at each of them and see if you can find one that, in your opinion, holds the most promise for the future. Feel free to see if you can find articles on the Web which compare and contrast the alternative approaches to support your conclusions.

1. RosettaNet: http://www.rosettanet.org
2. BizTalk: http://www.Biztalk.org
3. eCo Framework: http://www.commerce.net/projects
4. Electronic business XML (EbXML): http://ebxml.org
5. XML EDI Group: http://xmledi-group.org ❖

---

cal Markup Language), a powerful language used for the production of technical documents for many years. XML uses tags as well, but the big advantage it has over HTML is that you can insert words into the tags that let both computers and human beings understand the meaning of data contained between the tags (see Figure 5.12). This holds great potential for improving the effectiveness of search engines and, importantly, great potential for making the exchange of business documents between large and small companies much easier. EDI will be around for a long time because it has become a legacy system in large companies. Legacy systems are IT systems that were installed many years ago and still continue to perform well even though they become increasingly difficult for programmers to maintain as they get older. In the near future, at least, we expect to see large companies continue to use private networks or VANs for transmitting EDI transactions because they believe they are more secure and reliable than the Internet. As more and more small companies join the next generation EDI bandwagon, we expect them to use the Internet instead of the more expensive private networks and VANs. The next generation of EDI, whatever form(s) it eventually takes, should truly make the benefits of electronic exchange of standard business documents available to companies of all sizes, all over the world. The *On Your Own* project in this section asks you to compare some of the current ideas for next generation EDI that are currently in the works.

Purchasing of Indirect Materials (MRO)

As described in the accompanying Transportation Industry Perspective box (page 212), corporate purchasing departments do not want to be bothered with the paperwork required to process purchase orders for MRO materials, but at the same time, they do not want to let MRO purchases go completely uncontrolled. While the amounts on individual MRO purchase orders are small, collectively they can add up. To deal with this problem, many purchasing departments negotiate with MRO providers for discounted prices on a range of items. What used to be done is that the MRO supplier would print a custom catalog for the company showing the items that could be ordered and insert a price sheet showing the prices. If an administrative assistant needed to order supplies, he or she would find the item in the catalog, call the MRO supplier, and the item would be delivered the next day. E-commerce solutions for MRO do about what you would expect them to do. The paper catalog is replaced by an electronic catalog available through a Web browser on the PCs located on desktops throughout the corporation. Powerful search engines locate the items needed, and they are ordered using shopping cart technologies similar to the typical B2C retailer, sent to the MRO supplier electronically, and delivered to the desktop the next morning. Many of the same advantages previously discussed with Web retailing are present here as well: Ordering can be faster and more convenient, offerings and prices can be changed instantaneously, call centers can be integrated with the Web site, and broadband technologies can enhance the buying experience.

INDUSTRY PERSPECTIVE

Transportation

BNSF: Making the Trains Run on Time

One of North America's largest railroads, BNSF had negotiated a contract with Boise Cascade Office Products, arranging to purchase pens, pencils, paper, paper clips, and other goods at discounted prices. But many employees were still purchasing such products from local retailers and spending much more than was necessary.

BNSF did an analysis and found they were spending $3 million a year with Boise and $8 million with others. Clearly, the discounted arrangement with Boise Cascade was not working the way it was intended to work as employees bypassed the system.

BNSF has recently installed a new automated system to fix the problem. Employees are now required to buy office supplies over the company Intranet, where their browsers interface with the new system. When an order for office supplies is entered, it is routed electronically to Boise Cascade and products are shipped.

The system is working as planned. Company officials note that the corporatewide deployment of the new system has resulted in great savings. Paying list price or even 10 or 20 percent off with local shops just does not compare with buying from the corporate catalog online at 50 to 60 percent off.[25] ❖

B2B Marketplaces

B2B marketplaces seem to be a natural for the Web. *B2B marketplaces* are Internet-based services which bring together buyers and sellers. They have the potential to bring together large numbers of buyers and sellers, thereby giving buyers more choices and aggregating demand for the sellers. Transaction costs can be reduced, resulting in potential savings for both buyers and sellers. The operator of the marketplace often has software that facilitates matching buyers and sellers and helps them with the transaction. For example, one commonly used technique is to have the marketplace conduct a reverse auction. *Reverse auction* is the process in which a buyer posts its interest in buying a certain quantity of items, and sellers compete for the business by submitting successively lower bids until there is only one seller left. Marketplaces usually make their money by charging a transaction fee for their services.

In a recent *Harvard Business Review* article,[26] Kaplan and Sawhney analyzed the B2B marketplace landscape and observed that there are at least four variations on the common theme, depending on whether a company is buying direct or indirect materials (Kaplan and Sawhney call them manufacturing inputs and operating inputs, respectively) and whether or not the purchasing is systematic (i.e., repetitive) or spot, where the buyer needs to fulfill an immediate need at the lowest possible cost. The four categories of B2B marketplaces they identified, as illustrated in Figure 5.13, are

1. *MRO Hubs.* **MRO hubs** facilitate the sourcing of MRO materials without focusing on one particular industry.
2. *Yield Managers.* **Yield managers** create spot markets for operating resources such as manufacturing capacity, labor, and advertising. For example, if a radio station has some unsold advertising time slots it could post them on a yield management Web site and sell them to the highest bidder. In a way, it is similar to what airlines do with unsold airline seats at the last minute.
3. *Online exchanges.* **Online exchanges** make it easy for purchasing managers to purchase commodities or near-commodities needed for production when demand peaks all of a sudden or a traditional source of supply is disrupted. The marketplace makes it easy for buyers and sellers to conduct transactions without the need for negotiating contracts or establishing longer-term relationships.
4. *Catalog Hubs.* **Catalog hubs** are like MRO hubs except that they are industry-specific.

B2B marketplaces are still evolving. We expect that *Digital Darwinism* will be at work here as well, and not all of them will succeed. They seem to hold the most

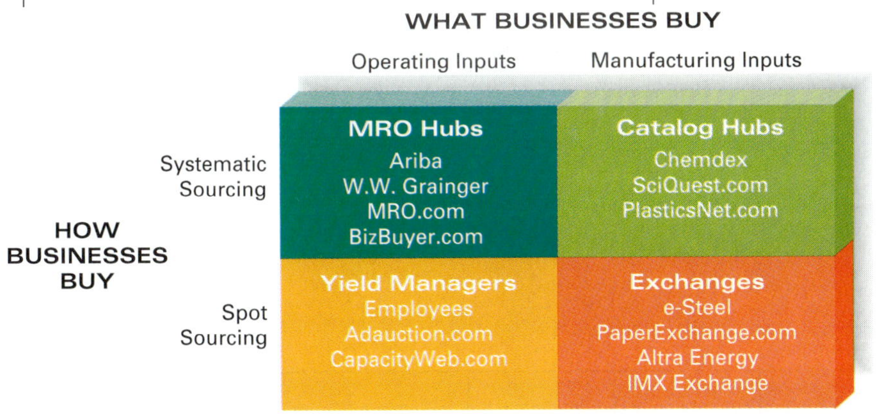

FIGURE 5.13

The B2B Matrix

promise in the MRO space inasmuch as relationships are often not as important here. The risks of doing business with a new supplier are lower. Working with a new direct materials supplier presents risks of shutting down an assembly line because of late delivery or quality problems. In addition, you have to remember that the legacy EDI systems of many large companies are the way that the supply chain is managed, and these systems, while complicated to set up, are working well. Finally, many suppliers will try to avoid letting anyone get between them and their customers. (Remember in Chapter 2 how we described all the tactics the airlines are using to recapture their best customers from travel agents and cybermediaries.)

Intranets and Extranets

An *intranet* is an internal organizational Internet that is guarded against outside access by special security software called a firewall (see Figure 5.14). *Extranets* are intranets that are restricted to an organization and certain outsiders, such as customers and suppliers. In contrast to intranets and extranets, the Internet can be accessed by anyone, although, of course, many Web sites require user names and passwords for access.

The Way Intranets Are Used

Intranets are used to facilitate communication within an organization and to manage many internal business processes. It would be hard for you to go into a modern office today and not see a PC on almost every desk. Giving employees access via their Web browsers to information that used to be available on paper can result in tremendous cost savings as well as provide assurance that the information on the corporate Intranet is the most current information available. For example, just about every organization of any size has an employee handbook in which the human resources department expounds policies regarding fringe benefits, vacations, sick leave, and the like. Putting the handbook on the corporate intranet makes it readily accessible to most employees, and when changes are made, a broadcast e-mail can be sent out asking employees to take notice. Intranet applications can range from simple ones such as these to putting expense reports and other forms online, newsletters, employee feedback, and sophisticated knowledge management systems.

Extranets

Extranet applications really follow the same principles as intranets except that the audience is expanded to include persons external to the organization, most often customers and suppliers. Extranets are used to share product and inventory information with customers and suppliers, news and information, and as a collaboration platform for joint projects. Extranets can be a vehicle for implementing more advanced supply chain management and customer relationship management systems. *Supply chain management systems* are interorganizational systems that drive time and cost out of the supply chain by fostering closer collaboration between trading partners. CPFR, discussed in Chapter 2, is a good example of a supply chain management system.

IDC, of Framingham, Massachusetts, divides customer relationship management applications into three segments: sales automation software, marketing automation software, and customer support and call center software. Sales software is designed to manage sales functions, from high-end processes such as account/contact management and list management, to low-end processes such as simple contact management. Marketing software assists with such things as campaign management and execution and list management and telemarketing. Customer support and call center applications are designed to enhance the management of relationships with existing customers.[27]

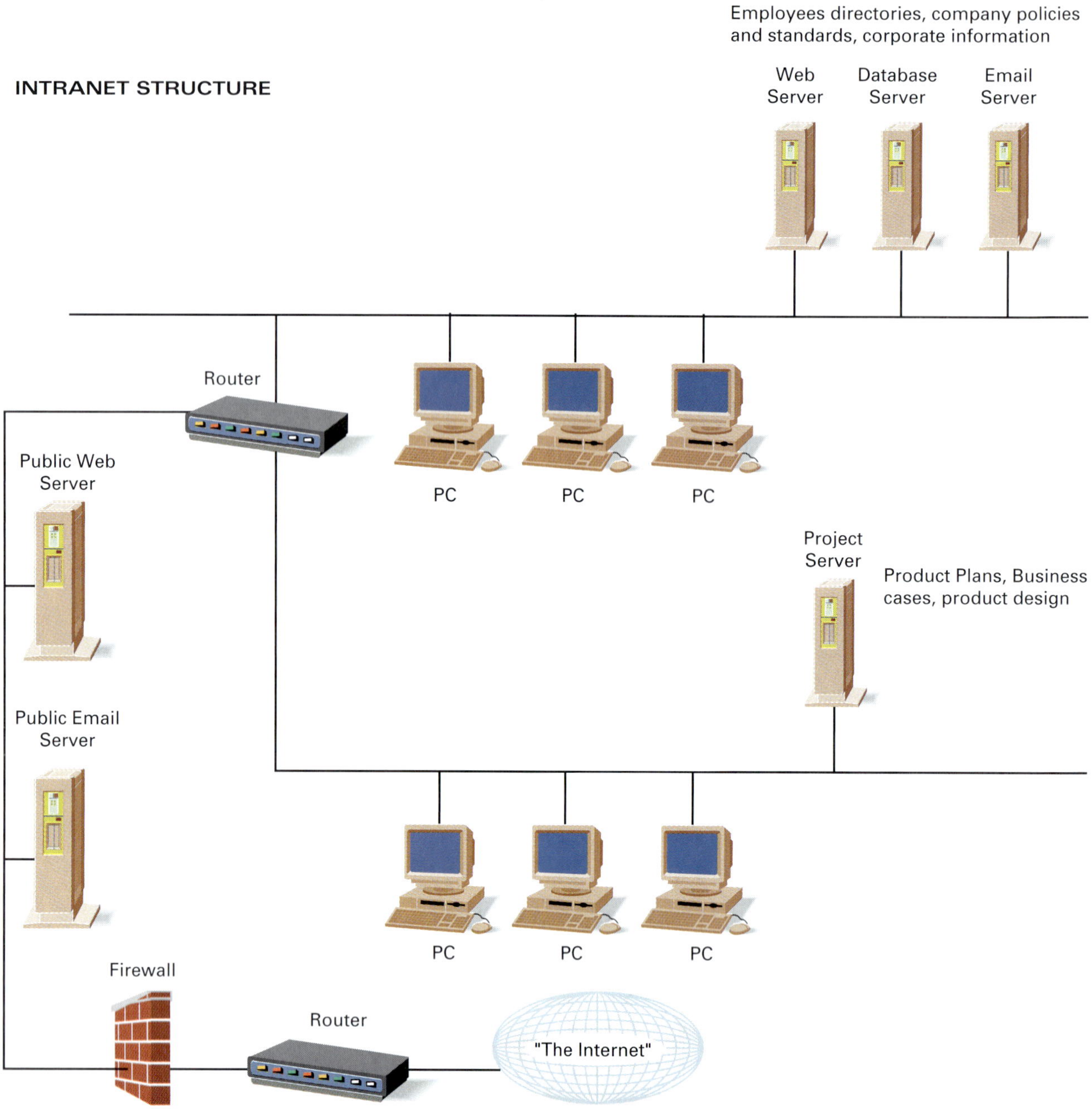

CHAPTER FIVE Electronic Commerce

INTRANET STRUCTURE

FIGURE 5.14
Intranet Structure

The Role of Government in Promoting E-Commerce

Local, regional, and national governments can play a key role in promoting the adoption of e-commerce technologies among consumers and businesses. You know by now that effective telecommunications networks are a requirement for conducting e-commerce. In many parts of the world, the telecommunications company is either owned by or controlled by the government, although there has been a trend toward privatization in recent years. The growth of e-commerce can be hurt by unenlightened government telecommunications policies. For example, networks can be subpar in performance, but low on a government's priority list for upgrading. In some countries, Internet access can be very expensive. For example, in the United States and several other countries, the cost of a local telephone call to connect you to your ISP is the same, whether you surf the Net for hours or just log on to quickly check your e-mail and then log off. In other countries, users are charged by the minute, which discourages Internet usage.

Perhaps most important is whether or not governments "walk the e-commerce talk." Governments in most countries are the largest single buyer of goods and services. If they adopt purchasing and payment policies that encourage the use of e-commerce, as the United States and other governments have done, they foster the spread of e-commerce throughout the nation.

Some local and regional governments are making it easier for citizens to conduct their affairs with governmental bodies over the Internet. For example, as illustrated in Figure 5.15, the State of Maryland in the United States permits businesses and private citizens to do many things over the Internet that used to involve getting in your car, driving to a state office, and standing in line. You can even get a fishing or hunting license or a boat registration form online.

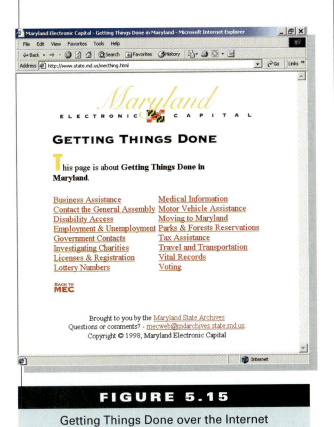

FIGURE 5.15

Getting Things Done over the Internet in Maryland

E-Commerce Payment Systems and Digital Cash

In order to complete an EC transaction, the seller must be paid. There are many possibilities for how this may be accomplished. Three possibilities are discussed below:

1. Traditional and next-generation EDI
2. Credit Cards and Smart Cards
3. Electronic Bill Presentment and Payment

Traditional and Next-Generation EDI

Just as there are traditional EDI transactions for purchase orders and other standard business documents, there are EDI transactions for payments. The use of EDI for payments is called *Financial EDI (FEDI)*. Financial EDI has not gained the same acceptance as EDI for one simple reason. Corporate treasurers, who are responsible for managing corporate cash, have not seen it to be advantageous to speed up payments to suppliers. When a payment is dropped into the mail, the payer can earn interest on the money until the check is cashed by the supplier. Oftentimes, corporate treasurers will see that a payment is mailed in time to reach the supplier by the due date, but the check will be drawn on a bank in another part of the country that will take days to clear. An electronic payment would clear much faster, and the payer would lose the use of that money for those extra few days.

Next-generation EDI approaches include FEDI transactions as a part of their proposed solutions. Still, the obstacle to more widespread acceptance of FEDI is not technical, but the reluctance of human beings to change their business processes. In the United States, the federal government is moving forward aggressively with electronic payments, encouraging them for businesses and even for direct deposits to the bank accounts of Social Security recipients.

Credit Cards and Smart Cards

In many countries, credit cards are the most common method of payment for e-commerce transactions, particularly in the B2C space. In the early years of B2C, consumers were reluctant to enter their credit card numbers on a Web site for fear that they would be stolen. Then it was pointed out that you were much more likely to have your credit card number stolen by a waiter in a restaurant than by a thief lurking on the Internet. Still, the lack of widespread use of credit cards by consumers in some countries, such as China and India, creates hurdles that B2C e-commerce companies in such countries will need to overcome.

Smart cards are one option that has been experimented with for some time. Smart cards are plastic cards the size of a credit card that contain an embedded chip on which digital information can be stored. When the stored digital information is monetary, the smart card is called a stored value card. One of the best-known smart card initiatives is Mondex (see http://www.mondex.com in Figure 5.16). The Mondex chip contains an "electronic purse" that can be loaded with electronic cash and then spent at retailers who have a Mondex card reader. Electronic cash is transferred from the buyer's Mondex card to the seller's device. Electronic cash can be added to a Mondex card by using a telephone connection to your bank. The Mondex solution is one possible answer to the micropayments issue we discussed earlier in this chapter, making it possible to purchase low-value items on the Internet. We discuss more about Internet digital cash and smart cards in the next chapter.

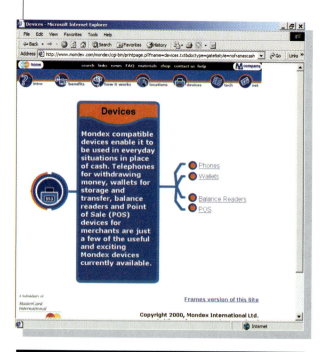

FIGURE 5.16

How Mondex Works

Electronic Bill Presentment and Payment

We all get bills in the mail every month, from the gas and electric company, the telephone company, the cable TV provider, department stores, and credit card companies. It costs money for the companies to print and mail the bills, and it costs us money to put a check in the mail. A technique called Electronic Bill Presentment and Payment is just beginning to take hold to reduce the time and paper in this process (and save us some trees in the process). *Electronic Bill Presentment and Payment (EBPP)* systems send us our bills over the Internet and give us an easy way to pay them if the amount looks correct. Electronic bill payment systems available through our local banks or such services as Checkfree and Quicken have been around for a while. What is different with EBPP systems is that our bills appear on a Web site or arrive in our e-mail inboxes instead of our home mail boxes.

Security and Privacy Issues

Security

Effective security is essential for e-commerce to succeed. If you're not comfortable with the security of e-commerce transactions, you'll avoid them. Most people would. Therefore, it is important that adequate security measures be in place to assure that the e-commerce environment is safe from external threats.

The subjects of e-commerce security and, more generally, IT security are quite extensive. Entire books have been written on the subject. Highly trained information system security professionals specialize in the area, working to be sure that computers and telecommunication networks are safe. In this section, we're able to give you just a brief overview of this very important topic, focusing on the special issues related to e-commerce security.

Internet Security Issues

Although computer and communications security issues have been around years, the Internet introduced some new concerns:

1. In contrast to private networks and VANs, the Internet is an open network with worldwide connectivity. In Table 5.1 of this chapter we showed a survey that estimated there are currently

Corporate Computer Security Risks

A survey conducted for the FBI by Computer Security Institute found that 75 percent of the responding companies said they had been victims of a computer-related crime with an average loss of more than $400,000.

A *New York Times* article cited employees as the biggest threat to a company's security. Employees have been found to do everything from unauthorized reading of private e-mails, to attacking computer systems to shut down the entire business.[28] ❖

407 million users of the Internet worldwide. Security threats come from people, from external hackers and disgruntled employees. Hacker and cracker are terms that are often confused. Hacker is the term used by computer programmers to describe a programmer who lacks formal training, although the popular press uses it to describe a computer criminal. Cracker is the more precise term to describe a programmer who gains unauthorized access to a computer system. Security experts will ask you to imagine that "what if just 1 percent of Internet users were potential crackers." That would mean that there were 4.7 million of them worldwide, and their numbers are growing rapidly!

2. As you have seen, the Internet is great for forming communities and for sharing digital information. There is a worldwide cracker community complete with Web sites that share cracking tips. They even hold conventions, which incidentally are also attended by security consultants wearing black T-shirts to blend in with the crowd.

3. The Internet was not designed with security in mind, making it more vulnerable to attacks from viruses and denial of service attacks. Denial of service attacks generate high volumes of phony transactions directed to popular Web sites, thus effectively denying access to legitimate users. Sites such as eBay and Amazon.com have been victims.

E-Commerce Security Concepts

Protection of e-commerce sites from security attacks is built around the following key concepts:

1. *Confidentiality.* Information stored in a Web site's database must be protected from unauthorized disclosure. Access to information must be on a "need to know" basis. Customer credit card numbers is an example of the kind of information that must be protected.

2. *Integrity.* Care must be taken to see that information in databases is accurate and not changed without proper authorization.

3. *Availability.* Information must be made available when needed and protected from accidental destruction (e.g., fires or floods) or from deliberate destruction by unauthorized persons.

4. *Authentication.* Systems must be in place to verify that a user seeking access to a computer system is who she says she is. Typically, this is accomplished through user names and passwords. In the future, we'll see more secure means such as those that employ biometrics (discussed in the next chapter).

5. *Nonrepudiation/auditability.* Procedures should be developed so that the origin and destination of electronic transactions can be verified. For example, if your company receives a purchase over the Internet, you would want to verify that it actually came from GM before you shipped a couple of truckloads of material. Digital signatures are the most promising techniques to deal with nonrepudiation. **Digital signatures** are digital codes that can be attached to an electronic document to uniquely identify the sender, much the same as your handwritten signature uniquely identifies you.

Some Common Security Tools

Security professionals have software tools available to help them protect sites. You're familiar with antivirus software packages and, we hope, have one installed on your PC and keep the virus files up to date. Two common techniques used to protect corporate sites are firewalls and intrusion detection software.

Firewalls are designed to protect private networks, typically intranets and extranets, from unauthorized intrusion. Firewalls can be either hardware or software, or a combination of both. (Figure 5.14 shows how a firewall is positioned in an intranet.) **Intrusion detection**

Honeypots

Computer security experts sometimes use "honeypots" to lure and trap crackers. They are called honeypots because honeypots are used to attract wild animals such as bears who are coming too close to people's homes and need to be trapped and set free in remote locations.

In the computer security setting, a honeypot is a computer on your network the sole purpose of which is to look and act like a legitimate computer although it actually is configured to interact with potential crackers in ways to capture details of their attacks. The more realistic the honeypot can be made to appear, the longer the attackers will stay occupied on the honeypot and away from your production systems. Also, the longer the cracker stays using the honeypot, the more you'll learn about the cracker's techniques. You may be able to use this information to identify the attackers and what they are looking for. This information could be used to apprehend them or, at a minimum, improve your defenses against future intrusions.[29] ❖

---

software attempts to detect when a security breach has occurred so that the intruder can be either observed and identified or expelled.

Designing Corporate Security Procedures

IT security professionals will tell you that 100 percent security is unattainable. Even the Web site of the Federal Bureau of Investigation (FBI) is cracked from time to time. Security professionals suggest that the approach to take is to undertake a risk assessment and then pick from the selection of available protective measures. Your organization will need to decide how much it should spend on IT security, and this is dependent on your risks. The greater the risks, the more that should be spent on protective measures. Finally, it is highly recommended that security audits be undertaken from time to time, which involves hiring computer security professionals to employ all the techniques that computer criminals would to break into your site, from technical tricks to using various schemes to discover employee passwords. Sometimes all it takes is to go into an office and look for passwords attached to PCs with yellow stickies.

Privacy

Like security, privacy has been an issue in the IT world for some time. (See Table 5.5 for Web sites of some privacy advocates.) The Internet and e-commerce, however, have magnified the potential problems. The central issue of e-commerce privacy is how marketers can use information collected on individuals for personalized marketing appeals without violating the privacy rights of individuals. At its core, the e-commerce privacy issue is an ethical issue. You should have the right to know what information is collected about you,

TABLE 5.5 Privacy Advocates Web Sites

Name of Organization	Web Address
Center for Democracy and Technology	www.cdt.org
Electronic Frontier Foundation	www.eff.org
Privacy Foundation	www.privacyfoundation.org
Privacy International	www.privacyinternational.org
Privacy Rights	www.privacyrights.org

THE GLOBAL PERSPECTIVE

European Privacy Laws

Privacy laws were passed in Europe more than five years ago that prohibit data stored in databases in the EU from being transferred to other countries unless the other countries have similar privacy protection laws. The United States is one of the countries that does not have similar laws.

In 2000, a "safe harbor" agreement was negotiated between the United States and the EU which permits U.S. companies to transfer data from EU databases in the absence of similar laws as long as they complied with the EU regulations.

Some experts believe that U.S. citizens will soon demand the same sort of protection from U.S. companies that U.S. companies give to residents of Europe. This will happen when U.S. customers and employees see that your company is providing a higher level of protection to European residents than they are to people in the United States.[30] ❖

---

to review it periodically to be sure it is accurate, and to determine whether or not it can be shared with others.

According to a report issued by the U.S. Federal Trade Commission,[31] the five core principles of IT privacy are

1. *Notice/Awareness.* Consumers should be given notice of an entity's privacy protection policies before any information is collected from them. Many e-commerce sites have privacy policies posted, but critics say that many of them are so long and filled with legal language that the average person does not take the time to read them.

2. *Choice/Consent.* The principle of choice or consent gives you the chance to consent to any other uses of the information that a Web site collects from you. Often, when you are registering for a Web site, it will tell you that it would like permission to send you special offers from time to time either from itself or from other companies with whom it would like to share information about you. You have the choice, then, of "opting in or opting out." ***Opting in*** is the term e-marketers use for your giving permission for alternative uses of your personal information. ***Opting out*** is when you say no.

3. *Access/Participation.* Access and participation refers to your right to view the information a company has collected about you so that you can verify that it is appropriate and correct. This is particularly important in an e-commerce environment since so much information can be collected about you without your knowledge. Cookies are one widespread technique for doing this. ***Cookies*** are small records deposited on your hard drive by a Web site containing information about you. Sometimes it's personal information such as your user name and password for the site that lets you log on faster. Sometimes it is information about your behavior on the site. While originally used to save you time and to keep you from seeing the same ad over and over, cookies are now used extensively for target marketing.

4. *Integrity/Security.* You have the right to expect that a Web site is maintaining adequate controls over personal information stored about you in its database. There have been many instances of Web sites being cracked and personal information stolen.

5. *Enforcement/Redress.* The fifth principle is that there be adequate enforcement mechanisms in place in the event that a company breaches any of the previous four principles. This is an area of much controversy. In Europe, for example, there are explicit regulations in force to protect the privacy of individuals. In the United States, e-businesses are lobbying for self-regulation. The Children's Online Privacy Protection Act (COPPA), which specifically addresses acceptable information collection and use practices for children under age 13, was enacted in the United States in 1998. There are many strong supporters in the United States for additional laws to protect individual privacy, and we will probably see such laws enacted in the near future.

KNOWLEDGE WORKER'S -LIST

The Growth of Global E-Commerce. Experts who are in the business of forecasting the growth of global e-commerce may differ in their estimates, but all agree that we can expect to see tremendous growth in the next few years. Forrester Research estimates that e-commerce will make up 8.6 percent of worldwide goods and services by the year 2004, and Goldman Sachs estimates that B2C e-commerce could amount to as much as 15 to 20 percent of total U.S. retail sales by the year 2010, up from 1 percent in 1999. Most experts agree that 85 to 90 percent of e-commerce sales will be in the B2B space.

Business to Consumer (B2C) Business Models. What Works and What Doesn't Work. Selling products over the Internet, e-tailers have found that commodity-like products work best, and digital products work the best of all, because these can be bought, paid for, and—most of all—delivered immediately. Successful e-tailers have learned the importance of good Web site design and marketing to attract consumers, the importance of merchandising, and the importance of fulfillment to get repeat customers. E-tailing has become more difficult to succeed in now that the easy money early days of the Internet are behind us. Now, investors are looking for profitable ventures.

The Variety of Options for Business to Business (B2B) Business Models. While relationships can be important in the B2C space, they tend to be more important in the B2B space because of the interdependencies that exist among trading partners, particularly for direct materials. EDI has facilitated the smooth operation of trading partner relationships by driving paper out of many interorganizational business processes. EDI has not spread beyond large "hub" companies and their smaller "spoke" trading partners because it can be difficult to set up and administer. Next-generation EDI techniques hope to address this problem. Internet-based B2B marketplaces are beginning to appear. They hold out the promise of cost savings by making it easier for buyers and sellers to find each other and for buyers to obtain better prices. Their future, however, is as yet unclear.

CLOSING CASE STUDY

Who Needs Disappearing Inc.?

You probably already know this, but you should be very careful about what you write in your e-mail messages because someone else may be reading them. In the first place, the courts in the United States have established that companies have the right to read e-mails transmitted on corporate networks. Responsible corporations will be sure that employees are notified that such a policy is in place, but not all corporations are responsible. Also, hackers can always find a way to see what you're saying in your e-mail messages if they want to. So be careful.

Most e-mails don't disappear. They are copied onto every computer they touch to be sure they aren't lost. Most messages pass through several computers on their path across the Internet (or even a corporate intranet) from sender to receiver. Even if both sender and receiver delete their e-mail messages, several other copies will be around for a while.

The concern to corporations is the possibility that e-mail will be read by unwelcome prying eyes, especially attorneys in lawsuits filed against the corporation.

A start-up company based in San Francisco, Disappearing Inc., hopes to solve this problem for corporations with software that makes e-mails legible to only the sender and recipient. Its software encrypts the messages so that only the sender and recipient can understand them. The software is available for free on the Web. Companies that want to use it for document retention pay $4 per user per month.

With the document retention feature, the sender can also put a time limit on the e-mail so that e-mails can be maintained for legally specific time periods, after which they disappear.

One of Disappearing Inc.'s first corporate clients is an international accounting and consulting firm, which

The Role of Government in Promoting E-Commerce. National, regional, and local governments can play a significant role in promoting the adoption of e-commerce by businesses in several ways. First, they can help to see that the necessary telecommunications infrastructure is in place and is priced to encourage e-commerce in those instances in which the government owns the telecommunications company. They can also encourage businesses to do business with them electronically by using e-commerce techniques to purchase goods and services. Finally, they set an example for businesses by offering improved essential governmental services to citizens over the Internet.

E-Commerce Payment Systems. In the B2C space, most e-commerce transactions are paid for with credit cards in the United States. Credit card payments have limitations for e-commerce because they are not suitable for small amounts and because there are many countries where the use of credit cards is not as well accepted as in the United States. Smart cards and digital cash have been proposed as alternatives, but they have not yet achieved widespread acceptance. Electronic Bill Presentment and Payment is an emerging technique that holds the promise of driving paper out of the B2C billing process for companies such as utilities, department stores, and credit card companies. Although Financial EDI has been available for B2B payments for some time, it has not attained wide acceptance, partly because of corporate treasurers' reluctance to employ it.

The Importance of Security and Privacy Issues. The number of Internet users is increasing rapidly, and if only a very small percentage of them are inclined toward computer crime, the threat to e-commerce businesses is still great. Part of the problem is that the Internet was not designed with security in mind, the way private networks were. Security threats must be taken seriously by e-businesses. Risk assessment should be made and appropriate security measures installed. Periodic security audits should be conducted as well.

The protection of individual privacy in e-commerce is a contentious issue. Using information obtained about individuals with their full knowledge and using it responsibly permits e-businesses to provide us with more personalized service. Concerns that some sites will not use personal information in a responsible manner has brought calls for legislation in the United States, along the lines of what has been in place in Europe for some time. ❖

---

is offering the software to its clients so that e-mails can be destroyed as effectively as paper documents are destroyed by shredders. This helps them reduce risks associated with old e-mail messages.

Disappearing Inc.'s challenge is to convince more corporations that there is a need for its software in order to avoid doing a disappearing act themselves.[32] ❖

◀ Questions ▶

1. Assume you are an associate with a venture capital firm. You have been approached by the founders of Disappearing Inc. who have asked your firm to consider making an investment in their company. What information would you want them to provide on possible competition before you take their request to the managers of your firm?
2. Do you think Disappearing Inc. has a product that will appeal to corporations? Why or why not? Is their product one that might be attractive to consumers as well as corporations? Why or why not?
3. Can you think of additional features that could be added to the software to make it more appealing to potential users?
4. Like all e-commerce start-ups, Disappearing Inc. will need to ramp up sales to reach profitability before it runs out of cash. What do you think would be effective marketing strategies for the company in the B2C and B2B spaces?
5. Assume that management will try to sell its software in other countries as soon as possible. How might the marketing strategies used in the United States change when approaching the European market? In Asia? How might they remain the same?

Electronic Commerce
Business and You on the Internet

Getting Your Business on the Internet

Let's say you've decided it might be fun (and profitable) to become an e-tailer and establish an Internet-based business. You know that many e-tailers don't make it. You'd like to be one of the ones that's successful. There are a lot of resources on the Internet that can help you with the task of selecting the right business in the first place, getting the site up and running, deciding who should host your site, marketing your site, understanding privacy issues, and obtaining the funds you need to pay your expenses until your business begins to show a profit. In this section, we've included a number of Web sites that can help you with setting up your business on the Web. On the Web site that supports this text (http:www.mhhe.com/haag select "Electronic Commerce Projects"), we've provided direct links to all these Web sites plus many, many more. These are a great starting point for completing this Real HOT section. We also encourage you to search the Internet for others.

Competitive Intelligence

The first thing you need to have is an idea for the business. What is that you would like to sell? Is it a product or a service? Make sure you have expertise, or something special to offer. After you've come up with a candidate, it's time to see how much competition is out there and what they're up to. One of the things many new business owners fail to do is to see how much competition is out there before they launch their business. They just get what they think is a great idea and then move ahead with it. A better idea is to look at what competitors are in the space you're considering. You may find there are too many and that they would be tough competition for you. Or, you may find that there are few competitors and the ones who are out there aren't doing a terrific job.

The Web sites we've listed below give you some guidance on how to perform an analysis of the competition before you start. After you've looked at them to get an idea of how to perform a competitive analysis, look at some of the Web sites of businesses in the competitive space you're thinking of entering. As you do, answer the following questions.

A. How many sites did you find that are offering the same product or service as you're planning to offer?

B. How many are in your country and how many are in other countries?

C. Did you come across a site from another country that has a unique approach that you did not see on any of the sites within your own country?

D. Evaluate the competitor sites based on some of the criteria listed in Table 5.4 (page 200).

E. Try to determine how successful the competitor sites are.

F. Either abandon your initial choice because it would be too risky to enter, or formulate a strategy for your site that would enable you to have a competitive advantage.

Storefront Software

If you decide to sell products, there is software that you can use to make it easy to create a Web site. There are many products to choose from. Some will cost you a lot of money, but others are free. FreeMerchant.com, for example, has a Totally Free Merchant, a Bronze Package for $29.95 per quarter, a Silver Package for $19.95 per month, and a Gold Package for $29.95 per month. What you get in each of these packages is listed in detail on the FreeMarket.com Web site. Even the Totally Free Merchant has such features as Internet Store Hosting, a catalog Importer, and a Secure Shopping Cart. Since there are many options to choose from, it would be worth your while to do a little research to see if you can find an article that compares current versions of storefront software. A site like ZDNet.com (http://www.

Electronic Commerce: Getting Your Business on the Internet   **223**

zdnet.com) would be a good place to start your search. Build up a list of features that you will need for your e-tailing site, and then compare your needs with the features offered by the various software packages. They all sound good when you read about them on the vendors' Web sites so be sure you take a "test drive" of the software before you sign up.

Another possibility would be to sign up for a shopping mall. Find your way to Amazon.com's zShops or Yahoo!Store and see what you think of these alternatives. Web sites of some of the available storefront software packages as well as the Amazon.com and Yahoo.com home pages are listed on page 225.

Finally, you'll need a way for your customers to pay you for what they buy. This involves getting a merchant account which permits you to accept credit cards. Most of the storefront sites we've listed will explain how merchant accounts work and will help you get a merchant account (see http://www.bigstep.com, for example). Hosting services can help you with this as well. As you continue to consider your new business, answer the following questions.

A. What features have you decided your storefront software must provide?

B. How have you evaluated the pros and cons of using a storefront software package versus the options offered by Amazon.com and Yahoo!? Why did you choose one and not the other?

C. Just about all of the software and services offer to provide you with additional features at an additional cost. Which additional features have you decided you need?

D. Whenever you're considering buying an IT product or service, it's a good idea to ask current users what they think about it. See if you can track down users of your preferred selection, send them an e-mail, and ask them what they like and dislike about it. You might be surprised at their answers.

Hosting Services

You've got some options here. You can decide to acquire the necessary computer and communications hardware and software to manage your own technical infrastructure or you can let a specialist firm do it for you. Unless you're really into the technical side of things, it's probably better to work with a firm that specializes in it. They are called *Web hosting services* and there are plenty of them around to choose from. Cost, reliability, security, and customer service are some of the criteria you might want to use in selecting a hosting service. If you're planning to have your business located in a country with poor telecommunications services, don't forget that you can choose a hosting service located in a country with a more reliable telecommunications infrastructure, anywhere in the world. In the table on page 225, we've included the Web sites of several hosting services from the United States and other countries. You might want to check out WebHostDirectory and TopHosts. com first. They're like shopping malls for Web hosting services. As you consider Web hosting services, answer the following questions.

A. Compare the costs of the various hosting services. Were you able to find one that seems to be within your budget?

B. How can you evaluate the reliability of the various Web hosting services?

C. How can you be sure that a candidate Web hosting service will provide adequate security for your business?

D. How can you evaluate the quality of a Web hosting service's customer service? What do you have a right to expect from them in the way of customer service?

E. This is another instance of its being a good idea to ask current users what they think about the service they're getting from your selection. See if you can track down users of your preferred selection, send them an e-mail, and ask them what they like and dislike about it. Once more, you may be surprised at their answers.

Marketing the Site

In this chapter, we discussed several options for marketing a Web site: registering with search engines, banner ads, viral marketing, affiliate programs, and marketing to existing customers, as well as using traditional media. Deciding on the marketing mix that will be most effective and still permit you to stay within a reasonable budget will be critical to the success of your venture. We've provided some sites on page 225 that should be helpful to you. Some of them explain how to use some of the techniques we've listed in greater detail. You may want to consider employing an Internet marketing consultant to help you lay out a marketing plan. We've listed a couple of them. Also, your storefront software or Web hosting service may also offer to help you market your site. You may want to evaluate their offerings as well. As you consider how to market your site, answer the following questions.

A. How have you defined your target market? Who are the people that will be most interested in your product or service?

B. Which of the available marketing techniques have you selected as being most appropriate to market your site? Why have you selected this particular marketing mix?

C. Is there a place for traditional media in marketing your site? If so, what is it, and how did you justify it?

D. What marketing methods are competitive or similar sites using? Can you learn from them? Can you do better?

E. What have you decided about using the services of a marketing consultant? How did you justify your decision?

F. Are there marketing services offered by your storefront software or hosting service that are appropriate for you to use?

Privacy Issues

You should develop a privacy policy and post it on your Web site. This will assure your customers and potential customers that you will treat personal information obtained about them with the utmost care and respect. There are third party services that you can use which will review your security and privacy practices periodically. You'll pay for such services, but when you use them you're permitted to put their icon on your site. This is further assurance to your customers that yours

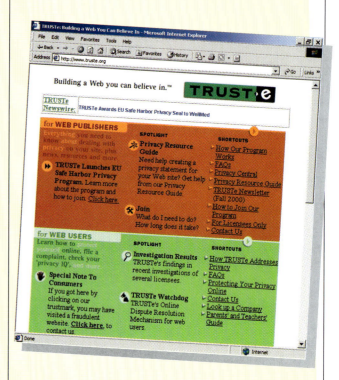

is a safe and responsible site. Some sites who highlight their privacy policies and sites of assurance services are listed in the table on page 225. As you consider privacy, answer the following questions.

A. Draft a privacy policy appropriate for your site. What does it say?

B. Do you feel you need the services of a company such as Truste or WebTrust? Why or why not?

C. Do you feel you need the services of Verisign? Why or why not?

Getting Funding

Now comes the hard part. It used to be the case that anyone with a business plan with the word Internet in it would have lots of investors ready to throw money at them. A little bit of healthy reality has set in, and now investors want to see your "path to profitability." There are five basic types of investors you might approach to fund your business. Traditional lenders, such as banks, are not very likely candidates for you unless they are one of the few that also operates a venture fund. Banks are not known for taking risks with their depositors' money and like to lend to businesses that have a track record. They also like to have collateral in case a loan goes bad. Venture capitalists typically do not invest in raw start-ups (although some do), so they're probably not a good bet. Besides, they're notorious for taking a big chunk of your company and getting seats on your board of directors so they can fire you if necessary. Angel investors are one good place to look. Angel investors are wealthy individuals who like to help budding entrepreneurs. Oftentimes, they are successful e-commerce entrepreneurs themselves, and want to give a little back. E-commerce incubators are another good possibility. They provide a supportive environment for start-ups and offer either direct venture funding or access to funds. Incubators don't accept every start-up, so if you can get into one, it can be a good thing. Finally, you can always fall back on friends and family. This is how many start-ups get their initial funding, along with the maxed-out credit cards of the founders. Some advice on funding can be found at the sites below. As you begin to look for funding, answer the following questions.

A. Develop a rough estimate of the amount of funding your company will need from the time of inception until it hits breakeven. What is that point?
B. On the basis of this estimate, which of the possible funding sources do you think you might approach first? Why?
C. What questions would you ask if you were being approached as a potential investor in your business idea?
D. What are the key things that have to come together in the right way in order for your business idea to be successful?
E. See if you can list the advantages and disadvantages of each funding source and make a list of which ones to approach in priority sequence. What does your list look like?

Web Sites for Help in Starting a Web-Based Business

Competitive Intelligence	Address
Society of Competitive Intelligence Professionals	http://www.scip.org
Fuld & Company, Inc.	http://www.fuld.com
Competia Global CI Community	http://www.competia.com
Fast Company	http://www.fastcompany.com

Storefront Software	Address
Amazon.com	http://www.amazon.com
Bigstep.com	http://www.bigstep.com
Digital StoreFronts	http://www.digitalstorefronts.com
ECongo.com	http://www.econgo.com
Freemerchant	http://www.freemerchant.com
Iconomy.com	http://www.iconomy.com
Yahoo!	http://www.yahoo.com

Hosting Services	Address
Ameritech	http://www.ameritech-hosting.com
Miditech.com	http://www.miditech.com
TopHosts.com	http://www.tophosts.com
Verio	http://www.verio.net
Web@access	http://www.webaccess.com
WebFusion	http://www.webfusion.co.uk
WebHostDirectory	http://www.webhostdir.com

continued

Web Sites (concluded)

Marketing Your Site	Address
AdDesigner.com	http://www.addesigner.com
Atavia	http://www.atavia.com
Bannerite.com	http://www.bannerite.com
Daniel Janal: Internet Mkt.	http://www.janal.com
Google	http://www.adwords.google.com
Microsoft bCentral	http://www.submit-it.com
Wilson Internet Services	http://www.wilsonweb.com

Privacy Issues	Address
AICPA	http://www.aicpa.org
Engage, Inc.	http://www.engage.com
PrivacyChoices	http://www.privacychoices.org
Truste	http://www.truste.org
Verisign	http://www.verisign.com
WebTrust	http://www.cpawebtrust.org

Getting Funding	Address
Business Plan Preparation Service	http://www.bizplanprep.com
European Business Angels Network	http://www.eban.org
Growth Ventures Group	http://www.growthventures.com
HerAssistant.com	http://www.herassistant.com
National Business Angels Network	http://www.nationalbusangels.co.uk
Softbank Venture Capital	http://www.sbvc.com

KEY TERMS AND CONCEPTS

Affiliate Programs, 202
ANSI X12, 186
Asynchronous Transfer Mode (ATM), 186
Bandwidth, 182
Banner Ads, 201
Bluetooth, 171
Bridge, 185
Bus Topology, 181
B2B Marketplaces, 212
Cable Modem, 167
Catalog Hubs, 212
Category 3, 168
Category 5, 168
Clicks-and-Mortar, 192
Click-throughs, 201
Client/Server Network, 171
Coaxial Cable (Coax), 183
Communications Media, 181
Communications Processors, 185
Communications Satellites, 184
Communications Service Providers, 177
Complementors, 206
Computer Network, 165
Conversion Rate, 203
Cookies, 219
Demand Aggregation, 190
Digital Divide, 191
Digital Signatures, 217
Digital Subscriber Line (DSL), 165
Direct Materials, 206
Directories, 201
E-commerce, 190
EDI, 207
EDIFACT, 186
Electronic Bill Presentment and Payment (EBPP), 216
E-tailer, 192
Ethernet, 186
Ethernet Card, 168
Extranets, 213
Financial EDI (FEDI), 215
Firewalls, 217

Gateway, 185
Global Digital Divide, 191
Home PNA, 168
Indirect Materials, 206
Infrared, 183
Integrated Services Digital Network (ISDN), 186
Interactive Chat, 194
Intermediaries, 205
International Virtual Private Network (International VPN), 179
Internet Virtual Private Network, 179
Intranets, 213
Intrusion Detection Software, 217
Local Area Network (LAN), 179
Marketing Mix, 200
M-commerce, 192
Meta Tags, 201
Micropayments, 199
Microwave Transmission, 183
MRO, 206
MRO Hubs, 212
Multiplexors, 185
Network Hub, 169
Network Interface Card (NIC), 168
Network Topology, 179
Online Exchanges, 212
Optical Fiber, 183
Opting In, 219
Opting Out, 219
Peer-to-Peer Network, 167
PNA Adapter Card, 168
Private Network, 178
Public Network, 178
Pure Plays, 192
Repeaters, 184
Reverse Auction, 212
Ring Topology, 181
Router, 185
Satellite Modem, 167
Spam, 202
Star Topology, 181
Supply Chain Management Systems, 213
Switch, 169
Telephone Modem, 165
Transmission Control Protocol/Internet Protocol (TCP/IP), 186
Value Network, 206
Value-Added Network (VAN), 178
Viral Marketing, 202
Virtual Private Network (VPN), 179
Wide Area Network (WAN), 179
WiFi (Wireless Fidelity), 183
Wired Communications Media, 181
Wireless Access Point (WAP), 169
Wireless Communications Media, 181
XML, 210
Yield Managers, 212

SHORT-ANSWER QUESTIONS

1. What is the digital divide? What is the global digital divide?
2. List four advantages of B2C e-commerce over traditional retailing.
3. What is meant by the phrase "Digital Darwinism"?
4. Why are digital products the best to sell over the Internet?
5. What is the attraction of affiliate programs to e-tailers?
6. What is the essential difference between XML and HTML?
7. What is the difference between an intranet and an extranet? How are each of them used?
8. What are two or three examples of how governments can promote the adoption of e-commerce techniques?
9. Why has Financial EDI been slow to gain acceptance?
10. What is the difference between a hacker and a cracker?

SHORT-QUESTION ANSWERS

For each of the following answers, provide an appropriate question:

1. Business to Business (B2B), Business to Consumer(B2C), Consumer to Business (C2B), and Consumer to Consumer (C2C).
2. 407 million.
3. Pure Plays.
4. Interactive chat.
5. Micropayments.
6. Conversion rate.
7. 85 to 90 percent.
8. MRO hubs, yield managers, online exchanges, and catalog hubs.
9. Mondex.
10. Firewalls and intrusion detection software.
11. Cookies.

DISCUSSION QUESTIONS

1. In what ways can shopping over the Internet be more convenient for consumers? In what ways can it be less convenient?
2. Why is the ability to change prices instantaneously considered an advantage for e-tailers? Can you think of an instance in which personalized pricing could be a disadvantage for an e-tailer?
3. There have been a string of e-tailers running out of cash, not being able to attract more from investors, and going out of business. What are some of the main reasons for this? What are the keys to success in B2C e-commerce?
4. Under what circumstance would it be appropriate to consider using viral marketing? What are some of the other marketing techniques available for an e-tailer to use? Why is it important to consider a mix of techniques rather than just relying on a single one?
5. Why are relationships between companies so important in the B2B space? Give an example of an instance in which you might need to rely on a long-term relationship with a supplier to help you out with a business problem. Give an example of the risks a company might be taking if they chose to buy direct materials from a supplier they had never done business with before simply on the basis of price.
6. Why has traditional EDI been so slow to gain acceptance with small and medium-sized companies? How do some of the ideas for next-generation EDI intend to address this issue?
7. Describe the services provided by Value-Added Networks that make it easier for companies to exchange EDI transactions with each other. Why don't more companies use the Internet for EDI since it is much cheaper than using a Value-Added network?
8. What are the advantages and disadvantages of B2B marketplaces for buyers? For sellers? Why do some observers say that B2B marketplace operators have to be on the alert for Digital Darwinism in their space?
9. What is a denial of service attack? Why are denial of service attacks and other types of security breaches considered to be a threat to e-commerce? What approach should companies take to protect themselves from security threats to their e-commerce systems?
10. E-commerce businesses are lobbying for industry self-regulation on privacy, while many public interest groups and lawmakers are saying that legislation is required. What are the pros and cons of each point of view?

CHAPTER OUTLINE

INDUSTRY PERSPECTIVES

Retail
237
Growing Up with Speech Recognition

Health Care
239
Virtual Reality for the Betterment of People and Society

IT & Telecommunications
245
EZfone Makes Internet Phone-Calling "EZ"

".com"
247
Storage Space and Software for Rent/Free on the Internet

Manufacturing
250
OnStar Is Always Onboard while You Drive

IN THE NEWS

- **234** 3-D technologies on the Internet (Figure 6.3).
- **235** "Fruit flies like a banana." What does that sentence mean?
- **236** The automatic speech recognition market is expected to more than triple in revenue between 1992 and 1997.
- **240** Volvo's virtual reality system lets you experience a car wreck and the deployment of air bags.
- **241** Biometrics may use your breath as a password.
- **243** How electronic cash will work on the Internet (Figure 6.7).
- **244** Making almost-free long-distance phone calls over the Internet.
- **249** Almost 100 percent of 18-year-olds in Finland have cell phones.

FEATURES

- **238** **On Your Own** Understanding the Speed of Automatic Speech Recognition
- **244** **Team Work** Finding Electronic Cash on the Internet
- **249** **The Global Perspective** Buy Soft Drinks with Your Phone? They Do in Finland
- **249** **On Your Own** Which Internet Appliance Is Right for You?
- **253** **Team Work** Finding Home Appliances with a Brain
- **254** **The Global Perspective** Staying in Touch with Your Home from around the World
- **257** **Electronic Commerce** Finding Freeware and Shareware on the Internet

KNOWLEDGE WORKER'S CHECKLIST

In the Information Age, Knowledge Workers Understand . . .

1. Why some technologies are categorized as "emerging"
2. How emerging technologies are beginning to incorporate more of the senses
3. The dramatic changes occurring as a result of and on the Internet
4. The role of the wireless revolution in mobilizing people and technology
5. How emerging technologies will affect their personal lives

WEB SUPPORT

http://www.mhhe.com/haag

- 3-D Web sites
- Automatic Speech Recognition Systems
- Internet-Based Phone Calling Services
- Antivirus Software
- Games
- Screen Savers and Desktop Themes
- Shareware/Freeware Search Resources
- Messaging and E-Mail Software

Emerging Technologies
Innovations for Tomorrow

CHAPTER 6

CASE STUDY
High-Tech Hollywood Creates High-Quality Films

What do all these movies have in common—*Broken Arrow*, *Terminator 2: Judgment Day*, *Casper*, *Toy Story*, *Free Willy*, *Apollo 13*, *Forrest Gump*, *Braveheart*, *Die Hard 3*, *Roger Rabbit*, and *The Matrix*? Well, other than the fact that they were all Hollywood blockbuster movies, they all contained footage that was computer-generated or enhanced. It's true—many of the scenes you saw were never really filmed with a camera.

And that's true for almost all Hollywood movies today. Instead of actually filming scenes, producers capture certain images and use computer technology to enhance the scenes or combine portions of several scenes. In Hollywood today, screen sensation is all about visual effects. Of the over $1 billion spent on production costs for movies in the summer of 1995, $150 million went to visual effects costs. According to Greg Estes, product and technical marketing manager at Silicon Graphics, "Visual effects have become one of the main drivers in the business." Think about these scenes from some of the movies mentioned above:

- *Terminator 2: Judgment Day.* In this movie, producers used a technique called "morphing" to transform the bad terminator into different people—a woman, a police officer, and a security guard.
- *Free Willy* and *Apollo 13*. In these movies, a technique called "transparency" was used to create Willy's huge splashes in the water and the beautiful sunset view from the Apollo 13 capsule.
- *Die Hard 3*. If you think Bruce Willis was lying on the street when a car nearly hit him, think again. Using a technique called "digital recasting," producers were able to combine two scenes: (1) Bruce as he lay on the ground and (2) a car in the middle of the street just inches away from where Bruce wasn't.
- *Casper*, *Toy Story*, and *Roger Rabbit.* In these movies, producers developed three-dimensional characters and scenes to combine with real people and animated characters.
- *The Matrix.* Producers shot many scenes in this movie in true three-dimensional imagery. This imagery made many of the scenes seem more real than life and to jump off the screen.

Creating visual effects is not cheap. Many scenes that incorporate visual effects cost as much as $10,000 per second to create. Couple that with the fact that desktop graphics workstations capable of performing such techniques as morphing and digital recasting cost as much as $60,000 each, and you can see that Hollywood is spending a lot of money to get you into a movie theater.[1,2,3,4] ❖

Introduction

Hollywood truly has embraced high tech; for that matter, so have most businesses around the world, regardless of industry. Hollywood's high-tech focus includes some relatively new technologies, or what we refer to as *emerging technologies*. For example, digital recasting, morphing, and transparency are all important components of multimedia. You may be wondering why multimedia would be called an "emerging technology," especially when you can go to virtually any grade school anywhere in the country and see hundreds of young children learning to read, spell, and perform arithmetic using multimedia applications. Well, the term "emerging" doesn't necessarily mean brand new. We call a technology emerging if it falls into one of two categories:

- It is a technology that is so new that most businesses haven't exploited it.
- It is a technology that is fairly well-established, but businesses haven't fully exploited it.

In the first instance, we include such technologies as electronic cash, which facilitates Internet cash transactions. This is a very new technology. In fact, it's so new that many organizations still aren't certain how it will work or whether they even want their customers to make electronic cash purchases. These types of emerging technologies, for the most part, really are **new** technologies.

In the second instance, we include technologies such as automatic speech recognition (ASR). You can find many current uses of ASR—in cell phones, when you call for directory assistance, and in airline flight arrival and departure systems. But few organizations are exploiting the full benefit that ASR offers. We refer to these types of technology as *emerging* because the business world in general has yet to exploit their full potential.

Regardless of which technologies we describe as emerging or why, it's important for you to learn about them so you can determine how best to use them. And that's the focus of this chapter—emerging technologies, what they are, how they are being used, and how they may be used in the future. To facilitate our discussion of emerging technologies, we've grouped them into four categories (see Figure 6.1):

- **Emerging technologies for all the senses.** These include applications that incorporate one or more of the following features: three-dimensional images, automatic speech recognition, virtual reality, and/or biometrics. These emerging technologies enhance the presentation of information to you and allow you to interact with your computer beyond just using a mouse and keyboard.
- **Emerging technologies for the Internet explosion.** You may think that the Internet is a standard technology, buy many new technologies for and uses of the Internet are emerging. These include electronic cash, Internet telephones, high-speed Internet access, and Internet appliances.
- **Emerging technologies for the wireless revolution.** These include global positioning systems and wireless local area networks.
- **Emerging technologies for your personal life and home.** These include smart cards, intelligent home appliances, and a completely Internet-connected home. These will surely change how you live.

As you explore the emerging technologies we present in this chapter, you should constantly ask yourself two questions. First, are these technologies still emerging or have they become standard? After all, this book was available in 2001—maybe things have changed since then. Second, have other technologies surfaced that could be classified as emerging? Information technology is one of the most rapidly changing and dynamic aspects of the business world. How many new technologies have you seen in the last six months? What are

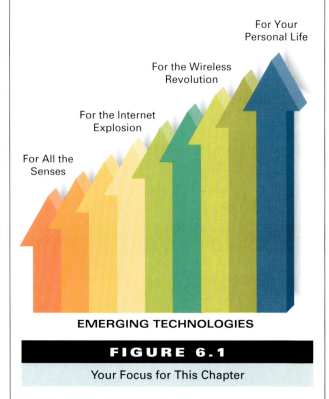

FIGURE 6.1

Your Focus for This Chapter

they? Which of the four categories would you place them in? Or do you need to create a new category?

Emerging Technologies for All the Senses

Throughout this text we've described information technology as a set of tools that helps you work with information and perform tasks related to information processing. It's a simple and accurate description, but some people forget that there are many types of information and that information can be presented in numerous different forms. Until recently, people working with technology have been content to work with information in traditional ways—entering text on a keyboard, viewing a graph on the screen, printing a document, and so on. But several technologies are emerging that promise to radically change that and allow you to work with information that appeals to the senses: three-dimensional imaging, automatic speech recognition, virtual reality, and biometrics.

3-D Technology for Real Sight

Traditionally, we have viewed information displays in two dimensions or pseudo three dimensions. In two dimensions, you see only length and width—for example, the first graph in Figure 6.2 is two-dimensional. In pseudo three dimensions, shades and shadows are added to create a display that is somewhat realistic (second graph in Figure 6.2). Because it's not truly three-dimensional, it's called "pseudo." Most personal productivity software packages available today are capable of producing pseudo three-dimensional views of graphs, photos, and artwork. But what they can't do is generate real three-dimensional images.

Real *three-dimensional (3-D)* technology presentations of information give you the illusion that the object you're viewing is actually in the room with you. You can see the depth of the image, turn it to reflect different angles to see its various perspectives, and in some ways understand the density of the object. Although 3-D technology is still in its infancy, it's already turning up in a number of areas—medicine, movies, video games, data visualization, science, education, and many others (see Figure 6.3). In the opening case study you saw how Hollywood is incorporating 3-D technologies into movies such as *Toy Story, Casper,* and *The Matrix.*

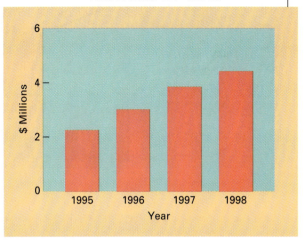

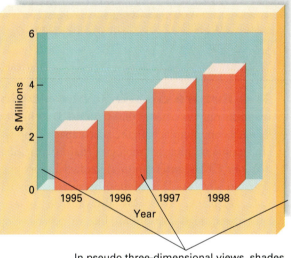

In pseudo three-dimensional views, shades and shadows are added to images.

FIGURE 6.2

Two Dimensions and Pseudo Three Dimensions

3-D technology is not really a stand-alone technology; instead, it's incorporated into other types of technology and IT systems. For example, a number of Web sites include 3-D representations of photos. The number is growing to the extent that many people believe we'll all be surfing the Internet in 3-D in just a few short years. This, of course, would increase the allure of the Internet for electronic commerce. 3-D will allow consumers to get a great real-life view of products before they buy them. 3-D technologies are also showing up in multimedia and virtual reality applications (which we'll discuss later in this chapter).

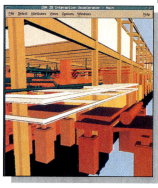

Like many Web sites, Lightscape (http://www.lightscape.com) generates 3-D images for your viewing. Soon all Web sites (even your personal one) will make use of 3-D technologies.

FIGURE 6.3
Three-Dimensional Applications

The Future of 3-D Technologies

It's really only a matter of time before 3-D technologies become commonplace. In the past, capacity and speed constraints of other technologies (hard disks, internal memory, CPUs, and monitors) made 3-D very expensive and slow. As Dan Mapes, president of Synergy-Labs, explains, "3-D was always seen as a very specialized, high-cost option, like an expensive spice from China. That day is passing fast."[5] Even today's inexpensive home computers have sufficient capacity and speed to generate 3-D images. It's just a matter of time before 3-D becomes a standard technology.

Automatic Speech Recognition

Conversing with Your Computer

People and computers have been engaging in normal conversation for many years now—in the movies. First, the computer captures and understands the words of the person; second, the computer generates speech in response to the words spoken by the person. For this to occur, two IT systems are needed, one for each phase. We refer to the first phase as automatic speech recognition and the second phase as speech synthesization. Of the two, automatic speech recognition is the real emerging technology that promises to forever change how people enter information and commands.

An *automatic speech recognition (ASR)* system not only captures spoken words but also distinguishes word groupings to form sentences. We refer to ASR as a system because it contains a number of IT components that work together. For example, an ASR system contains an input device (a microphone), software to distinguish words, and databases containing words to which your spoken words are matched. To distinguish words and sentences and match them to those in a database, an ASR system follows three steps (see Figure 6.4).

- **Step 1: Feature Analysis.** The first step of ASR is called *feature analysis.* Feature analysis captures your words as you speak into a microphone, eliminates any background noise, and actually converts the digital signals of your speech into phonemes. A phoneme is simply the smallest unit of speech, something most people equate with syllables. In Figure 6.4, you can see that the ASR system distinguished two phonemes in the word "tonight": "tə" and "nit." This is exactly what you would see if you looked up the word "tonight" in the dictionary to determine how to pronounce it. The feature analysis step then passes the phonemes to step 2.

- **Step 2: Pattern Classification.** The second step is called *pattern classification.* In it, the ASR system attempts to recognize your spoken phonemes by locating a matching phoneme

Emerging Technologies for All the Senses   235

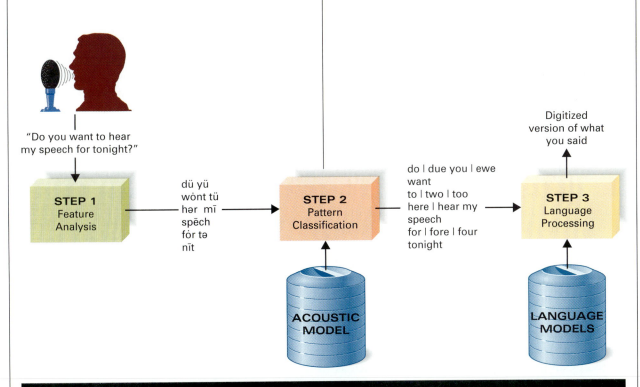

FIGURE 6.4

The Three Steps in Automatic Speech Recognition

sequence among the words stored in an acoustic model database. The acoustic model database is essentially the ASR system's vocabulary. In doing so, the ASR system is attempting to determine if it recognizes the words you spoke. Figure 6.4 shows that the system found two possible matches for "dü," the words "do" and "due." It also found multiple matches for "tü," "hər," and "fòr." So, it sends all these possibilities to language processing—step 3.

- **Step 3: Language Processing.** The third step is called *language processing*. In it, the ASR system attempts to make sense of what you're saying by comparing the possible word phonemes (generated in step 2) with a language model database. The language model database includes grammatical rules, task-specific words, phrases, and sentences you might frequently use. If a match is found, what you said is stored in digital form.

Step 3—language processing—is by far the most complicated step, because the ASR system must attempt to determine your exact words. For example, did you begin your sentence with the word "do" or "due," was your second word "you" or "ewe," and so on. This is definitely not a simple process for a computer; it may be for you, but it's not for a computer. Throughout this process, the ASR system must perform a number of tasks, including evaluating the inflection of your voice. In our example, you're asking a question. So the ASR system recognizes the inflection for a question and, thus, determines that your first word is "do," rather than "due."

Our example illustrates why ASR systems are called "recognition" systems instead of "understanding" systems. While conversing with another person, you can easily distinguish "do" from "due," "you" from "ewe," and so on, according to the context of the sentence in which the word is used. However a computer has a difficult time with this because it possesses limited interpretative capabilities. Consider this sentence: "Fruit flies like a banana." What does it mean? Well, in the context of gardening Olympics, it implies that if you were to toss a piece of fruit into the air, it would "fly" through the air in the same way a banana would if you were to throw it. More realistically, though, it means that a winged insect called a fruit fly is particularly fond of the taste of a banana. So, while an ASR system would be able to correctly recognize your words, it certainly couldn't determine whether you were talking about the gardening Olympics or the taste preferences of certain insects.

Types of Automatic Speech Recognition Systems

If you survey the current ASR systems that are available today, you'll find four different types—discrete, continuous, speaker-independent, and speaker-dependent. ***Discrete ASR*** systems require you to pause between each spoken word. This may seem a bit cumbersome, but even with pauses, speaking is faster than typing, and most people adapt quickly to providing a pause between each word. ***Continuous ASR*** systems can process continuous streams of words—that is, normal speech patterns. Of these two, discrete ASR systems are the most prevalent. Continuous ASR systems have a long way to go before they can distinguish individual words in rapid, continuous speech.

Speaker-independent ASR systems can be used by anyone, but their vocabularies are often limited, and some lack expansion capabilities. For example, a number of speaker-independent ASR systems work in conjunction with personal productivity software such as word processing applications. They allow you to speak, rather than type or point at, certain commands (such as file, save, print, and so on). However, you can't use these systems to actually enter text by speaking. Finally, a ***speaker-dependent ASR*** system lets you "train" it to recognize your voice. You train these systems by reading a lengthy text, such as a Mark Twain novel, into a microphone. As you read, the system begins to recognize your voice and build its vocabulary. However, a speaker-dependent system recognizes only the speech of the person who trained it.

Ultimately, everyone would like ASR systems to be continuous and a combination of both speaker-dependent and speaker-independent. That is, the best ASR system would allow you to speak normally (continuous), allow you to expand its vocabulary (speaker-dependent), and allow multiple users (speaker-independent). Such a system is in the future—perhaps five years—but ASR systems are definitely moving in that direction. If you'd like to learn more about today's ASR systems, connect to the Web site for this text at http://www.mhhe.com/haag, select "Emerging Technologies," and then choose "ASR Systems."

Some Interesting Uses of Automatic Speech Recognition

Can you imagine that one day you'll sit in front of a computer to type a term paper, and instead of typing, you'll actually speak your paper? That possibility is just around the corner. In fact, many people believe that ASR systems will be standard technology on home computers within the next few years. That's only a small portion of the real potential of ASR systems. Imagine driving in your car and adjusting the temperature by simply saying, "make it hotter," or watching television and saying, "ESPN," to switch the channel. This will become a reality in your lifetime. Not to be outdone, businesses are seeking innovative ASR implementations to gain advantage in the marketplace. Some of those organizations are listed below:[6]

- Sprint, US West, Southwestern Bell, and many other telephone service providers already offer voice dialing to their customers. By simply saying "dad" or "pizza," your telephone will automatically dial the number from a list of predefined numbers.

- KitchenAid recently demonstrated voice-controlled refrigerators, ovens, dishwashers, washing machines, and dryers. With a voice-controlled oven, for example, all you have to say is "prime rib, 8 pounds," and the oven will automatically set the temperature and notify you when dinner is ready.

- Thomas Cook Travel is working on a voice-controlled travel agency system that you can use over the phone. When you call for plane reservations, a computer will ask you for your destination and decipher your response to determine where and when you want to go and when you want to return.

Many organizations are even exploring "interviewerless interviews." With this type of system, marketing research firms will be able to perform telemarketing activities without human operators.[7] The possibilities really are limitless—anything you can communicate by typing, pointing, or speaking can probably benefit from an ASR system.

The Future of Automatic Speech Recognition

ASR is an emerging technology because it has a long way to go before it becomes a standard business application. Nonetheless, the ASR market was expected to exceed $751 million in revenue by the end of 1997, up from $189.3 million in 1992.[8] ASR will not become a standard business technology until the following conditions are met.

- **Greater storage for an expandable vocabulary.** Sounds, even when phonetically digitized, require

INDUSTRY PERSPECTIVE

Retail

Growing Up with Speech Recognition

People today are excited about and fascinated by automatic speech recognition. Tomorrow, they won't be. And not because ASR will slowly dwindle away, but rather because today's young children are growing up with speech recognition as a normal part of their everyday lives. If you don't think so, just look at the toys they play with.

MGA Entertainment has created a voice-controlled doll called My Dream Baby. My Dream Baby actually moves through four growth stages and indeed grows by two inches during the process. When a child starts playing with My Dream Baby, he or she can name it. From then on, My Dream Baby will respond to commands that are associated with her name. My Dream Baby can sing songs, recite the ABCs, play peek-a-boo, and eventually gain a 500-word vocabulary. Parents can program My Dream Baby with a unique birth date, the current date and time, and holidays.

This is the sort of toy that children play with today. They are voice-activated and voice-controlled, and they are valuable learning and development tools for children.

Automatic speech recognition is emerging and will become a part of our everyday lives. We'll look back someday and recall a time when speech recognition was emerging. Younger people may look oddly at us and simply state that we are "old."[9] ❖

---

more storage space than a word in text form. If you need an ASR system with a large vocabulary, you'll need more storage for an acoustic model.

- **Better feature analysis to support continuous speech.** The most notable drawback to continuous ASR systems is their limited ability to distinguish words that are quickly and continuously spoken. One of the problems is that we tend to drop consonants when we speak, making it difficult for an ASR system to determine where one word ends and another begins. This process is handled by feature analysis (step 1), which must become more sophisticated, because some people don't want to pause between each spoken word (as a discrete ASR system requires).

- **More dynamic language models to support speech understanding.** Speech recognition is great, but true speech understanding would be much better. For this to happen, language models that understand words in context must become more dynamic, understanding your words not only within the context of a sentence, but also in a paragraph or even in an entire conversation.

- **More flexible pattern classification to support many people.** For ASR to become truly viable in the workplace, a given system must be usable by anyone, in the same sense that anyone can use a keyboard or mouse. With the exception of speaker-independent systems, which usually have a limited vocabulary, ASR systems lack this quality. The proliferation of ASR systems that can interpret the speech of anyone—even those suffering from a head cold or speaking in a dialect—will define the true success of automatic speech recognition in business.

Virtual Reality

Making You Feel Like You're There

Imagine a time when you can experience a roller coaster ride, snow skiing, and sky diving without ever going to a theme park, visiting the slopes of Colorado, or getting in an airplane. Sound too good to be true? Not actually. On the horizon is a new technology that will virtually place you in any experience you desire. That new technology is *virtual reality*—a three-dimensional computer simulation in which you actively and physically participate. Let's look again at that definition and note several key features of virtual reality.

- Virtual reality incorporates 3-D technologies to give you a real-life illusion.

ON YOUR OWN

Understanding the Speed of Automatic Speech Recognition

Consider the following paragraph:

> There truly will come a time when knobs and dials are no longer present on any home appliance. Instead, people will simply speak commands and the appliance will respond appropriately. For couch potatoes, this represents a real problem. The only exercise for most couch potatoes occurs while operating the remote control—with automatic speech recognition, their thumbs won't even get a workout.

Now time yourself while you type that paragraph using word processing software and compare that time to those listed below:

- How long does it take you to say that paragraph using a continuous flow of words?
- How long does it take you to say that paragraph if you pause after each word?

What were your results? How much time did you save by speaking the paragraph instead of typing it? Based on the length of the typed paragraph, how much time would you save if you spoke a 10-page term paper instead of typing it? By the way, how many spelling errors did you make while typing the paragraph? ❖

- Virtual reality creates a simulation of a real-life situation.
- In virtual reality, special input devices capture your physical movements and special output devices send physical responses back to you.

That last feature is what truly distinguishes virtual reality from other types of technology. For example, multimedia incorporates many media such as sound, video, and animation. So does virtual reality. But virtual reality goes one step further by incorporating physiological input and output (the sense of touch). In fact, taste and smell are the only senses that aren't usually represented in virtual reality; and even those might one day be incorporated.

To incorporate physiological input and output, virtual reality makes use of several special input and output devices—most commonly gloves, headsets, and walkers (see Figure 6.5). A *glove* is an input device that captures and records the shape and movement of your hand and fingers and the strength of your hand and finger movements. A *headset* is a combined input and output device that serves two purposes. As an input device, a headset captures and records the movement of your head—side to side, up and down. As an output device, a headset contains a screen that covers your entire field of vision and displays various views of an environment, based on your movements. Finally, a *walker* is an input device that captures and records the movement of your feet as you walk or turn in different directions. In some virtual reality systems, walkers also act as output devices by changing the tension of the rollers, to simulate walking through sand or mud, or even changing their angle, to simulate walking up or down a hill.

To illustrate how these work, consider a virtual reality environment in which you're trying to shoot mon-

FIGURE 6.5

Input and Output Devices in Virtual Reality

INDUSTRY PERSPECTIVE

Health Care

Virtual Reality for the Betterment of People and Society

Imagine a world in which the color blue feels like sandpaper, a world in which the only furniture you can sit on must be green, or a world in which the sound of a pin dropping on the floor sounds like the cracking of thunder. Most of us can't. Unfortunately, that's the real world for a person with autism. Autism is a disease that interferes with the development of the part of the brain that processes sensory perceptions. And, in many instances, autistic people may feel sandpaper grinding across their skin when they see a color or they may be unable to correlate similar objects, such as chairs, bar stools, couches, and love seats (all items on which you can sit).

For autistic people, the world is a mishmash of objects that make no sense to them when they have to deal with them all at once. That makes teaching autistic people very difficult. For example, if you place two differently colored chairs in front of an autistic person and tell him or her that they are both chairs, that person may become confused and disoriented.

A simple world is the best world for individuals suffering from autism. Unfortunately, the real world is not simple. So researchers are finding ways to use virtual reality to teach people with autism. In a virtual reality simulation, researchers can eliminate all forms of background noise, colors, and objects. As the autistic person becomes comfortable with the virtual reality simulation, new objects or colors can be introduced without the usual adverse effects.

Researchers are also using *virbots* to teach autistic people in a virtual reality environment. These virbots are simulations of people that can instruct autistic people and help them reason with new objects.

Technology is great in the business world. But the greatest uses of technology may never make anyone rich; instead those uses will allow mentally and physically challenged individuals to cope with daily life.[10,11] ❖

---

sters in a swamp. When you put on your headset, you see the swamp in front of you. As you move your head, you see different views of the swamp. Don't forget—your views of the swamp would be in 3-D, giving you the illusion that you're really in a swamp. As you begin to walk on the walker, the headset adjusts your view so that it looks as if you're walking into the swamp. And, as you proceed into a marshy bog, the walker adjusts its tension to make it more difficult for you to walk. There's a glove on your hand and a gun in the glove. As you move your hand, the headset adjusts its view so you can virtually see your hand and the direction in which you're pointing the gun. So, when you finally see a monster, you move your hand in the appropriate direction and squeeze the trigger. On your screen you see the gun fire and, you hope, vaporize the monster.

Applications of Virtual Reality

In 1995 revenues for virtual reality were estimated at $275.8 million, which is not really that much.[12] Nonetheless, virtual reality applications are popping up everywhere, sometimes in odd places. One of the more common applications of virtual reality is found in the entertainment industry. There are a number of virtual reality games on the market, including downhill Olympic skiing, racecar driving, golfing, air combat, and marksmanship (similar to our example of monsters in a swamp). Some require special input and output devices (more than just gloves, headsets, and walkers). For example, virtual reality racecar driving uses a clutch, brake, gas pedal, and gear shift; and virtual reality skiing uses a huge fan to give you the illusion of wind blowing in your face as you race down a ski slope.

Also in the area of entertainment, virtual reality is appearing in many movies. In *Disclosure* Michael Douglas enters a virtual reality environment that simulates a large room with filing cabinets full of information. In *Virtuosity* virtual reality gets so real that Denzel Washington must track down a virtual reality killer who figured out how to exit the virtual environment and enter the real world. And, if you saw the movie *Congo*, you might have noticed that Amy (the gorilla) uses sign language and virtual reality gloves to communicate with humans.

In business, many organizations are exploring virtual reality to create numerous simulated environments. Consider these examples:

- Matsushita Electric Works has devised a virtual reality system to help you select new kitchen appliances. You simply provide Matsushita with the layout of your kitchen, which is scanned into a virtual reality system. Once you enter the virtual reality environment, you can change your refrigerator or dish washer, see how they fit, and even request color changes.

- Volvo has a virtual reality system to demonstrate the safety features of its cars. In this virtual reality system, you virtually experience a car wreck to learn how air bags work.

- Many airlines use virtual reality to train pilots how to react effectively in adverse conditions. In this environment, pilots are faced with bad weather, defective engines, and malfunctioning landing gear.

Think about the last example. Is it really possible for airlines to provide anything but a simulation of real-life conditions? Not really—and that's one of the greatest advantages of virtual reality. It can create simulations of environments without the presence or incorporation of physical objects. Thus pilots can virtually crash a plane while they learn to cope with adverse conditions. Yet no one is injured, no planes are lost.

Motorola discovered this benefit of virtual reality when training assembly line workers.[13] Traditionally, Motorola had spent hundreds of thousands of dollars to build replica assembly lines to facilitate training. With virtual reality assembly line training, however, Motorola simply created a "virtual" assembly line that presents different situations to each worker with the press of a button. By using virtual reality, Motorola has realized a tenfold increase in savings. But it doesn't stop there—Motorola has found that virtual reality–trained employees learn more efficiently than employees who were trained on real assembly lines. As Art Paton, instructional design manager at Motorola, explained, "They [employees] become totally immersed in the virtual environment and seem to absorb concepts much faster." That, coupled with cost savings, is a substantial advantage of virtual reality training.

The health care industry, likewise, is exploring virtual reality for a variety of applications. Using virtual reality, doctors can now practice surgery, explore the human body, and diagnose diseases, all without touching a cadaver.[14] Some doctors are even using virtual reality to perform long-distance triage. In this instance, a doctor in one location slips into virtual reality gloves and a special head-mounted camera to examine a patient. Another doctor—who can be located halfway around the world—also wears virtual reality gloves and a headset. Whatever the first doctor sees and feels is electronically communicated to the second doctor who, in turn, sees and feels the same thing. This health care application of virtual reality will soon be widely used for disaster area triage when it's impossible to transport doctors quickly to the location.

Cybersickness
The Downside of Virtual Reality

Every coin has two sides. Virtual reality, like all technologies, has associated disadvantages as well as advantages. People who participate in virtual reality environments sometimes experience *cybersickness*, including eyestrain, simulator sickness, and flashbacks.[15] You may experience eyestrain if you remain too long in a virtual reality system that uses a low-resolution headset for displaying views. Because of the low resolution, your eyes must work harder to distinguish images. Some people experience simulator sickness when the physiological inputs and outputs of the system are out of sync. For example, if you move your head and the headset takes an extra second to adjust your view, you may experience nausea or dizziness. Finally, some people experience virtual reality flashbacks several hours after using virtual reality. This occurs because virtual reality systems cannot yet provide you with a wholly "virtual" physical experience. So your brain must compensate for this while you use virtual reality. Later, your brain may also try to compensate while you're experiencing real life. This may cause you to experience déjà vu or a temporary disassociation with reality.

The Future of Virtual Reality

Virtual reality is part of your future, regardless of its disadvantages. Researchers are working daily to solve the problems that produce cybersickness. Further, researchers are suggesting innovative uses for virtual reality—some that may dramatically alter both your business and personal life. In business, for example, some people are exploring virtual reality as a tool to illustrate corporate downsizing.[16] In this instance, a CEO can define the new structure of an organization (fewer employees, new business processes, and less building space) in virtual reality. Other top managers can then virtually view and experience the effects of the proposed organizational changes. One day, virtual reality may be the first tool individuals and groups reach for when they want to create or reorganize a business—and it may simulate the fact that you no longer have a job.

On the home front, you may soon be able to experience the company of friends and family members through virtual reality piped over the Internet.[17] These types of virtual reality applications make use of **Cave automatic virtual environments (CAVEs)**, which are special 3-D rooms spread across the world. You enter a CAVE, as would your friends or family members in another location. Once inside, your image (including sound and movement) would be projected into the other CAVE; likewise, the images of the people in the other CAVE would be projected into your CAVE. All of you would simply have the illusion of carrying on a conversation while sitting in the same room. Someday, grandparents may be able to enjoy their distant grandchildren in a playground through the use of CAVEs.

Biometrics

No More Passwords

Today, the standard security mechanism is a password. You have to create it, you have to remember it, and you need to change it frequently. But that will soon change with the emerging technology of biometrics. **Biometrics** is the use of physical characteristics—such as your fingerprint, the blood vessels in the retina of your eye, the sound of your voice, or perhaps even your breath—to provide identification. Already, biometrics is widely used in high-security environments such as military installations.

The concept is quite simple. You can copy someone's password, but you can't copy a fingerprint or retina scan. The banking industry is currently converting all its ATMs to use biometrics, specifically a retina scan. When you open an account and request ATM use, the bank doesn't issue you an ATM card. Instead, the bank scans your retina and captures a copy of it. To use an ATM, you allow the machine to scan your retina and it matches you to your account. You can then perform whatever transaction you want.

Home computers may someday be devices that commonly use biometrics. You can already find keyboards that have a special scanning device for your fingerprint (see Figure 6.6). You can't turn on and use your machine until you provide a fingerprint scan. Apple's latest operating system also uses voice recognition as a password mechanism. When you turn on your Apple, you must speak your password. The system will

FIGURE 6.6
Fingerprint Scanning on a Keyboard

then verify not only your password but also your voice. It makes a lot of sense when you think about it.

Some Final Thoughts about Emerging Technologies for All the Senses

Emerging technologies such as automatic speech recognition and virtual reality encompass most of the senses except taste and smell. Smell may be incorporated sooner than you think. Researchers are already working on special aroma-producing systems that use combinations of perfumelike substances to create virtually any smell. Just think about it—while using virtual reality to surf the waves of Hawaii, the system may also produce a salt smell (and splash water in your face when you fall).

Taste, unfortunately, has a long way to go. Although researchers can reproduce literally any taste, most people are wary of placing something in their mouths and swallowing any residue. If we do get to the point where IT systems actually reproduce tastes for us, one question will be on everyone's mind: "If it's a virtual taste, does that mean the calories are also virtual?" It'll be interesting to see (or rather taste).

The Internet Explosion

Emerging All Around You

Undoubtedly, the Internet is the most visible, rapidly changing, dynamic, mind-boggling, and exciting emerging technology. Perhaps we shouldn't just say "the Internet." More appropriately, what's really most exciting and emerging about the Internet is the way in which the business world and individuals are exploiting it. For example, in Chapter 5 we explored how organizations are establishing their own private Internets, called "intranets." We also looked at other topics such as extranet applications, Internet virtual private networks, and competitive intelligence gathering—all of which have something to do with exploiting the Internet and its worldwide connectivity.

In this section, we will look at four more emerging aspects of the Internet: (1) electronic cash, which you can use to purchase products on the Internet, (2) using the Internet to make free long-distance phone calls, (3) high-speed Internet access, and (4) Internet appliances.

Electronic Cash
Virtual Money on the Internet

Currently, we have three major methods of paying for products and services—cash, debit card or check, and credit card. For every purchase you make, you use one of these methods of payment. The same will be true when you make purchases over the Internet. Let's briefly explore these methods of payment, and then we'll see how they'll work on the Internet, especially Internet cash transactions. Everyone is familiar with *cash transactions*. You buy a product or service in exchange for real cash, either folding or coins. Cash is a tender backed by the federal government. So we all know that we can accept a $10 bill from someone today and that it will be worth $10 tomorrow when we use it to make purchases.

Debit and credit transactions are different. Like cash, *debit transactions* require that you gather money in advance and then spend it. When you make a purchase using a personal check or your checking account debit card, you complete a debit transaction. That is, you build up a pool of money in your checking account, and then you spend it. *Credit transactions*, on the other hand, give you the ability to make purchases first and pay for them later. When you charge products on a store charge account or your credit card, for example, you're creating a balance that you must later pay.

On the Internet, debit and credit transactions occur similarly. For example, you can use your checking account debit card or credit card to make purchases on the Internet. When you locate a product you'd like to purchase, you simply provide the merchant with your account number. If you use a debit card, the merchant will notify your bank of the transaction. Your bank simply debits your account and credits the account of the merchant. If you use a credit card, the merchant will notify your credit card issuer of the transaction. The credit card issuer will pay the merchant for the transaction and bill you for the transaction amount.

Internet cash transactions, however, are very different from real-life cash transactions. When you cruise the Internet in search of products to buy, you can't carry around or use hard cash—you need electronic cash. ***Electronic cash*** (also called ***e-cash*** or ***digital cash***) is exactly what its name implies—an electronic representation of cash. This electronic representation of cash is nothing more than a file (similar to a word processing or spreadsheet file) that says you have a certain denomination of money in electronic form. You can then buy products and services on the Internet by sending the e-cash file to a merchant. It may sound simple (and it is in theory), but e-cash is the subject of much debate.

Figure 6.7 demonstrates how e-cash will someday work on the Internet. To use e-cash to make purchases on the Internet, the first thing you have to do is obtain e-cash from an electronic bank on the Internet. You can buy e-cash in a variety of ways—you can send real cash through the mail, provide your debit or credit card number as if you were making a regular product purchase, or actually open an account with an electronic bank and request that an amount of e-cash be deducted from your account balance and sent to you. Whatever the case, the electronic bank will electronically send you e-cash files. For example, you could request $100 in e-cash in $20 increments. What you would end up with is 5 e-cash files, each representing $20 on your hard disk.

Once you have your e-cash, all you have to do is find a product to purchase on the Internet and send the appropriate number of e-cash files to the merchant (for example, a $40 purchase would require two e-cash files). In turn, the merchant can use the e-cash to purchase products and services from other merchants or return it to the electronic bank for real money.

What's Holding Up Electronic Cash?

E-cash is deceptively simple—instead of using real money, you simply use an electronic form of money. And indeed, someday it will be simple and commonplace. First, however, there are many hurdles to overcome. We describe some of these below.

- **Anyone can be an electronic bank.** Currently, there are no governmental regulations defining who can become an electronic bank. In fact, you as an individual can open your own electronic bank

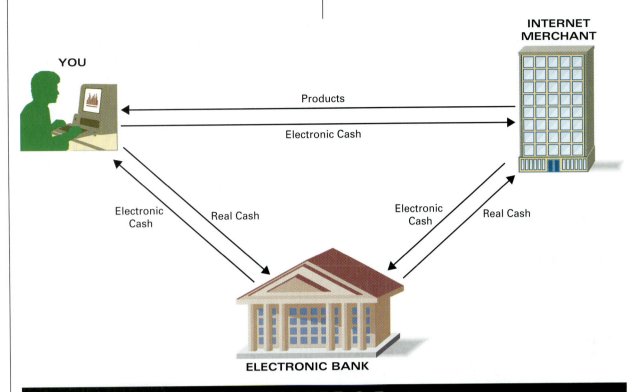

FIGURE 6.7

How Electronic Cash Will Work on the Internet

on the Internet. You don't need the government's permission, and you don't need to be backed by the FDIC or FSLIC.

- **There are no standards for how e-cash should look.** Many electronic banks are surfacing on the Internet, and none of them agree on what an e-cash file should look like. So e-cash from one electronic bank doesn't necessarily look like e-cash from another electronic bank. This has many merchants wary—dealing with different forms of e-cash is almost like accepting different forms of international currency.

- **Merchants must have accounts with electronic banks.** Most electronic banks require that merchants establish accounts with them to facilitate real-money and e-cash exchange. For example, the Mark Twain Bank in St. Louis is an electronic bank from which you can purchase e-cash.[18] Unfortunately, a merchant to whom you send e-cash must also have an account with the Mark Twain Bank in order to convert your e-cash into real money.

- **E-cash makes money laundering easy.** E-cash is completely anonymous. It contains no information about you—only about the denomination and electronic bank provider. Thus e-cash can easily be used for money laundering. Illegally obtained real cash can easily be traded in for e-cash; the owner of the e-cash can then spend it without anyone's knowing its origination.

- **E-cash is easy to lose.** E-cash is simply an electronic file on your hard disk; so, if your hard disk crashes, you may lose your money, and it is unlikely that your electronic bank will replace it. Likewise, you could accidentally erase your e-cash files, or they could be destroyed by some glitch that occurs while you transmit them to an Internet merchant.

What Will It Take for Electronic Cash to Become a Reality?

In spite of its drawbacks, e-cash is coming and it will be widely used in a matter of a few years. For e-cash to become a reality, two major things must happen. First, standards are needed to define how e-cash will look and work. One organization working on these standards is the Joint Electronic Payments Initiative (JEPI), headed by such businesses as Cybercash, IBM, and Microsoft.[19]

CHAPTER SIX Emerging Technologies

Finding Electronic Cash on the Internet

Do a little cruising around the Internet to find electronic banks that provide e-cash and merchants who accept e-cash. To find electronic banks, you might want to start at the sites for the Mark Twain Bank and Cybercash. Those sites will probably provide you with a list of additional sites that accept e-cash for purchases.

How many electronic banks did you find? Are some of these "real" banks or simply organizations that convert your hard money into electronic money? Did you happen to find any electronic banks that looked a little "shady," as though you couldn't trust them?

What about merchants who accept e-cash—how many of those did you find, and what type of merchandise are they selling? Do these merchants offer payment forms other than e-cash? ❖

Several other organizations are also working on standards. All these organizations will have to unite and agree on a common standard. Second, the federal government must become involved in developing regulations for electronic banks. Most merchants are wary of electronic banks because there are no formal rules governing their operation or liquidity. You should be wary as well. Research an electronic bank before you send it money; you may be sending your money to a "mom and pop" shop that runs away with it.

CAREER OPPORTUNITY

Is there a career opportunity associated with e-cash? You bet. Now it's easier than ever to open your own business on the Internet. You'll reach millions of people daily by setting up shop on the Internet, and e-cash will soon be an easy, convenient method for your customers to make purchases.

Once these two problems are solved, e-cash will become a standard Internet technology. As merchants gain confidence in and begin accepting e-cash, more consumers will use it. Acceptance of e-cash will follow the same pattern as the recent and increasing acceptance of non-Visa or non-MasterCard credit cards; as more merchants accept them, more consumers will use them.

Free Internet Telephone Use

No More Long-Distance Charges

One of the greatest advantages of the Internet is worldwide connectivity, which allows you to access information resources and communicate with people all over the world (for example, through e-mail or in chat rooms). What's even better, these communications are paid for through the monthly fees you pay your Internet service

THE BASICS

A Computer with a Sound Card, Microphone, and Set of Speakers

GETTING STARTED

MAKING THE CALL

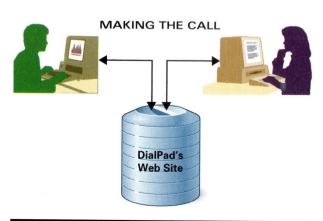

FIGURE 6.8
Making an Internet Phone Call

INDUSTRY PERSPECTIVE

IT & Telecommunications

EZfone Makes Internet Phone-Calling "EZ"

We will someday in a completely seamless and simple fashion make all our phone calls over the Internet. It doesn't matter if a phone call is local, is to a cell phone, is a U.S. long-distance phone call, or even is an international call, all our phone conversations will probably occur over the Internet. Right now, we're in a period of transition. Some Internet phone-calling services require that the parties be connected to the Internet. Others, such as EZfone, allow you to make the Internet connection after you've made the call.

EZfone requires you to purchase a special plug-and-play card for your computer. Once installed (it takes only a few minutes), you plug your telephone into that card. When you want to make a call, you simply use that telephone. When the other person answers, you can carry on a normal conversation. But if that person also subscribes to EZfone's service and is talking on a phone also connected to a plug-and-play card on his or her computer, you (as the calling party) press the # key.

Then, both of you hang up from your call and wait. While you wait, both computers establish an Internet connection. Once this is done, your computers will ask you to pick up your phones.

Now, your phone call is absolutely free through the Internet.

Again, we are in a transition period. So, EZfone's system does require that both parties have the plug-and-play card and that both parties use phones connected to those cards. But this will soon change. Traditional telephone service providers, Internet service providers, and Internet phone-calling providers are working in conjunction with each other to develop the technologies that will allow you to make free long-distance phone calls over the Internet with no hassles. You won't need special plug-and-play cards, and you won't have to wait while your computer establishes an Internet connection. ❖

---

provider, such as America Online. In other words, these connections are made without long-distance charges accruing to your monthly phone bill. If these worldwide connections are basically free, then why not use them to make long-distance phones for free? You can.

This emerging technology of making free long-distance phone calls over the Internet requires a few basic technology tools, which your computer probably already has. You need

1. Access to the Internet through an Internet service provider
2. A set of speakers
3. A microphone

Let's consider using DialPad (http://www.dialpad.com), an Internet provider of free long-distance phone calls (see Figure 6.8). When you connect to DialPad the first time, you'll have to register yourself as a user (the registration is free too) and download some software.

When you want to make a phone call over the Internet, you go through a series of simple steps. First, you connect to the Internet and DialPad. At DialPad, you then browse through a listing of people who are currently on the Internet and also have Internet phone-calling capabilities through DialPad. From the list, you click on the name of the person you want to speak with. DialPad will call that person for you. Then, it's just a regular conversation—you speak into your microphone and hear the other person through your speakers.

And it gets even better. Some Internet phone providers even allow you to call regular phone numbers. So, the person you want to speak to doesn't have to be connected to the Internet. In short, you call that person's regular phone number and he or she answers using a regular phone (which can be a cell phone).

High-Speed Internet Access

No More Waiting

Most cable TV service providers and telephone service providers aren't content just to offer you standard services at standard speeds. Indeed, most can now offer you high-speed access to the Internet. To do this, these

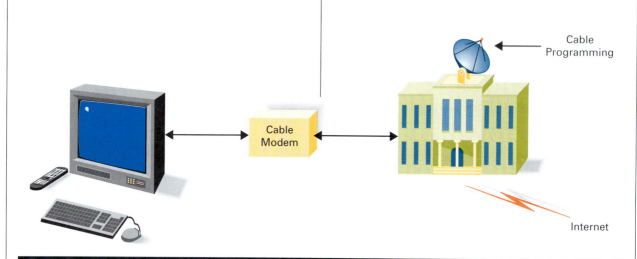

FIGURE 6.9
Connecting to the Internet through a Cable Modem

companies are bringing DSL and ISDN lines into your home, as we discussed in *Extended Learning Module C*. DSL and ISDN connections give you the ability to access and use the Internet at speeds up to 100 times faster than a traditional phone line. With most of these types of connections, you can establish local area networks (LANs) in your home and connect all your computers to the one high-speed line.

Many cable TV providers are also offering you the ability to use these high-speed lines and use your TV as your monitor (see Figure 6.9). In this instance, you don't even need a computer to access the Internet. If your cable TV service provider does offer you this ability, it will also provide you with a wireless mouse and keyboard. So, you can sit across the room in the comfort of your favorite chair and cruise the Internet on your TV.

This type of service may come to you in the form of a cable modem (as we discussed in *Extended Learning Module C*). In this instance, your cable modem connects your television to a cable TV service provider. But it isn't anything like your cable TV box. Traditional cable boxes support only a one-direction flow of information from your cable TV service provider to you. Cable modems, on the other hand, are bidirectional. This simply means that you can enter information and commands (using your wireless mouse and keyboard) and the information and commands will flow back to your cable TV service provider, who passes them on to the Internet.

Internet Appliances
Just for Cruising the Internet

Some people today want Internet access but not a fully functional computer. That is, they want a device that includes just the basics of Internet use—a modem, a keyboard, a mouse, and a monitor. These people don't really care about storage devices, a large amount of RAM, or a fast CPU; they simply want to cruise the Internet and gather whatever information they need.

For these people, an Internet appliance may be just the answer. An ***Internet appliance*** (or ***Web appliance***) is a scaled-down computer or newly developed device that supports access to the Internet and possibly a few other basic functions such as note taking and maintaining an address book. Internet appliances truly are emerging, so who knows how they'll shake out over the next few years.

Internet appliances range from scaled-down tower PCs that do include disk drives to Web-enabled cell phones that allow you to view Web sites on their small display screens. So, let's break them down into four categories:

1. Scaled-down PCs
2. Internet-only appliances
3. Web-enabled personal digital assistants
4. Web-enabled cell phones

In the first category, almost every computer manufacturer, Dell, Gateway, Compaq, HP, IBM, is offering a scaled-down, cheaper version of its PC line. Compaq has created the iPAQ, a 500Mhz machine with CD-ROM and hard drive and Internet-connection capabilities for about $600. IBM offers its NetVista 566Mhz machine for $699, Dell the OptiPlex 600Mhz machine for $930, Gateway its E-1400 566Mhz machine for $1,100, and HP its e-pc 600Mhz machine for about $1,000.

All these are scaled-down versions of previously fully functional PCs offered by the manufacturers, who

INDUSTRY PERSPECTIVE ".com"

Storage Space and Software for Rent/Free on the Internet

As Internet appliances become more prevalent, the question becomes one of how you use your appliance for information processing, where you store your software, and where you store your information. While Internet appliances that are basically scaled-down versions of PCs include disk drives, other Internet appliances such as cell phones and PDAs do not. But what if you want to use one of those devices to build and save a spreadsheet? Where will you store your spreadsheet software and where will you store your spreadsheet?

The answer is on the Internet. Internet appliances are designed to use the Internet. Wouldn't it be nice if you could connect to a Web site that would allow you to rent software and storage space, or better yet have it for free? Well, those types of sites are emerging. One such site is Visto.com (http://www.visto.com). At Visto.com, you can store files for free on the Internet, and you can use Visto.com's calendar software to maintain your appointments and Visto.com's address book to maintain your list of contacts.

Beyond the basic functions such as maintaining appointments and lists of contacts, other Web businesses plan on letting you rent more sophisticated software. For example, Microsoft will soon roll out "pay-per-use" of its Microsoft Office suite. So, you won't need to buy PowerPoint if you create only a couple of presentations per year. Instead, you'll just rent it as you need it.

With these types of sites Internet appliances will proliferate. With no storage capabilities at all, you'll soon be able to use your cell phone to create a spreadsheet document and save that document on the Internet. ❖

---

are attempting to reach a market of people who want Internet access but also basic processing capabilities. For example, on each of these machines you can load Microsoft Office XP and perform tasks related to word processing, spreadsheet, database, Web development, and task management. What you can't do with them is power-intensive tasks such as video editing and production. These machines are cheaper than their counterparts and attract a large market.

The second category of Internet appliances really are just that—Internet appliances—which are designed basically to help you access the Internet and use e-mail. Beyond that, they may include some limited capabilities such as task management and maintaining an address book. But they are really designed just to help you access the Internet. When you purchase one of these devices, you must also purchase Internet access, the same as you would through a typical Internet service provider such as America Online. So, the devices themselves may be cheap, but the monthly Internet access fee makes them more expensive.

Internet appliances in this category include: MSN Companion for $78, iPAQ Home Internet Appliance for $199, ICEBOX for free (that's $0), i-opener for $299, WebTV Plus for $199, ePodsOne for $199, and NIC for $330. Again, don't let the prices fool you. For example, ICEBOX is free, but you must sign a three-year Internet access contract at $21.95 per month, bringing its total three-year cost to roughly $790.

The third category of Internet appliances includes Web-enabled personal digital assistants. A personal digital assistant (PDA) is a small hand-held computer that supports note taking, maintaining an address book, and managing finances and tasks. A PDA comes equipped with a unique writing stylus and touch-sensitive screen. You use the writing stylus to write and select icons on the touch-sensitive screen. So, basically you don't have a traditional keyboard on a PDA.

Today's PDAs also come equipped with a wireless modem that allows you to access the Internet. However, only a small percentage of Web sites are PDA-enabled. The reason is simple. If you want your Web site to be viewed on a PDA, you must "recast" your content so that it can be displayed on a small PDA screen (not a typical large monitor). Nonetheless, more and more Web sites every day are recasting their content so it can be displayed on PDAs.

Finally, many cell phones are Web-enabled, and we call them Web phones. A **Web phone** is a special type of cell phone that allows you to access the Internet. Right

248 CHAPTER SIX Emerging Technologies

A Scaled-Down PC

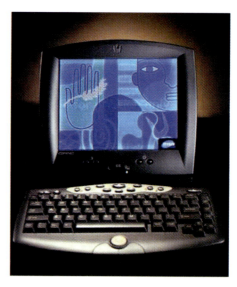

An Internet-Only Appliance

A Web-Enabled Personal Digital Assistant (PDA)

A Web-Enabled Cell Phone

FIGURE 6.10

What's Your Choice of Internet Appliance?

now, these are not the cell phones you get free with a calling plan. Many of today's better Web phones can cost as much as $500. Most important, Web phones include a microbrowser. A ***microbrowser*** is Web browser software for Web phones that can display text information and a limited amount of graphics in a small space.

Don't buy a Web phone if you want to enjoy hours of Internet surfing with graphics, animation, and sound. Web phones are ideal for fast access to bits and pieces of information—flight schedules, weather reports, sports scores, and news. This information will come to you mainly in text form only (but expect that to change soon).

The Wireless Revolution

Virtual Connectivity

In *Extended Learning Module C* we introduced you to unguided communications media, which are also called wireless communications media. These communications media connect people and technology without physical cables—what you might refer to as "virtual connectivity." For the most part, these types of commu-

THE GLOBAL PERSPECTIVE

Buy Soft Drinks with Your Phone? They Do in Finland

In Finland, home of Nokia, the most successful cell phone company in the world, cell phones are more than just talking devices. Finns exchange text messages with their phones on a regular basis, but they also use their phones to buy goods and services.

Vending machines are equipped to accept the dialing of codes on your cell phone, in lieu of money, to dispense snacks and soft drinks. The charge for the junk food is then added to your phone bill. If you want to play a tune on a juke box or play a video game, you use your phone. If you want to wash your car, you don't need cash, just a cell phone. If you want to play golf, you can pay for the balls with your cell phone. Nokia even has a phone that you can use in a very high-temperature and high-humidity environment. This phone is for use while enjoying a sauna—a favorite Finnish activity.

The Finnish word for cell phone means "little hand" and a cell phone is almost as indispensable to Finns as the hands they were born with. Sixty-five percent of Finns have cell phones as opposed to 25 percent of Americans. Almost 100 percent of 18-year-olds in Finland have cell phones. Young children use cell phones before they can read.

Finland is the most advanced nation in the world—telephonically speaking. It was the first country to have more cell phones than wired phones. Public phone boxes are almost completely a thing of the past.

Nokia, which most people think is a Japanese company, used to be a manufacturer of toilet paper and rubber boots. In 1992 Nokia's management decided to change direction and entered the phone market. Since then the company has met with spectacular success, having left Motorola, the largest American cell phone company, in the dust (but not in the sauna). ❖

ON YOUR OWN

Which Internet Appliance Is Right for You?

You have many choices when it comes to Internet appliances—from scaled-down PCs to cell phones. Which is right for you is a function of how, when, and where you plan to use it.

First, decide which of the four categories of Internet appliances is best for you. Provide a couple of reasons why you believe this to be true.

Second, do some research in that particular category. Find at least three devices in that category. Record their prices and their functionality. On the basis of that information, which would you choose and why?

Finally, are you ready to purchase an Internet appliance right now? Or will you wait until they become better and cheaper? ❖

---

nications media are fairly well established, but the business world has yet to truly exploit their full potential or use them in innovative ways. In the future, however, you can expect organizations and people everywhere to join the wireless revolution, using wireless technologies for virtually all their connectivity needs. Indeed, as you just read in the previous section, many people are beginning to use PDAs and cell phones to access the Internet. These devices are wireless and do provide virtual connectivity, literally anywhere in the world. In this section, we will explore two more aspects of the wireless revolution: (1) the global positioning system and (2) wireless local area networks.

Global Positioning System

Knowing Where You Are while You Roam

Wireless technologies, such as digital pagers, smart phones, and laptop computers with cellular modems, indeed seem to solve many problems. These technologies allow you to contact friends, family members, and offices, regardless of your proximity to a phone line. But "where you are" could still present problems. You've undoubtedly encountered this problem while traveling a lonely stretch of highway—what highway you are on, where the nearest town is, and many other questions have probably crossed your mind. You've got a road map, but it doesn't show farm-to-market road 358 near Boise, Idaho.

Well, fortunately, a new technology—the global positioning system—is available that will help you always know where you are. The ***global positioning system (GPS)*** is a collection of 24 earth-orbiting satellites that continuously transmit radio signals you can use to determine where you are (see Figure 6.11). A GPS receiver—a small hand-held device—picks up the radio signals from four of the satellites and can pinpoint your exact position within a few hundred feet. The GPS receiver also contains maps that you can then use to determine where that nearest town is or on what road you're traveling.

For many years, GPS receivers have been used commercially. Airplane pilots, sea captains, and military personnel constantly use GPS receivers to determine their

INDUSTRY PERSPECTIVE — **Manufacturing**

OnStar Is Always Onboard while You Drive

Imagine driving one night and being completely lost in a town you know nothing about. You reach up for your rearview mirror, push a button, and hear a voice say, "Good evening. I see that you're driving on Third Street in Amarillo, Texas. How may I help you?" The voice is not one of a robot-controlled car direction system, but rather a person located anywhere in the United States.

That's how OnStar's in-vehicle safety, security, and information system works. When you push the button, your car actually makes a phone call to OnStar's call service center. And your car—equipped with a GPS—also communicates your exact location to the service center. An OnStar representative answers your call and can help you find directions. Even if you're not lost, the representative can help you with directions to the nearest gas station, ATM, or restaurant.

What if your car gets stolen? Just call the OnStar service center. The service center will use your car's GPS to find its location and inform the nearest local law enforcement agency of its whereabouts.

These types of capabilities are still emerging, but they will become common very soon. General Motors already uses OnStar's technology and services in about 10 of its car lines, most notably the Cadillac. Other car manufacturers are quickly doing the same.

Of course, there are some ethical questions here. What if you want to know where your son, daughter, husband, or wife is? Will you be able to call OnStar and find the location of their car? Should you be able to or is that an invasion of privacy? Can you justify doing that if it's four o'clock in the morning and your child hasn't come home yet? Can you justify doing that if your spouse is 30 minutes late coming home from work?

What about nonfamily members? Should you be able to use this service to track your nanny who is out with your children? As technology—such as GPS—becomes more pervasive and invasive, we'll have to deal with these ethical questions. And they are not simple to answer.[20,21] ❖

location and the distance to certain destinations. That same technology is also available to you. A personal GPS receiver costs only about $300. If you're an airplane pilot, you can order a special GPS receiver that includes maps of air spaces and airports. Many organizations have found interesting and innovative applications of GPS receivers, including OnStar (see "Manufacturing Industry Perspective").

Wireless Local Area Networks
Mobilizing Technology

Wireless technologies such as GPSs, cell phones, PDAs, and wireless keyboards and mice can do more than just make people mobile; they can make technology itself mobile. One such wireless technology that's emerging is a wireless local area network. A *wireless local area network (wireless LAN)* is a network that covers a limited distance in which all components or computers are connected without physical cables.

In a wireless LAN, a central access point is established through which all wireless communications travel (see Figure 6.12). This access point is usually physically connected to a LAN server that provides information and software to all the wireless clients. The wireless clients can include computers and peripheral devices such as scanners and printers. What's really significant about wireless LANs is that they allow computers and peripheral devices to move easily without moving a cable (pulling cable for a network is a major business expense). So, if you were to rearrange your office, you could move your computers without concern for cables and cable outlets.

Listed below are several organizations that have realized benefits from wireless networks.

- IBM has developed a new wireless service for real estate agents. For less than $200 a month, real estate agents gain wireless access to a Multiple Listing Service (MLS) database.[22]
- Karolinski Hospital (Stockholm, Sweden) is using a wireless LAN to mobilize nurses to increase the

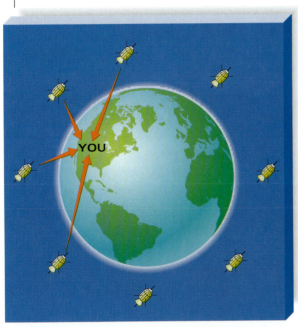

Wherever you are, your GPS receiver will pick up the transmissions from four of the satellites to determine your exact location.

FIGURE 6.11

Knowing Where You Are with the Global Positioning System

Information and Software

FIGURE 6.12

A Wireless Local Area Network (LAN)

efficiency of patient prescription distribution. Nurses move through the hospital with a wireless laptop, dispensing prescription drugs.[23]

- At Stanford University, students no longer go to labs to use computers. Instead, they can access them wirelessly, regardless of whether they're in the student union building, sitting on the lawn, or eating in a cafeteria. Stanford's students can access the wireless network from anywhere within a 15-mile radius of the campus.[24]

Addressing the "ility" Issue of Wireless Technologies

In business, communication by means of wireless technologies—whether for people or technology—addresses the key "ility" issue. That is, port**ability** and mob**ility.** Just think about it—if you require a mobile workforce, you must provide them with portable technologies connected to a network. If your employees are meeting in a hotel room, network connections can be achieved through the phone line. But what about line personnel on a factory floor? They can't very well stop what they're doing and find the nearest phone line. These people require the portability and mobility of wireless technologies.

In Figure 6.13, you can see that wireless LAN revenues are expected to increase by almost 250 percent from 1995 to 1997. This is only for wireless LANs—it doesn't include cellular phones, digital pagers, smart phones, microwaves, or satellites. If you include these, total wireless revenues will probably exceed $10 billion in 1997. It all goes back to the "ility" issue—making your workforce mobile with portable technologies that allow them to communicate with others, regardless of location.

> ### CAREER OPPORTUNITY
> Wireless technologies give people the ability to work anywhere anytime without accessing telephone lines or cables. The use of these technologies is definitely on the rise—revenues for wireless office products (simple digital pagers and cellular phones) are expected to exceed $3.3 billion in 1998, up from $394 million in 1995.[26] Your career opportunity lies in determining if, how, and where wireless technologies can increase your productivity in more places. If they can, join the wireless revolution.

Emerging Technologies for Your Personal Life

Many of the emerging technologies we've discussed will significantly affect not only your personal life, but also your internal business operations and market interactions. The business world is also producing technologies that simplify your personal life. And where's the competitive advantage in developing emerging technologies that make your personal life easier? Think about it for a moment. You've probably purchased such items as an answering machine, a digital alarm clock, and a microwave oven just because they make your life easier. These purchases generate revenues for the product manufacturer. Of the many emerging technologies that will make your personal life easier, we highlight three in this section—smart cards, intelligent home appliances, and your Internet-connected home.

Smart Cards
Electronic Cash in Your Wallet

Many people are predicting that paper currency and metal coins will become obsolete with the growing acceptance and use of electronic versions of money. In the previous section, we explored the use of electronic cash

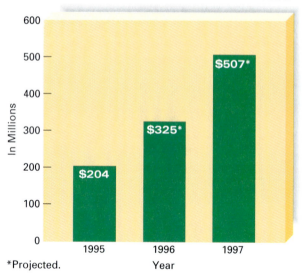

FIGURE 6.13

Wireless LAN Revenues on the Rise[25]

on the Internet. Another form of electronic cash is the *smart card*—a small plastic card (about the size of a credit card) that contains a memory chip on which a sum of money can be recorded and updated (see Figure 6.14). It's really just a simple matter of buying a smart card for a certain denomination and then using it for buying clothes, paying for gas, making long-distance calls on pay phones, or even riding on public transportation.

To make a purchase with a smart card, you insert the card into a card reader device that (1) reads the amount of money you have stored on your card, (2) deducts the amount of your purchase, and (3) tells you your balance. When you've spent the balance, you can take the smart card back to where you bought it and purchase more electronic money to replenish it.

Smart cards have been around for several years in a variety of forms. For example, toll road administrators have made them available to commuters in an effort to relieve congestion at toll booths. And the sponsors of the 1996 Summer Olympics experimented with smart cards, allowing people to use them for purchasing soft drinks, food, and Olympics-related items such as clothing. The Tran$cash Consortium is even developing a public transportation smart card that can be read while still in your wallet.[27] The Tran$cash system uses a wireless technology that will communicate with your smart card when you board the bus. The wireless technology emits a signal that locates your card, deducts the fare, and updates your balance—you never have to present your card to the driver.

Intelligent Home Appliances

Getting the Computer to Do Your Work (Almost)

Wouldn't it be great to have a full-time maid to cook your meals, wash the dishes, and launder your clothes? You'd probably pay dearly for such a service; unfortunately, your budget probably won't allow such an expenditure. And don't expect a computer robot to show up at your doorstep that will perform all those functions. In spite of what you may have seen on *The Jetsons* or *Lost in Space*, it'll be a long time before the technology industry develops a robot to take over your household chores. But don't despair. There is a growing number of home appliances that can ease your burden. These appliances are called **intelligent home appliances**—appliances that contain an embedded IT system that controls numerous functions and is capable of making some decisions. Consider these examples:

- Smart vacuum cleaners that automatically adjust settings based on naps or densities of your carpet, varying densities and weights of dirt, and collection bag fullness.[28]

- Hand-held camcorders that make sure your movie never jumps around. For example, Matsushita has

Finding Home Appliances with a Brain

Visit several local appliance stores, find intelligent home appliances, then answer the following questions:

1. What intelligent home appliances did you find?
2. What was the cost of each appliance?
3. What functions do the appliances perform?
4. Which, if any, are voice-controlled?
5. Is there a difference between the cost of the intelligent appliance and the same appliance with no intelligence? ❖

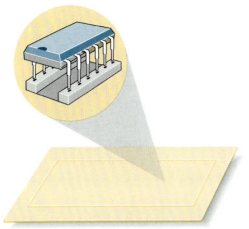

A smart card contains a memory chip on which electronic money can be stored and updated.

FIGURE 6.14

The Anatomy of a Smart Card

THE GLOBAL PERSPECTIVE

Staying in Touch with Your Home from around the World

When our homes become completely Internet-connected, think of what you'll be able to do while you're away from home. From anywhere in the world, you'll be able to adjust the heat, turn on and off lights, check your voice mail, and hundreds of other activities.

Right now, we can't even conceive of everything we'll be able to do. While on vacation in the south of France, you'll be able to connect to the Internet and see a live video of your children at home. You'll be able to talk with your refrigerator and see (or smell) food that's about to spoil. You'll be able to check the water content of your soil and start the water for the lawn sprinklers.

You'll be able to do this from anywhere in the world. Connections won't matter because we'll all be using wireless devices connected to a GPS system in the sky. Speed won't matter because we'll have solved the last-mile bottleneck problem.

As you continue your studies of technology, we encourage you to think "beyond your ears." That's our version of asking you to think outside the box. ❖

---

developed a camcorder that compares each frame to the previous one, determines if the movement of objects is caused by hand movement jitters, and, if so, eliminates the problem.[29]

- Gas ranges that detect when water is about to boil, regulate simmering, and adjust temperature settings for a variety of cookware and foods.[30]
- Clothes washers that automatically balance loads to avoid stoppage, determine dirt content to add detergent, determine type of clothes for the appropriate cycle, and determine clothes weight for the amount of water.[31,32]
- Dishwashers that can save you as much as $44 annually in electricity and water consumption by evaluating dirt content and shutting off the wash cycle when your dishes are clean.[33]

You may be using many intelligent appliances and not even know it. As each day passes, home appliances with embedded IT systems are becoming more commonplace. Many of these intelligent appliances make use of automatic speech recognition. So, when you say "boil water," an intelligent gas range will adjust its settings based on the amount of water you have to boil and the type of cookware you're using. You may even be able to tell your microwave oven to "pop popcorn." It will adjust the settings and even shut itself off when all the kernels are popped—no more burned popcorn in the microwave.

Behind these new types of intelligent home appliances is an emerging technology called fuzzy logic. *Fuzzy logic* is a method of working with "fuzzy" information; that is, information that is incomplete, ambiguous, or imprecise. For example, fuzzy logic can analyze information such as *hot, cold, tall, short, medium, reasonable,* or even *somewhat*. As opposed to most types of IT systems that require crisp, discrete information (such as a specific number or measurement), fuzzy logic systems work with information that is often a matter of interpretation. For example, if you were describing professional basketball players, would you describe a 6-foot 5-inch player as "tall"? What about a 6-foot 4.5-inch player—would that person be "short"?

Fuzzy logic is actually a subfield of artificial intelligence (AI), which we discussed in Chapter 4. Recall that AI is the science of making machines imitate human thinking and behavior. Human thinking and behavior almost always deal with a type of fuzzy information. Intelligent home appliances must incorporate fuzzy logic (such as determining the boiling point of water) to make decisions.

Your Internet-Connected Home

As we close this chapter, you should consider the "big picture" and how your home life will change. Someday, your home will be completely connected and Internet-connected. First, that is, every electronic device in your home will be connected to all others. From anywhere in your home, using wireless speech recognition, you'll be able to start and stop any device, lower the lights, play music, and a host of other activities.

Second, your home will be completely connected to the Internet. So, you may have an intelligent toilet that can take your blood pressure and pulse and evaluate your bodily wastes to see if you're getting sick. This information will be sent—via the Internet—to your doctor's office. Your doctor will have an AI-based computer that can determine your health and perhaps even send you an e-mail message that your vitamin C is getting low.

These are not far-fetched ideas. You can probably expect to see them on a widespread basis by the year 2015. The Internet will be the driving force behind all this. The Internet is becoming important and ubiquitous to the point that in the not too distant future our entire society and business world will depend on it completely every day. Think about electricity—we depend on it completely every day. Someday, we will depend on the Internet in the same way.

CLOSING CASE STUDY

Self-Scanning, Multimedia, and Wireless Grocery Shopping

From Lands' End to Sharper Image, retailers of all kinds are embracing emerging technologies. Shoe retailers can capture a computer image of your foot and customize shoes to fit you exactly. Wedding accessories retailers create full images of a bride's physique and fashion the perfectly fitting wedding dress.

Grocery stores, wanting to make your shopping experience more enjoyable and easier, while hoping you'll buy more food and food-related products, are not to be outdone. Grocery stores are already using emerging technologies such as self-scanning checkout lines, multimedia kiosks, and wireless grocery carts.

Self-Scanning Checkout Lines

Checking out at a grocery store is always the worst aspect of shopping, especially if you have only a couple of items and the lines are long. So, most grocers now have self-scanning checkout lines where you do your own scanning and perform your own transaction processing (essentially, a form of a customer integrated system). In these lines, you simply pass each grocery item across a scanner and place each item in a bag. The bag device actually weighs your items to ensure that the weight of the item you place in the bag is the same as the weight of the item you just scanned. If you have produce, you place it on a scale and then enter a unique code for the item.

Then you scan your own coupons if you have some and enter your method of payment. If by card, you swipe your card and then verify your amount. If by cash, you insert bills and coins into a machine. That's about all—except for walking out with your groceries and preparing them for dinner.

Multimedia Kiosks

Have you ever tried to find certain small or peculiar items in a grocery store? How about toothpicks? How about fruit bars? Where *are* those items located? Perhaps you wander through the aisles until you find them. But most people prefer to go directly to the items they need for a quick and efficient grocery shopping experience.

What about comparison shopping? What are the nutritional differences between canned peaches, dried peaches, and fresh peaches? Which is the best to use in peach pie or homemade peach ice cream? Does it make a difference?

Well, many grocery stores now have multimedia kiosks to help you find items and find the right kind of items. If you were hunting for the right peaches, the kiosk would compare the nutritional values of fresh, canned, and dried peaches. It would also inform you of their cost and offer you a map showing their locations. Some grocery multimedia kiosks also give you the ability to print recipes.

Wireless Grocery Carts

Using wireless technologies and a form of a global positioning system attached to your grocery shopping cart, you can now move through the store, entering items you wish to find, and have the system display directions for you. With some of these systems, you can even enter your grocery list to have the system respond with the most efficient way to move through the store to pick up what you need.

In the information age and the coming digital age, all forms of businesses will fiercely embrace such emerging technologies, because of the value these technologies provide. And, behind the scenes, these technologies will help businesses learn more about you. ❖

KNOWLEDGE WORKER'S -LIST

Why Some Technologies Are Categorized as "Emerging." Categorizing a technology as emerging doesn't necessarily mean that it's brand new. Technologies can be called emerging because

- The technology is so new that most businesses have really yet to begin using it
- The technology is fairly well-established, but businesses have yet to fully exploit it

In the first instance, you can include such technologies as electronic cash. In the second instance, you can include such technologies as multimedia.

How Emerging Technologies Are Beginning to Incorporate More of the Senses. Emerging technologies that are beginning to incorporate more of the senses include

- ***3-D*** Technologies that present images realistically enough that you may believe the object is in the room with you
- ***Automatic speech recognition*** Technologies that can capture what you say and distinguish between words and sentences
- ***Virtual reality*** Technologies that present a three-dimensional computer simulation in which you actively and physically participate
- ***Biometrics*** Technologies that use physical characteristics—such as your fingerprint, the blood vessels in the retina of your eye, the sound of your voice, or perhaps even your breath—to provide identification

The Dramatic Changes Occurring as a Result of and on the Internet. Changes surrounding the Internet are undoubtedly the most visible, rapidly changing, dynamic,

◀ Questions ▶

1. Find a grocery store that offers one or more emerging technologies and try shopping there. What was your experience? Did you have trouble, perhaps, scanning your own groceries or spelling items correctly at a multimedia kiosk?

2. By providing self-scanning, grocery stores are hoping to achieve two goals. The first is to give you a more efficient shopping experience. The second is to employ fewer checkout clerks. What are the legal, ethical, and social ramifications of replacing people with technology? In your view, do grocery stores have an obligation to retrain employees displaced by technology? Why or why not?

3. What about security? Is it possible for you to scan one item and then place another of equal weight in your bag? Doesn't automation actually make stealing easier? What other measures can grocery stores take to minimize if not eliminate theft?

4. What about fraudulent use of someone else's credit card? If you pay by credit card, a clerk is supposed to match your signature with the signature on the back. But not in self-scanning. You swipe your card and process your transaction, all without ever providing a signature. How can grocery stores overcome this problem? Or can they?

5. As you move through a grocery store with a wireless and GPS-enabled cart, the grocery store will be tracking your every move. They will then be able to determine, for instance, that you buy milk first and then breakfast cereal. Grocery stores plan to use such information to send you marketing material. How does that make you feel? Is it an invasion of your shopping privacy? Why or why not?

6. What other emerging technologies could grocery stores employ to making your shopping experience more enjoyable and efficient? What about speech recognition or perhaps biometrics? Will the proliferation of technology in the retail environment in general have a positive or negative effect on consumers? Justify your answer.

mind-boggling, and exciting of all the emerging technologies. Four such changes include

1. *Electronic cash* An electronic representation of cash that you can use to make purchases on the Internet
2. *Internet telephones* The technology tools necessary for carrying on a phone conversation over the Internet
3. *High-speed Internet access* Technologies such DSL and ISDN lines offered by cable TV service providers and telephone service providers and cable modems offered by cable TV service providers
4. *Internet appliances* Scaled-down computers or newly developed devices that support access to the Internet and possibly a few other basic functions such as note taking and maintaining an address book

The Role of the Wireless Revolution in Mobilizing People and Technology. Wireless communications media connect people and technology without physical cables—what you might refer to as *virtual connectivity*.

1. *Global positioning system (GPS)* 24 earth-orbiting satellites that continuously transmit radio signals that you can use to determine your location
2. *Wireless local area networks (wireless LANs)* Networks that cover a limited geographic distance in which all components or computers are connected without physical cables

How Emerging Technologies Will Affect Their Personal Lives. Many emerging technologies will simplify your personal life. Two such emerging technologies include

- *Smart cards* A small plastic card that contains a memory chip on which a sum of money can be placed and updated
- *Intelligent home appliances* Appliances in your home that contain an embedded IT system that controls numerous functions and is capable of making some decisions

Finally, all emerging technologies will come together to create your completely Internet-connected home. ❖

Electronic Commerce
Business and You on the Internet

Finding Freeware and Shareware on the Internet

When you buy your first computer, software seems a secondary decision since most computers come preloaded with software. But after a while you begin to feel a need for other software and that's when sticker shock sets in. Even upgrading to the latest version of your existing software can make a real dent in your pocketbook. And after installing new software, you may find it simply doesn't meet your needs. That's when you notice that you can't return opened software, you can only exchange it for a new copy. So if it doesn't meet your needs you're out of luck with commercial consumer software.

An alternative to commercial software that you might consider is shareware or freeware. Shareware is sometimes called "try before you buy" software because users are permitted to try the software on their own computer system (generally for a limited time) without any cost or obligation. Then you make a payment if you decide you want to keep using the software beyond the evaluation (trial) period. Freeware is software available at no charge to users for as long as they choose to use the software.

Using Your Computer for More than Work

By far the most popular freeware/shareware applications are games. The quality of these software titles is truly amazing for software that is free to download and begin playing immediately whenever you want. Shareware/freeware games are so numerous on the Internet that you'll often find games grouped by categories. Common categories are action/adventure, board, card, casino, educational, role-playing, simulation, sports, strategy and war, and word games.

When you're looking over the games available, remember that you should first ascertain whether the software is shareware or freeware. In some cases the Web site is not really clear on this issue. For example, some game descriptions make no mention of money, yet after you've downloaded the game it talks about registering your game for a price. At the other end of the spectrum you'll encounter traditional software that lists a price next to the description and requires a credit card to download and purchase, and often these games will describe themselves as shareware. Remember though, true shareware permits you to download the software and try it for free. So, in this case, the term shareware is a bit of a misnomer.

Connect to the Internet and several sites that offer freeware and shareware games. Pick at least two games and download them. For each, answer the following questions:

A. Is a description of the game provided?
B. Are system requirements listed?
C. Can you tell if the game is freeware or shareware without downloading it?
D. Are any of the games you selected really commercial software that requires a purchase before you download the game?
E. If the game is shareware, how long may you use it until registration is required?
F. If the game is shareware, does the game cease to function after the free period is over? How can you tell without waiting that long?
G. How long does it take to download the game? Is it worth it?

Animating Your Computer Screen

Wander through most any office or even your school computer lab and you'll see a variety of screen savers in action. Screen savers—the software that occupies your screen when the computer is unused for a period of time—are very common utilities. Sometimes the screen saver provides a beautiful scene with a recurring action. Others provide a different look every time they activate. Microsoft Windows includes several standard screen savers. In Windows 95 and beyond you'll also find *desktop themes* that do include a screen saver but go much further than that. In addition to providing software that activates when your computer is inactive, themes alter the look of the basic screen you see when you are working. Borders, standard application icons, and even the cursor are changed with desktop themes.

Connect to a couple of different sites that offer screen savers. Download at least two screen savers and answer the following questions:

A. Is a description of the screen saver provided?
B. Is the screen saver available for other operating systems?
C. Can you tell if the screen saver is freeware or shareware without downloading it?
D. Do any of the screen savers include desktop themes for Windows?
E. Are any other screen savers or desktop themes available at the site?
F. Does it work as advertised?

Protecting Your Computer Investment

Have you ever been frantically typing away, desperately trying to make an assignment deadline, when all of a sudden something goes wrong with your computer? If you're lucky the problem is something easy to identify, so you correct the problem and go on about your work. Other times the solution eludes you. Most of the time these problems have nice logical explanations such as hardware or software conflicts or failures of some kind.

In a few rare instances, the problem may have been caused intentionally—by a computer virus—a program which someone develops with malicious intent to harm an IT system.

So how does a computer virus get into your system? Anytime you download software, open a file attachment to an e-mail, or read a file off a diskette from another computer, you stand the chance of contracting a computer virus. And access to the Internet increases your opportunity to download files from many different sources. So on every computer it owns virtually every company installs antivirus protection software that scans new files for known viruses and purges them from the system. The catch is that traditional antivirus software can find only viruses that it knows about. As new viruses come along, antivirus software must be updated. The deviant minds that develop viruses seem to find more and better ways to infiltrate your system every day.

Connect to a site that allows you to download antivirus software, download the software, and answer the following questions:

A. Is the antivirus software shareware, freeware, or traditional retail software?

B. What viruses does the software detect?

C. Does the software remove the virus as well as detect it?

D. Are updates for the software available to detect new viruses? How often are they available? At what cost?

E. Does the software detect viruses not yet created? How does it do that?

F. Does the software site offer recommendations to reduce your chance of contracting a virus?

G. Does the site tell you what to do if you have already contracted a virus?

Searching for Shareware and Freeware

So maybe the shareware/freeware software concept appeals to you. You'd like to be able to try the software before you buy. If you want software such as screen savers or antivirus software you're in luck. Just look through the table on the next page or go to the Web site that supports this text. But what if you want some shareware to help you compose music or to keep track of your soccer team's schedule? Well, then you'll have to go searching for that software. You could use a general-

purpose search engine such as Yahoo! and type in shareware and music or soccer. If you do this you will find a few shareware software titles to download. But suppose those few titles don't meet your needs.

Finding shareware/freeware titles can be daunting for two reasons. First, currently there are over 1 million shareware and freeware titles available to you. Unless a search engine is designed specifically for this type of software, you'll probably miss many of these titles using a general-purpose search engine. Second, most shareware/freeware developers don't have their own Web sites. As many don't develop their software as a business, they can't justify the cost of supporting their own Web sites. To address both of these challenges, Web sites have been created that maintain databases of thousands of shareware/freeware software titles. Most also include a search engine to help you navigate through these thousand of titles.

Find a site that maintains a database of freeware and shareware software. As you peruse it, answer the following questions:

A. How does the site group the software?

B. Can you search by operating system or platform?

C. Does the site provide descriptions of the software?

D. Can you search by file size?

E. Are screen captures from the software provided?

F. Are reviews and/or ratings of the software provided?

G. When was the last update for the site?

Communicating over the Internet

Have you ever sent an e-mail to a friend and had her or him respond right away? It's often a little surprising and raises the question, Wouldn't it be great if you always knew just which of your friends were on the Internet at the same moment as you? One way to know is always to check a predesignated chat room somewhere on the Internet for your friends, but that's cumbersome and there's another way. Instant messaging freeware applications allow you and your friends to watch for each other and to tell instantly when you log onto the Internet. Once you see each other, you can send messages (that arrive faster than e-mail and need not be opened), request real-time chats, include more than one friend in these chat sessions (that are also private), and find new friends who are on the Internet when you are. Instant messaging applications require you to register yourself and receive either a "handle" (a name you pick for yourself) or a registration number. Your friends will look for your handle or number to tell if you are on the Internet when they are.

One problem you or your friends may have if you use your school's or company's e-mail system is that when you travel or are away from school or work you must dial back into the school or work system to retrieve your e-mail. If you travel, this can mean long-distance charges. Or maybe the number of phone lines to dial into the system are limited. Either way, retrieving your e-mail can be a hassle. Enter browser-based free e-mail. A number of companies now offer free e-mail accounts that can be accessed through your Web browser just by accessing the Internet. Many of the larger Internet service providers offer toll-free phone numbers for Internet access. This means wherever you are you have quick, cheap access to your e-mail.

Find one instant messaging software site, download the software, and have a classmate do the same. Register with the service and try communicating. Also, pick one free e-mail provider, register with it, notify a classmate, and practice sending and receiving e-mail through the service. Then, answer the following questions:

A. How easy was the messaging software to download, install, and register?

B. Were you able to see and communicate with a classmate using the messaging software?

C. How quickly did the instant messages arrive using the messaging software?

D. Were you able to find other new friends on the messaging software? Could you qualify them by similar interests?

E. What other services does the messaging software offer? Are any of interest to you?

F. How easy was it to register and use the free e-mail? Was it completely free?

G. Does the free e-mail service allow you to attach files to your e-mails? If so, do they limit the size of these files?

Web Sites for Downloading Freeware and Shareware

Antivirus Software	Address
F-Prot	http://www.datafellows.com
ViruSafe	http://www.virusafe.com
VirusScan	http://www.mcafee.com
Sophos	http://www.sophos.com

Games	Address
Hotgames.com	http://www.hotgames.com
Free Games Net	http://www.free-games-net.com
Freegames.org	http://www.freegames.org
Jumbo	http://www.jumbo.com
Free Games 4 Fun	http://www.freegames4fun.com

continued

Web Sites (concluded)

Screen Savers and Desktop Themes	Address
Top100ScreenSavers.com	http://www.top100screensavers.com
ScreensaverShot.com	http://www.screensavershot.com
Bonanzas Online	http://www.bonanzas.com/ssavers
Screens and Themes	http://www.screensandthemes.com
Screensavers.com	http://www.screensavers.com

Shareware/Freeware Search Resources	Address
ZDNet Downloads	http://www.zdnet.com/downloads
Shareware Stockpile	http://www.stockpile.com
Freeware Hall of Fame	http://www.freewarehof.org
FreewareArena	http://www.freewarearena.com
FreewareFilez	http://www.freewarefilez.com

Messaging and E-Mail Software	Address
Microsoft Hotmail	http://www.hotmail.com
AOL Instant Messenger	http://www.aol.com/aim
Yahoo! Mail	http://www.mail.yahoo.com
ICQ	http://web.icq.com
Lycosmail	http://www.lycosmail.com

Go to the Web site that supports this text:
http://www.mhhe.com/haag
and select "Electronic Commerce Projects."

We've included links to over 100 Web sites for finding freeware and shareware.

KEY TERMS AND CONCEPTS

Automatic Speech Recognition (ASR), 234
Biometrics, 241
Cave Automatic Virtual Environment (CAVE), 241
Continuous Automatic Speech Recognition, 236
Cybersickness, 240
Discrete Automatic Speech Recognition, 236
Electronic Cash (E-Cash; Digital Cash), 242

Emerging Technology, 232
Feature Analysis, 234
Fuzzy Logic, 254
Global Positioning System (GPS), 250
Glove, 238
Headset, 238
Intelligent Home Appliances, 253
Internet Appliance, 246
Language Processing, 235
Microbrowser, 248
Pattern Classification, 234

Smart Card, 253
Speaker-Dependent Automatic Speech Recognition, 236
Speaker-Independent Automatic Speech Recognition, 236
Three-Dimensional (3-D), 233
Virtual Reality, 237
Walker, 238
Web Appliance, 246
Web Phone, 247
Wireless Local Area Network (Wireless LAN), 251

SHORT-ANSWER QUESTIONS

1. Why are some technologies considered to be "emerging"?
2. What three steps are involved in automatic speech recognition?
3. How do the four types of automatic speech recognition systems differ?
4. What is virtual reality? What are the key features of virtual reality?
5. What type of cybersickness sometimes occurs when people use virtual reality?
6. How does electronic cash work on the Internet?
7. What are the key "ility" issues that wireless technologies address?
8. What are intelligent home appliances? What can they do for you?
9. What is biometrics?
10. What are the four categories of Internet appliances? How do they differ?

SHORT-QUESTION ANSWERS

For each of the following answers, provide an appropriate question:

1. 3-D, automatic speech recognition, virtual reality, and biometrics.
2. Pattern classification.
3. My fingerprint, for example.
4. These are all examples of cybersickness.
5. Because it's easy to lose.
6. A cable modem.
7. A microbrowser.
8. It can help me find where I am.
9. One reason is because pulling cable is expensive.
10. Intelligent home appliance.

DISCUSSION QUESTIONS

1. Of the technologies we've presented in this chapter, which do you consider to be emerging and which do you consider now to be standard? Also, make a note of any emerging technologies we discussed that simply fizzled out and never became a reality.
2. What new emerging technologies have you noticed in recent months that we did not include in this chapter? Are they considered emerging because the technology is so new that most businesses have really yet to begin using them, or are they fairly well-established but businesses have yet to fully exploit them?
3. Throughout this chapter, we've discussed many issues related to privacy and ethics. Which emerging technologies do you believe have the greatest potential for increasing the invasion of a person's privacy? For each technology, what actions must society take to prevent this invasion of privacy? What actions must the government take to prevent this invasion of privacy?
4. Based on the emerging technologies in this chapter, what do you believe the "home of the future" will look like? Think about every facet of a home, from lawn and garden sprinklers to garbage disposals and trash compactors.
5. With free long-distance calling through the Internet, many traditional telephone service providers will have to change their business plans. In what ways will their plans have to change? Can these traditional telephone service providers continue to stay in business or are they doomed to go out of business? Why?

CHAPTER OUTLINE

INDUSTRY PERSPECTIVES

Financial Services
270
Disaster Recovery Plans Are More than One Plan

Retail
273
For Sears, Planning for the Future was Essential

Manufacturing
287
Prototyping with Software Is a Must in Manufacturing

".com"
299
JD Edwards' OneWorld Enterprise Software Prepares Your Organization for the Web

IN THE NEWS

- **283** Ninety-five percent of all projects incur cost and time overruns. And 65 percent of those eventually incur costs two to three times greater than originally planned.
- **286** Selfsourcing—developing systems for yourself as a knowledge worker—is one more aspect of knowledge worker computing.
- **292** Revenues from IT-related outsourcing are expected to exceed $120 billion in the year 2000.
- **292** Forty-five percent of businesses have outsourced some major portion of their IT environment.
- **295** Duke Power Co. officially "turned the lights out" on a systems development project after spending over $12 million.

FEATURES

- **276** **Photo Essay 7-1** ITW Enterprises at Work
- **284** **The Global Perspective** Hiring Programmers from around the World
- **284** **Team Work** Your Responsibilities during Each Step of the SDLC
- **291** **On Your Own** How Have You Selfsourced?
- **295** **On Your Own** A Request for Proposal and the Systems Development Life Cycle
- **296** **The Global Perspective** Outsourcing at a Global Level
- **299** **Team Work** Matching IT Systems to the *Who* of Systems Development
- **303** **Electronic Commerce** Building the Perfect Web Page

KNOWLEDGE WORKERS' CHECKLIST

In the Information Age, Knowledge Workers Understand . . .

1. The importance of planning and how to plan for IT systems in an organization
2. Why their participation is important in the development of IT systems
3. How organizations traditionally develop IT systems through insourcing and their role during that process
4. What selfsourcing and outsourcing are and how they affect the way organizations develop systems
5. How to take a holistic organizational view using enterprise resource planning and enterprise software

WEB SUPPORT

http://www.mhhe.com/haag

- Enterprise Software
- Case Tools
- Web Development Tools
- Web Page References
- Free Images and Backgrounds
- Web Hosting Services

Developing IT Systems

Bringing IT Systems to Life

CHAPTER 7

CASE STUDY

HomeBase Buys Software to Move beyond EDI

Electronic data interchange (EDI) is certainly a cost-saving technology. HomeBase relied heavily on EDI to move documents between itself and its suppliers, in late 1998 issuing 90 percent of its purchase orders and 70 percent of its invoices using EDI. But HomeBase found that EDI simply wasn't enough for two reasons.

First, HomeBase moved its EDI transactions over a value-added network (VAN). The VAN charged a fee for each transaction, and those fees began to add up. HomeBase split the fees with its partners, but came to realize that its partners were passing those costs back to HomeBase in the form of higher prices.

Second, many of HomeBase's smaller suppliers couldn't afford the up-front investment in technology for EDI. Those smaller suppliers accounted for over 200 of HomeBase's 1,500 suppliers, and for them HomeBase was forced to process documents manually, a painstaking, error-ridden, and expensive process.

Clearly, HomeBase needed a new software solution beyond EDI that (1) had no fees and (2) its smaller suppliers could afford.

Instead of developing its own new software, HomeBase went shopping and found eBizness Transact, a component of IPNet eBizness Suite. Although eBizness Transact isn't exactly cheap, Glen Hamilton, manager of quick response at HomeBase, explained, "We were confident we would not have to wait long for our investment to pay for itself."

HomeBase didn't have to wait long. It was able to install eBizness Transact in about a half day. After two weeks of integrating eBizness Transact with its current systems, HomeBase began testing it with seven of its largest suppliers. The test was a complete success. Most importantly, HomeBase had found its software solution that required no fees and could easily be used by smaller suppliers.

HomeBase and all its suppliers are realizing immediate benefits from eBizness Transact. According to Glen, many of HomeBase's larger suppliers are saving as much as $50,000 per year. As many as 10 smaller suppliers are switching from paper documents to eBizness Transact every week.

HomeBase's acquisition of eBizness Transact is a form of software outsourcing, in which your organization buys software that has been developed by another organization. As HomeBase found, software acquired in this manner is often very easy to install, test, and begin using. Outsourcing is just one of the many facets of software development that we'll explore in this chapter.[1] ❖

Introduction

HomeBase acquired vitally important software through outsourcing. Outsourcing is one of the three *whos* (as in *who* will *do* it) of systems development, the other two being insourcing (developing software in-house) and selfsourcing (developing software for yourself as a knowledge worker). Today, organizations all over the world are spending billions of dollars to acquire or develop software and IT systems. Some are buying, or outsourcing, it (as did HomeBase) and others are insourcing it, developing it in-house.

Why should you learn about the systems development process? As a knowledge worker in today's information age, you and your work will definitely be affected by IT systems. Those systems that effectively meet your needs will help you be more productive and make better decisions. Systems that don't meet your needs may have a damaging effect on your productivity. So it's crucial that you help your organization develop the best systems possible.

As we move through the systems development process in this chapter, we'll focus on how the process works and what roles you may play. We don't expect to make you into a systems development expert. Students majoring in IT or MIS often take as many as seven courses that deal with a different aspect of systems development. But even if you're not majoring in IT or MIS, and don't plan to be an expert, you'll still have systems development roles and responsibilities in your career.

IT Systems
Aligning Organizational Goals and IT

Before we look at specific processes for implementing the systems development effort in your organization, it's worthwhile to take a step back and look at planning. Planning is the most fundamental and critical step of any effort your organization undertakes, regardless of whether you're developing a system that allows your customers to order products over the Internet, determining how to create the best logistical structure for warehouses around the world, or developing a strategic information alliance with another organization. If you don't carefully plan your activities (and determine why they're necessary), you're doomed to failure. If you don't believe that, revisit some of the dot-com failure stories in the chapter on electronic commerce (Chapter 5).

Planning takes on an especially strong organizational focus for new IT systems. For example, you already have systems in place that will affect or be affected by new systems (we call these older systems *legacy systems*), and you have to plan for this. Moreover, new IT systems support the concept of business process reengineering; that is, you may be able to create more efficient and streamlined business processes as a result of developing new IT systems. This takes planning. Everyone in your organization wants new and better IT systems. Unfortunately, your organization has limited resources and cannot develop all proposed IT systems, so you must carefully plan for which proposed IT systems will be developed, when, how, and by whom.

As your organization goes about this vitally important planning process, it will follow four general steps (see Figure 7.1). The goal is to create an *IT systems plan,* a document that outlines (1) what systems you

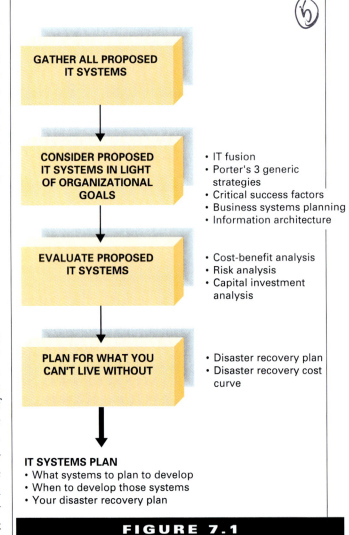

FIGURE 7.1

The IT Systems Planning Process

plan to develop, (2) when to develop those systems, and (3) your disaster recovery plan. Below, we highlight some of the major issues and challenges in creating an IT systems plan.

Gathering All Proposed IT Systems

Many of the IT systems proposed for development will be suggested by your organization's overall planning process. For example, your organization may decide to create an Internet presence, in which case it may need systems for allowing customers to order products on the Internet or perhaps even an extranet that allows your customers to tap into valuable resources on your intranet.

Your organization also needs to provide a mechanism that allows knowledge workers to suggest what new systems need to be developed. Many organizations today have formal procedures and forms that allow knowledge workers to do so. However you go about it, you must first gather all requests for new systems development.

Considering Proposed IT Systems in Light of Organizational Goals

In first considering all proposed IT systems development efforts, you need to do so in light of organizational goals and the strategic direction of your organization. Here, you can employ many techniques and methods such as IT fusion, Porter's three generic strategies (discussed in Chapter 2), critical success factors, business systems planning, and the development of an information architecture.

IT fusion is an idea originally developed by Peter Keen.[2] *IT fusion* occurs when the information technology within your organization is indistinguishable from the business processes and the people who exploit the information technology. That's a powerful statement. Your organization should strive to make technology such an integral part of its business dealings that your customers can't distinguish when technology starts and stops in a business process. If you can achieve this, you've achieved IT fusion. IT fusion should definitely be a part of your overall organizational plan, and IT systems should be developed to support it.

You should also evaluate proposed IT systems in light of your critical success factors. A *critical success factor (CSF)* is a factor simply critical to your organization's success. AT&T used the CSF method to help its long-distance service business.[3] AT&T's customer reps had found it difficult to communicate the advantages of using AT&T over the competition as small-business owners complained of increasingly complicated rate structures. As a result, the reps simply weren't successful in converting small businesses to AT&T's service, a CSF for the firm. So, AT&T examined the sales process and found that its rate information was not in a form that was helpful to its customers (a customer moment of value facet). AT&T then created a new system called 1-800-COMPARE, which it implemented with sophisticated data mining technologies that search through a caller's phone records to provide a side-by-side comparison of the caller's current carrier to AT&T. This information was all the reps needed to succeed and execute a CSF for the firm.

Evaluating Proposed IT Systems

At this point in the planning process, you've identified potential systems development efforts according to your organizational goals. However, because of limited resources, your organization can seldom develop every IT system it needs. To further refine which systems you'll develop, you need to use such techniques as a cost-benefit analysis method, a risk analysis method, and various capital investment analysis methods.

The *cost-benefit analysis* is the process of evaluating prospective IT systems for development by comparing system costs with system benefits. Costs and benefits include:

- Cost estimates for the actual systems development process
- Cost estimates for systems operation, maintenance, and support
- Cost estimates for systems adoption at different times in the future
- Costs for the organizational change required
- *Tangible benefits*—systems benefits that can be monetarily quantified (a form of objective information)
- *Intangible benefits*—systems benefits that cannot be monetarily quantified (a form of subjective information).

Typically, you compare costs and benefits by charting the quantifiable costs and benefits over time. In Figure 7.2a, you can see that costs are high during development while benefits remain at zero. Over time, benefits should surface and costs should drop to a level required to support the system.

IT systems risk (measured with the risk analysis method) is the possibility that a system will not achieve the benefits you predict. Figure 7.2b identifies general categories of systems you want to develop and ones you might want to avoid, based on the degree of risk compared to the magnitude of benefit.

Finally, the most quantitative of the evaluation methods is *capital investment analysis,* which calculates a quantitative measure of IT systems value using any number of different financial models including payback method, cost-benefit ratio, return on investment, net present value, and internal rate of return. In Table 7.1 you'll find a list of these different capital investment models, along with a description of how to perform the calculations.

We recommend that you use all of these methods when evaluating proposed IT systems for development. The more analysis you perform, the better your chances are of identifying the right systems to develop.

Planning for What You Can't Live Without

Last, but certainly not least, you need to determine which IT systems (and the information they support) you can't live without. If you truly achieve IT fusion, then many of your systems will be vital to your success and everyday operations. Unfortunately, disasters—such as power outages, floods, and even harmful hacking—occur all the time. Given that, your organization needs to develop a disaster recovery plan. A ***disaster recovery plan*** is the documentation of the possibility of losing an IT system and the formulation of procedures to minimize the damage.

A part of your disaster recovery plan should be a disaster recovery cost curve (see Figure 7.3). A ***disaster recovery cost curve*** charts (1) the cost to your organization of the unavailability of information and technology and (2) the cost to your organization of recovering from a disaster over time. Where the two intersect is in fact the best recovery plan in terms of cost and time.

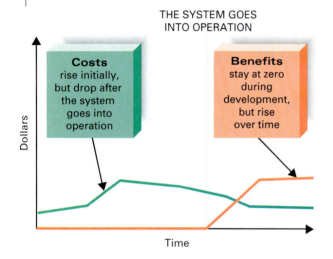

FIGURE 7.2A

Cost-Benefit Analysis

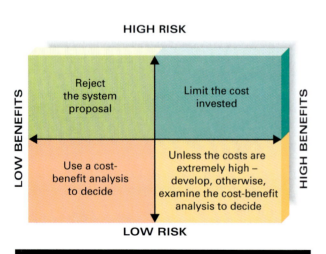

FIGURE 7.2B

Risk Analysis

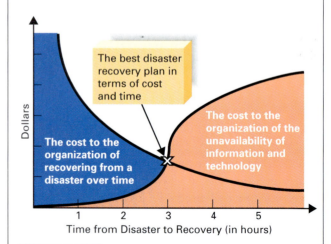

FIGURE 7.3

Deciding How Much to Spend on Disaster Recovery

TABLE 7.1 Capital Analysis Financial Models

Financial Model	Formula	Type of Result
Payback method (in years)	$\dfrac{\text{Original investment}}{\text{Annual net cash flow}}$	= time to pay back
Cost-benefit ratio (as a factor)	$\dfrac{\text{Benefits}}{\text{Costs}}$	= cost-benefit ratio
Return on investment (ROI, as a percent)	$\dfrac{\text{(Benefits-cost-depreciation)}}{\text{useful system life}}$	= net benefit
Net present value (NPV, in $)	Total net present value of all cash flows*	= value today of return in future
Internal rate of return (IRR, as a percent)	The NPV represented as a percentage return*	= expected return

*The net present value and internal rate of return calculation are too complex to summarize above. So both are defined completely below:

Net present value = sum of the present value of all future payments less the initial cost
 = $-CF_0 + \Sigma[CF_t/(1 + r)^t]$ where CF_0 = the initial cost
  CF_t = each future payment
  r = the discount rate
  t = the number of the time payment

Internal rate of return = the rate that completes the following summation equation
Cost = $\Sigma[CF_t/(1 + IRR)^t]$ where CF_t = the future payments
  IRR = the internal rate of return
  t = the number of the payment

The Goal—The IT Systems Plan

The culmination of all your systems planning efforts is the IT systems plan. It should carefully document which systems you plan to develop, the justification for developing those systems, when you plan to develop those systems, and the nature of your disaster recovery plan. Armed with your IT systems plan, you're ready to begin the actual systems development process.

Systems Development Is a Question-and-Answer Session

When people approach systems development, they ask questions such as: "*What* systems should we develop?" "*When* should we develop those systems?" "*Who* should develop the systems?" and "*How* should we go about developing systems?" The most important question people always ask is, "*Why* is my participation important during the systems development process?" These are all great questions and your answers to them will determine the success of the systems development process. Let's address *why* your participation is important, and then we'll look at the *who* and *how* aspects of systems development (we've already addressed *what* and *when* in the previous section on planning).

Why Is Your Participation Important?

Many people who have come before you and undoubtedly many who will follow say, "I'm not going to be an IT specialist—so why should I learn about the systems development process?" If you're asking that same question, congratulations—you're well on your way to becoming an information-literate knowledge worker. How so? Because you're asking, "Why is this material important to *me*? What does it mean? How can I use it?"

INDUSTRY PERSPECTIVE

Financial Services

Disaster Recovery Plans Are More than One Plan

It is possible to carry disaster recovery planning too far in the business world. Consider the merger of U.S. Bancorp and Firstar Bank, which created the nation's eight-largest bank holding company. At the time of the merger, the two separate entities had a combined total of almost 1,500 different disaster recovery plans. These plans ranged from what a particular branch bank would do in the event of a major disaster all the way to what another would do in the event it lost its janitorial services.

Even worse, there was only one technology disaster recovery plan in place for all branch banks to follow. And that single plan was housed within each branch bank, meaning that an update to it required updates at every location.

So, the manager of business continuity at U.S. Bancorp Kevin Donovan purchased a software package called Revolution, a product published by Comdisco. Revolution uses scenario-based planning to take into account various types and lengths of electrical outages and other disasters and then recommends the best disaster recovery plan depending on how fast a branch bank needs to recover. Revolution deploys the disaster recovery plan on the firm's intranet, giving access to all branches but maintaining only one central source so updating is simpler.

Today, the firm has only two disaster recovery plans for branch banks—one for rural branches and one for urban branches.

Most large organizations need more than one disaster recovery plan. But 1,500 is too many. If you're developing and maintaining that many disaster recovery plans, you're probably spending more on disaster recovery planning than what any particular disaster would cost.[4] ❖

Your participation in the systems development process is vitally important because you are (or will be)

1. A business process expert
2. A liaison to the customer
3. A quality control analyst
4. A manager of other people

First and foremost, in business you **are** the business process expert. For example, if you're an administrator at a hospital and the development of a new nursing allocation system is under way, who knows best how nursing allocation should occur? That's right—you do. During systems development, business process experts (which we refer to as knowledge workers throughout this text) know how things should work, what things should happen, how to handle exceptions, and so on. It would be ludicrous to tell a group of IT specialists to develop a new nursing allocation system without telling them how nurses should be allocated according to certain criteria such as expertise, overload hours, and time of year. In business, you are a business process expert. Without your input, the new system will never meet your needs.

Second, your knowledge of and participation in the systems development process is vitally important because you're a liaison to the customer. That is, you know what a certain customer segment wants, and you can relay that information to the project team. For example, if you work for a telephone company and manage a call center that fields billing questions, aren't you qualified to provide information pertaining to the appearance and content of new phone bills? Of course you are. And, if you want to make your customers happy, you have to act as a liaison between them and the project team.

Third, your participation is important because you'll act as a quality control analyst during the systems development process. Once you help define the logical requirements of a new system, you can't simply walk away and expect a system that meets your needs. For example, you still need to help review alternative technical solutions, acting as a quality control analyst to assure that the chosen technical alternative meets your logical needs.

Finally, your participation in the systems development process is important because you have ultimate responsibility for the work and productivity of others. In short, you will be a manager of other people, and it's your responsibility to see that new systems will improve the productivity of those you manage.

Systems Development
Who and *How*?

In the previous section, we dealt with the *what* and *when* questions of the systems development process during the planning step. These two questions always come first because they are the most important and they deal with all proposed systems development projects in your organization. Your organization should always determine *what* systems to develop and *when* to develop those systems within the strategic direction and goals of your organization.

Let's now turn our attention to the *who* and *how* questions of systems development. That is, (1) *who* will be responsible for the development of a specific system and (2) *how* or what tools and methods should you use to develop a specific system? You should notice that these two questions deal with a specific system. Your organization must consider each of these questions for each new systems development project. Many organizations today choose different *whos* and different *hows* for different projects.

Answering the *Who* Question of Systems Development

When approaching systems development as a knowledge worker, you have three choices for answering the *who* question—IT specialists within your organization, knowledge workers such as yourself, and another organization (see Figure 7.4). First, you can choose IT specialists within your organization to develop a new system. If this is your decision, you're choosing to *insource* the development of a new system. Second, you can ask knowledge workers (one of which may be you) to develop their own respective systems, which is *selfsourcing*. This is becoming quite common in most organizations and is part of the overall concept of knowledge worker computing. Finally, you can choose another organization to develop a new system, which is *outsourcing*.

Determining *who* is critical in systems development. In the box entitled "Asking Questions to Make the *Who* Decision," we've highlighted important issues to help you make that decision. As we explore the various *whos* throughout this chapter, we'll discuss these issues in more detail.

Answering the *How* Question of Systems Development

The *how* question of systems development relates to the tools and methods you choose for the development of a new system. The *how* question has numerous alterna-

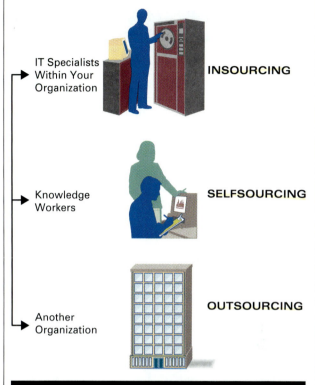

FIGURE 7.4

Options for Answering the *Who* Question

tives. For example, in *Extended Learning Module A*, we introduced groupware; and in *Extended Learning Module B*, we looked at how to develop a system using a personal productivity software package (a DBMS package for creating a personal database). In this chapter, we want to look mainly at three more *how* options, which include the following:

- *Traditional systems development life cycle.* A structured approach to systems development in which you, as a knowledge worker, tell IT specialists within your organization what you want
- *Prototyping.* The process of building models of systems to determine requirements and express functionality
- *Enterprise resource planning (ERP)* and *enterprise software.* A holistic view of your organization, its processes, and the supporting IT systems

As we explore various *hows* throughout this chapter, we'll discuss issues that will help you decide which *how* is best for a given systems development project.

Combining *Who* and *How*

The *who* and *how* answers to the systems development questions are definitely interrelated. For example, if you

Asking Questions to Make the *Who* Decision

	Answer	Choices Insource	Selfsource	Outsource
1. Will the system support a unique core competency?	Yes	Yes	Maybe	No
2. Is cost an overriding consideration?	Yes	No	Maybe	Yes
3. Is time critical?	Yes	No	Maybe	Yes
4. Do you possess the necessary technical expertise?	Yes	Yes	Maybe	No
5. Is organizational control of the system critical?	Yes	Yes	Maybe	No
6. Will the system support a common business or industry function?	Yes	Maybe	No	Yes
7. Is gaining or having the necessary technical expertise part of your strategic plan?	Yes	Yes	Maybe	No
8. Will the system support only a small number of knowledge workers? ❖	Yes	Maybe	Yes	Maybe

choose IT specialists within your organization (insourcing), they'll most often use the traditional systems development life cycle. If you choose to develop your own system (selfsourcing), you'll most often use prototyping. Whatever the case, decisions that you'll face during systems development are not simple, and making the wrong decision can cost your organization millions of dollars and a strategic or competitive advantage in the marketplace.

Insourcing and the Traditional Systems Development Life Cycle

Separating Duties among IT Specialists and Knowledge Workers

Most organizations today still choose insourcing as the *who* and the traditional systems development life cycle as the *how* for systems development. Recall that *insourcing* involves choosing IT specialists within your organization to develop the system. The ***traditional systems development life cycle (traditional SDLC)*** is a structured step-by-step approach to developing systems that creates a separation of duties among IT specialists and knowledge workers. In the traditional SDLC (which we'll simply refer to as the SDLC), knowledge workers are the business process experts and quality control analysts, whereas IT specialists are responsible for the actual design, implementation, and support of the system. Using the SDLC, your organization follows six steps (see Figure 7.5), including

1. *Planning* Establish an IT plan to meet the strategic plans of the organization.
2. *Scoping* Define the scope of the proposed system.
3. *Analysis* Determine the logical requirements for the proposed system.
4. *Design* Convert the logical requirements into a technical system design.
5. *Implementation* Create the new system.
6. *Support* Provide ongoing support.

Throughout this section, we highlight ITW Enterprises as it proceeded through the SDLC. ITW Enterprises (ITW) serves the metropolitan area of Detroit by assisting business executives in finding temporary apartment housing while they work in Detroit. In late 2000, ITW found itself in somewhat of a dilemma. Business was booming, which was good. Unfortunately, ITW found that it had quickly outgrown its supporting IT infrastructure. The IT systems at ITW simply could not handle the huge volume of information that flowed

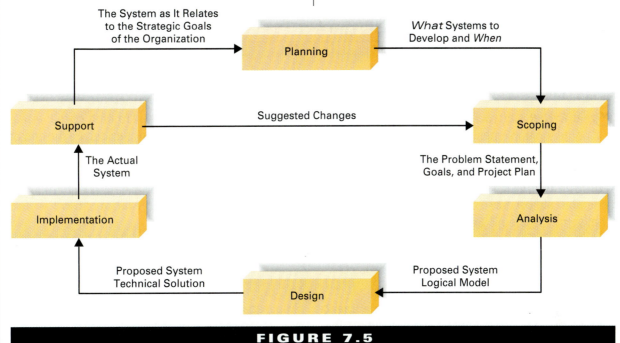

FIGURE 7.5

The Six Steps in the Traditional Systems Development Life Cycle

INDUSTRY PERSPECTIVE

Retail

For Sears, Planning for the Future Was Essential

In 1990, Sears, Roebuck & Co., one of the most well-known retailers in the world, spent two years and millions of dollars developing a software system to support the work of field technicians. At the time, wireless devices were truly an emerging technology. But Sears realized the potential value of wireless devices and developed a system based on wireless technologies, planning that the company's return on investment would be substantial over time.

And its planning has paid off. Today, Sears employs nearly 13,000 field technicians, repairing everything from dishwashers to lawn mowers at customers' homes. About 8,500 field technicians are working at any particular time, accounting for 72,000 work orders per day.

With its wireless technology–based system developed 10 years ago, Sears has eliminated all forms of paper flowing to and from the field. Using their handheld devices, field technicians can access Sears's database of 5 million parts for ordering and availability. This alone has reduced back office expenses by 70 percent. Field technicians no longer fill out time cards. Instead, they use mobile computers to send time information to Sears's payroll system. Sears can also alter routes for the day and instantly notify each technician of new jobs or changes to the existing job schedule.

Today, planning is fundamental. But don't just plan for today's technologies. Instead, look out on the horizon and seek emerging technologies for systems development.[5] ❖

We've Got a Problem . . .

No Wait—We've Got Many Problems!

Reid Becker started ITW 3 years ago from his home to supplement his income. "Supplement" is no longer the correct term. Reid's business now represents over 50 apartment complexes, works with over 300 business executives per month, and generates almost $250,000 in profit annually. So what's the problem? Business is great, and the money is even better. How could there be a problem? Let's listen to what some employees (and a customer) have to say.

"One of my biggest jobs is to find new apartment complexes to represent. But I never know what type of apartment complexes we need to represent. I can go look in the master client workbook, but it takes me hours to determine that we need more apartment complexes with workout facilities or more complexes with three-bedroom apartments."
—*Mark from Apartment Services*

"The daily reports we receive from Apartment Services were okay when I was only working with a few clients. Today I worked with over 40 clients, all of whom had different desires. I'm tired of requesting 40 different reports every day. Besides, by the end of the day many units in some apartment complexes are gone. Too much information—much of which is already old—does me no good."
—*Nash from Client Services*

"Last week I received a folder from Client Services that didn't include the name of the apartment complex a client had chosen. I spent almost an hour tracking down the right person who could tell me a simple apartment complex name. I lost valuable time and had to come in on the weekend to make it up."
—*Julia from Finance*

"I really appreciate the service you provide. But I asked to see several photos of each apartment complex before making my decision. It took several days for those photos to arrive. When I finally chose an apartment complex, it was already full."
—*Rhonda (an unhappy customer)* ❖

---

through the organization. ITW had a real problem; without access to timely and correct information, employees couldn't perform their jobs effectively, which meant that customers were unhappy and revenues were lost. The owner of ITW, Reid Becker, recognized that a new system was badly needed.

Photo Essay 7–1 details ITW prior to the new system, including customers, the organizational structure, how processes worked, and the supporting IT infrastructure.

Step 1: Planning

Establishing an IT Plan to Meet the Strategic Plans of the Organization

Planning is the first step in any systems development process—regardless of your answer to *who* or *how*. During the planning step of systems development, your goal is to forge an important alliance between the strategic direction of the organization and the IT systems

plan (what we have referred to as IT fusion). Again, we cannot stress enough the importance of the planning step in systems development. Proper planning not only helps your organization define new systems but also helps align the IT systems plan with the strategic organizational plan; aids in determining whether the development of systems should be insourced, selfsourced, or outsourced; and helps you develop guidelines for technology use throughout the organization.

Step 2: Scoping

Defining the Scope of the Proposed System

The goal of step 2—*scoping*—is to lay the foundation for the systems development process of a specific system. Recall that step 1 deals with identifying all systems that your organization needs to develop. Starting with step 2, you focus on one specific system and its development. Most important, you want to very clearly define the problem in step 2. That may seem simple and straightforward, but you'd be surprised how many systems development efforts are unsuccessful because people focus on only a symptom of the problem, and not the real problem.

At ITW, for example, Reid gathered several people from different departments to determine exactly what the problem was and to develop a plan for proceeding with the systems development process. In the first meeting, everyone was quite vocal and aggressive in blaming others for specific problems. But, in reality, no one was to blame. The real problem was that the current IT infrastructure no longer supported the business processes. Things were fine with a small number of apartment complexes and only a handful of clients. But as the business grew the IT infrastructure didn't. It was time to change, and it was time to change the technology, not the people. Once employees realized this, they began to focus more on their jobs and how technology failed to support their efforts. In the end, the group created a problem statement and a plan of action (see Figure 7.6).

CAREER OPPORTUNITY

Did ITW plan for its new system and systems development process? Unfortunately, no. ITW recognized that a problem existed, determined that the problem was important enough to solve, and then set out to develop a new IT system. Many small organizations such as ITW do not have a good IT systems plan in place; they simply react to problems as they arise. Regardless of the size of your organization, you should always have some sort of IT systems plan in place.

Key Tasks during Scoping

Determine Which Business Units the New System Will Affect Scoping not only involves obtaining a better grasp of the proposed system but also how the proposed system will affect your organization. The proposed system at ITW affected all areas, so the project team included members from each department.

Gather the Project Team The *project team* should include a manager (usually an IT person), management people within the organization who will act as champions of the proposed system, management people of business units that the proposed system will affect, several IT specialists, and several knowledge workers. Each of these people brings special expertise and knowledge to the project team. At ITW, everyone

---

Problem Statement

The current structure does not support information sharing among departments. In some instances, there are automated portions that allow Apartment Services and Finance to share needed information. However, Client Services needs not only access to that information, but also the ability to provide access to its information to the other departments.

The Goals of the New System

1. Automate information gathering and tracking by Client Services.
2. Allow Apartment Services to view but not update any information in Client Services.
3. Support a mechanism that will allow clients to access apartment information, including photos and apartment complex layouts.
4. Allow Client Services to view but not update any information in Apartment Services.
5. Support electronic distribution of the "folder" from Client Services to Finance and from Finance to Apartment Services.

How Current Systems Will Be Affected

1. *Apartment information gathering and tracking* The system that allows Apartment Services to gather and track apartment information works well for that department. The new system should interface with that system without requiring significant changes.
2. *Fee for services* The system that allows Finance to access the appropriate fee also works well, but the new system should generate the fee for services statements.

Project Plan

Time Table: One year for entire project
- 1 month   Model the current system
- 2 months Create a model of the new system
- 3 months Create the technical design of the new system
- 3 months Program the new system
- 1 month   Install and test any new hardware or software
- 2 months Convert to the new system

Budget: $100,000

Project Development Team:
- ITW owner
- Manager of Client Services and 2 Client Services employees
- Manager of Apartment Services and 1 Apartment Services employee
- 1 employee from Finance
- Project manager (from IT) and 2 IT employees
- Consultant

FIGURE 7.6

Problem Statement and Project Plan for ITW

PHOTO ESSAY 7-1 ITW Enterprises at Work

OVERVIEW

ITW Enterprises (ITW) serves the metropolitan area of Detroit by assisting business executives (*clients*) in finding temporary apartment housing. ITW generates cash flow by charging a fee to each apartment complex in which it places a client. Clients are not charged for the services ITW provides.

Each apartment complex that ITW represents provides information concerning available apartments for rent and general information about amenities, including swimming pools, workout facilities, on-site security, and so on. When ITW places a client with an apartment complex, ITW generates a fee for services statement for that apartment complex.

When a client contacts ITW, a client profile is built that details client requirements and projected length of stay. ITW then matches the client with the apartment complex that meets most—if not all—of his or her needs. Again, clients are not charged a fee.

ITW has two sets of customers—apartment complexes and business executives who need temporary housing. People who need temporary housing are called "clients."

ITW represents apartment complexes to clients. When a new apartment complex is signed, information concerning location, rental price, size, furnished or unfurnished, leasing price, and so on, is gathered. This information can be changed at any time. Also, ITW can terminate its relationship with any current apartment complex, at which time the information is removed.

Clients of ITW fall into one of two categories:
1. Business executives who need temporary housing while they work in Detroit for 6 months or less. These executives then return to their permanent residences in other cities.
2. Business executives who have been permanently transferred to Detroit and need temporary housing while they find permanent housing.

ORGANIZATIONAL STRUCTURE*

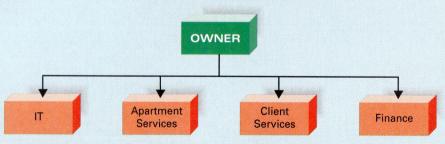

*Description of the organizational structure is at the top of the next page.

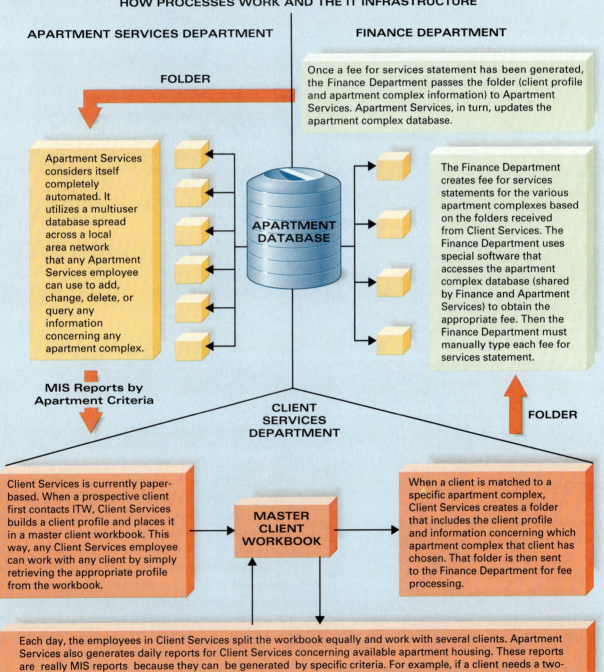

Photo Essay 7-1: ITW Enterprises at Work **277**

agreed that the proposed system would affect Client Services the most and Finance the least. So the project team included the manager and two employees from Client Services and only one employee from Finance.

Review Existing Applications to Which an Interface Will Be Required Essentially, no IT system is an island. Rarely will you find a stand-alone system in an organization—that is, one that doesn't interface in some way with another system. The same is true for new systems. More than likely, each new system will have to interface with one or more existing systems. At ITW, the project team determined that the proposed system would have to interface with the two current systems. So the project team discussed interface requirements in the problem statement and project plan.

Perform an Initial Feasibility Review *Feasibility reviews* are important to the systems development effort, especially during the early steps. When you perform an initial feasibility review, you can't simply look at it from a cost versus benefit point of view. You must also consider technical and time feasibility. *Technical feasibility* simply asks, "Is there hardware and software for what we want to do, and do we have the expertise to work with that hardware and software?" If the answer is no to either question, then developing the proposed system through insourcing may be technically impossible.

Time feasibility asks the question, "Do we have the time to devote to the development of the proposed system?" Organizational resources are scarce, and systems development requires time and people. It may be that your IT specialists simply don't have time to devote to a new system. At ITW, the project team agreed that the IT department had sufficient time to devote to the proposed system, that the proposed system was probably technically feasible, and that it could be developed for about $100,000—an amount Reid was willing to pay.

Develop a Plan for Proceeding The final task of scoping is to develop a plan for proceeding. The *project plan* includes a list of people who will participate on the project team, a preliminary budget, and a time frame for completing each major step or task. As you proceed, you'll probably have to update many of these estimates and add new members to the project team.

Your Role during Scoping

Define the Exact Problem or Opportunity We cannot stress this task enough. Systems development is aimed specifically at either solving a problem or taking advantage of an opportunity. Your new system will only be successful if it solves the right problem or takes advantage of the right opportunity.

Participate in Developing a Plan for Proceeding The project plan includes people, project milestones, and a preliminary budget. Each of these will have a great impact on your area. Many of the people will be knowledge workers from your area. Project milestones include dates by which you need certain tasks performed and the budget will most probably include monetary allocations from your departmental budget.

> **CAREER OPPORTUNITY**
> You should notice that ITW's plan includes a consultant. Many people hesitate to hire consultants because they believe that hiring a consultant is an insult; that is, "I don't know enough, so I have to bring in someone smarter than I am." That's a bad attitude. In business, you can't know everything. Hiring a consultant is a smart move if you need one. You should view hiring a consultant as, "I'm smart enough to know I need help. And if I get the right person to help, my organization will benefit, and so will I."

Step 3: Analysis
Determining the Logical Requirements for the Proposed System

The goal of step 3—*analysis*—is to determine the logical requirements for the proposed system. The key in this step is logical, not physical. At this point, you're not concerned with any implementation or technical details. You simply focus on your information and processes from a logical point of view. For example, you would identify what information you need but not how to store that information in the form of a file or database.

At ITW, the consultant suggested that the best way to proceed was, first, to model how processes currently worked and, second, to model how everyone would like those processes to work. Most important, he noted that these models should deal only with logical aspects, not physical. Creating logical models, however, is not simple. You must detail each piece of information carefully and define each process in excruciating detail. To help with this, the consultant introduced the project team to a number of modeling tools, one of which was flowcharting—a graphic tool for depicting the steps in a process. The project team first tackled the process of what happened after a match was found. This process included completing the folder, generating the fee for services statement, and updating the apartment database to reflect that a specific unit was no longer available at an apartment complex. Figure 7.7 shows the project team's flowchart for this process.

Although everyone knew what happened, it was alarming to see it laid out step-by-step. The seemingly simple process involved all three departments and 12 steps. The next task facing the project team was to create the best way the process should occur. And it didn't take long. After a few attempts at a drawing board, the team came up with a new process (see Figure 7.8).

The analysis step results in a complete logical model of how the proposed system will work and an updated project plan (which includes a new justifiable feasibility review). The complete logical model of the proposed system must include a step-by-step description of the processes as well as thorough documentation of all the information the proposed system will work with.

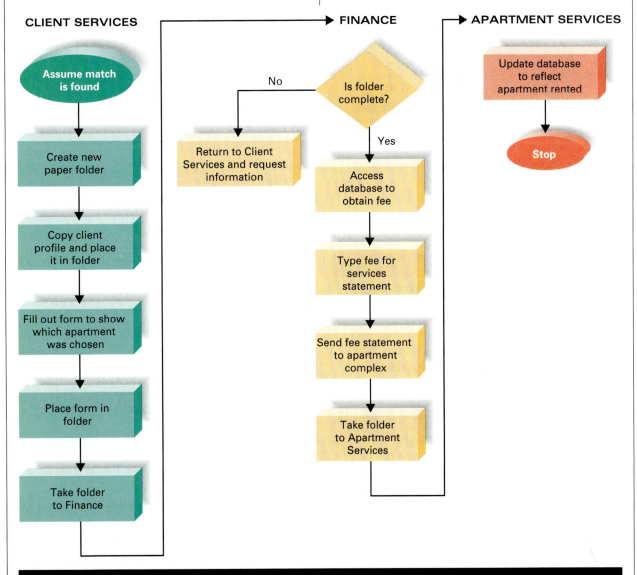

FIGURE 7.7

The Current Process at ITW

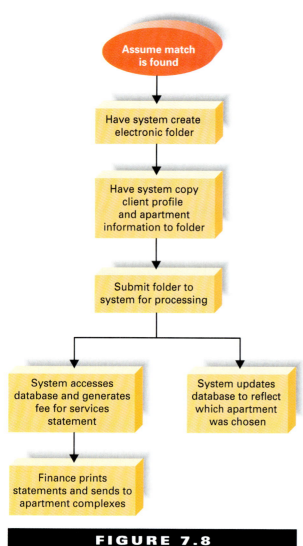

FIGURE 7.8

Proposed Process at ITW

Key Tasks during Analysis

Model, Study, and Analyze the Current System and Business Processes Before you can develop a new system, you must first understand how the current system and business processes work. Although you've already defined the problem in scoping, in analysis you explore it in more detail. This includes modeling in detail each process step-by-step and each piece of information you work with. As the project team at ITW found out, modeling the current system prior to creating the proposed system can be an eye-opening experience.

Define New Information and Processing Requirements The goal of any systems development effort is to create a system that works with new information and/or

performs new processes. As with the current system model, you must define each of these in great detail.

Model the New System Once you've defined the current system and new processes and information, it's time to combine the two to create a new system model. This new model will be created from a logical point of view and will provide the foundation for developing a technical model in step 4.

Update the Project Plan and Scope Once you perform all tasks in analysis, you must revise the project plan and scope. This involves updating the preliminary budget, the feasibility review, and the time frame for development. It may also involve adding new people to the project team and revising the problem scope.

Your Role during Analysis

Provide Information Concerning How the System Currently Works You're the business process expert—that means you know how current processes and the system work. It's vitally important that you provide this information as the current system model will become the foundation for developing the new system model.

Provide Information Concerning New Information and Processing Requirements You're still the business process expert. You know how things need to change—what new business processes and information you need. At ITW, the members of the project team from the various departments played a key role in providing information concerning how the current system worked and what new information and processing were needed.

Monitor and Justify the New Feasibility Review Again, much of the money for the new systems development will come from your budget. It's your responsibility to justify the expenditure.

Step 4: Design

Convert the Logical Requirements into a Technical System Design

The goal of step 4—*design*—is to build a technical blueprint of how the proposed system will work. In this step, your role becomes that of quality assurance. IT specialists complete most of the tasks in design, but you must still review their recommendations and assure that the proposed technical solution meets your logical requirements. The recommendations of the IT specialists will address hardware, software, telecommunications, information, people, and procedures, as well as user interfaces (screens, reports, and so on).

At ITW, the IT specialists spent two months exploring many options, evaluating their worth, and determining their cost. Their final recommendation to the team seemed to satisfy everyone's needs and meet the stated goals. Let's review their recommendations for the hardware, software, telecommunications, and information building blocks of the system.

Hardware The new system would require a local area network on which each employee had a workstation (see Figure 7.9). This would involve purchasing workstations for each person in Client Services. The local area network would contain two important features: first, a server on which apartment and client information would reside; and second, an all-important connection to the Internet that would allow the clients of ITW to view apartment information, including photos and complex layouts (a form of an extranet).

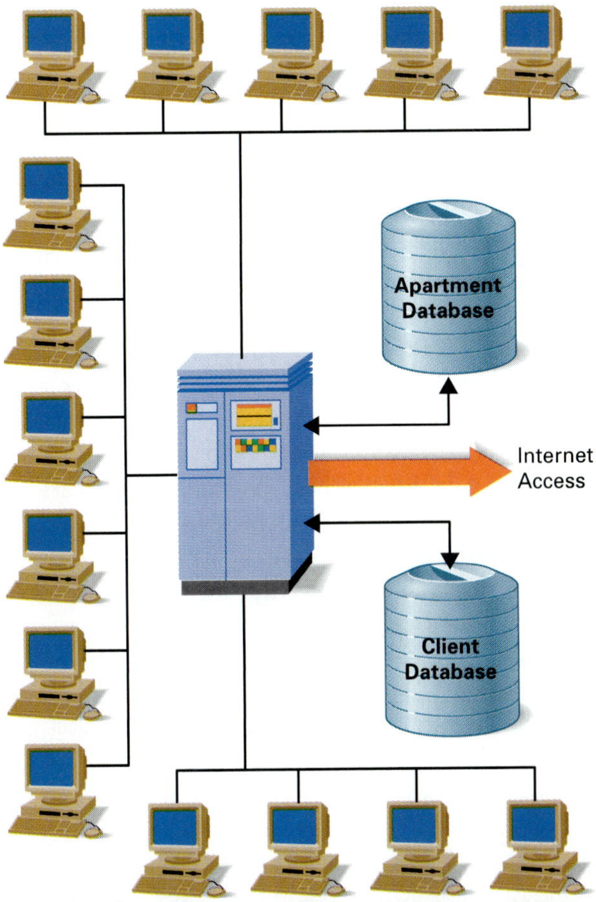

Software For an operating system, the IT specialists recommended using Windows NT. This would provide security features that would limit access to information to only those who required it. For example, when a Client Services employee logged on, the security features of Windows NT would allow them view and query access only to apartment information, but it would also allow them to add, change, and delete client profile information.

For application software, the IT specialists determined that necessary interfaces to the two existing systems would not be required. The application software currently used for those two systems would continue to be used without modifications for the new system. In fact, the IT specialists even decided that the software used to create and maintain the database for the apartment complexes could also be used to create and maintain the client profiles. The proposed system, however, included requirements for matching a client profile to a list of potential apartment complexes. The IT specialists determined that they would have to write special application software to do this. This new application software would take a specific client profile and query the apartment database to create a list of potential complexes, based on ranking criteria that the client provided.

Telecommunications The link to the Internet would create a substantial marketplace advantage. If clients wanted to see information concerning specific apartments, they could simply access ITW's Web site and query available apartments based on key field information that Client Services would provide. Some people initially thought that would mean creating two copies of all apartment information—one for the apartment database and one for the Web site. The IT specialists explained, however, that they could easily write utility software that would extract information from the apartment database and place it on the Web site every hour. The system would handle everything.

Information Information is at the center of ITW's proposed system. More important, the ability to freely access and communicate information is vital. The proposed system included two databases—apartment and client—that would reside on the local area network. For determining the exact content of these databases and their structures, the IT specialists created E-R diagrams,

FIGURE 7.9

The Proposed Hardware Solution at ITW

employed normalization, and created a data dictionary that specified the attributes. They also built sample screens and reports for the rest of the project team to review. During its review, the project team requested a few changes and added an additional query screen.

Key deliverables of design include a recommended technical model of how the proposed system will work and function and an updated project plan. As with all steps, the updated project plan may include new project milestones and an updated and justifiable feasibility review.

Key Tasks during Design

Identify Alternative Technical Solutions Because the goal of design is to build a technical blueprint of how the proposed system will work, you'll probably have to explore many different options. Technology today offers a variety of hardware and software platforms. It's important that you explore all of them. At ITW, the IT specialists explored a number of alternative technical solutions and evaluated the worthiness of each.

Analyze the Alternative Solutions and Choose the Best Once you've developed several technical alternatives, you must analyze each in terms of time, cost, and technical feasibility. This will allow you to recommend the best solution. Again, IT specialists, for the most part, perform this function, but it's still your responsibility to analyze and question various technical alternatives.

Update the Project Plan and Scope Once you've chosen the best technical solution, you have to update the project plan. Again, this will include revising the time frame, performing an updated feasibility review, and identifying new project team members to carry out step 5.

Your Role during Design

Ensure that the Recommended Technical Solution Meets the Logical Requirements During design, your role decreases as a business process expert and increases as a quality control analyst. The IT specialists will develop several alternative technical solutions. It's your job to analyze each and ensure that the recommended solution best meets your logical requirements.

Monitor and Justify the Project Plan Again, at the end of each step you must update and justify the project plan, including the new time frame and the feasibility review.

Step 5: Implementation
Creating the New System

The goal of step 5—*implementation*—is to bring the proposed system to life and place it in the organization. This step involves writing and testing any necessary software and acquiring and installing any new hardware. IT specialists perform most of these tasks, but quality assurance is still a key role for you. The IT specialists involved in implementation are charged with delivering an operational system complete with documentation. Your organization will use this documentation during support if any changes are necessary.

Key Tasks during Implementation

Programming Programming involves writing any necessary software. IT specialists perform this function and may take months or even years to write the software. At ITW, the programming was relatively simple—the IT specialists had to write only the software that matched clients to apartment complexes and the utility software that extracted apartment information from the apartment database and loaded it into ITW's Web site.

Hardware Acquisition and Installation Most new systems require new hardware. It may be as simple as adding internal memory to workstations or as complex as setting up a wide area network across several states. Whatever the case, the IT specialists, for the most part, are responsible for hardware acquisition and installation. At ITW, the IT specialists purchased and installed workstations for each Client Services employee and connected everyone by way of a local area network.

Testing Once the new hardware and software are in place, your responsibility increases dramatically. It's now time for you to test the new system to ensure that it works correctly and meets your logical needs. Many people overlook testing or do it hurriedly. Never sacrifice the time it takes to test the system completely. At ITW, for example, the project team loaded the new databases with fictitious information, generated hundreds of queries, and created numerous fee for services statements to ensure that the new system worked perfectly.

Training Once you determine that the new system works correctly, you must provide training for the people who will use it.

Conversion Conversion is simply moving from the old system to the new system. There are a variety of conversion methods, including

- *Parallel conversion* Using both the old and new system until you're sure that the new system performs correctly
- *Plunge conversion* Discarding the old system completely and immediately using the new system
- *Pilot conversion* Having only a small group of people use the new system until you know that it works correctly and then adding the remaining people to the system
- *Piecemeal conversion* Converting to only a portion of the new system until you're sure that it works correctly and then converting to the remaining portions of the new system

At ITW, the project team chose to use a parallel conversion method for moving Client Services from the old system to the new system. This gave them a backup if the new system failed.

Your Role during Implementation

Determine the Best Training Method All knowledge workers must learn how the new system works, and you can train those people in a variety of ways, including classes and one-to-one training.

Determine the Best Method of Conversion Conversion is critical. Parallel conversion is the safest, but most expensive, method because it may require that some people perform the same task on two systems. Plunge conversion, on the other hand, is the quickest and cheapest, but the most dangerous, method. If the new system fails, your organization is without an operational backup system. Your choice is critical and will depend on the nature of the system and its importance to daily operations.

Provide Complete Testing of the New System Testing is critical. You must thoroughly test each portion of the system as well as the entire system. Never sacrifice testing time or your system may not work correctly all the time.

Monitor the Budget and Schedule and Look for "Runaway" Projects Most systems development projects become "runaway" projects during implementation because not enough time or money was allocated to the programming function. Programming is not a simple task, and it can become even more difficult if some requirements weren't defined. You should monitor the programming function carefully and ensure that programming dates are met.

Runaway projects are a serious problem in today's business environment. According to a *Computerworld* survey, 95 percent of all projects incur costs and time overruns.[6] And 65 percent of those eventually incur costs two to three times greater than originally planned. As an example, the Federal Aviation Administration (FAA) set out in 1983 to develop a completely new automated air traffic control system. After spending over $7.6 billion on the proposed five-year project, the FAA still isn't finished, putting the project at least 12 years behind schedule.[7]

Step 6: Support
Providing Ongoing Support

Support is the final sequential step of any systems development effort. The goal of this step is to ensure that the system continues to meet stated goals. Once a system is in place, it must change as your business changes. Constantly monitoring and supporting the new system involves making minor changes (for example, new reports or information capturing) and reviewing the system to ensure that it continues to move your organization toward its strategic goals.

Key Tasks during Support

React to Changes in Information and Processing Needs As changes arise in the business environment, you must react to those changes by assessing their impact on the system. It might very well be that the system needs to change to meet the ever-changing needs of the business environment. If so, you need to notify the IT specialists of those changes.

Assess the Worth of the System in Terms of the Strategic Plan of the Organization After several years, it's entirely possible that an existing system may no longer meet the strategic needs of your organization. In this instance, the system may require a major overhaul, or you may have to scrap it in favor of a new system.

Your Role during Support
Provide a Mechanism for People to Request Changes To create the best support environment, you need to

THE GLOBAL PERSPECTIVE

Hiring Programmers from around the World

The numbers are staggering no matter which report you read. According to a study released by Georgetown University and the Information Technology Association of America, 840,000 IT jobs were to go unfilled in 2000. And the Bureau of Labor Statistics reported 480,000 IT openings and said that the United States would require an average of 140,000 new skilled IT workers per year between 2000 and 2006.

Many of these unfilled jobs are for skilled programmers, especially for Web-based applications that require expertise in XML, UML, and Java. So, many U.S. companies are responding by hiring outside the United States. Popular countries for obtaining skilled programmers include Japan, Taiwan, India, and Pakistan, and most Middle Eastern countries.

Potential employees from outside the U.S. can obtain H-1B visas to work in this country. Companies here can pay as little as $1,000 to petition for an H-1B visa for a foreign employee. That's a small amount compared to having an IT job go unfilled. Many U.S. companies are even willing to pay as much as $20,000 to help foreign workers relocate.

What does this mean for you? Does it mean you won't have a job when you graduate if you're majoring in IT or MIS? Quite the contrary. Your skills as a domestic knowledge worker will be in high demand.[8]

TEAM WORK

Your Responsibilities during Each Step of the SDLC

During insourcing, you have many responsibilities because you're a business process expert, liaison to the customer, quality control analyst, and manager of other people. However, according to which step of the SDLC you're in, your responsibilities may increase or decrease. In the table below, determine the extent to which you participate in each SDLC step according to your four responsibilities. For each row you should number the SDLC steps from 1 to 6, with a 1 identifying the step in which your responsibility is the greatest and a 6 identifying the step in which your responsibility is the least.

	SDLC Step					
	Planning	Scoping	Analysis	Design	Implementation	Support
Business process expert						
Liaison to the customer						
Quality control analyst						
Manager of other people						

TABLE 7.2 The Pros and Cons of Insourcing and the SDLC

Advantages	Disadvantages
Allows your organization to tailor a system to your exact needs.	It takes time to get exactly what you want.
Uses a structured step-by-step approach.	Some smaller projects suffer from a structured approach.
Creates a separation of duties among IT specialists (technical responsibility) and knowledge workers (business process responsibility).	IT specialists and knowledge workers speak different languages, which can create a communications gap.
Requires key deliverables before proceeding to the next step.	If you omit a requirement early, it can be costly to correct that mistake later.

provide a way for knowledge workers to request changes. You could develop a form that knowledge workers could fill out to request changes or have weekly meetings to discuss any needed changes.

Assess the Worth of Proposed Changes before Passing Them on to the IT Specialists Once you receive requested changes, you must assess their worth before passing them on to the maintenance team. Again, changes cost money that will probably come from your departmental budget. You must carefully weigh each requested change for merit and monetary worth.

As you can see, the SDLC is a structured, step-by-step process that creates a separation of duties among knowledge workers and IT specialists. In design, for example, IT specialists are responsible for developing several alternative technical solutions. Your responsibility is to evaluate the alternative solutions. And, in implementation, the IT specialists are responsible for programming, while you're responsible for testing the software to make sure it works correctly.

Insourcing (as the *who*) and the SDLC (as the *how*) are among the many ways to develop IT systems and offer your organization many advantages. But, as with everything, each advantage can also be a disadvantage. Table 7.2 highlights many of the advantages of insourcing and the SDLC and points out how these advantages can sometimes be disadvantages.

Does that mean your organization should abandon insourcing and the SDLC and find better ways to develop systems? Absolutely not. In many instances, the best way to develop systems is to allow your organization's IT specialists to use a structured step-by-step approach. In other instances, though, alternative *who*s and *how*s are more appropriate.

> **CAREER OPPORTUNITY**
> In the remainder of this chapter, we explore two alternatives to the *who* question—selfsourcing and outsourcing. We also explore a number of alternatives to the *how* question. For you, the real key to success is the ability to determine which *who* and which *how* is most appropriate for a given systems development project.

ITW Ongoing Support

"Today, we couldn't survive without our new system. And we realize that, as our business changes, the system must change as well. So, we created a project maintenance team that meets every Friday to evaluate the effectiveness of the system, identify any changes, and assess whether the changes are worth making."

—*Reid Becker* ❖

Selfsourcing and Prototyping

Empowering Knowledge Workers to Develop Their Own Systems

Throughout this text, we've elaborated on the concept of knowledge worker computing—knowledge workers taking an active role in developing and using their own systems to support their efforts in personal and workgroup environments. What we want to look at now is how you, as a knowledge worker, go about developing systems, which we call selfsourcing. **Selfsourcing** (also called *knowledge worker development*) is the development and support of IT systems by knowledge workers with little or no help from IT specialists. So selfsourcing is simply one more aspect of knowledge worker computing.

You should understand that some selfsourcing projects still involve support from IT specialists. For example, Eaton Corp., located in Minnesota, actively encourages the selfsourcing of systems development in Lotus Notes by providing training classes to knowledge workers.[9] In these training classes knowledge workers learn how to set up a document database; use built-in templates to develop applications quickly; and create customized forms, views, and macros. And, when Eaton's knowledge workers actually begin creating their own systems, IT specialists are available to answer questions and handle more complicated technical issues, such as installing software on a client/server network or creating a local area network from scratch.

When a group of knowledge workers decides to create an IT system through selfsourcing, they most often employ a technique called prototyping, or building a model of the system before creating the final system. You'll also find that prototyping is a popular technique when IT specialists in your organization follow the SDLC. So, before we explore the steps in selfsourcing, let's take a look at prototyping.

Prototyping
Building Models

Prototyping is the process of building a model that demonstrates the features of a proposed product, service, or system. A *prototype,* then, is simply a model of a proposed product, service, or system. If you think about it, people prototype all the time. Automobile manufacturers build prototypes of cars to demonstrate safety features, aerodynamics, and comfort. Building contractors construct models of homes and other structures to show layout and fire exits. Your instructor may give you sample test questions for an upcoming exam. These sample questions are a model of what you can expect.

In systems development, prototyping can be a valuable tool to you. Prototyping is an iterative process in which you build a model from basic requirements, have other knowledge workers review the prototype and suggest changes, and further refine and enhance the prototype to include suggestions. Most notably, prototyping is a dynamic process that allows knowledge workers to see, work with, and evaluate a model and suggest changes to that model to increase the likelihood of success of the proposed system.

You can use prototyping to perform a variety of functions in the systems development process. Some of these include the following:

Gathering requirements Prototyping is a great requirements gathering tool. You start by simply prototyping the basic systems requirements. Then you allow knowledge workers to add more requirements (information and processes) as you revise the prototype. Most people use prototyping for this purpose.

Helping determine requirements In many systems development processes, knowledge workers aren't sure what they really want—they simply know that the current system doesn't meet their needs. In this instance, you can use prototyping to help knowledge workers determine their exact requirements.

Proving that a system is technically feasible Let's face it, there are some things to which you cannot apply technology. And knowing whether you can is often unclear while scoping the proposed system—that's why scoping includes a technical feasibility review. If you're uncertain about whether something can be done, prototype it first. A prototype you use to prove the technical feasibility of a proposed system is a **proof-of-concept prototype**.

Selling the idea of a proposed system Many people resist changes in IT. The current system seems to work fine and they see no reason to go through the process of developing and learning to use a new system. In this case, you have to convince them

INDUSTRY PERSPECTIVE

Manufacturing

Prototyping with Software Is a Must in Manufacturing

Most manufacturers today prototype more with software than they actually prototype the software itself. The manufacturing environment was the first to give birth to prototyping. The concept was quite simple—don't build a working product and then test it; rather, build a model of the product and test the model as it's being developed.

That was the approach—and a good one—for many years. Today, however, manufacturers aren't building physical models for testing. Instead, they're building virtual models with software. For example, the automobile manufacturing industry used to spend five years developing physical models and testing them in a variety of settings, such as wind tunnels. Now, that process has been cut to three years, with another year expected to go away soon.

How? Well, think about it for a moment. If you can use a computer to build a virtual prototype of a product such as a car, perhaps you can build a prototype of the testing environments as well on a computer. And that's what's happening today. Manufacturers are building virtual models of products and testing them in virtual environments (this is a common application for virtual reality).

At Chrysler, for example, designers build virtual prototypes of engines and the amount of space under the hood. According to Charles Sestock, manager of technical operations for Chrysler International, "It dramatically reduces the engineering time for locating components in 'the battle for real estate' under the hood and behind the dash."

Prototyping was born in manufacturing. And software developers constantly look toward manufacturing for best business practices of prototyping use and implementation.[10] ❖

---

that the proposed system will be better than the current one. Because prototyping is relatively fast, you won't have to invest a lot of time to develop a prototype that can convince people of the worth of the proposed system. A prototype you use to convince people of the worth of a proposed system is a *selling prototype*.

The Prototyping Process

Prototyping is an excellent tool in systems development. However, who uses prototyping and for what purpose determines how the prototyping process occurs. Most often, IT specialists use prototyping in the SDLC to form a technical system blueprint. In selfsourcing, however, you can often continue to refine the prototype until it becomes the final system. The prototyping process for either case is almost the same; only the result differs. Figure 7.10 illustrates the difference between insourcing and selfsourcing prototyping. Regardless of *who* does the prototyping, the prototyping process involves four steps:

1. *Identify Basic Requirements* During the first step, you gather the basic requirements for a proposed system. These basic requirements include input and output information and, perhaps, some simple processes. At this point, however, you're typically unconcerned with editing rules, security issues, or end-of-period processing (for example, producing W-2s for a payroll system at the end of the year).

2. *Develop Initial Prototype* Based on the basic requirements, you then set out to develop an initial prototype. Most often, your initial prototype will include only user interfaces, such as data entry screens and reports.

3. *Knowledge Worker Reviewing* Step 3 starts the truly iterative process of prototyping. When knowledge workers first enter this step, they evaluate the prototype and suggest changes or additions. In subsequent returns to step 3 (after step 4), they evaluate new versions of the prototype. It's important to involve as many knowledge workers as possible during this step.

288 CHAPTER SEVEN Developing IT Systems

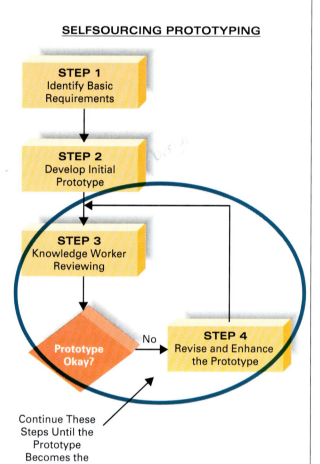

FIGURE 7.10

Prototyping Steps for Insourcing and Selfsourcing

This will help resolve any discrepancies in such areas as terminology and operational processes.

4. *Revise and Enhance the Prototype* The final sequential step in the prototyping process is to revise and enhance the prototype according to any knowledge worker suggestions. In this step, you make changes to the current prototype and add any new requirements. Next, you return to step 3 and have the knowledge workers review the new prototype.

For either insourcing or selfsourcing, you continue the iterative processes of steps 3 and 4 until knowledge workers are happy with the prototype. What happens to the prototype after that, however, differs.

During selfsourcing, you're most likely to use the targeted application software package or application development tool to develop the prototype. This simply means that you can continually refine the prototype until it becomes the final working system. For example, if you choose to develop a customer service application using Lotus Notes, you can prototype many of the operational features using Lotus Notes development tools. Because you develop these prototypes using the targeted application development environment, your prototype can eventually become the final system.

That process is not necessarily the same when insourcing. Most often, IT specialists develop prototypes using special prototyping development tools. Many of these tools don't support the creation of a final system—you simply use them to build prototypes. Therefore, the finished prototype becomes a blueprint or technical design for the final system. In the appropriate stages of the SDLC, IT specialists will implement the prototypes in another application development environment better suited to the development of production systems.

The Advantages of Prototyping

Encourages Active Knowledge Worker Participation First and foremost, prototyping encourages knowledge workers to actively participate in the development process. As opposed to interviewing and the reviewing of documentation, prototyping allows knowledge workers to see and work with working models of the proposed system.

Helps Resolve Discrepancies among Knowledge Workers During the prototyping process, many knowledge workers participate in defining the requirements for and reviewing the prototype. The "many" is key. If several knowledge workers participate in prototyping, you'll find it's much easier to resolve any discrepancies the knowledge workers may encounter.

Gives Knowledge Workers a Feel for the Final System Prototyping, especially for user interfaces, provides a feel for how the final system will look, feel, and work. When knowledge workers understand the look, feel, and working of the final system, they are more apt to determine its potential for success.

Helps Determine Technical Feasibility Proof-of-concept prototypes are great for determining the technical feasibility of a proposed system.

Helps Sell the Idea of a Proposed System Finally, selling prototypes can help break down resistance barriers. Many people don't want new systems because the old one seems to work just fine, and they're afraid the new system won't meet their expectations and work properly. If you provide them with a working prototype that proves the new system will be successful, they will be more inclined to buy into it.

The Disadvantages of Prototyping

Leads People to Believe the Final System Will Follow Shortly When a prototype is complete, many people believe that the final system will follow shortly. After all, they've seen the system at work in the form of a prototype, how long can it take to bring the system into production? Unfortunately, it may take months or years. You need to be sure that people understand that the prototype is only a model—not the final system missing only a few simple bells and whistles.

Gives No Indication of Performance under Operational Conditions Prototypes very seldom take all operational conditions into consideration. This problem surfaced for the Department of Motor Vehicles in a state on the East Coast.[11] During prototyping, the system—which handled motor vehicle and driver registration for the entire state—worked fine for 20 workstations at two locations. When the system was finally installed for all locations (which included over 1,200 workstations), the system spent all its time just managing communications traffic—it had absolutely no time to complete any transactions. This is potentially the most significant drawback to prototyping. You must prototype operational conditions as well as interfaces and processes.

Leads the Project Team to Forgo Proper Testing and Documentation You must thoroughly test and document all new systems. Unfortunately, many people believe they can forgo testing and documentation when using prototyping. After all, they've tested the prototype, and why not use the prototype as the documentation for the system? Don't make this mistake.

Again, prototyping is most probably a tool that you will use to develop many knowledge worker computing systems. Let's now take a look at the set of steps you would go through to develop a knowledge worker computing system using prototyping.

The Selfsourcing Process

You can probably create most smaller knowledge worker computing systems in a matter of hours, such as interfacing a letter in a word processing package with a customer database to create individualized mailings. More complicated systems, however, require that you follow some sort of formal process during development. In Figure 7.11 we've illustrated the selfsourcing process and in the box entitled "Key Tasks in Selfsourcing" we've summarized the key tasks within some of the selfsourcing steps. As you can see, the selfsourcing process is very similar to the steps in the SDLC. However, you should notice that the selfsourcing process does include prototyping. This is key—when you develop a system for yourself, you will most often go through the process of prototyping. As you consider the box "Key Tasks" and Figure 7.11, we would alert you to several important issues.

CHAPTER SEVEN Developing IT Systems

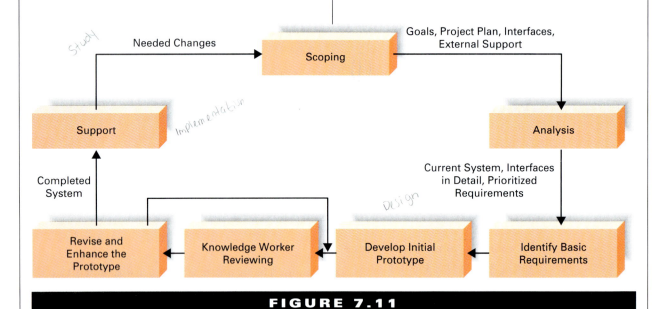

FIGURE 7.11
The Selfsourcing Process

Key Tasks in Selfsourcing

Scoping
- Define system goals in light of organizational goals
- Create a project plan
- Identify any systems that require an interface
- Determine what type of external support you will require

Analysis
- Study and model the current system
- Understand the interfaces in detail
- Define and prioritize your requirements

Support
- Completely document the system
- Provide ongoing maintenance ❖

Aligning Your Selfsourcing Efforts with Organizational Goals

When your first begin scoping a system you want to develop, you must consider it in light of your organization's goals. If you're considering developing a system for yourself that's counterintuitive to your organization's goals, then you should abandon it immediately. And that doesn't necessarily mean that you want an IT system that will reduce sales or decrease your number of customers. Perhaps you could be spending your time more wisely. You obviously have a full work week and developing a system through selfsourcing takes time—your time.

So, your first task should always be to consider what you want to develop in conjunction with what your organization expects you to do.

Determining What External Support You Will Require

As we've already stated, some selfsourcing projects will involve support from IT specialists within your organization. Your in-house IT specialists are a valuable resource during the selfsourcing process. Don't forget about them and be sure to include them in the scoping activity.

Documenting the System Once Complete

Even if you're developing a system just for yourself, you still need to document how it works. If you ever get promoted, other people will come in behind you and probably use the system you developed. And they may even want to make changes. So, you need to document how your system works from a technical point of view as well as create an easy-to-use operation manual.

ON YOUR OWN

How Have You Selfsourced?

You've probably performed the selfsourcing process many times. For example, if you've created a resume, you probably prototyped it using a word processing package. And, if you've prepared a presentation for a class, you may have prototyped it using a presentation graphics software package.

Think about the many other instances when you've selfsourced and used personal productivity software. For each, identify your goal, what personal productivity software you used, and how you performed the prototyping process. Do some types of personal productivity software packages lend themselves better to prototyping than others? What are they? What types of personal productivity software packages do not lend themselves well to prototyping? Why is this true? ❖

Providing Ongoing Support

When you develop a system through selfsourcing, you must be prepared to provide your own support and maintenance. For example, if you develop a customer relationship database using Microsoft Office XP, you must be prepared to convert it to Microsoft Office 2004 when it becomes available and your organization adopts it. The systems development process doesn't end with implementation and use—it continues on a daily basis with support and maintenance.

The Advantages of Selfsourcing

Improves Requirements Determination During insourcing, knowledge workers tell IT specialists what they want. In selfsourcing, knowledge workers essentially tell themselves what they want. This greatly improves the effectiveness of capturing requirements, which helps ensure the success of the new system.

Increases Knowledge Worker Participation and Sense of Ownership No matter what you do, if you do it yourself, you always take more pride in the result. The same is true when developing an IT system through selfsourcing. If knowledge workers know that they own the system because they developed and now support it, they are more apt to actively participate in its development and have a greater sense of ownership.

Increases Speed of Systems Development Many small systems do not lend themselves well to insourcing. These smaller systems may suffer from "analysis paralysis" because they don't require a structured step-by-step approach to their development. In fact, insourcing may be slower than selfsourcing for smaller projects.

Potential Pitfalls and Risks of Selfsourcing

Inadequate Knowledge Worker Expertise Leads to Inadequately Developed Systems Many selfsourcing systems are never completed because knowledge workers lack the real expertise with IT tools to develop a complete and fully working system. It may seem like no big deal. The system couldn't have been that important if the people who needed it never finished developing it. But that's not true. If knowledge workers choose to develop their systems, they must spend time away from their primary duties within the organization. This diverted time may mean lost revenue.

Lack of Organizational Focus Creates "Privatized" IT Systems Many selfsourcing projects are done outside the IT systems plan of an organization. This simply means that there may be many "private" IT systems that do not interface with other systems and possess uncontrolled and duplicated information. These types of systems serve no meaningful purpose in an organization and can only lead to more problems.

Insufficient Analysis of Design Alternatives Leads to Subpar IT Systems Some knowledge workers jump to immediate conclusions about the hardware and software they should use without carefully analyzing all the possible alternatives. If this happens, knowledge workers may develop systems that are processing inefficiently.

Lack of Documentation and External Support Leads to Short-Lived Systems When knowledge workers develop systems, they often forgo documentation of how the system works and fail to realize that they can expect little or no support from IT specialists. All systems—no matter who develops them—must change over time. Knowledge workers must realize that those changes are their responsibility. They also need to realize that making those changes is easier if they document the system well.

> **CAREER OPPORTUNITY**
>
> Managing selfsourcing when other knowledge workers perform it is vitally important. But so is managing selfsourcing when you're the knowledge worker doing the developing. Make sure that **you** follow a good set of steps and the guidelines set forth by your organization. No matter what you think, you are not immune to the potential pitfalls and risks of selfsourcing.

Outsourcing

Developing Strategic Partnerships

Consider MasterCard International and the following astounding numbers that MasterCard's network supports:

- 22,000 financial institutions in 30 countries
- Settlement of $500 million per day on the average in credit and debit card transactions
- Over 16 million transactions on its busiest days during December
- Almost 11 million transactions on a typical day.[12]

But MasterCard's primary business isn't telecommunications, so it has outsourced the development and maintenance of its network to AT&T Solutions. AT&T always guarantees availability, security, and speed of MasterCard's network. And MasterCard would literally go out of business if AT&T failed on its promises. So, MasterCard has done more than simply outsource its networking to AT&T. It has created a strategic outsourcing partnership with AT&T, knowing full well that it might very well lose hundreds of millions of dollars in revenue if its partner (AT&T) doesn't hold up its end of the bargain.

MasterCard's choice of *who* to develop its IT networking system is an example of outsourcing. ***Outsourcing*** is the delegation of specific work to a third party for a specified length of time, at a specified cost, and at a specified level of service (the guarantee of perfect delivery). IT outsourcing today represents a significant opportunity for your organization to capitalize on the intellectual resources of other organizations by having them take over and perform certain business functions in which they have more expertise than you. Outsourcing is becoming so big in the IT area that revenues from IT-related outsourcing were expected to exceed $120 billion in the year 2000 (up from $80 billion in 1995).[13] According to a Yankee Group survey of 500 companies, 90 percent have outsourced at least one major business function and 45 percent have outsourced some major portion of their IT environments.[14]

IT outsourcing for software development can take on one of four forms (See Figure 7.12):

1. Purchasing existing software
2. Purchasing existing software and paying the publisher to make certain modifications
3. Purchasing existing software and paying the publisher for the right to make modifications yourself
4. Outsourcing the development of an entirely new and unique system for which no software exists

In these instances, we're not talking about personal productivity software you can buy at a local computer store. We're talking about large software packages that may cost millions of dollars. For example, i2 has developed an inventory management system called Rhythm,

FIGURE 7.12

Major Forms of Outsourcing Systems Development

which sells for about $500,000.[15] Solectron Corp., for example, purchased Rhythm and credits it with moving inventory 30 percent faster than its previous in-house-developed inventory management software and reducing carrying costs by 25 percent. Why? Because i2 possesses significant intellectual expertise in inventory management, while Solectron focuses on manufacturing. Essentially, Solectron capitalized on the intellectual expertise of i2 by buying its software.

The Outsourcing Process

The outsourcing process is both similar to and quite different from the SDLC. It's different in that you turn over much of the design, implementation, and support steps to another organization (see Figure 7.13). It's similar in that your organization begins with planning and scoping. It is during one of these steps that your organization may come to understand that it needs a particular system but cannot develop it in-house. If so, that proposed system can be outsourced. Below, we briefly describe the remaining steps of the outsourcing process.

Select a Target System

Once you've identified a potential system for outsourcing, you still have some important questions to answer. For example, will the proposed system manage strategic and sensitive information? If so, you probably wouldn't consider outsourcing it. That is, you don't want another organization seeing and having access to your most vital information. You should also consider whether the system is small enough to be selfsourced. If so, let knowledge workers within your organization develop the system instead of outsourcing it. On the other hand, if the proposed system is fairly large and supports a routine, nonsensitive business function, then you should target it for outsourcing.

Establish Logical Requirements

Regardless of your choice of insourcing or outsourcing, you must still perform step 3 of the SDLC—*analysis*—or establishing the logical requirements for the proposed system. If you choose to outsource, the statement of your logical requirements becomes your request for proposal.

Develop a Request for Proposal

Outsourcing involves telling another organization what you want. *What you want* is essentially the logical requirements for a proposed system, and you convey that information by developing a request for proposal. A *request for proposal (RFP)* is a formal document that describes in detail your logical requirements for a proposed system and invites outsourcing organizations (which we'll refer to as "vendors") to submit bids for its development. An RFP is the most important document

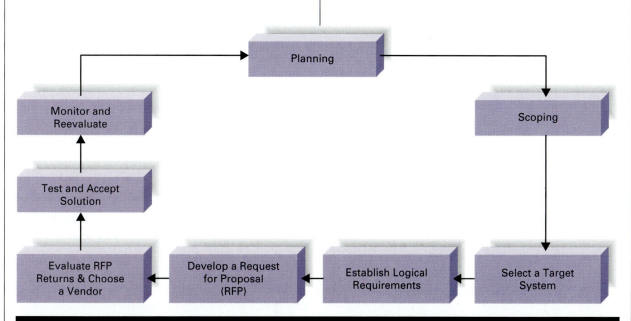

FIGURE 7.13

The Outsourcing Process

in the outsourcing process. For systems of great size, your organization may create an RFP that's literally hundreds of pages long and requires months of work to complete.

It's vitally important that you take all the time you need to create a complete and thorough RFP. Eventually, your RFP will become the foundation for a legal and binding contract into which your organization and the vendor will enter. At a minimum, your RFP should contain the elements in Figure 7.14. Notice that an RFP includes key information such as an overview of your organization, underlying business processes that the proposed system will support, a request for a development time frame, and a request for a statement of detailed outsourcing costs.

All this information is vitally important to both your organization and the vendors. For your organization, the ability to develop a complete and thorough RFP means that you completely understand what you have and what you want. For the vendors, a complete and thorough RFP makes it easier to identify a proposed system that will meet most, if not all, your needs.

Evaluate Request for Proposal Returns and Choose a Vendor

Your next task in outsourcing is to evaluate the RFP returns and choose a vendor. You perform this evaluation of the RFP returns according to the scoring method you identified in the RFP. This is not a simple process. No two vendors will ever provide RFP returns in the same format. And the RFP returns you receive will almost always be longer than the RFP itself.

Once you've thoroughly analyzed the RFP returns, it's time to rank them and determine which vendor to use. Most often, you rank RFP returns according to cost, time, and the scoring mechanism you identified. Again, ranking RFP returns is not simple. One vendor may be the cheapest, but requires the longest time to develop the new system. Another vendor may be able to provide a system quickly, but without some of the features you identified as critical.

Once you've chosen the vendor, a lengthy legal process follows. Outsourcing is serious business—and serious business between two organizations almost always requires a lot of negotiating and the use of lawyers. Eventually, your organization has to enter a legal and binding contract that very explicitly states the features of the proposed system, the exact costs, the time frame for development, acceptance criteria, and criteria for breaking the contract for nonperformance or noncompliance.

Test and Accept Solution

As with all systems, testing and accepting the solution is crucial. Once a vendor installs the new system, it's up to you and your organization to thoroughly test the solution before accepting it. This alone may involve months of running the new system while operating the old one (the parallel conversion method).

When you "accept" a solution, you're saying that the system performs to your expectations and that the vendor has met its contract obligations so far. Accept-

---

1. Organizational overview
2. Problem statement
3. Description of current system
   3.1 Underlying business processes
   3.2 Hardware
   3.3 Software (application and system)
   3.4 System processes
   3.5 Information
   3.6 System interfaces
4. Description of proposed system
   4.1 New processes
   4.2 New information
5. Request for new system design
   5.1 Hardware
   5.2 Software
   5.3 Underlying business processes
   5.4 System processes
   5.5 Information
   5.6 System interfaces
6. Request for implementation plan
   6.1 Training
   6.2 Conversion
7. Request for support plan
   7.1 Hardware
   7.2 Software
8. Request for development time frame
9. Request for statement of outsourcing costs
10. How RFP returns will be scored
11. Deadline for RFP returns
12. Primary contact person

FIGURE 7.14

Outline of a Request for Proposal (RFP)

A Request for Proposal and the Systems Development Life Cycle

If you review Figure 7.14 on the previous page closely, you'll notice that an RFP looks very similar to the steps of the SDLC. In the table below, identify which steps of the SDLC correspond to each element of an RFP. ❖

Elements of a Request for Proposal	Step(s) of the SDLC
1. Organizational overview	
2. Problem statement	
3. Description of current system	
4. Description of proposed system	
5. Request for new system design	
6. Request for implementation plan	
7. Request for support plan	
8. Request for development time frame	
9. Request for statement of outsourcing costs	
10. How RFP returns will be scored	
11. Deadline for RFP returns	
12. Primary contact person	

ing a solution involves "signing off" on the system, which releases the vendor from any further development efforts or modifications to the system. Be careful when you do this—modifications to the system after sign-off can be extremely expensive. In 1996, Duke Power Co., a utility company based in Charlotte, North Carolina, continually tested but never accepted an outsourced system.[16] Duke officially turned the lights out on a $23 million customer information system project after investing over $12 million in its development. Duke Power outsourced the development of the customer information system and had no choice but to terminate the project when the vendor requested an additional two years to make necessary modifications.

Monitor and Reevaluate

Just like systems you develop using the SDLC, systems you obtain through outsourcing need constant monitoring and reevaluation. In outsourcing, you also have to reassess your working relationship with the vendor. Is the vendor providing maintenance when you need it and according to the contract? Does the system really perform the stated functions? Do month-end and year-end processes work according to your desires? Does the vendor provide acceptable support if something goes wrong? These are all important questions that affect the success of your outsourcing efforts. The most important question, though, is, "Does the system still meet our needs and how much does it cost to update the system?" In many outsourcing instances, if the system needs updating you must contract with the original vendor. This is potentially one of the greatest drawbacks to outsourcing. When you outsource a system, you create a heavy dependency on that vendor to provide updates to the system, and updates are not inexpensive.

The Advantages and Disadvantages of Outsourcing

Throughout our discussions of outsourcing, we've directly or indirectly described many of the advantages and disadvantages of outsourcing. Below we summarize the major advantages and disadvantages of outsourcing the systems development process.

- **Advantages: Allows your organization to**

    Focus on Unique Core Competencies By outsourcing systems development efforts that support

THE GLOBAL PERSPECTIVE

Outsourcing at a Global Level

According to Greg Quesnel, president and CEO of CNF, "Projects don't get bigger or more complex than what we've been awarded by GM." Why? Because General Motors agreed to outsource its entire $5 billion annual expenditures on global logistics services to CNF.

In the deal, CNF will take over all operations related to global logistics for GM, including logistical information systems. GM believes this outsourcing deal will help cut in half its $40 billion in inventory costs and reduce the time to deliver vehicles from 13 days to 8 days or less.

CNF will be responsible daily for moving 180 million pounds of freight from 12,000 suppliers to 70 assembly plants, which ship approximately 8.3 million vehicles per year. To do this effectively, CNF will develop software to consolidate and manage GM's contracts with third-party logistics providers. This will enable GM to get a better picture of its complete supply chain, while reducing costs substantially.

If you don't think outsourcing is big business, think again.[17] ❖

---

noncritical business functions, your organization can focus on developing systems that support important, unique core competencies.

Exploit the Intellect of Another Organization Outsourcing allows your organization to obtain intellectual capital by purchasing it from another organization. Says John Halvey, a partner specializing in outsourcing deals at the law firm Millbank, Tweed, Hadley, and McCloy, "People want to buy knowledge, not develop it themselves."[18]

Better Predict Future Costs When you outsource a function, whether systems development or some other business function, you know the exact costs. Zale Corp., a discount jewelry store, outsourced some of its IT systems and tied payments to the vendor according to how well Zale's stores perform.[19] After all, the new IT systems will affect a store's performance, so why not tie a vendor's payment to it?

Acquire Leading-Edge Technology Outsourcing allows your organization to acquire leading-edge technology without technical expertise and the inherent risks of choosing the wrong technology.

Reduce Costs Outsourcing is often seen as a money saver for most organizations. And, indeed, reducing costs is one of the important reasons organizations outsource.

Improve Performance Accountability Outsourcing involves delegating work to another organization at a specified level of service. Your organization can use this specified level of service as leverage to guarantee that it gets exactly what it wants from the vendor.

- **Disadvantages: Your organization may suffer from outsourcing because it**

Reduces Technical Know-How for Future Innovation Outsourcing is a way of exploiting the intellect of another organization. It may also mean that your organization will no longer possess that expertise internally. If you outsource because you don't have the necessary technical expertise today, you'll probably have to outsource for the same reason tomorrow.

Reduces Degree of Control Outsourcing means giving up control. No matter what you choose to outsource, you are in some way giving up control over that function.

Increases Vulnerability of Strategic Information Outsourcing systems development involves telling another organization what information you use and how you use that information. In doing so, you could be giving away strategic information and secrets.

Increases Dependency on Other Organizations As soon as you start outsourcing, you immediately begin depending on another organization to perform many of your business functions. For example, GE was set to introduce a new washing machine—but it didn't happen on time.[20] It seems that GE outsourced some of its parts development and the vendor was late, resulting in a delayed product introduction that cost GE money.

CAREER OPPORTUNITY

Why is it important for you to understand the outsourcing process? Two reasons. First, outsourcing is a part of most organizations today, including yours. Second, outsourcing probably means more work for you, and you should be aware of this. If you choose outsourcing, you'll still be responsible for tasks such as providing key information about the current system and the requirements of the new system. You'll also be responsible for outsourcing-related tasks such as creating an RFP, evaluating RFP returns, and choosing a vendor.

Enterprise Resource Planning and Enterprise Software

Taking the Holistic View

Today, many organizations are taking a very holistic view of their structure and processes as they develop IT systems. That is, these organizations have come to realize that the development of a particular system without regard to the organization as a whole has serious disadvantages. To move toward a more holistic view, organizations are adopting the concept of enterprise resource planning (in conjunction with IT fusion) and using enterprise software to develop all systems in a coordinated fashion.

Enterprise resource planning (ERP) is the coordinated planning of all an organization's resources involved in the production, development, selling, and servicing of goods and services. ERP may sound like a solid concept that all organizations should follow, but it just isn't that easy. In organizations of any size, seeing and understanding the whole corporate picture is difficult. Even more so, to be able to plan for all the required resources needed for any initiative is even more difficult.

Further complicating the problem is that processes and IT systems are already in place supporting a particular business function, but perhaps not the organization as a whole. So, just adopting ERP requires that most organizations undertake numerous reengineering efforts to ensure that the entire organization is operating as a single entity.

Enterprise software directly supports the concept of ERP. *Enterprise software* is a suite of software that includes (1) a set of common business applications, (2) tools for modeling how the entire organization works, and (3) development tools for building applications unique to your organization (see Figure 7.15).

To use enterprise software effectively in support of ERP, your organization must first model its existing structure, divisions and departments, and processes, such as inventory procurement, accounts receivable, customer service, and so on (see Figure 7.16). In parallel, it must also develop a model of all IT systems, how they work together, and perhaps how they conflict with each other. Armed with that information, your organization can then undertake the process of ERP to determine how best to streamline processes and develop the appropriate underlying IT systems that will support those processes through decentralized computing and shared information.

The goal in using enterprise software to support ERP is also shown in steps 3 and 4 in Figure 7.16. That is, once you use enterprise software to develop a holistic view of your organization and how its processes work and the underlying IT systems, you can use your enterprise software to make changes to your organizational model and then regenerate (with some effort) how your new processes will work and the IT systems that support those processes.

Leading enterprise software vendors include SAP, Oracle, PeopleSoft, JD Edwards, Computer Associates, and Baan. As you can see from the graph in Figure 7.15, SAP is the dominant vendor of enterprise software (its R/3 enterprise software accounts for 30 percent), followed by Oracle (10 percent), and JD Edwards (9 percent).

In the future, it looks as if enterprise software suites will replace CASE tools. *Computer-aided software engineering (CASE) tools* are software suites that automate some or all steps in the SDLC. Categories of CASE tools include:

- ■ *Integrated CASE tools,* which support the entire SDLC
- ■ *Upper CASE tools,* which support the front-end steps of the SDLC, including planning, scoping, analysis, and design
- ■ *Lower CASE tools,* which support the back-end steps of the SDLC, including design, implementation, and support.

Integrated CASE tools most closely parallel enterprise software. However, CASE tools were originally developed just to support the SDLC, which focuses

Common Applications of Enterprise Software

- Payroll
- Customer Service
- Logistics
- Accounts Payable
- Accounts Receivable
- Customer Relationship Management
- Supply Chain Management
- Electronic Data Interchange
- Intranet Development and Support
- Extranet Development and Support
- Invoicing
- Sales Order Processing
- Manufacturing
- Product Design and Testing
- Human Resource Management
- Marketing

Top Enterprise Software Vendors

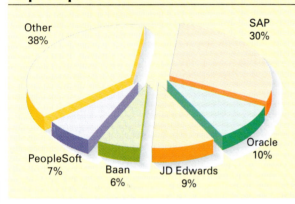

Other 38%
SAP 30%
Oracle 10%
JD Edwards 9%
Baan 6%
PeopleSoft 7%

FIGURE 7.15

Enterprise Software Vendors and Common Applications

ENTERPRISE SOFTWARE HELPS YOU

1. Model your entire organization
   - Structure
   - Divisions and departments
   - Goals
   - Processes and information
   - IT systems

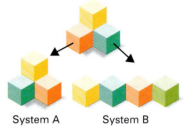

Your Organization

System A   System B

2. Generate processes and IT systems based on your organizational model

Your New Organization

3. Make changes to your organizational model

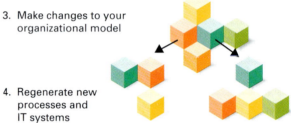

New System A   New System B

4. Regenerate new processes and IT systems based on your new organizational model

FIGURE 7.16

Using Enterprise Software to Support Enterprise Resource Planning

The Reality of Enterprise Resource Planning and Enterprise Software

ERP and enterprise software almost sound too good to be true. They are, however, a reality, and many organizations are exploiting them. In spite of their tremendous advantages, many organizations are either not using ERP and enterprise software or only partially implementing them. Below, we list a few reasons why.

The Existence of Legacy Systems

Legacy systems are IT systems previously built using older technologies such as mainframe computers and programming languages such as COBOL. Legacy systems may work well in isolation but they tend to be very difficult to interface with when your organization develops new systems based on state-of-the-art technologies such as the Internet, client/server computing, and programming languages such as Java.

only on the development of a single system. Later, planning capabilities were added to some integrated CASE tools, but it seemed to be more an afterthought than a well-defined plan. So, CASE tools—even integrated CASE tools—do not really require your organization to take a holistic view through ERP. For that reason, we see enterprise software suites replacing CASE tools in the future.

INDUSTRY PERSPECTIVE

".com"

JD Edwards' OneWorld Enterprise Software Prepares Your Organization for the Web

Simply put, it's time to extend the concept of enterprise resource planning (ERP) beyond the four walls of your organization. Why? Because electronic commerce is here and here to stay. And electronic commerce requires that your organization works in well-defined collaboration with all its business partners—suppliers, distributors, alliances, and customers.

So, your organization can no longer consider ERP as only an internal initiative—you must extend it and its planning and development activities to include your external partners. Fortunately, JD Edwards may have the enterprise software answer. Its new suite, called OneWorld Xe, includes over 300 Internet-ready applications which support everything from customer ordering to collaborative efforts in which your organization and another can design a new product in the privacy of an extranet.

OneWorld Xe creates unique "databots." These databots are XML-based and Java-based applets that are intelligent enough within themselves to support electronic commerce activities such as invoicing and EDI. Using these databots as building blocks for your applications, you can quickly develop Windows, HTML, or Java front-end interfaces. Moreover, these databots are designed in such a way that they can interface with back-end office functions that could very well be supported by legacy systems.

Perhaps the "E" in ERP now stands for e-commerce.[21] ❖

TEAM WORK

Matching IT Systems to the *Who* of Systems Development

In this chapter, we discussed three alternative *whos* for systems development—IT specialists within your organization (insourcing), knowledge workers (selfsourcing), and another organization (outsourcing). In *Extended Learning Module A,* we looked at seven different types of IT systems that support your organization's business processes and how they work with information.

Complete the table below by identifying which of the alternative *whos* are most appropriate for developing the seven different types of IT systems. In some instances, you may find that different groups of people can develop these systems. For each that you identify (even if it's only one), be prepared to give a business example. ❖

IT Systems	Insourcing	Outsourcing	Selfsourcing
TPS			
CIS			
MIS			
WSS			
DSS and AI			
EIS			
IOS			

CHAPTER SEVEN Developing IT Systems

KNOWLEDGE WORKER'S -LIST

The Importance of Planning and How to Plan for IT Systems in an Organization. Planning is the most fundamental undertaking of any organization for any effort. In systems development, organizations use planning to develop an *IT systems plan,* a document that outlines (1) what systems you plan to develop, (2) when to develop those systems, and (3) your contingency plan for disasters. Creating an IT systems plan involves four steps:

1. Gathering all proposed IT systems
2. Considering proposed IT systems in light of organizational goals using such techniques as
   - IT fusion
   - Porter's three generic strategies
   - Critical success factors
3. Evaluating proposed IT systems using such methods as
   - Cost-benefit analysis
   - Risk analysis
   - Capital investment analysis
4. Planning for what you can't live without by developing a disaster recovery plan

Why Their Participation Is Important in the Development of IT Systems. No matter *what* systems your organization chooses to develop, *when* it chooses to develop those systems, *who* will develop those systems, or *how* your organization will develop those systems, you participation is important because you are

- A business process expert
- A liaison to the customer
- A quality control analyst
- A manager of other people

How Organizations Traditionally Develop IT Systems through Insourcing and Their Role during that Process. Insourcing involves using IT specialists within your organization to develop a system. In this case, the *how* is the *traditional systems development life cycle*—a structured step-by-step approach to developing systems that creates a separation of duties among knowledge workers and IT specialists. In the six steps of the SDLC, your roles are outlined in the table on page 301.

What Selfsourcing and Outsourcing Are and How They Affect the Way Organizations Develop Systems. *Selfsourcing* is the development and support of IT systems by knowledge workers with little or no help from IT specialists. So selfsourcing is an important aspect of *knowledge worker computing*. During selfsourcing, knowledge workers basically forgo IT specialists and the use of the SDLC in favor or developing their own systems, mainly by using *prototyping* (the building of models).

Outsourcing is the delegation of specific work to a third party for a specified length of time, at a specified cost, and at a specified level of service. In systems development, your organization can outsource literally everything, with the exception of planning, scoping, and analysis. In outsourcing, the most important document is a request for proposal. A *request for proposal (RFP)* is a formal document that outlines your logical requirements of a proposed system and invites outsourcing organizations or vendors to submit bids for its development.

But organizations have invested literally billions of dollars in developing and maintaining legacy systems. That makes it difficult for them to simply throw away those systems and develop new ones using enterprise software to support ERP.

The Cost of Ownership

Enterprise software is among the most expensive software your organization can purchase (essentially, a form of outsourcing). Complete enterprise software suites can easily cost millions of dollars. After you purchase an enterprise software suite, you have only a common set of prebuilt applications and the tools for developing your organization's unique applications. The development of those unique applications can easily cost you millions of dollars more.

The Cost of Reengineering

Fundamental to the concept of ERP is business process reengineering. Let's face it—organizations that have

How to Take a Holistic Organizational View Using Enterprise Resource Planning and Enterprise Software. *Enterprise resource planning (ERP)* is the coordinated planning of all an organization's resources involved in the production, development, selling, and servicing or goods and services. So, ERP requires that an organization consider the organization as a whole in the development of IT systems. To support ERP, many organizations employ enterprise software. *Enterprise software* is a suite of software that includes (1) a set of common business applications, (2) tools for modeling how the entire organization works, and (3) development tools for building applications unique to your organization. ❖

Your Roles during the SDLC

Planning (from Chapter 8):

- Understand how the strategic direction of the organization will affect your area.
- Provide information requirements for your area.
- Identify proposed IT systems needed in your area.
- Participate in developing an IT systems plan.

Scoping:

- Define the exact problem or opportunity.
- Participate in developing a plan for proceeding.

Analysis:

- Provide information concerning how the system currently works.
- Provide information concerning new information and processing requirements.
- Monitor and justify the new feasibility review.

Design:

- Ensure that the recommended technical solution meets the logical requirements.
- Monitor and justify the project plan.

Implementation:

- Determine the best training method.
- Determine the best method of conversion.
- Provide complete testing of the new system.
- Monitor the budget and schedule and look for "runaway" projects.

Support:

- Provide a mechanism for people to request changes.
- Assess the worth of proposed changes before passing them to the IT specialists.

---

evolved over time have inefficient processes, redundant processes, and processes that do not work well together. To rectify this, your organization must undergo numerous business process reengineering efforts. *Business process reengineering (BPR)* is the reinventing of processes within a business. Many people today characterize BPR as a "knee breaking" initiative in which you completely disregard what you're doing in favor of processes that are streamlined and completely integrated. This, again, represents a huge expense, which some organizations are not willing to undertake.

The Expertise Needed for Enterprise Software

Finally, to use enterprise software, your organization must provide extensive training for its IT staff. Developing IT systems within an enterprise software suite requires expertise unique to that particular suite. Enterprise software vendors such as SAP and JD Edwards provide months and even years of training to your organization if you choose to purchase one of their suites. This expertise is in such high demand that you can actually become a certified developer using different enterprise software suites. If you do, your career will be long, prosperous, and full of money.

CLOSING CASE STUDY

Co-Developing Enterprisewide Systems in the Medical Field

Let's first set the stage in the medical field, centered specifically around the patient, and use HCA as an example. HCA is a complete healthcare delivery organization (HDO) that includes a vast network of participating hospitals and physician offices. Depending on need, a given HCA customer goes to the most appropriate hospital for care. Perhaps a customer goes to one hospital in the spring to be treated for allergies, and then goes to another hospital in the winter to be treated for a skiing accident.

A given customer (patient) may be covered under multiple insurance plans and may use any of those plans under a variety of circumstances. Each insurance provider has its own unique set of forms and procedures, as well as different terms for the same type of information. For example, as the primary method of identification, one insurance provider may provide a PIN (patient identification number), which is 10 digits long, while another provides a CPN (customer policy number), which is 8 digits long.

Physician offices represent yet another challenge. Customers (patients) visit different physician offices depending on their need, and the physicians have a variety of identification numbers. For example, most physicians have a UPIN, state license number, tax ID, DEA number, and even identification numbers that distinguish them within a particular practice management system (HCA often refers patients to providers outside its system).

If there ever was an industry that needed an integrated IT system to effectively consolidate and track information, the medical industry is it.

So, HCA partnered with Healthcare.com Corp. to implement its industry-leading Emerge enterprisewide master patient index (EMPI). With Emerge, a patient has only a master EMPI module, which contains a complete medical history and insurance plan. The master module contains information about all the customer's insurance plans as well as detailed information concerning all physician and hospital visits. With Emerge centralizing this information and giving everyone access to it, each physician knows the complete history of a patient, each hospital can see what other procedures have been performed, and even the insurance providers have up-to-date medical information.

The EMPI module concept required some development effort. As Paul Joyce, project manager in the IT&S Enterprise MPI for HCA, explained, "We wanted to integrate our patients' medical records across the bridge between the hospital and the physician offices, and between the hospital and the health plans. We wanted to be able to index among those communities since they have a variety of identifiers. At that time no one had an EMPI that would do that, so we codeveloped these two areas with Healthcare.com."

Providing quality care is a critical success factor (CSF) at HCA, and supporting the achievement of that CSF is the EMPI. Prior to implementing the system, HCA surveyed five physician offices. Of the 97,000 patient records it found, 75 percent of those patients had also visited an HCA hospital. That meant that for 72,000 patients the medical staff in the hospitals was looking at only a part of their demographic and insurance information.

During implementation of the EMPI, HCA found over 80,000 duplicate medical records between the legacy systems for hospitals and physician offices. By combining these, the quality of care increased through the minimization of errors. As Paul further explained, "By having a more complete patient medical record available, the doctor has more information during the treatment of the patient, and minimizes the possibility of duplicate medical records causing medication errors."[22] ❖

◄ Questions ►

1. According to the *who* of systems development, how did HCA go about the systems development process for the EMPI system? Within that *who*, further explain how the systems development process worked.

2. To implement the EMPI system, HCA first deployed it in five HCA hospitals and five physician offices in Richmond, VA. What type of conversion method is this? Why do you think HCA chose this particular conversion method? For each of the other methods, identify at least one advantage and one disadvantage that HCA might have considered.

3. Privacy of information in the medical field is a key issue. Are there any privacy issues associated with

HCA's use of an EMPI master module for each patient that is shared among all hospitals, physician offices, and insurance providers? Would you like to have a single master module that contains all your medical information? What would be the advantages of having one? What would be the disadvantages?

4. HCA's approach to developing the EMPI really supported the concept of enterprise resource planning (ERP). Why was using ERP so important to the success of HCA's system? How did it consider not only internal operational aspects when using ERP but also the needs of partnering organizations?

5. Disaster recovery planning is also key in the medical field. If you go to a hospital for an emergency, an IT system suffering from some sort of disaster could also have disastrous consequences for you. Visit a medical care provider in your area and determine its disaster recovery plan. What does it look like? What is the time frame for getting systems back up and running?

6. "Quality of care" includes both tangible and intangible benefits. What are some of those benefits? Consider it from two points of view—benefits to the patients and benefits to the internal efficiencies of a medical care provider.

Electronic Commerce
Business and You on the Internet

Building the Perfect Web Page

Almost every business is doing it—some are doing it better than others, but almost every business you can name is building a Web page. Businesses are building Web pages for a variety of reasons—to create a presence on the Internet, to provide an electronic storefront for displaying products and services, and to give customers the ability to order those products and services (B2C electronic commerce).

About one of every 50 people is doing it too. Some want to build a Web page because it's the "in thing," others want to show off their pets, and still others hope to meet people (called *e-friends*) around the world.

Building a Web page really is a process of "building" something, just as we discussed building IT systems in this chapter. You have a variety of building tools (called Web development tools) available to you, you must consider the target audience for whom you're building your Web page, there are good ways and bad ways to build a Web page, and Web pages always require maintenance and updating.

In this electronic commerce section, we'd like to alert you to the many facets of building a Web page. These facets include

- HTML—the language for creating a Web page
- Web development tools for accelerating the process of creating a Web page
- Online references and books for creating a Web page
- Free stuff on the Internet for building a Web page such as backgrounds and counters
- Web hosting services

This is not the place to specifically take you through all the steps of building a Web page. Instead we will point you to some great references to help you with that, one of which is the Website that supports this text. What you will gain by reading this electronic commerce section is insights into the process of building a good

Web page. Thus, you won't find a lot of exercises to complete here or questions to answer. Rather we hope you'll be excited about building your own Web page after reading this electronic commerce section, and that you will go on to further reading to help you do just that.

In this section, we've included a number of Websites related to building the perfect Web page. On the Website that supports this text (http://www.mhhe.com/haag, select "Electronic Commerce Projects"), we've provided direct links to all these Websites as well as many, many more. These are a great starting point for completing this *Real HOT* section. We would also encourage you to search the Internet for others.

HTML—The Language of Web Pages

Hypertext markup language (***HTML***) is the language used to create Web pages on the Internet. Using HTML, you simply specify (1) what information you want on your Web page such as your name or a photo of your pet and (2) how that information is supposed to look. Like all other programming languages and software such as Word or Excel, new versions of HTML become available from time to time, with the most recent versions offering you more capabilities and flexibility.

In HTML you specify how information is supposed to look by using tags. A tag in HTML is (for the most part) a formatting statement. For example, consider the following HTML statement:

<CENTER><B><I>Web Page Heading</I></B></CENTER>

That HTML statement contains some information for a Web page (Web Page Heading) along with three tags that determine how the information will be displayed. In this instance, the three tags are CENTER, B, and I. The CENTER tag will display the information centered on the screen, the B tag will bold the information, and the I tag will italicize the information.

Notice also that these tags have a beginning and ending point. For the CENTER tag, <CENTER> starts centering information and </CENTER> stops centering information. So, all information between the beginning and ending CENTER tag is centered. The same is true for the bold tag (<B> and </B>) and the italicize tag (<I> and </I>). Most—but not all—tags in HTML have a beginning and ending point.

So, to create a Web page using HTML you simply need to learn the tags in HTML (there are several hundred). Then, you determine what information you want

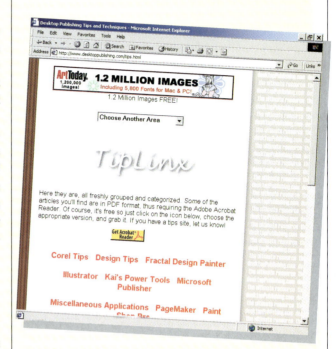

your Web page to contain and what tags you need to use to affect the presentation of that information when someone accesses and views your Web page.

Web Development Tools

There are a variety of ways in which you can build your Web page. Most notably, you can (1) write your own HTML code, (2) use a word processing package, (3) purchase and use a Web development tool, or (4) download and use a free Web development tool. Of course, many issues will affect your decision. If you want a really elaborate Web page, you should write your own HTML code or purchase a Web development tool. If price is a concern, then purchasing a Web development tool may not be an option. If you're just interested in getting a simple Web page up and running, you should probably consider using a word processing package or downloading a free Web development tool.

If you choose to write your own HTML code, then you'll need to become very familiar with HTML and its tags. You may also need to be prepared to learn and use a graphics package such as PhotoShop or CorelDraw. Writing your own HTML code requires the most expertise (and usually time), but it also gives you the greatest flexibility and capability. If you really become an HTML expert, you can expect to get a job writing HTML and make a salary in excess of $50,000 per year in many cases.

Perhaps the simplest way to create a Web page is to use a word processing package such as Microsoft Word.

To do so in Word, create a document that represents what you want your Web page to look like. As you do, add all the necessary formatting (color, bolding, centering, and the like), make use of tables and lists, and insert any clip art you want. When you're done, choose "File" from the menu bar and then "Save as HTML." Word will automatically generate the HTML code necessary to produce a Web page just as your document looks. Afterward, you can choose "View" from the menu bar and "HTML Source" to see what the code looks like (you can also change the code at that point, which will automatically change the look of your Web page).

Your third option for creating a Web page is to purchase and use a Web development tool (some people refer to these as Web authoring tools). A Web development tool is simply a piece of software that facilitates your building a Web page. Using one of these tools—most of which come with easy point-and-click interfaces— you define what you want your Web page to look like (much as you would using Word). Then the software takes over and generates the HTML code for you.

The real advantage of Web development tools lies in Website management. Most Websites actually contain more than one Web page. For example, once you connect to the main page of a Website, it will probably contain links or buttons that you click on to view additional information or explore other parts of the Website. Each part is actually called a Web page, with all the Web pages making up a Website. And using a Web development tool, you can easily create, manage, and maintain a huge Website that may have as many as a thousand separate pages.

If you're going to purchase a Web development tool, you should make your decision carefully. We recommend you consider the following issues:

- How much will it cost?
- How widely is the product used?
- How easy is it to create a simple Web page?
- How easy is it to create a complex Web page?
- Does the product support good site management?

As a final alternative, you may want to consider using a free Web development tool. This category of software is often called freeware (which typically is free) or shareware, which may require you to pay a nominal fee. For more on freeware and shareware, revisit the *Real HOT Electronic Commerce* section for Chapter 6. Of course, many people will tell you that you get what you pay for. So if it's free, don't get your hopes too high that you'll be able to do everything you want using one of these

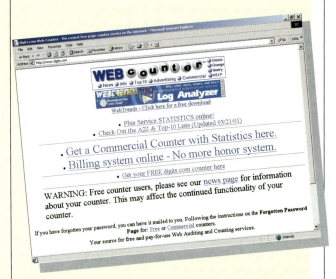

tools. Many of these free Web development tools don't support easy point-and-click interfaces; rather, they are simply text editors that help you write HTML code.

References for Creating a Web Page

As you consider building a Web page, you'll need to learn how to write HTML or use a Web development tool. What do you do when you want to learn how to do something? You take a class, perhaps buy a book, or even ask a professional. If you're really serious about building a great Website, you should probably do all of the above. Perhaps your school offers a course in building Web pages or you can enroll in a weekend conference on building Web pages taught by a professional.

If you're interested in purchasing some books, here is a recommended list below, separated into two categories—one for designing Web pages and one for writing HTML. If you choose to use a Web development tool, you'll be able to find a variety of books devoted to the software of your choice.

Designing Web Pages:

- *Guide to Web Content and Design* (Roger Parker)
- *Creating Killer Web Sites* (David Siegel)
- *Web Page Design* (Mary Morris and Randy Hinrichs)
- *Teach Yourself Great Web Design* (Anne-Rae Vasquez-Peterson and Paul Chow)

Writing HTML:

- *<Creative HTML Design>* (Lynda Weinman and William Weinman)

- *Using HTML 4, Java 1.1, and JavaScript 1.2* (Eric Ladd)
- *Web Programming Unleashed* (Bob Breedlove)
- *The Complete Reference HTML* (Thomas Powell)

You can also find a variety of sources on the Internet for writing HTML and designing Web pages. We would encourage you to seek those out— they're quite good.

Free Stuff on the Internet

The Internet is full of free stuff, and you can use much of it to build your Web page. Most notably, you can find free (1) images and backgrounds and (2) counters. You can find hundreds of sites on the Internet that provide free images and backgrounds that you can download and incorporate into your Web page. To do so, you simply connect to one of the sites, find the image or background you want, and then follow the procedures for downloading. If you find a site that doesn't provide downloading instructions, try pointing at the image or background you want and right-clicking on the mouse. That usually opens a "Save As" window that allows you to save the image or background to your client machine.

Once you build your Web page, you might want to keep track of how many people visit you. When someone accesses your Web page, it's called a *hit*, and you keep track of hits using a counter. You've probably seen a lot of Web pages that contain a counter stating the number of people who have visited there. Just like images and backgrounds, you can find free counters for download all over the Internet (we've provided a list of a few in the table at the end of this section).

Web Hosting Services

Writing HTML (or using a Web development tool) to create a Web page is only part of the equation. After you build your Web page, you need to transfer your Web page to a Web server. Why? Because the computer that you use to build your Web page is most probably a client—a computer you use to move around the Internet and access information and services provided by a server. For example, if you build your Web page on your home computer, no one on the Internet can access your machine because it's a client and not a server.

What you have to do is transfer your Web page to a server computer of your Internet service provider. And who's your Internet service provider? Well, that differs from person to person. At the University of Denver (DU), for example, all students and faculty can use DU as their Internet service provider. So, once a DU student builds a Web page, he or she follows a simple process to transfer the Web page to DU's server. Then, anyone anywhere in the world can access that student's Web page.

Your school may provide the same service. Answer the following questions. To find the answers, you may need to talk to your instructor or your school's computer help desk:

A. Can you build your own Web page and place it on your school's Web server?

B. What Web development tools are available at your school to use?

C. What is the transfer process you must go through to move your Web page from your client computer to your school's Web server?

D. Does your school have any limitations on the size of your Web page? If so, what are those limitations?

E. What is your Web page address on your school's Web server?

Some schools may not offer all students the ability to build a Web page and place it on a Web server. If that's true, you can still build a Web page for the whole world to see. To do so, you simply use a more traditional Internet service provider (ISP) such as AOL, Prodigy, or perhaps a local ISP. These ISPs—in addition to providing you access to the Internet—also give you the ability to build a Web page and place it on their Web servers.

Of course how you do that, the cost the ISP will charge you, and limitations differ for each ISP. If you're interested, you should contact an ISP and inquire about how to build a Web page, how the transfer process works, and how much it costs. We leave that up to you. Many ISPs today offer free Web site hosting— you should definitely contact them.

Final Thoughts

You must address the issue of placing information on the Internet for all to see. You need to keep in mind that *everyone* (over 900 million people) on the Internet will be able to access your Web page. Obviously it is impossible to estimate the trustworthiness of many of these individuals, no more than all those who would see your name in a phone book. We encourage you to think seriously before placing the following information on your Web page:

- Your full name
- Address
- Phone number
- Date of birth
- Social security number
- Student ID number
- Home town

Today, the Internet is almost as accessible as directory assistance. Think carefully about what information you want people to know about you.

Web Sites for Building a Web Page

Web Product (Manufacturer)	Address
PageMill (Adobe Systems)	http://www.adobe.com
HotDog Pro (Sausage Software)	http://www.sausage.com
HoTMetaL Pro (SoftQuad)	http://www.softquad.com
Dreamweaver (Macromedia)	http://www.macromedia.com
FrontPage (Microsoft)	http://www.microsoft.com

Web Reference Content	Address
Creating graphics using graphics packages	http://www.desktoppublishing.com/tips.html
Design tips and techniques	http://www.desktoppublishing.com/tipsweb.html
HTML code and tips	http://www.1accessweb.com/optic1/backgrounds.html
10 steps to building your own Web page	http://www.1accessweb.com/optic1
HTML reference guide	http://www.ecn.bgu.edu/users/gallery/webwork/www.html#notbasics

Free Images and Backgrounds	Address
	http://web-star.com/botd/botd.html
	http://www.netreach.net/people/edpenland/anim.html
	http://desktoppublishing.com/backgrounds.html
	http://www.celtique-boutique.com/animal.htm
	http://www.desktoppublishing.com/cliplist.html

Counters	Address
	http://www.digits.com
	http://www.ace.net.au/images/counters/count2.htm
	http://purgatory.ecn.purdue.edu:20002/JBC/david/how.html
	http://www.asoftware.com
	http://www.geocities.com/members/tools/counter.html

Go to the Web site that supports this text: **http://www.mhhe.com/haag** and select "Electronic Commerce Projects."

We've included links to over 100 Web sites for building a Web page, including the dos and don'ts of building a good Web page and service provider requirements.

CHAPTER SEVEN Developing IT Systems

KEY TERMS AND CONCEPTS

Business Process Reengineering (BPR), 301
Capital Investment Analysis, 268
Computer-Aided Software Engineering (CASE) Tools, 297
Cost-Benefit Analysis, 267
Critical Success Factor (CSF), 267
Disaster Recovery Cost Curve, 268
Disaster Recovery Plan, 268
Enterprise Resource Planning (ERP), 297
Enterprise Software, 297
Feasibility Review, 278
Hypertext markup language (HTML), 304
Insourcing, 272
Intangible Benefit, 267
Integrated CASE Tools, 297
IT Fusion, 267
IT Systems Plan, 266
IT Systems Risk, 268
Knowledge Worker Development, 286
Legacy System, 298
Lower CASE Tool, 297
Outsourcing, 292
Parallel Conversion, 283
Piecemeal Conversion, 283
Pilot Conversion, 283
Plunge Conversion, 283
Project Plan, 278
Project Team, 275
Proof-of-Concept Prototype, 286
Prototype, 286
Prototyping, 286
Request for Proposal (RFP), 293
Selfsourcing, 286
Selling Prototype, 287
Tangible Benefit, 267
Traditional Systems Development Life Cycle (Traditional SDLC), 272
Upper CASE Tools, 297

SHORT-ANSWER QUESTIONS

1. Why is your participation important in the systems development process?
2. What are the six steps of the traditional SDLC? What are their goals?
3. What are the steps in the outsourcing process?
4. What is IT fusion? Why is it important?
5. What should an IT systems plan include?
6. How does enterprise software support enterprise resource planning?
7. What are the three categories of CASE tools?
8. How is selfsourcing an important aspect of knowledge worker computing?
9. What are the advantages and disadvantages of prototyping?
10. What is a request for proposal? Why is it the most important document in the outsourcing process?

SHORT-QUESTION ANSWERS

For each of the following answers, provide an appropriate question.

1. It includes what systems to develop and when.
2. When technology is indistinguishable from people and processes.
3. One is return on investment.
4. Because I'm a business process expert.
5. Insourcing, outsourcing, and selfsourcing.
6. When programming occurs.
7. Testing a system on a select group of people.
8. What I do when I develop systems for myself.
9. Buying existing software is one example.
10. Starting over with a clean slate.
11. Software that support enterprise resource planning.

DISCUSSION QUESTIONS

1. Our discussion of ITW Enterprises in this chapter focused on the traditional systems development life cycle. What other tools and methods could ITW have used to increase the efficiency and quality of the systems development process?
2. If you view systems development as a question-and-answer session, another question you could ask is, "Why do organizations develop IT systems?" Consider what you believe to be the five most important reasons organizations develop IT

systems. How do these reasons relate to topics in the first six chapters of this book?

3. Why is it important to develop a logical model of a proposed system before generating a technical design? What potential problems would arise if you didn't develop a logical model and went straight to developing the technical design?

4. On page 272, we listed questions you should ask when considering the *who* of systems development. Which question do you believe to be the most important? The least important? Justify your answers.

5. What tools and methods have had the greatest impact on the increase in selfsourcing? What would happen to IT specialists if these methods and tools became so good that organizations completely eliminated the SDLC and just used outsourcing and selfsourcing? Is this actually a possibility?

6. In the box on page 272, we developed a set of questions to help you answer the *who* question of systems development. Develop a similar set of questions to help answer the *how* question of systems development. How many questions did you create? Based on how your questions are answered, what seems to be the most popular *how* for systems development? The least popular?

7. If your friends were about to start their own business and asked you for planning and development advice with respect to IT systems, what would you tell them? What if their business idea was completely Internet-based? What if their business idea didn't include using the Internet at all? Would your answers differ? Why or why not?

CHAPTER OUTLINE

INDUSTRY PERSPECTIVES

Manufacturing **317**
Don't Send Suggestive E-Mail from Your Place of Work!

Health Care **318**
Employee Monitoring That Makes People Happy

Entertainment and Publishing **326**
Bounce and *Toy Story 2*: Playing Digitally at a Cinema Near You

".com" **327**
eCampus Is Security Conscious

Financial Services **335**
The Bank Was in Danger of Collapse

IN THE NEWS

- **313** Your ethical structure can change over time.
- **316** Your employer can find out what you say in chat rooms.
- **316** E-mail is about as private as a postcard.
- **321** Cultural Diversity: It takes all kinds to make a world.
- **323** Ergonomics: A cure for a pain in the neck.
- **324** No organization can survive without information.
- **324** You can sell information—keep it too.
- **325** Information: A capital idea.
- **327** Script bunnies are not the cute kind.
- **328** Worms wiggle their way into IT systems.
- **333** Encryption: An electronic key.
- **334** Disaster Recovery: Ka-Boom! Now what chief?

FEATURES

- **314** **Team Work** What Would You Do?
- **319** **On Your Own** Who Knows about You?
- **321** **The Global Perspective** Britain's E-Mail Privacy—RIP
- **323** **On Your Own** Is Your Computer a Health Hazard?
- **324** **The Global Perspective** Going to College without Going to College
- **325** **Team Work** Could You Work a Help Desk?
- **338** **Electronic Commerce** Making Travel Arrangements on the Internet

KNOWLEDGE WORKER'S CHECKLIST

In the Information Age, Knowledge Workers Understand . . .

1. The importance of ethics
2. Privacy
3. Accommodating Diversity
4. Information and its Protection

WEB SUPPORT

http://www.mhhe.com/haag

- Airlines
- Trains and Busses
- Rental Cars
- Road Conditions and Maps
- Lodging
- One-Stop Travel Sites
- Destination Information

Protecting Information and People

Threats and Safeguards

CHAPTER 8

CASE STUDY

Payless—Shoes with Information behind Them

Payless ShoeSource, Inc., is North America's largest family footwear retailer. In 2000, Payless sold about $3 billion worth of shoes (average price about $12) at its 4,900 stores in the United States, Canada, Puerto Rico, Central America, and Guam.

Payless replenishes inventories and ships new models of shoes to its stores automatically. In a giant warehouse, a computer-controlled conveyer belt system reads the barcodes on the boxes and sends the shoes off to the right bin where they're picked up and shipped all over the world.

The entire system relies on a data center in Topeka, Kansas. All the data analysis, decision-making, and control are based on the information that the Topeka data center collects and stores daily. Payless has a mainframe, several minicomputers, and thousands of PCs. The entire corporate network is controlled from the Topeka data center. Even if there is a network problem in Taiwan, the people in Topeka handle it. Since Kansas is located in "Tornado Alley," the data center is underground—all 16,000 square feet of it.

Every night, the data center polls all the stores, domestic and overseas, for information about their sales for that day. The company has a data warehouse with two years' worth of information on every shoe type and size sold in every store that's available for online analytical processing (OLAP). Since losing this information would be disastrous, Payless has lots of safeguards in place. Here are some examples.

- The primary communications provider for nightly polling of the stores is AT&T, but should there be a problem, the phone system will automatically switch to Sprint to continue the information download.

- If the power goes out, an array of 120 heavy-duty batteries take over briefly while the power generator fires up, and there are two of those—just in case. The generators each have 10,000 gallon diesel fuel tanks.

- The data center also has two backup air conditioning systems in case the original one goes out.

- If fire breaks out, fire-fighting gas (FM 2000) sprays down from the ceiling to suffocate the flames within seconds. If that doesn't work, water sprinklers kick in as a last resort—water isn't good for computer equipment.

- All information is backed up onto high capacity cassette tapes. The company has about 30,000 of these. Each day the backup tapes are sent off site by truck, so that if anything should happen to the information stored at the data center, the backups will be available.

- The company has an agreement for the use of a hot site in Philadelphia, where the entire data center can relocate and continue operations if a very major disaster such as an earthquake were to occur. Every year all the IT staff practice a disaster drill.

Payless knows that without its information it can't survive because the company won't be able to manage its inventory. Information is the engine of the business and so must be protected at all costs. ❖

Introduction

As you've already learned, the three components of an IT system are information technology, information, and knowledge workers. Most of what you've seen in previous chapters has dealt with IT and how it stores and processes information. In this chapter we're going to concentrate on people, who are, after all, the reason that we have IT systems in the first place; and the information itself (see Figure 8.1).

It's been said that the only constant in life is change. Change, certainly, is an inescapable aspect of IT systems today and it will be so in the foreseeable future. You can't always control change but you can create an atmosphere in which change is not disruptive either for people or for systems. The best environment for an IT system and the people who use it is one that has stability without stagnation and change without chaos.

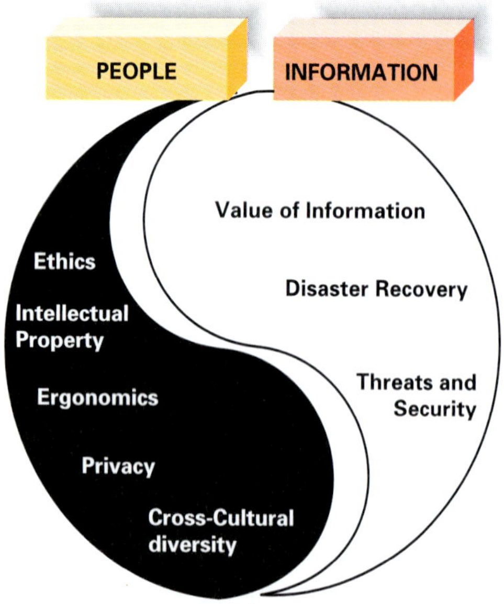

To provide continuity and comfort for people in a changing technical world you must understand:

- The importance of ethics
- People's need for privacy
- Cultural differences (cross-cultural diversity)
- The need for a healthy workplace (ergonomics)

To provide the best environment for information in a changing world you must understand:

- The value of information to the organization
- Threats to information and how to protect against them (security)
- The need to plan for the worst case scenario (disaster recovery)

People

An Organization's Most Important Resource

The most important part of any IT system is the people who use it and are affected by it. How people treat each other has always been important, but in an electronic age, with huge power at our fingertips we can affect people's lives in ways never before possible. How we act toward each other is largely determined by our ethics.

Ethics

Doing What's Right

Ethical people have integrity. They're people you can definitely trust. They're people who are just as enthusiastic about the rights of others as they are about their own rights. They have a strong sense of what's fair and right and what isn't. But even the most ethical people sometimes face difficult choices.

Ethics are the principles and standards that guide our behavior toward other people. Acting ethically means behaving in a principled fashion and treating

FIGURE 8.1

Your Focus for This Chapter

other people with respect and dignity. It's simple to say, but not so simple to do since some situations are complex or ambiguous. The important role of ethics in our lives has long been recognized. As far back as 44 B.C., Cicero said that ethics are indispensable to anyone who wants to have a good career. Having said that, Cicero, along with some of the greatest minds over the centuries, struggled with what the rules of ethics should be.

Our ethics, rooted in our history, culture, and religions remain the same over time at important levels, but our sense of ethics shifts over time, and from culture to culture. In Europe in past centuries, women who had just given birth sometimes smothered the new baby out of desperation. These were women who already had more children than they could feed and had nowhere and no one to go to for help. Faced with an impossible situation, they took what seemed to them the only reasonable way out. Many of their contemporaries didn't consider this to be unethical—it was simply a sad but necessary act to save the older children from starvation. Today, in our society, this would be criminal, of course.

This is an extreme example of people facing a difficult decision, but it illustrates the murky area ethics can be. It's a perennial question for philosophers whether there's an underlying core of ethics that's eternal or whether ethics are relative to the place and time. Without a doubt, however, each society has its own set of standards. As times and circumstances change, some standards change too. Making moral choices can be a hard challenge. While there's a basic sense of right and wrong in our society, there's plenty of room for ambiguity and tough decisions too.

Two things affect how you make your decision when you're faced with an ethical dilemma. The first is your basic ethical structure, which you developed as you grew up. The second is the set of practical circumstances involved in the decision that you're trying to make—that is, all the shades of gray in what are rarely black or white decisions.

Your ethical structure and the ethical challenges you'll face may be said to exist at several levels (see Figure 8.2).[1] At the outside level are things that most people wouldn't consider bad, taking paper clips or sending an occasional personal e-mail on company time. Do these things really matter? At the middle level are more significant ethical challenges. One example might be accessing personnel records for personal reasons. Could there ever be personal reasons so compelling that you would not feel ethical discomfort doing this? Reading someone else's e-mail might be another "middle" example. At the innermost ethical level are ethical violations that you'd surely consider very serious, embezzling funds or selling company records to a competitor. And yet over time, your ethical structure can change so that even such acts as these seem more or less ethical. For example, if everyone around you is

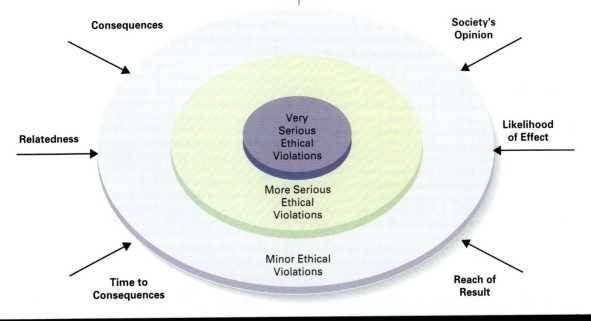

FIGURE 8.2
Your Ethical Structure

TEAMWORK

What Would You Do?

Analyze the following situation. You have access to the sales and customer information in a flower shop. You discover that the boyfriend of a woman you know is sending roses to three other women on a regular basis. The woman you know is on the flower list, but she believes that she's the only woman in his romantic life. You really think you should tell the woman. Your dilemma is that you have a professional responsibility to keep the company's information private. However, you also believe that you have a responsibility to the woman. Do you tell her?

Are there factors that would change your decision? Each team member should individually consider the additional information below. Then indicate whether any one or more of these factors would change your decision. Then form a consensus with your team. ❖

Additional Facts	Yes	No	Why?
1. The woman is your sister.			
2. The man is your brother.			
3. The woman is about to give the man her life savings as a down payment on a house in the belief that they will soon be married.			
4. The woman is already married.			

accessing confidential records for their own purposes, in time you might come to think it's no big deal. And this might spell big trouble for you.

The practical circumstances surrounding your decision always influence you in an ethical dilemma.[2] It might be nice if every decision were crystal clear and considerations such as these needn't be taken into account, but decisions are seldom so easy.

1. **Consequences.** How much or how little benefit or harm will come from a particular decision?
2. **Society's opinion.** What is your perception of what society really thinks of your intended action?
3. **Likelihood of effect.** What is the probability of the harm or benefit that will occur if you take the action?
4. **Time to consequences.** What length of time will it take for the benefit or harm to take effect?
5. **Relatedness.** How much do you identify with the person or persons who will receive the benefit or suffer the harm?
6. **Reach of result.** How many people will be affected by your action?

Let's hope your basic sense of right and wrong will steer you in the right direction, but no matter what your sense of ethics is or how strong it is, such practical aspects of the situation may affect you as you make your decision, perhaps unduly, perhaps quite justifiably. Ethical dilemmas usually arise, not out of simple situations, but from a clash between competing goals, responsibilities, and loyalties. Ethical decisions are complex judgments that balance rewards for yourself and others against responsibilities to yourself and others. Inevitably, your decision process is influenced by uncertainty about the magnitude of the outcome, by your estimate of the importance of the situation, sometimes by your perception of conflicting "right reactions," and two socially acceptable "correct" decisions.

What do you do then if you're faced with a choice that is not perfectly ethically clear? If you feel you are in an ethical quandary—you probably are. If you find you're giving the situation a whole lot of thought, the situation may deserve it. You may wish to talk to a friend, a teacher, a supervisor, or a mentor. We can't tell you what to do here, except to remind you that we're all faced with such dilemmas, they are real, and they have consequences.

Let's look at an example. Say your organization is developing a decision support system (DSS) to help formulate treatments for an infectious disease. Other companies in the industry are working on similar projects. The first system on the market will most likely reap huge profits. You may know that your DSS doesn't yet work properly—it's good, but not yet totally reliable. But you're feeling extreme pressure from your boss to get the system onto the market immediately. You're worried about the harm that might come to a patient because of your DSS; but, on the other hand, it does work well most of the time. Is it up to you or not? You have a family to support and student loans to repay. And you like being employed. Can you hold out and get more information on the system's reliability? What do you do? Can you ask for advice in so sensitive a situation?

Your company may well have an office or person whose job it is to give advice on work-related ethical dilemmas. Many companies do. Failing that, you could look up your company's code of ethics. If you can't find that or don't think it's taken seriously in your place of work, you can check your profession's ethical code. The ACM, for example, has a code of ethics for IT employees. However, in the end, what you finally decide to do will depend on your ethics.

Intellectual Property
Product of the Mind

One area in which your ethics will surely be tested is in the question of copying proprietary software. Will you take care to do the right thing? Software is a type of intellectual property. **Intellectual property** is intangible creative work that is embodied in physical form.[3] Music, novels, paintings, and sculptures are all examples of intellectual property. Music, novels, and so on are worth much more than the physical form in which they are delivered. For example, a single song is worth far more than the CD you purchased. Intellectual property is covered by copyright law.

As a form of intellectual property, software is usually protected by copyright law, although sometimes it falls under patent law, which protects an idea, such as the design of a kitchen appliance or an industrial pump valve. Copyright law protects authorship of literary and dramatic works, musical and theatrical compositions, and works of art. **Copyright** is the legal protection afforded an expression of an idea, such as a song or a video game. Having a copyright means that no one can use your song or video game without your permission.

Copyright law doesn't forbid the use of intellectual property completely. It has some notable exceptions. For example, a TV program could show your video game without your permission. This would be an example of the use of copyrighted material for the creation of new material, i.e. the TV program. And that's legal; it falls under the Fair Use Doctrine. The **Fair Use Doctrine** says that you may use copyrighted material in certain situations—for example, in the creation of new work or, within certain limits, for teaching purposes. One limit is on the amount of the copyrighted material you may use. Generally, the determining factor in copyright disputes is whether the copyright holder has been or is likely to be denied income because of the infringement. Courts will consider factors such as how much of the work was used and how, and when and on what basis the decision was made to use it.

Remember that copyright infringement is *illegal*. That means it's illegal outside of a "fair use" situation to simply copy a copyrighted picture, text, or anything else, for your own purposes, without permission, whether the copyrighted material is on the Internet or not. In particular, it's illegal to copy copyrighted software. But there's one exception to that rule. You may always make one copy of copyrighted software to keep for backup purposes. When you buy copyrighted software, what you're paying for is the right to use it—and that's all.

How many other copies you may make depends on the copyright agreement that comes with the software package. Some software companies say emphatically that you may not even put the software on more than one computer—even if they're both yours and no one else uses either one. Other companies are a little less strict, and agree to let you put a copy of software on multiple machines—as long as only one person is using that software package at any given time. In this instance, the company considers software to be like a book, in that you can have it in different places and you can loan it out, but only one person at a time can use it.

If you copy copyrighted software and give it to another person or persons, you're pirating the software. **Pirated software** is copyrighted software that is copied and distributed without permission of the owner. Software piracy cost businesses $12 billion in 1999. The biggest losers (in rank order) were the United States, Japan, United Kingdom, Germany, China, France, Canada, Italy, Brazil, and the Netherlands. The Software and Information Industry Association (SIAA) and the Business Software Alliance (BSA) say that this means lost jobs, wages, tax revenues, and a potential barrier to success for software start-ups around the globe.[4]

> **CAREER OPPORTUNITY**
> Help is available if you have questions or concerns about what is appropriate behavior for a knowledge worker. The following organizations have formulated codes of ethics regarding the use of computers and the handling of information. Information about these organizations is available on the Internet:
>
> - Computer Professionals for Social Responsibility (CPSR) (http://www.learncd.com/%7Ejgraves/cpsr.htm)
> - Association for Computing Machinery (ACM) (http://www.acm.org)
> - Association of Information Technology Professionals (AITP)—formerly Data Processing Managers Association (DPMA) (http://negaduck.cc.vt.edu/DPMA)
> - Institute of Electrical and Electronics Engineers (IEEE) (http://www.ieee.org)

Privacy

Who Wants Your Personal Information?

In Chapter 5 you learned the core principles of IT privacy. In this section we'll examine some specific areas of privacy—employers' collection of information about employees; businesses' collection of information about consumers; government collection of personal information; and privacy in international trade.

Privacy and Employees

Companies need information about their employees and customers to be effective in the marketplace. But people often object to having so many details about their lives available to others. If you're applying for a job, you'll most likely fill out a job application, but that's not the only information a potential employer can get about you. For a small fee, employers, or anyone else, can find out about your credit standing, your telephone usage, your insurance coverage, and many other interesting things. An employer can also get information on what you said on the Internet from companies who collect and collate chat room exchanges. An employer can also ask a job applicant to take drug and psychological tests, the results of which are the property of the company. After you're hired, your employer can monitor where you go, what you do, what you say, and what you write in e-mails—at least during working hours.

Businesses have good reasons for seeking and storing personal information on employees. (1) They want to hire the best people they can, and then they want to ensure that staff members are conducting themselves appropriately and not wasting or misusing company resources. (2) Businesses can be held liable for the actions of employees. They can be sued for failing to adequately investigate the backgrounds of employees.

In the year 2000, 40 million e-mail users are estimated to have sent 60 billion electronic messages.[5] The American Management Association in New York estimates that 45 percent of large U.S. companies monitor electronic communications including e-mail, voice mail, and fax machine traffic.[6] One reason that companies monitor employees' e-mail is that they can be sued for what their employees send to each other and to people outside the company.

Chevron Corporation and Microsoft settled sexual harassment lawsuits for $2.2 million each because employees received offensive e-mail (see the Manufacturing Industry Perspective in this section). Other companies such as Dow Chemical Company, Xerox, the New York Times Co., and Edward Jones took preemptive action by firing people who sent or stored pornographic or violent e-mail messages.[7]

Numerous vendors sell software products that scan e-mail, both incoming and outgoing. The software can look for specific words or phrases or sexually offensive messages in the subject lines or in the body of the text. It can also flag unsolicited ads and newsletters.

Some employees welcome e-mail monitoring. For example, 20th Century Fox directors and producers find that e-mail monitoring protects them from the rantings of unhappy writers whose screen plays may have been rejected.[8]

Another reason employers monitor their workers' use of IT resources is to avoid wasting resources. In May 2000, Victoria's Secret had an online fashion show at three o'clock in the afternoon on a weekday. About 2 million people watched the show, presumably many of them on their companies' computers. One employee watching the fashion show used as much bandwidth as it would take to download the entire *Encyclopedia Britannica*.[9] So, not only is the employee wasting company time, the employee is also slowing down the work of others.

INDUSTRY PERSPECTIVE

Manufacturing

Don't Send Suggestive E-Mail from Your Place of Work!

Do you send jokes to people over the Internet? If you got a joke giving 25 reasons "why beer is better than women," or pornographic pictures, would you be offended? Twenty-eight women who worked at Chevron Information Technology Co., a Chevron operating company based in California, were. They wrote to the company's management asking them to look into what they perceived as sexual harassment. The women said that, far from the company's helping them, four of the women were singled out for retaliation.

The four women filed suit charging the company with tolerating a sexually hostile working environment. In the end, Chevron settled out of court, paying the women $2.2 million. This sum didn't cover the company's costs in the matter. There were lawyer fees to be paid and the cost of hundreds of hours spent by employees and outside experts trying to discover the identity of the senders of the offensive material. Despite their best efforts, including fingerprinting and DNA testing, they weren't able to ascertain who was responsible.

Chevron isn't alone in footing the bill for the lack of management control of electronic traffic. Microsoft Corp. also settled a sexual harassment suit for allowing pornographic messages to be sent through the company's e-mail system. Microsoft settled out of court for $2.2 million. A West Coast company paid $250,000 to settle an age discrimination suit when the CEO wrote an e-mail directing the human resource department to "get rid" of a female employee.

Other companies didn't let similar situations get as far as the courts. They took action by firing employees who exchanged inappropriate e-mail.

- The New York Times Co. fired more than 20 people for sending or forwarding e-mail the paper considered to be offensive.
- The First Union Bank fired seven employees for the same reason.
- Dow Jones Chemical launched a massive investigation on the basis of employee complaints. Fifty employees were fired, some of whom had worked for Dow for more than 10 years.
- Nissan Motor Corp. fired two people for receiving and storing sexually suggestive messages.[10] ❖

About 70 percent of Web traffic occurs during work hours, and this is reason enough for companies to monitor what, and for how long, employees are viewing on the Web. Again, various software packages are available to keep track of people's Web surfing. Some software actually blocks access to certain sites.

Privacy and Consumers

Businesses face a dilemma. Customers want businesses to know who they are, but at the same time they want them to leave them alone. To provide what customers want, businesses have to know what customers want. To do this they need to know about customers' lifestyles, habits, and preferences. Massive amounts of information are available to businesses. A relatively large Web site may get about 100 million hits per day. The site gets about 200 bytes of information for each hit. That's about 20 gigabytes of information per day.[11] This level of information load has made electronic customer relationship (eCRM) systems the fastest-growing area of software development. Part of managing customer relationships is personalization. Web sites greeting you by name, and Amazon.com's famous recommendations that "people who bought this also bought . . ." are examples of personalization, which is made possible by the Web site knowing about you.[12]

Apart from being able to collect its own information about you, a company can readily access consumer information elsewhere. Credit card companies sell information, so does the Census Bureau, and so do mailing list companies. Web traffic tracking companies such as DoubleClick follow you around the Web and then sell the information about where you went and for how long. DoubleClick can get to know you over time and

INDUSTRY PERSPECTIVE

Health Care

Employee Monitoring That Makes People Happy

You'll hear a lot of complaints about employee monitoring systems, but not from the nurses and nurses' aides at Freeman Hospital in Joplin, Missouri. Freeman put a system into its acute care facility that instantly finds where nurses are in the building. The objective of the system is to improve patient care and service.

The patients in the acute care facility where people who undergo surgery stay until they get well enough to go home are often in a lot of pain. Minutes count when you're a patient who's really hurting and the system gets help to you fast.

The way it works is that nurses and nurses' aides wear badges that send out infrared signals which are picked up by sensors in the ceilings. A box on the wall with a display lets you see who's where. When a patient presses the buzzer, or a staff member needs to find a nurse, the system knows where the nurse is and relays the call to that location. This saves the staff precious time and energy since the person on duty at the nurses' station no longer has to run around trying to find the right nurse. It also prevents messages from getting lost in the fast-paced routine of the staff, since the call for help stays in the system until the nurse enters the patient's room, at which time the room sensor detects the nurse's arrival and turns off that call.

If the nurse is already busy when a call comes in, he or she can talk to the patient about the urgency of the call and can summon help if necessary. An additional benefit is that patients don't have to put up with a continuous stream of intercom announcements calling for this or that nurse to report to the nurses' station.

A total of about 250 people are on the system, which logs in staff when they come to work and keeps track of which nurse is assigned to which patients. That's how the system knows who to route a call to when a patient needs help. ❖

---

provide their customers with a profile on you that is highly refined. Some companies are really sneaky. For example, the first release of RealNetworks' RealJukebox sent information back to the company about what CDs the people who downloaded the software were playing. This information collection was going on when the customer wasn't even on the Web.[13]

If as a consumer you want to protect personal information about yourself, you can use various software packages to do so.

- ***Anonymous browsing.*** You can get software that hides your identity from the Web sites you visit.
- ***E-Mail encryption.*** You can get software like Pretty Good Privacy (PGP) to encrypt your e-mail. There is also software that causes your messages to self-destruct after a certain period of time. Certain Web sites such as PrivacyX let you send and receive anonymous and encrypted e-mail messages.
- ***Cookie stoppers.*** A cookie is a small file that a Web site places on your computer which contains information about you and your Web activities.

The next time you visit the site, it recovers this information. Browsers accept cookies by default. But you can set your browser to reject cookies or to inform you when a site wants to place one on your hard disk. You can also buy cookie management software that identifies and blocks certain types of cookies.

Privacy and Government Agencies

Government agencies have about 2000 databases containing personal information on individuals.[14] The various branches of government need information to administer entitlement programs, social security, welfare, student loans, law enforcement, and so on.

Law Enforcement You've often heard about someone's being apprehended for a grievous crime after a routine traffic stop for something like a broken taillight. The arrest most likely ensued because the arresting officer ran a check on the license plate and driver's license. The officer probably checked the NCIC

People **319**

ON YOUR OWN

Who Knows about You?

Make a table of information you have freely given to:

- Employers
- Click stores
- Brick stores
- Government agencies.

Answer the following questions:

- What did you get from giving this information? State your answer in general terms.
- Recall the last three times you provided someone or an organization with information. What information did you provide and what did you get in return? ❖

---

database and found the outstanding warrant there. This is how the culprits responsible for the Oklahoma City bombing were caught.

The *NCIC (National Crime Information Center)* is a huge database with information on the criminal records of more than 20 million people. The NCIC also contains information on outstanding warrants, missing children, gang members, juvenile delinquents, stolen guns and cars, and so on. The NCIC has links to other private and government databases. Police all over the country can access information on the NCIC database. Sometimes they do so in response to something suspicious, and other times it's just routine. For example, Americans returning from outside the country are routinely checked through the NCIC when they come through customs.

It's not surprising that NCIC information has been abused. Several police departments have found that a significant number of employees illegally snooped for criminal records on people they knew or wanted to know.

Actions of the Tampa Police Department at the 2001 Super Bowl caused an outcry from privacy advocates. Police, with the agreement of the NFL, focused video cameras on the faces of tens of thousands of spectators as they entered the stadium. The images were sent to computers which, using face recognition software, tried to match the images to a database of pictures of suspected criminals and terrorists. The police spokesperson said that their actions were legal since it's permissible to take pictures of people in public places. The American Civil Liberties Union (ACLU) protested the surveillance of people without cause. Such surveillance of patrons is usual at gambling casinos and other businesses in the private sector. The ACLU's objection was to the surveillance by a government agency without authorization.[15]

IRS The IRS (Internal Revenue Service) gathers income information on all taxpayers. The IRS has access to other databases too. For example, the IRS keeps track of vehicle registration information so that it can check up on people buying expensive cars and boats to make sure they're reporting an income level that corresponds to their purchases. The IRS can, of course, access other databases. Bell Atlantic says that it gets 22,000 requests for phone records from the IRS, FBI, and other government agencies per year. It seldom informs the customer.[16]

Census Bureau The Census Bureau collects information on all the U.S. inhabitants it can find every 10 years. All citizens are requested to fill out a census form, and some people get a very long and detailed form requiring them to disclose a lot of personal information. The information that the Census Bureau collects is available to other government agencies and even to commercial enterprises. The Bureau doesn't link the information to respondents' names, but sells summarized information on geographic regions. Some of these regions are relatively small, however, consisting of less than 100 blocks.

It's fairly safe to assume that anytime you have contact with any branch of government, information about you is subsequently stored somewhere. For example, if you get a government-backed student loan, you provide personal information such as your name, address, income, parents' income, and so on. Some of the information nuggets attached to the loan would be the school you're attending, the bank dispersing the loan, your repayment schedule, and later your repayment history.

What Does the Law Say?

The United States doesn't have a consistent set of laws protecting citizens from misuse of information. However, some laws are in place. Here's a sampling.

- The **Privacy Act** restricts what information the federal government can collect; allows people to access and correct information on themselves; requires procedures to protect the security of personal information; and forbids the disclosure of name-linked information without permission.
- The **Freedom of Information Act** says that citizens have the right to access the information that federal agencies have collected on them.
- The **Computer Matching and Privacy Protection Act** says that government agencies can't compare certain records trying to find a match. However, most records are not covered by this act.
- The **Bork Bill** (officially known as the **Video Privacy Protection Act**) prohibits the use of video rental information on customers for any purpose other than that of marketing goods and services directly to the customer.
- The **Communications Assistance for Law Enforcement Act** requires that telecommunications equipment be designed so that authorized government agents are able to intercept all wired and wireless communications being sent or received by any subscriber. The Act also requires that subscriber call-identifying information be transmitted to a government agency when and if required.
- The **Health Insurance Portability and Accountability Act** gives the health-care industry until April 2002 to formulate and install policies and procedures to keep patient information confidential.
- The **Financial Service Modernization Act** requires that financial institutions protect personal customer information and that they have customer permission before sharing such information with other businesses. ❖

Privacy and International Trade

If a customer in Europe buys books from Amazon.com's United Kindgom division, you'd probably be surprised to find out that Amazon may not transfer the customer's credit card information to Amazon in the United States without being in compliance with "safe-harbor principles." *Safe-harbor principles* are a set of rules to which U.S. businesses that want to trade with the European Union (EU) must adhere. You probably wouldn't think twice about sending customer information, such as a name and address, via e-mail from one part of the company to another. But if you're in a subsidiary in an EU country and the recipient is in the United States you might have a problem.

The EU has very stringent rules about the collection of personal information and has implemented a Directive on Protection of Personal Data. In 1998, the EU set privacy goals and each country had to make laws to achieve those goals according to its own culture and customs. So there are still differences in privacy laws among European countries. In general, the rights granted EU citizens include the right to know the marketer's source of information, the right to check your personal information, the right to correct it, and the right to specify that your information can't be used for direct marketing.

The United States and the European Union began negotiations on the heels of the EU directive to create safe-harbor principles for U.S.-based companies to be able to transfer personal information out of European countries. The safe-harbor rules cover every industry and almost all types of personal information. After extensive negotiations, in June 2000, the United States became the first country outside the EU to be recognized as meeting information privacy requirements of EU states.[17] Without this agreement, disruption of the $120 billion in trade between the United States and Europe would have been a distinct possibility.

So for your company, or Amazon.com, to be able to transfer personal information out of EU countries, you'd have to first register with the U.S. Department of Commerce and agree to adhere to the safe-harbor principles. Although participation is theoretically voluntary, if you transfer personal information without having registered,

THE GLOBAL PERSPECTIVE

Britain's E-Mail Privacy—RIP

In the United States, laws on privacy tend to be focused on keeping Big Brother, or Big Government, in check. In Europe, laws tend to be more strict against Big Business. In Great Britain, for example, despite strict personal privacy laws imposed on business, Parliament granted itself extraordinary powers to intercept e-mail. The law, called the **Regulation of Investigatory Powers (RIP)**, came into effect in October 2000. Following are some of its provisions.

- The Act grants certain government agencies the right to demand encryption keys and access to e-mail traffic, although they can do this only with the authorization of a Secretary of State or a judge.
- The person under surveillance doesn't have to be the target of an investigation, just somehow related to it.
- It's a criminal offense for anyone asked to surrender an encryption key to disclose the fact to anyone else, including superiors. Even the company under surveillance won't know.
- The Act allows government agencies to install a "black box" at an ISP location to trap e-mail and any other communications.
- The law applies to all companies operating in Britain, not just British ones.

Many people believe that the Act is well named RIP, since it may spell the death of business. They fear that RIP will curtail investment and encourage British companies to locate off shore.

Great Britain isn't the only European country "listening in" on e-mail. The Dutch government admitted that its security service has been collecting e-mail messages sent abroad by companies in that country.[18] ❖

---

you're risking punitive action from the U.S. Federal Trade Commission as well as from the European country from which you transferred the information.[19]

Cultural Diversity

A Mile or Two in Different Shoes

Although we may rejoice in the uniqueness of the peoples of the world, find endless enchantment in exploring our different identities, and understand the value of cultural diversity in the workplace, it's necessary to recognize that the journey of cultural discovery can be troublesome. If you go to live or work in another country for any length of time, you're likely to suffer a profound reaction called culture shock. **Culture shock** is the disorientation and confusion that you experience when you're accustomed to one culture and suddenly find yourself in another where signals, behavior, and beliefs are different. You feel rather like Alice did in Wonderland—nothing seems to make sense. You experience culture shock when you first encounter a huge change and suffer from the absence of familiarity and predictability.

Here's a story to illustrate the point. A young woman, who spoke very little German, went to Germany to work. She had a job in an office where people were as nice to her as they could be without much verbal communication. One day, just weeks after her arrival, which happened to coincide with the grape harvest season, a colleague brought her a basket of grapes. He walked up to her desk with a big smile and the grapes. She, appreciative of the welcoming gesture and the prospect of grapes, said one of the few German words that she knew. She said "Danke" (thanks). The man's smile vanished, he shrugged, turned on his heel and walked off with the grapes. The young woman was bewildered and distraught at having caused the disappointment she saw in the man's face. The man was equally confused. What had happened was that the man had understood her to say "No, thanks" instead of "Yes, thanks" which was what she had meant. Because she had no idea of what had just happened, she didn't know how to rectify the situation.

Did you leave your hometown to go to school? Did you feel sort of lost and lonely? Did the people act differently or have a different accent? Was the weather significantly different? If the differences you encountered made you feel unsettled, you already know something about culture shock. The distinction is one of degree. The farther away you go, the more intense the culture shock.

Vive La Difference

- In Germany, a wedding ring on the left hand means that the wearer is engaged to be married. During the wedding ceremony the ring is transferred to the right hand. So a wedding ring on the right hand means the person is married.
- In Japan, sneezing or blowing your nose in public is considered offensive, whereas slurping your food is considered to be a sign of appreciation.
- In China, it's perfectly acceptable to give someone a photo of him or herself, but if you write the person's name on the photo as identification or in a dedication it is taken to mean that you consider that person to be dead.
- In Russia, and many other countries, commas and decimal points are reversed. For example, the number 12,345.67 would be written as 12.345,67.
- In predominantly Christian cultures, the Sabbath is Sunday, Israel celebrates the Sabbath on Saturday, and the Moslem countries have their holy day on Friday.
- In England, an ATM is referred to as a "hole in the wall" machine. Germans refer to collecting money from an ATM as "pulling money." ❖

In today's mobile world, it's quite likely that you'll have to go to another country or have contact with people who didn't grow up the same way you did. You might be sent abroad to manage IT systems and, if so, you'll be likely to encounter unexpected social customs. You might want to promote certain knowledge workers or assign them duties that are contrary to their social norms. You might run into problems just setting up human resource information. For example, if you're in Nigeria, your personnel database will need to accommodate up to four wives per male employee.

You might find yourself embarrassing people when you meant only to encourage them. In the United States, it's generally considered an honor to be singled out for praise. However, in many cultures, notably in Asia, where the group is more important than the individual, it may be humiliating. In the United States, giving a family member a job merely because that person is a family member is called nepotism and is frowned upon. In many cultures, not giving a job to a family member would be considered disloyal, offensive, and a dishonor to the family.

Phases of Adjustment Culture shock usually has three distinct phases.

- The first is the initial *joy phase* when you're enamored with the newness and novelty of your surroundings.
- The second phase is the *aversion phase* when the novelty wears off and you become disillusioned and disoriented. In this phase you may become depressed or aggressive and the feelings can become severe.
- The third and last phase is the *adjustment phase* when you gradually get used to your new surroundings. You make friends and learn what is expected of you and what the signals mean.

In the last phase you adjust and come to appreciate your new environment. If you make it to the third phase, you're lucky, because you can then embrace the new without losing the best of the old. Unfortunately some people never make it past the second phase and leave the new location feeling disgruntled, angry, and disdainful.

Being aware of the possible effects of culture shock can help you adjust more quickly to being away from home and help minimize any negative effects on your productivity. Visiting knowledge workers will find it helpful if you understand what they're experiencing.

Alleviating the Symptoms In preparation for relocation, it helps to learn all you can about the new culture—especially the language. Language encompasses much of the identity of a society, and people appreciate your making at least a good try at their language. You could read the history of the country you're going to, learning about what molded the society. You'll find lots of information on the Internet. If you're going to manage IT systems in another country, be sure to investigate laws that pertain to collecting, storing, and accessing information. If you're transferring information out of the country, you should also investigate laws concerning what can and can't be taken out. In Canada, for exam-

ON YOUR OWN

Is Your Computer a Health Hazard?

Find five computers in different places and measure

- The distance from your eyes to the monitor
- The angle of your hands when they're on the keyboard
- The height of the mouse in relation to the keyboard

1. When you work at a computer for a long time, do you ache in any particular spot? If so, where?
2. If you feel discomfort, are the keyboard and monitor arranged according to the guidelines in Figure 8.3?
3. Do you take a rest periodically? Experts recommend that you do so about once every hour. ❖

---

ple, there are laws prohibiting banking information from being processed outside the country.

Ergonomics

Are You Sitting Comfortably?

The physical arrangement of electronic equipment is very important to the well-being of the people using it. **Ergonomics** is the study of how to design and arrange your workplace so that you can achieve maximum productivity and reduce discomfort and adverse health effects. Microsoft Corp.'s Bill Gates and other celebrities use chairs designed to position their bodies at the same angle that the body naturally assumes in a zero-gravity environment.[20] The chairs have 10 different adjustments geared to align your spine at a 128-degree angle. The design of the chairs is based on NASA's studies showing the relaxation posture that astronauts assume when floating around in space. Ergonomics actually involves much more than having a good chair. It deals with all types of work areas and machinery, but we will limit the discussion here to IT equipment.

Improperly arranged computer components can cause physical injuries. **Repetitive strain injury (RSI)** is characterized by headache, neck ache, eyestrain, wrist pain, fatigue, and stress caused by repetitive actions. Carpal tunnel syndrome is one type of RSI. Known as "the industrial disease of the information age," RSI is the leading cause of injury, productivity loss, and financial strain on small businesses, costing hundreds of thousands of dollars a year in work-related injuries.[21] Some victims even become disabled, temporarily or permanently. The U.S. Bureau of Labor Statistics says that, nationwide, the number of RSI-related illnesses and injuries was 22,600 in 1982 and 322,000 in 1994. These figures correspond to the huge increase in the use of computers during that period. Remember that in 1982 the IBM PC was introduced. An estimated 4.4 million people in the United States suffer from various computer-related disorders. When an employee is out with an injury, the company may have to pay overtime for workers to assume the job of the absentee and, perhaps, train someone else.

So how can you, as a knowledge worker or a manager of IT systems, avoid becoming part of the RSI statistics? Basically, your computer should be an extension of your body as you work. Ergonomic experts have developed guidelines for the safe use of computers. Note in Figure 8.3 the upright, right-angled posture of the

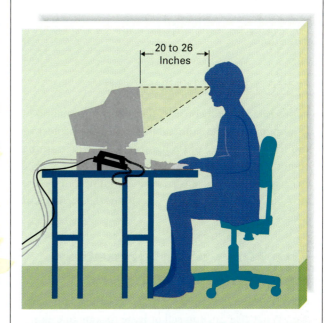

FIGURE 8.3

What the Experts Say

THE GLOBAL PERSPECTIVE

Going to College without Going to College

The largest and most innovative education and training organization in Europe is Britain's Open University, which has 218,000 students—141,000 at the undergraduate level and 10,000 at the graduate level. The remaining 67,000 students are not pursuing a specific degree. The university's oldest student thus far was a 93-year-old; its youngest, a 9-year-old prodigy studying mathematics. Many more students audit courses. This huge university lacks a physical campus. It has a small central administration facility, but most faculty and students telecommute—they teach and learn from home.

Students receive course materials by mail or e-mail. Courses are taught (about 700 hours per year) on TV outside prime time. Radio courses (about 150 hours per year) are also available. Students studying science receive home-experiment kits and work through their lab courses at home. Seven thousand tutors and counselors provide help and support to the students through 13 regional centers.

Since the university opened in 1971, about 172,000 undergraduate degrees have been awarded and almost 8,000 master's and Ph.D.-level degrees. Because of the high standards exacted by the Open University, these degrees are respected throughout Europe.

Because of its virtual nature, the Open University is accessible to people in countries outside Britain. All European Union citizens are eligible for admission. But the university also has partnerships with countries outside the European Union including Russia, Hungary, Singapore, and Hong Kong.

Although the Open University in the United Kingdom is the largest in the world, it's not the only one. For example, Israel also has an Open University with an enrollment of 25,000 where the language of instruction is Hebrew. In the United States the idea is becoming popular for graduate degrees.[22,23] ❖

---

person using the computer. You should look straight, or a little down, at the monitor, and your mouse and keyboard should be positioned to keep your arms parallel to the floor.

Information

In this section we'll consider the role of information in an organization, its vulnerabilities, how to protect it, and the importance of preparing for the worst. In the opening case study, you saw that Payless ShoeSource takes great pains to ensure that its information—the life's blood of the company—gets to the data center and is kept safe.

The Role of Information

Raw Material and Capital

Nothing else is as universal or as versatile as information. What else can you sell or lease to someone else—and simultaneously retain for yourself? This unique resource called "information" has two functions in an organization: as raw material and capital.

Information as Raw Material

Raw materials are the components from which a product is made. For example, the raw materials for a chair might be wood, glue, and screws. But almost anything you buy has information as part of the product. If you doubt this, wander through a store and see how many products incorporate absolutely no information. Even bananas have stickers telling you something about their distributor. Of course, the amount of information varies. You get a lot more information if you buy a jet airplane than if you buy a cake mix. Sometimes it's the information that makes a product particularly valuable. Take the example of two identical pairs of sports shoes that were originally made by the same company but sold under different logos. It's very likely that the shoes with the more widely known or prestigious logo will sell for a higher price than those with the lesser logo. The more desirable logo doesn't increase the functional value of the shoes. They're the same shoes! But the information (in this case the logo) proclaims something to the world that the wearer wants to be associated with. For that statement, whatever it is, the customer is prepared to pay extra.

Could You Work a Help Desk?

For knowledge workers to be effective they need their IT systems to function well. Every now and then, someone will have problems and will need help. Some of the questions they might ask are listed below. Do some research and answer them.

1. I just got a brand new printer. The instructions talk about a "driver." What does that mean?
2. How do I put a folder on my desktop so that I won't have to drill down through subdirectories?
3. What does "General Protection Fault" mean? What can I do about it?
4. My toolbar for formatting my document is gone from my Word screen. How do I get it back?
5. I can't find a file and I know I saved it. How can I find it?
6. Why should I use the shut-down feature before I turn off my computer?
7. I'm going to be telecommuting. How do I know what settings my modem should have?
8. If I buy a computer for my home, will I automatically get Internet access? ❖

The most successful companies place the highest value on information. United Parcel Service (UPS) is an example. The company's IT budget is second only to its expenditures on aircraft.[24] This is because UPS is selling not only a shipping service, but also information. You can connect to the UPS Web site and track your package—every single package. As UPS Chief Information Officer (CIO) Frank Ergbrick puts it, "A package without information has no value."

General Motors doesn't just sell vehicles. As we've described elsewhere in this text, its Cadillacs feature an option called OnStar that combines a global positioning system (GPS)—which identifies your position anywhere on earth—with networked sensors, a cell phone, and a link to customer support centers. With the OnStar system you can get directions to any destination and even advice on where to dine. OnStar also contributes to your safety. If the car's air bag inflates, the sensor sends a signal to the customer support center, which tries to contact you on the car phone. If there's no response, the support center uses the GPS component to locate your car, then alerts the emergency service nearest to you. The OnStar system can help track your car if it's stolen. So a Cadillac is not just a car—it's an IT system on wheels.

Information as Capital

Capital is the asset you use to produce a product or service. Buildings, trucks, and machinery are examples of capital. For our chair manufacturer, the capital would be the factory building, the saw, the glue dispenser, screw drivers, and so on. These items are not part of the chair, but they're necessary to build it. You incur a cost in acquiring capital, and you expect a return on your investment. Additionally, you can sell or lease capital assets.

You can think of information as capital. It's used by companies to provide all products. Organizations need information to provide what their target market wants. They need information in the form of manufacturing schedules, sales, marketing, and accounting information, and so on.

Information capital is one of the most important and universal types of capital in an organization. Not every company has a building or a truck, but every single one has information. We cannot state the case too strongly; an organization cannot exist without information any more than you can survive without oxygen.

Security
Is Your Information Safe?

Now that you've spent huge amounts of time, money, and energy on capturing, generating, and processing the information that's so vital to your organization, you'd better protect it from loss and damage. What can happen? It might be easier to answer the question "what can't happen." Hard disks can crash, computer parts can fail, hackers and crackers can gain access and

INDUSTRY PERSPECTIVE

Entertainment & Publishing

Bounce and Toy Story 2: Playing Digitally at a Cinema Near You

The movie *Bounce* was the first major motion picture to be delivered digitally via satellite. *Titan AE* was the first to be delivered and distributed via the Internet. *Toy Story 2* was the first to be completely created, mastered and exhibited digitally. Most people who went to see *Toy Story 2* watched it projected from film. However, the audiences at six theaters—four in California, and one each in Texas and Florida—saw a digital version.

What all these firsts have in common is QuVIS, a company in Topeka, Kansas, that designed and manufactures the QuBit. The system digitally records, stores, and plays back motion images for film production and other types of video. In all, there are 31 digital cinema theaters in the world and all of them use the QuVis system. Information doesn't just drive business at QuVis—it *is* the business. Repackaging and presenting information is what QuVis does.

Digital movies are the wave of the future. The quality of digital movies is much better with no scratches or grainy patches. There's no film to wear out. There are no shipping charges since digital film can be transmitted via communications media. And each frame can be uniquely encoded so that theft can be easily traced.

The movie goes to the QuBit on tape or a DVD-ROM. It's then transferred to a set of four hard disk drives with a total capacity of 75 gigabytes inside the QuBit. There's even a backup copy of the movie kept on the hard drives in case something goes wrong. If it does, the QuBit seamlessly switches over to the backup so that the viewers never know there's a problem.

The QuBit has more applications than just movies. It can handle computer animation, projection applications, television broadcast, virtual entertainment rides, scientific applications, and medical/industrial applications. The QuBit image is clear enough to decipher facial features of the people in a crowd at a football game. It's good enough for NASA to be able to examine a space shuttle liftoff frame by frame. ❖

---

do mischief, thieves engaged in industrial espionage can steal your information, and disgruntled employees or associates can cause damage.

The FBI estimates that computer sabotage costs businesses somewhere close to $10 billion every year. Companies are increasing their spending on Internet security software, already having spent more than $4 billion in 2000; this figure is expected to double by 2003.[25] "There's no Fortune 500 company that hasn't been hacked, I don't care what they tell you," says one hacker.[26] "Hacking" means unauthorized access to computers and computer information. There are "white hat" hackers who claim not to do any damage and "black hat" hackers who cause damage. 3Com gets "thousands of attacks a week. From kids to criminals to foreign governments," says David Starr, senior VP.[27] Even Microsoft's computers have been hacked.

The Players

People who break into computer systems are called hackers. **Hackers** are very knowledgeable computer users who use their knowledge to invade other people's computers. They're usually under 25 years of age and are generally very talented individuals. There are essentially five types.

White-Hat Hackers follow a "hackers' code" and, while they break into computers they have no right to access, they often report the security leaks to the victims. Their thrill is in being able to get into someone else's computer. Their reward is usually the admiration of their fellow hackers. There's plenty of information on the Web for those who want to know how to hack into a system—about 2,000 sites offer free hacking tools, according to security experts.[28]

Information 327

INDUSTRY PERSPECTIVE

".com"

eCampus is Security Conscious

If you're a regular viewer of MTV you've seen the ad for eCampus.com where the college student burps the alphabet. But eCampus.com has a very serious side. And that side is concerned about protecting its Web site. eCampus.com, launched in 1999, is in the PC Data's list of the 20 most frequently accessed Web sites. Not surprisingly, the site's busiest time is when school sessions start.

eCampus.com's security initiative is two-pronged. First, the site protects itself from curious and malicious intruders, and second, from network failure.

The site attracts a young, computer-literate, and very curious clientele—the same population that is most feared by security-conscious Web administrators everywhere.

eCampus.com uses Enterprise Security Manager (ESM) software, which provides them with enterprisewide security. The software defines, manages, and enforces security policies.

The site also has two types of firewalls (NetScreen and Checkpoint) and two intrusion-detection software packages called Intruder Alert and Netprowler. The intruder-detection software can tell eCampus.com if anyone is scanning the network trying to find a way in. If the potential intruder returns two or three times in a row, the site figures it has someone who is serious about breaking into their network. Along with detecting breaches of security, the software will also help create a digital trail for prosecution of the offenders.

Perhaps you think this is overkill. In response, eCampus.com would tell you that it gets at least two hack attempts per week. The number in any given week is directly proportional to the number of people accessing the site.

To protect the network from failure, eCampus.com has a second data center in a nearby town. Both sites have redundant routers, software, uninterruptible power supply systems, and a complete and updated duplicate database.[29] ❖

Black-Hat Hackers go further than just looking. They're cyber vandals. They exploit or destroy the information they find, steal passwords, or otherwise cause harm. They deliberately cause trouble for people just for the fun of it. They create viruses, bring down computer systems, and so on, for no reason other than the dubious satisfaction of having wasted the time and money of people they've probably never met and never will.

Crackers are hackers with malicious intent. They might break into a system to blackmail, bribe, or get revenge with the information they find. Crackers are the people who engage in corporate espionage.

Hacktivists, or *cyber terrorists*, are politically motivated hackers who use the Internet to send a political message of some kind. The message can be a call to end world hunger—or it can involve an alteration of a political party's Web site so that it touts another party's candidate, or it can be slogans for a particular cause or diatribes inserted into a Web site against a particular religious or national group.

The hacktivists' idea is that the bigger the company they break into, the more likely the attack will be publicized and the more attention their message will get. For example, pro-Muslim hackers based in Pakistan vandalized 20 Web sites and threatened to embark on an Internet attack against AT&T. Pro-Palestinian hackers attacked Lucent Technology's Web site during the same week. Security experts believe that AT&T and Lucent were targets because they do a lot of business in and with Israel.[30]

Script Bunnies are people who would like to be hackers but don't have much technical expertise. They download click-and-point software that automatically does the hacking for them. An example of this was the young man who started the Kournikova worm (we'll discuss viruses and worms later in this section) in Holland. It was very similar to the Love Bug worm in that it sent itself to all the people in the Outlook address book. He said he found the toolkit to make the virus on the Internet, and when asked about the people whose computers were affected, said that it was "their own fault if they got infected." Tens of millions of people got the virus, a large portion of whom opened the attachment hoping to see a picture of Anna Kournikova.[31]

Types of Cyber Crimes

Cyber crimes range from electronically breaking and entering to cyber stalking and murder. In October 1999, 21-year-year-old Amy Boyer was shot and killed outside the building where she worked. Her killer, Liam Youens, had been electronically stalking her for two years. Youens became obsessed with Amy and had even posted a Web site dedicated to her on which he announced his intention to kill her. He got her social security number online, found out where she worked, tracked her down and shot her, after which he shot himself.[32]

Most cyber crimes are not as bad as murder, but they can be serious nonetheless. Viruses and denial-of-service attacks are the two most common types of cyber crime.

Viruses The term "computer virus" is a generic term for lots of different types of destructive software. A ***computer virus*** is software that was written with malicious intent to cause annoyance or damage. There are two types of viruses. The first type of virus is benign. This type of virus displays a message or slows down the computer but doesn't destroy any information.

The second kind of virus is malignant. These viruses do damage to your computer system. Some will scramble or delete your files. Others shut your computer down, or make your Word software act funny, or damage flash memory in your digital cameras so that it won't store pictures any more.

One of the most prevalent types of computer viruses is the macro virus. This type of virus is usually spread by e-mail attachments. ***Macro viruses*** spread by binding themselves to software such as Word or Excel. They can make copies of themselves and spread from file to file destroying or changing the file in some way. Some viruses leave markers behind to mark that computer as "done."

This type of virus needs human help to move to another computer. If you have a macro virus on your system and you e-mail an infected document as an attachment, the person who gets the e-mail sets the virus loose as soon as he or she opens up your attachment.

A worm is another type of virus. A ***worm*** is a computer virus that spreads itself, not only from file to file, but from computer to computer via e-mail and other Internet traffic. Worms don't need your help to spread themselves. They find your e-mail address book and help themselves to the addresses, sending themselves to your contacts.

One of the more famous recent viruses is a worm called the Love Bug virus. It arrives in your e-mail as an attachment to an e-mail message. The subject of the e-mail is "I LOVE YOU"—a very alluring message to be sure. The text says to open the attached love letter, the name of which is, appropriately, LOVE LETTER. However, what's attached is anything but love. It's a mean piece of software that gets into your computer system as soon as you open it, and is ready to launch the next time you restart your computer. The Love Bug virus caused the Massachusetts state government to shut down its e-mail, affecting 20,000 workers. The virus also caused problems on Capitol Hill and shut down e-mail at the British Parliament. Companies as diverse as Ford Motor Co., H. J., Heinz, Merrill Lynch & Co., and AT&T were affected.[33] All in all, the Love Bug and its variants affected 300,000 Internet host computers and millions of individual PC users causing file damage, lost time, and high-cost emergency repairs totaling about $8.7 billion.[34,35]

The Love Bug has two objectives—to spread itself as far and as fast as it can, and to destroy your files (see Figure 8.4). First, it spreads itself by mailing itself to everyone in your Outlook address book, and, as if that weren't enough, it also uses Internet chat software to spread itself to chat rooms. A previous worm of the same type named Melissa sent itself only to the first 50 people listed in Outlook's address book.

Second, the Love Bug locates files on your computer that have certain extensions, .MP3 music files, .jpg picture files, .doc Word files, .xls Excel files, .wav sound files, .html browser files, and many others. Having found these files it wipes them out and puts itself in their place by appending .vbs to the end of the file name. For example, if you had a file called MySong.wav on your hard disk drive, the Love Bug virus would change the name to MySong.wav.vbs after it had done its dirty work.

There are at least 29 versions of the Love Bug virus. After people knew not to open the LOVE LETTER attachment, the hackers changed the name of it to some-

1 Virus arrives in an e-mail marked "I LOVE YOU"

2 When you open the attachment, you turn virus loose in your computer

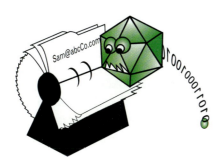
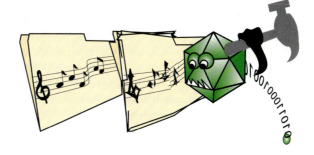

3 It goes to your address book to mail itself to all your friends

4 The virus starts destroying files

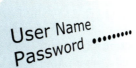

5 Virus looks for passwords that it can send back to its creator

FIGURE 8.4
Love Bug Virus

thing else. For example, one version is "MOTHER'S DAY," and the body of the text says that the receiver has been charged hundreds of dollars for a Mother's Day "diamond special." You have to open the attachment to print the invoice—and then the virus goes into action.

A virus can't hurt your files unless the virus instructions are executed. That means that you have to run or launch the software with the virus, that is, the attach-

ment. So be very careful about opening an attachment if you're not sure what it is and where it came from.

There are even virus hoaxes. This is e-mail sent intending to frighten people about a virus threat that is, in fact, bogus. People who get such an alert will usually tell others, who react in the same way. The virus is nonexistent, but the hoax causes people to get scared and lose time and productivity. Within companies the losses can be very severe since computer professionals must spend precious time and effort looking for a nonexistent problem.

As well as knowing what viruses can do, you need to know what they can't do. Computer viruses can't

- Hurt your hardware, your monitor or processor.
- Hurt any files they weren't designed to attack. A virus designed for Microsoft's Outlook generally doesn't infect Qualcomm's Eudora, or any other e-mail application.
- Infect files on write-protected disks.
- Infect compressed files unless the files were infected before they were compressed.

Denial-of-Service Attacks Many e-businesses have been hit with denial-of-service attacks. ***Denial-of-service attacks*** flood a Web site with so many requests for information that it slows down or crashes. The most common is the "Ping of Death," in which thousands of computers try to access a Web site at the same time, overloading the target site and shutting it down. The objective is to prevent legitimate customers from getting into the site to do business. A Ping attack can also bring down the firewall server (the computer that protects the network), giving free access to the intruders. E*Trade, Amazon.com, and Yahoo!, among others, have been victims of this nasty little game.

The process is actually very simple (see Figure 8.5). The plan starts with the hackers planting a program in networks that aren't protected well enough. Then, on a signal sent to the networks from the hackers, the program activates. What it does is "ping" every computer on its network. A ping is a standard operation that networks use to check that all computers are functioning properly. A ping is a sort of roll call for the network computers. The server says "are you there?" and each computer in turn answers "yes, I'm here."

But the hacker ping is different in that the return address of the are-you-there message is not the originating server, but the intended victim's server. So on a signal from the hackers, thousands of computers repetitively try to access E*Trade or Amazon.com, saying "yes, I'm here." The flood of calls overloads the online companies' computers and they can't conduct business.

For an online stockbroker, denial-of-service attacks can be disastrous. It may make a huge difference whether you buy shares of stock today or tomorrow. And since stockbrokers need a high level of trust from customers to do business, the effect of having been seen to be so vulnerable is very bad for business.

Creating and Implementing a Security Plan

It has been said that while in years past managers used to have nightmares about takeover bids, they now have nightmares about teenagers with computers and Internet access. Lloyd's of London says that 70 percent of risk managers see the Internet and e-commerce as the biggest emerging risks in the new century.[36] Given the extraordinary importance of information in an organization, it's imperative that companies make their best efforts to protect that information; that is, they should practice risk management. ***Risk management*** consists of the identification of risks or threats, the implementation of security measures, and the monitoring of those measures for effectiveness. The first step in the process is establishing what the potential threats are and what parts of the system are vulnerable. That process is called risk assessment. ***Risk assessment*** is the process of evaluating IT assets, their importance to the organization, and their susceptibility to threats, to measure the risk exposure of these assets. In simple terms, risk assessment asks (1) what can go wrong? (2) how likely is it to go wrong? and (3) what are the possible consequences if it goes wrong?[37]

Implementing the correct amount and type of security is not an easy matter. Too much security can hamper employees' ability to do their jobs, resulting in decreased revenue. Too little security leaves your organization vulnerable. You need strong enough security to protect your IT systems but not so much that the right people can't access the information they need in a timely fashion. Generally, security consists of a combination of measures such as backup procedures, firewalls, encryption, security software of various kinds, and system auditing.

Backups As always, an ounce of prevention is worth a pound of cure. The easiest and most basic way to prevent loss of information is to make backups of all your information. There's no action you can take that's more rudimentary or essential than making copies of important information methodically and regularly (at least once a week). Employee carelessness and ignorance cause about two-thirds of the financial cost of loss or damaged information.[38] Take the example of one company whose accounting server went down the day that paychecks should have been distributed. The crisis arose during an administration transition. The people who had been temporarily running the system thought that backup occurred automatically. It didn't, so all payroll information was lost. To get the system up and run-

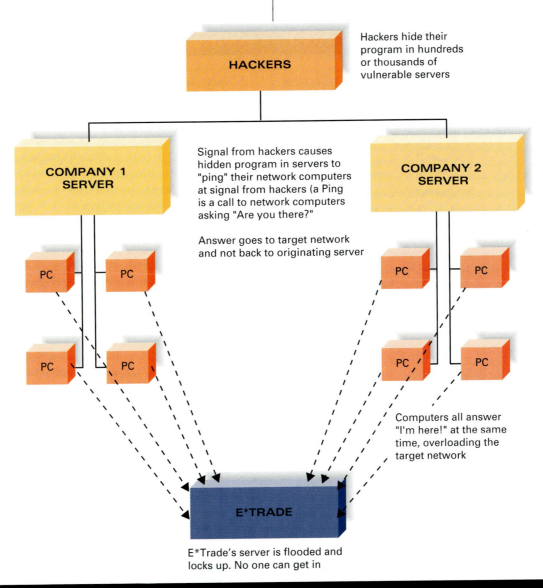

FIGURE 8.5

Denial of Service

ning again, the company had to pay thousands of dollars to consultants to restore the network application, and had to pay four people for 300 hours of overtime to reenter information. In addition, it cost $48,000 for a disk-recovery company to retrieve the information from the damaged disk drive.[39] And all this trouble and expense could have been avoided if backup procedures had been followed.

Make sure you back up ALL information. It's easy to forget about the information that's not stored in the main computer system or network, such as correspondence and customer information kept only by administrative assistants and receptionists, and private information not kept in the main organizational databases or data warehouses. Your backup schedule should include not only your information, but also your software.

You have several options when backing up information. You can use removable hard disks, a hard disk on another computer, or CD-Rs, CD-RWs, and tapes.

- *Safe:* Should you choose to store your backups in a safe, make sure that the safe is not only fireproof, but also heatproof. Floppy disks and CDs suffer damage at temperatures above 125 degrees Fahrenheit. Also remember that water causes damage too, so get a safe that's waterproof.

Top 10 Dot-Cons According to the FTC

The U.S. Federal Trade Commission (FTC) is on the trail of Internet crime. It has published a list of the top 10 online frauds. The following information came from their site at http://www.ftc.com.

- Online auction fraud: In this case you get something less valuable than what you paid for, or you might even get nothing at all.
  FTC says: Always use a credit card or an escrow service.

- Internet service provider scams: You get a check for a small amount ($3 or $4) in the mail and cash it. Then you find you're trapped into long-term contracts with ISPs which exact huge penalties if you cancel.
  FTC says: Read ALL the information about the check before you cash it and watch for unexpected charges.

- Credit card fraud: You get an offer which says you can view adult-oriented Web sites for free if you provide a credit card number—just to prove you're over 18. Then your credit card bill appears with charges for goods and services you never purchased.
  FTC says: Always examine your credit card carefully for unauthorized charges. You only have to pay up to $50 of the charges if your card was misused.

- Web cramming: You get a promotion which offers you a free custom-designed Web site for a trial period with no obligation. Then you find you've been charged on your phone bill, even though you never agreed to continue or even accept the offer in the first place.
  FTC says: Check your phone bill carefully.

- International modem dialing: You're offered free access to adult material if you download "viewer" or "dialer" software. The software also disconnects your modem and reconnects through an international long-distance number without your knowledge.
  FTC says: Before you download anything "free," read all the disclosures carefully. Also, check your phone bill carefully.

- Multilevel marketing/pyramid schemes: You're told you can get rich by recruiting other people to sell products and services. But then you find that you're selling only to other distributors like yourself, and you can't make money that way.
  FTC says: Don't buy into schemes that require you to recruit distributors, buy inventory, or commit to a minimum sales level.

- Business opportunities: You see an offer to stay at home, be your own boss, and earn big bucks. But then you find that the scheme is a bust and you're no better off than before.
  FTC says: Check with others who have started business with the company. Get all promises in writing and get an attorney or accountant to check the contract.

- Investment schemes: You're offered an opportunity to invest in a day trading system or service and you're promised big returns that don't materialize.
  FTC says: Check with state and federal securities and commodities regulators. Also ask other people who invested with this program for information on how well they did.

- Health care products and services: You get an offer for items not sold through traditional outlets, which are miracle cures for all sort of illnesses. But you find that you're not healthier—just poorer.
  FTC says: Know that if the cure were that good, it wouldn't be such a secret.

- Travel/vacation fraud: You're offered a luxury trip with all sorts of "extras" at very low prices. Then you find that what you get is much lower quality or nothing at all. Or you're hit with hidden charges after you've paid.
  FTC says: Insist on seeing references before you part with any money. Also, get details on the deal in writing before you sign up. ❖

- *Different location:* Most experts recommend that you store your backups in a separate building in case the whole building is threatened. Many accounting firms, banks, and other financial institutions send information off the premises at the end of every work day.
- *Televault:* You can store a copy of your information with a security company that specializes in encrypting and storing backups. This is known as televaulting. Several Internet sites offer this service. Many will store backups for individuals too. Sometimes you get a certain amount of space free, perhaps about 20 Megabytes, and then you have to pay for any more you need.

Firewalls A firewall, which you learned about in Chapter 5, is hardware and/or software that protects computers from intruders. The firewall examines each message as it seeks entrance to the network, like a border guard checking passports. Unless the message has the "right" markings, the firewall blocks the way and prevents it from entering.

Encryption If you want to protect your messages and files, you can encrypt them. **Encryption is the process of scrambling a message so that it can't be read until it's unscrambled again.** There are various ways of encrypting messages. You can switch the order of the characters, replace characters with other characters, or insert or remove characters. All of these methods make the message look incomprehensible, but used alone, each one is fairly simple to figure out. So most encryption methods use a combination of methods.

Companies that get sensitive information from customers, such as credit card numbers, need some way of allowing all their customers to use encryption to send the information. But they don't want everyone to be able to decrypt the message, so they might use public key encryption. **Public key encryption (PKE)** is an encryption system that uses two keys: a public key that everyone can have and a private key for only the recipient. So if you do online banking, the bank will give you the public key to encrypt the information you send them, but only the bank has the key to decrypt your information.

Security Software Security software comes in many forms, which include antivirus, intrusion-detection, authentication, and security-auditing software.

- *Antivirus software* detects and eliminates viruses that are trying to enter your system either from another computer on your network, the Internet, or a storage medium. The important thing to remember is to update your antivirus software frequently since new viruses come along every day. Some antivirus vendors have an automatic update option. That means that you can set up the antivirus software to go out to the Web and download updates automatically to your computer. With other antivirus software you must go to the vendor's Web site to get the update.
- *Intrusion-detection* software looks for people on the network who shouldn't be there or who are acting suspiciously. For example, someone might be trying lots of passwords trying to gain access. "Honey pots" are a type of intrusion-detection software that create attractive, but nonexistent, targets for hackers. What actually happens is that hackers' keystrokes are recorded instead.
- *Authentication software* is an ID-checking tool. It's there to make sure that people logging onto the network are who they say they are. There are three basic ways of showing your identification: (1) what you know, like a password; (2) what you have, like an ATM card; (3) what you look like, or rather what your fingerprint or your hand's bone structure looks like. The tools that check such biological characteristics are called biometric devices. You can get a biometric mouse which checks the fingerprints of the person who tries to use it before granting access to secure computer files. A newer type of what-you-have authentication device is a digital certificate, which is a sort of electronic credit card. Agilent Technologies, a Hewlett-Packard company, uses digital certificates for its 15,000 employees all over the world.[40]
- *Security auditing software* checks out your computer or network for potential weaknesses. The idea is to find out where hackers could get in and to plug up the hole. Many third parties, such as accounting firms or computer security companies, also provide this service.

Disaster Recovery
Murphy's Law Applies

So far you've seen some of the threats that are out there and the security measures you can take to protect your information and IT system. But what if something catastrophic happens? Annually about 250 natural disasters occur worldwide. This is only an interesting statistic unless you're slap bang in the middle of such a disaster—then it's much more than interesting. But natural disasters aren't the only danger on the IT system horizon. Fires, burst water pipes, gas leaks, power outages, and other infrastructure breakdowns can all cause serious damage to your IT system and information. Of the companies hit with a catastrophic loss of computerized records, 43 percent never reopen, 51 percent close within two years, and only 6 percent survive long term.[41]

To make sure your organization is in that slim 6 percent, you need to be prepared. Banks are required by law to have a disaster recovery plan. General Motors demands that all of its dealers have one. A disaster recovery plan is the documentation of the possibility of losing an IT system and the formulation of procedures to minimize the damage. A well-managed disaster recovery plan is aimed at anticipating and recovering from a major disaster.

FIGURE 8.6

Disaster Recovery Plan

CAREER OPPORTUNITY

The business world of today is complex and fast-moving. To remain effective and marketable, you have to keep learning. Learning is not a spectator sport; you must be proactive. It's hard to keep up, but opportunities are available:

- Videotapes are available which are effective for skills training, like learning about software packages.
- You can teach yourself by reading and experimenting with software packages.
- Trade journals are always a good way to learn what's happening in your industry.
- Find out what incentives or financial support your company provides for knowledge workers who want to complete education and training courses.
- Volunteer for on-the-job training programs offered by your company.

The Plan

A good disaster recovery plan will take the following into consideration: customers, facilities, knowledge workers, business information, computer equipment, and communications infrastructure (see Figure 8.6).

- **Customers**: You're more likely to retain the business of people who know what's going on. Customers will be reassured if you inform them what's happening so that they can plan accordingly.
- **Facilities**: You'll most likely need to move operations to another facility if disaster strikes. One option is a ***hot site***, which is a separate and fully equipped facility to which you can move immediately after the disaster and resume business. Hot sites are popular with financial firms, who spend about $300 million a year to rent them. The Chubb Contingency Trading Facility, near Wall Street, is one such hot site. This facility has 10 trading rooms with faxes, copy machines, printers, backup generators, 1,000 phone lines, a local area network with PCs, and so on.[42] Another alternative is a ***cold site*** which doesn't have computer equipment installed, but is ready for the refugee company to move in.

INDUSTRY PERSPECTIVE Financial Services

The Bank Was in Danger of Collapse

The headquarters building of a large bank, which shall remain nameless, had uneven surfaces on the fifth and seventh floors of the 70,000-square-foot facility. They called in a construction firm to fix the problem. While there, workers discovered large cracks that revealed corroded tension cables. Tension cables are what hold the building and its prestressed concrete together. Corroded cables meant that the building could collapse at any minute. It was definitely a potential disaster. To avoid the worst, everything and everyone had to be moved out of the building—immediately.

This was no small task since the building was the center of a banking enterprise that covered five states. The 300 people in the building were responsible for core bank operations and keeping all the branches operating.

But bank personnel were ready for a disaster—they thought. They had a disaster plan that included two disaster sites that had computers, monitors and hubs, backup servers, and network connections. In one location, 80 computers with monitors, phones, cables, fax machines, printers, hubs, paper, and other supplies were stored in closets. At the other site, 20 workstations were already connected to the network and ready for business.

The bank's standard operating procedure was to do full backups every night and store the backup tapes in a fireproof safe. Bank personnel practiced disaster recovery drills on a regular basis and each person had a copy of the master plan.

However, when disaster actually struck, it was the little things that tripped them up. The first person to arrive at the backup site couldn't find a key to get into the building. When he did get inside, he had trouble disabling the alarm. At the second site, they got into the building, but didn't have a key to the room with the servers.

When they started moving equipment, they found that they didn't have enough tables and chairs since they had only practiced moving the contents of one room. They also hadn't planned where each department would be set up. They needed duct tape to tidy up all the wiring so no one would trip and suffer injury. As employees started arriving, they discovered that they didn't have enough parking places. The swimming pool next door asked them to please move their vehicles. They found themselves moving their cars every two hours to avoid getting tickets.[43]

- **Knowledge Workers:** Disaster recovery usually involves long working days. Before your employees can concentrate on your business they may have to make arrangements for the care of family members. You may have to make sleeping and eating arrangements for your employees too.

- **Business Information:** You've already seen how important it is to back up your business information. Actually, this should be a regular part of daily operations. You'll see its value very clearly during times of disaster.

- **Computer Equipment**: Most companies have complex networks with a mixture of software and hardware from various vendors. This makes the networks hard to duplicate for third party recovery services. So some companies develop their own recovery plan. NationsBank of Charlotte, North Carolina, did just that, with 118 software applications running on 77 platforms, with equipment from Digital Equipment, Hewlett-Packard, IBM, Stratus, and Tandem. Although being disaster-ready costs the bank millions of dollars a year it's still the lesser of two evils.[44]

CHAPTER EIGHT Protecting Information and People

KNOWLEDGE WORKER'S -LIST

The Importance of Ethics. *Ethics* are the principles and standards that guide our behavior toward other people. The decisions you make when faced with ethical dilemmas depend on two factors. These are your basic ethical structure and the set of practical circumstances involved in the decision. *Intellectual property* is intangible creative work that is embodied in physical form. *Copyright* is the legal protection afforded an expression of an idea, like a song or a video game. The *Fair Use Doctrine* says that you may use copyrighted material in certain situations. *Pirated software* is copyrighted software that is copied and distributed without permission of the owner.

Privacy. Privacy deals with issues of who has the right to collect and keep personal information about you. Employers need information on their employees before and after they're hired to protect their business. Businesses need information on consumers to be able to offer them what they want. Government agencies need information on citizens to carry out their duties. The European Union (UE) has rather strict privacy laws and U.S. companies that want to do business with the EU must comply with those laws.

Accommodating Diversity. *Culture shock* is the disorientation and confusion that you experience when you're ac-

As the quality of telecommunications improves with more bandwidth at a lower cost, disaster recovery plans will most likely change, says Bob Roth, Disaster Recovery Coordinator at Payless ShoeSource. In the future, companies will most likely simply mirror all of their information to a second site so that if one goes down, the other one can carry on business as usual. Some companies already do this.

CLOSING CASE STUDY

Arriving for Work in Your Fuzzy Slippers

Would you like to have a job where you didn't have to go to work every day or even at all? About 24 million Americans work that way—as telecommuters. In Europe the number is about 10 million. In 16 Asia-Pacific countries the number of telecommuters is up 27 percent from 1999 to about 3.3 million people. Here are some examples of telecommuters and how they work.

Extreme Telecommuter

At age 26 Paolo Conconi, who grew up in a small town in Italy, opened an electronic parts manufacturing business called MPS Electronics in Hong Kong. He's been getting the parts made in Asia and selling them in Europe since 1992. He's a very busy man and spends his day on the phone and computer getting things done. But he doesn't wear a business suit. He goes far beyond business casual by conducting business in his bathing suit—beside his swimming pool at his home in Bali, Indonesia. Paolo is what is called an "extreme" telecommuter, in that he works several time zones away from where his business is located.

Paolo got tired of life in the crowded, workaholic atmosphere of Hong Kong, so he moved to Indonesia when he fell in love with a woman who lived there. Now his swimming pool is larger than his Hong Kong apartment, and his villa, which is built around the pool, garden, and Hindu temple costs $650 a month—half of what his tiny home in Hong Kong cost.

However, it's not all sunshine, so to speak. Paolo says that to be such an extreme telecommuter, you need a lot of discipline and patience. For example, the electricity supply in Bali is unreliable and he often has problems with data connections.[45]

Moderate Telecommuter

Amy Hammingh is a change management consultant for Andersen Consulting and lives near Seattle. On Monday through Thursday she works at a client's of-

customed to one culture and suddenly find yourself in another where signals, behavior, and beliefs are different. Generally people go through three phases of adjustment in a new culture. *Ergonomics* is the study of how to design and arrange your workplace so that you can achieve maximum productivity and reduce discomfort and adverse health effects. *Repetitive strain injury (RSI)* is characterized by headache, neck ache, eyestrain, wrist pain, fatigue, and stress caused by repetitive actions.

Information and its Protection. Information has two functions in an organization: as raw material and capital. Threats to information include attacks from five different types of hackers, viruses, denial-of-services attacks, hard disk crashes, and so on. A security plan is essential. *Risk management* consists of the identification of risks or threats, the implementation of security measures, and the monitoring of those measures for effectiveness. *Risk assessment* is the process of evaluating IT assets, their importance to the organization, and their susceptibility to threats, to measure the risk exposure of these assets. Safety measures include backups, firewalls, encryption, and security software. A *disaster recovery plan* is the documentation of the possibility of losing an IT system and the formulation of procedures to minimize the damage. ❖

fice. On Friday, however, she's a telecommuter and works at home rather than driving the two hours to the corporate office. She set up her office in the second bedroom of her two-bedroom home. She and her husband have back-to-back desks and share devices they bought themselves such as printers, scanners, and so on. Amy uses a laptop that Andersen Consulting bought for her.

This sort of informal telecommuting arrangement is very common according to International Data Corporation, a company that tracks telecommuting trends.[46]

Minimal Telecommuter

When he went looking for a job, Tom Selfridge wanted a special perk. He wanted to able to work from home when his wife was away on business trips so that he could take care of their two young children. He accepted a job with Wolf Technologies Inc. in Jacksonville, Florida, a geology consulting firm that promised him just that.

The company got a great employee, and Tom has peace of mind knowing that he can look after his little ones when he needs to without a lot of hassle.[47] ❖

◄ Questions ►

1. What characteristics do all three telecommuters in this case have in common? Would you like to be a telecommuter? Why or why not?

2. What sort of person would potentially make a good telecommuter? What sort of qualities should he or she have?

3. What sorts of jobs would lend themselves to telecommuting? Think of three careers you could have that would allow you to be an extreme telecommuter and live anywhere in the world; three jobs in which you could be a moderate or minimal telecommuter; and three jobs you couldn't do as a telecommuter.

4. If you were to set up a home office, apart from rent and heat and cooling of the room, how much would it cost you to outfit it for doing your job and sending your output to the office electronically?

5. Many telecommuting experts believe that employers should pay all costs that an employee would incur by telecommuting. Is this reasonable? Why or why not?

6. Consider the advantages and disadvantages of telecommuting from three angles: to the employer, the employee, and society in general. Make six lists.

Electronic Commerce
Business and You on the Internet

Making Travel Arrangements on the Internet

It's very likely that in the course of business you'll be expected to travel either within the United States or abroad. You can use the Internet to check out all aspects of your journey, from mode of travel to the shopping opportunities that are available. The Internet can also give you pointers and direction about aspects of the trip you might not even have thought about.

In this section, we've included a number of Web sites related to making travel arrangements on the Internet. On the Web site that supports this text (http://www.mhhe.com/haag, click on "Electronic Commerce Support," select "Real Hot Electronic Commerce Project Support," and then select "Making Travel Arrangements on the Internet"), we've provided direct links to all these Web sites as well as many, many more. This is a great starting point for completing this Real Hot section. We would also encourage you to search the Internet for other sites.

Transportation

If you're not taking your own transportation—your private jet, or your car— you'll have to find flights, buses, trains, and/or rental cars to suit your needs. Let's look at sites where you can get this kind of information.

Air Travel

Some people are happy to travel with whatever airline provides the flight that fits into their schedule. Others insist on certain airlines, or won't travel on particular airlines. No matter how you feel, the Internet can help you find a flight. On the Internet, you can even get maps of the airports you'll be using. Many airports have sites on the Internet, such as Dallas/Ft. Worth International Airport at http://www.dfwairport.com. These sites can help you with provisions at the airport for disabled people, among other available services.

The Federal Aviation Authority site (http://www.faa.com) has a comprehensive list of airlines in this country and all over the world. Look at five of the sites below and choose five more (you can use some of the links listed on our text's Web site) and answer the following questions.

A. Can you make a flight reservation online at this site?

B. If you can book flights, does the site ask you to type in your departure and destination cities, or can you choose from a menu?

C. Again, if you can book flights at this site, on a scale of 1 to 10, rate how difficult it is to get to the flight schedule. That is, how many questions do you have to answer, how many clicks does it take, how much do you have to type in?

D. Is there information on when the lowest fares apply (for example, three-week advance booking, staying over Saturday night, etc.)?

E. Does the site offer to send you information on special deals via e-mail?

F. Does the site offer information on frequent flier mileage? Can you check your frequent flier account online?

G. Does the site offer you a map of the airports you will be using?

Trains and Busses

If you want to travel by rail or long distance bus, you can find many helpful sites. Here is a taste of what's available:

- Monterey Salinas Transit System at http://www.mst.org has information on bus travel in the United States.

- Amtrak at http://www.amtrak.com has a site that lets you look up train travel times and fares and buy tickets online for train travel in the United States.

- RailEurope at http://www.raileurope.com offers comprehensive coverage of all modes of travel in Europe, including, of course, rail travel.

- The Orient Express site at http://www.orient-expresstrains.com is a great help if you're interested in traveling by rail in Asia or Australia.

Look at two of these sites and see whether you can book tickets online. Do you need a password to see schedules?

Incidentally, when you're looking up sites outside the United States, remember that the date is often expressed with the day first, then the month, then the year, so that September 10, 1998, would be 10.9.98 or 10-9-98. Also, most of Europe uses 24-hour time, so that 2:15 P.M. would be 14:15.

Rental Cars

When you arrive at your destination, you may need a car. Some sites such as Rental Car Info's site at http://www.bnm.com have information on multiple companies, and all the large car rental companies have sites on the Internet. Check out three of the car rental Web sites on page 341, find three others (don't forget the good links on the Web site that supports this text), and answer the following questions.

A. Can you reserve a car at the Web site?
B. Can you search by city?
C. Is there a cancellation penalty? If so, how much?
D. Can you get a list of car types? Does this company rent sports utility vehicles?
E. Are there special weekend rates?
F. What does the site say about collision insurance purchased from that company in addition to your own insurance?
G. Can you get maps from the site?
H. Are special corporate rates specified on the site?

Road Conditions and Maps

You can generate maps online at several sites. MapQuest at http://www.mapquest.com is one of the most popular. Its TripQuest section has city-to-city and turn-by-turn directions, and its Map Shortcuts module gives you a list of cities and countries for which you can get maps. Other map sites are listed on page 341 and you can find additional sites on our Web site. Examine three map sites and answer the following questions.

A. Do these sites all give turn-by-turn driving directions?
B. Will they provide a map of an area without start and end points?
C. Do they have zoom in and zoom out capabilities?
D. Can you customize the map, perhaps by inserting a landmark or circling an area?
E. Are hotels, restaurants, etc., marked on the map?
F. If the site offers driving directions, can you specify whether you want the scenic route or the main highways?
G. Are the maps restricted to the United States? If not, what other countries are included?

Lodging

Hotels, especially the larger chains, usually have Web sites. Here you have access to a wealth of information about rates, amenities, and sometimes even information about the hotel's surroundings. The National Hotel Directory at http://www.evmedia.com has lists of a variety of hotels and also trade shows. The Hotel Guide site at http://www.hotelguide.com has information on 60,000 hotels all over the world, and The Trip.com (http://www.thetrip.com) has hotel reviews and promises discounted prices for certain hotels. On page 341 are Web sites for five hotel chains. You'll find many more links on our Web site. Choose two of these and two others and answer the questions below.

A. Can you search for a particular city?
B. Can you book a room online?
C. Are there properties belonging to this hotel chain outside the United States?
D. Can you see a picture of the room on the Internet?
E. Does the site tell you about special deals or promotions?

340 CHAPTER EIGHT Protecting Information and People

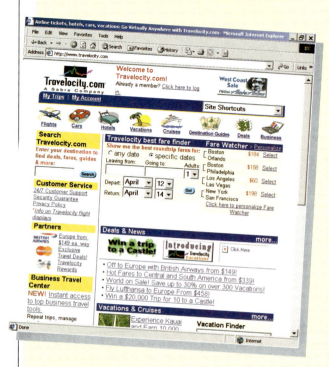

F. Is there information about perks you can get by staying there frequently?

G. Do you get a discount for booking online?

One-Stop Travel Sites

Some travel sites on the Internet allow you to book your entire trip from start to finish, offering a combination of airline, hotel, and other helpful information. Two of the most widely used are Microsoft's Expedia at http://expedia.msn.com and Preview at http://www.preview-travel.com. On the next page you'll find seven more sites. Choose five of these and find five more (don't forget to look for good links at the Web site that supports this text) and answer the following questions.

A. How many different booking services are offered from this site (airlines, hotels, rental cars, rail travel, etc.)?

B. If the site offers flight booking, how many flight alternatives does it offer? 3? 10? 20? 30? More than 30?

C. Does the site have information on low-cost specials for airlines, hotels, and/or rental cars?

D. Is there a traveler's assistance section?

E. Will the site answer your specific questions?

F. Can you search by destination or company for flights and lodging?

Destination Information

You might like to know before you get to your destination what restaurants, museums, shows, shopping, and special attractions are available. Many of the sites previously mentioned have this kind of information. MapQuest (http://www.mapquest.com) is an excellent example of such a site, as are many of the one-stop travel sites.

No matter what your interest or hobby, the Internet has a site for you. You can find sites dedicated to bird watching, bungee jumping, golf, or anything else that takes your fancy. Many others cater to entertainment events such as concerts. You can find destination information sites in the Table below and at the following sites:

- Excite's Travel site (http://city.net), which has destination information from Fodor's Travel.
- The Trip at http://www.thetrip.com includes restaurant reviews among its services.
- Restaurant Row (http://www.restaurantrow.com) has a list of 100,000 restaurants in 25 countries. You can search by country, city, and cuisine.
- The Open World site at http://www.openworld.co.uk/cityguides has information on 100 of the most popular cities to visit.

Web Sites for Travel Information

Airlines	Site
Southwest	http://www.southwest.com
Singapore Airlines	http://www.singaporeair.com
American Airlines	http://www.americanair.com
Delta	http://www.delta-air.com
Aer Lingus	http://www.aerlingus.ie

Airlines (continued)	Site
Japan Airlines	http://www.jal.co.jp/english/index_e.html
Northwest Airlines	http://www.nwa.com
South African Airways	http://www.saa.co.za
Alaska Airlines	http://www.alaska-air.com

Rental Cars	Address
Hertz	http://www.hertz.com
Avis	http://www.avis.com
Alamo	http://www.goalamo.com
Dollar	http://www.dollar.com
Rent-a-Wreck	http://www.rent-a-wreck.com

Maps	Address
MapsOnUs	http://www.mapsonus.com
AutoPilot	http://www.freetrip.com
MapBlast	http://www.mapblast.com
Excite Maps	http://city.net/maps
DeLorme's CyberRouter	http://route.delorme.com

Hotels	Address
Hilton Group	http://www.hilton.com
Embassy Suites	http://www.embassy-suites.com
Motel 6	http://www.motel6.com
Holiday Inn	http://www.holiday-inn.com
Hotel Choice	http://www.econolodge.com

One-Stop Travel Sites	Address
Travelocity	http://www.travalocity.com
FLIFO	http://www.flifo.com
Traveler	http://www.traveler.net
TravelLinks	http://www.trvltips.com/travellinks.html
Web Surfers Travel Guide	http://pages.prodigy.net/webtravels
Earthlink	http://www.earthlink.net/travel
Travel.org	http://www.travel.net

Site	Address
Kansas City	http://www.kansascity.com
New York City	http://www.ny.com/nyc
Las Vegas	http://www.pcap.com
Shaw Guides	http://www.shawguides.com
Music-Cal	http://www.musi-cal.com
Chicago Tribune	http://www.chicagotribune.com
Miami Herald	http://www.miamiherald.com/florida

Go to the Web site that supports this text: **http://www.mhhe.com/haag** and select "Electronic Commerce Projects."

We've included links to over 100 Web sites for making travel arrangements on the Internet.

CHAPTER EIGHT Protecting Information and People

KEY TERMS AND CONCEPTS

Anonymous Browsing, 318
Black-Hat Hackers, 327
Cold Site, 334
Computer Virus, 328
Cookie Stoppers, 318
Copyright, 315
Crackers, 327
Culture Shock, 321
Cyber Terrorists, 327
Denial-of-Service Attacks, 330

E-Mail Encryption, 318
Encryption, 333
Ergonomics, 323
Ethics, 312
Fair Use Doctrine, 315
Hackers, 326
Hactivists, 327
Hot Site, 334
Intellectual Property, 315
Macro Virus, 328

National Crime Information Center (NCIC), 319
Pirated Software, 315
Public Key Encryption, 333
Repetitive Strain Injury, 323
Risk Assessment, 330
Risk Management, 330
Safe-Harbor Principles, 320
Script Bunnies, 327
White-Hat Hackers, 326
Worm, 328

SHORT ANSWER QUESTIONS

1. What are ethics? How do ethics apply to business?
2. Why do employers monitor employees?
3. What is the dilemma that businesses face regarding customer privacy?
4. Name three government agencies that have information about citizens and give examples of the kind of information they have.
5. What is culture shock?
6. What is ergonomics? Why is it important?
7. What are the five types of hackers?
8. What's a virus? A worm?

SHORT QUESTION ANSWERS

For each of the following answers, provide an appropriate question.

1. Fair Use Doctrine
2. As capital and raw material
3. Slows down or crashes a business Web site
4. A plan of what to do in case the worst happens
5. Cracker
6. Risk assessment
7. Hot site
8. Repetitive strain injury

DISCUSSION QUESTIONS

1. When selling antiques, you can usually obtain a higher price for those that have a provenance, which is information detailing the origin and history of the object. For example, the property owned by Mrs. Jacqueline Kennedy Onassis sold for much more than its face value. What kinds of products have value over and above a comparable product because of such information? What kind of information makes products valuable? Consider both tangible (resale value) and intangible value (sentimental appeal).
2. Personal checks that you use to buy merchandise have a standard format. Checks have very few different sizes, and almost no variation in format. Consider what would happen if everyone could create his or her own size, shape, and layout of personal check. What would the costs and benefits be to business and the consumer in terms of buying checks, exchanging them for merchandise, and bank check processing?
3. Consider society as a business that takes steps to protect itself from the harm of illegal acts. Discuss the mechanisms and costs that are involved. Examine ways in which our society would be different if no one ever broke a law. Are there ever benefits to our society when people break the

law—for example, when they claim that the law itself is unethical or unjust?

4. Many European countries have very strict laws about what you can and can't do with name-linked information. In France, for example, the law stipulates that no information may be saved, electronically or on paper, about a person's religious or political affiliation. Discuss the implications of such laws for an open-information society such as the United States. What kind of information might be appropriate for such laws here, and how would they affect the management of IT systems?

5. Consider some movies and TV shows that deal with culture shock. Examples are *Moscow on the Hudson, Coming to America,* and *Third Rock from the Sun.* Can you think of any others? Film plots involving culture shock are often comedies, because cross-cultural diversity can lead to very amusing (as well as disastrous) situations, and perhaps the subject is best dealt with on the light side. Think of a film or show you have seen that deals with cross-cultural diversity. What sorts of misunderstandings occur and why?

6. Can you access all the IT systems at your college or university? What about payroll or grade information on yourself or others? What kinds of controls has your college or university implemented to prevent the misuse of information?

7. You know that you can't use a Macintosh to access information stored on a disk using a PC (unless you have a PowerPC or special software). What other instances of the lack of interoperability have you experienced personally or heard of? For example, have you used different versions of PowerPoint or MS Access that won't work on all the PCs that you have access to?

8. Have you experienced computer problems caused by a virus? What did the virus do? Where do you think you got it? How did you fix the problem?

9. If a major disaster such as a tornado or flood were to strike your college or university in the middle of the semester, who would be impacted and how? Consider all stakeholders.

10. Say you had a small business and you were considering buying expensive ergonomically designed office furniture such as chairs and desks for your knowledge workers. What would the intangible benefits be to your company of having employees who are comfortable?

11. What laws do you think the United States should pass to protect personal information? None? Laws such as the EU has? Stricter laws than the EU? Why? Should some personal information be more protected than other information? Why? Why not?

CHAPTER OUTLINE

INDUSTRY PERSPECTIVES

".com"
350
Who's Afraid of the Big, Bad Dot-Coms?

Hospitality & Leisure
350
Backup Servers Serve Up Domino's Pizza

IT & Telecommunications
352
Using Wireless Fiber Optics to Solve the Last-Mile Bottleneck Problem

IN THE NEWS

346 The 10 hottest jobs of the future.

346 The 10 most-likely-to-disappear jobs of the future (Table 9.1).

348 What it will take for B2C dot-coms to survive.

351 What is the last-mile bottleneck problem?

352 You are the most important business resource of the future.

FEATURES

347 On Your Own What's Your Future Job and the Skills You Need?

353 Team Work Gaze into Your Crystal Ball

356 Electronic Commerce Continuing Your Education through the Internet

KNOWLEDGE WORKER'S CHECKLIST

In the Information Age, Knowledge Workers Understand . . .

1. How jobs of the future will change
2. What it will take for B2C dot-coms to survive
3. The hurdles to overcome to achieve technology transparency
4. The most important business resource of the future

WEB SUPPORT

http://www.mhhe.com/haag

- The Best MBA Programs
- Graduate School Information
- Tele-Education (Distance Learning)
- Ph.D. Programs

Preparing for the Future

It's Your World

CHAPTER 9

CASE STUDY
Will You Allow History to Repeat Itself?

In the past few years, we've been witness to unbelievable shake-ups, shakeouts, rises to glory, and falls to bankruptcy in the technology arena. What's important for you about all this turmoil is to learn from other people's mistakes and not doom yourself to repeat the past.

When asked, "What's the single biggest lesson you'd pass on to someone just starting out in this business," here's what some people had to say.

> Prepare to dedicate more hours than you planned to the startup. If it is successful, it will consume bazillions of hours. If it is not, ditto.
> —Scott McNealy, founder, chairman, and CEO of Sun Microsystems

> I think that always in business you need to expect the worst. In the end, that's what separates the survivors from those who don't.
> —Halsey Minor, founder of CNET

> The single biggest lesson I learned early was, you focus on growing the pie, not on how big your personal piece of the pie is.
> —Dave Perry, founder and CEO of Ventro

> Being too risk-averse and being afraid to make mistakes. We probably need to make a few more.
> —Mike Eskew, vice chairman of UPS

> Not evaluating every aspect of our business often enough. We should have, every month, dissected our business from the top down, but we were moving too fast.
> —Marc Schiller, cofounder and CEO of ElectricArtists

> Spending money on unmeasured marketing to grow the brand.
> —George Bell, chairman and CEO of Excite@home

> Running TV advertising in 1999. We couldn't even handle the demand we had, and we ran TV.
> —John Barbour, CEO of Toysrus.com

Those are some pretty telling statements. In reality, they're just sound business advice that any organization should follow.[1] ❖

Introduction

If you don't usually read the opening case studies associated with each chapter, we'd really encourage you to go back and read this one. You've probably heard the age-old expression, "Those who don't know history are destined to repeat it." Believe us when we say that you don't want to repeat many of the mistakes made by some of the leading entrepreneurs in the technology field. Some were lucky enough to survive their mistakes. Others weren't.

As we close this text, we'd like to take a look at the future, while keeping the past (and present) in mind. Specifically, we'd like to help you prepare for the future. Your field of study doesn't matter nor whether you plan to work for a company or be an entrepreneur; you can always benefit from looking forward while keeping an eye on the past.

So, let's start by looking at what the future may hold in terms of jobs for you. After all, that's probably why you're in school. Then, we'll turn our attention specifically toward technology and discuss a couple of questions—Will B2C dot-coms survive? and When will we achieve technology transparency?

We'll conclude with two sections that focus very specifically on you. In the first of these sections, we'll ask you to make some predictions concerning the future. Then, we address one very important question: "In the future, what will be the most important business resource?" We hope you can already answer that question (and the answer is not technology).

What Are the Jobs of the Future?

Your Employment Possibilities

In a recent issue of *Time*, the famed Tom Peters gave his prediction concerning the 10 hottest jobs of the future and the 10 jobs mostly likely to disappear (see Table 9.1). Some of his predictions are quite wild (and you really need to read his justifications). Below, we list Tom's 10 hottest jobs of the future, along with excerpts concerning his rationale.[2]

1. **Tissue engineers**—"With man-made skin already on the market and artificial cartilage not far behind, 25 years from now scientists expect to be pulling a pancreas out of a Petri dish."

2. **Gene programmers**—"Digital genome maps will allow lab technicians to create customized prescriptions, altering individual genes by rewriting lines of computer code."

3. **Pharmers**—"New-age Old MacDonalds will raise crops and livestock that have been genetically engineered to produce therapeutic proteins."

TABLE 9.1 What's Hot and What's Not

The 10 Hottest Jobs of the Future	The 10 Most-Likely-Jobs-to-Disappear in the Future
1. Tissue engineers	1. Stock brokers, auto dealers, mail carriers, insurance and real estate agents
2. Gene programmers	2. Teachers
3. Pharmers	3. Printers
4. Frankenfood monitors	4. Stenographers
5. Data miners	5. CEOs
6. Hot-line handymen	6. Orthodontists
7. Virtual-reality actors	7. Prison guards
8. Narrowcasters	8. Truckers
9. Turing testers	9. Housekeepers
10. Knowledge engineers	10. Fathers

4. **Frankenfood monitors**—"With a little genetic tinkering, fast-growing fish and freeze-resistant fruits will help feed an overpopulated world."

5. **Data miners**—"…research gurus will be on hand to extract useful tidbits from mountains of data, pinpointing behavior patterns for marketers and epidemiologists alike."

6. **Hot-line handymen**—"Remote diagnostics will take care of most of your home electronics, but a few repairmen will still make house calls…via video phone."

7. **Virtual-reality actors**—"Pay-per-view will become pay-per-play, allowing these pros to interact with you in cyberspace dramas."

8. **Narrowcasters**—"Today's broadcasting industry will become increasingly personalized, working with advertisers to create content just for you."

9. **Turing testers**—"By the time you can't tell the difference [between human and machine intelligence], these human simulators will be used as unflappable customer service reps as well as Internet attaches who can summarize your e-mails and even write back: 'Hi Mom, sorry I missed your call…'"

10. **Knowledge engineers**—"Artificial-intelligence brokers will translate your expertise into software, then downsize you."

How's that for a futuristic look at jobs on the horizon. It's actually somewhat scary when you think about it. But don't despair—many of those jobs (and what they'll do) won't surface for many years to come.

However, you should take notice of how many of those jobs involve technology in some way. Even narrowcasters take advantage of many of the technologies and technology-related issues we've discussed in this text—personalization (Chapter 2) and data mining (Chapter 3). Many of the others take advantage of artificial intelligence, which we discussed in Chapter 4.

You should also notice that many of these future jobs incorporate the medical field in some way. The medical field, in many respects, is as growing and dynamic as the field of technology. No one ever really thought we would be able to completely break the DNA coding of a human being. But technology helped us do just that.

As you move forward with your career plans, you need to think "outside the box." Many of today's traditional and stable jobs simply won't be plentiful in the future. On the other hand, new jobs that incorporate

ON YOUR OWN

What's Your Future Job and the Skills You Need?

One of the best ways to prepare for the future is to do a little research. For this project, write down what job you'd like to have in the future. Then, go out on the Internet and find that job in various job databases (or do the same with the newspaper classified ads). Write down specific skills you need in order to land that job. As you do, categorize those skills into either computer-related, general, or discipline-specific. ❖

YOUR FUTURE JOB: _____

Skills You Need

Computer-Related	General	Discipline-Specific

technology (and perhaps medicine) will have high demands.

Will B2C Dot-Coms Survive?

Commodity-Like and Digital Products

Around the middle of 1999, the entire business and financial world decided that B2C (business to consumer) dot-com companies were to be the next hugely successful business endeavor. During that time, literally hundreds of thousands of B2C dot-com companies popped up on the Internet. Those companies obtained billions of dollars in venture capital and even billions more through initial public offerings (IPOs). With no signs to be seen of ever making a profit or providing a path to profitability, investors nevertheless poured untold sums of money into B2C dot-com companies.

Then, reality set in. Investors began to demand that those companies start to break even and show well-defined paths to profitability. Unfortunately, most B2C dot-coms couldn't do either, and the NASDAQ (the market on which most dot-coms were listed) dropped some 50 percent during the year 2000. During the surge upward, everyone seemed to dismiss solid business principles that had been used for many years to value the worth of a company. During the surge downward, we once again embraced those business principles and required dot-coms to follow them.

So, natural questions arose like, "Will B2C dot-coms survive? And, if so, which ones specifically?" The answer to the first question is definitely yes. B2C dot-com companies as a group will survive. However, the answer to the second question is a bit more elusive. We can't tell you for sure which B2C dot-com companies will survive in the long run, but we can tell you something of their characteristics.

In Chapter 5, we discussed the lessons learned by B2C entrepreneurs during the decline of B2C dot-com companies. We believe two of those lessons will become key characteristics that define surviving B2C dot-coms. They are (1) the selling of commodity-like products and (2) the selling of digital products. Let's consider those two characteristics within the context of an example of how we believe part of your future life will play out.

In the future, traditional radio stations will fight fierce competition from B2C dot-com companies that provide on-demand music selections. While driving your car, you'll simply say something like, "Computer, I want to hear the current top-five R&B hits." The computer in your car will connect to the Internet (using wireless technologies of course) and then search the Internet for a site that offers the best price on the music you want (see Figure 9.1). Your car's computer will then use your credit card to purchase the music and download it to your car stereo system, through which you'll hear exactly the music you want.

This is an excellent example of a surviving B2C dot-com company that will provide you with commodity-like digital products. It doesn't matter how or from where you obtain a particular music selection—it sounds the same (i.e., a commodity-like item). And music is digital, so it can be easily moved to and from the Internet. We truly believe that you'll someday listen to music in your car in this fashion. You'll probably do the same with your cell phone, your PDA, and even your desktop home computer.

Other examples of B2C dot-com companies that will survive because they offer commodity-like digital products include news and information sites, video and movie sites, and electronic textbook sites. As for B2C dot-com companies that sell products in other arenas, such as clothing, we believe some will survive and flourish and some will not. What will distinguish the winners from the losers? Well, it goes back to the other five lessons learned by B2C entrepreneurs that we discussed in Chapter 5—attracting and retaining customers, the importance of merchandising, executing well, picking your sector carefully, and watching the competition. Those that adhere to these solid business principles will survive; those that don't . . . well, you know the story.

When Will We Achieve Transparency?

Technology as a Part of Everyday Life

In Chapter 7, we discussed the concept of transparent technology or IT fusion. These occur when the technology is indistinguishable from the people and processes that exploit the technology. In this environment, you literally can't tell when technology is being used and when it isn't. Within that, we discussed how electricity is transparent. It is so common and wide-

When Will We Achieve Transparency? **349**

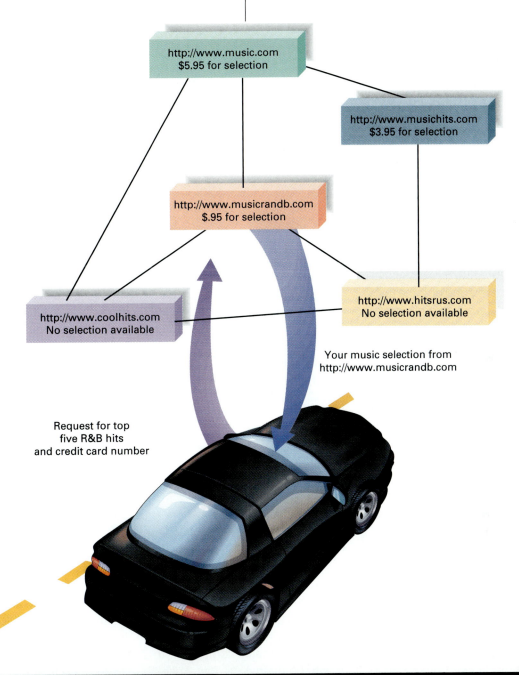

FIGURE 9.1

Pay-Per-Listening Music in Your Car

spread that we don't even think about it as being integral to what we do. Someday, technology will be the same. Some people say that we are many, many years away from transparent technology; we believe, on the other hand, that technology will be transparent within 10 years or so. For that to happen, we must overcome two hurdles—(1) the unreliability of technology and (2) the last-mile bottleneck problem.

The Unreliability of Technology

As much as we may hate to admit it, technology today is still somewhat unreliable. Computers malfunction and break down. It's a simple fact of life. Of course, you may lose electricity every now and then because a tree branch falls on a power line. But that occurs less often

INDUSTRY PERSPECTIVE

".com"

Who's Afraid of the Big, Bad Dot-Coms?

Commodity-like and digital products include books, specifically college textbooks. When the dot-com rage really kicked in, many traditional textbook publishers began to take notice of dot-com companies selling e-textbooks (or e-texts) on the Internet. After all, there's a huge expense associated with creating, distributing, and selling a paper-based book. However, you can create, distribute, and sell an e-text on the Internet for very little money. Most notably, on the Internet you have nominal distribution costs and print, paper, and bindery (PP&B) costs are almost zero.

Today, though, traditional textbook publishers aren't afraid of the dot-coms. Why? Because the publishing world realized that content is at the core of a textbook, and traditional publishers have contracts with authors who create the content. Those contracts state that an author cannot create content for another publisher if it's in direct competition with the author's existing content with the first publisher. As one analyst put it, "Dot-com, schmot-com! Content was king, and then content was crap, and now it's king again."

Accordingly, e-texts are expected to control only about 6.5 percent of the college textbook sales in 2005 and less than 2 percent of consumer-book sales. If you own the digital product (textbook content in this case), you may not have to fear dot-coms....Then again, you should always watch the competition.[3] ❖

INDUSTRY PERSPECTIVE

Hospitality & Leisure

Backup Servers Serve Up Domino's Pizza

According to Glen Mueller, president of Domino's franchisee RPM Pizza in Gulfport, Mississippi, Domino's expects that 50 percent of its business will be conducted over the Internet or interactive TV (such as WebTV) in the next five years. To many, that seems counterintuitive to the rapid fall of dot-coms (some of which were food-related businesses). But Domino's is betting the kitchen on it.

Working from that electronic assumption, Domino's is seeking ways to ensure that Internet-ordering is as reliable as phone-ordering (the major competitor to Internet-ordering). As Ray Anderson, president of QuikOrder, explains it, "We wanted dial-tone reliability, just like the telephone company offers. We can't have any downtime. In fact, if a user was on the system and something failed, we wouldn't want the user to know it."

So, Domino's went straight to Ray and QuikOrder and began outsourcing its Internet-ordering system. QuickOrder then installed a fault tolerant cluster of servers in its Chicago headquarters, on which it has already logged over 10,000 orders for Domino's. QuikOrder's fault tolerant server cluster (sometimes called a server farm) runs Domino's Internet-ordering system on two computers simultaneously. If one goes down, the other continues to process orders—and the user never knows it.

Who would have thought that fault tolerant and backup computers would help Domino's deliver your pizza on time?[4] ❖

than computer failures (and some of those occur because of that same tree branch).

To achieve technology transparency, technology must become more reliable. Your operating system can't "freeze up" for no reason. If it does, your computer should automatically save whatever you're doing so you don't lose any time or information. We also need fault tolerant or redundant computer systems. **Fault tolerant** or **redundant computer systems** have built-in backup systems that take over when a primary component fails. In many instances, organizations run two systems simultaneously—one as the primary and one as the redundant, with both processing the same transactions. The business world already has these in large-scale systems, but your PDA certainly doesn't. As technology becomes smaller, you can expect that all forms of technology tools will include fault tolerant and redundant components. Until then, technology transparency is not possible.

The Last-Mile Bottleneck Problem

While cruising the Internet, you may often find it slow presenting Web pages or downloading files. But do you know why that happens? For the most part, it's because of the last-mile bottleneck problem (see Figure 9.2). The **last-mile bottleneck problem** occurs when information is traveling on the Internet over a very fast line for a certain distance (from NAP to NAP) and then comes near your home where it must travel over a slower line. For example, the majority of the Internet backbone (discussed in *Extended Learning Module E*) operates on high-speed media such as fiber optics and satellite transmissions.

Unfortunately, the portion of the Internet from a network access point (NAP) to your home may use a medium (such as a twisted-pair phone line) that operates at a much slower speed. So, as information travels on the Internet backbone, it does so at great speeds, enabling you to request large video and audio files. However, during the so-called "last mile" to your home, that large amount of information must travel at a much slower speed.

For technology to become transparent, the "last mile" must be as fast as the Internet backbone. Then and only then, you'll be able to cruise the Internet just as fast as you can watch and change channels on your television. Much research is currently being performed in this area. In *Extended Learning Module C*, for example, we discussed such high-speed technologies as DSL and ISDN. When these types of technologies become widespread and affordable, you'll see literally no delays while cruising the Internet. Until then, you may perceive technology as being slow and "clunky" (definitely not transparent).

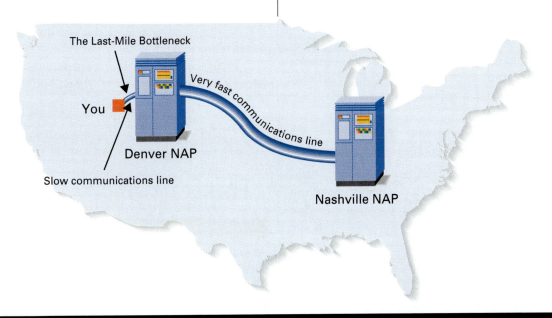

FIGURE 9.2
The Last-Mile Bottleneck Problem

INDUSTRY PERSPECTIVE

IT & Telecommunications

Using Wireless Fiber Optics to Solve the Last-Mile Bottleneck Problem

In early 2000, Lucent Technologies announced a joint venture with TeraBeam Internet Systems. The goal of the joint venture is simple—solve the last-mile bottleneck problem.

The newly formed company will deploy wireless fiber optics in the so-called "last mile" of Internet communications. The new system uses lasers to carry network traffic through the air. The small sending and receiving device can actually be placed inside an office building or home behind a window. So, the system doesn't even require rooftop installations that often require rooftop permissions or cable right-of-ways.

According to Chris Nicoll, an analyst at Current Analysis, "We're not just talking wireless from a customer to a base station. You could [network] a whole metro area in a matter of days. Municipalities like Boston and Washington would probably appreciate using TeraBeam instead of tearing up streets [to bury fiber-optic cable]."

It's hoped that this new and emerging technology will completely eliminate the last-mile bottleneck problem.[5]

Any Last Predictions?

Some Things to Think About

Here's a section you may find interesting. Instead of telling you what we think, we ask you to consider what *you* think will happen in the future.

Will We Close the Digital Divide?

The digital divide defines technology "haves" and "have nots." Generally, the digital divide also defines economic "haves" and "have nots." Can less fortunate groups of people acquire and use technology? In doing so, will that lead them to economic prosperity?

Will Technology Truly Become "Intelligent"?

The keyword in artificial intelligence right now is "artificial." We have to program how computers perform and what actions they take. Will that change? What research is under way to create computers that are truly intelligent? If we can someday create intelligent computers, what sort of impact will that have on our lives?

Will Coins and Cash Disappear?

Electronic forms of money are already a reality, and their use is becoming more widespread every day. Will we someday completely replace folding cash and coins with electronic forms of payment? In Scandinavian countries they already use cell phones to buy products from vending machines. Is a cashless society good or bad? Will it further widen the digital divide? How?

Will Wireless Be the Only Way?

Currently, we have trillions of dollars invested in the wired infrastructure of our society. But we're finding that we need a wireless infrastructure for high-speed transfers and mobility. Will the world someday become completely wireless? What sort of implications will that have for electronic security and personal privacy?

What Will the Key Future Business Resource Be?

Knowledge Workers

As we close this chapter that begins your future, you should walk away, at a minimum, with one key thought. The future success of the business world really depends on only one asset—knowledge workers. Throughout the history of the business world, people (today we call them knowledge workers) have always been the key resource. That will certainly not change in the future. As a knowledge worker—no matter what

TEAM WORK

Gaze into Your Crystal Ball

Here's an opportunity for you to make some further predictions of the future (and they don't all have to be technology-specific). As a group, come up with five of the most dramatic and far-reaching predictions of the future you can imagine. As you present these, discuss the role of technology.

Prediction	The Role of Technology
1.	
2.	
3.	
4.	
5.	

your profession or in which industry you work—**you are the key business resource.**

As technology becomes more transparent and intelligent and more business is conducted in cyberspace, your individual success will define the success of your organization. Your ability to work with customers, create new products and services, define the strategic direction of your organization, make decisions, work with information, and perform a host of other activities is really at the heart of any business undertaking.

So, given that you will be an organization's most important asset, how do you prepare for the future? Below, we've listed some ways in which you can better position yourself.

- **Learn Solid Business Principles**—We quickly determined from the rise and fall of the dot-com B2C market that solid business principles were the guiding light for any undertaking, even in cyberspace. So, regardless of your major or future job aspirations, take seriously your core business classes—human resource management, accounting, finance, marketing, business management, economics, IT and MIS, production and operations management, and business law. To be successful, you need an area of expertise, but you also need to be a "jack of all trades" in the business world.

- **Learn to Be an Effective Communicator**—If you poll potential employers and ask what skills any new employee should have, one that will always come up is *effective communicator*. More broadly, we say you need "interpersonal skills." You must learn to create well-written documents, prepare well-rehearsed and persuasive presentations, and resolve conflicts in a group environment. We cannot stress this enough—*effective communicators* are successful in business.

- **Learn to Be Productive with Technology**—Technology can definitely make you more efficient in what you do. Take the time (and it doesn't take much time) to learn all the functionality within such personal productivity tools as word processing, spreadsheet, database management, Web authoring, presentation graphics, and communications software. Today, we spend much more time at work than we ever have in the past. Forty-hour work weeks have gone by the wayside. Leisure time has been reduced to a minimum. But you don't want to spend all your time working. You can spend less time working if you become more productive through technology.

- **Learn to Think Globally**—The world is a global one. Daily, technology is helping us overcome national, political, and cultural barriers. Someday, intelligent translation software will allow you to have a phone conversation with anyone anywhere in the world while they use a different language. Remember—the optimist sees the donut while the pessimist sees the hole. The global market is definitely a very big "donut."

KNOWLEDGE WORKER'S ✓-LIST

How Jobs of the Future Will Change. Jobs in the future will definitely change, just as they have dramatically changed in the past. According to Tom Peters, the 10 hottest jobs of the future will be:

1. Tissue engineers
2. Gene programmers
3. Pharmers
4. Frankenfood monitors
5. Data miners
6. Hot-line handymen
7. Virtual-reality actors
8. Narrowcasters
9. Turing testers
10. Knowledge engineers

Almost all these new jobs are technology-related (as well as medical-related).

What It Will Take for B2C Dot-Coms to Survive. B2C dot-coms as a group will definitely survive. Most of the ones that survive will offer commodity-like digital products such as music, news, videos, and books. Others will survive because they've learned their business lessons well— the importance of attracting and retaining customers, merchandising, executing well, picking a sector carefully, and watching the competition.

The Hurdles to Overcome to Achieve Technology Transparency. The two important hurdles to overcome to achieve technology transparency include:

- **Learn to Act Ethically**—An overriding concern in the future will always be ethics, just as it is today. If you always act ethically, you will stay out of trouble and the world will be a much better place. Enough said.

CLOSING CASE STUDY

You and Your Information

In our final case study, we want to take a look at information pertaining to the most important person in your life—you. Today's business environment is not only information-based, so is all of society. No matter what you do or where you go, your information travels with you and is eventually captured and stored by a number of organizations. In this all-encompassing information environment, let's consider two issues—trust and accuracy. As you'll see, both are very related.

First, answer the questions below, which pertain to your every day life.

1. Do you keep a paper record of all your long-distance phone calls—when you placed them by date and time, to whom, and the length—and then compare that list to your monthly phone bill? ☐ Y ☐ N

2. Do you meet with the meter reader to verify the correct reading of your water, gas, or electricity usage? ☐ Y ☐ N

3. As you shop, do you keep a record of the prices of your groceries and then compare that record to the register receipt? ☐ Y ☐ N

4. Do you frequently ask to see your doctor's medical record on you to ensure that it's correct? ☐ Y ☐ N

5. When you receive a tuition bill, do you pull out your calculator, add up the amounts, and verify that the total is correct? ☐ Y ☐ N

6. Have you ever purchased a credit report on yourself to make sure your credit information is accurate? ☐ Y ☐ N

7. Have you ever called the police department to verify that no outstanding traffic violations have been inadvertently assigned to you? ☐ Y ☐ N

8. Do you count your coin change when you receive it from a store clerk? ☐ Y ☐ N

9. Do you verify your credit card balance by keeping all your credit card receipts and then matching them to charges on your statement? ☐ Y ☐ N

10. Do you keep all your paycheck stubs to verify that the amounts on your W-2 form at the end of the year are correct? ☐ Y ☐ N

To how many questions did you answer yes? To how many did you answer no? More than likely, you probably answered no to almost all the questions (if not all of them). What does that have to say about your trust that organizations are maintaining accurate information about you? Well, it basically says that you trust organi-

1. The unreliability of technology—which will be solved through ***fault tolerant*** and ***redundant computer systems***, which have built-in backup systems that take over when a primary component fails.
2. ***The last-mile bottleneck problem***—which occurs when information is traveling on the Internet over a very fast line for a certain distance (from NAP to NAP) and then comes near your home where it must travel over a slower line.

The Most Important Business Resource of the Future. The single most important business resource of the future will be **you** as a knowledge worker. You can prepare for this role by:

1. Learning solid business principles
2. Learning to be an effective communicator
3. Learning to be productive with technology
4. Learning to think globally
5. Learning to act ethically ❖

---

zations to keep accurate information about you. The real question is, "Is that necessarily the case?"

Now answer the set of questions below, which relate to the level of confidence organizations have in the accuracy of information you give them.

1. When interviewing with potential employers, do they take your word that you have a college degree? ☐ Y ☐ N
2. If you deposit several checks into your checking account at once, does the bank trust you to correctly add the amounts? ☐ Y ☐ N
3. When you register for a class that has a prerequisite, does your college or university assume that you have actually taken the prerequisite class? ☐ Y ☐ N
4. When you make a deposit at an ATM and enter the amount, does the bank assume that you entered the correct amount? ☐ Y ☐ N
5. When you're buying a house and negotiating a loan, does the bank assume that the price you're paying for the house is correct and not inflated? ☐ Y ☐ N
6. When insuring your car, does the insurance company assume that you have a good driving record? ☐ Y ☐ N
7. When you apply for a parking permit at your college or university, does it assume that the car belongs to you? ☐ Y ☐ N
8. When you file your taxes, does the IRS assume that you've reported all your income over the past year? ☐ Y ☐ N

The answer to each of those questions is probably no. And what does that say about the extent to which organizations trust you to provide accurate information? In this instance, it may not be strictly a matter of trust. Organizations today can't afford to have *dirty information*—information that's not accurate. Because organizations base so many of their decisions on information, inaccurate information creates a real problem that may equate to inefficient processes and lost revenue.

So, on the one side, you're probably very trusting in your assumptions that organizations are maintaining accurate information about you. On the other side, organizations don't really depend on you to provide accurate information. ❖

◄ Questions ►

1. Should you really trust organizations to maintain accurate information about you? In many instances, is it even worth your time and energy to verify the accuracy of that information?
2. What other examples can you think of in which you simply trust that your information is accurate? What other examples can you think of in which specific organizations don't assume that you're providing accurate information?

3. What sort of impact will cyberspace business have on the issues of trust and accuracy? Will it become easier or more difficult for cyberspace business to assume that you're providing accurate information? Will you trust cyberspace business to maintain your information more accurately than traditional organizations?

4. What are the ethical issues involved in organizations sharing information about you? In some instances it may be okay and in your best interest. But what if the shared information about you is inaccurate? What damage could it cause? What recourse do you have, if any?

5. It's a real dilemma—most people think that credit card offerers charge extremely high interest rates. But how many people do you know who actually go through the process of calculating their average daily balances, applying the interest rates, and then verifying that the interest charged on their accounts is correct? Why do people complain that they are being charged excessive interest rates and then fail to check the accuracy of the interest calculations?

6. What about the future—as more organizations maintain even more information about you, should you become more concerned about accuracy? Why or why not?

Electronic Commerce
Business and You on the Internet

Continuing Your Education through the Internet

For many of you, this course may mark the end of your endeavors in higher education. Indeed, you may be preparing right now to enter the business world by sending out resumes and participating in job interviews. If so, we certainly hope you're letting the Internet help (see the Real HOT Electronic Commerce section in Chapter 1, "Using the Internet as a Tool to Find a Job"). For others of you, you may still have another year or two before completing your education. Whatever the case, you need to consider the current landscape of the business world and what it's going to take for you to compete now and in the future.

To be perfectly honest, it's a dog-eat-dog world out there. The competitive landscape of business is more intense than it ever has been. And that competitiveness spills into your personal life. Many of you are in school right now to get an education to better compete in the job market. But many knowledge workers are finding out that an undergraduate degree is simply not enough to compete in the business world.

So, many people are turning once again to higher education to obtain a master's degree, professional certification such as a CPA or CFP (certified financial planner), or perhaps even a Ph.D. in business. You may also be considering the same, either immediately upon graduation or sometime in the near future.

And, just like businesses, graduate schools (and all schools in general) are using the Internet as a way to communicate information to you. Many of these schools are even offering online courses you can complete through the Internet to further your education.

In this section, we've included a number of Web sites related to continuing your education through the Internet. On the Web site that supports this text (http://www.mhhe.com/haag, "Electronic Commerce Projects"), we've provided direct links to all these Web sites as well as many, many more. These are a great starting point for completing this Real HOT section.

MBA Programs

Many of you will undoubtedly choose to continue your education by obtaining an MBA. And you probably should. The market for the best business positions is extremely competitive, with hiring organizations seeking individuals who can speak more than one language, have job experience, and have extended their educational endeavors beyond just getting an undergraduate degree. Indeed, there are over 400,000 people in the United States seeking an MBA right now (that's an all-time high), and you must compete against some of those people in the job market.

Each year, the *U.S. News & World Report* ranks the top business schools in the nation. In the table on page 358, we've provided a list of the top 5 business schools in the nation and where you can find them on the Internet. On the Web site that supports this text, you'll also find a list of the remaining Web sites for the top 50 business schools in the nation.

Choose a couple of different business schools from the list of 50, visit their Web sites, and answer the following questions for each:

A. What business school did you choose?
B. Does that school offer a graduate program in your area of interest?
C. Does the graduate program Web site contain biographical sketches of faculty?
D. Can you apply online?
E. Is there a major benefactor for the business school? If so, who is it?
F. Does the site list tuition and fee costs?
G. Does the site contain a list of the graduate courses offered in your area of interest?

As you prepare to enter the workforce and perhaps think about pursuing a master's in business, we would encourage you to return to the Web site that supports this text and visit the list of the top 50 business schools. On a yearly basis, we will update that list to include any new schools among the most elite offering graduate programs in business.

Specialized MBA Programs

In the previous section, you explored a few of the top 50 business schools in the nation. Those schools were ranked irrespective of any specialization, focusing rather on overall academic reputation. *U.S. News & World Report* also compiles an annual list of the best

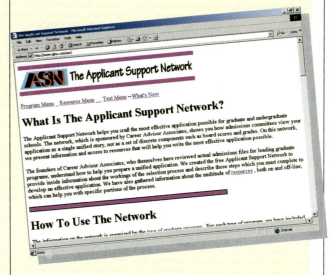

business schools in 10 specializations: accounting, entrepreneurship, finance, health services administration, management information systems, international business, general business, marketing, nonprofit organizations, and production/operations. And if you're interested in a specialized MBA, you should consider viewing schools in these lists.

In the table on pages 359 and 360, we've provided a list of 30 of the best business schools in the above areas (3 for each) and where you can find them on the Internet. In that table, we've added any schools that did not appear in the top schools from the previous section. In health services administration, for example, the top-ranked school is Wharton, and we included the University of Minnesota (ranked fifth) and University of California–Irvine (ranked ninth) because they did not appear in the list of the top 5. And on the Web site that supports this text, you'll find the complete lists of the top 10 business schools in each area.

Choose at least 3 schools that offer a specialization in your area of interest and visit their Web sites. Based on what you find, rank those 3 schools according to your first, second, and third choice. What factors did you consider? Was cost an overriding concern? Before you began your analysis, did you already have a preconceived notion of the best school? Did you change your mind once you visited the schools' sites?

Graduate School Information and Tips

Before you begin your decision-making process concerning which graduate school to attend, you should gather a variety of material. For example, obtaining a directory of universities (both domestic and interna-

tional) would be helpful. Perhaps even more important, you should ask yourself several questions. Are you ready for graduate school? Why are you considering going to graduate school? How do you determine which school is best for you based on such issues as price, location, and area of specialization?

Many of these questions are very personal to you. For example, we can't help you determine if you're really ready for graduate school or answer why you're considering going to graduate school. But what we can do is point you toward some valuable resources on the Internet to help you answer some of your questions and find a wealth of information relating to universities. In the table below, we've provided a list of sites on the Internet that either provide school information or help you work through some of your questions. Like most people choosing to continue their education, you'll find these types of sites to be very helpful.

At your leisure, we recommend that you connect to several of these sites and see what they have to offer. Some simply provide a list of universities, whereas others may be particularly useful as you make that all-important decision.

Tele-Education (Distance Learning)

Throughout this text, you've explored the concept of 24-hour connectivity through information technology. Using IT (part of which is the Internet), organizations today are sending out telecommuting employees, and medical and health facilities are establishing telemedicine practices. And your school may be doing the same—using IT to develop the environment of tele-education.

Tele-education—which goes by a number of terms including e-education, distance learning, distributed learning, and online learning—enables you to get an education without "going" to school. Quite literally, you can enroll in a school on the East Coast and live in Denver, enjoying great winter skiing. Using various forms of IT (videoconferencing, e-mail, chat rooms, and the Internet), you can take courses from schools all over the world. Some of those schools even offer complete degree programs via IT.

And these schools definitely include graduate programs in business. For example, the Massachusetts Institute of Technology and Duke University have graduate programs that combine traditional classroom instruction courses and computer-delivered courses. In 1997, Ohio University (Athens) introduced *MBA without Boundaries,* an MBA program that is completely online except for a required six-week orientation session.

As well, many for-profit organizations offer courses on the Internet that range from preparing for the CPA exam to IT-focused courses such as Windows NT and COBOL programming. In the table below, we've provided a list of sites that have something to do with providing online courses for the Internet. You should definitely connect to the Web site that supports this text and view the list of other sites related to tele-education. And if you're interested in taking online courses from a specific school, we recommend you connect to its Web site to determine if it offers courses over the Internet.

Connect to at least 5 of these sites and explore the possibilities of tele-education. As you do, consider the issues that follow the table below.

Web Sites for Continuing Your Education

University MBA Programs	Address
Harvard University	http://www.hbs.edu
Stanford University	http://www.gsb.stanford.edu
University of Pennsylvania (Wharton)	http://www.wharton.upenn.edu/mba
Massachusetts Institute of Technology (Sloan)	http://mitsloan.mit.edu
Northwestern University (Kellogg)	http://www.kellogg.nwu.edu

Web Sites for Continuing Your Education

Accounting	Address
University of Chicago	http://www.chicagogsb.org
Stanford University	http://www.gsb.stanford.edu
University of Texas–Austin	http://www.texasinfo.bus.utexas.edu

Entrepreneurship	Address
Babson College	http://www.babson.edu/mba
University of Pennsylvania (Wharton)	http://www.wharton.upenn.edu/mba
Harvard University	http://www.hbs.edu

Finance	Address
University of Pennsylvania (Wharton)	http://www.wharton.upenn.edu/mba
University of Chicago	http://www.chicagogsb.org
New York University (Stern)	http://www.stern.nyu.edu

Quantitative Analysis	Address
Massachusetts Institute of Technology (Sloan)	http://mitsloan.mit.edu
Carnegie Mellon University	http://www.gsia.cmu.edu
University of Chicago	http://www.chicagogsb.org

Management Information Systems	Address
Massachusetts Institute of Technology (Sloan)	http://mitsloan.mit.edu
Carnegie Mellon University	http://www.gsia.cmu.edu
University of Minnesota (Carlson)	http://www.carlsonmba.csom.umn.edu

International Business	Address
Thunderbird Graduate School	http://www.t-bird.edu
University of South Carolina (Moore)	http://www.business.sc.edu
University of Pennsylvania (Wharton)	http://www.wharton.upenn.edu/mba

General Business	Address
Harvard University	http://www.hbs.edu
Stanford University	http://www.gsb.stanford.edu
University of Michigan–Ann Arbor	http://www.bus.umich.edu

Marketing	Address
Northwestern University (Kellogg)	http://www.kellogg.nwu.edu
University of Pennsylvania (Wharton)	http://www.wharton.upenn.edu/mba
Harvard University	http://www.hbs.edu

Nonprofit Organizations	Address
Yale University	http://www.yale.edu/som
Harvard University	http://www.hbs.edu
Northwestern University (Kellogg)	http://www.kellogg.nwu.edu

continues

Web Sites (concluded)

Production/Operations	Address
Massachusetts Institute of Technology (Sloan)	http://mitsloan.mit.edu
Carnegie Mellon University	http://www.gsia.cmu.edu
Purdue University (Krannert)	http://www.mgmt.purdue.edu/programs/masters

Graduate School Information	Address
List of American universities	http://www.clas.ufl.edu/CLAS/american-universities.html
List of universities all over the world	http://www.mit.edu:8001/people/cdemello/univ.html
List of community colleges	http://www.mcli.dist.maricopa.edu/cc
Gradschools.com	http://gradschools.com
Application Support Network	http://www.iglou.com/asn

Tele-Education (Distance Learning)	Address
eCollege	http://www.ecollege.com
University of Phoenix	http://onlikne.uophx.edu
Adult University	http://www.adultu.com
Open University	http://www.open.ac.uk
Online @ Syracuse University	http://www.suce.syr.edu/online

Ph.D. Programs	Address
Harvard University	http://www.hbs.edu
Princeton University	http://www.princedton.edu/index.shtml
University of Wisconsin–Madison	http://wiscinfo.doit.wisc.edu/bschool
John Hopkins University	http://www.jhu.edu/www/academics/graduate.html
University of Maryland College Park	http://www.rhsmith.umd.edu/default.asp

A. Can you just take courses or enroll in a complete degree program?
B. What is the cost of tele-education?
C. What process do you go through to enroll in a tele-education program?
D. How would you feel about staying at home instead of going to class?
E. How do tele-education programs foster interactivity between students and teachers?
F. How much do you think you would learn in a tele-education program compared to a traditional in-class program?
G. For what type of individual is a tele-education program best suited?

Ph.D. Programs

Several years ago, people wanting to gain an advantage in the job market pursued an MBA; and that trend still holds true. But a new trend may be on the horizon—that of developing an even more significant advantage in the job market by obtaining a Ph.D. The thought process is simple. If more people are entering the job market with an MBA, the next logical step is to obtain a Ph.D.

Of course, earning a Ph.D. requires several more years of school beyond an MBA, but a growing number of people are willing to make that investment. In business programs, Ph.D. graduates have two main options: entering the private sector or choosing to stay in academia as a professor. Either option certainly yields tremendous benefits, including significantly higher salaries and great flextime (primarily in academia).

In the table above, we've provided a list of some of the top institutions in the country offering Ph.D. programs in business and where you can find them on the Internet (you can find a list of others on the Web site that supports this text). Connect to a few of these school sites and explore what it takes to enter a Ph.D.

program. Can you see this as a realistic possibility in your lifetime? Can you find a Ph.D. program for your area of interest (e.g., finance, marketing, and so on)? If obtaining a Ph.D. is a new trend for gaining an advantage in the job market, what's next? If you do choose to pursue a Ph.D., how important is it for you also to have some work experience?

As a final note, we would encourage you to keep learning. The business world changes on a daily basis, and you need to change with it. For example, there's always new information technology entering the marketplace everyday. If you don't know how to use it, you've placed yourself behind the eight ball. However you choose to continue your education—through online courses, by obtaining some sort of professional certification, by completing a master's or Ph.D. program, or by simply reading books and learning on your own—never stop learning. Your career depends on it.

Go to the Web site that supports this text: **http://www.mhhe.com/haag** and select "Electronic Commerce Projects."

We've included links to over 100 Web sites for continuing your education through the Internet, including the best business schools in the nation according to *U.S. News & World Report.*

KEY TERMS AND CONCEPTS

Fault Tolerant Computer System, 351

Last-Mile Bottleneck Problem, 351

Redundant Computer System, 351

SHORT-ANSWER QUESTIONS

1. In what key areas will jobs of the future be found? What are a few of the hottest jobs of the future?
2. Many B2C dot-coms will survive because they offer what type of products?
3. What two hurdles must we overcome to achieve technology transparency?
4. What is the last-mile bottleneck problem?
5. What will the key future business resource be?

SHORT-QUESTION ANSWERS

1. Virtual-reality actor.
2. Narrowcaster.
3. Commodity-like and digital products.
4. Fault tolerant or redundant computer system.
5. The last-mile bottleneck problem.
6. You.

DISCUSSION QUESTIONS

1. Many people believe that the business world will eventually "return to the basics" and forgo doing business in cyberspace. What are your feelings on this issue? Is there room in the future for traditional brick-and-mortar businesses as well as clicks-and-mortar businesses?
2. Besides interpersonal skills, what other general skills will people need to succeed in the future? Which of those skills can be facilitated by technology?
3. How long do you think it will be before technology truly becomes transparent? In addition to overcoming the unreliability of technology and the last-mile bottleneck problem, what else must occur for us to achieve technology transparency?

CASE 1

Assessing the Value of Information

Trevor Toy Auto Mechanics

Trevor Toy Auto Mechanics is an automobile repair shop in Phoenix, Arizona. Over the past few years, Trevor has seen his business grow from a two-bay car repair shop with only one other employee to a 15-bay car repair shop with 21 employees.

Up to now, Trevor has always advertised that he will perform any work on any vehicle. But that's becoming problematic as cars are becoming increasingly more complex. Trevor has decided he wants to create a more focused repair shop, and is asking for your help. He has provided you with a spreadsheet file that contains a list of all the repairs his shop has completed over the past year. The spreadsheet file contains the fields provided in the table below.

Column	Name	Description
A	MECHANIC #	A unique number assigned to the mechanic who completed the work.
B	CAR TYPE	The type of car on which the work was completed.
C	WORK COMPLETED	What type of repair was performed on the car.
D	NUM HOURS	How long in hours it took to complete the work.
E	COST OF PARTS	The cost of the parts associated with completing the repair.
F	TOTAL CHARGE	The amount charged to the customer for the repair.

Trevor is open to any suggestions you might have. So, your analysis could include any combination of (1) keeping only certain mechanics, (2) repairing only certain types of cars, and/or (3) performing only certain types of repairs.

It is your responsibility to analyze the list and make a recommendation to Trevor concerning how he should focus his business.

Some Particulars You Should Know

1. As you consider the information provided to you, think in terms of what information is important—you might need to use the existing information to create new information.
2. All mechanics are paid the same hourly wage.
3. Disregard any considerations associated with downsizing such as overhead—simply focus on the information provided to you.

4. Disregard any considerations for potential competition located near Trevor.
5. Upon completing your analysis, please provide concise yet detailed and thorough documentation (in narrative, numeric, and graphic forms) that justifies your recommendations.
6. File: TREVOR.xls (Excel file)

CASE 2

Assessing the Value of Information

Affordable Homes Real Estate

In late 1995 a national study announced that Eau Claire, Wisconsin, was the safest place to live. Since then housing development projects have been springing up all around Eau Claire. Six housing development projects are currently dominating the Eau Claire market—Woodland Hills, Granite Mound, Creek Side Huntington, East River Community, Forest Green, and Eau Claire South. These six projects each started with 100 homes, have sold all of them, and are currently developing phase 2.

As one of the three partners and real estate agents of Affordable Homes Real Estate, it is your responsibility to analyze the information concerning the past 600 home sales and choose which development project to focus on for selling homes in phase 2. Because your real estate firm is so small, you and your partners have decided that the firm should focus on selling homes in only one of the development projects.

From the Wisconsin Real Estate Association you have obtained a spreadsheet file that contains information concerning each of the sales for the first 600 homes. It contains the following fields:

Column	Name	Description
A	LOT #	The number assigned to a specific home within each project.
B	PROJECT #	A unique number assigned to each of the six housing development projects (see table below).
C	ASK PRICE	The initial posted asking price for the home.
D	SELL PRICE	The actual price for which the home was sold.
E	LIST DATE	The date the home was listed for sale.
F	SALE DATE	The date on which the final contract closed and the home was sold.
G	SQ. FT.	The total square footage for the home.
H	# BATH.	The number of bathrooms in the home.

The following numbers have been assigned to each of the housing development projects:

Project Number	Project Name
23	Woodland Hills
47	Granite Mound
61	Creek Side Huntington
78	East River Community
92	Forest Green
97	Eau Claire South

It is your responsibility to analyze the sales list and prepare a report that details which housing development project your real estate firm should focus on. Your analysis should be from as many angles as possible.

Some Particulars You Should Know

1. You don't know how many other real estate firms will also be competing for sales in each of the housing development projects.
2. Phase 2 for each housing development project will develop homes similar in style, price, and square footage to their respective first phases.
3. As you consider the information provided to you, think in terms of what information is important and what information is not important. Also, don't forget about the time and content dimensions discussed in Chapter 1. Be prepared to justify, by time and content, how you went about your analysis.
4. Upon completing your analysis, please provide concise, yet detailed and thorough, documentation (in narrative, numeric, and graphic forms) that justifies your decision. In this instance, consider the form dimension of information as you prepare your presentation.
5. File: REALEST.xls (Excel file)

CASE 3

Executive Information System Reporting

B&B Travel Consultants

Benjamin Travis and Brady Austin are co-owners of B&B Travel Consultants, a medium-sized travel agency located in Seattle, Washington, that specializes in cruises. Currently, B&B Travel has five different offices in Seattle. At the present time, Ben and Brady are considering various executive information system packages that can show them overall information views of their organization as well as give them the ability to access more detailed information. Ben and Brady have hired you to make recommendations about what reports should be available through the soon-to-be-purchased executive information system.

The table below is a list of the information that will be the foundation for the reports in the proposed executive information system. These five items comprise a record that is created each time a sale is made. To help you develop realistic reports, Ben and Brady have provided you with a spreadsheet file that contains specific sales over the last six months.

Name	Column	Description
LOCATION #	A	A unique number that identifies which office location recorded the sale.
TRAVEL AGENT #	B	A unique number that identifies which travel consultant recorded the sale.
CRUISE LINE	C	The name of the cruise line for which the package was sold.
TOTAL PACKAGE PRICE	D	The price charged to the customer for the package.
COMMISSION	E	The amount of money B&B made from the sale of the package.

What Ben and Brady are most interested in is viewing several overall reports and then being able to request more detailed reports. So, as a consultant, your goal is to develop different sets of reports that illustrate the concept of drilling down through information. For example, you should develop a report that shows overall sales by location (each of the five different offices) and then also develop more detailed reports that show sales within each location by agent.

Some Particulars You Should Know

1. Ben and Brady would much rather see information graphically than numerically. So as you develop your reports do so in terms of graphs that illustrate the desired relationships.
2. As you consider the information provided to you, think in terms of overall views first and then detailed views second. This will help you develop a logical series of reports.
3. If you wish, you can explore a variety of software tools to help you create the reports. When complete, prepare your presentation using a presentation graphics package that lets you create a really great presentation of your recommendations.
4. Again your goal is not to create reports that point toward a particular problem or opportunity. Rather you are to design sets of logical series of reports that illustrate the concept of drilling down.
5. File: TRAVEL.xls (Excel file)

CASE 4

Building Value Chains

StarLight's Customers Define Value

StarLight, Inc., is a Denver-based retailer of high-quality apparel, shoes, and accessories. In 1915, with money earned in the Colorado gold mines, Anne Logan invested in a small downtown Denver shoe store. A few years later, Anne expanded her business by adding fine apparel. Today, StarLight has 97 retail stores and discount outlets throughout the United States. Since the beginning, StarLight's business philosophy has reflected its founder's beliefs in exceptional service, value, selection, and quality. To maintain the level of service StarLight's customers have come to expect, the company empowers its employees to meet any customer demand—no matter how unreasonable it may seem. With so many stores, it's difficult for Cody Sherrod, StarLight's VP for Business Information and Planning, to know the level of service customers receive, what customers value, and what they don't. These are important questions for a retailer striving to provide the finest customer experience and products while keeping costs to a minimum.

Cody decided a value chain analysis would be helpful in answering these questions. So, customer surveys were designed, distributed, completed, collected, and compiled into a database. Customers were asked to value their experience with various processes in the StarLight value chain. Specifically, for each value chain process customers were asked whether this area added value to their experience or reduced the value of their experience. Customers were asked to quantify how much each process added or reduced the value of the services they received. Using a total of 100 points for the value chain, each customer distributed those points among StarLight's processes. The survey results in the database consist of the fields shown in the accompanying table (on page 366).

Cody has asked you to gather the raw survey material into two value chains, the value-added chain and the value-reducing chain. You'll create chains that summarize the survey information and size the process areas proportionately as described in Chapter 2. Specifically, your job is to perform the following:

1. Create queries or reports in the provided database to summarize the value-added amounts and the value-reducing amounts for each process.

2. Draw two value chains using that summary information to size the depicted area for each process. Use the value chains in Chapter 2 as reference.

3. Compare the value-added and value-reducing process percentages. Do they correlate in any way? If so, why do you think that is? If not, why not?

4. In the table description provided, a dashed line is drawn between the "purchasing" process and the "receive and greet customers" process. Processes above the line are considered support processes, while processes below are considered primary processes. Create a database query to compare how customers value the total of support processes versus primary processes. Do this for both value-added and value-reducing processes. Do the results make sense or are they surprising? Explain why you think either way.

Field Name	Description
Survey ID	An ID number uniquely identifying the survey.
VA/VR	A field that identifies whether the current row of information reflects a value-added response or a value-reducing response.
Date	Survey response date.
Mgmt/Acctg/Finance/Legal	Customer value experience, if any, with management, accounting, finance, and the legal departments.
HR Mgmt	Customer value of the attitude and general personnel environment.
R&D/Tech Dev	Customer perceived value of the quality of research and technology support.
Purchasing	Customer value placed on the quality and range of product selection.
----------	----------
Receive and Greet Customers	Customer value placed on initial contact with employees.
Provide Direction/Advice/Info	Customer value placed on initial information provided by employees.
Store Location/Channel Availability & Convenience	Customer value placed on location, availability, and convenience.
Product Display/Site or Catalog Layout	Customer value placed on aesthetic appeal of merchandise display and layout.
Sales Service	Customer value placed on quality of service provided by sales associates.
Marketing	Customer value placed on the effectiveness of marketing material.
Customer Follow-up	Customer value placed on post-sales service and follow-up.

Some Particulars You Should Know

1. Remember that the total value-added/value-reducing amount for each process must equal 100 percent.

2. The survey values in the database are not percentages although the sum of all responses for a given survey equals 100.

3. File: STARLIGHT.mdb (Access file)

CASE 5

Using Relational Technology to Track Technology

REMO Fashions

REMO Fashions is a manufacturer and provider of bicycle accessories located in Phoenix, Arizona. Because of the boom in bicycle sales over the last several years, REMO has been providing its staff with personal computer systems to handle the abundance of paperwork. REMO, however, has little idea of who is using which personal computer systems and what those computer systems are composed of.

Figure RH.1 shows a basic report that REMO's managers would like to see every month concerning who has what technology on their desks. REMO has four different departments—Manufacturing (1011), Advertising (1124), Customer Service (1111), and Distribution (1139). Each of these departments is overseen by a manager. Within each department, each employee has a personal computer system made up of a CPU, a monitor, and one or two printers. Each personal computer system has a unique number that describes it, as does each CPU, monitor, and printer.

```
                        REMO Fashions
                     Technology Utilization
                        March 13, 2001

System:      11379-A
Price:       $3590                    Department:    1124—Advertising
Employee:    11439—Samson, Beverly    Manager:       Davies, John

        CPU:     11367                Monitor:       4089
                 80586                               Packard Bell
                 120 MHz                              640 × 1028
                 16 MB RAM                            $540
                 $1800

        Printers: 337                                338
                  Hewlett-Packard                    Hewlett-Packard
                  LaserJet 4L                        LaserJet 5L
                  $500                               $750


System:      11363-B
Price:       $2390                    Department:    1139—Distribution
Employee:    11470—Williams, Bill     Manager:       Ko, Julie

        CPU:     11368                Monitor:       5011
                 80486                               Packard Bell
                 75 MHz                               640 × 1028
                 8 MB RAM                             $540
                 $1400

        Printers: 341
                  Epson
                  Stylus Color II Ink Jet
                  $450
```

FIGURE RH.1

Technology Report for REMO Fashions

REMO decided to implement a relational database model to track technology use in the organization. Originally, REMO decided to let one of its employees handle the construction of the database. However, that employee has not had the time to completely implement the project. REMO has asked you to take over and complete the construction of the database.

The entity classes and primary keys for the database have been identified:

Entity Class	Primary Key
Department	Department Number
Employee	Employee Number
System	System Number
Monitor	Monitor Number
Printer	Printer Number
CPU	CPU Number

The following rules have also been identified:

1. A department can have many employees and must have at least one.
2. An employee must be assigned to one and only one department.
3. An employee is not required to have a system but may have up to two systems.
4. A system can be assigned to only one employee but need not be assigned to any employee.
5. A system must have one and only one CPU and one and only one monitor.
6. A system must have at least one printer and may have two printers.
7. A monitor must be assigned to one and only one system.
8. CPUs and printers need not be assigned to any systems but cannot be assigned to more than one system.

Your job is to be completed in the following phases:

1. Develop and describe the entity-relationship diagram.
2. Use normalization to assure the correctness of the tables.
3. Create the database using a personal DBMS package.
4. Use the DBMS package to create the basic report in Figure RH.1.

Some Particulars You Should Know

1. You may not be able to develop a report that looks exactly like the one in Figure RH.1. However, your report should include the same information.
2. Complete personnel information is tracked by another database. For this application, include only the minimum employee information—number, last name, first name, and department.
3. Information concerning all employees, departments, and systems is not readily available. You should, however, create information for several fictitious systems to include in your database.
4. File: Not applicable

CASE 6

Building a Decision Support System

Creating an Investment Portfolio

Most experts recommend that if you're devising a long-term investment strategy you should make the stock market part of your plan. You can use a DSS to help you decide on what stocks to put into your portfolio. You can use a spreadsheet to do the job. The information you need on 10 stocks is contained in a Word file called STOCKS.doc. This information consists of

- Two years of weekly price data on 10 different stocks.
- Stock market indices from
  - The Dow Jones Industrial Average
  - NASDAQ Composite
- Dividends and cash flow per share over the last 10 years (Source: Value Line).

Using this information, build a DSS to perform stock analysis consisting of the following tasks:

1. **Examine Diversification Benefits**
   A. Calculate the average return and standard deviation (σ) of each of the 10 stocks.
   B. Form 15 different portfolios: five with 2 stocks each; five with 5 stocks each; five with 10 stocks each.

Answer the following questions using your DSS:

- How does the standard deviation of each portfolio compare to the (average) standard deviation of each stock in the portfolio?
- How does the average return of the portfolio compare to the average return of each stock in the portfolio?
- Do the benefits of diversification seem to increase or diminish as the number of stocks in the portfolio gets larger?
- In the two-stock and five-stock portfolios what happens if you group your stocks toward similar industries?

2. **Value Each of the Stocks**
   A. Estimate the dividend growth rate based on past dividends.
   B. Estimate next year's dividend using this year's dividend and the estimated growth rate.
   C. Generate two graphs, one for past dividends and one for estimated dividends for the next five years.

Some Particulars You Should Know

1. When performing your calculations, use the weekly returns. That is, use the change in the price each week rather than the prices themselves. This gives you a better basis for calculation because the prices themselves don't usually change very much.
2. File: STOCKS.doc (Word file)

CASE 7

Advertising with Banner Ads

HighwaysAndByways.com

Business is booming at HighwaysAndByways, a dot-com firm focusing on selling accessories for car enthusiasts (e.g., floor mats, grill guards, air fresheners, stereos, and so on). Throughout the past year, HighwaysAndByways has had Web site management software tracking what customers buy, the Web sites from which customers came, and the Web sites customers went to after visiting HighwaysAndByways. That information is stored in a spreadsheet file and contains the fields in the accompanying table (on page 370). Each record in the spreadsheet file represents an individual visit by a customer that resulted in a purchase.

Column	Name	Description
A	CUSTOMER ID	A unique identifier for a customer who made a purchase
B	TOTAL PURCHASE	The total amount of a purchase
C	PREVIOUS WEB SITE	The Web site from which the customer came to visit HighwaysAndByways
D	NEXT WEB SITE	The Web site the customer went to after making a purchase at HighwaysAndByways.

HighwaysAndByways is interested in determining three items and has employed you as a consultant to help. First, HighwaysAndByways wants to know on which Web sites it should purchase banner ad space. Second, HighwaysAndByways wants to know which Web sites it should contact to determine if those Web sites would like to purchase banner ad space on the HighwaysAndByways Web site. Finally, HighwaysAndByways would like to know which Web sites it should develop reciprocal banner ad relationships with; that is, HighwaysAndByways would like a list of Web sites on which it would obtain banner ad space while providing banner ad space on its Web site for those Web sites.

Some Particulars You Should Know

1. As you consider the information provided to you, think about the levels of information literacy. In other words, don't jump to conclusions before carefully evaluating the provided information.
2. You don't know if your customers made purchases at the Web site they visited upon leaving HighwaysAndByways.
3. Upon completing your analysis, please provide concise yet detailed and thorough documentation (in narrative, numeric, and graphic forms) that justifies your recommendations.
4. File: CLICKSTREAMS.xls (Excel file)

CASE 8

Evaluating Requests for Proposal

ITW Enterprises

In Chapter 7 we followed ITW Enterprises (ITW) as it proceeded through the SDLC to develop its new system. Let's suppose that ITW decided to outsource the development of the new system and hired you to evaluate the request for proposal (RFP) returns.

When we discussed the outline of an RFP, we stated that you'd want to include how the RFP returns will be scored. One method of scoring is to list the information and processes you want, assign each a weight, and ask the vendors to check off which ones their systems support. In Figure RH.2, we include a sample scoring mechanism for ITW's supposed outsourcing concerning information it would like to capture about clients. Notice that each information attribute has been categorized as required, would be nice, or optional. Required information attributes are worth 5 points, would be nice information attributes are worth 3 points, and optional information attributes are worth 1 point.

	INFORMATION ATTRIBUTE CATEGORY			DOES YOUR SYSTEM HANDLE THIS ATTRIBUTE?		
INFORMATION ATTRIBUTE	REQUIRED (5)	WOULD BE NICE (3)	OPTIONAL (1)	YES (1)	NO (−1)	SCORE
Last Name	X			X		5
First Name	X			X		5
Middle Initial			X	X		1
Pet? (Y/N)	X			X		5
Desire tennis court? (Y/N)	X				X	−5
Desire pool? (Y/N)	X				X	−5
Desire on-site security? (Y/N)	X			X		5
Smoker? (Y/N)			X		X	−1
Age		X		X		3
Number bedrooms	X			X		5
Children? (Y/N)			X		X	−1
Floor (top or bottom)		X			X	−3
Desire covered parking? (Y/N)	X				X	−5
Income level			X	X		1
Desire washer/dryer in apt? (Y/N)		X		X		3
Desire vaulted ceiling? (Y/N)			X		X	−1
Max rent	X			X		5
YOUR TOTAL SCORE FOR THESE INFORMATION ATTRIBUTES:						17

FIGURE RH.2

Sample Scoring Mechanism

If a vendor says its system will handle a particular information attribute, we multiply its point value by 1. If a system does not handle a particular information attribute, we multiply its point value by −1. We then sum the scores to determine an overall score.

In a file called RFP.doc we have provided a portion of the RFP that ITW sent to potential vendors. In that file you'll find a complete list of ITW's information requirements. ITW received three back; these returns are in files called VENDOR1.doc, VENDOR2.doc, and VENDOR3.doc. Your task is to develop a spreadsheet that compares how each vendor scored concerning ITW's information requirements.

Some Particulars You Should Know

1. Each vendor has recommended a system that will work. The only difference is what information is and is not supported by each vendor.
2. In ITW's RFP document, you'll find a complete description of the scoring mechanism. This will help you develop your comparative spreadsheet.

3. When you've completed your analysis, prepare a presentation using a presentation graphics package.
4. File: RFP.doc, VENDOR1.doc, VENDOR2.doc, VENDOR3.doc (Word files)

CASE 9

Demonstrating How to Build Web Sites

With HTML

Building a good Web site is simple in some respects and difficult in others. It's relatively easy to learn to write HTML code. Building an effective and eye-catching Web site is a horse of a different color. That is to say, there is a stretch between just using the technology and using the technology to your best advantage.

Your task in this project is to build a presentation (using presentation graphics software such as Microsoft PowerPoint) that achieves two goals. First, your presentation should show your audience how to write simple HTML code to create a Web site. Your presentation should include the HTML code for:

- Text formatting (bold, italicize, and the like)
- Font families and sizing
- Font colors
- Background colors and images
- Links
- Images
- Numbered and bulleted lists

Next, your presentation should provide the audience with a list of guidelines for creating an effective Web site. For this, you should definitely embed links into your presentation that go to Web sites that illustrate good Web site design, displaying examples of both effective and ineffective designs.

Some Particulars You Should Know

1. In a file called HTML.doc, we've provided many links to Web sites that teach you how to write HTML code.
2. In a file called DESIGN.doc, we've provided many links to Web sites that teach you how to effectively design Web sites.
3. Files: HTML.doc and DESIGN.doc (Word files)

CASE 10

Making the Case with Presentation Graphics Software

Information Technology Ethics

Management at your company is concerned about the high cost of computer crime, from lawsuits over e-mail received to denial-of-service attacks and crackers breaking into the corporate network to steal information. You've been asked to make a presentation to inform your colleagues. Develop a presentation using a presentation package such as Microsoft's PowerPoint.

You can choose your presentation's emphasis from the following topics.

- Ethics as it relates to IT systems.
- Types of crime aimed at IT systems (such as viruses).
- Types of crime that use IT systems as weapons (such as electronic theft of funds from one account to another).
- Security measures, how good they are, what they cost, how expensive they are to implement.
- Electronic monitoring of employees (from employer and employee standpoints).
- Collection and use of personal information on consumers.

Sources of Information

- In the file ETHICS.doc, you'll find sources for the topics listed above.
- The Web is a great place to find lots of information.
- Most business publications, such as *Business Week, InformationWeek, Fortune,* and *The Wall Street Journal,* frequently have good articles on ethics, cybercrime, and security. You can get some of these articles on the Web.
- General news publications such as *Newsweek* and *USA Today* print articles on these topics.

Your task is to weave the information you find into a coherent presentation using graphs and art where appropriate.

Some Particulars You Should Know

1. Content Principles
   - Each slide should have a headline.
   - Each slide should express one idea.
   - Ideas should follow logically.

2. Design Principles
   - Follow the "Rule of 7"—no more than 7 lines per slide and 7 words per line.
   - Keep it simple.
   - Keep it organized.
   - Create a path for the eye.
   - Divide space in an interesting way.
   - Use at least 30 point type.
   - Use color and graphics carefully, consistently, and for a specific purpose.
   - Use high-contrast colors (black/white, deep blue/white, etc.).

3. File: ETHICS.doc (Word file)

EXTENDED LEARNING MODULE D

HARDWARE AND SOFTWARE

If you have discussions with people concerning computers and technology, some common questions always surface:

- What technology do I need?
- What software should I buy?
- Do I need an ink jet or laser printer?
- How do hardware and software work together?

In fact, you may be asking some of these very questions yourself. If so, this extended learning module will answer those questions. And if you're already well adept at computer terminology, this extended learning module will help you create categories of technology so you can better remember them.

Everything in the technology environment is either hardware or software (see Figure D.1). *Hardware* is the physical devices such as your printer, monitor, CPU chip, and disk. *Software* is the set of instructions that your hardware executes to carry out a particular task for you. For example, Microsoft Word can help you write letters and term papers and Lotus Freelance Graphics can help you create art and manipulate photos.

No matter what you do with your computer, you need both hardware and software. If you want to surf the Internet, for instance, you need hardware that would include a modem (for connecting to the Internet), a mouse and keyboard (for navigating), and a monitor or screen (for viewing Web sites). You also need software that would include connectivity software (for connecting to the Internet) and Web browser software (for visiting and viewing Web sites). This is an obvious but important point—no matter what you want to do with your computer, you need both hardware and software.

In this *Extended Learning Module D*, we'll first look at specific types of hardware. Then we'll look toward specific types of software. Finally, we'll combine them all, see how they work together, and discuss issues related to your buying a personal computer.

Hardware
Physical devices
- Monitor
- Mouse
- Disks

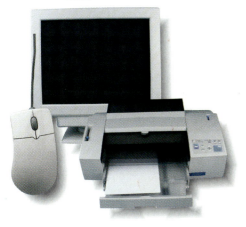

Software
Instructions that your hardware executes
- Payroll
- Word processing
- Spreadsheet

IMPORTANT POINTS TO REMEMBER:
1. No matter what you want to do with your computer, you need both hardware and software.
2. We often say that hardware is the *physical interface* to your computer. Why?
3. We often say that software is the *intellectual interface* to your computer. Why?

FIGURE D.1

Technology Hardware and Software

Computer Hardware: Physical Devices

In Chapter 1 we suggested that the best way to consider hardware is in a set of five categories supporting five information-processing tasks. Those five Cs of information-processing tasks are

1. Capturing information
2. Conveying information
3. Creating information
4. Cradling information
5. Communicating information

In Table D.1, you can find those five information-processing tasks as well as some examples of IT tools that support them. Let's explore these categories further.

Capturing Information: Input Technologies

Input technologies are tools you use to capture information or commands at the point of origin; they include such tools as a keyboard, mouse, touch screen, and bar code reader. The best input technology for a given situation is one that captures information or commands at the **point of origin**. Consider the following example. As a CEO of a major corporation, you need to send out a letter. You call in your assistant, who writes the letter on paper as you dictate. Your assistant then types the letter and sends it out. Seems straightforward enough but, in reality, the content of the letter was not captured at its point of origin; rather it was captured three times.

TABLE D.1 The 5 Cs of Information-Processing Tasks and IT Tools That Support Them

Information-Processing Task	Description	IT Tools
CAPTURING information	Obtaining information at its point of origin	Input technologies: • Mouse • Keyboard • Bar code reader
CONVEYING information	Presenting information in its most useful form	Output technologies: • Screen • Printer • Monitor
CREATING information	Processing information to create new information	Computer's brain: *Processing or software* • CPU • RAM
CRADLING information	Storing information for use at a later time	Storage technologies: • Hard disk • CD-ROM • DVD
COMMUNICATING information	Sending information to other people or another location	Telecommunications technologies: • Modem • Satellite • Digital pager

Let's review the process. As you dictated the letter, your assistant heard it—that's capture #1. After your assistant heard it, he or she recorded it on paper—that's capture #2. Then your assistant typed it—that's capture #3. Now that seemingly straightforward process doesn't make so much sense, does it? Businesses cannot afford to perform the same task three times. Always remember, capturing information or commands at the point of origin is key.

There are many different types of input technologies. Some, such as automatic speech recognition systems—which should have been used in the above example—capture information and commands that originate as sounds; others capture information that has already been recorded on paper; still others capture information and commands that are physiological in form.

As you begin to consider which input technologies would be best for a given situation, ask yourself the following two questions (see Table D.2):

Am I trying to capture information, commands, or both?

In what form is the information and/or commands I'm trying to capture?

By answering those two questions, you can determine which input technologies are best according to what you're trying to capture (information, commands, or both) and in what form the information and/or commands originate. For a good review of specific input technology tools, take a look at the accompanying photo essay "Input Technology Tools."

TABLE D.2 Which Input Technologies Should You Use?

	Information	Commands	Both	Audio	Direct	Screen Representation	Text & Images on Paper	Physiological
Keyboard			✓		✓			
POS system			✓		✓			
Sound input	✓			✓				
Touch-tone			✓	✓				
ASR			✓	✓				
Mouse		✓				✓		
Trackball		✓				✓		
Pen mouse		✓				✓		
Pointing stick		✓				✓		
Touch pad		✓				✓		
Touch screen		✓				✓		
Light pen			✓			✓		
Bar code reader	✓						✓	
OMR	✓						✓	
MICR	✓						✓	
OCR	✓						✓	
Personal scanner	✓						✓	
Glove			✓					✓
Headset			✓					✓
Walker			✓					✓
Biometric device	✓							✓

PHOTO ESSAY

Input Technology Tools

A **keyboard** is today's most popular input technology. It looks similar to a typewriter keyboard, but contains many special keys. Keyboards capture direct input and are effective for both information and command capturing.

A **point-of-sale system (POS system)** captures information and commands at the point of a transaction, typically in a retail environment. POS systems capture direct input and are good for both information and command capturing.

A **sound input** device captures information that originates in audio form. Using sound input devices, you can capture any type of sound (a dog barking, a doorbell ringing, and so on) and record it for later reproduction. Sound input devices capture information only in an audio form.

A **Touch-Tone input** device captures information and commands that originate in audio form from a telephone keypad. Many universities today allow students to register for classes using Touch-Tone–based telephone registration systems. Touch-Tone input devices can capture both information and commands that originate in audio form.

An **automatic speech recognition system (ASR system)** not only captures spoken words but also distinguishes word groupings to form sentences. Your speech can then be used as information (for example, the contents of a letter) and commands (for example, save and print the letter). ASR systems capture both information and commands that originate in audio form.

A **mouse** is the most popular type of pointing input device for capturing mainly commands. You move the mouse on a flat surface that causes the pointer on the screen to move accordingly. Once you have positioned the screen pointer appropriately, you can click icons (screen representations) to initiate certain functions or tasks. Mice capture mainly commands that originate in a screen representation form.

A **trackball** is an upside-down, stationary mouse in which you move the ball instead of the device. Trackballs are popular for use on portable systems when there is limited room for moving a mouse. Trackballs capture mainly commands that originate in a screen representation form.

A **pen mouse** looks like a fountain pen and performs similarly to mice and trackballs. A pen mouse has a ball at the tip that causes the pointer on the screen to move as you move the pen mouse across a flat surface. Pen mice capture mainly commands that originate in a screen representation form.

A **pointing stick** is a small rubberlike device that causes the pointer to move on the screen as you apply directional pressure. Pointing sticks are used almost exclusively on portable systems and most often appear in the middle of the keyboard. Pointing sticks mainly capture commands that originate in a screen representation form.

A **touch pad** is another form of a stationary mouse on which you move your finger to cause the pointer on the screen to move. Like pointing sticks, touch pads are used almost exclusively on portable systems. Touch pads mainly capture commands that originate in a screen representation form.

A ***touch screen*** is a special screen that lets you use your finger to literally point at and touch a particular function you want to perform. Touch screens are popular for use in make-your-own greeting card systems and information centers. Although you can enter information using a touch screen, most touch screens capture mainly commands that originate in a screen representation form (icons).

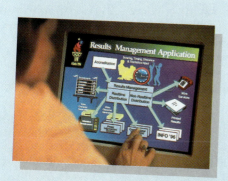

A ***light pen*** is a special light-producing input device used in conjunction with a light-sensitive (photoelectric) screen or pad. With a light pen, you point to the screen where you want more information to appear or where a function is located that you want to perform. Air traffic controllers use light pens to point at aircraft on a screen to make more information appear, including the aircraft type and altitude. Light pens capture mainly commands that originate in a screen representation form.

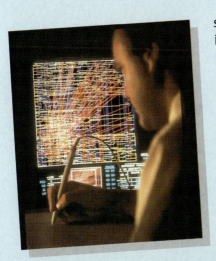

A ***bar code reader*** captures information in a predetermined format that exists as a series of vertical bars whose width and distance apart determine a number. Bar code readers

are a popular device in retail environments for capturing universal product code (UPC) information. Bar code readers mainly capture information that must exist in a predetermined format on paper.

An ***optical mark recognition (OMR)*** input device detects the presence or absence of a mark in a predetermined place. Most collegiate aptitude examinations are graded using OMR devices, and many professors grade true/false and multiple-choice exams using OMR devices. Optical mark recognition devices mainly capture information that must exist in a predetermined format on paper.

A ***magnetic-ink character recognition (MICR)*** input device reads a set of preprinted electronic symbols, usually numbers and characters. The banking industry originally used MICR devices to process the billions of checks each month written by consumers and businesses. Magnetic-ink character recognition devices capture information that exists in a predetermined format on paper.

An ***optical character recognition (OCR)*** input device can capture information that exists in both predetermined and non-predetermined formats. For information that exists in a predetermined format, optical character recognition devices (called ***formatted OCR devices***) read a set of symbols (usually just characters and numbers) whose format has been standardized by the American National Standards Institute (ANSI). Formatted OCR devices are often used in retail environments for scanning price tags. Formatted optical character recognition devices capture information that must exist in a predetermined format on paper.

Some types of optical character recognition input devices can capture information that exists on paper but not in a predetermined format (such as handwriting and text generated by a printer). These types of OCR devices are called **unformatted OCR devices.** Unformatted OCR devices capture information and then put it into an editable format so that you can change the information. Personal digital assistants (PDAs), which we discussed in Chapter 6, use unformatted OCR. To record information with your PDA, you use a special writing stylus and a touch-sensitive screen. The touch-sensitive screen captures your handwriting as you write with the writing stylus. So, unformatted OCR devices mainly capture (1) information that already exists on paper but not in a predetermined format or (2) handwriting information that you record on a touch-sensitive screen.

An **image scanning** input device captures information (usually pictures, diagrams, and graphs) that is not in a predetermined format. Image scanning devices differ from unformatted OCR input devices in that they usually just capture the information for inclusion in a document and do not give you the ability to make changes to the captured information. Image scanning devices capture information that does not exist in a predetermined format on paper.

A **glove** input device captures the movement of your hand and fingers, including dexterity and strength of movement. Glove input devices are used in computer-based puppetry, computer-based sign language systems, and most often in virtual reality systems. Glove input devices capture information and commands that originate in physiological form.

A **headset** input device captures the movement of your head, side to side and up and down. As with gloves, headsets are mainly used in virtual reality systems. Headsets capture information and commands that originate in physiological form.

A **walker** input device captures the movement of your legs and feet, including speed of travel and directional movement. A walker looks similar to an exercise treadmill. As with headsets and gloves, walkers are mainly used in virtual reality systems. Walkers capture information and commands that originate in physiological form.

Biometrics, which we discussed in Chapter 6, is the use of physical characteristics—such as your fingerprint, the blood vessels in the retina of your eye, the sound of your voice, or perhaps even your breath—to provide identification. To perform biometric-based identification, there are corresponding devices that capture information such as your fingerprint or the sound of your voice. This type of information is in a physiological form. ❖

Conveying Information: Output Technologies

Output technologies are the tools you use to see, hear, or otherwise accept the results of your information-processing requests. The best output technology for a given situation is one that presents information in its most useful form. Output form, then, should be your most important question (see Table D.3):

In what form do I need to convey information?

The answer to that question will lead you to one of three categories of output technologies—audio, on-screen, and printed.

Although the most appropriate form of presentation is the key to determining the correct output technology, you can't stop there. You must also determine the quality of the information produced by an output technology. This issue relates most directly to on-screen output technologies (called screens or monitors) and printed technologies (printers and plotters). For an overview of output technologies, including the issue of quality for on-screen and printed output technologies, review the accompanying photo essay "Output Technology Tools."

TABLE D.3 Which Output Technologies Should You Use?

	In what form do I need to convey information?		
	Audio	**On-Screen**	**Printed**
Sound output	✓		
Speech synthesis	✓		
Screen/monitor		✓	
Printer			✓
Monitor			✓

PHOTO ESSAY

Output Technology Tools

A **sound output** device reproduces previously recorded and stored sounds. Sound output devices are the output equivalent to sound input devices. Sound output devices simply convey prerecorded information in audio form.

A **speech synthesis** output device creates speech output from text. Speech synthesis output devices are the flipside of automatic speech recognition input devices. Speech synthesis devices convey information in audio form.

A **plotter** is a special type of printer that draws output on paper. That is, a plotter uses a writing instrument attached to a moveable arm that moves over the paper and positions the writing instrument appropriately. Many plotters let you use different colors to create output. Make-your-own greeting card systems most often use a plotter as the output device for creating the card. Plotters convey information in printed form.

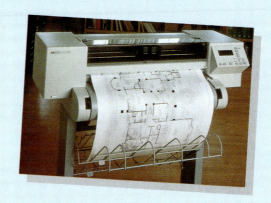

Quality of on-screen output technologies is affected by the graphics adapter card, color, resolution, size, and the flicker question.

A **graphics adapter card** connects the monitor to the rest of the hardware. The quality of the graphics adapter card determines, to a large extent, the number of pixels that will be displayed on the screen and the number of colors used. Monitors that use only one color are called **monochrome monitors**. Other monitors can produce up to 17 million different colors.

Resolution is determined by the number of pixels on a screen. A **pixel** is the smallest display element on a screen that can be turned on or off and made different shades of colors. For example, a monitor whose resolution is 1,024 × 768 has 1,024 rows and 768 columns of pixels (over 750,000 total pixels). Thus the more pixels the higher the resolution.

Size definitely affects presentation quality. Most people are moving toward using 17-inch and 21-inch monitors as opposed to the standard 12-inch monitors.

A pixel is a screen element that can be turned on or off and made different shades of colors.

Some monitors make two passes to produce information on the screen—these are called *interlaced monitors.* Monitors that make only one pass to produce information are called *noninterlaced monitors.* Interlaced monitors seem to flicker and can be hard on your eyes and can adversely affect presentation quality.

On-screen technologies for portable systems are called *flat panel displays.* Because of the technology used to con-

vey information on flat panel displays, their quality is less than that of a standard monitor with the same resolution, color capability, and graphics adapter card. You can also now find flat panel displays for desktop systems (see photo at left). Soon, flat panel displays will be the only type of monitors you find, even for desktop systems. Flat panel display technology quality is increasing every day and will soon be as good as (if not better than) traditional monitors.

Quality of print technologies is affected by impact versus nonimpact, use of preformed character sets, color, dot matrix versus letter quality, graphics, and special printing needs.

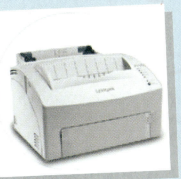

Printers that strike the page with some sort of mechanism are called *impact printers,* whereas printers that do not strike the page are called *nonimpact printers.* Nonimpact printers are quieter, cleaner, and typically provide better-quality output than impact printers. Nonimpact printers are also the choice for most color printing needs.

Many printers are equipped with preformed character sets. If they are, they have a difficult time creating graphics, but provide high-quality output of the preformed character sets.

Color affects the presentation quality of print technologies. Some printers work with no color (called *monochrome printers*), whereas others support up to 16 colors.

Dot matrix printers use a matrix of pins to form characters and then strike those pins through a printer ribbon onto a page. Dot matrix printer quality is near but not letter quality. *Letter quality printers,* on the other hand, use other technologies to create images on a page. For example, preformed character set printers are letter quality printers, *ink jet printers* spray ink onto a page to create letter quality output, and *laser printers* use a special laser technology and inklike toner to create letter quality output.

"A picture is worth a thousand words." That's especially true for print technologies. Laser and ink jet printers provide the best graphics, followed by dot matrix printers. Most preformed character printers produce little or no graphics because they have to use already-formed characters (dashes, periods, and the like) to create a "pseudo" graphic image.

Some printers work with one size of paper and lack extended functional capabilities. Other printers allow you to use different sizes of paper and such special output forms as gum labels and envelopes. ❖

Dot matrix printer

High-resolution laser printer

Creating Information: Computer's Brain

At the heart of the 5 Cs of information-processing tasks and associated IT tools is the task of creating information by your computer's brain (sometimes called the processing engine). Your computer's brain contains two components—the internal memory and the central processing unit. The internal memory is the common connection in your IT system hardware. The central processing unit is the part of the hardware that actually executes the software instructions and coordinates the interaction of all the other hardware devices.

The Central Processing Unit The *central processing unit (CPU)* is the hardware in an IT system that interprets and executes the software instructions and coordinates how all the other hardware devices work together. The CPU has two components—the control unit and the arithmetic/logic unit (see Figure D.2). The *control unit* interprets software instructions and literally tells the other hardware devices what to do, based on the software instructions. As you might guess, the *arithmetic/logic unit (A/L unit)* performs all arithmetic operations (for example, addition and subtraction) and all logic operations (such as sorting and comparing numbers).

The Internal Memory The *internal memory* (its common name is *random-access memory* or *RAM*) is temporary storage that holds three things:

1. Information you are working with
2. The application software you are using
3. The operating system software

The internal memory takes on the role of a notepad that the CPU uses to temporarily store information and instructions.

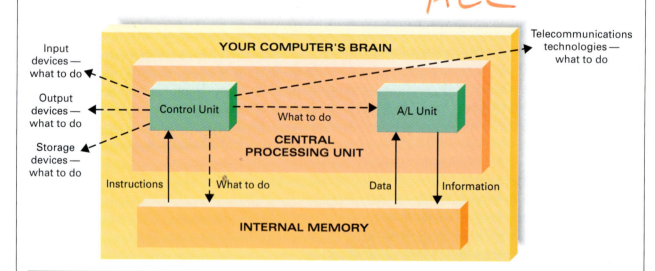

FIGURE D.2
The Components of Your Computer's Brain

Cradling Information: Storage Technologies

Storage technologies are the tools you use to more permanently store information for use at a later time. Although we use the term "permanent" for storage technologies, most storage technologies give you the ability to change your information or erase it altogether. When considering the use of storage technologies, ask two questions to determine which storage technology is best for your needs. (see Table D.4):

Will I need to update my information later?

How much information do I have to store?

The answer to the first question will lead you to one of three types of storage technologies: (1) those that provide easy updating capabilities, (2) those that provide updating capabilities that are sometimes slow, and (3) those that do not allow you to update your information. The answer to the second question will lead you to one of two categories of storage technologies—limited and massive.

For a good review of specific storage technologies, take a look at the accompanying photo essay "Storage Technologies."

TABLE D.4 Which Storage Technologies Should You Use?

	\multicolumn{3}{c}{Will I need to update my information later?}	\multicolumn{2}{c}{How much information do I have to store?}
	Easy Updating	**Slow Updating**	**No Updating**	**Limited**	**Massive**
Floppy disk	✔			✔	
Hard disk	✔				✔
CD-ROM			✔		✔
DVD	??	⟵⟶	??		✔
Tape		✔			✔

PHOTO ESSAY
Storage Technologies

Magnetic Tape Storage Technologies

Magnetic tape storage technologies store information on and retrieve it from a tape using a sequential method of access. That is, in order to read information halfway through the tape, the first half of the tape must be passed over (using something similar to fast-forward with a cassette tape). Magnetic tapes are primarily used for backing up information and software that exist on another storage technology.

For small computer systems, such as your personal computer, magnetic tapes are about one-half the size of a standard VCR tape. On larger systems, a magnetic tape looks like a large reel-to-reel tape.

The amount of storage on a tape is referred to as tape density. **Tape density** is measured in **bytes per inch** or **BPI**. So a tape with a density of 9,600 BPI can hold 9,600 bytes or characters per inch.

Magnetic tape for large systems.

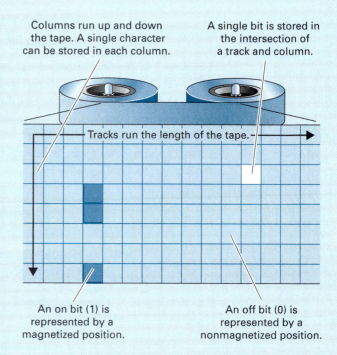

Columns run up and down the tape. A single character can be stored in each column.

A single bit is stored in the intersection of a track and column.

Tracks run the length of the tape.

An on bit (1) is represented by a magnetized position.

An off bit (0) is represented by a nonmagnetized position.

Disk Storage Technologies

Disk storage technologies separate the storage medium (called the "disk") into tracks, with each track divided into several sectors. Disk storage technologies use a direct method of access, which means you can move directly to the information you need without passing over the previous information. Disk storage technologies comprise the majority of the storage technologies used today and include magnetic floppy disks, magnetic hard disks, optical disks, and magneto-optical disks.

Magnetic hard disk storage technologies store information on multiple disks called platters. Magnetic hard disks come in a variety of forms, including internal hard disks, external hard disks, hard disk cartridges, and hard cards.

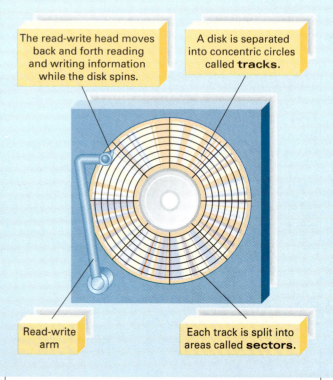

The read-write head moves back and forth reading and writing information while the disk spins.

A disk is separated into concentric circles called **tracks**.

Read-write arm

Each track is split into areas called **sectors**.

Hard disk pack for large systems

An ***internal hard disk*** rests inside the cabinet of your computer. From the front you can't even tell an internal hard disk is present.

An ***external hard disk*** sits outside the cabinet of your computer.

Hard disk cartridges are storage technologies in which the multiple disks or platters can be easily removed from the disk drive and replaced with another cartridge of disks or platters. Hard disk cartridges for large computer systems are called ***hard disk packs***.

Hard cards are storage technologies that exist on a board that can be inserted into an expansion slot on your computer.

Optical Disk Storage Technologies

O***ptical disk storage technologies*** use a laser beam to read and write information to an optical disk. Because of the precision of laser technology, optical disks can hold more information than a magnetic disk. When the laser creates information on an optical disk, it burns ***pits*** into the disk surface to represent an off bit (bit 0). The areas between the pits are called ***lands*** and represent an on bit (bit 1).

When the laser reads information from an optical disk, the laser penetrates the bottom layer of protective plastic and emits a light source against the layer of reflective aluminum. If the light strikes a pit, the light is scattered and isn't reflected back. If the light strikes a land, it is reflected and interpreted as an on bit.

The most common type of optical disk is ***CD-ROM***. And because the laser must physically alter the surface of the disk (by creating pits), information cannot be

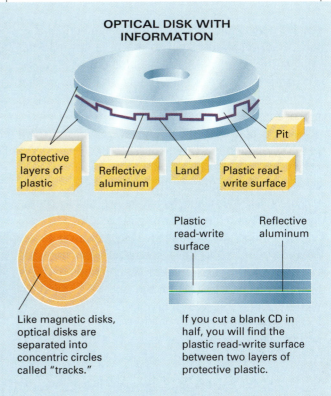

OPTICAL DISK WITH INFORMATION

Protective layers of plastic • Reflective aluminum • Land • Pit • Plastic read-write surface

Like magnetic disks, optical disks are separated into concentric circles called "tracks."

Plastic read-write surface • Reflective aluminum

If you cut a blank CD in half, you will find the plastic read-write surface between two layers of protective plastic.

changed once written to the disk. That's why CD-ROMs are ROM, or read-only memory.

Most MP3 players use a form of CD-based storage technology to write information called CD-recording (or CD-R). ***CD-R*** is an optical storage device on which you can write information, but only once. We often refer to these types of storage devices as WORM (write once, read many) devices. So, you can use CD-R to create a traditional-size CD or a disk that you can use in an MP3 player.

Magneto-Optical Disk Storage Technologies

M***agneto-optical disk storage technologies*** use a laser for reading and writing information and a form of magnetization to give you the ability to alter the stored information. The disks used in magneto-optical disk storage technologies are often called ***erasable optical disks.***

An erasable optical disk has a crystalline alloy that contains crystal-like objects and can be heated, which allows the crystal-like objects to move. To write information, the laser heats the alloy, and the crystals are adjusted to represent information through a form of magnetization. To read information, a laser source is emitted against the crystals. A given alignment of crystals can (1) block the light so that it is not reflected against the layer of reflective aluminum or (2) allow the light to pass through the crystals and reflect against the layer of reflective aluminum and back to the laser.

Most people would place **digital video disks (DVD)** in the category of magneto-optical technologies. Technically, that may be correct sometimes and incorrect in others. First-generation DVD technologies, for example, are still read-only (ROM) but have an initial capacity of 4.6GB with a possible upgrade to 17GB. As well, first generation DVDs can read CD-ROM. Newer generations of DVD (DVD-RAM and DVD+RW) truly are erasable optical disks. These generations possess rewritable capabilities, but often are not compatible with existing CD-ROM technologies.

Whatever the case, CD-ROM is on its way out, and DVD is its successor. ❖

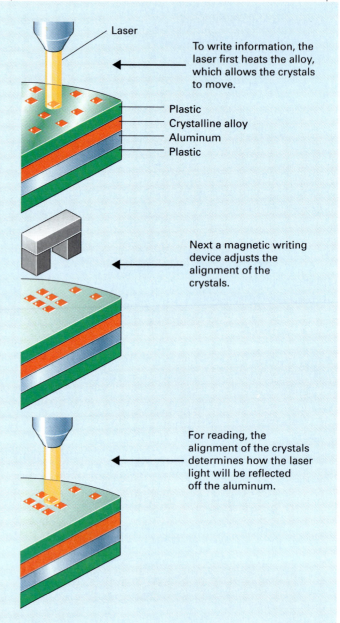

Communicating Information: Telecommunications Technologies

Telecommunications technologies are the tools you use to send information to and receive it from another person or location. Telecommunications technologies represent the fastest growing and most widely varied of all the technology tools. Telecommunications technologies are often associated with the term network. A ***network*** is two or more computers connected so that they can communicate with each other and share information, software, peripheral devices, and/or processing power. Examples of a network include two computers connected to the same printer or the literally millions of computers connected all over the world that make up the Internet.

We devoted all of *Extended Learning Module C*, parts of Chapter 5, and parts of Chapter 6 to telecommunications technologies and the business activities they support. So we won't discuss them in any detail here. For you personally, the most important telecommunications technologies are connectivity software and a modem. ***Connectivity software*** enables you to use your computer to "dial up" or connect to another computer (see Figure D.3). You probably use connectivity software to dial into your school's computer system so you can gain access to the Internet. If you use an ISP such AOL, it has provided the necessary connectivity software you need.

A ***modem*** is a device that connects your computer to your phone line so that you can access another computer or network. Of course, if you're lucky, you may have a high-speed connection to the Internet through DSL, ISDN, or a cable modem.

Again, we would encourage you to read *Extended Learning Module C* and Chapters 5 and 6 for more detailed discussions of telecommunications technologies.

FIGURE D.3
Connecting with Connectivity Software

Computer Software: Intellectual Interfaces

Software is the set of instructions that your hardware executes to carry out a particular task for you. Like hardware, there are categories of software, with the most important two being system software and application software.

System Software: Technology Management

System software handles tasks specific to technology management and coordinates the interaction of all your IT components. System software can be further broken down into two categories—operating system software and utility software.

Operating system software is system software that controls your application software and manages how your hardware devices work together. So, your operating system software helps you perform such functions as multitasking (work with more than one piece of application software at a time), writing information to a storage device, and formatting a disk. It also is your primary interface when you turn on your computer. For example, if you use a Microsoft operating system, the first screen you see is called your Windows desktop screen (see Figure D.4), which is essentially your operating system.

FIGURE D.4
Your Windows Desktop Screen

Popular personal operating system software today includes:

- **Microsoft Windows XP**—Microsoft's newest operating system
- **Microsoft Windows 2000 Millennium (Windows 2000 Me)**—Microsoft's home computer user operating system
- **Microsoft Windows 2000 Professional (Windows 2000 Pro)**—Microsoft's recommendation for people who have a personal computer connected to a network
- **Microsoft Windows NT Workstation**—Microsoft's operating system for high-end personal computers and workstations
- **Linux**—an open-source operating system that seems destined to work better in Internet-based environments as opposed to purely personal environments
- **Mac OS**—Apple's operating system for its personal computers

The second category of system software includes utility software. **Utility software** is software that provides additional functionality to your operating system. However, don't get the idea that utility software is simply "optional" and not required. You definitely need several pieces of utility software—some will come with your operating system and some you'll need to purchase.

The most important utility software today is antivirus software. **Antivirus software** is utility software that scans for and often eliminates viruses in your RAM and on your storage devices (see Figure D.5). Viruses are everywhere today, with 200 to 300 new ones surfacing each month. Viruses can be very destructive to your computer, and you should definitely have antivirus software to combat them.

Other important pieces of utility software include

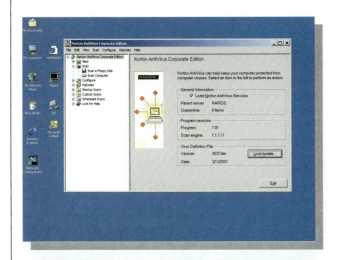

FIGURE D.5
Antivirus Software

- **Connectivity software**—enables you to use your computer to "dial up" or connect to another computer
- **Crash proof software**—saves information if your system crashes and you're forced to turn it off and then back on again
- **Uninstaller software**—removes software you no longer want
- **Disk optimization software**—organizes your information on your hard disk in the most efficient way

You can also buy utility suites. Most utility suites include all the software we just mentioned plus a lot more. The three dominant utility suites today are McAfee Office Pro, Norton SystemWorks Professional Edition, and Ontrack SystemSuite.

Application Software: Your Productivity

Application software is the software designed to help you solve specific problems (personal or business) or perform specific tasks (again, personal or business). Throughout this text, we focus on many types of business application software such as groupware and customer relationship management software. Here, we'll take a brief look at personal productivity software, probably your most immediate need within application software.

Personal productivity software helps you do things that you could otherwise probably do manually. Personal productivity software includes such tools as word processing, spreadsheet, desktop publishing, presentation graphics, personal information management, database management systems, and Web authoring.

These are the software tools that you use on a daily basis to be more efficient and effective. For example, you could write a term paper with a typewriter, but word processing software makes it much faster and includes additional functionality such as colors, borders, automated table of contents, and footnote formatting. You could prepare a home budget with a pencil and paper, but spreadsheet makes it much faster, especially if you want to play the "what if" game or generate graphs of your monthly expenses.

Most people choose to purchase personal productivity software in the form of a suite. A suite is simply a collection of software that costs much less than if you purchased each software package individually. In Table D.5, you can see the major personal productivity software suites and what they include.

We won't go into detail here concerning the exact features of various types of personal productivity software. More than likely, you'll take classes that teach you how to use personal productivity software, namely word processing, spreadsheet, database, presentation graphics, and Web authoring. If not, we would encourage you to search for classes offered in your community that teach these types of software. For that matter, you can learn most of them on your own with a good instruction book.

TABLE D.5 Popular Suites and What They Include

	Microsoft Office XP Pro	Microsoft Office XP Premium	Corel WordPerfect Office 2000 Standard	LotusIBM SmartSuite Millennium
Word processing	Word	Word	WordPerfect	Word Pro
Spreadsheet	Excel	Excel	Quattro Pro	Lotus 1-2-3
Presentation	PowerPoint	PowerPoint	Presentations	Freelance Graphics
Desktop publishing	Publisher	Publisher	Trellix	
Personal finance	Money	Money		
Personal information management			Central	Organizer
Web authoring	FrontPage	FrontPage	Trellix	FastSite
Graphics		PhotoDraw		

Hardware And Software Working Together: Perfect Harmony

Now, that we've looked at hardware and software and categories within each, let's turn our attention to how they work together. Remember first, that no matter what you want to do with your computer, you need both hardware and software. For our example, let's consider that you have an icon on your Windows desktop for a special program that you use frequently. That program allows you to enter two numbers and then it displays the result of adding them together. Of course, we realize that you would never use such a piece of software, but it suits our illustration just fine.

When you double-click on that icon, your mouse sends that command to your CPU. Using the operating system instructions which reside in your internal memory (RAM), your control unit (inside your CPU) determines that you want to launch and use a program—it knows that because you double-clicked on the icon. So, your control unit determines the path to that program and sends a message to your hard disk. That message includes where the program is located on your hard disk and instructions that tell your hard disk to get it and transfer it to your RAM. Then, your control unit tells your RAM to hold the program for processing.

With that stage set, let's look at the software as well as what appears on your screen. The software is shown in Figure D.6 and what appears on your screen is shown in Figure D.7. Looking at Figure D.6, you can see the program contains six lines of code. The first line of code is line 10, with the last being 60. What you need to understand first about how your computer executes a line of code is that one line of code isn't usually a single instruction to your computer; rather, your computer must execute a series of internal instructions to execute a single line of code. Below, we list each line of code and the corresponding series of internal instructions that your computer must perform.

```
10   CLS
20   PRINT "Please enter two numbers"
30   INPUT A, B
40   C = A + B
50   PRINT "The result is:"; C
60   STOP
```

FIGURE D.6

Software Program for Adding Two Numbers

10 CLS

10.1 Your control unit must first send a message to your RAM telling it to pass the first line of code.

10.2 Your control unit interprets the line of code and determines what each hardware device needs to do.

10.3 Your control unit sends a message to your screen, telling your screen to build a small window with no contents.

20 PRINT "Please enter two numbers"

20.1 Your control unit sends a message to your RAM telling it to pass the next line of code.

20.2 Your control unit interprets the line of code (which is a display function) and determines what each hardware device needs to do.

20.3 Your control unit takes what is between quotes (Please enter two numbers), passes it to your screen, and tells your screen to display it.

30 INPUT A, B

30.1 Your control unit sends a message to your RAM telling it to pass the next line of code.

30.2 Your control unit interprets the line of code (which is a data entry function) and determines what each hardware device needs to do.

30.3 Your control unit sends a message to your screen telling it to display a question mark (?).

30.4 Your control unit sends a message to your keyboard telling it to accept two numbers and pass those numbers to RAM.

30.5 Your control unit sends a message to your RAM telling it to accept two numbers from your keyboard and store them in memory positions A and B. (Are you beginning to get the idea?)

40 C = A + B

40.1 Your control unit sends a message to your RAM telling it to pass the next line of code.

40.2 Your control unit interprets the line of code (which is an arithmetic function) and determines what each hardware device needs to do.

40.3 Your control unit sends a message to RAM telling it to pass the contents of A and B to your A/L unit.

40.4 Your control unit sends a message to your A/L unit telling it to accept the two numbers from RAM, add the two numbers together, and pass the result back to RAM.

40.5 Your control unit sends a message to your RAM to accept the result from the A/L unit and store the result in memory position C.

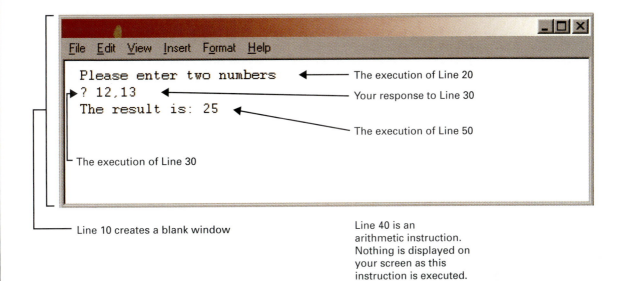

FIGURE D.7

What Appears on Your Screen

50 PRINT "The result is:"; C

50.1 Your control unit sends a message to your RAM telling it to pass the next line of code.

50.2 Your control unit interprets the line of code (which is another display function) and determines what each hardware device needs to do.

50.3 Your control unit sends a message to your RAM telling it to pass the contents of memory position C to your screen.

50.4 Your control unit sends a message to your screen telling it to display the text between quotes (The answer is:) and the contents of memory position C (that was passed to it by RAM).

60 STOP

60.1 Your control unit sends a message to your RAM telling it to pass the next line of code.

60.2 Your control unit interprets the line of code (which is a termination function) and determines that each hardware device needs to do nothing.

That is a very realistic example of what goes inside your computer while you use software. And it's not really that complicated—basically, your control unit interprets each instruction and tells all the other devices what to do. What is amazing is that most software packages include millions of lines of code and require that images, buttons, and icons appear on the screen.

So, now you've read a fairly complete review of both hardware and software. You need them both, no matter what you do. In Figure D.8, you can see how all the technology hardware tools work together as well as the role of software.

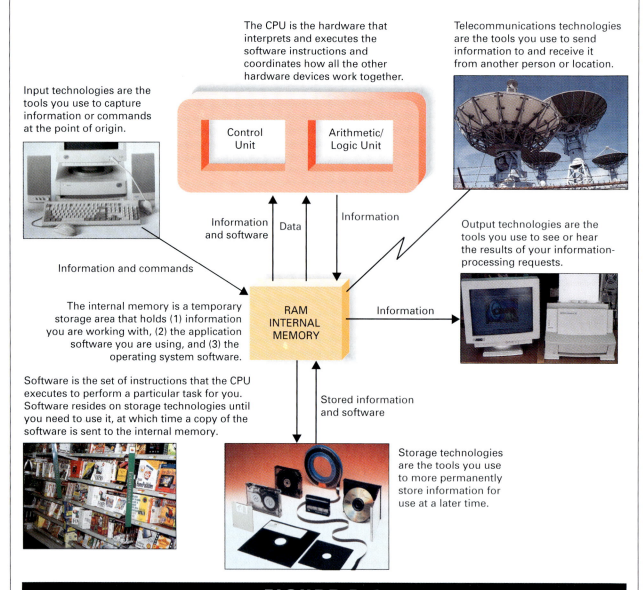

FIGURE D.8

The Complete Technology Tool Set

Buying Your Personal Computer System: What Do You Really Need?

Let's wrap up *Extended Learning Module D* with some helpful tips, hints, and strategies for buying a personal computer. As you go through these, keep in mind that these are our personal recommendations and not set in stone. As you cover them in class, always ask about your particular situation. Both your instructor and classmates can help.

Buy as Much RAM as You Can

RAM holds the application software you're using, your operating system, and the information you're working with. The more RAM you have, the more applications you can run at once and the more information you can work with without performance degradation. You'll especially need a lot of RAM if you want to work with audio and video. We recommend a minimum of 128Mb, but 256Mb is better.

Buy as Fast a CPU as You Can

As we illustrated in the earlier example of what your computer must go through to execute a small program that adds two numbers, the speed of your CPU is essential. We recommend that you always buy the fastest CPU you can. Right now, that may be a CPU with a speed of 1Ghz to 1.5Ghz—buy it if you can.

Buy Personal Productivity Software in a Suite

Even if you won't use all the software in a personal productivity suite, it's still much cheaper than buying the packages individually. Your school's bookstore may have software available at an educational discount. Check there first, then go to the Internet.

Standard Input Devices Are Usually Enough

Most computer systems today come with all the input devices you need—mouse, keyboard, microphone, and scanner. Those will definitely get you started. However, you may want to consider upgrading their quality. For example, you may want to buy a three-button mouse with a scroll ball built in. You may want a better keyboard. These are all inexpensive items. We recommend that you try what you get and then upgrade. Upgrading usually amounts to unplugging one and plugging in another.

Consider the Quality of Your Printer

Many systems today come with free printers. Be careful here—"free" usually means low quality. Even if you're just using your system for school, consider getting a printer with a higher dpi and perhaps even a laser printer.

Buy the Fastest Modem You Can

Modem speed is important if you surf the Internet a great deal. However, check with your ISP first before buying a fast modem. It may be that your ISP supports only speeds up to 56k. If so, there's no need to get a faster modem.

Desktop versus Laptop—Who Knows?

This is a common question—Do you need a desktop computer or a laptop that offers you mobility? Think carefully here—many people buy a laptop because they think it would be "cool" to carry around a computer. But if you use your computer only at home, buy a desktop. Don't tell yourself that you'd use your computer on vacation if you had a laptop—you probably won't. Buy a laptop only if you can really justify using it in more than one location. Why? Because laptops are more expensive than desktops.

Buying a Used Computer—Beware

Computers aren't terribly expensive, but they're also not cheap. To cut expenses, many people look toward buying a used computer. If cost is an overriding concern, then you should consider a used computer; however, used computers have two drawbacks. First, "used" means that the computer is already old and will become obsolete faster. Second, you seldom get any sort of warranty with a used computer. Computers do break down, and they are expensive to repair.

Consider Ergonomics

Finally, you need to consider ergonomics—which includes not only your computer but also your workspace. With respect to your computer, buy a high-resolution monitor that will be less stressful on your eyes and consider various types of keyboards and mice. For your workspace, buy a good chair and desk, which will create less stress on your back and your joints. For a further discussion of ergonomics, review Chapter 8.

Questions and Projects

1. We mentioned that laptops are more expensive than desktop computers. Find a new laptop and a new desktop that have similar features (CPU speed, amount of RAM, and so on). What's the price difference? Why do you think laptops cost more than desktops?

2. What are the storage devices of the computers you evaluated in the first question? How much information does each hold? Is this storage capacity fairly "standard" or high or low?

3. For the personal productivity software suites presented in Table D.5, do a little research. Which is the most popular? What is the cost of each? Does your school offer an educational discount for a particular personal productivity software suite? If so, how much cheaper is it than retail?

4. Does your school have a recommended or required personal productivity software suite? Why or why not?

5. What's the difference in price between an ink jet and a laser printer that have the same dpi? What are the advantages (beyond price) of having an ink jet printer as opposed to a laser printer?

6. New computer systems today often come with price breaks as high as $400 if you subscribe to a particular ISP. How does this work? What are the advantages and disadvantages of this type of price break?

EXTENDED LEARNING MODULE E

THE INTERNET AND THE WORLD WIDE WEB

Perhaps the most visible and explosive information technology tool is the Internet. No matter where you look or what you read, someone always seems to be referring to the Internet. On television commercials, you find Internet addresses displayed (such as http://www.ibm.com for an IBM commercial or http://www.toyota.com for a Toyota commercial). In almost every magazine these days, you'll find articles about the Internet because of its growing significance to our society. Most major business publications, such as *Fortune*, *Forbes*, and *Business Week*, devote entire issues each year to the Internet and how to use it for electronic commerce.

Need further evidence? There were 25 major college football Bowl Games in late 2000 and early 2001. Of those, four were sponsored by dot-com companies, including the micronpc.com Bowl, insight.com Bowl, crucial.com Bowl, and galleryfurniture.com Bowl. Another Bowl Game was the Silicon Valley Football Classic.

The Internet really is everywhere—and it's here to stay. What's really great about the Internet is that it takes only a couple of hours to learn. Despite what you may think, it is undoubtedly one of the easiest technologies ever invented. If you've never cruised or surfed the Internet, the next few pages explain how to do it. After reading those pages and participating in one of the Internet scavenger hunts, you'll be a skilled Internet cruiser (or surfer if you prefer the ocean to the highway). The Internet is so easy and fun that you may find yourself not wanting to leave cyberspace. Of course, beyond being fun to use this technology, the Internet connects you to a world of information to give you leverage in the real world of everyday life, school, and business.

PHOTO ESSAY

A Tour of the Internet

The **Internet** is a vast network of computers that connects millions of people all over the world. Schools, businesses, government agencies, and many others have all connected their internal networks to the Internet, making it truly a large network of networked computers.

The Internet is different from the Web (which we'll discuss in a moment). The Internet is really what makes the Web possible. Think of the Internet as a city's vast plumbing system—the water treatment facility, the pipes, valves, and stations that move water throughout the city, and even the sewer lines. And think of the Web as your water faucet, sink, tub, and drain. You need what's in your house to take a shower as well as the vast plumbing system underneath it. So, the Internet is the backbone of technologies (both hardware and software) that makes it possible for you to use the Web as you see fit.

The **Internet backbone** is the major set of connections for computers on the Internet (see Figure E.1). A **network access point (NAP)** is a point on the Internet where several connections converge. At each NAP is at least one computer that simply routes Internet traffic from one place to another (much like a water station in your city's plumbing system). These NAPs are owned and maintained by a network service provider. A **network service provider (NSP)**, such as MCI or AT&T, owns and maintains routing computers at NAPs and even the lines that connect the NAPs to each other. In Figure E.1, you can see that Dallas is an NAP, with lines converging from Atlanta, Phoenix, Kansas City, and Austin.

At any given NAP, an Internet service provider may connect its computers to the Internet. An **Internet service provider (ISP)** is a company that provides individuals, organizations, and businesses access to the Internet. ISPs include AOL, Juno (which is free), and perhaps even your school. In turn, you "dial up" and connect your computer (called a *client* computer) to an ISP computer (called a *server* computer). So, your ISP provides you access to the Internet (and thus the Web) by allowing you to connect your computer to its computer (which is already connected to the Internet).

FIGURE E.1

The Internet Backbone in the United States

Types of Computers on the Internet

There are many kinds of computers on the Internet—namely, router (which we've already discussed), client, and server computers (see Figure E.2). Your computer that you use to access the Internet and surf the Web is called a *client computer*. Your client computer can be a traditional desktop or laptop computer, a Web or Internet appliance, a PDA, or perhaps even a cell phone.

Internet server computers are computers that provide information and services on the Internet. There are four main types of server computers on the Internet—Web, mail, ftp, and IRC servers. A **Web server** provides information and services to Web surfers. So, when you access http://www.ebay.com, you're accessing a Web server with your client computer. Most often, you'll be accessing and using the services of a Web server.

A **mail server** provides e-mail services and accounts. Many times, mail servers are presented to you as a part of a Web server. For example, Hotmail is a free e-mail server and service provided by MSN. An ***ftp (file transfer protocol) server*** maintains a collection of files that you can download. These files can include software, music files (many in MP3 format), and games. An **IRC (Internet Relay Chat) server** supports your use of discussion groups and chat rooms. IRC servers are popular hosting computers for sites such as http://www.Eopinions.com. There, you can share your opinions about various topics, and the site will even pay you if people read the product reviews you write.

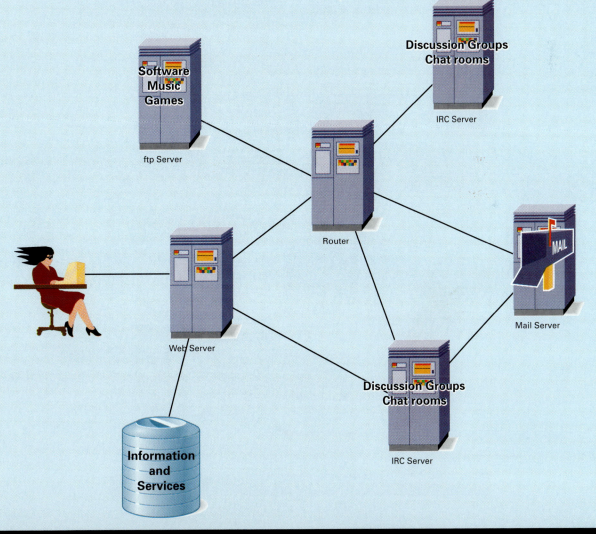

FIGURE E.2

Computers on the Internet

The World Wide Web

The **World Wide Web (Web)** is the Internet in a linked multimedia form. Before the Web, the Internet was all text-based; you saw no icons, you couldn't use a mouse, and sound, animation, and video were an impossibility. In pre-Web days, you had to know where exactly to go on the Internet to find what you needed; cruising, surfing, and searching were not terms associated with the Internet. Now, because of the Web, the Internet supports information in a variety of forms (sound, video, graphics, text, and so on). That information can also be linked to other places that may have similar information.

A **Web site** is a specific location on the Web where you visit, gather information, and perhaps even order products. Each Web site has a Web site address. A **Web site address** is a unique name that identifies a specific site on the Web. Technically, this address is called a domain name. A **domain name** identifies a specific computer on the Web and the main page of the entire site. Most Web sites include several and perhaps hundreds of Web pages. A **Web page** is a specific portion of a Web site that deals with a certain topic (it also has a unique address called a Web page address).

For example, the Web site address for *The USA Today* is http://www.usatoday.com (see Figure E.3). Within that site, you can visit many different pages. For example, you can click on the *Sports* link, which will take you to the sports section (or Web page) within *The USA Today* site. The Web page address for *The USA Today* sports section is http://www.usatoday.com/sports/sfront.htm (see Figure E.3).

FIGURE E.3

The USA Today Web Site and Pages

Interpreting Addresses

Most addresses start with http://www, which stands for hypertext transfer protocol (http) and World Wide Web (www). The remaining portion of the address is unique to each Web site or page. If you visit http://www.etrade.com, for example, you know you're visiting the Web site for the organization Etrade. You can also tell it's a commercial organization by the last three letters—com. This three-letter extension can take on many forms—edu, gov, mil, and many others—and is referred to as the top-level domain (see Figure E.4). So, http://www.ucla.edu is the site address for UCLA, an educational institution.

Some site addresses have two characters that follow after that. In this case, it's identifying the country location of the site. For example, http://www.uts.edu.au is the site address for the University of Technology in the city of Sidney—in Australia.

That's a pretty succinct but thorough introduction to the Internet, the Web, Web sites and pages, and Web addresses. The Web is really easy to use and navigate. With Web browser software, you can go anywhere in the world with a click of your mouse. And it's extremely difficult—if not impossible—to mess up the Web. So, let's get surfing.

Domains	Description
Com	Commercial or for-profit business
Edu	Educational institution
Gov	U.S. government agency
Mil	U.S. military organization
Net	Internet administrative organization
Org	Professional or non-profit organization
Int	International treaties organization

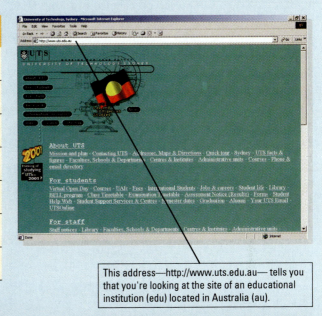

This address—http://www.uts.edu.au— tells you that you're looking at the site of an educational institution (edu) located in Australia (au).

FIGURE E.4

Interpreting Addresses

Navigating the Web with Web Browser Software

The most important software you need to surf the Web is Web browser software. **Web browser software**—as its name implies—is software that allows you to browse or surf the Web. Popular Web browser software today includes Internet Explorer and Netscape Communicator. If you use an ISP such as Juno, it will provide you with its own proprietary Web browser software. It really doesn't matter which you use—all have the same basic functionality and features.

For our purposes, let's use Internet Explorer (see Figure E.5). Across the top of Internet Explorer, you'll find a menu bar. If you click on **File** for example, you can find functions that allow you to save a Web site to your computer (**Save As . . .**) and print a Web site (**Print**). Under **Edit** you can find functions that allow you to copy and paste information. Although we don't have the space to do so here, you should definitely explore all the menu bar features.

Below the menu bar, you'll find a button bar that contains many useful features. For example, the **Back** button will take you back through the list of Web sites you've visited, the **History** button will let you see a list of Web sites you've visited over the last three weeks, and the **Search** button will allow you to find Web sites by key word or words.

Below the button bar, you'll find the **Address** field, which displays the address of where you are on the Web. If you know the address of a site or page you'd like to visit, you can simply click in the **Address** field, type in the address, and hit the enter key or click on the **Go** button.

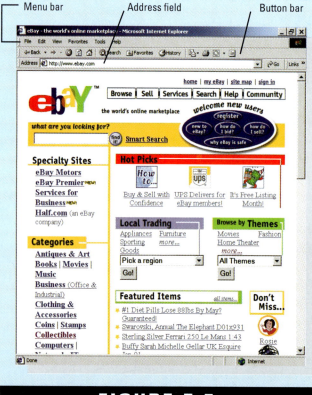

FIGURE E.5

Anatomy of a Web Browser Screen

The majority of your Web browser screen displays the contents of the site or page you're viewing. It also includes a scroll bar to the right that allows you to move up and down to view all the contents. In Figure E.6, you can see that we're currently viewing fatbrain.com (http://www.fatbrain.com). fatbrain.com is a popular site for finding books of a technical nature (as opposed to fiction books).

Within that site, you'll see many links. A **link** (often called a *hypertext link*) is either clickable text or images that take you to a different site or page. For example, if you click on (only once for links) the text "Company Overview," you'll be taken to a Web page that describes the company. This link is in text form, which most often is displayed in blue and underlined. You can also see links in the form of images. For example, the checkered-flag image is a link that will take you to a Web page that lists bestsellers. If you can't readily determine if an image is a link or simply present for aesthetic purposes, move your pointer over it. If it's a link, your pointer will change from an arrow to a hand pointing with one finger.

Once you've linked to a new page or site, it's easy to get back to your original page. All you have to do is click once on the **Back** button in the menu bar.

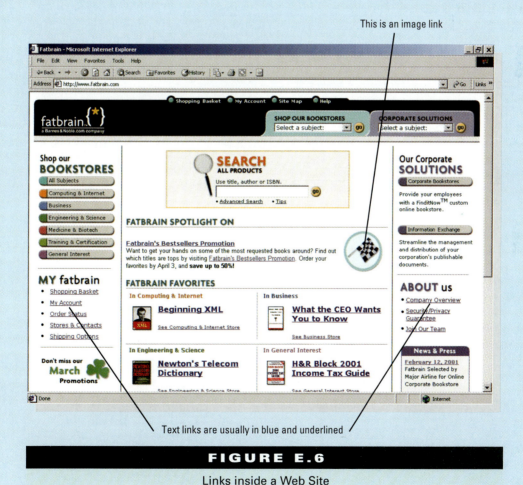

FIGURE E.6
Links inside a Web Site

Finding Sites with a Search Engine

The Web currently includes millions of different sites. Often, you may not know exactly where you want to go, and if this is the case, you can use a search engine. As we discussed in Chapter 5, there are two main types of search engines—directories and true search engines. Directory search engines organize listings of Web sites into hierarchical lists. True search engines, on the other hand, use software agent technologies to search the Internet for key words and place them into indexes.

Suppose, for example, that you wanted to find out who is up for an Academy Award in the year 2001. To do so, you might use a directory-based search engine such as Yahoo! (see Figure E.7). You would first go to the Yahoo! site by typing http:// www.yahoo.com into the address field. Then, you would click on **Arts & Humanities**, **Awards**, **Movies**

FIGURE E.7

Using a Directory-Based Search Engine

and Films@, **Academy Awards**, and **73rd Annual Academy Awards (2001)**. You can then select whatever Web site seems to offer the information you want.

On the other hand, you could use a true search engine, such as Ask Jeeves, to find the same information. Ask Jeeves is a search engine that allows you to enter a question concerning information you'd like to find. To do so, you would first go to Ask Jeeves by typing http://www.askjeeves.com into the address field. Then, you would enter the question, "Who is up for an academy award in 2001" (without the quote marks), and click on **Ask** (see Figure E.8). As you can see in the second screen in Figure E.8, Ask Jeeves then provides a list of Web sites with the information you want.

So, which is better—a directory-based search engine or a true search engine? Well, that depends on you. Some people think in hierarchical terms and prefer directory-based search engines. Besides, directory-based search engines often provide lists of related areas that might be of interest. Other people think in terms of questions and answers and don't care about related areas. Therefore, they use true search engines such as Ask Jeeves. We definitely recommend that you become acquainted with both. Other popular search engines that you might want to explore include Mamma.com (http://www.mamma.com), AltaVista (http://www.altavista.com), Excite (http://www.excite.com), HotBot (http://www.hotbot.com), Lycos (http://www.lycos.com), and WebCrawler (http://www.webcrawler.com).

To help you better learn how to use these and other search engines, try your hand at the scavenger hunts on the next three pages.

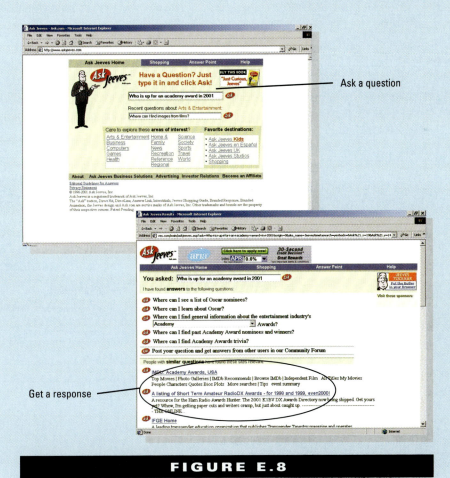

FIGURE E.8

Using a True Search Engine

Scavenger Hunts

For each of the scavenger hunt exercises you find on these pages, find a Web site that provides the appropriate information to answer the question. Record the answer to the exercise and the Web address of the site you found it at in the spaces provided. (You cannot use encyclopedia Web sites such as the one for *Encyclopedia Britannica*.)

Scavenger Hunt 1

1. The color Johnny Cash wears on stage.
   Answer: _____
   http:// _____
2. The location of the convolutions of Broca.
   Answer: _____
   http:// _____
3. The northernmost Scandinavian country.
   Answer: _____
   http:// _____
4. The author of *Stranger in a Strange Land*.
   Answer: _____
   http:// _____
5. What a pluviometer measures.
   Answer: _____
   http:// _____
6. Sergeant Schultz's standard cop-out.
   Answer: _____
   http:// _____
7. The title of Richard Nixon's presidential memoirs.
   Answer: _____
   http:// _____
8. Which pole tilts toward the sun between June 21 and September 21.
   Answer: _____
   http:// _____
9. Who starred in the 1965 Broadway hit *Golden Boy*.
   Answer: _____
   http:// _____
10. Tomorrow's forecast for Dublin.
    Answer: _____
    http:// _____

Scavenger Hunt 2

1. What broccoli and cauliflower were developed from.
   Answer: _____
   http:// _____
2. The author of *Roll Over Beethoven*.
   Answer: _____
   http:// _____
3. The first pope to visit Africa.
   Answer: _____
   http:// _____
4. The location of the pituitary gland.
   Answer: _____
   http:// _____
5. The largest U.S. state east of the Mississippi.
   Answer: _____
   http:// _____
6. The element whose chemical symbol is Pb.
   Answer: _____
   http:// _____
7. In what sports bombs are thrown.
   Answer: _____
   http:// _____
8. How many tusks an Indian rhinoceros has.
   Answer: _____
   http:// _____
9. The world's largest island.
   Answer: _____
   http:// _____
10. The first city with more than one TV station.
    Answer: _____
    http:// _____

Scavenger Hunt 3

1. The boxer whose life story was titled *Raging Bull*.
   Answer: _____
   http:// _____
2. The weight of the moon.
   Answer: _____
   http:// _____
3. The highest mountain in Africa.
   Answer: _____
   http:// _____
4. The Beatles movie that featured the Blue Meanies.
   Answer: _____
   http:// _____
5. Which ear most people can hear better with.
   Answer: _____
   http:// _____
6. What a lacrosse ball is made of.
   Answer: _____
   http:// _____
7. Where L'il Abner and Daisy Mae live.
   Answer: _____
   http:// _____
8. What park contains Firehole River and Fairy Falls.
   Answer: _____
   http:// _____
9. The patron saint of England.
   Answer: _____
   http:// _____
10. Who lives at 39 Stone Canyon Drive.
    Answer: _____
    http:// _____

Scavenger Hunt 4

1. The first woman to race in the Indianapolis 500.
   Answer: _____
   http:// _____
2. The location of Alhambra Palace.
   Answer: _____
   http:// _____
3. The river by which Pocahontas is buried.
   Answer: _____
   http:// _____
4. The color of the first mover in chess.
   Answer: _____
   http:// _____
5. What Jim Henson created.
   Answer: _____
   http:// _____
6. The first domesticated bird.
   Answer: _____
   http:// _____
7. The color of The Maltese Falcon.
   Answer: _____
   http:// _____
8. The most frequently broken bone in the human body.
   Answer: _____
   http:// _____
9. The cathedral in which Prince Charles and Lady Diana were married.
   Answer: _____
   http:// _____
10. The color of Mr. Spock's blood.
    Answer: _____
    http:// _____

Scavenger Hunt 5

1. How many times John Glenn orbited the earth.
   Answer: _____
   http:// _____

2. Bertie Wooster's butler.
   Answer: _____
   http:// _____

3. Where the sport of caber-tossing originated.
   Answer: _____
   http:// _____

4. The state in which John F. Kennedy is buried.
   Answer: _____
   http:// _____

5. What a prestidigitator is.
   Answer: _____
   http:// _____

6. The world's largest news agency.
   Answer: _____
   http:// _____

7. Who took dictation from Perry Mason.
   Answer: _____
   http:// _____

8. What the Seine river empties into.
   Answer: _____
   http:// _____

9. The father of the Declaration of Independence.
   Answer: _____
   http:// _____

10. The colors of the Italian flag.
    Answer: _____
    http:// _____

Scavenger Hunt 6

1. The only U.S. president born on July 4.
   Answer: _____
   http:// _____

2. The author of *Marjorie Morningstar*.
   Answer: _____
   http:// _____

3. The largest city in Alaska.
   Answer: _____
   http:// _____

4. The first U.S. billionaire.
   Answer: _____
   http:// _____

5. What is added to water to make tonic water.
   Answer: _____
   http:// _____

6. The baseball player known as "Charley Hustle."
   Answer: _____
   http:// _____

7. The age at which adolescence is considered to end.
   Answer: _____
   http:// _____

8. Olive Oyl's brother.
   Answer: _____
   http:// _____

9. The winner of the 1968 California Democratic primary.
   Answer: _____
   http:// _____

10. The world's largest cathedral.
    Answer: _____
    http:// _____

EXTENDED LEARNING MODULE F

OBJECT-ORIENTED TECHNOLOGIES

Object-oriented—it's one of the hottest topics in information technology right now, and it's destined to occupy the spotlight for many years to come. Every computer person and IT specialist is scrambling to learn how to write software in object-oriented programming languages, create databases using object-oriented database management systems, and design new systems using object-oriented analysis and design. Every software provider—such as Netscape, Microsoft, Borland, Corel, and IBM—is in the midst of changing its personal productivity software so that it's *object-oriented*. Below, you can review the object-oriented representation for the video rental store we discussed in Chapter 3.

But what is object-oriented? Why are object-oriented concepts and techniques becoming so popular? Why is knowing something about object-oriented concepts and techniques important to you as a knowledge worker? These are all great questions, and we hope to answer them here. We certainly don't claim that you'll be an object-oriented expert just by reading the next few pages, but you will have a good understanding of the whole object-oriented environment and why everyone seems to be moving toward objects.

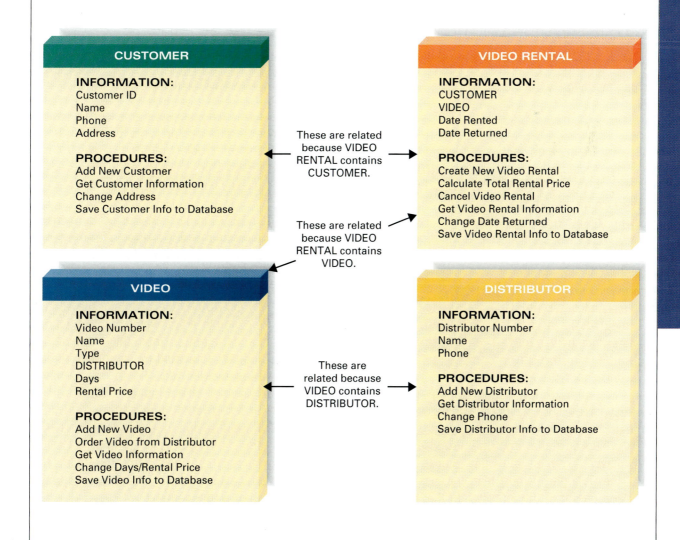

PHOTO ESSAY

What Does It Mean to Be Object-Oriented?

An ***object*** is a software module containing information that describes an entity class along with a list of procedures that can act on the information describing the entity class. So an ***object-oriented (O-O) approach*** is any approach—perhaps a programming language or a DBMS—that combines information and procedures into a single object. For example, the STUDENT object at your school contains information about you as well as the procedures to work with your information. Some of these procedures include the ability to change your address, assign you a major, and specify a graduation date.

Combining information and procedures is quite different from other approaches. Most often, information is stored separately from procedures. In other approaches it's possible to have the information but not be able to do anything with it (because you may not have the procedures). Likewise, you could have the procedures (in the form of software) but not be able to do anything with them because you don't have any information to work with.

A Home Stereo System

For a good analogy think of a home stereo system as an object-oriented system with each of the components being an object. The objects in a typical home stereo include an amplifier, a DVD player, a cassette deck, an equalizer, and a set of speakers. Each of these objects works with one specific group of information and has procedures for working with just that information. The information for the DVD player, for example, is the DVD itself. The methods in the DVD player include how to read the music from the DVD, in what order to play songs according to how you programmed it, and so on. But what the DVD player can't do is actually output the music for you to hear.

Why? Because that's not the responsibility of the DVD player. So, when you want to hear music on a DVD, the DVD player must read the music from the DVD and pass it to the amplifier. In that object, you can manipulate the volume. In fact, manipulating the volume of the music is a primary method of the amplifier object. From there the music is passed to the speakers with associated volume information.

Thus each component in a home stereo system really is an object. As an object, each component works with only certain information and performs certain functions. If one component needs another function performed, it must send a message to another object (or component) that can perform that function.

One other thing you should notice about objects is that a complete system needs only one object of each kind. Consider the speakers. You don't need one set of speakers for the DVD player, one set for the amplifier, and one set for the cassette player. Instead, each of those components can use the speaker object by simply sending to it the music to be played (through the amplifier object).

A Resort Rental Agency

As a business example, let's consider the use of O-O concepts for a resort rental agency. In Figure F.1, you can see three object representations for a resort rental agency that rents vacation properties to renters on a weekly basis—RENTER, RENT CONTRACT, and VACATION PROPERTY. Let's take a closer look at the RENT CONTRACT object. This object contains information concerning a rent contract and the procedures that allow you to perform such functions as creating a new rent contract, calculating total rent, and saving contract information to a database. Notice also that the RENT CONTRACT object contains the RENTER object. So, for example, if you were completing a new rent contract and the renter stated that his or her address had changed, you could easily change the address while using the RENT CONTRACT object. Objects as a part of another object makes logical business sense. For our resort rental agency from a technical point of view, we're saying that the RENT CONTRACT object contains both the RENTER and VACATION PROPERTY objects. In business terms, this means that our resort rental agency rents a vacation property to a renter by creating a rent contract.

Photo Essay: What Does It Mean to Be Object-Oriented? **413**

To see how this works, let's examine the procedures list more closely for RENTER and RENT CONTRACT. In Figure F.2, we've detailed what some of those procedures involve. When you begin creating a new rent contract (using the RENT CONTRACT object), the first step in that procedure involves calling the *Get Renter Info* procedure in the RENTER object. You are then prompted to enter the renter's name, after which the *Get Renter Info* procedure attempts to find a match in the database. When a match is found, *Get Renter Info* sends the renter's information back to *Create New Rent Contract* in the RENT CONTRACT object. You then see the renter's information on the screen and are asked if the information is correct. If it's not, the next step is to call the *Change Address* procedure in the RENTER object which would prompt you for the new address and then store the renter's new information (by calling the *Save Renter Info to Database* procedure). ❖

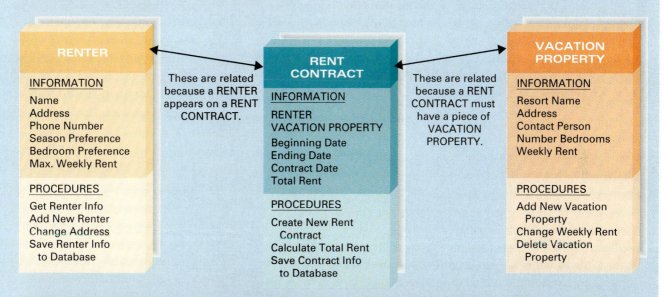

FIGURE F.1
An Object Representation of a Resort Rental Agency

RENTER OBJECT PROCEDURES

GET RENTER INFO
1. Accept renter name from user
2. Retrieve renter info from database
3. If no match found
   3.1 Display "Invalid renter name"
   3.2 Go to 1
4. Return renter info

CHANGE ADDRESS
1. Accept new address from user
2. Call **Save Renter Info to Database**

SAVE RENTER INFO TO DATABASE
1. Write renter info to database

RENT CONTRACT OBJECT PROCEDURES

CREATE NEW RENT CONTRACT
1. Call **Get Renter Info** in *RENTER* object and return information
2. Display information and ask user if address is correct
3. If answer is no
   3.1 Call **Change Address** in *RENTER* object ...
9. Call **Calculate Total Rent**
10. Ask user if total rent is okay
11. If answer is yes
   11.1 Call **Save Contract Info to Database**

CALCULATE TOTAL RENT
1. Number weeks = (ending date – beginning date) /7
2. Total rent = number weeks * weekly rent

SAVE CONTRACT INFO TO DATABASE
1. Write contract info to database

FIGURE F.2
Object Interaction through Procedures

Why Are Object-Oriented Concepts and Techniques Becoming So Popular?

PHOTO ESSAY

O-O Concepts Closely Model How You View the World

In business you actually view a given business process as a combination of information and the procedures that you need to act on that information. In a payroll environment for example, you view employees (which would be an object) as information—name, salary, number of dependents, and so on—and procedures that act on that information. Some of these procedures include adding a new employee, changing an employee's salary, calculating gross pay, and making the necessary deductions to calculate net pay. So, O-O concepts basically provide the same technical view as your logical business view.

O-O concepts make good business sense, and they also make sense in your personal life. Have you ever purchased a product that requires "some assembly" such as a mountain bike or gas grill? Upon opening the box and spreading out the contents you immediately reach for the instruction booklet (which is an example of an object-oriented approach). In the instructions you'll find a detailed set of steps concerning assembly along with a description of the various parts. You won't find the set of instructions separate from the description of the parts—they are combined because it makes the most sense to do so.

Reuse Leads to Productivity

From our rental resort agency example, you can easily see another reason why people are beginning to use an object-oriented approach—*reuse*. In an O-O environment, you simply define a procedure once and then allow any other object to use it as necessary. This reuse principle has significantly reduced the time it takes to develop software because procedures are only defined once and then literally reused time and time again. A good analogy here is that of our amplifier in a home stereo. You just need one amplifier; all other components—the DVD player, cassette deck, and equalizer—share in the use of the amplifier.

According to a survey of the 30 largest insurance companies in the United States, more than two-thirds include objects in their IT strategy. Why? Because a significant percentage of IT budgets in the insurance industry goes toward maintaining and modifying existing systems. For insurance companies, object technologies promise to reduce the time it takes to modify and maintain existing systems through code reuse. This is true not only for the insurance industry, but also for most other industries.

O-O Databases Support Complex and Unique Data Types

Besides combining information and procedures into a single object, O-O databases (discussed in Chapter 3) also work better with complex data types than other database models. Complex data types include diagrams, schematic drawings, video, sound, and text documents. The relational database model, although it may allow you to store and view such data types, does not include good mechanisms for allowing you to manipulate and change information within those data types. For example, you can include a CAD drawing of a part as a field in a relational database table, but it's literally impossible to work with any specific information in the drawing (such as cuts, specific components, and the ordering of assembly) without having that information also stored in other fields of the same table. O-O databases don't restrict information storage to two-dimensional tables, which gives you greater flexibility in storing and defining procedures that work with complex data types. In fact, most of today's multimedia applications rely on the use of objects and object-oriented databases.

Most other database models also restrict you to working with specific data types—alphabetic, numeric, decimal, currency, date, and so on. In an O-O database environment, however, you can create and work with data types that may be unique to a certain business process. In our earlier example of the resort rental agency, the VACATION PROPERTY object includes information concerning address. With an O-O database, you could easily define that this field includes not only a street address but also a unit number. You could then define a procedure that requires the entry of both. This is an example of a unique data type that requires not only a street address, but also a unit number.

O-O Concepts Support Reengineering Efforts

Many businesses today are seeking to reengineer business processes (we discuss business process reengineering in Chapter 7). Many of the "traditional" IT systems that support business processes separate information from procedures. Often, this separation is not closely aligned with how many people view the supported business processes. The Commercial Airline Group at Boeing, for example, has decided to use object technologies to reengineer its business processes—including manufacturing, procurement, finance, and sales. When complete, the new object-based system will be used by more than 55,000 Boeing employees.

O-O Technologies Are Becoming More Prevalent

One of the most significant drawbacks to the use of O-O concepts in recent years has been the lack of O-O technologies that are specifically designed to work with objects. Traditional third-generation programming languages such as COBOL and FORTRAN and database query languages such as SQL are designed to treat information and procedures separately. Today, however, a growing number of fourth- and fifth-generation languages, natural languages, and DBMS packages directly support the use of objects. Some of these new programming languages include C++, Smalltalk, OOCOBOL, Eiffel, Objective-C, CLOS, Actor, Object Pascal, and Java. Of all these, you can expect Java to have the most widespread use.

O-O Concepts Are Well-Suited to Client/Server

In *Extended Learning Module C*, we explore client/server as the emerging blueprint for organizational networks, and most organizations are choosing to develop client/server networks through object-oriented technologies. Formally defined, a **client/server network** is a network in which one or more computers are servers and provide services to the other computers which are called clients. Spreading objects across a client/server network makes logical sense: client workstations contain objects with local procedures for working with local information, and servers contain objects with global procedures for working with global information. To see how objects work in a client/server environment, let's look at the example of a client/server model 3 implementation found in *Extended Learning Module C.*

In a model 3 client/server implementation model, the server handles the entire data management function, the client handles the entire presentation function, and both share in processing the logic or business rules. So the server object contains procedures for retrieving and storing information (data management) and for processing some of the logic or business rules. Likewise, the client object contains procedures for some of the logic or business rules and for presenting information (the presentation function). To demonstrate the model 3 implementation, we assume that you are the manager of the manufacturing division in an organization and need to give pay raises to each of your employees. For assigning pay raises, you also have to follow several rules—some for just your division and some for all organizational employees.

In an object-oriented environment, your client workstation contains an object for assigning pay raises to manufacturing division employees according to manufacturing division rules and formatting and presenting information to you. The server contains an object for assigning pay raises according to organizational rules and for retrieving information from and saving information to the database. In Figure F.3, you can see how this actually works.

First, your MANUFACTURING DIVISION EMPLOYEE object (which we'll call the client object) asks you for an employee and sends a message to the ORGANIZATIONAL EMPLOYEE object (which we'll call the server object) to retrieve that employee's information from the database and return it. Your client object then executes the rules for determining pay raises for manufacturing employees, displays that information to you, and sends the proposed pay raise to the server object. The server object then executes the organizational rules for assigning pay raises and returns the modified pay raise to your client object. Your client object then displays that information to you and allows you to submit the finalized pay raise for processing to the

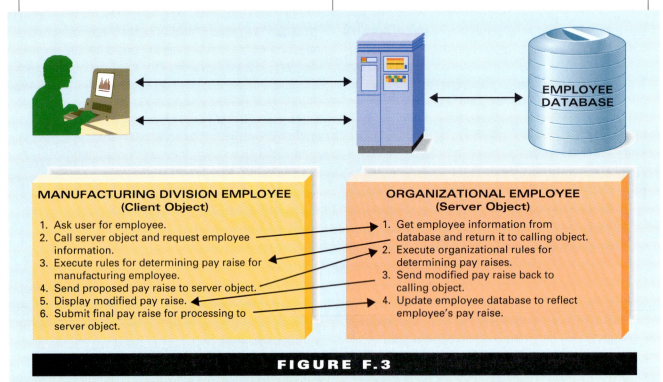

FIGURE F.3

Object-Oriented Technologies and Client/Server—The Perfect Match

server object. Finally, the server object updates the Employee database to reflect the employee's pay raise.

And while you're assigning pay raises to manufacturing division employees, other managers could be doing the same for their employees. In this instance, you and the other managers essentially share the server object—another excellent example of reuse. ❖

So Why Are Object-Oriented Concepts and Techniques Important to You?

As we close our discussion of O-O concepts and techniques, let's address the most important question of all; that is, "Why is knowing something about O-O concepts and techniques important to you as a knowledge worker?" After all, we've already stated that the use of objects is really transparent to you. For example, when you access a Web page with animated movement, you actually get an object that contains information (a description of the animated figures, their color, shape, and so on) and procedures that act on that information (how the figures are supposed to move, their speed, and so on). But if this is transparent to you, why is it important that you understand it?

Well, recall from Chapter 1 that an important part of knowledge worker computing includes developing some systems for yourself or a group. That's why you learned how to build your own database in *Extended Learning Module B*. The simple fact of the matter is that you will—in all probability—develop some of your own systems. And as you do, you'll probably do so using object-oriented technologies.

Some of the tools you might use in the future to develop your own systems are called enterprise software, which we discussed in Chapter 7. Right now, they are indeed "enterprise" in nature; however, you can expect that to change over time. Eventually, we believe that enterprise software will be widely used by knowledge workers to develop their own systems. And it makes sense. Enterprise software supports enterprise resource planning (ERP), which takes a holistic view of your organization and its specific information technology needs. Using enterprise software, then, your organization can build objects that can be reused in all departments and business units. And you can reuse those objects to build your own applications (knowledge worker computing).

GLOSSARY

A

Ad hoc decision also called a **nonrecurring decision**; a decision that you make infrequently (perhaps only once) and you may even have different criteria for determining the best solution each time.

Ad hoc report a report you can generate whenever you want.

Adaptivity the ability of an intelligent agent to discover, learn, and take action independently.

Affiliate program an arrangement made between e-commerce sites that directs traffic from one site to the other and by which, if a sale is made as a result, the originating site receives a commission.

Alliance partner company that you do business with on a regular basis in a cooperative fashion, usually facilitated by IT systems.

Antivirus software utility software that scans for and often eliminates viruses in your RAM and on your storage devices.

Application development facility a wealth of building blocks that you can use to create applications quickly, so teams can literally "get to work."

Application generation subsystem facilities to help you develop transaction-intensive applications in a database environment.

Application software the software designed to help you solve specific problems (personal or business) or perform specific tasks (again, personal or business).

Arithmetic/logic unit (A/L unit) the part of the central processing unit that performs all arithmetic operations and all logic operations.

Artificial intelligence (AI) the science of making machines imitate human thinking and behavior.

Asynchronous transfer mode (ATM) is a transmission mode that divides long messages into smaller units called cells.

Atomic primary key a primary key that uses only one field to create a unique description.

Automatic speech recognition (ASR) not only captures spoken words, but also distinguishes word groupings to form sentences.

Autonomy the ability of an intelligent agent to act without your telling it every step to take.

B

B2B marketplace an Internet-based service which brings together many buyers and sellers.

Bandwidth (capacity) refers to the amount of information that a communications medium can transfer in a given amount of time.

Banner ad a little ad that appears on Web sites.

Bar code reader captures information in a predetermined format that exists as a series of vertical bars whose width and distance apart determine a number.

Biometrics the use of physical characteristics – such as your fingerprint, the blood vessels in the retina of your eye, the sound of your voice, or perhaps even your breath – to provide identification.

Black-hat hacker a hacker who exploits or destroys information, steals passwords, or otherwise causes harm.

Bluetooth a technology that provides entirely wireless connections for all kinds of communication devices.

Bridge an internetworking unit that connects two networks of the same kind.

Bus topology a network topology in which all computers are connected to a single communications medium over which all communications travel.

Business process a standardized set of activities that accomplishes a specific task, such as processing a customer's order.

Business process reengineering (BPR) the reinventing of processes within a business.

Business to business (B2B) companies whose customers are primarily other businesses.

Business to consumer (B2C) companies whose customers are primarily individuals.

Buyer agent also called a shopping bot; an intelligent agent that looks on the Web for the product of your choice and brings the information back to you.

Buyer power high when buyers have many choices of whom to buy from and low when their choices are few.

C

Cable modem device that uses your TV cable to deliver an Internet connection.

Capital investment analysis calculating a quantitative measure of IT systems value.

Cat 3 (Category 3) ordinary phone cable.

Cat 5 (Category 5) a better-constructed version of the Cat 3 twisted-pair cable used for the telephone system.

Catalog hub similar to an MRO hub except that it is industry-specific.

Cave automatic virtual environment (CAVE) a special 3-D, virtual reality room that can display images of other people located in other CAVEs all over the world.

CD-R an optical storage device on which you can write information, but only once.

CD-ROM the most common type of optical disk.

Central processing unit (CPU) the hardware in an IT system that interprets and executes the software instructions and coordinates how all the other hardware devices work together.

Centralized database a database that maintains all database information in one location.

Character the smallest logical unit of information for a knowledge worker.

Chief information officer (CIO) the strategic level IT manager who directs all IT systems and personnel while communicating directly with the highest levels of the organization.

Choice the third step in the decision-making process where you decide on a plan to address the problem or opportunity.

Click-throughs a count of the number of people who visit one site and click on a banner ad and are taken to the site of the advertiser.

Clicks-and-mortar a retailer, like Nordstrom, which has both an Internet presence and physical stores.

Client/server network a network in which one or more computers are servers and provide services to the other computers which are called clients.

Coaxial cable (coax) one central wire surrounded by insulation, a metallic shield, and a final case of insulating material.

Cold site an alternative site where a company sets up its IT system in case of a disaster. A cold site does not have computer equipment installed but has backup power generators, a sprinkler system, a security system, and so on.

Collaborative filtering a technique to enable a Web site to support personalization.

Collaborative planning, forecasting, and replenishment (CPFR) a concept that encourages and facilitates collaborative processes among members of a supply chain.

Communications media the paths, or physical channels, in a network over which information travels from one place to another.

Communications processor a hardware device that facilitates the flow of information between networks or computers.

Communications satellite microwave repeaters in space.

Communications service provider a third-party who furnishes the conduit for information.

Comparative report a report that shows two or more sets of similar information in an attempt to illustrate a relationship.

Competitive advantage providing a product or service in a way that customers value more than the competition's.

Complementor a company that provides products and services that complement the offerings of another company and thereby extends its value-adding capabilities to its customers.

Composite primary key a primary key that uses more than one field to create a unique description.

Computer-aided software engineering (CASE) tool software that automates some or all steps in the systems development life cycle.

Computer network also called a network; two or more computers connected so that they can communicate with each other and share information, software, peripheral devices, and/or processing power.

Computer virus software that is written with malicious intent to cause annoyance or damage.

Connectivity software enables you to use your computer to "dial up" or connect to another computer.

Contingency plan the documentation of the possibility of losing an IT system and the formulation of procedures to minimize the damage.

Continuous automatic speech recognition an automatic speech recognition system that can process continuous streams of words—that is, normal speech patterns.

Control unit the part of the central processing unit that interprets software instructions and literally tells the other hardware devices what to do, based on the software instructions.

Conversion rate the percentage of customers who visit a site who actually buy something.

Cookie a small record deposited on your hard drive by a Web site containing information about you.

Copyright legal protection afforded an expression of an idea, like a song or a video game.

Cost-benefit analysis the process of evaluating prospective IT systems by comparing system costs with system benefits.

Cracker a hacker with malicious intent.

Crash proof software utility software that saves information if your system crashes and you're forced to turn it off and then back on again.

Creative design one that solves the business problem in a new and highly effective way rather than the same ways others have solved it.

Critical success factor (CSF) a factor critical to organizational success.

Cross-cultural diversity the difference in behavior and attitude between people from different cultures.

Crossover part of a genetic algorithm where portions of good outcomes are combined in the hope of creating an even better outcome.

Culture the collective personality of a nation or society, encompassing language, traditions, currency, religion, history, music, and acceptable behavior, among other things.

Culture shock the disorientation and confusion that you experience when you're accustomed to one culture and suddenly find yourself in another, where signals, behavior, and beliefs are different.

Customer integrated system (CIS) a system which is an extension of a transaction processing system that places technology in the hands of an organization's customers and allows them to process their own transactions.

Customer moment of value providing service when the customer wants it (time), where the customer wants it (location), how the customer wants it (form), and in a manner guaranteed to the customer (perfect delivery).

Cybersickness eyestrain, simulator sickness, and flashbacks that many people experience who participate in virtual reality environments.

D

Data any raw facts or observations that describe a particular phenomenon.

Data administration the function in an organization that plans for, oversees the development of, and monitors the information resource.

Data administration subsystem helps you manage the overall database environment by providing facilities for backup and recovery, security management, query optimization, reorganization, concurrency control, and change management.

Data definition subsystem helps you create and maintain the data dictionary and define the structure of the files in a database.

Data dictionary contains the logical structure of information in a database.

Data management the component of a decision support system (DSS) that performs the function of storing and maintaining the information that you want your DSS to use.

Data manipulation subsystem helps you add, change, and delete information in a database and mine it for valuable information.

Data mart a subset of a data warehouse in which only a focused portion of the data warehouse information is kept.

Data mining tool a software tool you use to query information in a data warehouse.

Data-mining agent an intelligent agent that operates in a data warehouse discovering information.

Data warehouse a logical collection of information—gathered from many different operational databases—that supports business analysis activities and decision-making tasks.

Database a collection of information that you organize and access according to the logical structure of that information.

Database administration the function in an organization that is responsible for the more technical and operational aspects of managing the information contained in operational databases.

Database management system (DBMS) the software you use to specify the logical organization for a database and access it.

Database management system engine (DBMS engine) accepts logical requests from the various other DBMS subsystems, converts them to their physical equivalent, and actually accesses the database and data dictionary as they exist on a storage device.

Decentralized computing an environment in which an organization splits computing power and locates it in functional business areas as well as on the desktops of knowledge workers.

Decision support system (DSS) a highly flexible and interactive IT system that is designed to support decision making when the problem is not structured.

Demand aggregation combines purchase requests from multiple buyers into a single large order which justifies a discount from the business.

Denial-of-service an attack that floods a Web site with so many requests for information that it slows down or crashes.

Design the second step of the decision-making process. It's where you consider possible ways of solving the problem, filling the need, or taking advantage of the opportunity.

Digital divide the fact that different peoples, cultures, and areas of the world or within a nation do not have the same access to information and telecommunications technologies.

Digital signature a digital code that can be attached to an electronic document to uniquely identify the sender, much the same as your handwritten signature uniquely identifies you.

Digital subscriber line (DSL) high-speed Internet connection using phone lines, which allows you to use your phone for voice communication at the same time.

Digital video disk (DVD) a form of magneto-optical disk storage technologies.

Direct material a material that is used in production in a manufacturing company or is placed on the shelf for sale in a retail environment.

Directory a search engine that organizes listings into hierarchical lists.

Disaster recovery cost curve charts (1) the cost to your organization of the unavailability of information and technology and (2) the cost to your organization of recovering from a disaster over time.

Disaster recovery plan is the documentation of the possibility of losing an IT system and the formulation of procedures to minimize the damage.

Discrete automatic speech recognition an automatic speech recognition system which requires that you pause between each spoken word.

Disintermediation by using the Internet as a delivery vehicle, intermediate players in a distribution channel can be bypassed.

Disk optimization software utility software that organizes your information on your hard disk in the most efficient way.

Disk storage technology a storage technology that separates the storage medium (called a "disk") into tracks, with each track divided into several sectors.

Distributed database a database in which information is distributed to various locations.

Distribution chain the path followed from the originator of a product or service to the end consumer.

Domain expert the person who provides the domain expertise in the form of problem-solving strategies.

Domain name identifies a specific computer on the Web and the main page of the entire site.

Dot matrix printer a printer that uses a matrix of pins to form characters and then strikes those pins through a printer ribbon onto a page.

E

E-tailer an Internet retail site.

EDIFACT protocol for transmitting commonly formatted information in electronic data interchange (EDI) transactions.

Electronic bill presentment and payment (EBPP) send us our bills over the Internet and give us an easy way to pay them if the amount looks correct.

Electronic cash (e-cash; digital cash) an electronic representation of cash.

Electronic commerce is commerce, but it is commerce accelerated and enhanced by IT, in particular, the Internet. It enables customers, consumers, and companies to form powerful new relationships that would not be possible without the enabling technologies.

Electronic data interchange (EDI) is the direct computer-to-computer transfer of transaction information contained in standard business documents such as invoices and purchase orders, in a standard format.

Electronic meeting software lets a team have a "virtual" meeting through information technology.

Electronic meeting support the component of groupware that helps you schedule meetings and carry out those meetings.

Emerging technology a technology that falls into one of the two following categories: (1) it is so new that most businesses haven't exploited it or (2) it is fairly well-established, but businesses haven't fully exploited it.

Encryption the process of scrambling a message so that it can't be read until it's unscrambled.

Enterprise resource planning (ERP) the coordinated planning of all an organization's resources involved in the production, development, selling, and servicing of goods and services.

Enterprise software a suite of software that includes (1) a set of common business applications, (2) tools for modeling how the entire organization works, and (3) development tools for building applications unique to your organization.

Entity class a concept—typically people, places, or things—about which you wish to store information and that you can identify with a unique key.

Entity-relationship (E-R) diagram a graphic method of representing entity classes and their relationships.

Entry barrier a product or service feature that customers have come to expect from companies in a particular industry.

Erasable optical disk the disks used in magneto-optical disk storage technologies.

Ergonomics the study of how to design and arrange your workplace so that you can achieve maximum productivity, reducing discomfort and adverse health effects.

Ethernet the most common protocol for connecting components in a LAN.

Ethernet card the most common type of network interface card.

Ethics sets of principles or standards that help guide behavior, actions, and choices.

Exception report a report that shows only a subset of available information based on some selection criteria.

Executive information system (EIS) a highly interactive management information system combined with decision support systems and artificial intelligence for helping managers identify and address problems and opportunities.

Expert system an artificial intelligence system that applies reasoning capabilities to reach a conclusion.

Explanation module the part of an expert system where the "why" information, supplied by the domain expert, is stored to be accessed by knowledge workers who want to know why the expert system asked a question or reached a conclusion.

External database a database that exists outside the organization.

External hard disk sits outside the cabinet of your computer.

External information information that describes the environment surrounding the organization.

Extranet an intranet that is restricted to an organization and certain outsiders, such as customers and suppliers.

F

Fair Use Doctrine allows you to use copyrighted material in certain situations.

Fault tolerant computer also called a redundant computer; a computer that has built-in backup systems that take over when a primary component fails.

Feasibility review the reviewing of a proposed system to determine if it is feasible from a cost, technical, and time point of view.

Feature analysis the first step in automatic speech recognition; it captures your words as you speak into a microphone, eliminates any background noise, and actually converts the digital signals of your speech into phonemes.

Fiber distributed data interface (FDDI) a communications standard for connecting high-speed local area networks or links among geographically dispersed LANs.

Field a logical grouping of characters.

Financial EDI the use of EDI for payments.

File a logical grouping of records.

Firewall designed to protect private networks, typically intranets and extranets.

First mover the company first to market with a new IT-based product or service.

Five forces model a model developed to determine the relative attractiveness of an industry.

Flaming the distribution of an online communication that offends someone because of the use of obscene, derogatory, or inappropriate language.

Flat panel display on-screen technology for portable systems that is now also being used for desktop systems.

Foreign key a primary key of one file that also appears in another file.

Formatted OCR a device that reads a set of symbols whose format has been standardized by the American National Standards Institute (ANSI).

ftp (file transfer protocol) server a computer that maintains a collection of files that you can download.

Fuzzy logic a method of working with "fuzzy" information; that is, information that is incomplete, ambiguous, or imprecise.

G

Gateway an internetworking unit that connects networks that are completely dissimilar with respect to how they work and communicate internally.

Genetic algorithm an artificial intelligence system that mimics the evolutionary, survival-of-the-fittest process to generate increasingly better solutions to a problem.

Geographic information system (GIS) a decision support system designed specifically to work with spatial information.

Global positioning system (GPS) a collection of 24 earth-orbiting satellites that continuously transmit radio signals you can use to determine where you are.

Global digital divide the term used specifically to describe differences in IT access and capabilities between different countries or regions of the world.

Global reach the ability of an organization to extend its reach to customers anywhere there is an Internet connection, and at a much lower cost.

Globalization a characteristic of today's business environment. It simply states that business today is global business; customers, suppliers, distributors, retailers, and competitors exist all over the world for any type of business.

Glove an input device in virtual reality that captures and records the shape and movement of your hand and fingers and the strength of your hand and finger movements.

Graphics adapter card connects the monitor to the rest of the hardware.

Group decision support system (GDSS) a type of decision support system that facilitates the formulation of and solution to problems by a team.

Group document database a powerful storage facility for organizing and managing all documents related to specific teams.

Group scheduling software provides facilities for maintaining the day-to-day electronic calendars of team members and evaluating those calendars to schedule optimal meeting times.

Groupware the popular term for the software component that supports the collaborative efforts of a team.

H

Hacker a very knowledgeable computer user who uses his/her knowledge to invade other peoples' computers.

Hacktivist (cyber terrorist) a politically motivated hacker.

Hard card a storage technology that exists on a board that can be inserted into an expansion slot on your computer.

Hard disk cartridge a storage technology in which multiple disks or platters can be easily removed from the disk drive and replaced with another cartridge of disks or platters.

Hard disk pack a hard disk cartridge for large computer systems.

Hardware the physical devices in technology such as your printer, monitor, CPU chip, and disk.

Headset a combined input and output device in virtual reality that (1) captures and records the movements of your head and (2) displays various views of an environment on a screen that covers your entire field of vision.

Hot site a separate and fully equipped facility to which you can move immediately after a disaster and resume business.

I

Image scanning an input device that captures information (usually pictures, diagrams, and graphs) that is not in a predetermined format.

Impact printer a printer that strikes the page with some sort of mechanism.

Implementation the final step in the decision-making process where you put your plan into action.

Indirect material a material that is necessary for running a modern corporation, but does not relate to the company's primary business activities.

Inference engine the processing component of an expert system. It reasons through your problem facts and the domain expertise in the knowledge base to reach a conclusion.

Information data that has a particular meaning within a specific context.

Information age how today's business environment is characterized. It is a time when businesses depend on their information and when knowledge is power.

Information-literate knowledge worker a knowledge worker who can define what information is needed, knows how and where to obtain that information, understands the meaning of the information once received, and can act appropriately, based on the information, to help the organization achieve the greatest advantage. In all instances, an information-literate knowledge worker always uses information according to ethical and legal constructs.

Information partnership two or more companies cooperating by integrating their IT systems, thereby providing customers with the best of what each can offer.

Information technology (IT) any computer-based tool that people use to work with information and support the information and information-processing needs of an organization.

Information technology fusion (IT fusion) this occurs when the information technology within your organization is indistinguishable from the business processes and the people who exploit the information technology.

Information technology systems risk the possibility that a system will not achieve the predicted benefits.

Infrared an unguided communications medium that uses a red light (below the visibility of the human eye) to transmit information.

Ink jet printer a printer that sprays ink onto a page to create letter quality output.

Innovation the process of devising new ways to do things in new and creative ways.

Input technologies the tools you use to capture information or commands at the point of origin.

Instance an occurrence of an entity class that can be uniquely described.

Intangible benefit a systems benefit that cannot be monetarily quantified.

Integrated CASE tool a CASE tool which supports the entire systems development life cycle, from planning through support.

Integrated services digital network (ISDN) a plan and an international communications protocol for converting the world's public telephone system from analog to digital.

Integrity constraint a rule that helps assure the quality of information.

Intellectual property intangible creative work that is embodied in physical form.

Intelligence the first step in the decision-making process where you find or recognize a problem, need, or opportunity (also called the diagnostic phase of decision making).

Intelligent agent software that assists you, performing repetitive tasks and adapting itself to your preferences.

Intelligent home appliance an appliance that contains an embedded IT system that controls numerous functions and is capable of making some decisions.

Interactive chat lets you engage in real-time typed exchange of information between you and one or more other individuals over the Internet.

Interlaced monitor a monitor that makes two passes to produce information on the screen.

Intermediary a specialist company that adds services.

Internal hard disk rests inside the cabinet of your computer.

Internal information information that describes specific operational aspects of the organization.

Internal memory a temporary storage area that holds three things: (1) information you are working with, (2) the application software you are using, and (3) the operating system software.

International virtual private network (international VPN) a virtual private network that depends on services offered by phone companies of various nationalities.

Internet a vast network of computers that connects millions of people all over the world.

Internet appliance also called a Web appliance; scaled-down computer or newly-developed device that supports access to the Internet and possibly a few other basic functions such as note taking and maintaining an address book.

Internet backbone the major set of connections for computers on the Internet.

Internet server computer a computer that provides information and services on the Internet.

Internet service provider (ISP) a company that provides individuals, organizations, and businesses access to the Internet.

Internet virtual private network (Internet VPN) a network that gives you a way to establish a virtual Internet network that consists of you, your customers, and suppliers.

Interorganizational system (IOS) a system that automates the flow of information between organizations to support the planning, design, development, production, and delivery of products and services.

Intersection relation a relation you create to eliminate a repeating group.

Intranet an internal organizational Internet that is guarded against outside access by special security software called a firewall.

Intrusion detection software software that attempts to detect when a security breach has occurred so that the intruder can be either observed and identified or expelled.

IRC (Internet Relay Chat) server a computer that supports your use of discussion groups and chat rooms.

IT systems plan a document that outlines (1) what systems you plan to develop, (2) when to develop those systems, and (3) your contingency plan for disasters.

J

Just-in-time (JIT) an approach that produces or delivers a product or service just at the time the customer wants it.

K

Keyboard today's most popular input technology.

Knowledge acquisition the component of the expert system that the knowledge engineer uses to enter the rules.

Knowledge base the part of the expert system that stores the rules.

Knowledge-based system also called an **expert system,** is an artificial intelligence system that applies reasoning capabilities to reach a conclusion.

Knowledge engineer the person who formulates the domain expertise into an expert system.

Knowledge worker a person who works with and produces information as a product.

Knowledge worker computing places technology, technology power, software, information, and technology knowledge in the hands of those who need it—knowledge workers.

Knowledge worker database a database designed and maintained by a knowledge worker to support his or her personal information needs.

Knowledge worker development the development and support of IT systems by knowledge workers with little or no help from IT specialists.

L

Land a representation of an on bit (bit 1) on an optical disk.

Language processing the third step of automatic speech recognition; it attempts to make sense of what you're saying by comparing the possible word phonemes (generated in step 2) with a language model database.

Laser printer a printer that uses a special laser technology and inklike toner to create letter quality output.

Last-mile bottleneck problem occurs when information is traveling on the Internet over a very fast line for a certain distance (from NAP to NAP) and them comes near your home where it must travel over a slower line.

Legacy system IT systems previously built using older technologies such as mainframe computers and programming languages such as COBOL.

Letter quality printer a printer that uses a technology to create high-quality output on a page.

Levels of information literacy different levels or stages that describe your understanding of information. These levels include professional (only understanding information at its face value), expert, and innovator (understanding what information truly means).

Light pen a special light-producing input device used in conjunction with a light-sensitive (photoelectric) screen or pad.

Link (hypertext link) either clickable text or images that take you to a different site or page.

Local area network (LAN) a network that covers a limited geographic distance, such as an office, office building, or a group of buildings within close proximity.

Logical view focuses on how you as a knowledge worker need to arrange and access information to meet your particular business needs.

Lower CASE tool a CASE tool which supports the back-end steps of the systems development life cycle, including design, implementation, and support.

M

M-commerce e-commerce conducted over a wireless device such as a cell phone or personal digital assistant (PDA).

Macro virus a virus that spreads by binding itself to software like Word or Excel.

Magnetic hard disk storage technology stores information on multiple disks, called platters.

Magnetic tape storage technology stores information on and retrieves if from a tape using a sequential method of access.

Magnetic-ink character recognition (MICR) an input device that reads a set of preprinted electronic symbols, usually numbers and characters.

Magneto-optical disk storage technology uses a laser for reading and writing information and a form of magnetization to give you the ability to alter the stored information.

Mail server a computer that provides e-mail services and accounts.

Management information systems (MIS) a system that provides periodic, predetermined, and/or ad hoc reporting capabilities.

Management information systems (MIS) deals with the planning for, development, management, and use of information technology tools to help people perform all tasks related to information processing and management.

Management information systems (MIS) challenge a challenge that all businesses must strive to meet. That challenge deals with how to coordinate the use of a business's three most important resources—information, information technology, and people—while providing products and services at the customer's moment of value.

Marketing mix the set of marketing tools that a firm uses to pursue its marketing objectives in the target market.

Mass customization when a business gives its customers the opportunity to tailor its product or service to the customer's specifications.

Meta tag a part of a Web site text not displayed to users but accessible to browsers and search engines for finding and categorizing Web sites.

Micro-payment a technique to facilitate the exchange of small amounts of money for an Internet transaction.

Microbrowser Web browser software for Web phones that can display text information and a limited amount of graphics in a small space.

Microwave an unguided communications medium that uses a high-frequency band of radio broadcast transmission and dish-shaped antennae for sending and receiving information.

Model management the part of the decision support system that consists of both the DSS models and DSS model management system.

Monochrome monitor a monitor that uses only one color.

Monochrome printer a printer that produces output in only black.

Mouse the most popular pointing input device for capturing mainly commands.

MRO hub facilitates the sourcing of MRO materials without focusing on one particular industry.

Multidimensional analysis (MDA) tool a slice-and-dice technique that allows you to view multidimensional information from different perspectives.

Multiplexor a device that collects the transmissions from several communications media and sends them over a single line that operates at a higher capacity.

Mutation part of a genetic algorithm; it's the process of randomly trying combinations and evaluating the success (or failure) of the outcome.

N

National Crime Information Center (NCIC) huge database with information on the criminal records of more than 20 million people.

Network also called a computer network; two or more computers connected so that they can communicate with each other and share information, software, peripheral devices, and/or processing power.

Network access point (NAP) a point on the Internet where several connections converge.

Network hub a device that connects multiple computers into a network but which allows only one communication link at a time.

Network interface card (NIC) an expansion card or a PC card (for a laptop) that connects your computer to a network and allows information to flow between your computer and the rest of the network.

Network service provider (NSP) owns and maintains routing computers at network access points and even the lines that connects the NAPs to each other.

Network topology the physical arrangement of computers in a network.

Neural network an artificial intelligence system which is capable of learning to differentiate patterns.

Nonimpact printer a printer that does not strike the page with some sort of mechanism.

Noninterlaced monitor a monitor that makes only one pass to produce information on the screen.

Nonrecurring decision also called an **ad hoc decision,** is a decision that you make very infrequently (perhaps only once) and you may even have different criteria for determining the best solution each time.

Nonstructured decision decisions for which there may be several "right" answers, and there is no precise way to get a right answer.

Normalization a process of assuring that a relational database structure can be implemented as a series of two-dimensional tables.

Object a software module containing information that describes an entity class along with a list of procedures that can act on the information describing the entity class.

Object-oriented approach any approach—perhaps a programming language or a DBMS—that combines information and procedures into a single object.

Object-oriented database (O-O database or OODB) a database model that brings together, stores, and allows you to work with both information and procedures that act on the information.

Object-oriented database management system (O-O DBMS or OODBMS) the DBMS software that allows you to develop and work with an object-oriented database.

Objective information information that quantifiably describes something that is known.

Online analytical processing (OLAP) the manipulation of information to support decision making.

Online database a database that exists outside an organization.

Online exchange a marketplace which makes it easy for purchasing managers to purchase commodities or near-commodities needed for production when demand peaks all of a sudden or a traditional source of supply is disrupted.

Online transaction processing (OLTP) involves gathering transaction information, processing that information, and updating existing information to reflect the gathered and processed transaction information.

Operating system software system software that controls your application software and manages how your hardware devices work together.

Operational database a database that supports online transaction processing.

Operational management the level of management that manages and directs the day-to-day operations and the implementation of goals and strategies.

Optical character recognition (OCR) an input device that captures information that exists in both predetermined and non-predetermined formats.

Optical disk storage technology uses a laser beam to read and write information to an optical disk.

Optical fiber a communications medium that uses a very thin glass or plastic fiber through which pulses of light travel. Optical fiber is the fastest and most reliable guided communications medium.

Optical mark recognition (OMR) an input device that detects the presence or absence of a mark in a predetermined place.

Opting in the term e-marketers use for your giving permission for alternative uses of your personal information.

Opting out the term e-marketers use for your not giving permission for alternatives uses of your personal information.

Output technologies the tools you use to see, hear, or otherwise accept the results of your information-processing requests.

Outsourcing the delegation of specific work to a third party for a specified length of time, at a specific cost, and at a specified level of service.

P

Parallel conversion moving from the old system to the new system by using both the old and new systems until you're sure that the new system performs correctly.

Partitioned database a database that maintains certain files of information in different locations—usually where that information is most often used.

Pattern classification the second step of automatic speech recognition; it attempts to recognize your spoken phonemes by locating a matching phoneme sequence among the words stored in an acoustic model database.

Peer-to-peer network a network in which a small number of computers share hardware (such as a printer), software, and/or information.

Pen mouse a device that looks like a fountain pen and performs similarly to mice and trackballs.

Perfect delivery understanding a customer's moment of value in terms of time, location, and form and taking the necessary steps to assure that those characteristics can be met.

Periodic report a report that is produced at a predetermined time interval—daily, weekly, monthly, yearly, and so on.

Permission marketing when marketers get your permission to send your way only offers you're very likely to find attractive.

Personal productivity software helps you do things that you could otherwise probably do manually.

Personalization when an Internet site can know enough about your likes and dislikes that it can fashion offers that are more likely to appeal to you.

Physical view deals with how information is physically arranged, stored, and accessed on some type of secondary storage device.

Piecemeal conversion moving from the old system to the new system by converting to only a portion of the new system until you're sure that it works correctly and then converting to the remaining portions of the new system.

Pilot conversion moving from the old system to the new system by having only a small group of people use the new system until you know that it works correctly and then converting the remaining people.

Pirated software copyrighted software that is copied and distributed without permission of the owner.

Pit a representation of an off bit (bit 0) on an optical disk.

Pixel the smallest display element on a screen that can be turned on or off and made different shades of colors.

Plotter a special type of printer that draws output on paper.

Plunge conversion moving from the old system to the new system by discarding the old system completely and immediately using the new system.

PNA adapter card an expansion card that you use to network multiple computers with ordinary phone cable.

Point-of-sale system (POS system) captures information and commands at the point of origin of a transaction, typically in a retail environment.

Pointing stick a small rubberlike device that causes the pointer to move on the screen as you apply directional pressure.

Primary key a field in a database file that uniquely describes each record.

Private network consists of the communications media that your organization owns or exclusively leases to connect networks or network components.

Project plan includes a list of people who will participate on the project team, a preliminary budget, and a time frame for completing each major step or task.

Project team a team designed to accomplish specific one-time goals which is disbanded once the project is complete.

Proof-of-concept prototype a prototype you use to prove the technical feasibility of a proposed system.

Prototype a model of a proposed product, service, or system.

Prototyping the process of building a model that demonstrates the features of a proposed product, service, or system.

Public encryption key (PKE) an encryption system that uses two keys: a public key that everyone can have and a private key for only the recipient.

Public network a network on which your organization competes for time with others.

Pure play an Internet retailer such as Amazon.com that has no physical stores.

Q

Query-by-example (QBE) tool helps you graphically design the answer to a question.

Query-and-reporting tool found in a data warehouse environment. These tools are similar to query-by-example tools, structured query language, and report generators in a typical database environment.

R

Random access memory (RAM) the internal memory that holds your information and the operating system and application software you're working with.

Record a logical grouping of fields.

Recurring decision a decision that you have to make repeatedly, and often periodically, either weekly, monthly, quarterly, or yearly.

Redundant computer also called a fault tolerant computer; a computer that has built-in backup systems that take over when a primary component fails.

Relation a two-dimensional table in the relational database model.

Relational database model a database model that uses a series of two-dimensional tables or files to store information.

Repeater a device which takes a message, strengthens it, and passes it along.

Repetitive strain injury (RSI) also referred to as cumulative trauma disorder (CTD), is characterized by headache, neckache, eyestrain, wrist pain, fatigue, and stress caused by repetitive actions.

Replicated database a database that maintains multiple copies of information in different locations.

Report generator helps you quickly define formats of reports and what information you want to see in a report.

Request for proposal (RFP) a formal document that describes in detail your logical requirements for a proposed system and invites outsourcing organizations (which we refer to as "vendors") to submit bids for its development.

Resolution for a screen, that is determined by the number of pixels.

Reverse auction the process in which a buyer posts its interest in buying a certain quantity of items, and sellers compete for the business by submitting successively lower bids until there is only one seller left.

Ring topology a network topology in which all computers are connected to a single communications medium (similar to a bus), and that communications medium is connected at both ends to form a closed loop.

Risk assessment the process of evaluating IT assets, their importance to the organization, and their susceptibility to threats, to measure the risk exposure of those assets.

Risk management consists of the identification of risks or threats, the implementation of security measures, and the monitoring of those measures for effectiveness.

Rivalry among existing competitors is high when an industry is less attractive to enter into and low when an industry is more attractive to enter into.

Router an internetworking unit that connects networks that are somewhat dissimilar with respect to certain communications aspects, such as how computers are addressed and the size of messages sent.

Rule-based expert system the type of expert system that expresses the problem-solving process as rules.

S

Safe-harbor principle a set of rules to which United States business that want to trade with the European Union (EU) must adhere.

Satellite modem a modem that allows you to get Internet access from your satellite dish.

Script bunny a person who would like to be a hacker but doesn't have much technical expertise.

Selection part of a genetic algorithm which gives preference to better outcomes.

Selfsourcing the development and support of IT systems by knowledge workers with little or no help from IT specialists.

Selling prototype a prototype you use to convince people of the worth of a proposed system.

Shared information an environment in which an organization's information is organized in one central location, allowing anyone to access and use it as they need to.

Shopping bot also called a buyer agent; an intelligent agent that looks on the Web for the product of your choice and brings the information back to you.

Smart card a small plastic card (about the size of a credit card) that contains a memory chip on which a sum of money can be recorded and updated.

Sociability the ability of an intelligent agent to confer with other agents.

Software the set of instructions that your hardware executes to carry out a particular task for you.

Sound input a device that captures information that originates in audio form.

Sound output a device that reproduces previously recorded and stored sounds.

Spam unsolicited e-mail from a company you have never done business with.

Speaker-dependent automatic speech recognition an automatic speech recognition system that lets you "train" it to recognize your voice.

Speaker-independent automatic speech recognition an automatic speech recognition system that can be used by anyone, but often contains a limited vocabulary that cannot be expanded.

Speech synthesis an output device that creates speech output from text.

Star topology a network arrangement which has a central hub or switch from which all computers radiate.

Storage technologies the tools you use to more permanently store information for use at a later time.

Strategic management the level of management that provides an organization with overall direction and guidance.

Structured decision a decision where processing a certain kind of information in a specified way will always provide the right answer.

Structured query language (SQL) a standardized fourth-generation query language found in most database environments.

Subjective information information that attempts to describe something that is currently unknown.

Summarized report a report that aggregates information in some way.

Supplier power high when buyers have few choices of whom to buy from and low when there are many choices.

Supply chain the paths reaching out to all suppliers of parts and services to a company.

Supply chain management system an interorganizational system that drives time and cost out of the supply chain by fostering closer collaboration between trading partners.

Switch a device that connects multiple computers into a network in which multiple communication links can be in operation simultaneously.

Switching costs the costs that can make customers reluctant to switch to another product or service.

System software handles tasks specific to technology management and coordinates the interaction of all your IT components.

T

Tactical management the level of management that develops the goals and strategies outlined by strategic management.

Tangible benefit a systems benefit that can be monetarily quantified.

Tape density the amount of information that can be stored in one inch of a magnetic tape.

Telecommunications technologies the tools you use to send information to and receive it from another person or location.

Telecommuting the use of communications technology to work in a place other than a central location.

Telephone modem device that connects your computer to your phone line so that you can access another computer or network.

Temporary advantage an advantage that, sooner or later, the competition duplicates or even leap-frogs you with a better system.

Threat of new entrants high when it is easy for competitors to enter the market and low when it's difficult for competitors to enter the market.

Threat of substitute products or services alternatives to using a product or service.

Three generic strategies cost leadership, differentiation, or a focused strategy.

Three-dimensional (3-D) a technology presentation of information that gives you the illusion that the object you're viewing is actually in the room with you.

Touch pad another form of a stationary mouse on which you move your finger to cause the pointer on the screen to move.

Touch screen a special screen that lets you use your finger to literally point at and touch a particular function you want to perform.

Touch-tone input a device that captures information and commands that originate in audio form from a telephone keypad.

Trackball an upside-down, stationary mouse in which you move the ball instead of the device.

Traditional systems development life cycle (traditional SDLC) a structured step-by-step approach to developing systems that creates a separation of duties among IT specialists and knowledge workers.

Transaction processing system (TPS) a system that processes transactions that occur within the organization.

Transmission control protocol/Internet protocol (TCP/IP) the primary protocol for transmitting information over the Internet.

Transnational firm a firm that produces and sells products and services in countries all over the world in coordinated cooperation.

U

Unformatted OCR a device that captures information and then puts it into an editable format so that you can change the information.

Uninstaller software utility software that removes software you no longer want.

Upper CASE tool a CASE tool that supports the front-end steps of the systems development life cycle, including planning, scoping, analysis, and design.

User agent intelligent agent that helps an individual perform computer-related tasks.

User interface management the part of the decision support system that allows the user, or knowledge worker, to communicate with the DSS.

Utility software software that provides additional functionality to your operating system.

V

Value-added network (VAN) a semipublic network that provides services beyond the movement of information from one place to another.

Value chain a tool that views the organization as a chain—or series—of processes each of which adds value to the product or service for the customer.

Value network all of the resources behind the click on a Web page that the customer doesn't see, but that together create the customer relationship-service, order fulfillment, shipping, financing, information brokering, and access to other products and offers.

Videoconferencing software allows a team to have a "face-to-face" meeting when members are geographically dispersed.

View allows you see the content of a database file, make whatever changes you want, perform simple sorting, and query to find the location of specific information.

Viral marketing encourages users of a product or service supplied by a B2C company to ask friends to join in as well.

Virtual private network (VPN) a public network that promises availability to your organization, but doesn't provide you with a dedicated line or communications media.

Virtual reality a three-dimensional computer simulation in which you actively and physically participate.

Virtual workplace a technology-enabled workplace. No walls. No boundaries. Work anytime, anyplace, linked to other people and information you need, wherever they are.

W

Walker an input device in virtual reality that captures and records the movement of your feet as you walk or turn in different directions.

Web appliance also called an Internet appliance; scaled-down computer or newly-developed device that supports access to the Internet and possibly a few other basic functions such as note taking and maintaining an address book.

Web browser software software that allows you to browse or surf the Web.

Web page a specific portion of a Web site that deals with a certain topic.

Web phone special type of cell phone that allows you to access the Internet.

Web server a computer that provides information and services to Web surfers.

Web site a specific location on the Web where you visit, gather information, and perhaps even order products.

Web site address a unique name that identifies a specific site on the Web.

White-hat hacker a hacker who breaks into computers they have no right to access and often report the security leaks to the victims.

Whiteboard software allows you to make a presentation to your team members and electronically captures any notes you may write on a large whiteboard.

Wide area network (WAN) a network that covers large geographic distances, such as a state, a country, or even the entire world.

WiFi (Wireless Fidelity) a well established medium for local network access.

Wired communications media transmit information over a closed, connected path.

Wireless communications media transmit information through the air.

Wireless local area network (wireless LAN) a network that covers a limited distance in which all components or computers are connected without physical cables.

Wireless Network Access Point (Wireless Access Point, WAP) a device that allows computers to access a wired network using radio waves.

Workgroup support system (WSS) a system that is designed specifically to improve the performance of teams by supporting the sharing and flow of information.

World Wide Web (Web) is the Internet in a linked multimedia form.

Worm a computer virus that spreads itself, not only from file to file, but from computer to computer via e-mail and other Internet traffic.

X

X.12 (also ANSI X12) a protocol for transmitting commonly formatted information in electronic data interchange (EDI) transactions.

XML (eXtensible Mark-up Language) a language coming into use for the production of Web documents and as the basis for the exchange of business documents.

Y

Yield manager creates spot markets for operating resources such as manufacturing capacity, labor, and advertising.

PHOTO CREDITS

Module A
Photo A.1, p. 33, © Corbis CB045952.
Photo A.2, p. 33, © Corbis CB038105.
Photo A. 3, p. 33, © The Stock Market RF4472158.
Photo A.4, p. 33, © Michael Schwarz/The Image Works.

Chapter 2
Figure 2.1, p. 48, © Michael Newman/PhotoEdit.
Figure 2.3a, p.51, © Mark Richards/Photo Edit.
Figure 2.3b, p.51, © Bob Daemmrich/The Image Works.
Figure 2.3c, p.51, © Davis Barber/PhotoEdit.
Figure 2.3d, p.51, © Bonnie Kamin/PhotoEdit.
Figure 2.3e, p.51, © Spencer Grant/PhotoEdit.
Figure 2.3f, p.51, © Ryan McVay/PhotoDisc.
Figure 2.3g, p.51, © Leslye Borden/PhotoEdit.

Chapter 6
Figure 6.3a, p. 234, Courtesy of International Business Machines Corporation. Unauthorized use not permitted.
Figure 6.3b, p. 234, Image courtesy of Stone & Webster.
Figure 6.5, p. 238, Roger Russmeyer/Corbis.
Figure 6.6, p. 241, Courtesy of Secugen Corporation.
Figure 6.10a, p. 248, Courtesy of International Business Machines Corporation. Unauthorized use not permitted.
Figure 6.10b, p. 248, Courtesy of Compaq Corporation.
Figure 6.10c, p. 248, Courtesy of Handspring Inc.
Figure 6.10d, p. 248, Courtesy of Nokia.

Module D
Figure D.1, p. 375, Courtesy of International Business Machines Corporation. Unauthorized use not permitted.
Photo D.1, p. 378, Courtesy of International Business Machines Corporation. Unauthorized use not permitted.
Photo D.2, p. 378, Courtesy of International Business Machines Corporation. Unauthorized use not permitted.
Photo D.3, p. 379, Courtesy of International Business Machines Corporation. Unauthorized use not permitted.
Photo D.4, p. 379, © David Young-Wolf/PhotoEdit.
Photo D.5, p. 380, Courtesy of Intermec Technologies Corporation.
Photo D.6, p. 380, Courtesy of International Business Machines Corporation. Unauthorized use not permitted.
Photo D.7, p. 382, Courtesy of Hewlett-Packard.
Photo D.8, p. 382, Courtesy of International Business Machines Corporation. Unauthorized use not permitted.
Photo D.9, p. 383, Courtesy of International Business Machines Corporation. Unauthorized use not permitted.
Photo D.10, p. 383, Courtesy of Lexmark International, Inc.
Photo D.11, p. 383, PhotoDisc/CMCD/ST002437.
Photo D.12, p. 383, © Steven Lunetta/Page to Page.
Photo D.13, p. 386, Image Courtesy of Hewlett-Packard.
Photo D.14, p. 387, Courtesy of International Business Machines Corporation. Unauthorized use not permitted.
Photo D.15, p. 387, Courtesy of International Business Machines Corporation. Unauthorized use not permitted.
Photo D.16, p. 396, Courtesy of International Business Machines Corporation. Unauthorized use not permitted.
Photo D.17, p. 396, © Steven Lunetta/Page to Page.
Photo D.18, p. 396, Courtesy of International Business Machines Corporation. Unauthorized use not permitted.
Photo D.19, p. 396, © Steven Lunetta/Page to Page.
Photo D.20, p. 396, © Gail Meese/Meese Photo Research, Created on 5/14/01 3:38 P.M.

NOTES

Chapter 1

1. McMaster, Mark, "Cutting Costs with Web-Based CRM," *Sales & Marketing Management*, Nov. 2000, pp. 26-30.
2. Zuckerman, Mortimer, "America's Silent Revolution," *U.S. News & World Report*, July 18, 1994, p. 90.
3. Verity, John, "A Trillion-Byte Weapon," *Business Week*, July 31, 1995, pp. 80-81.
4. Naughton, Keith, "Ford Opens the Throttle," *Business Week*, September 18, 1995, pp. 66-68.
5. Lubove, Seth, "The Berserk-ley Boys," *Forbes*, August 14, 1995, pp. 42-43.
6. Johnson, John, "On the GO at USCO," *Warehousing Management*, Sept. 2000, pp. 26-30.
7. Arnst, Catherine, "The Networked Corporation," *Business Week*, June 26, 1995, pp. 86-89.
8. *Fortune*: August 1975; August 11, 1980; August 19, 1985; July 30, 1995; and August 7, 1995.
9. Schlender, Brent, "Sony Plays to Win," *Fortune*, May 1, 2000, pp. 142-157.
10. Baig, Edward, "Welcome to the Officeless Office," *Business Week*, June 26, 1995, pp. 104-106.
11. Keohan, Martin, "The Virtual Office: Impact and Implementation," *Business Week*, September 11, 1995, pp. 95-98.
12. Langhoff, June, "Telecommute America," *Fortune*, October 30, 1995, pp. 229-235.
13. Baxter, Andrew, "Smart Response to a Changing Market," *Financial Times*, March 1, 1995, p. 13.
14. Novack, Janet, "The Data Edge," *Forbes*, September 11, 1995, pp. 148-152.
15. Donnell, Anthony, "Solutions: Provident Agents Dump Paper for Automation," *Insurance & Technology*, Oct. 2000, p. 23.
16. Sprout, Alison, "The Internet Inside Your Company," *Fortune*, November 27, 1999, pp. 161-168.
17. Ladika, Susan, "Paperless Payoff," *Hospitals & Health Networks*, Oct. 2000, pp. 20-24.
18. Manes, Stephen, "That's Intertainment!," *Forbes*, July 3, 2000, p. 146.
19. Kallman, Ernest, and John Grillo, *Ethical Decision Making and Information Technology*, McGraw-Hill, San Francisco, 1993.
20. Stewart, Thomas, "What Information Costs," *Fortune*, July 10, 1995, pp. 119-121.
21. Peyser, Marc, and Steve Rhodes, "When E-Mail Is Ooops Mail," *Newsweek*, October 16, 1995, p. 82.
22. Novack, Janet, "The Data Miners," *Forbes*, February 12, 1996, pp. 96-97.
23. Orr, Alicia, "Clothing Retailer Uses Database to Serve Executive Clientele," *Target Marketing*, July 2000, p. 68.

Chapter 2

1. WARE, LORRAINE COSGROVE, "CAD System Puts Wind in Cup Challenger's Sails", *Computerworld*, June 5, 2000, http://www.computerworld.com/cwi/story/0,1199,NAV47_STO45421,00.html.
2. "UPS worldwide Logistics 'Tunes Up' Fender Guitar's European Supply Chain", UPS Logistics Group News Release (May 1999).
3. Korzenowski, Paul and McDougall, Paul, "Dell Finds Success In Its Custom-Build Strategy: Vendor looks to enterprise-systems business to continue its high rate of growth. *InformationWeek Online*, November 15, 1999.
4. "Internet Business Solutions from Cisco and Ariba: The Impact of the Internet for Buyers and Suppliers", informational posting on Cisco Web site, www.cisco.com, August 1, 2000.
5. Adams, Scott, *The Dilbert Future: Thriving on Stupidity in the 21st Century*, New York. Harper Publishing, 1997, p. 55.
6. *BusinessWeek Online*, September 18, 2000. www.businessweek.com.
7. *BusinessWeek Online*, November 29, 2000. www.businessweek.com
8. "Singapore TradeNet: A Tale of One City", Harvard Business School Case 191-009, John King and Ben Konsynski, Copyright 1990 by the Fellows of Harvard College.
9. www.sedb.com.sq/home.html
10. www.siebel.com
11. Weinberg, V., *Structured Analysis*, New York. Yourdan Press, 1980, pp. 3-4.
12. www.cpfr.org
13. Conners, Mary, "Baxter's Big Makeover in Logistics", *Fortune*, July 8, 1996, pp. 106C-106N.
14. Applegate, Lynda M.; McFarlan, F. Warren; and McKenney, James L; *Corporate Information Systems Management: Text and Cases*, Fifth Edition, New York. Irwin/McGraw-Hill 1999, p. 64.
15. Holohan, Meghan, "Roll Over, Gutenberg", *Computerworld Online*, August 28, 2000, adapted.
16. www.covisint.com
17. Kontzer, Tony, *InformationWeek Online*, August 25, 2000.
18. Edwards, Owen, "Bow Tech: ASAP Case Study, *Forbes ASAP*, June 3, 1996, pp. 54-58.
19. http://www.fcc.gov/3G/
20. McFarlan, F. Warren; Copeland, Duncan G, Note on Airline Reservations Systems (Revised), Part II, Harvard Business School Product Number 189099, 10/31/88.
21. McCubbrey, Donald J. "Disintermediation and Reintermediation in the US Air Travel Distribution Industry: A Delphi Study", Communications of the Association for Information Systems, Volume 1, Article 1 June 1999.
22. www.pharmacyconnects.com/content/ph-post/1998/07-98/ppo079801.html
23. Hoffman, Thomas, "Prescription for Savings", *Computerworld*, July 1, 1996, p. 37.
24. *Computerworld Online*, April 17, 2000 (adapted)

Chapter 3

1. Whiting, Rick, "Profile: Geon Co.—Geon Leads Chemical Industry in E-Business Changes," *Informationweek*, September 11, 2000, p. 146.
2. Zulman, Shelley, "Dressing Up Data," *Oracle Magazine*, January–February 1995, pp. 46–49.
3. "The Chain Store Age 100," *Chain Store Age*, August 1996, p. 3A.
4. Lais, Sami, "Satellite Ho!," *Computerworld*, May 29, 2000, pp. 70-71.
5. Diltea, Steve, "Managing Sales with Software," *Nation's Business*, March 1996, pp. 29-31.
6. Convey, Mary, "Controversy Heats Up Over Malpractice Database Access," *National Underwriter*, October 30, 2000, pp. 9, 12.
7. Cash, James, "Gaining Customer Loyalty," *InformationWeek*, April 10, 1995, p. 88.
8. O'Leary, Mick, "NEXIS Finally Goes Dot-Com," *Information Today*, November 2000, pp. 32-33.
9. Anthes, Gary, "Car Dealer Takes the Personal out of PCs," *Computerworld*, August 14, 1995, p. 48.
10. Hamilton, Joan, "Medicine's New Weapon: Data," *Business Week*, March 27, 1995, pp. 184-188.
11. Wendy Knight & Associates, "Think You Know Your Health Plan? Think Again," *Newsweek*, September 16, 1996, special advertising section.
12. Watterson, Karen, "A Data Miner's Tools," *BYTE*, October 1995, pp. 91-96.
13. Kling, Julia, "OLAP Gains Fans among Data-Hungry Firms," *Computerworld*, January 8, 1996, pp. 43, 48.
14. Hutheesing, Nikhil, "Surfing with Sega," *Forbes*, November 4, 1996, pp. 350-351.
15. Cafasso, Rosemary, "OLAP: Who Needs It?" *Computerworld*, February 2, 1995, p. 12.
16. Radding, Alan, "Blue Cross Climbs Mountain of Data with OLAP," *InfoWorld*, January 30, 1995, p. 64.
17. Nash, Kim, "MasterCard Extends Its Limit," *Computerworld*, July 31, 1995, p. 6.
18. Whiting, Rick, "Borders Wants to Read Its Customers Like a Book," *Informationweek*, Aug. 21, 2000, p. 34.
19. LaPlante, Alice, "Big Things Come in Smaller Packages," *Computerworld*, June 24, 1996, pp. DW/6-7.
20. Babcock, Charles, "Slice, Dice, & Deliver," *Computerworld*, November 13, 1995, pp. 129-132.
21. Karthaus, Ed, "At the Fingertips," *Canadian Insurance*, April 2000, pp. 22-24.
22. Phillips, Ben, "Ice Service's Data Warehouse Goes with the Flow," *PC Week*, January 22, 1996, pp. 45-46.
23. Shewmake, Brad, "SAS Helps Scientists Decipher Human Genetic Code," *InfoWorld*, June 12, 2000, p. 80.
24. "Mining the Data of Dining," *Nation's Restaurant News*, May 22, 2000, pp. S22–S24.

Chapter 4

1. "When Intelligence Rules, the Manager's Job Changes," *Management Review*, July 1994, pp. 33-35.
2. Gambon, Jill, "A Database That 'Ads' Up," *InformationWeek*, August 7, 1995, pp. 68-69.
3. Maynard, Roberta, "Leading the Way to Effective Marketing," *Nation's Business*, October 1996, pp. 10-11.

4. McCartney, Scott, "Airlines Catch Technology Tailwind: Computers Discover Ways to Cut Costs to Offset Higher Fuel, Labor Expenses," *Star Tribune* (Minneapolis, MN), p. 1d.

5. Simon, Herbert, *The New Science of Management Decisions,* rev. ed., Prentice-Hall, Englewood Cliffs, NJ, 1977.

6. Maslakowski, Carla, "Cut Adverse Drug Reactions with Clinical Decision Support," *Health Management Technology,* August 1996, pp. 28–30.

7. Scheier, Robert L., "Timing Is Everything," *Computerworld,* August 5, 1996, pp. 62–63.

8. "Turning Data into Useful Information," *Progressive Grocer,* July 1994, p. 14.

9. Hoffman, Thomas, and Mitch Wagner, "Visions of Holiday $ugarplums," *Computerworld,* December 4, 1995, pp. 1, 147.

10. "HEALTHvision Supports Patient Care with Diagnostic Decision-Support Too: DXplain Provides Quality of Clinical Diagnoses at the Point of Care." *PR Newswire Association, Inc.,* January 12, 2000.

11. Townsend, Anthony M., Michael E. Whitman, and Anthony R. Hendrickson, "Computer Support System Adds Power to Group Processes," *HR Magazine,* September 1995, pp. 87–90.

12. Jackson, Neal, et al., "Support Group Decisions via Computer Systems," *Quality Progress,* May 1995, pp. 75–78.

13. Connors, Daniel P., and David D. Yao, "Methods for Job Configuration in Semiconductor Manufacturing," *IEEE Transactions on Semiconductor Manufacturing,* August 1996, pp. 401–410.

14. McDougall, Paul. "IBM Unveils a Way to Make Faster Chips," *Information Week,* April 10, 2000, p.40.

15. Nunamaker, J.F., Jr., et al., "Electronic Meeting Systems to Support Group Work: Theory and Practice at Arizona," Working paper, College of Business, University of Arizona, March 1990.

16. Fabris, Peter, "Felon Television," *CIO,* September 1, 1996, pp. 24–26.

17. Gillooly, Caryn, "Bright Light," *InformationWeek,* November 20, 1995, p. 56.

18. Keefe, Mari, "GIS Technology Builds Infrastructure to Aid Fair, Fast Elections," *Computerworld,* June 5, 2000, pp. 42–43.

19. Patterson, David, "Mapping Out Your Future," *Nursing Homes,* October 1995, pp. 34–35.

20. Bird, Jane, "Computers versus Crime," *Management Today,* April 1996, pp. 66–68.

21. Swenson, John, "GIS Software Goes Corporate," *InformationWeek,* June 3, 1996, p. 103.

22. Woodbury, Carol, "GIS Software," *Journal of Property Management,* September–October 1996, pp. 60–62.

23. Duenas, Mark, "Ada County Rewrites the Book with GIS," *American City & County,* February 1995, p. 84.

24. Dunkin, Amy, "The Quants May Have Your Numbers," *Business Week,* September 25, 1995, pp. 146–147.

25. Clerking, Daniel, Peter J. Fox, and Frederick E. Petty, "A Decision Support System for Hospital Bed Alignment," *Hospital and Health Services Administration,* Fall 1995, pp. 386–400.

26. Port, Otis, "Computers that Think Are Almost Here," *BusinessWeek,* July 17, 1995, pp. 68–71.

27. Cossack, S., "Expert System Offers Relief for Child Abuse," *Computerworld,* July 29, 1991, p. 37.

28. Stuart, Ann, "A Dose of Accuracy," *CIO,* May 15, 1996, pp. 22–24.

29. "Smartsources.com Signs Up Sony Electronics to Use Its Origin Pro Software," *Canadian Corporate News,* September 7, 2000.

30. Marsan, Carolyn Duffy. "Car-Shopping Service Adds Voice to Its Web Site," *Network World,* June 12, 2000, P. 37.

31. Glatzer, Hal, "Neural Networks Take On Real-World Problems," *Computerworld,* April 18, 1994, pp. 133–135.

32. Perry, loc. cit.

33. McCartney, Laton, "Technology for a Better Bottom Line," *Information Week,* February 26, 1996, p. 40.

34. Malhorta, Manish, et al., "Artificial Neural Systems in Commercial Lending," *Bankers Magazine,* November–December 1994, pp. 40–44.

35. Mandelman, Auker, "The Computer's Bullish!" *Barron's,* December 14, 1992, pp. 16–17.

36. Punch, Linda, "Battling Credit Card Fraud," *Bank Management,* March 1993, pp. 18–22.

37. "Cigna, IBM Tech Tool Targets Health Care Fraud," *National Underwriter Property & Casualty-Risk & Benefits,* October 1994, p. 5.

38. Perry, William, "What Is Neural Network Software?" *Journal of Systems Management,* September 1994, pp. 12–15.

39. Port, Otis, "Diagnoses That Cast a Wider Net," *Business Week,* May 22, 1995, p. 130.

40. Baxt, William G., and Joyce Skora, "Prospective Validation of Artificial Neural Network Trained to Identify Acute Myocardial Infarction," *The Lancet,* January 6, 1997, pp. 12–15.

41. Hoffman, Thomas, "Swamp Thing," *Computerworld,* August 7, 1995, pp. 83–84.

42. Warren, P., "Police to Pinpoint 'Problem' Kids with Neural Technology," *Computing,* October 19, 1995, p. 16.

43. Begley, S., "Software au Naturel," *Newsweek,* May 8, 1995, pp. 70–71.

44. Goldberg, David E., "Genetic and Evolutionary Algorithms Come of Age," *Communications of the ACM,* March 1994, pp. 113–119.

45. Baumohl, Bernard. "Can You Really Trust those Bots? *Time,* December 11, 2000, p. 80.

46. Coopee, Todd. "WebCriteria Helps Bolster Customer's Online Experiences," *InfoWorld,* November 27, 2000, p. 56.

47. Dobbs, Sarah Boehle Kevin, Donna Gordon Goldwasser and Jack Stamps. "The Return of Artificial Intelligence, *Training,* November 2000, p. 26.

48. Wolinsky, Howard. "Advisa Helps Companies Get More From Their Data: Helps managers to Understand Market," *Chicago Sun-Times,* December 20, 2000, p. 81.

49. Allen, Maryellen Mott, "The Myth of Intelligent Agents," *Online,* November/December 2000, pp. 45–51.

50. Stepanek, Marcia. "Weblining," *BusinessWeek,* April 3, 2000, pp. 25–33.

Module C

1. Baig, Edward, C. "Eyeing Smarter New Products at Demo 2001," *USA Today,* February 14, 2001, p. 3D.

2. "How to Revitalize Host Systems for Client/Server Computing Today and Tomorrow," *Datamation,* April 1, 1995, pp. S1–S24.

3. Schalon, Lisa, "Sales Automation Systems Increase Sales, Productivity," *Best's Review-Life-Health Insurance Edition,* January 1996, pp. 100–102.

Chapter 5

1. Neuborne, Ellen "Pepsi's Aim Is True: The cola giant's Web strategy finds the new generation of customers", *BusinessWeek Online,* January 21, 2001.

2. Rayport, Jeffrey F. and Jaworski, Bernard J., *e-Commerce,* New York. McGraw-Hill/Irwin MarketspaceU, 2001, p. 4.

3. www.nua.ie/surveys/how_many_online/index.html, January 15, 2001.

4. "Internet Hosts", *www.Economist.com,* November 23, 2000.

5. Forrester Research, October 26, 2000, quoted at www.nua.com/surveys.

6. "Survey: The New Economy. Elementary My Dear Watson", *www.Economist.com,* September 23, 2000.

7. McDonald, Time, "UN Urged To Close Global Digital Divide", *E-Commerce Times,* June 20, 2000, http://www.ecommercetimes.com/news/articles2000/000620-5.shtml

8. "Survey: E-Commerce, Shopping around the web", *www.Economist.com,* February 24, 2000.

9. Kelley, Joanne, "The Right Tool. Ace Hardware's online community makes dealers far more productive. *Context Magazine,* December 2000/January 2001, www.contextmag.com.

10. Gartner Group, January 24, 2001, quoted at http://www.nua.ie/surveys/?f=VS&art_id=905356379&rel=true.

11. Schwartz, Evan I., *Digital Darwinism,* Broadway Books, 1999, book jacket.

12. "Fire Alarm" Barrons Table, *Barrons Online,* March 20, 2000.

13. Songini, Marc L. and Copeland, Lee. "Toyota Web-enables dealers, supply chain. Following rivals, carmaker projects huge savings in transportation, inventory." www.Computerworld.com, October 16, 2000.

14. "Europe to lead world in online grocery sales", Newsbytes.com, 06/26/00, quoted at http://uk.iplanet.com/center/ecnews/markettrends/onlinesaleswe.html

15. Kotler, Philip, *Marketing Management: Analysis, Planning, Implementation and Control", Ninth Edition,* Upper Saddle River, New Jersey, Prentice Hall, 1997. p. 92.

16. Toni Will-Harris www.efuse.com/Design/top_10_do_s_and_don_ts.html

17. http://www.bcentral.com/tb/search.asp

18. Weintraub, Arlene, "Online Pet-Suppliers Are Howling in Pain. Layoffs, retrenchments, consolidation: Trouble is brewing in this overcrowded market". *BusinessWeek Online,* June 7, 2000 (adapted).

www.businessweek.com/bwdaily/dnflash/jun2000/nf00607f.htm

19. Murphy Kathleen, "Fulfillment Gaffes Plague Sites, Study Says" *INTERNET WORLD NEWS*, Tuesday, January 23, 2001 Vol. 3, Issue 14, (www.internetworld.com), adapted.

20. "Survey: Business and the Internet", *The Economist*, June 26, 1999.

21. Keen, Peter, and McDonald, Mark, *"The eProcess Edge"*, Berkeley, California, Osborne/McGraw-Hill, 2000. p. 96.

22. Henderson, John C. "CEO Users Guide: Shall We Dance?" *Context Magazine*, July-August 1999. www.contextmag.com/magazine/setMagazineMain.asp

23. Ibid, p. 97.

24. Cope, James "Dairy Industry Gets Set for B2B Exchange: Dairy.com to use spot-market model for perishables" www.computerworld.com/cwi/story/0,1199,NAV47_STO56627,00.html, January 21, 2001 (adapted).

25. Metz, Cade, "BNSF: Making the Trains Run on Time, *PC Magazine*, October 31, 2000. www.zdnet.com/ibizmag/stories/reviews/0,10472,2645869,00.html

26. Kaplan and Sawhney; "E-Hubs: The New B2B Marketplaces", *Harvard Business Review*, May-June 2000 p. 99.

27. Evans, James "CRM Market to Grow: Customer Relationship Management Segment will soar to $12.1 Billion by 2004." *WebBusiness*, August 2000. http://webbusiness.cio.com/archive/082400_crm.html

28. "IBM Security Services. Enabling e-commerce while managing risk". IBM Global Services. http://www.ibm.com/services/files/security1.pdf

29. Bandy, Phil, Money, Michael and Worstell, Karen, "What is a honeypot? Why do I need one?" SANS Institute Resources, www.sans.org/newlook/resources/IDFAQ/honeypot2.htm

30. Thibodeau, Patrick, "Privacy Legislation raises questions: Will Americans envy strong EU protections" *Computerworld Online*, November 6, 2000. http://www.computerworld.com/cwi/story/0,1199,NAV47_STO53367,00.html

31. "Fair Information Practice Principles", U.S. Federal Trade Commission, http://www.ftc.gov/reports/privacy3/fairinfo.htm

32. Brown, Jeanette, "Making Disappearing Inc. More Visible: Even with nifty software that can force sensitive e-mail to self-destruct, the startup needs to persuade more big companies that its product is worth the trouble" *Business Week Online*, November 29, 2000. www.businessweek.com/technology/content/0011/ec1128.htm (adapted).

Chapter 6

1. Guttman, Monika, "Hollywood Falls in Love with Technology," *U.S. News & World Report*, February 16, 1996, pp. 73-74.

2. Kim, Albert, "Hollywired," *Entertainment Weekly*, October 13, 1995, pp. 21-22, 26, 30, 32.

3. Daly, Steve, "Don't Believe Your Eyes," *Entertainment*, July 16, 1995, p. 279.

4. http://www.movie-page.com/1999.matrix.htm

5. Coy, Peter, "3-D Computing," *Business Week*, September 4, 1995, pp. 70-77.

6. Mannes, George, "Machines That Listen," *Popular Mechanics*, July 1995, pp. 46-49.

7. Syedain, Hashi, "Technology Finds a New Voice," *Marketing*, November 17, 1994, p. XIV.

8. Remich, Norman, "Speech Market Growing 35% Annually," *Appliance Manufacturer*, July 1993, pp. 57-58.

9. Higgins, Amy, "Talky Toys Listen Up!," *Machine Design*, December 7, 2000, pp. 60-68.

10. McConnaughey, Janet, "Virtual Reality Used to Treat Autism," *The Denver Post*, October 20, 1996, p. 39A.

11. Setton, Dolly, "Invasion of the Virbots," Forbes.com, Fall 2000, pp. 22-26.

12. Dataquest, 1995.

13. Adams, Nina, "Lessons from the Virtual World," *Training*, June 1995, pp. 45-47.

14. Flynn, Laurie, "VR and Virtual Spaces Find a Niche in Real Medicine," *The New York Times*, June 5, 1995, p. C3.

15. Gross, Neil, "Seasick in Cyberspace," *Business Week*, July 10, 1995, pp. 110, 113.

16. Queenan, Joe, "Getting (Virtually) Real," *Chief Executive*, November 1995, p. 70.

17. Maney, Kevin, "High-Tech Rooms with 3-D View," *USA Today*, May 11, 1995, pp. 1B-2B.

18. Zeiger, Dinah, "A Digital Wallet in Your Computer," *The Denver Post*, September 9, 1996, pp. 7G, 12G.

19. Bloom, Jennifer, "Web Pioneers Unite to Seek Open Standard for Payments," *American Banker*, April 18, 1996, pp. 1, 17.

20. Vasilash, Gary, "Computing Power on the Road and at Work," *Automotive Manufacturing & Production*, November 2000, pp. 66-68.

21. Brown, Carolyn, "A Smooth Ride," *Black Enterprise*, November 2000, p. 194.

22. Blodgett, Mindy, "A Wireless LAN Landslide," *Computerworld*, April 1, 1996, p. 59.

23. Larsen, Amy, "Wireless LANs: Worth a Second Look," *Data Communications*, November 1995, pp. 95-100.

24. Bozman, Jean, "Practicality of Wireless Applications Grows," *Computerworld*, January 16, 1995, pp. 53, 58.

25. Blodgett, loc. cit.

26. Murphy, Elena, "Telecom Growth Leaps," *Purchasing*, April 25, 1996, pp. 86-87.

27. Zeiger, Dinah, "Smart Card Technology to Get Boost," *The Denver Post*, October 10, 1996, p. 2C.

28. "Vacuum Cleaner Features a Smart Analog Controller," *Appliance Manufacturer*, February 1995, pp. 91-93.

29. Rao, Srikumar, "Good Morning, Hal," *Financial World*, October 10, 1995, pp. 92-93.

30. "First Fuzzy Logic for Cooktop Controller," *Appliance Manufacturer*, February 1996, pp. 86-87.

31. Nairn, Geoff, "Washer Features Fuzzy Logic, Virtual Sensors," *Design News*, September 25, 1995, p. 50.

32. Rogers, Dale, "A Case for Fuzzy Thinking: The Fuzzy Logic Algorithm Will Make the Logistics Professional's Job Go a Lot Smoother in the Near Future," *Transportation & Logistics*, March 1996, pp. 108-110.

33. Baker, Andrea, "Intelligent Dishwasher Outsmarts Dirt," *Design News*, April 4, 1995, pp. 69-72.

Chapter 7

1. "Tool Talk," *Chain Store Age*, Nov. 2000, pp. 10B-11B.

2. Keen, Peter, "Information Technology and the Management Difference: A Fusion Map," *IBM Systems Journal*, 1993, pp. 17-39.

3. Morrison, Ian, *The Second Curve*, Ballantine Books, New York, 1996.

4. Middlemiss, Jim, "U.S. Bankcorp Streamlines Business Continuity Process," *Bank Systems & Technology*, December 2000, p. 56.

5. Albright, Brian, "Come See the Software Side of Sears," *Frontline Solutions*, October 2000, pp. 36-38.

6. Garner, Rochelle, "Why JAD Goes Bad," *Computerworld*, April 25, 1994, pp. 87-88.

7. Lane, Randall, "FAA, Inc." *Forbes*, August 26, 1996, p. 48.

8. Ruber, Peter, "The Great Foreign IT Worker Debate," *Informationweek*, Nov. 27, 2000, pp. 153-160.

9. Fryer, Bronwyn, "When Users Take Notes," *Computerworld*, August 8, 1994, p. 82.

10. Oliver, Richard, "AutoIntelligence," *Management Review*, Feb. 2000, pp. 12-13.

11. Haag, Stephen, and Peter Keen, *Information Technology: Tomorrow's Advantage Today*, McGraw-Hill, New York, 1996.

12. Girard, Kim, "MasterCard Upgrade Gives Network a Charge," *Computerworld*, May 6, 1996, p. 86.

13. Verity, John, "Let's Order Out for Technology," *Business Week*, May 13, 1996, p. 47.

14. Anderson, Howard, "Innovators in Outsourcing," *Forbes*, October 23, 1995, pp. 1-45 (special advertising supplement).

15. McHugh, Josh, "Bowling Ball, Marbles, and Garden Hose," *Forbes*, October 21, 1996, pp. 84-92.

16. Hoffman, Thomas, and Julia Kling, "Utility Unplugs Object Project," *Computerworld*, February 26, 1996, pp. 1, 125.

17. Gilbert, Alorie, "GM Joint Venture to Track In-Transit Inventory," *Informationweek*, December 2000, p. 26.

18. Verity, loc. cit.

19. Caldwell, "The New Outsourcing Partnership," loc. cit.

20. Byrne, John, "Has Outsourcing Gone Too Far?" *Business Week*, April 1, 1996, pp. 26-28.

21. Gould, Lawrence, "The 'E' in ERP Is Going Electronic," *Automotive Manufacturing & Production*, December 2000, pp. 64-67.

22. Keener, Ronald, "Bridge the Patient-Provider Gap," *Health Management Technology*, November 2000, pp. 44-49.

Chapter 8

1. Fogliasso, Christine and Donald Baack, "The Personal Impact of Ethical Decisions: A Social Penetration Theory Model," *Second Annual Conference on Business Ethics Sponsored by the*

Vincentian Universities in the United States, New York, 1995.

2. Jones, T.M., "Ethical Decision Making by Individuals in Organizations: An Issue-Contingent Model," *Academy of Management Review,* 1991, pp. 366-395.

3. Baase, Sara, *The Gift of Fire: Social, Legal and Ethical Issues in Computing,* Prentice-Hall, Upper Saddle River, NJ, 1997.

4. www.siaa.net/sharedcontent/press/.2000/5-24-00.html

5. Adams, Hall III, "E-Mail Monitoring in the Workplace: The Good, the Bad and the Ugly," *Defense Counsel Journal,* January 2000, pp. 32–46.

6. York, Thomas, "Invasion of Privacy? E-Mail Monitoring is on the Rise," *InformationWeek,* February 21, 2000, pp.142–146.

7. Corbin, Dana, "Keeping a Virtual Eye on Employees," *Occupational Health & Safety,* November 2000, pp. 24–28.

8. York, loc. cit.

9. Corbin, loc. cit.

10. Verespej, Michael A., "Internet Surfing," *Industry Week,* February 7, 2000, pp. 58–64.

11. Medford, Cassimir, "Know Who I Am," *PC Magazine,* January 16, 2001, pp. 136–137.

12. Medford, loc.cit.

13. Graven, Matthew P., "Leave Me Alone," *PC Magazine,* January 16, 2001, pp. 151–152.

14. Baase, loc. cit.

15. Carey, Jack, "ACLU Decries Super Bowl Surveillance," *USA Today,* February 2, 2001, p. 1C.

16. Baase, loc. cit.

17. De Bony, Elizabeth, "EU Overwhelmingly Approves U.S. Data-Privacy Regulations," *Computerworld,* June 5, 2000, p.28.

18. Rohde, Laura, "U.K. E-Mail Law Reaches U.S.," *InfoWorld,* September 4, 2000, pp. 28–29.

19. Banham, Russ, "Share Data At Your Own Risk," *World Trade,* November 2000, pp. 60–63.

20. "Ergonomic Posturing," *CIO,* March 15, 1996, p. 22.

21. Dessoff, Alan L., "What's Wrong with Your Computer Workstation?" *Safety & Health,* October 1995, pp. 60–63.

22. Web, www.open.ac.uk/OU/Intro/WhatIs.html.

23. Carswell, Linda, "Distance Education Via the Internet: The Student Experience," *British Journal of Educational Technology,* January 2000, pp. 29–46

24. Caldwell, Bruce, "We Are the Business," *InformationWeek,* October 28, 1996, pp. 36–50.

25. Mogelefsky, Don, "Security Turns Inward," *Incentive,* May 2000, p. 16.

26. Radcliff, Deborah, "Hackers, Terrorists, and Spies," *Software Magazine,* October 1997, pp. 36–47.

27. Hulme, George V. and Bob Wallace. "Beware Cyberattacks," *InformationWeek,* November 13, 2000, pp. 22–24.

28. Mogelefsky, loc.cit.

29. Hulme, George V., "Ecampus.com Sets Sights on 'Campus' Security," *InformationWeek,* June 5, 2000, p. 132.

30. Hulme and Wallace, loc. cit.

31. Kornblum, Janet, "Kournikova Virus Maker: No Harm Meant," *USA Today,* February 14, 2001, p. 3D.

32. Karp, Jack, "The Year in CyberCrime," www.techtv.com/cybercrime/story/0,23158,3303045,00.html, December 25, 2000.

33. Meserve, Jason, "People Around the World Bitten by 'Love Bug,'" *Network World,* May 8, 2000, pp. 14, 28.

34. "Fast Times," *Fortune,* Summer 2000, pp. 35–36.

35. Zemke, Ron, "Tech-Savvy and People-Stupid," *Training,* July 2000, pp. 16–18.

36. Spencer, Vikki, "Risk Management: Danger of the Cyber Deep," *Canadian Underwriter,* September 2000, pp. 10–14.

37. Paul, Brooke, "How Much Risk is Too Much?" *InformationWeek,* November 6, 2000, pp. 116–124.

38. Eastwood, Alison, "End-Users: The Enemy Within?" *Computing Canada,* January 4, 1996, p. 41.

39. Sharp, Kevin R., "When Disaster Strikes," *Computerworld,* September 5, 1994, pp. 97–99.

40. Breidenbach, Susan, "Security Tools: Keeping Ahead of the Cybercrooks," *InformationWeek,* August 21, 2000, pp. 136-138.

41. Hoffer, Jim, "Backing Up Business," *Health Management Technology,* January 2001, p. 70.

42. Kahan, Stuart, "Hot Sites: The Solution When Business Interruption is Fatal," *The Practical Accountant,* July 1994, pp. 58–63.

43. "Disaster Diary," *Network World,* January 15, 2001, pp. 42–46.

44. DePompa, Barbara, "Averting a Complete Disaster," *InformationWeek,* July 15, 1996, pp. 40-50.

45. Voigt, Kevin, "For 'Extreme Telecommuters,' Remote Work Means Really Remote," *Wall Street Journal,* January 31, 2001, p. B1.

46. Dannhauser, Carol Leonetti, "Who's in the Home Office?" *American Demographics,* June 1999, cover story.

47. "Remote Control," *BusinessWeek Online* at www.businessweek.com/smallbiz/content/apr2000/ma3674054.htm April 4, 2000.

Chapter 9

1. Bazdarich, Colleen, et al, "If I Knew Then What I Know Now," *eCompany,* March 2001, pp. 71–80.

2. Rawe, Julie, "What Will Be the Ten Hottest Jobs?," *Time,* May 22, 2000, pp. 70–71.

3. Brown, Eryn, "Who's Afraid of E-Books?," *Fortune,* February 5, 2001, pp. 159–162.

4. Connor, Deni, "QuikOrder Brings Domino's Pizza to You in 30 Minutes or Less," *Network World,* March 6, 2000, p. 20.

5. Cope, James, "Lucent, TeraBeam Plan to Clear Last-Mile Bottleneck," *Computerworld,* April 17, 2000, p. 26.

INDEX

Access
    high-speed, to the Internet, 245–246
    to medical malpractice databases, industry perspective on, 88
Ace Hardware, industry perspective on, 194
Acxiom Corp., 24–25
Ad hoc
    decisions, 130, 417, 421
    reports, 38, 417
Adaptivity, 154–155, 417
Addresses, interpreting, 403
Adtrack, 128
AFC Enterprises, 109
Affiliate programs, 202, 417
Affordable Homes Real Estate, 363–364
Aging schedules, 39
AI. *See* Artificial intelligence
Air travel, 338
Airline industry, 69–71, 240
    disintermediating the travel agent, 71
    frequent flyer programs, 70
    helping the little guy compete, 70
    reservation systems, 69–70
    yield management systems, 70–71
A/L unit. *See* Arithmetic/logic unit
Alliance partner, 50, 417
Allright Distributors, 208
Amazon.com, 4, 67, 152
Anonymous browsing, 318
ANSI X12 protocol, 186, 424
Antivirus software, 391, 417
APOLLO, 70
Appliances, Internet, 246–248, 424
Application development facilities, 41, 417
Application generation subsystems, 93–94, 110, 417
Application software, 391–392, 417
    developing, 41
Arithmetic/logic (A/L) unit, 384, 417
Artificial intelligence (AI), 42, 143–144, 156, 417
ASR. *See* Automatic speech recognition
Asynchronous transfer mode (ATM) protocol, 186, 417
Atomic primary keys, 97, 417
Attracting and retaining customers, 200–203
    affiliate programs, 202
    banner ads, 201–202
    email and viral marketing, 202
    registering with search engines, 201
    selling to existing customers, 202–203
Auction houses, on the Internet, 77
Autism, 239
Autobytel.com, 148
Automatic speech recognition (ASR), 234–237, 256, 378, 417
    continuous, 236, 418
    conversing with your computer, 234–235
    future of, 236–237
    types of, 236
Automobiles, buying on the Internet, 77
Autonomy, 154, 417

Backup servers, Domino's Pizza example, 350
Backups, 330–331, 333
    facilities for, 94
Bandwidth (capacity), 182, 417
Banks in danger of collapse, industry perspective on, 335
Banner ads, 201–202, 417
Bar code reader, 379, 417
Bass Brewery, 14
Baxter International, 58
B&B Travel Consultants, 363–364
B2B. *See* Business to business e-commerce
B2C. *See* Business to consumer e-commerce
Benefits. *See also* Cost-benefit analysis
    intangible, 267, 420
    tangible, 267, 423
Biometrics, 241, 256, 380, 417
Black-hat hackers, 327, 417
Blue Plus, 97
Bluetooth, 171, 417
BNSF, making the trains run on time, industry perspective on, 212
Books and music, buying on the Internet, 75–76
Borders Group Inc., 105
Bottleneck problem, 351–352
Bounce, industry perspective on, 326
BPI. *See* Bytes per inch
BPR. *See* Business process reengineering
Brainpower, for your business, 126–164
Bridging, 185, 417
    gap between business people and technical people, 52–53
Broadband telecommunications, enhancing buying experience, 195
Browsing. *See also* Microbrowsers
    anonymous, 318
Building a database, 117–125
    defining entity classes and primary keys, 118–119
    defining information for each relation, 122–124
    defining relationships among entity classes, 119–122
    designing and building a relational database, 118
    using a data definition language to create your database, 125
Building models, 286–287
Built-in integrity constraints, 89
Bus topology, 181, 417
Business
    activities of, 4–5
    changing the face of, 2–31
    characteristics of today's new, 8–12
    e-commerce, 10–11
    and globalization, 8–9
    knowledge worker computing, 12
    personal information gathering by, 23–25
    Sony example, 9
    team work, 10
Business networks, 171–176
    client/server—a business view, 171–175
    client/server—a physical view, 175–176
Business principles, 353
Business process reengineering (BPR), 301, 417
Business processes, 63, 417
Business resources
    effective communication, 353
    ethical action, 353
    global thinking, 353
    information as key for the future, 9–10, 352–354
    productivity with technology, 353
    solid business principles, 353
Business reviews, 45. *See also* individual examples

Business to business (B2B) e-commerce, 50, 205–214, 417
    Allright Distributors example, 208
    BNSF trains example, 212
    corporate purchasing segments, 206
    dairy industry example, 207
    extranets, 213
    intranets, 213–214
    marketplace, 60, 212–213, 417
    new EDI, 211
    purchasing of direct materials, 206–211
    purchasing of indirect materials, 211
Business to consumer (B2C) e-commerce, 50, 192–205, 417
    Ace Hardware example, 194
    advantages of, 192–195
    attracting and retaining customers, 200–203
    betting on, 195
    broadband telecommunications enhancing buying experience, 195
    call centers integrated with Web site, 194–195
    for commodity-like items, 198–199
    for digital products, 199
    end of the beginning in, 196–197
    executing well, 204
    instantaneous changes in offerings and price, 193–194
    merchandising, 203–205
    online grocery sales example, 199
    sector selection, 204
    for services, 195
    speed and convenience, 192–193
    survival of dot-coms, 348
    Toyota example, 198
    watching the competition, 204–205
Buyer agents, 152, 417
Buyer power, 58, 60, 417
Buying experience, broadband telecommunications enhancing, 195
Bytes per inch (BPI), 386

Cable modems, 166–167, 417
Call centers, integrated with Web site, 194–195
Capacity issues, 182, 417
Capital investment analysis, 268, 417
CASE. *See* Computer-aided software engineering tools
Catalina Supermarkets, 158
Catalog hubs, 212, 417
Category 3 cable, 168, 417
Category 5 cable, 168–169, 417
Cave automatic virtual environments (CAVEs), 241, 417
CD-ROMs, 387, 417
CD-Rs, 387, 417
Census Bureau, privacy issues involving, 319
Central processing unit (CPU), 384, 417
Centralized databases, 107, 111, 417
CEO. *See* Chief executive officers
Change management facilities, 96
Characters, 84, 417
Chase Manhattan Bank, 151, 154
Chief executive officers (CEO), 107, 111, 417
    attitude toward information technology, 52
Chief information officers (CIO), 107, 111, 417
Children's Online Privacy Protection Act (COPPA), 219
Choice, 130, 156, 417
    of a vendor, 294
Chrysler, 287

Cigna Corp., 151
CIO. *See* Chief information officers
CIS. *See* Customer integrated systems
Cisco Systems, 50, 52
Citibank, 151
Classification, pattern, 234–235, 422
Cleanscape software, 3
Click-throughs, 192, 417
Clicks-and-mortar, 192, 204, 417
Client/server networks, 171–175, 415, 417
    distributed data management, 172
    distributed logic, 172
    distributed presentation, 171
    divisional rules, 173
    organizational rules, 173
    a physical view, 175–176
    remote data management, 172
    remote presentation, 171
Clothing and accessories, buying on the Internet, 76
Coaxial cable (coax), 183, 417
Coins and cash, disappearance of, 352
Cold site, 334, 417
Collaborative filtering, 67, 417
Collaborative planning, forecasting, and replenishment (CPRF), 57, 417
Collecting information, 87
".com" industry perspectives
    dairy industry gets set for B2B exchange, 207
    fear of the big, bad dot-coms, 350
    free long-distance phone calls on the Internet, 16
    JD Edwards' OneWorld enterprise, 299
    keeping an eye on the competition, 62
    making the move to .com, 91
    security consciousness of eCampus, 327
    storage space and software for rent/free on the Internet, 247
Combining information from different databases, 100–101
Commodity-like items, selling by e-commerce, 198–199
Communicating
    information, 389
    over the Internet, 260
Communications media, 181, 417
    key considerations for, 184–185
Communications processors, 185, 417
Communications satellites, 184, 417
Communications service providers, 176–179, 417
    private network, 178
    public network, 178
    value-added network, 178
    virtual private network, 179
Company financials, finding sources of, 160
Comparative reports, 38, 417
Competition, 204–205
Competitive advantage, 46–79, 417
    airline industry example, 69–71
    CAD Prep AmericaOne for the America's Cup example, 47–48
    Cisco Systems example, 50, 52
    Dell Computer example, 50–51
    in e-commerce, 65–69
    Federal Express example, 48–49
    GM luring customers with OnStar example, 74
    knowledge workers checklist, 72–73
    opportunities close to home, 50
    ordering products on the Internet, 75–77
    paperless payments, 72
    for smart companies using IT, 52–57
    tools that can help, 57–65
    UPS and Fender Guitar example, 49
Competitive intelligence, 222
Complementors, 206, 417
Composite primary keys, 97, 417
Composite relations, 121
Computer networks, 226, 417
Computer screen, animating, 258
Computer viruses, 328, 418
Computer-aided software engineering (CASE) tools, 297, 417
Computers. *See also* Hardware; Software
    buying accessories on the Internet, 76–77
    connecting with ethernet cards and dedicated network cable, 168–169
    connecting with wireless home networks, 169
Computing
    decentralized, 14, 418
    knowledge worker, 12
Concurrency control facilities, 95–96
Connecting to the Internet, 165–167
    cable modem, 166–167
    digital subscriber line, 165–166
    satellite modem, 167
    telephone modem, 165
Connectivity software, 389, 391, 418
Consumer information, 113
Consumer privacy, 317–318
Continental Airlines, decision support example, 127–128
Contingency planning, 268, 418
    industry perspective on, 270
Continuous automatic speech recognition, 236, 418
Control unit, 384, 418
Convenience, 192-193
Conversing with your computer, 234–235
    feature analysis, 234
    language processing, 235
    pattern classification, 234–235
Conversion
    piecemeal, 283, 422
    rate of, 203, 418
Cookie stoppers, 318
Cookies, 219, 418
Cooperation, 137
COPPA. *See* Children's Online Privacy Protection Act
Copyright issues, 315, 336, 418
Corporate purchasing segments, 206
Cost-benefit analyses, 267, 418
Costs
    of disaster recovery, 268, 418
    of ownership, 300
    of reengineering, 300–301
    of switching, 58, 423
CPFR. *See* Collaborative planning, forecasting, and replenishment
CPU. *See* Central processing unit
Crackers, 218, 226, 418
Cradling information, 385–388
Crash proof software, 391, 418
Creating
    electronic resumes, 27
    information, 384
Creating a security plan
    backups, 330–331, 333
    encryption, 333
    firewalls, 333
    security software, 333
Creative design, 54, 418
    demanding, 54–56
Credit cards, 215–216
Crimes. *See* Cyber crimes
Critical success factors (CSF), 267, 418
CRM. *See* Customer relation management systems
Cross-cultural diversity, 418
Crossover, 152, 157, 418
CSF. *See* Critical success factors
Cultural diversity, 321, 418
Culture shock, 321, 336, 418
Customer integrated systems (CIS), 37, 418
Customer knowledge, industry perspective on, 105
Customer moment of value, 5–6, 16–17, 418
    the form dimension, 17
    the location dimension, 17
    the time dimension, 16–17
Customer relation management (CRM) systems, 3
Cyber crimes, 328–330
    denial-of-service attacks, 330
    viruses, 328–330
Cyber terrorists, 327, 420
Cybersickness, 240, 418
Cybiko, 21

Dairy industry, moving to B2B exchange, industry perspective on, 207
Data, 15, 25, 418
Data administration, 107, 111, 418
Data administration subsystems, 94–96, 110, 418
    backup and recovery facilities, 94
    change management facilities, 96
    concurrency control facilities, 95–96
    query optimization facilities, 95
    reorganization facilities, 95
    security management facilities, 95
Data definition subsystems, 89–90, 110, 418
Data dictionary, 87–88, 418
Data management, 131–132, 418
    distributed, 172
    remote, 172
Data manipulation subsystems, 90–93, 110, 418
Data marts, 105, 418
Data mining, 100
    AFC Enterprises example, 109
    counting your customers, 106
    in dining establishments, 109–111
    Einstein/Noah Bagel example, 111
    getting to know your customers, 105
    Harrah's Entertainment example, 110
    Pizzeria Uno example, 110–111
    politically correct, 101
    Red Robin International example, 109–110
Data-mining agents, 154, 162, 418
Data-mining tools, 102–103, 111, 418
    described, 102–103
    intelligence agents, 103
    multidimensional analysis, 103
    need for, 105
    query-and-reporting, 102–103
Data warehousing, 100, 103–105, 107, 110–111, 418. *See also* Data mining tools; Databases
    already having a data warehouse, 104
    combining information from different databases, 100–101
    described, 100–102
    important considerations in, 103–105
    to know your customers, 105
    multidimensional, 101–102
    need for, 103–104

Index **433**

numbers of employees to involve in, 104–105
political correctness in, 101
supporting decision making, 102
timeliness of the information, 103, 105
Database administration, 108, 111, 418
Database and database management system environment, 86–96
information privileges during university registration example, 95
medical malpractice database example, 88
moving to .com, 91
Database applications, developing and maintaining, 109
Database management system (DBMS) engines, 89, 110, 418
Database management systems (DBMS), 89, 110, 418
application generation subsystems, 93–94
data administration subsystems, 94–96
data definition subsystems, 89–90
data manipulation subsystems, 90–93
described, 89–96
support for OLTP, OLAP, and information management, 96
Databases, 80–116, 418. *See also* Online databases and information repositories
built-in integrity constraints, 89
collections of information, 87
described, 86–89
dining data example, 109–111
environment of, 86–96
Green Bay Packer "Cheesehead" hat example, 81
important characteristics of, 87–89
information in an organization, 82–86
knowledge workers checklist, 110–111
logical structure, 87–88
logical ties in the information, 88–89
object-oriented database model, 99–100
in an organization, 106–109
partitioning, 107, 422
relational database model, 96–97
replicating, 107, 423
searching online, 112–114
DBMS. *See* Database management system
Decentralized computing, 14, 37, 418
Decentralized information, industry perspective on, 15
Decision support, 126–164
artificial intelligence in, 143–144
bank computer example, 157–158
Continental Airlines example, 127–128
expert systems in, 144–149
genetic algorithms, 151–152
geographic information systems, 140–143
group decision support systems, 135–140
intelligent agents, 152–156
investment opportunities example, 159–161
knowledge workers checklist, 156–157
neural networks, 150–151
Decision support systems (DSS), 42, 130–135, 156–157, 418
and artificial intelligence, 42
components of, 131–134
for data management, 131–132
ethical questions in, 134–135
health care example, 134
for model management, 132–133
for user interface management, 133

Decisions, 128–130
making, 130
nonrecurring, 130
nonstructured, 129
recurring, 130
structured, 129
Dedicated network cables, connecting computers with, 168–169
Dell Computer, 50–51
Demand aggregation, 190, 418
Demographics, 113–114
Denial-of-service attacks, 330, 418
Design, 130, 156, 280–282, 418
Designing corporate security procedures, 218
Desktop versus laptop, 397
Destination information, 340
Development tools, Web, 304–305
Digital cash. *See* Electronic cash
Digital cinema, industry perspective on, 326
Digital divide, 191–192, 418
closing, 352
global, 191, 419
Digital products, marketing, 199
Digital signatures, 217, 418
Digital subscriber lines (DSL), 165–166, 418
Digital video disks (DVD), 388, 418
Dilbert, 54
Direct materials, 206, 418
Directories, 201, 418
Disappearing Inc., 220
Disaster recovery plan, 333–337, 418
business information, 335
computer equipment, 335
cost curve, 268, 418
customers, 334
facilities, 334
knowledge workers, 335
Discrete automatic speech recognition, 236, 418
Disintermediation, 67–68, 418
travel agent example, 71
Disk optimization software, 391, 418
Disk storage technologies, 386–387, 418
Distributed data management, 172
Distributed databases, 107, 111, 418
Distributed logic, 172
Distributed presentations, 171
Distribution chains, 50, 418
Divisional rules, 173
Doctor's little helper, industry perspective on, 134
Document management, 41
Domain experts, 146, 418
Domain names, 402, 418
Domino's Pizza, industry perspective on backup servers in, 350
Dot matrix printers, 383, 418
DowElanco, 105
Dreyer's, 4
DSL. *See* Digital subscriber lines
DSS. *See* Decision support systems
DVD. *See* Digital video disks

E-cash. *See* Electronic cash
E-commerce. *See* Electronic commerce
E Ink, industry perspective on, 60
E-mail
encryption for, 318
and viral marketing, 202
E-R. *See* Entity-relationship diagram
E-tailers, 192, 418
EBPP. *See* Electronic bill presentment and payment

eCampus, security consciousness of, industry perspective on, 327
EDI. *See* Electronic data interchange
EDIFACT protocol, 186, 419
Education
graduate school information and tips, 357–358
through the Internet, 356–361
long-distance, 358–360
MBA programs, 357
Ph.D. programs, 360
specialized MBA programs, 357
Effective communication, 353
Egghead Software, 68
Einstein/Noah Bagel, 111
EIS. *See* Executive information systems
Electronic bill presentment and payment (EBPP), 216, 419
Electronic cash (e-cash; digital cash), 242–244, 257, 419
becoming a reality, 243–244
delays in implementing, 242–243
Electronic commerce (e-commerce), 10–11, 188–228, 419
business to business, 205–214
business to consumer, 192–205
buying Pepsi online, 189
credit cards and smart cards, 215–216
Disappearing Inc. example, 220
disintermediation, 67–68
European privacy laws, 219
getting your business on the Internet, 222–225
global reach, 68
growth of, 190–192
knowledge workers checklist, 220–221
mass customization and personalization, 65–67
new technologies for, 68–69
payment systems and digital cash, 215–216
role of government in promoting, 214–215
security concepts, 217
traditional and next-generation EDI, 215
uniqueness of, 65–69
Electronic data interchange (EDI), 207, 419
Electronic meetings
software, 41, 419
support, 40, 419
Electronic resumes, creating and posting, 27
Emerging technologies. *See* Technologies
Employees, privacy and, 316–317
Encryption, 323–324, 333, 419
Enterprise resource planning (ERP), 297–302, 419
cost of ownership, 300
cost of reengineering, 300–301
existence of legacy systems, 298, 300
expertise needed for enterprise software, 301–302
JD Edwards' OneWorld enterprise example, 299
preparing your organization for the Web, 299
Enterprise software, 298, 300–302, 419
Enterprisewide systems in the medical field, 302
Entertainment industry perspectives
Bounce and Toy Story 2, 326
customer knowledge, 105
digital cinema, 326
E Ink, 60
"Intertainment," 21
Entity classes, 97, 110, 118, 419
defining, 118–119
relationships among, 119–122

Entity-relationship (E-R) diagramming, 119, 419
    in building a database, 117–125
Entry barriers, 62, 419
Erasable optical disks, 387–388, 419
Ergonomic considerations, 323, 337, 398, 419
ERP. *See* Enterprise resource planning
Ethernet, 186, 419
Ethernet cards, 168, 419
    connecting computers with, 168–169
Ethernet protocol, 186
Ethical questions, 21, 419
    in decision support systems, 134–135
    in expert systems, 149
    in neural networks, 151
    in organizing and managing information, 108–109
Evaluating. *See also* Monitoring and reevaluating
    proposed IT systems, 267–268
    requests for proposals, 294, 370–372
Exception reports, 38, 419
Execution, 204
Executive information systems (EIS), 42–43, 419
Expert systems, 42, 144–149, 157, 419
    capabilities of, 148–149
    components of, 146–148
    ethical questions in, 149
    for getting goods safely across the border, 144
    information types, 146
    IT components, 147–148
    people in, 146–147
    for traffic lights, 150
Expertise needed for enterprise software, 301–302
Explanation modules, 148, 157, 419
eXtensible Mark-up Language. *See* XML
External databases, 107, 111, 419
External hard disks, 387, 419
External information, 18, 34, 419
Extranets, 213, 226, 419
Extreme telecommuters, 336
EZfone Internet phone-calling, industry perspective on, 245

Fair Use Doctrine, 315, 336, 419
Fault tolerant computers, 355, 419
FDDI. *See* Fiber distributed data interface
Fear of dot-coms, industry perspective on, 350
Feasibility reviews, 309, 419
Feature analyses, 234, 419
Federal Trade Commission (FTC), 332
FedEx, 15, 48–49
FEDI. *See* Financial EDI
Fender Guitar, 49
Fiber distributed data interface (FDDI), 419
Fields, 84–85, 419
Files, 85, 419
Financial aid resources, 113
Financial EDI (FEDI), 215, 419
Financial services industry perspectives
    access to medical malpractice databases, 88
    bank in danger of collapse, 335
    contingency plans, 270
    decentralized information, 15
    Web sites, 154
Find-and-retrieve agents, 152–153
Firewalls, 217, 419
First mover, 49, 419
First Union Bank, 158
Firstar Bank, 270
Five forces model, 58–62, 419
    buyer power, 58
    rivalry among existing competitors, 59

    supplier power, 58
    threat of new entrants, 59
    threat of substitute products or services, 58–59
Flaming, 22, 419
Flat panel displays, 383, 419
Flows of information in an organization, 17–18, 35
Ford, 4
Foreign keys, 89, 110, 419
Form dimension, 17
Formatted OCR devices, 379–380, 419
Free long-distance phone calls on the Internet, 244–245
    industry perspective on, 16
Free stuff on the Internet, 306
Freeware and shareware on the Internet, 257–260
    animating computer screen, 258
    communicating over the Internet, 260
    protecting computer investment, 258–259
    searching for shareware and freeware, 259
    using computer for more than work, 257–258
Frequent flyer programs, 70
FTC. *See* Federal Trade Commission
ftp (file transfer protocol) servers, 401, 419
Fulfillment, 204
Funding, 224–225
Fusion, information technology, 267, 420
Future
    achieving transparency, 348–349, 351
    of automatic speech recognition, 236–237
    of B2C dot-coms, 348, 350
    of coins and cash, 352
    continuing your education through the Internet, 356–361
    of the digital divide, 352
    gazing into your crystal ball, 353
    innovations for, 230–262
    of "intelligent" technology, 352
    jobs and skills for, 346–348
    key business resource of, 352–354
    knowledge worker's checklist, 354–355
    planning for, 273
    preparing for, 344–361
    of 3-D technologies, 234
    of virtual reality, 240–241
    of wireless, 352
    you and your information, 354–355
Fuzzy logic, 254, 419

Gates Rubber Company, 207–209
Gateways, 185, 419
Gathering all proposed IT systems, 267
GDSS. *See* Group decision support systems
GE, 178
    industry perspective on, 53
Generic strategies, 59, 423
Genetic algorithms, 42, 151–152, 157, 419
Geographic Information System (GIS), 42, 140–143, 156–157, 419
Getting business on the Internet, 222–225
    competitive intelligence, 222
    getting funding, 224–225
    hosting services, 223
    marketing the site, 224
    privacy issues, 224
    storefront software, 222–223
Getting funding, 224–225
GIS. *See* Geographic information system
Global digital divide, 191, 419
Global e-commerce growth projections, 191
Global perspectives, 7, 9, 55, 84, 106, 140, 144, 199, 219, 249, 254, 284, 296, 324

Global Positioning System (GPS), 68, 250–251, 419
Global reach, 68, 419
Global Village, 17
Globalization, 8–9, 9, 419
Gloves, 238, 380, 419
GM, 18, 34, 296, 325
Government agencies
    Census Bureau, 319
    IRS, 319
    law enforcement, 318–319
    privacy issues involving, 318–320
GPS. *See* Global positioning system
Graduate school information and tips, 357–358
Graphics adapter cards, 382, 419
Green Bay Packer "Cheesehead" hats, 81
Group decision support systems (GDSS), 42, 135–140, 156–157, 419
    IBM example, 137
    IT tools in, 136–137
    key components of, 136–137
    for meetings, 137–140
    people in, 136
    South African elections example, 140
    virtual meetings, 139
Group document databases, 419
Group projects, 362–373
    advertising with banner ads, 369–370
    assessing the value of information, 362–364
    building a decision support system, 368–369
    building value chains, 365–366
    demonstrating how to build Web sites, 372
    evaluating requests for proposals, 370–372
    executive information system reporting, 363–364
    making the case with presentation graphics software, 372–373
    using relational technology to track technology, 367–368
Group scheduling software, 40, 419
Groupthink, 138
Groupware, 40, 419
Growth of global e-commerce, 190–192

Hackers, 326, 420
    black-hat, 327, 417
    white-hat, 326, 424
Hactivists (cyber terrorists), 327, 420
Hard cards, 387, 420
Hard disk cartridges, 387, 420
Hard disk packs, 387, 420
Hardware, 375–389, 420. *See also* Software
    buying your personal computer system, 397–398
    capturing information, 376–380
    communicating information, 389
    conveying information, 381–384
    cradling information, 385–388
    creating information, 384
    input technologies, 376–380
    intellectual interfaces, 390–392
    output technologies, 381–384
    storage technologies, 385–388
    telecommunications technologies, 389
    working together with software, 393–396
Harrah's Entertainment, 110
Headset, 238, 380, 420
Health care industry perspectives
    cracking the human genetic code, 108
    doctor's little helper, 134

Index   **435**

intranet telephone directory, 18
just-in-time surgery, 58
virtual reality for the betterment of people and society, 239
High-speed Internet access, 245–246
High-tech Hollywood, 231
HighwaysAndByways, 369–370
History, repeating itself, 344
Hollywood, high-tech, 231
Home networks, 165–171
    connected to the Internet, 165–167
    with ethernet cards and dedicated network cable, 168–169
    with existing phone wiring, 168
    peer to peer, 167–171
    simple, 167–171
HomeBase, buying software to move beyond EDI, 264
Homes, Internet-connected, 254–255
Honeypots, 218
Hospitality & leisure industry perspectives, backup servers at Domino's Pizza, 350
Hosting services, 223
    Web, 306
Hot sites, 334, 420
HTML. *See* Hypertext markup language
Human genetic code, industry perspective on cracking, 108
Hypertext links, 405, 421
Hypertext markup language (HTML), 304

IBM, industry perspective on, 137
IDC, 213
"Ility" issue of wireless technologies, addressing, 252
Image scanning, 380, 420
Impact printers, 383, 420
Implementation, 130, 156, 282–283, 420
Implementing a security plan
    backups, 330–331, 333
    encryption, 333
    firewalls, 333
    security software, 333
Indirect materials, 206, 420
Industry perspectives
    ".com" companies, 16, 62, 91, 148, 207, 247, 299, 327, 350
    entertainment & publishing, 21, 60, 105, 326
    financial services, 15, 88, 154, 270, 335
    health care, 18, 58, 108, 134, 239
    hospitality & leisure, 350
    IT & telecommunications, 245, 352
    manufacturing, 53, 137, 198, 250, 287
    retail, 194, 237, 273
    transportation, 212
Inference engines, 147, 420
InfoBase, 24–25
Information, 14–19, 25, 34–35, 324–336, 420. *See also* Online databases and information repositories
    in banking, 335
    Bounce and Toy Story 2 examples, 326
    capturing, 376–380
    children's healthcare example, 18
    conveying, 381–384
    for customer moment of value, 16–17
    decentralized, 15
    digital movies example, 326
    disaster recovery plan for, 333–336
    eCampus example of securing, 327
    flows of in an organization, 17–18

free long-distance phone calls on the Internet, 16
going to college without going to college, 324
in help desk work, 325
intranet telephone directory example, 18
as a key resource, 9–10
logical ties in, 88–89
managing while it is used, 84–86
in an organization, 82–86
oversight of organizational, 107–108
ownership of, 108
partnerships involving, 49, 420
personal, 354–355
processing in the form of transactions, 82
role of, 18–19, 324–325
Royal Caribbean Cruises example, 84
security of, 325–333
supporting innovation, 14
using to make a decision, 82–83
Information age, 2–31, 420
    characteristics of today's new business, 8–12
    knowledge workers in, 19–25, 420
    management information systems challenge, 4–7
    managing customer relations in an electronic world, 3
Information literacy, levels of, 20, 421
Information technology (IT), 12–14, 24, 35, 420
    redefining business operations through innovation in, 15
    supporting decision-making tasks, 13
    supporting information-processing tasks, 12–13
    supporting shared information through decentralized computing, 14
Information technology (IT) fusion, 267, 420
Information technology (IT) industry perspectives
    EZfone makes Internet phone-calling "EZ," 245
    using wireless fiber optics to solve the last-mile bottleneck problem, 352
Information technology (IT) systems, 266–269. *See also* Customer integrated systems; Decision support systems; Executive information systems; Interorganizational systems; Management information systems; Transaction processing systems; Workgroup support systems
    and artificial intelligence, 42
    bringing to life, 264–309
    business examples of, 45
    developing, 264–309
    enterprise resource planning and enterprise software for, 297–302
    enterprisewide systems in the medical field example, 302
    evaluating proposed, 267–268
    gathering all proposed IT systems, 267
    HomeBase example, 264
    information in, 34–35
    insourcing, 272–285
    knowledge workers checklist, 300–301
    for organizations, 33–45, 267
    outsourcing, 292–297
    risks of, 268, 420
    selfsourcing and prototyping, 286–292
    Web page example, 303–307
    what you can't live without, 268
Information technology (IT) systems plans, 266–267, 269–270, 300, 420
Infrared media, 183, 420
Ink jet printers, 383, 420

Innovation, 52, 420
Innovations for the future, 230–262
Input devices, standard, 397
Input technologies, 376–380, 420
    tools using, 378–380
Insourcing, 266
    analysis, 278–280
    design, 280–282
    hiring programmers from around the world, 284
    implementation, 282–283
    ITW Enterprises example, 276–277
    planning, 274
    responsibilities during, 284
    scoping, 274–275, 278
    Sears example, 273
    support, 283, 285
    and the traditional systems development life cycle, 272–285
Instances, 97, 118, 420
Instantaneous changes, in offerings and price, 193–194
Intangible benefits, 267, 420
Integrated CASE Tools, 297, 420
Integrated services digital network (ISDN) protocol, 186, 420
Integrity constraints, 89, 420
Intellectual interfaces, 390–392
Intellectual property issues, 315, 336, 420
Intelligence, 130, 156, 420
Intelligent agents, 42, 103, 111, 152–157, 420
    adaptivity, 154–155
    autonomy, 154
    bargain hunting online, 153
    components of, 154–156
    components of an intelligent agent, 154–156
    data-mining agents, 154
    find-and-retrieve agents, 152–153
    monitoring and surveillance agents, 153–154
    selecting AI software, 155
    sociability, 155–156
    user agents, 153
    Web site example, 154
Intelligent home appliances, 253–254, 257, 420
Interactive chat capabilities, 194, 420
Interlaced monitors, 383, 420
Intermediaries, 205, 420
Internal hard disks, 387, 420
Internal information, 18, 34, 420
Internal memory, 384, 420
International trade, privacy and, 320–321
International virtual private network (VPN), 179, 420
Internet, 420
    auction houses on, 77
    buying on, 75–77
    electronic cash on, 242–244
    explosion in, 241–248
    finding sites with a search engine, 406–407
    free telephone use on, 244–245, 257
    navigating the Web with Web browser software, 404–405
    security issues on, 216–217
    server computers for, 401, 420
    storage space and software for rent/free on, 247
    tour of, 400–401
    and the World Wide Web, 399–416
Internet access, high-speed, 245–246
Internet appliances, 246–248, 257, 420
Internet backbone, 400, 420

Internet-connected homes, 254–255
Internet Relay Chat. *See* IRC servers
Internet service providers (ISP), 400, 420
Internet virtual private network (Internet VPN), 179, 420
Internships, locating, 28
Interorganizational systems (IOS), 42, 44–45, 429
Interpreting addresses, 403
Intersection relations, 121, 420
"Intertainment," industry perspective on, 21
Interviewing, 28
Intranet telephone directory, industry perspective on, 18
Intranets, 17, 213–214, 227, 420
Intrusion detection software, 217–218, 420
Investment opportunities on the Internet, 159–161
    finding other sources of company financials, 160
    learning about investing, 159
    making trades online, 161
    researching the company behind the stock, 160
    retrieving stock quotes, 161
IOS. *See* Interorganizational systems
IRC (Internet Relay Chat) server, 401, 420
IRS, privacy issues involving, 319
ISDN. *See* Integrated services digital network protocol
ISP. *See* Internet service providers
IT. *See* Information technology
ITW Enterprises, 274–283, 370–372

JD Edwards, industry perspective on OneWorld enterprise of, 299
JIT. *See* Just-in-time
JM Family Enterprises, 95
Job databases, 26–27
Jobs of the future, 346–348
Just-in-time (JIT), 56, 420
    industry perspective on surgery using, 58

Keyboard, 420
Knowledge acquisition, 147, 157, 420
Knowledge base, 147, 157, 421
Knowledge-based systems, 144, 421
Knowledge engineers, 147, 157, 421
Knowledge worker computing, 12, 421
Knowledge worker databases, 107, 111, 421
Knowledge worker development, 309, 421
Knowledge workers, 4, 19–23, 421
    information-literate, 19–20
    socially responsible, 20–23
Knowledge workers checklists, 24–25, 110–111, 156–157, 220–221, 256–257, 300–301, 336–337, 354–355

LAN. *See* Local area networks; Wireless local area networks
Lands, 387, 421
Lands' End, 105, 133
Language processing, 235, 421
Laser printers, 383, 421
Last-mile bottleneck problem, 351–352, 355, 421
Law enforcement agencies, privacy issues involving, 318–319
Legacy systems, 298, 300, 421
Letter quality printers, 383, 421
LEXIS-NEXIS, 91
Libraries, 113
Light pens, 379, 421

Links, 405, 421
Local area networks (LAN), 179, 421
Location dimension, 17
Lodgings, 339–340
Logical requirements, establishing, 293
Logical structures, 87–88
Logical ties, in information, 88–89
Logical view, 89, 421
Long distance communications, 184
Lower CASE Tool, 297, 421

Macro virus, 328, 421
Magnetic hard disk storage technologies, 386, 421
Magnetic-ink character recognition (MICR), 379, 421
Magnetic tape storage technology, 386, 421
Magneto-optical disk storage technologies, 387–388, 421
Mail servers, 401, 421
Management
    data, 131–132, 418
    document, 41
    model, 132–133, 421
    operational, 17, 34, 422
    risk, 330, 337, 423
    strategic, 17, 34, 423
    tactical, 17, 34, 423
    technology, 390–391
    user interface, 133, 424
Management information systems (MIS), 4–7, 24, 38–39, 421
    customer moment of value, 5–7
    role of information technology, 6–7
    and what businesses do, 4–5
Management systems
    database, 89–96, 110, 418
    supply chain, 213, 423
    yield, 70–71
Managing customer relations, in an electronic world, 3
Managing information, 106–109
    database models and databases appropriate to, 107
    developing and maintaining databases and database applications, 109
    effect of technological changes on, 106–107
    ethics involved in, 108–109
    human genetic code example, 108
    information ownership considerations, 108
    oversight of, 107–108
    while it is used, 84–86
Manufacturing industry perspectives
    finding what to fix at IBM, 137
    GE leadership in competitive IT, 53
    OnStar always onboard while driving, 250
    prototyping with software, 287
    Toyota getting moving on Web initiatives, 198
Marketing
    right mix of, 200, 421
    of sites, 224
Mass customization, 421
    and personalization, 65–67
MasterCard, 104, 151, 292
Matsushita Electric Works, 240
MBA programs, 357
MCI, 3–4
M-commerce, 192, 421
MDA. *See* Multidimensional analysis tools
Medical field, enterprisewide systems in, 302

Medium distance communications, 184
Meetings, 138–140
    asynchronous, 139–140
    different-time, 139–140
    same-time, 139
    synchronous, 139
    virtual, 139
Merchandising, importance of, 203–205
Mervyn's, 82–83
Meta tags, 201, 421
Metropolitan Life, 179–180
MICR. *See* Magnetic-ink character recognition
Micro-payments, 199, 421
Microbrowsers, 248, 421
Microwave transmission, 183, 421
Minimal telecommuters, 337
MIS. *See* Management information systems
Mitchells of Westport, 24
Model management, 132–133, 421
Modems, 389
    buying, 397
    cable, 167, 417
    satellite, 167, 423
    telephone, 423
Moderate telecommuters, 336–337
Mondex, 216
Monitoring and reevaluating, 295. *See also* Surveillance agents
Monochrome
    monitors, 382, 421
    printers, 383, 421
Motorola, 240
Mouse, 378, 421
MRO hubs, 206, 212, 421
Multidimensional analysis (MDA) tools, 101–103, 111, 421
Multimedia kiosks, 255
Multiplexors, 185, 421
Mutations, 152, 157, 421
My Dream Baby, 237
MySimon.com, 153

NAFTA. *See* North American Free Trade Agreement
NAP. *See* Network access point
National Crime Information Center (NCIC), 319, 421
Negotiation, 28
Net2Phone, 16
Network access points (NAP), 400, 421
Network hubs, 169, 421
Network interface cards (NIC), 168, 421
Network service providers (NSP), 400, 421
Network technologies, 179–186
    processors, 185
    telecommunications media, 181–185
    types of
        by geographic distance, 179
        by physical structure, 179, 181
Network topologies, 179, 421
    bus, 181
    ring, 181
    star, 181
Networks, 165–186, 389, 421
    business, 171–176
    communications service providers, 176–179
    by geographic distance, 179
    home, 165–171
    neural, 42, 150–151, 157, 421

Index

peer-to-peer, 167–171, 422
    by physical structure—topologies, 179, 181
Neural networks, 42, 150–151, 157, 421
    ethical questions in, 151
    training, 150–151
Next-generation EDI, 215
NIC. *See* Network interface cards
Nokia, 249
Nonimpact printers, 383, 421
Noninterlaced monitors, 383, 421
Nonrecurring decisions, 130, 156, 414, 421
Nonstructured decisions, 129, 156, 421
Normalization, 120–121, 422
North American Free Trade Agreement (NAFTA), 144
NSP. *See* Network service providers

Object-oriented database management systems (O-O DBMS or OODBMS), 100, 422
Object-oriented database models, 99–100
Object-oriented databases (O-O database or OODB), 100, 422
Object-oriented (O-O) technologies, 411–416, 422
    defined, 412–413
    importance of, 416
    popularity of, 414–416
Objective information, 18, 34, 422
Objects, 99, 422
OCR. *See* Optical character recognition
Offerings, making instantaneous changes in, 193–194
OLAP. *See* Online analytical processing
OLTP. *See* Online transaction processing
OMR. *See* Optical mark recognition
One Voice, 148
One-stop travel sites, 340
OneWorld Xe, 299
Online analytical processing (OLAP), 13, 35, 422
Online databases and information repositories, 107, 111–114, 422
    consumer information, 113
    demographics, 113–114
    financial aid resources, 113
    libraries, 113
    real estate, 114
    searching online databases and information repositories, 112
Online exchanges, 212, 422
Online transaction processing (OLTP), 13, 35, 82, 422
OnStar, industry perspective on, 250
OODB. *See* Object-oriented database
OODBMS. *See* Object-oriented database management systems
Open University, 324
Operating system software, 390, 422
Operational databases, 82, 107, 111, 422
Operational management, 17, 34, 422
Optical character recognition (OCR), 379, 422
    formatted devices for, 379–380, 419
Optical disk storage technologies, 387, 422
Optical fiber, 183, 422
Optical mark recognition (OMR), 379, 422
Opting in/opting out, 219, 422
Order entry, 36
Ordering products on the Internet, 75–77
    automobiles, 77
    books and music, 75–76
    clothing and accessories, 76

computers and accessories, 76–77
    Internet auction houses, 77
    ordering products on the Internet, 75
Organizational rules, 173
Organizations, 34
    information oversight in, 107–108
Organizing information
    effect of technological changes on, 106–107
    ethics involved in, 108–109
Output technologies, 381–384, 422
Outsourcing, 266, 292–297, 300, 422
    advantages and disadvantages, 295–296
    choosing a vendor, 294
    developing request for proposal, 293–294
    establishing logical requirements, 293
    evaluating request for proposal, 294, 370–372
    at a global level, 296
    monitoring and reevaluating, 295
    request for proposal and the systems development life cycle, 295
    selecting target system, 293
    testing and accepting solution, 294–295
Oversight, of the organization's information, 107–108

Parallel conversion, 283, 422
Partitioned databases, 107, 422
Pattern classification, 234–235, 422
Payless ShoeSource, Inc., 311–312
Peer-to-peer networks, 167–171, 422
Pen mouse, 378, 422
People issues, 312–324
    cultural diversity, 321–323
    e-mail privacy, 321
    employee monitoring, 318
    ergonomics, 323–324
    ethics, 312–315
    health hazards from computer use, 323
    intellectual property rights, 315–316
    privacy, 316–321
    suggestive e-mail, 317
Pepsi, buying online, 189
Perfect delivery, 6, 422
Periodic reports, 38, 422
Permission marketing, 69, 422
Personal business on the Internet, 26–28
    creating and posting an electronic resume, 27
    going right to the source—the organization you want, 28
    interviewing and negotiating, 28
    job databases, 26–27
    locating that "all important" internship, 28
    searching newspapers the new-fashioned way, 27–28
    using the Internet as a tool to find a job, 26
Personal computer system, 397–398
    buying personal productivity software in a suite, 397
    buying the fastest modem you can, 397
    caution about buying a used computer, 398
    considering ergonomics, 398
    desktops versus laptops, 397
    printer quality, 397
    standard input devices, 397
Personal computing
    AI software to use, 155
    automatic speech recognition, 238
    bargain hunting online, 153
    B2C services, 195

building on the state of the art, 63
    e-mail, 33
    Internet appliances, 249
    opportunities close to home, 50
    possibilities for new EDI, 211
    redefining business operations, 15
    request for proposal, and the systems development life cycle, 295
    selfsourcing, 291
    up-to-date information, 103
    your future job and the skills you need, 347
Personal information, that businesses know, 23–25
Personal life
    intelligent home appliances, 253–254
    smart cards, 252–253
    staying in touch with your home from around the world, 254
    technologies for, 252–255
    your Internet-connected home, 254–255
Personal productivity software, 391–392, 422
    buying in a suite, 397
Personalization, 66, 422
Ph.D. programs, 360
Phone wiring, using existing, 168
Physical devices, 376–389
Pilot conversion, 283, 422
Pirated software, 22, 315, 336, 422
Pits, 387, 422
Pixels, 382, 422
Pizzeria Uno, 110–111
Planning, 274
    for what you can't live without, 268
Plotters, 382, 422
Plunge conversion, 283, 422
PNA adapter cards, 168, 422
Point of origin, 376
Point-of-sale systems (POS), 378, 422
Pointing sticks, 378, 422
PolyOne Corp., 81
POS system. *See* Point-of-sale systems
Posting an electronic resume, 27
Price, making instantaneous changes in, 193–194
Primary keys, 88, 110, 118, 422
    defining, 118–119
Printer quality, 397
Privacy advocates, 218
Privacy issues, 218–219, 224, 316–321
    and consumers, 317–318
    and employees, 316–317
    European privacy laws, 219
    and government agencies, 318–320
    and international trade, 320–321
Private networks, 178, 422
Processing information, in the form of transactions, 82
Processors, 185
    Internet working units, 185
    multiplexors, 185
Productivity software, 391–392, 422
Productivity with technology, 353
Project plan, 278, 422
Project team, 52–53, 422
Proof-of-concept prototype, 286, 422
Proposed IT systems, considered in light of organizational goals, 267
Protecting
    computer investment, 258–259
    information and people, 310–343

Protocols, 186
    ANSI X12, 186
    ATM, 186
    EDIFACT, 186
    ethernet, 186
    ISDN, 186
    TCP/IP, 186
Prototyping, 286–289, 300, 422
    advantages and disadvantages of, 289
    building models, 286–287
    a must in manufacturing, 287
    process of, 287–289
    with software, industry perspective on, 287
Provident Mutual Life, 15
Public key encryption (PKE), 333, 422
Public networks, 178, 422
Purchasing direct materials, 206–211
    EDI, 207–209
    next-generation EDI, 209–211
Purchasing indirect materials (MRO), 211
Pure plays, 192, 422

QBE. *See* Query-by-example tools
Query-and-reporting tools, 102–103, 111, 422
Query-by-example (QBE) tools, 92, 422
Query optimization facilities, 95

Random access memory (RAM), 384, 423
Real estate, 114
Records, 84–85, 423
Recovery facilities, 94
Recurring decisions, 130, 156, 423
Red Robin International, 109–110
RedEnvelope, 203
Redundant computers, 355, 423
References, for creating a Web page, 305–306
Registering with search engines, 201
Regulation of Investigatory Powers Act, 321
Relational databases
    defining entity classes and primary keys, 118–119
    defining information for each relation, 122–124
    defining relationships among entity classes, 119–122
    designing and building, 118
    models of, 96–97, 110, 423
    using a data definition language to create your database, 125
Relations, 97, 110, 423
    defining information for each, 122–124
REMO Fashions, 367–368
Remote data management, 172
Remote presentations, 171
Rental cars, 339
Reorganization facilities, 95
Repeaters, 184, 423
Repetitive strain injuries (RSI), 323, 337, 423
Replicated databases, 107, 423
Report generators, 92, 423
Reports
    ad hoc, 38, 417
    comparative, 38, 417
    exception, 38, 419
    periodic, 38, 422
    summarized, 38, 423
Requests for proposals (RFP), 293, 300, 423
Researching, the company behind the stock, 160
Resolutions, 382, 423

Retail industry perspectives
    growing up with speech recognition, 237
    the right tool for Ace Hardware, 194
    for Sears, planning for the future was essential, 273
Retrieving stock quotes, 161
Reverse auctions, 212, 423
RFP. *See* Requests for proposals
Ring topology, 181, 423
Risk assessment, 330, 337, 423
Risk management, 330, 337, 423
Rival-Watch.com, 62
Rivalry, among existing competitors, 62, 423
Road conditions and maps, 339
Robert Talbott, 63
Robots, 143
Role of government, in promoting e-commerce, 214–215
Role of information, 324–325
    as capital, 325
    as raw material, 324–325
Role of information technology, 6–7
Routers, 185, 423
Royal Caribbean Cruises, 84
RSI. *See* Repetitive strain injuries
Rule-based expert systems, 147, 423

SABRE, 70
Safe-harbor principles, 219, 320, 423
Same city meetings, 139
Same planet meetings, 139
Same room meetings, 139
Same time meetings, 139
Satellite modems, 167, 423
Sausage Software, 68
Scoping, 274–275, 278
Script bunnies, 327–328, 423
SDLC. *See* Systems development life cycle
Search engines, registering with, 201
Searching
    newspapers, 27–28
    online databases and information repositories, 112–114
    for shareware and freeware, 259
Sears, Roebuck & Co., planning for the future, industry perspective on, 273
Sectors targeted for selling, picking carefully, 204
Security issues, 216–218, 325–333
    common security tools, 217–218
    creating and implementing a security plan, 330–331, 333
    designing corporate security procedures, 218
    e-commerce security concepts, 217
    Internet security issues, 216–217
    the players, 326–328
    types of cyber crimes, 328–330
Security management facilities, 95
Selection, 152, 157, 423
    of target systems, 293
Self-scanning checkout lines, 255
Selfsourcing, 266, 286, 289–292, 300, 423
    advantages and pitfalls of, 291–292
    aligning with organizational goals, 290
    determining what external support is required, 290
    documenting the completed system, 290
    providing ongoing support, 291
    on your own, 291

Selling prototypes, 287, 423
Selling to existing customers, 202–203
Servers
    backup, 350
    mail, 401, 421
    Web, 401, 424
Service providers
    communications, 176–179, 417
    Internet, 400, 420
Shared information, 14, 423
Shopping bots, 152, 423
Short distance communications, 183–184
Signet Corp., 14
Smart cards, 215–216, 252–253, 257, 423
Smart companies
    bridging the gap between business people and technical people, 52–53
    CEO's attitude toward information technology, 52
    demanding a creative design, 54–56
    GE leadership example, 53
    getting a competitive advantage from IT, 52–57
    looking beyond the four walls of the company, 56–57
    viewing the business problem from another perspective, 53–54
SNOOPE, 150
Sociability, 155–156, 423
Software, 375, 390–392, 423
    AI, 155
    antivirus, 391, 417
    application, 391–392, 417
    connectivity, 389, 391, 418
    crash proof, 391, 418
    disk optimization, 391, 418
    electronic meeting, 41, 419
    enterprise, 301, 419
    enterprise resource planning, 297–302
    group scheduling, 40, 419
    intrusion detection, 217–218, 420
    operating system, 390, 422
    personal productivity, 391–392, 397, 422
    pirated, 22, 315, 336, 422
    preparing your organization for the Web, 299
    for rent/free on the Internet, industry perspective on, 247
    security, 333
    storefront, 222–223
    system, 390–391, 423
    technology management, 390–391
    uninstaller, 391, 424
    utility, 391, 424
    videoconferencing, 41, 424
    Web browser, 404, 424
    whiteboard, 41, 424
    working together with hardware, 393–396
Sound input devices, 378, 423
Sound output devices, 382, 423
Spam, 202, 423
Speaker-dependent automatic speech recognition, 236, 423
Speaker-independent automatic speech recognition, 236, 423
Specialized MBA programs, 357
Speech recognition, industry perspective on, 237
Speech synthesis, 382, 423
Speed, 192–193
SQL. *See* Structured query language

Standard input devices, 397
Star topology, 181, 423
StarLight Inc., 365–366
Stock quotes, retrieving, 161
Storage space, free on the Internet, industry perspective on, 247
Storage technologies, 385–388, 423
Storefront software, 222–223
Strategic management, 17, 34, 423
Strategic opportunities, 46–79
    airline industry example, 69–71
    CAD Prep AmericaOne for the America's Cup, 47–48
    in e-commerce, 65–69
    GM luring customers with OnStar, 74
    knowledge workers checklist, 72–73
    ordering products on the Internet, 75–77
    paperless payments, 72
    smart companies getting a competitive advantage from IT, 52–57
    tools that can help, 57–65
Structured decisions, 129, 156, 423
Structured query language (SQL), 93
Subjective information, 18, 34, 423
Subsystems
    application generation, 93–94, 110, 417
    data administration, 94–96, 110, 418
    data definition, 89–90, 110, 418
    data manipulation, 90–93, 110, 418
Summarized reports, 38, 423
Supplier power, 58, 60–61, 423
Supply chain management systems, 213, 423
Supply chains, 56–57, 423
Support, 283, 285
    for decision-making tasks, 13, 102
    for information-processing tasks, 12–13
    for information sharing through decentralized computing, 14
    for innovation, 14
Surveillance agents, monitoring and, 153–154
Switching, 227, 423
    costs of, 58, 423
Systems development life cycle (SDLC)
    question-and-answer in, 269–272
    traditional, 272, 300, 424
Systems software, 390–391, 423

Tactical management, 17, 34, 423
Tangible benefits, 267, 423
Tape density, 386, 423
TCP/IP. *See* Transmission control protocol/Internet protocol
Team decision-making process, 136
Team dynamics, 40–41
Team work, 10
    Allright Distributors example, 208
    defining customers and their moment of value, 6
    defining information privileges during university registration, 95
    during each step of the SDLC, 284
    finding electronic cash on the Internet, 244
    finding home appliances with a brain, 253
    finding the best IT strategy for your industry, 61
    gazing into your crystal ball, 353
    helping the little guy compete, 70
    holding virtual meetings to complete a project, 139
    matching IT systems to the who of systems development, 299
    placing your bets, 195
    politically correct data mining, 101
    traffic lights, 150
    working a help desk, 325
Technologies. *See also* Information technology
    automatic speech recognition, 234–238
    biometric, 241
    for creating high-quality Hollywood films, 231
    emerging, 230–262
    finding freeware and shareware on the Internet, 257–260
    growing up with speech recognition, 237
    intelligent home appliances, 253–254
    the Internet explosion, 241–248
    Internet-connected homes, 254–255
    knowledge workers checklist, 256–257
    multimedia kiosks, 255
    personal, 252–255
    productivity with, 353
    for real sight, 233
    self-scanning checkout lines, 255
    for the senses, 233–241
    smart cards, 252–253
    staying in touch with home, 254
    that work with the Internet, 68–69
    3-D, 233–234
    truly "intelligent," 352
    unreliability of, 349, 351
    virtual reality, 237–241
    wireless grocery carts, 255
    the wireless revolution, 248–252
Technology management, 390–391
Tele-education, 358–360
Telecommunications industry perspectives
    EZfone making Internet phone-calling "EZ," 245
    using wireless fiber optics to solve the last-mile bottleneck problem, 352
Telecommunications media, 181–185
    bandwidth, 182
    key considerations for, 184–185
    wired, 182–183
    wireless, 183–184
Telecommunications technologies, 389, 423
Telecommuting, 11, 336–337, 423
    extreme, 336
    minimal, 337
    moderate, 336–337
Telephones
    modems for, 165, 423
    network, 227
    Web, 247–248, 424
Temporary advantage, 49, 423
Terrorists. *See* Cyber terrorists
Testing solutions, 294–295
Thinking globally, 353
Threats
    of new entrants, 59, 61–62, 423
    safeguarding against, 310–343
    of substitute products or services, 58–59, 61, 423
3-D technologies, 233–234, 256, 424
    future of, 234
Time dimension, 16–17
Tools, 57–65
    building on the state of the art, 63
    E Ink example, 60
    finding the best IT strategy for your industry, 61
    five forces model, 58–62
    just-in-time surgery, 58
    keeping an eye on the competition, 62
    three generic strategies, 59, 62–63
    value chain, 63–65
Topologies, 179, 421
Touch pads, 378–379, 424
Touch screens, 379, 424
Touch-tone input devices, 378, 424
Toy Story 2, industry perspective on, 326
Toyota, industry perspective on, 198
TPS. *See* Transaction processing systems
Trackballs, 378, 424
Trading online, 161
Traditional
    EDI, 215
    systems development life cycle, 272, 300, 424
Training neural networks, 150–151
Trains and busses, 338–339
Transaction processing systems (TPS), 36, 424
Transitional firms, 30, 424
Transmission Control Protocol/Internet Protocol (TCP/IP), 186, 424
Transparency
    achieving, 348–349, 351
    Domino's Pizza example, 350
    last-mile bottleneck problem, 351–352
    unreliability of technology, 349, 351
Transportation industry perspectives, BNSF: making the trains run on time, 212
Travel arrangements on the Internet, 338–340
    air travel, 338
    destination information, 340
    lodging, 339–340
    one-stop travel sites, 340
    rental cars, 339
    road conditions and maps, 339
    trains and busses, 338–339
Trevor Toy Auto Mechanics, 362–363
Twentieth Century Fox, 158

Unformatted OCR devices, 380, 424
Uninstaller software, 391, 424
Unreliability, of technology, 349, 351
Upper CASE Tools, 297, 424
UPS, 49
U.S. Bancorp, 270
US West, 17, 152
USCO Logistics, 7
Used computers, caution about buying, 398
User agents, 153, 163, 424
User interface management, 133, 424
User interfaces, 147, 157
Utility software, 391, 424

Value-added networks (VAN), 178, 424
Value chains, 63–65, 424
    identifying processes that add value, 64
    identifying processes that reduce value, 64–65
Value networks, 206, 424
VAN. *See* Value-added networks
Videoconferencing software, 41, 424
View, 91–92, 424
Viral marketing, 202, 424
Virtual meetings, 139
Virtual private networks (VPN), 179, 424

Virtual reality, 237–241, 256, 424
    applications of, 239–240
        for the betterment of people and society, 239
        and cybersickness, 240
        future of, 240–241
Virtual workplaces, 11, 424
Viruses, computer, 328, 418
Visa, 158
Visual effects, 231
Volvo, 240
VPN. *See* International virtual private networks;
    Virtual private networks

Walker, 238, 380, 424
Wal-Mart, 56–57
WAN. *See* Wide area networks
WAP. *See* Wireless access point
Web. *See* World Wide Web
Web appliances, 246, 424
Web initiatives, industry perspective on, 198
Web pages, 303–307, 402, 424
    browser software for, 404, 424
    development tools for, 304–305
    free stuff on, 306
    hosting services for, 306
    HTML, 304
    references for creating, 305–306

Web phones, 247–248, 424
Web servers, 401, 424
Web sites, 402, 424
    addresses of, 402, 424
    call centers integrated with, 194–195
    design tips, 200
    industry perspective on, 154
White-hat hackers, 326, 424
Whiteboard software, 41, 424
Wide area networks (WAN), 179, 424
WiFi (Wireless Fidelity), 183, 424
Wired communications media, 181–183, 424
    coaxial cable, 183
    optical fiber, 183
    twisted-pair, 182–183
Wireless Access Point (WAP), 169–170, 424
Wireless communications media, 181, 183–184, 424
    future of, 352
    long distance, 184
    medium distance, 184
    short distance, 183–184
Wireless fiber optics, using to solve the last-mile
    bottleneck problem, industry perspective
    on, 352
Wireless grocery carts, 255
Wireless home networks, 169

Wireless local area networks (LAN), 251–252, 257, 424
Wireless revolution, 248–252
    buying soft drinks with your phone, 249
    global positioning system, 250–251
    Internet appliances, 249
    OnStar onboard while you drive, 250
Wireless technologies, addressing "ility" issue of, 252
Workgroup support systems (WSS), 40–41, 424
    applications development, 41
    document management, 41
    team dynamics, 40–41
World Wide Web (Web), 402–410, 424
    interpreting addresses, 403
Worms, 328, 424
WSS. *See* Workgroup support systems

X.12 protocol, 186, 424
XML (eXtensible Mark-up Language), 210, 424

Yield management systems, 70–71
Yield managers, 212, 424